William Lonsdale Watkinson, und Andere

The Preacher's Commentary on the Book of Psalms

Vol. II.

William Lonsdale Watkinson, und Andere

The Preacher's Commentary on the Book of Psalms
Vol. II.

ISBN/EAN: 9783744778718

Printed in Europe, USA, Canada, Australia, Japan

Cover: Foto ©Lupo / pixelio.de

More available books at **www.hansebooks.com**

THE PREACHER'S COMMENTARY

ON THE

BOOK OF PSALMS.

THE
Preacher's Complete Homiletical
COMMENTARY

ON THE

OLD TESTAMENT

(ON AN ORIGINAL PLAN),

With Critical and Explanatory Notes, Indices, &c. &c.

BY

VARIOUS AUTHORS.

LONDON:
RICHARD D. DICKINSON, FARRINGDON STREET.
1879.

A

HOMILETIC COMMENTARY

ON THE BOOK OF

PSALMS.

VOL. II.

ON PSALMS LXXXVIII.—CIX.
By WILLIAM JONES;

ON PSALMS CX.—CXX.
By J. W. BURN;

ON PSALMS CXXI.—CXXX.
By GEORGE BARLOW;

ON PSALMS CXXXI.—CL.
By WILLIAM JONES.

LONDON:
RICHARD D. DICKINSON, FARRINGDON STREET.
1879.

Ballantyne Press
BALLANTYNE, HANSON AND CO.
EDINBURGH AND LONDON

INDEX OF SUBJECTS.

	PAGE
ABSOLUTE, the,	208
the incomprehensibleness of God is generally acknowledged,	208
men have universally striven to solve the mystery,	209
the Bible gives us a revelation of all that may be known of God in a manner suited to our faculties and saving to our soul,	209
Acceptable prayer, attributes and advantages of,	434
Advent, the features and effects of the King's,	90
the features of His advent—awful majesty, widest conspicuousness, perfect righteousness,	90
the effects of His advent,	90
it should occasion joy to all; it does occasion destruction to His foes, confusion to idolaters, and gladness to His people,	91
Adversity and God's salvation, man's,	289
man's adversity is often extreme in its intensity, duration, and danger,	289
God's salvation is the remedy for man's adversity,	289
Man's adversity should lead him to cry for God's salvation,	290
This remedy should be sought for holy ends,	290
Affliction,	297
The characteristics and consolations of,	297
The remedy for and the results of,	298
Affliction and its remedy,	268
God's children are afflicted,	268
Affliction should drive us to God for help,	268
God undertakes to apply the remedy for affliction,	268
Affliction: its comforts, duties, and dangers,	277
God's servants are permitted to suffer affliction,	277
God has special comforts for His afflicted servants,	277
Affliction should lead us to call upon God to fulfil His promises,	277
Affliction should not lead us to decline from God's law,	278
Afflictions of life, the, and the resource of the godly,	110

VOL. II.

	PAGE
Human life is characterised by great afflictions,	110
Great afflictions are characterised by great needs,	110
In great afflictions the godly man has a great resource,	110
Afflictions of man, the mercy of God in the,	125
Afflictions of the good, the,	340
The good in all ages have been greatly afflicted,	340
The good have always survived the cruelty of their tormentors,	341
The afflictions of the good are Divinely limited,	341
Affliction, the purpose and benefit of,	283
Age of piety, the old,	70
is the old age of a life of faith and communion with God,	70
is characterised by hope,	70
is one of cheerfulness,	70
is characterised by affection,	71
and to the last by usefulness,	71
All-important enumeration, an (See NUMERATION),	46
Analogies, grass and its moral (See GRASS),	445
Answer, an earnest prayer and an immediate (See PRAYER),	376
Apostate contrasted, the obedient and the,	334
Argument with God,	258
the fact; the argumentative value of the fact, and the prayer founded on the argument and fact,	258
Army, the royal,	177
Church weapons and character,	177
spirit, opportunity, and influence,	178
Aspects and expressions of humility (See HUMILITY),	344
Aspects of the Divine Being, inspiring (See DIVINE),	412
Aspirations, lofty,	304
Atheism, the folly of practical,	75
in supposing that God does not observe human conduct, and will not recompense it,	75
Attitude of the righteous towards the ungodly, the proper,	306
the ungodly are the subjects of the tenderest compassion and the bitterest grief,	307

b

	PAGE
the subjects of zealous evangelisation,	307
are pitied and evangelised not for sentimental but for practical reasons,	307
Attitude of the wicked towards the righteous, the, and the condition of the righteous under oppression,	292
the wicked described,	292
the righteous counselled,	293
Attitude towards the righteous and the wicked. God's,	303
Attributes and advantages of acceptable prayer,	434
Attributes of the upright (See UPRIGHT),	198
BATTLE, the day of, and the protection of God,	394
the period spoken of,	394
the protection acknowledged,	394
the encouragement to be deduced,	395
Beauties of holiness, the,	458
salvation promotes physical beauty,	458
salvation is spiritual beauty,	459
this beauty resembles the beauty of God Himself, is varied, immortal, and ever-increasing,	459
Benedictions,	252
the blessing supplicated,	252
the conditions of blessing fulfilled,	252
the blessing vouchsafed,	252
the place of blessing,	252
Benedictions, Divine,	224
the subjects of the blessing,	224
the characteristics of the blessing,	224
the conditions of the blessing,	225
Benefit and obligation of the Word of God, the,	291
Benefits, man's remembrance of the Lord's,	122
the benefits of God,	122
may be forgotten,	122
should not be forgotten,	122
Bible better than riches, the,	284
what wealth can do the Bible can do better,	284
what wealth cannot do the Bible can,	285
what wealth will do the Bible won't,	285
Bible duties,	276
to meditate upon it,	276
to love it,	276
to delight in it,	276
not to be ashamed of it,	276
to earnestly practise it,	277
Blessed life, the (See LIFE),	253
Blessed, the God in whom man is (See GOD),	421
Blessedness of knowing the joyful sound (See SOUND),	16
Blessedness of the Divinely-instructed man,	76
because of the instruction which he receives,	76
the faithfulness of God,	77
and the righteousness of His judgments,	77

	PAGE
Blessedness of the good, the,	339
is the result of a holy life,	339
consists in a happy livelihood,	339
is found in the joys of domestic life,	339
is augmented by witnessing the prosperity of Zion,	340
Blessedness of the people of God, the,	13
as worshippers of God,	13
as conscious of His favour,	14
as rejoicing in Him,	14
as exalted by Him,	15
as strengthened by Him,	15
as governed and protected by Him,	15
Blessedness, the source and means of,	260
God is the fountain of all blessedness,	260
man's blessedness consists in the enjoyment of God,	260
and is secured through instruction in His statutes,	260
Blessing man, God, and man blessing God,	120
God blessing man, with forgiveness,	120
healing,	120
redemption, coronation, satisfaction,	121
and invigoration,	121
man blessing God with His soul,	121
with His entire spiritual being,	121
with recollection of His benefits,	121
with reverent admiration of His character,	121
Blessing, the happiness of society dependent on the Divine (see HAPPINESS),	337
Blessings in human pilgrimage, Divine,	146
adapted to human needs, e.g., direction, protection, provision, possession,	146
adequate to human needs,	147
guaranteed by Divine faithfulness,	147
bestowed for the most worthy purpose,	147
call for devout praise,	147
Blessings of obedience, the,	279
protection, success,	280
manifestations of God's presence and favour,	280
growth in grace,	280
peace, joy, heaven,	280
Blessings on the sanctuary (See SANCTUARY),	349
Bondage and deliverance,	214
the bondage was degrading,	214
unnatural, exasperating,	214
followed by a Divine redemption,	215
Bounty and faithfulness of God, the,	189
God's bounty, His gifts are as varied as man's need,	189
as plentiful as man's need,	189
equal to all the emergencies of man's need,	189
God's bounty is based upon His faithfulness,	189
and is conditional on man's piety,	189
Builders, the song of the,	352
lessons touching preparatory work,	352
prayer for God's blessing on the builders' work,	353
the Divine answer to the prayer,	353

	PAGE
CALUMNY, the nature and doom of,	318
calumny is a terrible instrument of mischief,	319
productive of acute suffering,	319
drives the soul to seek redress in prayer,	319
involves its perpetrators in severest vengeance,	320
Captives, the afflicted, and their glorious Emancipator,	161
a picture of a painful captivity,	161
the reason of this painful captivity,	161
the design of this painful captivity,	161
the deliverance from this painful captivity,	161
Caring for souls, the duty of,	402
what it is,	402
on whom it devolves,	403
the great evil of neglecting it,	403
Cedar, the, an analogue of soul growth,	69
it grows not by repression, but by development,	69
by the appropriation and subordination of the outward elements,	69
slowly,	69
by ceaseless activities,	70
to immense size and magnificence,	70
during long ages,	70
Celebration, a noble, of the faithfulness and mercy of the Lord,	6
in the view of these attributes which is presented,	6
in the way in which they are celebrated,	7
in the basis on which the celebration rests,	7
in the circumstances in which it is made,	8
Celebration of the praise of God, the good man's (See PRAISE),	61
Character, the, and portion of God's people,	95
the character of God's people,	95
the portion of God's people,	96
Character, the, privileges, and duty of the King's subjects,	94
their character,	94
they are sincere and upright, devout,	94
they love the Lord,	94
their privileges,	95
preservation from evil,	95
deliverance from enemies,	95
bestowal of gladness,	95
their duty, to hate evil, and thankfully rejoice in the Lord,	95
Characteristics of the blessed people,	148
they are a worshipping people,	148
they are a righteous people,	148
they are the Lord's people,	148
Characteristics, the, and blessedness of true religion,	194
the characteristics—fear of the Lord,	194
delight in His commandments,	194
Divine praise,	194
the blessedness,	194
Chastisement,	249

	PAGE
its nature, limits, consolations, and effects,	249
Children the gift of God,	338
are to be judiciously trained,	338
are a source of domestic joy,	338
are the strength and defence of home,	339
Christ refreshing Himself (See REFRESHING),	182
Christ the corner-stone,	250
the only corner-stone,	250
the Divinely established corner-stone,	251
the rejected corner-stone,	251
the marvellous corner-stone,	251
Christ, the kingdom of,	93
Christ, the sovereignty of,	174
Christ reigns by Divine appointment,	175
by Divine right,	175
by a devout acknowledgment,	175
over a disputed empire,	175
by the enforced service of His foes,	175
and will reign over an undisputed universe,	176
Christ's triumph over tyranny,	180
all tyranny is the foe of Christ,	180
is subject to the wrath of Christ,	181
will be destroyed by Christ,	181
will be supplanted by Christ,	181
Christian progress,	271
the way of, is Divinely revealed,	271
is possible only under certain definite conditions,	271
is impossible without Divine assistance,	272
Christian union (See UNION),	356
Church and congregational worship (See WORSHIP),	184
Church, a revival of the, and symptoms which precede it,	115
Church-builders, encouragements for,	350
the presence of God in His Church,	350
the blessing of God in His Church,	351
the triumph and glory of the Head of the Church,	351
Church-builders, lessons for,	347
when churches are needed their erection is of great importance,	347
churches should be erected for the worship of God,	348
in the worship of God in the church the manifestation of His presence should be earnestly sought,	348
in seeking this manifestation of His presence we have powerful pleas which we may urge,	348
Church of God, Jerusalem a type of the (See JERUSALEM),	326
Church, Zion a type of the,	353
Comforts of Christians, the, under trials,	81
the distressing thoughts which are apt to oppress the mind of a good man,	81
the consolations of God opposed to these uneasy thoughts,	82
Communion of saints, the,	281
must have a religious basis,	281
is the spiritual intercourse between spiritual men, and between spiritual	

	PAGE
men and God, through the Divinely-appointed means,	281
is reasonable and natural when on this basis,	282
Compassion, human wretchedness and Divine,	365
the wretched condition of mankind in consequence of their apostasy from God,	365
the method of Divine compassion to man in his rescue from this state of guilt, &c.,	366
Compensations, contrasts and,	283
Complaint, prayer, and confidence,	172
A mournful complaint of mental distress, physical exhaustion,	172
approach to death and reproach of foes,	173
an earnest prayer,	173
the objects sought and the pleas urged,	173
an encouraging confidence,	173
assurance of salvation from God,	173
determination to offer praise to God,	173
Condescension of God, the majesty and,	379
Condition of the righteous under oppression, the,	292
	292
Conduct of a good man in a time of trial, the,	395
earnest prayer,	395
noble resolutions,	396
confident expectation,	397
and earnest prayer repeated,	397
Confidence, complaint, prayer, and (See COMPLAINT),	172
Confidence in God, a declaration of,	77
in the midst of enemies,	78
in the midst of anxious thoughts,	78
in the Divine support,	78
in the Divine protection,	78
in the Divine retribution,	79
a source of joy even in the midst of dangers and anxieties,	79
Consequences of idolatry, the moral (See IDOLATRY),	222
Consideration, the Divine,	311
Consistency, separation and (See SEPARATION),	302
Consolation, a great contrast and (See CONTRAST),	117
Constant praise (See PRAISE),	313
Contrast, a, God's mercy and man's frailty,	126
the frailty of man's life upon earth and the mercy of God,	126
the brevity of man's life upon earth and the eternity of the mercy of God,	126
the final departure of man from the earth, and the eternal mercy of God present with him wherever he may be,	126
the final departure of good men from the earth, and the eternal mercy of God resting upon their descendants,	126
Contrast and consolation, a great,	117
a great contrast,	117

	PAGE
the changefulness and transitoriness of human life and nature,	117
the eternity and immutability of God,	118
a great consolation,	118
as regards the Psalmist and the Church,	118
Contrasts and compensations,	283
Control over man's life, God's absolute,	36
a reason for acknowledging Him,	36
a reason for seeking His favour,	36
a consolation in bereavement,	36
an encouragement to labour,	36
an antidote against the fear of death,	37
Corner-stone, Christ the (See CHRIST),	250
Courage,	245
its source and manifestations,	245
Covenant of God, the, and the sins of men,	21
the sins of men are opposed to the covenant of God,	21
yet men who in the covenant of God are richly blessed may sin grievously against Him,	22
the sins of men will be punished by God,	22
the sins of men cannot frustrate the covenant of God,	23
Covenant of God, the, lamentation and expostulation by reason of the apparent failure of,	24
the lamentation,	24
the king was dethroned,	24
their defences were destroyed,	24
they were the prey of their neighbours,	24
they were defeated in battle,	24
their vigour and glory had ceased,	25
they attributed their sad condition to their rejection by God,	25
the expostulation is based upon the duration of their distresses,	26
the brevity of their life,	26
the vanity of their life,	26
the certainty of death,	26
the loving-kindness promised by God,	26
the reproaches which fell upon them,	27
Covenant with David, God's,	16
the election of David,	17
he was elected from the people,	17
to sovereignty and service, by God,	17
the promises made to David,	18
constant support,	18
victory over his foes,	18
conspicuous power,	18
enlarged dominion,	19
intimate and exalted relationship,	19
perpetual establishment of the covenant,	19
Creation a plea in prayer,	285
man is the creation of God,	285
was created for Divine service,	285
is not now as he was when created,	286
the necessity of a new creation,	286
desiring this new nature, no plea is more appropriate and powerful than the fact that we are God's creation,	286

	PAGE
Creation a revelation of the Lord (See REVELATION),	130
Creation, the, and the creature, the Creator,	225
Creation of God, man a wonderful (See MAN),	384
Creation, the majesty of God in (See MAJESTY),	128
Creation, voices of,	135
the Divine existence is to constitute the central fact in our contemplation of the universe,	136
the principle of dependence is everywhere developed in the universe,	136
a devout contemplation of the universe is calculated to increase man's hatred of sin,	136
Creator, the, the creation, and the creature,	225
Cry for judgment, a,	73
the complaint of the Church,	73
of its enemies, their character and triumph,	73
their cruel oppression and practical atheism,	74
the appeal of the Church for justice, judgment is the prerogative of God alone,	74
is sometimes apparently long delayed,	74
is earnestly invoked,	74
Cry, the, of a distressed servant of God,	404
a picture of great distress,	404
an exercise indicating great wisdom,	405
an appeal of great power,	405
a desire of great fervour,	406
Cynicism,	238
the Psalmist's consisted in a hasty conclusion and an uncharitable verdict,	238
was natural under the circumstances, although not justifiable,	238
was only a passing mood,	238
was successfully resisted and overcome,	238
DANGER and its remedy, a,	304
the danger consists in the lust of gain,	304
infidelity, sin,	305
the remedy is by "the expulsive force of a new affection" to make danger flee,	305
the danger is avoided and the remedy applied by earnest prayer,	305
Danger, the soul's escape from (See ESCAPE),	331
David, God's covenant with (See COVENANT),	16
Day, the constituents of a complete and holy,	311
it begins with prayer,	311
continues with obedience,	311
closes with meditation,	311
Day, the Lord's, and its duties,	251
Day, the world's most joyous,	87
a day when the relations of the Lord	

	PAGE
to the world shall be rightly apprehended,	87
He alone is God of the world,	87
His salvation is for all the world,	88
He is King of all the world,	88
He is Judge of all the world,	88
a day when the relations of the Lord to the world shall be duly celebrated,	88
He will be worshipped universally,	88
enthusiastically, joyously,	88
and reverently,	89
De Profundis (See PROFUNDIS),	342
Death, God's estimate of (See ESTIMATE),	240
Death, the philosophy of,	437
the destiny of all,	437
the peculiar privileges of the godly,	438
Death, two views of,	241
Declaration of confidence in God (See CONFIDENCE),	77
Deliverance,	234
of the soul from death,	234
of the eyes from tears,	235
of the feet from falling,	235
Deliverance a theme for joyous song,	335
because of the misery it emancipates from,	335
its unexpectedness,	335
its reviving effects,	335
the gladness it occasions,	335
its evidence of the Divine power,	335
Deliverance, bondage and (See BONDAGE),	214
Deliverance from their enemies, a prayer of the godly for,	416
his description of his enemies,	416
his prayer for deliverance from them,	417
his resolution to praise God for deliverance from them,	417
Dependence, universal, and Divine support,	433
the universality of dependence,	433
the infinitude of the Divine resources,	433
the timeliness of the Divine gifts,	433
the case of the Divine gifts,	433
the sufficiency of the Divine gifts,	434
Deprecated, Divine judgment (See JUDGMENT),	407
Desire of the wicked, the,	203
perishes because it is selfish,	203
has nothing to fall back upon in case of disappointment,	203
has no resources on which to rely,	203
is set on unsatisfactory objects,	203
the frown of God is upon it,	204
Desires, the granting of selfish, an injury to the soul,	153
Determination, a fourfold,	262
to meditate on God's precepts,	263
to have respect to God's ways,	263
to delight in God's statutes,	263
to remember God's Word,	263
Difficulty of singing songs in exile (See SONGS),	372
Diseases healed, spiritual,	122
why sin is called a disease,	122

	PAGE
the variety of these diseases,	123
the remedy by which God heals them,	123
Distress, a prayer of the godly man from the depths of (See PRAYER),	399
Distress to the good, the ferocity of the wicked a source of (See FEROCITY),	320
Distressed seamen and the Sovereign of the sea (See SEAMEN),	163
Distressed servant of God, the cry of a (See CRY),	404
Distressed servant of God, the prayer of a (See PRAYER),	408
Distressed travellers and the Divine Helper (See TRAVELLERS),	159
Divine Being, errors respecting the,	428
Divine Being, inspiring aspects of the,	412
the Author of human skill,	412
the Protector of human life,	413
the Source of human authority,	413
the Object of human trust,	413
the Supreme Good of human life,	413
the Recipient of human praise,	413
Divine benedictions (See BENEDICTIONS),	224
Divine dwelling-place, the (See DWELLING),	226
Divine education,	268
Divine guidance (See GUIDANCE),	411
Divine mercy, the (See MERCY),	243
Divine protection (See PROTECTION),	323
Divine protection, the (See PROTECTION),	302
Divine provisions (See PROVISIONS),	218
Divine relationships (See RELATIONSHIPS),	241
Doxology,	30
God is blessed in Himself,	30
God is blessed by His creatures,	30
God is blessed for ever,	31
Doxology,	158
Doxology, the,	461
the sphere of the Divine praise,	461
the reason of the Divine praise,	462
the measure of the Divine praise,	462
the manner of the Divine praise,	462
the offerers of the Divine praise,	462
Duties, Bible (See BIBLE),	276
Duty, law, prayer,	254
Dwelling-place, the Divine,	226
is exalted,	226
is holy,	226
is to be the dwelling-place of man,	226
EARTH, God's praise on the (See PRAISE),	453
Earth, the, God's gift and man's inheritance,	226
the earth is God's gift to man,	226
it is an equitable, a magnificent, a prepared, and,	226
an universal gift,	227
it is God's gift to man for definite uses,	227
for religious ends,	227
for the education of man's mind,	227
for man's use and enjoyment,	227
to be evangelised for Christ,	227
Education, Divine,	268

	PAGE
Effectual, fervent, and believing prayer (See PRAYER),	309
Emancipation, a glorious, a cruel persecution and (See PERSECUTION),	145
Emancipation, Divine, human imprisonment and (See IMPRISONMENT),	403
Emancipator, the afflicted captives and their glorious (See CAPTIVES),	161
Enclosure, the sacred,	249
the enclosure, its gates and keys,	249
its privileges and duties,	250
Encouragement to His people to trust in Him, the strength of God an (See STRENGTH),	11
Encouragements for church-builders (See CHURCH),	350
Encouragements for prayer (See PRAYER),	231
Encouragements to holy song (See SONG),	64
Enemies, the lamentable fate of the Church's (See FATE),	341
Enjoyment, the saint's, of the law of God,	294
the law of God is lovable,	294
God's saints possess a spiritual taste which enables them to appreciate His law,	294
they exercise that taste continually,	295
Errors respecting the Divine Being,	428
Escape from danger, the soul's,	331
the soul is surrounded by dangers,	331
these dangers are not invincible,	332
a way is divinely provided for the escape of the soul from all danger,	332
Estimate of death, God's,	240
a high, unusual, unexpected, and specific estimate.	240
Estimated by the light of heaven, sin,	40
Eternal praise,	193
the object and subjects of praise are eternal,	193
the worshippers have "life eternal,"	194
Exaltation, human,	211
in the spheres of daily life,	211
in God's method of redemption,	212
in the history of the Christian Church,	212
in the resurrection of the body,	212
Exalted, God's Word,	376
Examples of the holy sovereignty of God and the becoming worship of His people,	101
examples of the becoming worship of man,	101
in earnest prayer, in holy lives,	101
examples of the sovereignty of God in His answers to His servants' prayers,	101
Excellence and beauty of fraternal unity (See UNITY),	354
Excellence of praise to God, the (See PRAISE),	439
Exclamation, life an (See LIFE),	42
Exemplary humility (See HUMILITY),	345
Expostulation from the depth of misery (See MISERY),	4

INDEX.

	PAGE
Expostulation, lamentation and, by reason of the apparent failure of the covenant of God (See COVENANT),	24
Extremity, man's, God's opportunity,	245
man in distress,	245
man's duty in distress,	245
man's consolations in distress,	245
man's deliverance in distress,	245
Exultant hymn, an (See HYMN),	97
FAILURE of the covenant of God, lamentation and expostulation by reason of the apparent (See COVENANT),	24
Faith, fearlessness, fixedness, and (See FEARLESSNESS),	200
Faith, the nature and power of,	237
the nature of faith,	237
the power of faith is to find expression for itself,	237
constrains those who believe to confess their belief,	237
inspire loyalty to the truth we believe,	237
impress us with the necessity of its declaration,	237
is the power of loyalty to the Lord of faith,	237
and the power of successful enterprise,	237
Faithful Promiser, the (See PROMISER),	141
Faithfulness and mercy of the Lord, a noble celebration of the (See CELEBRATION),	6
Fate of the Church's enemies, the lamentable,	341
they are signally defeated,	341
their life-purpose is abortive,	341
they remain unblessed,	341
Favour of God desired, the,	149
Fear and its remedy,	273
the Christian has nothing to fear but sin,	273
the only safety from sin and its reproach is the life of righteousness,	274
the danger and the safety are revealed by the Word of God,	274
the danger is to be deprecated, and the safety sought by prayer,	274
Fearlessness, fixedness, and faith,	200
Fearlessness, what it consists in,	200
is impossible without fixedness,	200
no fixedness without faith,	200
Features and effects of the King's advent, the (See ADVENT),	90
Fellowship, religious,	286
is possible only to religious persons,	286
is to be desired by religious persons,	286
is profitable to religious persons,	287
Ferocity of the wicked, the, a source of distress to the good,	320
the good are brought into unavoidable contact with the wicked,	320
the attitude of the wicked is one of fierce antagonism to the good,	321
the ferocity of the wicked is a source of distress to the good,	321

	PAGE
Finite, the, and the infinite,	293
with regard to earthly life,	293
earthly greatness and grandeur,	293
the development of human character,	293
the acquisition of human knowledge,	293
human pleasures and satisfactions,	294
human institutions,	294
Fixedness and faith, fearlessness (See FEARLESSNESS),	200
Foes, the, and victory of the good,	57
the foes of the good,	57
are numerous, various, terrible,	57
the victory of the good,	57
is complete and certain,	57
Folly, the, of practical atheism (See ATHEISM),	75
Forgetfulness of the Divine works,	152
the works of God are worthy of an attentive review and thankful remembrance,	152
there is in human nature a tendency to forget the works of God,	153
the sinfulness and danger of forgetting them,	153
the best means of remembering them,	153
Frailty, human, and Divine greatness,	32
the greatness of God,	32
He existed before the world,	32
He created the world,	32
He is eternal,	32
the frailty of man,	33
the brevity of his life upon earth,	33
the mournful end of his life upon earth,	34
the great Sovereign of his life upon earth,	34
the relation between the great God and frail man,	34
we are weak, and rest in His omnipotence.	35
we are short-lived, and rest in His eternity,	35
Frailty, human, an incentive to seek the Divine blessing,	44
the Psalmist seeks for help in forming a correct estimate of life,	44
the mercy of God in life,	44
the manifestation of God's power and grace in life,	45
the establishment of human work in life,	46
Frailty, human, the result of human sin,	37
death is associated with physical sufferings, and these are a result of sin,	38
with mental sufferings, and these are a result of sin,	39
Frailty, man's, God's mercy and (See CONTRAST),	126
Freedom,	276
man's natural condition is one of bondage,	276
man walks at liberty when he seeks and finds God's precepts,	276
man walks permanently and securely	

	PAGE		PAGE
at liberty only as long as he seeks and finds God's precepts,	276	God, the incomparableness of (See INCOMPARABLENESS),	8
GIFT of God, children the (See CHILDREN),	338	God, the, in whom man is blessed,	421
		all peoples have a God,	421
		man must trust, love, and worship,	421
Gladness, religious,	65	that people only is blessed whose God is Jehovah,	421
gladness as the gift of God,	65	He is the only worthy object of man's trust,	421
arising from the contemplation of God's works,	65		
finding expression in devout song,	66	supreme love and worship,	421
Glance, the heavenward,	328	God, the living and true, idols and (See IDOLS),	221
is directed to One who is enthroned in majesty,	328	God, the majesty and condescension of,	210
who has supreme government,	328	the majesty of God,	210
who is rich in mercy,	329	He is throned above the realm of space,	210
this glance is persevering and triumphant,	329	above all duration,	211
Glory of Christ's kingdom,	430	the condescension of God,	211
is manifested in its origin,	430	He looks on physical laws, and employs them,	211
in the manner and spirit of its administration,	430	upon man, and visits him,	211
in the character of His subjects,	430	upon human governments, and employs them,	211
in the privileges attached to it,	431		
Glory of God, the sole, and the abnegation of man,	219	God, the mercy of, solicited,	47
		God, the omnipresence of, and its impressions upon man (See OMNIPRESENCE),	383
God's glory consists in His supreme perfection,	219		
is expressed in the mercy and truthfulness of His works and ways,	219	God, the reign of (See REIGN),	91
should be apprehended and acknowledged by man,	219	God, the rejoicing of the good man in the government of (See GOVERNMENT),	66
is not the object of God's solicitude, but man's,	219	God, the righteousness of nature's, nature's beauty and (See NATURE),	187
removes all ground of boasting on the part of man,	220	God, the servant of (See SERVANT),	272
God, argument with (See ARGUMENT),	258	God, the sole glory of, and the abnegation of man (See GLORY),	219
God blessing man and man blessing God (See BLESSING),	120	God, the Word of, its sphere and its service (See WORD),	259
God desired, the favour of,	149	God, the works of, the subject of soul-satisfying search (See WORKS),	185
God incomparable,	10		
God in creation, the majesty of (See MAJESTY),	128	God, trust in (See TRUST),	222
God in nature,	118	God, walking before (See WALKING),	235
four aspects of the Divine Being—as intimately acquainted with all portions of the universe,	119	God's absolute control over man's life (See CONTROL),	36
		God's attitude towards the righteous and the wicked,	303
the Sovereign Proprietor of the universe,	119	God's estimate of death (See ESTIMATE),	240
the all-transforming Spirit of the universe,	119	God's gift and man's inheritance, the earth (See EARTH),	226
the all-surveying Spirit of the universe,	119	God's goodness, its nature, and its relation to prayer and life (See GOODNESS),	282
God, mercy in, and in creation (See MERCY),	363	God's mercy, the greatness of (See MERCY),	168
God mindful of man (See MINDFUL),	223	God's omnipresence (See OMNIPRESENCE),	381
God, the bounty and faithfulness of (See BOUNTY),	189	God's people, the character and portion of),	95
God, the eternal truth of (See TRUTH),	106		
God, the goodness of nature's, the purpose of nature and (See NATURE),	188	God's perfect knowledge of man (See KNOWLEDGE),	379
God, the greatness and gentleness of,	442	God's salvation (See SALVATION),	314
the text reveals the constructive side of the Divine government, as seen in the building of the Church,	442	God's testimonies a ground of joy (See TESTIMONIES),	261
		God's treatment of different classes of character (See TREATMENT),	377
the gentle care of human hearts,	442		
the order, regularity, and stability of creation,	442	God's ways, though often inscrutable, are righteous and just,	92

	PAGE
God's Word a tried word and a loved word,	308
God's Word desired,	305
instructive, wonderful, kept,	306
God's works and God's words (See WORKS),	290
Godly, the angelic ministers of the (See MINISTERS),	54
Godly, the glorious privileges of the (See PRIVILEGES),	57
Godly, the inviolable security of the (See SECURITY),	51
Godly, the safe hiding-place of the (See HIDING-PLACE),	49
Godly, the trials of the (See TRIALS),	318
Godly under misrepresentation, the (See MISREPRESENTATION),	317
Golden mean, the (See MEAN),	198
Good resolutions (See RESOLUTIONS),	255
Good, the afflictions of the (See AFFLICTIONS),	340
Good, the blessedness of the (See BLESSEDNESS),	339
Good, the foes and victory of the (See FOES),	57
Goodness, God's, its nature and its relation to prayer and life,	282
its nature, it is Divine, and operative,	282
it is an encouragement to prayer,	282
our prayer having such encouragement should be of the largest kind and for the best things,	282
Goodness in nature, providence, and grace, the Divine,	450
Goodness, man's recognition of God's (See RECOGNITION),	242
Goodness, the Lord's, and man's sin,	149
man's sin notwithstanding the Lord's goodness,	149
the Lord's goodness notwithstanding man's sin,	150
Goodness, the praise of the Divine,	425
the manifestations of God's goodness,	425
the universality of God's goodness,	426
the praise of God's goodness,	427
Government of God, the rejoicing of the good man in the,	66
God is the Supreme Ruler,	66
His rule is unchangeably righteous,	66
this is manifest in the destruction of the wicked,	66
the salvation of the righteous,	67
Government of heaven, the Divine,	207
is acknowledged and obeyed universally, reverentially, swiftly,	208
comprehensively, continually,	208
willingly, perfectly,	208
Government of nations, the Divine,	207
is personal, exalted, benevolent,	207
suitable to the circumstances of all nations,	207
administered by Christ,	207
Grace and guidance, a good man's prayer for (See PRAYER),	410
Granting, the, of selfish desires an injury to the soul,	153

	PAGE
Grass and its moral analogies,	445
in grass we have an illustration of Christian humility and cheerfulness,	446
Gratitude,	205
there are grounds for,	205
these grounds are often ignored,	205
these grounds should be acknowledged by present thankfulness,	205
and by perpetual thankfulness,	206
Great, the supremely,	443
God is great in His essence,	443
in His power,	443
in His knowledge,	444
Greatness and gentleness of God, the (See GOD),	442
Greatness, human frailty and Divine (See FRAILTY),	32
Greatness of God's mercy, the (See MERCY),	168
Greatness of God, the, an incentive to praise Him,	359
the poet illustrates God's greatness by His judgments upon the heathen,	359
His regard for His people,	359
His eternity and unchangeableness,	360
Greatness, the praise of the Divine (See PRAISE),	423
Greatness, true,	309
may be consistent with external humiliation,	309
external humiliation should not belittle a man,	309
Growth, the cedar an analogue of soul (See CEDAR),	69
Guidance, Divine,	411
the prayer of one who felt his need of Divine guidance,	411
believed that God had a way marked out for him,	411
believed that God could reveal His way to Him,	411
had placed himself in the right attitude to receive Divine guidance,	412
HAPPINESS of society, the, dependent on the Divine blessing,	337
family greatness should be founded on the Divine blessing,	337
the safety of civil society is secured by the Divine blessing,	337
the prosperity of society is dependent on the Divine blessing,	337
Happy people, a picture of a (See PICTURE),	418
Happy people, the	422
Harmony of creation restored, the,	138
the glory of the Lord in His works,	138
the joy of the righteous in the Lord,	138
the desire of the righteous concerning the wicked,	138
Harps on the willows,	369
every man has a harp,	369
sometimes the harp has to be hung on the willows,	370
yet it needs not to be cast away,	371
Hate, love and,	300

	PAGE
Hatred, holy,	301
in its nature, causes, and specific objects,	301
Healed, spiritual diseases (See DISEASES),	122
Healing, human sickness and Divine (See SICKNESS),	162
Hear God's voice, sinners entreated to,	86
Heaven, the Divine government of (See GOVERNMENT),	207
Heavens, God's praise in the (See PRAISE),	452
Heavenward glance, the (See GLANCE),	328
Help of helplessness, the timely,	232
who are the helpless?	232
when are they helped?	232
how are they helped?	233
Helper of man, the mighty,	20
man's great need as a sinner,	20
Christ's great power as a Saviour,	21
Helplessness, the timely help of (See HELP),	232
Heritage of His people, God's Word the,	299
a heritage valuable and responsible,	299
Hiding-place of the godly, the safe,	49
an implication of danger,	49
an assurance of safety,	49
an expression of confidence,	50
Historical surprises (See SURPRISES),	143
History of a rebellious people, passages from the,	155
an incorrigibly rebellious people,	155
a brave man acting as minister of justice in a critical time,	155
a holy man sinning and suffering by reason of the sin of others,	155
the great God contending against human sin,	156
Holiness, the beauties of (See BEAUTIES),	458
Holy hatred (See HATRED),	301
Home of the soul, the,	35
the soul of man needs a home,	35
the soul of man may find a home in God,	36
Home, the picture of a pious,	107
its worship,	107
its head,	108
its servants,	108
the head of a pious house will do his utmost to banish wickedness from the world,	109
Hope of a distressed patriot, the,	113
the object and ground of his hope,	113
the strength of his hope,	114
the results anticipated from its fulfilment,	114
Hope of redemption, the,	343
is based on the revelation of the Divine Word,	343
rouses the most passionate longings of the human soul,	343
is encouraged by reflecting on the amplitude of the Divine mercy,	343
is strengthened by the assurance of the completeness of redemptive blessings,	343

	PAGE
Human exaltation (See EXALTATION),	211
Human frailty and Divine greatness (See FRAILTY),	32
Human frailty an incentive to seek the Divine blessing (See FRAILTY),	44
Human frailty the result of human sin (See FRAILTY),	37
Humility, aspects and expressions of,	344
humility in certain of its features,	344
as connected with contentment and rest,	344
growing into hope,	345
Humility, exemplary,	345
the humility which the poet displayed,	345
the methods in which the possession of this grace will be shown and attested,	346
the means of producing it,	346
Hymn, an exultant,	97
we have here exultation for the most excellent reasons,	97
with the fullest expression,	98
in the widest extent,	98
IDOLATRY, the moral consequences of,	222
the idolater becomes like his idols in mental incapacity,	222
in moral insensibility,	222
in deep degradation,	222
in malign harmfulness,	222
in spiritual death,	222
Idols and the living and true God,	221
idols vary, God remains the same,	221
idols are many and conflicting, God is one and in harmony with Himself,	221
idols are the work of men's hands, God is eternal and uncreated,	221
idols can only occupy temples made with hands, God is in the heavens,	221
idols are senseless, God is keenly sensitive of the wants of His creatures,	221
Idols, the vanity of, an incentive to praise the Lord God,	360
the innate religiousness of human nature,	360
the sad perversion of the religious element in human nature,	360
the grand Object of worship for man,	361
the chief place of worship for man,	361
Illustration of the renewal of the soul, the renewal of the face of the earth, an (See RENEWAL),	137
Immortality, the vanity of man apart from his (See VANITY),	27
Imprisonment, human, and Divine emancipation,	403
man's imprisonment as a sinner,	403
man's emancipation by the Saviour,	404
man's praise to the Emancipator,	404
Incentive to praise Him, the greatness of God, an (See GREATNESS),	359
Incentive to praise the Lord God, the vanity of idols, an (See IDOLS),	360
Incentive to seek the Divine blessing, human frailty an (See FRAILTY),	44

	PAGE		PAGE
Incident of the journey, a common,	81	KING, Jehovah the,	71
Incitements to praise the Lord,	358	the majesty of the King,	71
the persons to whom the exhortation is addressed,	358	the might of the King,	72
		seen in the stability of the world,	72
they have access to and serve God,	358	in the subjugation of His enemies,	72
the reasons by which the exhortation is enforced,	358	the eternity of the King and of His kingdom,	72
because of the holiness of God,	358	the truth of His testimonies,	72
the delight which the exercise yields,	358	Kingdom of Christ, the,	93
His special relation to Israel,	358	Kingdom, the glory of Christ's (See GLORY),	430
His sovereignty in nature,	358		
Incomparable, God,	10	Kingdom, the temple and the,	215
Incomparableness of God, the,	8	King's advent, the features and effects of the (See ADVENT),	90
heavenly beings are mighty,	8		
heavenly beings are holy,	9	King's subjects, the character, privileges, and duty of the (See SUBJECTS),	94
heavenly beings worship God,	9		
Inequalities readjusted, providential,	266		
the problem stated,	266	Knowledge of God, the sorrows of the soul and the (See SORROWS),	401
the prosperity of the wicked,	266		
the adversity of the righteous,	266	Knowledge of man, God's perfect,	379
the problem solved,	266	God knows all men,	379
the adversity of the wicked,	266	God knows all men thoroughly,	380
the prosperity of the righteous,	266	God knows all men constantly,	380
Infinite, the finite and the (See FINITE),	293	the practical influence of this knowledge on us and on our life,	380
Infinity, the, expressions and objects of the Divine mercy (See MERCY),	123		
Ingratitude,	171	LAMENT of a distressed patriot, the,	111
Inquiry, a godless, and a godly response,	220	his distress was very great,	111
the question,	220	absorbing, consuming, isolating,	111
why and by whom is it asked?,	220	occasioned reproaches from his enemies,	112
an all-sufficient answer,	220		
God exists; He exists in the heavens,	220	was regarded as an expression of the Divine anger,	112
He does according to His pleasure,	221	was not hopeless,	112
Insignificance, the, and greatness of man (See MAN),	414	was patriotic,	112
		Lamentation and expostulation by reason of the apparent failure of the covenant of God (See COVENANT),	24
Invitation to worship, an (See WORSHIP),	82		
		Law of God, the saint's enjoyment of the (See ENJOYMENT),	204
JEHOVAH the King (See KING),	71		
Jehovah the refuge of the distressed (See REFUGE),	321	Law, prayer, duty,	254
Jerusalem a type of the Church,	326	Lessons for church-builders (See CHURCH),	347
because it is securely founded,	326		
the place of general assembly,	326	Liberator, the Lord the,	439
the seat of universal government,	326	Liberality,	201
Journey, a common incident of the,	81	true liberality must have righteousness for its basis,	201
Joy of Divine worship, the,	325		
is realised in anticipation,	325	need for its object,	201
is enhanced when shared with others,	325	usefulness for its end,	202
is most fully realised in the sanctuary,	325	will have success and honour as its reward,	202
is abiding,	326		
Joys, spiritual,	140	Life a shadow, human,	416
it is God's will that His people should be happy,	140	Life an exclamation,	42
		life has the brevity of a cry,	42
His people have been for the most part a sad and sorrowing people,	140	life is a cry full of meaning,	43
		Life as the sphere of Divine service (See SERVICE),	227
how is this to be accounted for?	141		
Jubilant people of God, the,	456	Life, its sustenance and aim,	263
the reasons of their rejoicing,	456	Life, long,	60
the character of their rejoicing,	457	is desirable,	60
the expression of their rejoicing,	457	is promoted by true religion,	60
Judgment, a cry for (See CRY),	73	is not to be estimated by the number of its months and years,	60
Judgment deprecated, Divine,	407		
the truths implied,	407	a godly man will be satisfied with the length of his life as determined by God,	60
the petition offered,	407		
the reasons urged,	407		

	PAGE
Life of a godly man, the pitiable, the commendable, and the reprehensible in the troubled,	170
the pitiable; he complains of slander, malignity, and ingratitude,	170
the commendable; he committed his cause to the Lord in prayer,	171
the reprehensible; he manifests a revengeful spirit,	171
Life, the afflictions of, and the resource of the godly (See AFFLICTIONS),	110
Life, the blessed,	253
all men are not happy,	253
men can secure happiness only by a right state of the heart,	253
and maintain it only by a right state of the life,	254
provision is made for man's happiness in the Word of God,	254
Life, the complete triumph of the Christian (See TRIUMPH),	167
Light, God's Word a lamp and a,	295
the Word of God is a light,	296
a clear, full, and perennial light,	296
Light, to whom and when?,	197
to the upright,	197
who have their seasons of darkness,	197
in which light ariseth,	198
Long life (See LIFE),	60
Lord and His universe, the,	134
the Lord is the Creator of all things,	134
the Lord is the Proprietor of all things,	135
the Lord is the Sustainer of all things,	135
the Lord is the Sovereign of all things,	135
Lord, creation a revelation of the,	130
displays His absolute power,	130
displays His delight in beauty,	131
displays His great law of service,	132
displays His regard for all His creatures,	132
displays His supreme regard for man,	132
Lord in the Church and the state, the supremacy of the (See SUPREMACY),	99
Lord, the glorious reign and praise of the (See REIGN),	127
Lord, the liberator, the,	439
Lord, the praise of the,	130
Lord, the works and worship of the (See WORKS),	139
Lord's day, the,	251
Lord's goodness and man's sin, the (See GOODNESS),	149
Lord's time and ours, the (See TIME),	304
Lord's triumph, the (See TRIUMPH),	248
Lost sheep, the (See SHEEP),	315
Love and hate,	300
Love for God's Word,	300
what is it?	300
what degree of it should we have?	300
why should we love it?	300
how should we show our love to it?	301
what results will follow our love of it?.	301
MAJESTY and condescension of God, the (See GOD),	210

	PAGE
Majesty and condescension of God, the,	379
Majesty of God in creation, the,	128
the glorious vesture of the Lord,	128
the splendid palace of the Lord,	129
the sublime chariot of the Lord,	129
the wonderful messengers of the Lord,	129
the firm footstool of the Lord,	129
Man,	415
Man a wonderful creation of God,	384
man is a creation of God,	384
man is a wonderful creation of God,	384
therefore, man should celebrate the praise of his Creator,	386
Man blessing God, God blessing man, and (See BLESSING),	120
Man, the blessedness of the Divinely-instructed (See BLESSEDNESS),	76
Man, the insignificance and greatness of,	414
the insignificance of human life,	414
human life is unsubstantial,	414
human life is transitory,	415
the greatness of human life,	415
revealed by the regard of God for man,	415
Man, the mighty helper of (See HELPER),	20
Man, the vanity of, apart from his immortality (See VANITY),	27
Man's remembrance of the Lord's benefits (See BENEFITS),	122
Mean, the golden,	198
such circumstances will arise as to need and justify favour and loans,	198
that man is happy who is able wisely to afford those favours and loans,	199
that man is happy who can do good and no evil by his favours and loans,	199
Melchizedek, the order of,	179
Christ is a priest after,	179
that order was unique, righteous,	179
peaceful, royal, superior,	179
Christ's appointment to this priesthood is Divine,	180
Memory of the righteous, the stability and,	199
Men, a serious word for young (See WORD),	256
Mercy and man's frailty, God's (See CONTRAST),	126
Mercy in God and in creation,	362
in the Divine being and character,	362
in the Divine work in creation,	362
Mercy in human redemption and provision,	364
the mercy of God in redemption,	364
the mercy of God in provision,	365
Mercy in the revolutions of providence,	363
in the judgments upon Egypt,	363
in the destruction of tyrannical kings,	363
in the history of Israel,	364
Mercy of God in the afflictions of man, the,	125
Mercy of God solicited, the,	47
Mercy, the Divine,	243
the nature of,	244

	PAGE
the objects and manifestation of,	244
the recognition of,	244
Mercy, the greatness of God's,	168
this is seen in the blessings of daily life,	169
in the grand end for which it is manifested,	169
in the means by which it seeks to accomplish this end,	169
in the multitudes to whom it extends,	169
Mercy, the infinity, expressions, and objects of the Divine,	123
the infinity of the Divine mercy,	123
the expressions of the Divine mercy,	123
in His vindication of the oppressed,	123
in His general dealings with His people,	123
in the long delay of His anger,	123
in the transient duration of His anger,	123
in the forgiveness of sins,	124
in His fatherly compassion,	124
in His fatherly consideration,	124
in the revelation which He made to His people,	124
the objects of the Divine mercy,	124
Militant people of God, the,	460
the true spirit of,	460
the trusty weapon of,	460
the Divine warrant of,	461
the grand design of,	461
Mindful of man, God,	223
why is God mindful of man?	223
when and how is God mindful of man?	224
for what purpose is God mindful of man?	224
Ministers of the godly, the angelic,	54
are commissioned by God,	55
exercise their ministry for the godly as individuals,	55
only when the godly are in their true path,	55
always when the godly are in their true path,	56
by means of the exercise of their ministry the godly are enabled to surmount all the hindrances and conquer all the foes that beset their way,	56
Misery, expostulation from the depth of,	4
the Psalmist's extreme distress,	4
his misconception of God,	5
his nearness to death,	5
his belief that there are duties and privileges the discharge and enjoyment of which are limited to the present life,	5
his faith in God,	5
Misery, prayer from the depth of,	1
a great depth of affliction,	1
the Psalmist's troubles were spiritual,	1
his troubles were many,	2
were bringing him speedily to death,	2
isolated him from human society,	2
were from the hand of God,	3

	PAGE
were an expression of the wrath of God,	3
a great urgency of prayer,	3
his prayer was directed to God,	3
earnest and unceasing,	4
Misery to exultation, stages from (See STAGES),	157
Misrepresentation, the godly under,	317
the godly are not exempt from misrepresentation,	317
are distressed by misrepresentation,	317
should cry to God in misrepresentation,	317
God clears the godly from misrepresentation,	317
Morning prayer (See PRAYER),	310
Motherhood, its blessings and responsibilities,	212
children are the subject of fond and prayerful desire,	212
children are a mother's joy,	213
children are a mother's care,	213
children are Divine gifts,	213
Motive for persevering prayer, the,	230
this motive reveals God's condescension and anxiety to hear,	230
the determination based upon this motive,	230
the Divine intention that is suggested by the ground of this motive and the warrant of this determination,	230
NATIONS, the Divine government of (See GOVERNMENT),	207
Nature and advantages of true piety, the (See PIETY),	192
Nature and power of faith, the (See FAITH),	237
Nature, God in (See GOD),	118
Nature, the purpose of, and the goodness of nature's God,	188
the purpose of nature is to be remembered,	188
why? That we may have perpetual evidence of the goodness of God,	188
Nature's beauty and the righteousness of nature's God,	187
nature is beautiful,	187
nature's God is righteous,	187
nature is beautiful as the expression of the righteousness of God,	187
Near unto the Lord, a people,	455
Nearness and man's, God's,	311
Need, the, succour, and triumph of the soul (See SOUL),	201
Needful prayer, a (See PRAYER),	389
Nightly occupations of the godly, the (See OCCUPATIONS),	279
Noble people and a noble service, a,	204
the servants of God are a noble people,	204
they realise the noblest ideal of life,	204
have the noblest Master,	204
yield to the noblest claims,	204
have the noblest warrant for their service,	204
enjoy the noblest rewards,	204

xviii INDEX.

	PAGE
God's service is a noble service,	204
in the dignity of its sphere,	205
in the motive from which it springs,	205
in the instruments by which it is accomplished,	205
in the freedom of its consecration,	205
in the uses which it serves,	205
Numeration, an all-important,	46
the teacher,	46
the pupils,	47
the lesson,	47
the end,	47
OBEDIENCE, the blessings of (See BLESSINGS),	279
Obedient and the apostate contrasted, the,	334
the obedient are sustained by a consciousness of personal rectitude,	334
enjoy the Divine aid and blessings,	334
the apostates will be certainly punished,	334
Object, obligation, and expression of worship, the,	89
Obstacles are removed, why?	217
because of the omnipotent presence of the Lord,	217
covenant presence of the Lord,	217
merciful presence of the Lord,	217
righteous presence of the Lord,	217
Obstacles, the removal of,	216
antagonisms are quelled,	216
boundaries are removed,	216
difficulties are overcome,	217
Occupations of the godly, the nightly,	279
the duties of the night,	279
how they are to be performed,	279
why they are to be performed,	279
prepare us for the exercise of daily duties,	279
Omnipresence, God's,	381
He is personally present everywhere,	381
influentially present everywhere,	382
intelligently present everywhere,	382
His presence is everywhere realised by the godly soul,	382
Omnipresence of God, the, and its impressions upon man,	383
endeavour to realise God's omnipresence,	383
trace the impressions which it ought to produce on us,	384
Opportunity, man's extremity, God's,	245
Order of Melchizedek, the (See MELCHIZEDEK),	179
Orthodoxy,	288
what it implies,	288
what it consists in,	288
the result of,	289
PALM-TREE an analogue of the righteous, the,	68
in its resolute upward growth,	68
in its growth despite of hindrances,	68
in its perennial verdure,	68
in its fruitfulness,	69
Pardon with punishment,	102

	PAGE
forgiveness is the undisturbed communication of the love of God to sinful man,	102
such pardon does necessarily sweep away the one true penalty of sin,	102
yet leaves many penalties unremoved,	103
pardoning love so modifies the punishment that it becomes an occasion for thankfulness,	103
Passages from the history of a rebellious people (See HISTORY),	155
Pattern prayer, a (See PRAYER),	174
Patriot, the hope of a distressed (See HOPE),	113
Patriot, the lament of a distressed (See LAMENT),	111
Peace,	313
a qualification,	313
a process,	313
the result,	314
Peace and prosperity,	327
should be subjects of earnest prayer,	327
are correlative blessings,	327
are necessary for the cultivation of fraternal intercourse and affection,	327
should be sought for the sake of the Church of God,	328
People and a noble service, a noble (See NOBLE),	204
People and pleasure of the Lord, the,	458
People, a picture of a happy (See PICTURE),	418
People, characteristics of the blessed (See CHARACTERISTICS),	148
People near unto the Lord, a,	455
People of God, the blessedness of the (See BLESSEDNESS),	13
People of God, the jubilant (See JUBILANT),	456
People of God, the militant (See MILITANT),	460
People, the character and portion of God's,	95
People, the happy,	422
Persecution and a glorious emancipation, a cruel,	145
Israel persecuted in Egypt,	145
the root and manner of the persecution,	145
Israel emancipated from Egypt,	145
by human instruments,	145
by overcoming persistent resistance,	145
in favourable circumstances,	146
Perseverance,	270
steady,	270
rapid,	270
shameless,	270
Divinely assisted,	270
Personal and family piety (See PIETY),	247
Personal religion (See RELIGION),	252
Perversity, a sad picture of human,	154
despising the choicest inheritance,	154
disbelieving the best authenticated word,	154
murmuring against the Divine arrangements,	154

	PAGE
disobeying the commands of the Lord,	154
receiving deserved punishment,	154
entailing misery upon their posterity,	154
Petitions, the three,	47
for visible results from the work,	47
for the stability of the work,	48
for the succession of the work,	48
Philosophy of death, the (See DEATH),	437
Picture of a happy people, a	418
a noble offspring,	418
secular prosperity,	418
settled peace,	419
flowing from the favour of God,	419
Picture of a pious home, a (See HOME),	107
Picture of human perversity, a sad (See PERVERSITY),	154
Piety, personal and family,	247
piety is sadly wanting,	247
the want of piety is supplied,	247
piety must be personally appropriated,	247
piety is appropriated to be diffused,	248
piety alone will make home happy,	248
a happy home is a miniature of and a nursery for heaven,	248
Piety, the nature and advantages of true,	192
Piety, the old age of (See AGE),	70
Pilgrimage and the heavenly songs, the earthly,	278
God's people are on a pilgrimage,	278
delightful provisions are made for them on their pilgrimage,	278
Pilgrimage, Divine blessings in human (See BLESSINGS),	146
Pilgrims, strangers and (See STRANGERS),	265
Pitiable, the commendable, and the reprehensible, the, in the troubled life of a godly man (See LIFE),	170
Plea, an all-prevailing,	292
the plea,	292
the prayer based upon this plea,	292
the sources of the Psalmist's information as to both plea and prayer,	292
Pleasure of the Lord, the people and,	458
Portion, the soul's,	280
what it is,	280
how it is attained,	280
on what grounds it is given,	280
for what purpose it is given,	280
Power, the purpose of the revelation of God's (See REVELATION),	199
Practice, preaching and (See PREACHING),	275
Praise,	183
the true object of worship,	183
the true character of worship,	184
the true spirit of worship,	184
Praise, a psalm of universal,	104
the reasons of praise to the Lord,	104
the extent of praise to the Lord,	105
the character of praise to the Lord,	105
Praise, a summons to universal,	455
aspects of God's revelation of Himself;	

	PAGE
adapted to persons of all ranks and of the most varied duties,	455
adapted to persons of all ages,	455
fitted to inspire the praises of persons of all ranks and ages,	455
Praise, constant,	313
is due to God for the constancy of His judgments,	313
the beneficence of His judgments,	313
the clearness of His judgments,	313
the help He vouchsafes to keep His judgments,	313
the forgiveness He offers where we have broken His judgments,	313
Praise, eternal (See ETERNAL),	193
Praise from excellent society and for excellent reasons,	447
praise from excellent society,	447
they have a clearer knowledge of God,	447
they have a closer relation to God,	447
they have richer blessings from God,	447
praise for excellent reasons,	447
for the blessings of His providence,	447
for His agency in nature,	448
for the blessings of His revelation,	448
Praise in the heavens, God's,	452
by heavenly beings,	452
the praise which they offer to God is voluntary, constant, and thorough,	452
by heavenly bodies,	452
they are summoned to praise God because they were created by Him,	452
they are sustained by Him,	452
they are governed by Him,	452
the interest of godly men in God's praise in the heavens,	453
Praise of God, the good man's celebration of the,	61
the ground of this exercise,	61
the manner of this exercise,	62
the seasons of this exercise,	63
the excellence of this exercise,	63
Praise of the Divine goodness, the (See GOODNESS),	425
Praise of the Divine greatness, the,	423
the reasons of the Divine praise,	423
God is great in His deeds,	423
God is great in His majesty,	423
God is great in His goodness,	423
God is great in His righteousness,	423
the characteristics of the Divine praise,	423
it is constant, perpetual,	423
fervent and songful,	424
Praise of the Divine reign, the (See REIGN),	429
Praise of the Divine relation to different characters, the (See RELATION),	431
Praise of the Lord, the,	130
the Lord should be praised with the soul,	130
because of His attributes,	130
because of His work in creation,	130
both for what He reveals and what He conceals of Himself,	130
he is best qualified for this service "whose God is the Lord,"	130

	PAGE		PAGE
Praise of the Lord, the glorious reign and (See REIGN),	127	Prayer and confidence, complaint (See COMPLAINT),	172
Praise of time, the,	424	Prayer, an earnest, and an immediate answer,	376
as the decree of God,	424	the earnestness of his prayer,	376
as expressing the resolution and work of Christ's Church,	424	the effectual relief he gained,	376
Praise on the earth, God's,	453	the force of his example upon other minds,	377
the variety of,	453	Prayer, attributes and advantages of acceptable,	434
the Psalmist summons the inorganic creation to praise Him,	453	some attributes of acceptable prayer,	434
the Psalmist summons the vegetable creation to praise Him,	453	sincerity, reverence, faith,	434
the Psalmist summons the animal creation to praise Him,	453	some advantages of acceptable prayer,	434
the Psalmist summons the rational creation to praise Him,	454	the realisation of God's presence,	434
the universality of,	454	the fulfilment of their desires,	434
universal praise is God's right,	454	the attainment of His salvation,	434
the good man's desire,	454	Prayer, creation a plea in (See CREATION),	285
a fact which will be realised in the future,	454	Prayer, duty, law,	254
the rationality of,	454	Prayer, effectual, fervent, and believing,	309
it is manifestly and sublimely reasonable,	454	its object,	309
Praise the Lord, incitements to (See INCITEMENTS),	358	its reasons,	309
Praise, the subjects and expressions of,	463	its petitions,	310
Praise, the subjects and seasons of,	64	its characteristics,	310
the subjects of praise,	64	its warrants,	310
the loving-kindness of God,	64	its resolutions,	310
the faithfulness of God,	65	its basis,	310
the seasons of praise,	65	Prayer, encouragements for	231
in the morning,	65	pray because God is the Lord,	231
in the evening,	65	the Lord is our God,	231
Praise to God, the excellence of,	439	The Lord is gracious,	231
it is excellent in itself,	439	the Lord is righteous,	232
it is good,	439	our God is merciful,	232
pleasant and comely,	440	Prayer for grace and guidance, a good man's,	410
it is excellent in its reasons,	440	the Psalmist prays for God's distinguishing favour as a God of grace,	410
His relation to His Church,	440	God's daily guidance as a God of Providence,	410
His relation to troubled souls,	440	the constant acceptance of his devotions as a prayer-hearing God,	411
His relation to heavenly hosts,	440	Prayer from the depth of misery (See MISERY),	1
His retributive relation to men,	441	Prayer in trouble, and confidence in prayer, trouble in life (See TROUBLE),	392
Praise, trust and (See TRUST),	435	Prayer, its object and its value,	229
Praise, universal,	464	characteristics of,	229
the grand prerogative of God,	464	the object of,	229
the precious privilege of man,	465	the value of,	229
the fervent desire of the good,	465	Prayer, morning,	310
Praising Him, the providence and pleasure of God a reason for (See PROVIDENCE),	444	the Bible speaks much of,	310
Prayer,	306	morning is the most favourable time for,	310
the character of,	306	morning is the time God demands for,	311
the matter of,	306	morning is the most appropriate time for,	311
the manner of,	306	Prayer of a distressed servant of God, the,	408
the plea to be used in,	306	the blessings which are sought,	408
the purpose which should sustain,	306	the loving-kindness of God,	408
Prayer, a needful,	389	deliverance from distresses,	408
the need for such a prayer as this,	389	inward and spiritual blessings,	408
the manner in which such a prayer as this receives its answer,	390	the grounds upon which they are sought,	409
Prayer, a pattern,	174		
true in its direction,	174		
personal in its aim,	174		
submissive in its spirit,	174		
powerful in its plea,	174		

INDEX.

	PAGE
the sore needs of the Psalmist,	409
his personal relations to God,	409
the urgency with which they are sought,	410
Prayer of the godly for deliverance from enemies, a (See DELIVERANCE),	416
Prayer of the godly man from the depths of distress,	399
a picture of deep distress,	399
the persecution of his enemies,	399
the failure of human help,	399
the depression of his circumstances and condition,	400
a prayer of strong confidence,	400
God's accessibleness to him,	400
God's interest in him,	400
God's knowledge of him,	400
God's protection of him,	400
from this basis of faith the prayer rises,	400
Prayer of the upright, a,	389
for Divine examination,	389
for entire freedom from evil,	389
for Divine guidance in the way of righteousness,	389
Prayer preferred, the wicked way within us, and the,	391
Prayer, special,	230
the time for,	230
the subjects of,	231
the manner of,	231
Prayer, the motive for persevering (See MOTIVE),	230
Preaching and practice,	275
the Psalmist's prayer,	275
the Psalmist's purpose,	275
the Psalmist's consolation,	275
Preciousness and number of God's thoughts, the (See THOUGHTS),	386
Privilege and security of the good, the,	332
it is the privilege of the good to trust in the Lord,	332
it is the security of the good to be guarded by His presence,	332
their security is perpetual,	333
Privileges of the godly, the glorious,	57
some features in the character of the godly,	57
love to God,	57
knowledge of God,	58
prayer to God,	58
some of the privileges of the godly,	58
deliverance from danger,	58
exaltation and consequent safety,	58
answers to prayer,	58
the presence of God in trouble,	59
the conference of distinguished honours,	59
satisfaction with the duration of life,	59
full salvation,	59
Profession, religious,	296
should be of the most binding character,	296
the result of serious thought,	297
made with a free but resolute will,	297
faithfully and consistently kept,	297
Profundis, de,	342

VOL. II.

	PAGE
a consciousness of sin sinks the soul into depths of penitential sorrow,	342
from the depths of penitential sorrow the soul cries earnestly for pardon,	342
the penitential soul seeks pardon in order to serve God acceptably,	342
Progress, Christian,	271
the way of, is Divinely revealed,	271
is possible only under certain definite conditions,	271
is impossible without Divine assistance,	272
Promiser, the faithful,	141
the Lord's remembrance of His promises,	142
the perpetuity of His promises,	142
the confirmation of His promises,	142
the recipients of His promises,	142
the fulfilment of His promises,	143
Proper attitude of the righteous towards the ungodly, the (See ATTITUDE),	306
Prosperity and its qualifications,	196
what is prosperity?	196
what is calculated to produce it?	196
what objections can be urged against all this?,	197
Prosperity of the wicked, the temporal,	66
Prosperity, peace and (See PEACE),	327
Protection, Divine,	323
is ample and efficient,	323
shields from the most open assaults,	323
guards from the effects of secret treachery,	324
is a defence against every evil,	324
is realised amid the active duties of life,	324
overshadows the rest of home,	324
is unremitting,	324
Protection of God, the day of battle and the (See BATTLE),	394
Protection, the Divine,	302
where it is revealed,	302
the comfort this revelation brings,	302
Providence and pleasure of God a reason for praising Him, the,	444
the providence of God,	444
presiding over the elements,	444
creating vegetation,	444
providing for His creatures,	444
the pleasure of God,	444
is not in those who trust in their own resources,	444
is in those who trust in Him,	445
the praise of God,	445
a response for Divine favours,	445
an expression of gratitude for Divine favours,	445
Providence, mercy in the revolutions of (See MERCY),	363
Providential inequalities readjusted (See INEQUALITIES),	266
Provisions, Divine	218
are the result of the Divine presence,	218
contemplate real need,	218
come in unexpected forms,	218

c

	PAGE
flow with abounding fulness,	218
are constantly permanent,	218
Psalm of universal praise, a (See PRAISE),	104
Punishment, pardon with (See PARDON),	102
Purpose of the revelation of God's power, the (See REVELATION),	190
QUALIFICATIONS, prosperity and its (See PROSPERITY),	196
REAPING, sowing and (See SOWING),	336
Recognition of God's goodness, man's,	242
God's goodness is manifested to meet man's need,	242
shall be universally recognised,	243
such recognition will characterise the redeemed and glorified Church for ever,	243
Recollection and an encouraging anticipation, a devout resolution, grateful (See RESOLUTION),	374
Recollections, precious yet sorrowful,	367
of lost privileges,	367
their country,	367
their freedom,	368
their religious privileges,	368
of privileges which they had lost by reason of their non-appreciation of them,	368
Redeemed, the way of the,	160
Redemption and provision, mercy in human (See MERCY),	364
Redemption,	191
its sure foundations,	192
and its awful sanctions,	192
the hope of (See HOPE),	343
Refreshing Himself, Christ,	182
the Divine refreshment,	182
the consequence of that refreshment,	182
Refuge of the distressed, Jehovah the,	321
the soul is often in circumstances of distress,	322
in every time of distress Jehovah is an available refuge,	322
the most signal manifestations of Divine help are realised in the sanctuary,	322
the soul is delivered from distress only as it turns to Jehovah,	323
Reign and praise of the Lord, the glorious,	127
the reign of the Lord,	127
its stability,	127
its majesty,	127
its universality,	127
the praise of the Lord,	127
by holy angels,	127
by the unintelligent creation,	127
by redeemed men,	128
Reign of God, the,	91
the subjects of the Divine government,	91

	PAGE
certain characters which mark his administration,	92
the demand upon our grateful joy,	92
Reign, the praise of the Divine,	429
the characteristics of the Lord's,	429
glorious,	429
mighty,	429
perpetual,	429
the conversation on His reign,	429
delight in His reign,	429
praise of His reign,	429
desire for the extension of His reign,	429
Rejoicing of the good man in the government of God, the (See GOVERNMENT),	66
Relation to different characters, the praise of the Divine,	431
His relation to the weak and the burdened,	431
the dependent,	431
the prayerful,	432
His saints,	432
the wicked,	432
His righteousness and kindness in all His relations,	433
His praise because of all His relations,	433
Relationships, Divine,	241
a relationship of obedience yet friendship,	241
of friendship yet obedience,	242
must receive a formal and public acknowledgment,	242
Relief which the Gospel affords, the sufferings of God's servants, and the (See SUFFERING),	398
Religion, personal,	252
consists in the acknowledgment of a personal God,	252
acknowledgment of a personal God accessible to man,	252
apprehension of a personal God,	252
enjoyment of a Divine revelation,	253
personal sacrifices,	253
devout worship,	253
Religion, the characteristics and blessedness of true,	194
the characteristics of true religion,	194
fear of the Lord,	194
delight in God's commandments,	194
Divine praise,	194
the blessedness of true religion,	194
Religion, the posthumous results of,	195
what the text presupposes,	195
what the text declares,	195
what the text implies,	196
Religious fellowship (See FELLOWSHIP),	286
Religious gladness,	65
Religious profession (See PROFESSION),	296
Remedy, a danger and its (See DANGER),	304
Remembrance of the Lord's benefits, man's (See BENEFITS),	122
Removal of obstacles, the (See OBSTACLES),	216
Removed, why obstacles are (See OBSTACLES),	217

	PAGE
Renewal of the face of the earth an illustration of the renewal of the soul, the,	137
the renewal of the face of the earth, succeeds to the dreary and seemingly dead state of nature in winter,	137
is marked by life and freshness,	137
is very gradual,	137
is irresistible,	137
is initiatory to a glorious season of maturity,	137
Requital, spiritual,	238
God requites His saints for their prayers,	239
His requital is ample,	239
should be reciprocated by man's requital of God's love,	239
Resignation, its duties and usefulness,	287
resignation to the Divine will,	287
presupposes and includes prayer for comfort and support,	288
prayer for life is consistent with,	288
prolonged life is desired for the twofold influence that it may wield,	288
Resolution, a devout, grateful recollection, and an encouraging anticipation,	374
a devout resolution,	374
to praise God in the most excellent manner,	374
for the most excellent reasons,	375
a grateful recollection,	375
of speedy and gracious answers to prayer,	375
an encouraging anticipation,	375
Resolutions, good,	255
depend on the presence of God for their fulfilment,	255
have respect to Divine law,	256
their fulfilment depends on the right state of the heart and life,	256
and should be followed by gratitude,	256
Response, a godless inquiry and a godly (See INQUIRY),	220
Responsibility towards the young, our, a Sunday-school sermon,	116
Rest, the soul's return to its,	233
this rest is its rightful heritage,	233
man's lost rest may be regained,	234
Restored, the harmony of creation (See HARMONY),	138
Results of religion, the posthumous (See RELIGION),	195
Revelation of God's power, the purpose of the,	190
God's people have acquired the heritage of the heathen,	190
this acquisition is the result of Divine power,	190
and is for the benefit of humanity at large,	190
Revelation of the Lord, creation a,	130
displays His absolute power,	130
over the waters,	130
over the earth,	131
displays His delight in beauty,	131

	PAGE
His great law of service,	132
His regard for all His creatures,	132
His supreme regard for man,	132
Revival of the Church, a, and symptoms which precede it,	115
Revolutions, terrestrial,	165
revolutions in countries,	165
revolutions in human life,	166
the salutary impression of such,	166
Retribution,	373
an important feature of the Divine government of the world,	373
a cry for retribution,	373
an illustration of the nature of,	373
the desire for retribution is prone to develop into vindictiveness towards those who have injured us,	374
Reward of the wicked, the,	53
Riches, the Bible better than (See BIBLE),	284
Righteous, the palm-tree an analogue of the (See PALM),	68
Righteous, the stability and memory of the,	199
Road, the heavenly,	280
man is naturally in the wrong way,	280
reflection will lead men into the right way,	280
the choice of the right way must be followed by a deliberate change of habit,	281
the right way is to be pursued with alacrity,	281
this alacrity is not to be lessened by the dangers and privations of the road,	281
Royal army, the,	177
SACRED enclosure, the (See ENCLOSURE),	249
Sacrifices, spiritual,	298
a recognition of the spiritual priesthood of believers,	298
spiritual priests must have spiritual preparation,	298
must offer, and can only offer, spiritual sacrifices,	298
spiritual offerings must be free-will offerings,	299
free-will offerings are most acceptable to God,	299
Saints, the communion of (See COMMUNION),	281
Salvation,	274
the outcome of the Divine mercies,	274
not a human effort, but a Divine visitation,	274
the subject of Divine promise,	274
a witness to the steadfastness of the Divine word,	275
Salvation, God's,	314
its nature,	314
its conditions,	314
characteristics of the prayer for it,	315
its obligations,	315
Salvation, man's adversity and God's (See ADVERSITY),	289

	PAGE
Sanctuary, blessings on the,	349
the Temple is called the rest of God,	349
the Temple was incomplete without the ark,	349
the other blessings which are asked for,	350
School sermon, a Sunday,	116
Sarcasm the cause of pungent suffering, a common weapon of the enemies of God,	329
the cause of pungent suffering to His people,	330
this suffering is counterbalanced by the consolations of the Divine mercy,	330
Seamen and the Sovereign of the sea, distressed,	163
God's sovereignty over the sea,	163
man's impotency when the sea rebels against him,	163
man's resource when the sea rebels against him,	164
God's answer to man's cry,	164
man's obligation for God's interposition,	164
Seasons of praise, the subjects and,	64
Seasons, the uses of the (See USES),	132
Security of the godly, the inviolable,	51
as effected by God,	51
its tenderness and effectiveness,	51
as gloriously complete,	51
safe from all perils,	51
safe at all times,	52
raised above the fear of danger,	52
as conditionated by trust in God,	53
Security of the good, the privilege and (See PRIVILEGE),	332
Self-retributive character of slander, the (See SLANDER),	317
Separation and consistency,	302
the necessity of separation from evil-doers,	302
the duty of keeping God's commandments,	303
the importance of prompt resolution,	303
Serious word for young men, a (See WORD),	256
Sermon, a Sunday-school,	116
Servant of God, the,	272
God qualifies His servants,	272
those whom God qualifies for, He consecrates to His service,	272
those whom He consecrates He supports by special encouragements,	273
those whom He qualifies, consecrates, and encourages are expected to exhibit certain traits,	273
Service, a noble people and a noble (See NOBLE),	204
Service, life as the sphere of Divine,	227
the features of Divine service,	228
the sphere of Divine service,	228
exceptions to Divine service,	228
Shadow, human life a,	416
Sheep, the lost,	315
the wandering,	315
the search,	316

	PAGE
the recollection,	316
Sickness and Divine healing, human,	162
human sickness,	162
in its cause and effect,	162
Divine healing,	162
effected in answer to prayer,	162
effected with supreme ease,	162
demanding grateful acknowledgment,	163
Sin and folly of being unhappy, the (See UNHAPPY),	105
Sin estimated by the light of heaven,	40
Sin, human frailty the result of human (See FRAILTY),	37
Sin in its progress, pollution, and punishment,	156
sin in its progress,	156
disobedience,	156
evil associations,	156
idolatry,	156
offering human sacrifices,	156
sin in its pollution,	157
sin in its punishment,	157
punishment was long delayed,	157
an expression of Divine anger,	157
corresponded with the sin,	157
Sin in its root, expressions, and punishments,	151
in its root—forgetfulness of God,	151
in its expressions,	151
as regards the Divine provision,	151
as regards the Divinely-appointed leaders,	151
as regards the Divine Person,	151
in its punishments,	152
punishment corresponding with sin,	152
punishment averted by intercession,	152
Sin, the Lord's goodness and man's (See GOODNESS),	149
Sinners entreated to hear God's voice,	86
Sins of men, the covenant of God and the (See COVENANT),	21
Slander,	108, 170
Slander, the self-retributive character of,	317
the work of slander,	317
the retribution of slander,	318
Solicitude on behalf of sons and daughters,	419
the objects of this solicitude,	419
our sons,	419
our daughters,	420
the subjects of this solicitude,	421
Song, encouragements to holy,	64
Song of the Builders, the (See BUILDERS),	352
Songs in a strange land,	372
Songs in exile, the difficulty of singing,	371
what the world is to the Christian,	371
whence arises the difficulty of singing the Lord's song in a world like this,	372
what answer shall be returned to the inquiry—"How shall we sing?" &c.,	372
Songs of degrees,	316
Song, the earthly pilgrimage and the heavenly (See PILGRIMAGE),	278

	PAGE
Sons and daughters, solicitude on behalf of (See SOLICITUDE),	419
Sorrowful recollections, precious yet (See RECOLLECTIONS),	367
Sorrows of the soul and the knowledge of God, the,	401
a figure indicating great sorrow,	401
a fact affording great consolation,	402
Soul, the home of the (See HOME),	35
Soul, the need, succour, and triumph of the,	201
Soul's return to its rest, the (See REST),	233
Souls, the duty of caring for,	402
Sound, the blessedness of knowing the joyful,	16
what the Gospel is,	16
what it demands,	16
what it ensures,	16
Sovereign of the sea, distressed seamen and the (See SEAMEN),	163
Sovereignty of Christ, the	174
Christ reigns by Divine appointment,	175
by Divine right,	175
by a devout acknowledgment,	175
over a disputed empire,	175
by the enforced service of His foes,	175
will reign over an undisputed universe,	176
Sovereignty of God, examples of the holy, and the becoming worship of His people (See EXAMPLES),	101
Sowing and reaping,	336
the time of sowing is often attended with anxiety and sorrow,	336
the time of reaping is one of inexpressible joy,	336
Special prayer (See PRAYER),	230
Spirit, the wicked (See WICKED),	202
Spiritual joys (See JOYS),	140
Spiritual requital (See REQUITAL),	238
Spiritual sacrifices (See SACRIFICES),	298
Spiritual warfare (See WARFARE),	246
Stability and memory of the righteous, the,	199
Stages from misery to exultation,	157
misery leading to a cry for mercy,	158
a cry for mercy securing the Divine regard,	158
the Divine regard securing relief from trouble,	158
relief from trouble awakening prayer for complete salvation,	158
Strangers and pilgrims,	265
the stranger,	265
the stranger's prayer,	266
the stranger's longing,	266
Strength in weakness,	269
the Psalmist's case,	269
the Psalmist's prayer,	269
the Psalmist's plea,	269
Strength of God an encouragement to His people to trust in Him, the	11
the strength of God is manifested in His complete control over nature,	11
manifested in His subjugation of His foes,	12

	PAGE
ever exercised in harmony with righteousness, mercy, and truth,	12
an encouragement to trust Him,	13
Subjects and expressions of praise, the (See PRAISE),	463
Subjects and seasons of praise, the	64
Subjects, the character, privileges, and duty of the King's (See CHARACTER),	94
Succour and triumph of the soul, the need,	201
Suffering, sarcasm the cause of pungent (See SARCASM),	329
Sufferings of God's servants, the, and the relief which the Gospel affords,	398
God's most favoured servants have often been exposed to the utmost extremity and danger,	398
in the most hopeless circumstances the Gospel affords relief,	399
in proportion to the safety of God's children must be the misery of His enemies,	399
Summons to holy work, the,	79
review a few characteristics of the evil-doers,	79
consider the course which God has taken with these evil-doers, and what is involved in the appeal here uttered,	80
the response which is made to this appeal,	80
Summons to universal praise, a (See PRAISE),	455
Superior understanding (See UNDERSTANDING),	295
Support, universal dependence and Divine (See DEPENDENCE),	433
Supremacy of the Lord in the Church and the state,	99
His supremacy in the Church,	99
He dwells there,	99
He is supreme there,	99
His supremacy in the state,	99
characterised by power,	100
and righteousness,	100
His supremacy is a reason for worship,	100
Supremely great, the (See GREAT),	443
Surprises, historical,	143
a famine driving the people from the land promised to them, yet contributing to their possession of it,	143
a slave becomes the saviour of a country and of the chosen people,	143
a prisoner made the ruler over the land,	144
a subject people growing stronger than a sovereign people,	144
Symptoms which precede it, a revival of the Church, and,	115
TEMPLE and the kingdom, the,	215
Tenco et teneor,	267
how do we keep God's testimonies?.	267
how do God's testimonies keep us? .	267
Terrestrial revolutions (See REVOLUTIONS),	165

INDEX.

	PAGE
Testimonies a ground of joy, God's,	261
what the Psalmist did?	261
rejoiced in God's testimonies,	261
why he did it?	262
because of their suitability to his need,	262
because the greater covered the less,	262
Testimonies, the benefit of God's,	267
they are delights,	267
they are counsellors,	268
Testimony,	260
its subject,	260
its manner,	261
its reason,	261
Theme for joyous song, deliverance a (See DELIVERANCE),	335
Things and how to see them, wondrous (See WONDROUS),	264
Thoughts, the preciousness and number of God's,	386
the preciousness of them,	386
because of their originality,	386
their moral excellence,	386
their practicableness and utility,	387
their influence upon our thoughts,	387
their generosity,	387
the number of them,	387
the realisation of God's presence,	387
Three petitions, the (See PETITIONS),	47
Time and ours, the Lord's,	304
a time common to both to work,	304
a work common for both to do,	304
a time for God alone to work,	304
a work for God alone to do,	304
Time, the praise of (See PRAISE),	424
Travellers and their Divine Helper, distressed,	159
the distressed travellers,	159
through a pathless desert,	159
through a homeless desert,	159
through an inhospitable desert,	159
the all-sufficient Helper,	160
His help was granted in answer to prayer,	160
and was adequate to their need,	160
the manifest obligation,	160
to praise the Divine Helper,	160
Treatment of different classes of character, God's,	377
His treatment of the humble,	377
the proud,	377
His afflicted people,	378
His trustful people,	378
Trial, the conduct of a good man in a time of (See CONDUCT),	395
Trials of the godly, the,	318
uncongenial neighbours,	318
unrighteous contradictions,	318
Trials, the comforts of Christians under,	81
Triumph of the Christian life, the complete,	167
promoted by praise to God,	167
inasmuch as it honours God,	167
and strengthens faith,	167
promoted by consideration of the triumphs already achieved,	167
assured by God,	168

	PAGE
Triumph of the soul, the need, succour, and,	201
Triumph over tyranny, Christ's (See TYRANNY),	180
Triumph, the Lord's,	248
the personal triumph of Christ,	248
the triumphs of His Gospel in the human heart,	248
the triumphs of His Church in the world,	248
Trouble in life, prayer in trouble, and confidence in prayer,	392
trouble in life,	392
arising from enemies who were malignant,	392
confederate,	392
slanderous,	392
violent,	392
determined,	392
proud,	392
cunning,	392
prayer in trouble,	393
for preservation from enemies,	393
the overthrow of enemies,	393
confidence in prayer,	393
based upon his relation to God,	393
his ideas of God,	393
his experience of the protection of God,	393
his faith in the righteous rule of God,	393
True greatness (See GREATNESS),	309
Trust and praise,	435
the trust prohibited,	435
the trust encouraged,	436
the praise celebrated,	437
Trust, human and Divine,	246
man must trust,	246
whom should man trust?	246
who warrants that trust?	246
God offers Himself as the object of human trust,	246
Trust in God,	222
the nature of,	222
the grounds of,	223
those who,	223
the consequences of,	223
Truth of God, the eternal,	106
God is true,	106
in all generations,	107
Tyranny, Christ's triumph over,	180
all tyranny is the foe of Christ,	180
is subject to the wrath of Christ,	181
will be destroyed by Christ,	181
will be supplanted by Christ,	181
Tyranny of the wicked transient, the,	333
the rule of the wicked is tyrannical,	333
the tyranny of the wicked is transient,	333
the unchecked tyranny of the wicked would be a serious discouragement to the righteous,	333
UNBELIEF, a warning against (See WARNING),	84
Understanding, superior,	295
what in?	295
over whom?	295
through what power?	295
by what instrumentality?	295

with what results? . . . 295	what it implies, ... 235
Unhappy, the sin and folly of being, . 105	what it means, ... 236
God is happy, ... 105	where it takes place, . . . 236
angels are happy, . . . 105	Warfare, spiritual, . . . 246
forgiven men are happy, . . 105	danger, ... 246
we can only be unhappy by refusing pardon, ... 106	help, ... 247
	victory, ... 247
by refusing Christ, . . . 106	Warning against unbelief, a, . 84
by determining not to turn, . 106	the ensample of human sin, . 84
Union, Christian, ... 356	the ensample of Divine judgment, . 85
its nature, ... 356	the improvement to be made of these ensamples, ... 85
its importance, ... 356	
Unity, the excellence and beauty of fraternal, ... 354	Way of the redeemed, the, . . 160
	Way within us, the wicked, and the prayer preferred, . . . 391
its propriety, ... 354	
its comprehensiveness, . . 354	Ways, God's, though often inscrutable, are righteous, ... 92
its joyousness, ... 355	
its influence, ... 355	Ways, the two, ... 269
Universal praise (See PRAISE), . 464	there are two ways, . . . 269
Universal worship (See WORSHIP), . 206	these are open to man's deliberate choice, ... 269
Universe, the Lord and His (See LORD), 134	
Upright, a prayer of the (See PRAYER), 389	the false way is most natural to man, ... 269
Upright, the attributes of the, . 198	
the upright bend, . . . 198	to walk firmly in the true way Divine assistance is indispensable, . 269
yet they maintain their integrity, . 198	
Uses of the seasons, the, . . 132	continuance in the true way is conditional on the use of Divinely-appointed means, . . . 270
the uses of day, ... 133	
it is the season of work for man, . 133	
of retirement for wild beasts, . . 133	Weakness, strength in (See STRENGTH), 269
the uses of night, . . . 133	Wicked spirit, the, . . . 202
it is the season of rest for man, . 133	the character of the wicked, . . 202
of activity for wild beasts, . . 133	the inspection of the wicked, . . 203
the moral uses of the seasons, . . 134	the disappointment of the wicked, . 203
by them God teaches us, . . 134	the fate of the wicked, . . 203
the measurement of time, . . 134	Wicked, the desire of the (See DESIRE), 203
the preciousness of time, . . 134	Wicked, the insatiable voracity of the (See VORACITY), . . . 331
the fitness of certain times for certain duties, ... 134	
	Wicked, the poet's view of the, . 388
	the character of the wicked described, 388
VANITY of idols an incentive to praise the Lord God, the (See IDOLS), . 360	the end of the wicked predicted, . 388
	the companionship of the wicked avoided, ... 388
Vanity of man apart from his immortality, the, ... 27	
	Wicked, the reward of the, . . 53
the shortness of his life, . . 27	Wicked, the temporal prosperity of the, ... 66
the disorders and miseries of this world, 28	
the diseases of the body, . . 28	Willows, harps on the (See HARPS), . 369
the manual and mechanical labours, 28	Winter and its moral suggestions, . 449
the unsatisfactoriness of wealth, . 28	winter indicates the severity of God, 449
the unsatisfactoriness of knowledge, 29	suggests the retributiveness of the Divine arrangements, . . 449
the unsatisfactoriness of religion also, 29	
but this hypothesis is utterly false, . 30	some things which are peculiar to this season have special instruction for us, ... 449
Victory of the good, the foes and (See FOES), ... 57	
	is an emblem of old age, . . 450
View of the wicked, the poet's (See WICKED), ... 388	of the present state of the bodies of the departed, ... 450
Views of death, two, . . . 241	
Voice, sinners entreated to hear God's, 86	and of the present moral state of the world, ... 450
Voices of creation (See CREATION), . 135	
Voracity of the wicked, the insatiable, 331	Wondrous things, and how to see them, 264
the wicked are ever ready to devour the righteous, ... 331	man by himself cannot see wondrous things, ... 264
the Lord is the deliverer of the righteous, ... 331	there is a process by means of which man may see wondrous things, . 264
thanksgiving should be offered to the Lord for His deliverance, . . 331	when this process is complete wondrous things are seen in God's law, 264
	Word a lamp and a light, God's (See LIGHT), ... 295
WALKING before God, . . . 235	

	PAGE
Word a tried word and a loved word, God's,	308
Word exalted, God's,	376
Word for young men, a serious,	256
a serious question asked,	257
a satisfactory answer given,	257
sufficient reasons suggested,	257
Word, God's,	305
desired,	305
instructive,	306
wonderful,	306
kept,	306
Word, love for God's (See LOVE),	300
Word of God, the benefit and obligation of the	291
Word of God, the, its sphere and its service,	259
Word the heritage of His people, God's (See HERITAGE),	299
Word the object of reverence and joy, God's,	312
Word, the stability of God's, the rectitude of God's works, and	191
Word, the truth and endurance of God's,	312
God's word is based upon truth,	312
had its beginning in truth,	312
is true all through,	312
Work, the summons to holy (See SUMMONS),	79
Works and God's words, God's,	290
have immovable foundations,	290
continue,	291
are servants of the Divine faithfulness,	291
the heavens and the earth will some day cease to be; not so the promises,	291
Works and worship of the Lord, the,	139
the worship of the Divine Being,	139
the character of the Divine works,	139
the treatment of the Divine works,	140
the people of the Divine choice,	140
Works, forgetfulness of the Divine (See FORGETFULNESS),	152
Works of God, the, the subject of soul-satisfying search,	185

	PAGE
God's works are great,	185
should be the subject of study,	186
are promotive of soul-satisfaction,	186
Works, the rectitude of God's, and the stability of God's word,	191
World's most joyous day, the (See DAY),	87
Worship, an invitation to,	82
the method of worship,	82
joyfully,	82
readily,	83
gratefully,	83
reverently,	83
the motives of worship,	83
because Jehovah is supreme,	83
He is the creator and proprietor of all things,	83
because of His relations to His people,	84
Worship, church and congregational,	184
distinctions in worship,	184
places of worship,	184
manner of worship,	185
Worship of His people, examples of the holy sovereignty of God and the becoming (See EXAMPLES),	101
Worship of the Lord, the works and (See WORKS),	139
Worship, the highest,	11
is offered to God,	11
is offered by saints,	11
is reverent in spirit,	11
in it the presence of God is realised,	11
Worship, the joy of Divine (See JOY),	325
Worship, the object, obligation, and expression of,	89
Worship, universal,	206
God's name ought to be praised everywhere,	206
under all circumstances,	206
at all times,	206
Wretchedness and Divine compassion, human (See COMPASSION),	365
YOUNG, our responsibility towards the,	116
ZION a type of the Church,	353

INDEX TO AUTHORS QUOTED.

Very brief quotations are not indicated in this Index.

ADDISON, Joseph, 324, 424.
Alexander, J. A., 31.
Alford, Henry, 84, 129.
Allon, Henry, 462.
Amyraldus, 31.
Arvine, R., 85.
Augustine, 224.

BACON, L., 70.
Bailey, P. J., 60, 328, 465.
Bally, G., 75.
Barbauld, A. L., 39.
Barnes, Albert, 98, 114, 118, 238, 253, 256, 270, 281, 284, 312, 316, 318, 360, 374, 399, 419, 423, 432, 449.
Bayley, Emilius, 389.
Beecher, H. W., 95, 197, 213, 380.
Bevan, Ll.D., 369.
Bonar, Horatius, 44, 60, 105.
Bouchier, B., 74.
Boyle, Robert, 308.
Brooks, George, 353, 372, 379, 415, 455, 458.
Brown, J. Baldwin, 208.
Bruce, W. S., 424.
Buck, C., 385.
Burleigh, W. H., 389.
Burns, Jabez, 428, 437.
Bushnell, H., 134, 278.
Byron, Lord, 459.

CALVIN, John, 128, 380.
"Caravan and the Temple," the, 321, 328, 330, 333, 337, 342.
Carlyle, Thomas, 133, 319.
Chalmers, Thomas, 441.
Charnocke, Stephen, 32, 33, 100, 118, 380, 381.
"Christian Guardian," the, 416.
Clarke, Adam, 111, 257, 306, 312, 315, 340.
Clayton, George, 152.
Coleridge, S. T., 173.
Coley, Samuel, 210.

DALE, R. W., 227.
Darby, 3.
Dawson, W., 59.
Delitzsch, F., 460.
"Dictionary of Illustrations," 85.
D'Israeli, B., 177.

F——R, 122.
Finlayson, 238.
Fletcher, Joseph, 125.

GOADBY, J. J., 47.
Gray, Thomas, 111.
Griffin, R. A., 81.
Grindon, L. H., 38.
Gurnall, W., 109.
Guthrie, Thomas, 355.

HALL, John, 116.
Hall, Robert, 27, 81, 92, 430.
Hamilton, James, 31, 46.
Harmer, T., 329.
Havard, W., 319.
Hayman, Henry, 457.
Heber, Reginald, 90.
Hengstenberg, E. W., 48, 97, 151, 357, 409.
Henry, M., 59, 124, 156, 238, 270, 277, 306, 393.
Herbert, George, 359.
Hervey, A. C., 1.
Hibbard, F. G., 1.
"Homiletical Quarterly," the, 152, 411, 424.
Hood, E. P., 439.
Horsley, S., 114.
Horton, T., 79.
Howe, John, 7.

JENKINS, E. E., 236.

KEBLE, John, 332.

L., 93.
Lecky, W. E. H., 176, 178.
Liddon, H. P., 229, 248.
Lilley, W. O., 411.
Longfellow, H. W., 70.
Lovelace, 404.
L——s, 422.
Luther, M., 33, 34, 73, 355.

MACLAREN, A., 102, 180, 200, 240, 265, 352.
Mansel, H. L., 209.
Melville, H., 84.
Mill, J. S., 176.
Milton, John, 128, 131.
Moll, C. B., 204, 242, 284, 406.
Montgomery, J., 133, 345.
Moore, T., 112, 345, 351.

INDEX TO AUTHORS QUOTED.

Morris, A. J., 42, 235, 236.
M., W., 160.
N., 402.
Napoleon, 176, 182.
Newman, J. H., 385.

PARKER, Joseph, 73, 118, 135, 202, 221, 310, 442.
Pascal, B., 224.
Payson, E., 40, 86.
Peabody, 257.
Pearson, 225.
Perowne, J. J. S., 6, 71, 77, 82, 97, 99, 128, 138, 139, 142, 147, 148, 152, 158, 159, 165, 166, 170, 172, 194, 229, 344, 347, 354, 361, 367, 375, 379, 388, 392, 395, 396, 412, 413, 422, 451, 456, 461.
Plumptre, E. H., 210.
Pollok, R., 163.
"Preacher's Treasury," the, 356.
"Pulpit Analyst," the, 160.
Pulsford, J., 104, 121.
Punshon, W. M., 132, 349.

QUARLES, F., 160.

RAFFLES, T., 414.
Raleigh, A., 265.
Renan, E., 176.
Reynolds, H. R., 73, 79.
Robertson, F. W., 32, 108.
Ruskin, J., 131, 133, 445.
Rutherford, 192.

SAURIN, J., 382.
Sayer, J., 419.
Scott, W., 9.
Shakspeare, W., 110, 111, 117, 154, 170, 171, 172, 239, 317, 327, 330, 374, 415, 459.
"Skeletons of Sermons," 122.

"Sketches of Sermons," 93, 402.
Sleigh, W., 16, 149.
"Speaker's Commentary," the, 253, 284, 316.
Spenser, E., 55.
Spurgeon, C. H., 106, 108, 123, 439.
Stanley, A. P., 109, 237, 373.
Stewart, A., 227.
Stier, R., 250.
Strauss, 176.
Stuart, M., 118.
"Study," the, 115.

TENNYSON, A., 39, 228, 355.
Thodey, S., 345, 365, 371, 376, 383, 398, 410, 450, 463.
Thomson, J., 450.
Tillotson, J., 75.
Trapp, J., 341.
"Treasury of David," the, 64.

VAUGHAN, 183.
Vince, C., 194.

WALLACE, T., 391.
Waring, A. L., 344.
Watson, R., 75, 91.
Watts, I., 60, 138, 375, 437.
Wells, John, 64.
Wesley, C., 338.
Whitcomb, W. C., 356.
Wilberforce, S., 211.
Wileman, J., 115.
Wilkins, 443.
Wilson, G., 385.
Wythe, W. W., 376.

XAVIER, F., 58.

YOUNG, E., 369, 415, 418.
Young, J., 208, 219.

ERRATA.

Page 59a, line 51, *supply* "is" *before* "in."
,, 61, ,, 9, *for* "But" *read* "Both."
,, 61b, ,, 23, ,, "adduces" *read* "educes."
,, 72a, ,, 10, ,, "number" ,, "member."
,, 115a, ,, 2, ,, "our" ,, "one."
,, 359a, ,, 19, ,, "invite" ,, "incite."
,, 376b, ,, 1, ,, "transferred" ,, "transformed."
,, 386b, ,, 13, *delete* "is" *before* "drawn."
,, 389b, ,, 12, *for* "entranced" *read* "entrance."
,, 409a, ,, 54, ,, "Here" ,, "Hear."
,, 422a, ,, 24, ,, "omnipotence" *read* "omnipresence."
,, 437b, ,, 4, ,, "enemy is" ,, "enemies are."

ON THE
PSALMS.

PSALM LXXXVIII.
INTRODUCTION.

Superscription.—"*A Song or Psalm,*" i.e., combining the properties of both a Psalm and a song. "*For the sons of Korah,*" see Introduction to Psalm xlii. "The expression, 'To the Chief Musician,' amounts to a notice that we have before us a proper Church song." "*Upon Mahalath Leannoth.*" On "Mahalath," see Introduction to Psa. liii. "'*Leannoth*' is variously rendered, according as it is derived from ענה, *to suffer, be afflicted,* or from ענה, *to chant, sing.* Gesenius, De Wette, Dr. Davies, and others take the latter view; while Mudge, Hengstenberg, Alexander, and others take the former. Mudge translates, *to create dejection;* Alexander renders, *mahalath leannoth, concerning afflictive sickness;* Hengstenberg reads, *upon the distress of oppression.* The Septuagint (ἀποκριθῆναι) and the Vulgate (*respondendum*) indicate a *responsive song,* and Houbigant translates the words in question, *for the choirs that they may answer.* Many etymologists consider the primary idea of ענה, *to sing,* that of *answering.*

The tone of the Psalm in question, however, being decidedly that of *sadness and dejection,* it appears more probable that *leannoth* denotes the strictly elegiac character of the performance, and the whole title may read therefore, '*A Song or Psalm for the sons of Korah, to the chief musician upon the flutes* (or *the hollow instruments*) *to afflict* (or *cause dejection*) *a didactic Psalm of Heman, the Ezrahite.*'"—(F. G. Hibbard.) "*Maschil,*" an instruction, a didactic Psalm. "*Of Heman the Ezrahite.*" It is generally held that this Heman is the son of Joel, and grandson of Samuel the prophet, a Kohathite, one of the famous musicians of the time of David, who is several times spoken of in connection with Asaph and Ethan or Jeduthun, 1 Chron. vi. 33; xv. 17-19; xxv. 1, 3. "Ethan is the same as Jeduthun," says Hengstenberg. But Lord A. C. Hervey in *Smith's Dict. of the Bible* says, "Whether or no this Heman (i.e., the above-mentioned) is the person to whom the 88th Psalm is ascribed, is doubtful. The chief reason for supposing him to be the same is, that as other Psalms are ascribed to Asaph and Jeduthun, so it is likely that this one should be to Heman the singer. But on the other hand he is there called 'the Ezrahite;' and the 89th Psalm is ascribed to 'Ethan the Ezrahite.' But since Heman and Ethan are described in 1 Chron. ii. 6, as 'sons of Zerah,' it is in the highest degree probable that Ezrahite means 'of the family of Zerah,' and consequently that Heman of the 88th Psalm is different from Heman, the singer, the Kohathite. In 1 Kings iv. 31, again we have mention, as of the wisest of mankind, of Ethan the Ezrahite, Heman, Chalcol and Darda, the sons of Mahol, a list corresponding with the names of the sons of Zerah, in 1 Chron. ii. 6. The inference from which is, that there was a Heman, different from Heman the singer, of the family of Zerah the son of Judah, and that he is distinguished from Heman the singer, the Levite, by being called the Ezrahite. . . . If Heman the Kohathite, or his father, had married an heiress of the house of Zerah, as the sons of Hakkoz did of the house of Barzillai, and was so reckoned in the genealogy of Zerah, then all the notices of Heman might point to the same person, and the musical skill of David's chief musician, and the wisdom of David's seer, and the genius of the author of the 88th Psalm, concurring in the same individual, would make him fit to be joined with those other worthies whose wisdom was only exceeded by that of Solomon. But it is impossible to assert that this was the case."

There is nothing in the Psalm which marks clearly the time and occasion of its composition. The Psalm is very mournful and desponding in its character. There are other Psalms which are the utterance of the troubled heart, but they have in them some rays of light, some gleam of hope. But in this the darkness is unrelieved. It is, says Stier, "The most mournful of all the plaintive Psalms, yea, so wholly plaintive, without any ground of hope, that nothing like it is found in the whole Scriptures."

PRAYER FROM THE DEPTH OF MISERY.
(*Verses* 1-9.)

I. **A great depth of affliction.** In a very expressive manner the Psalmist sets forth his distresses.

1. *His troubles were spiritual.* "My soul is full of troubles." The Psalmist was probably suffering from some severe

and painful physical disease. He was certainly suffering in spirit. There is no trouble so sore and hard to bear as trouble in the soul. "The spirit of a man will sustain his infirmity; but a wounded spirit who can bear?" The poet's mind was troubled, his heart was sorrowful, he seems almost in despair. The severest anguish is not that of the body, but that of the spirit. When cherished hopes are blighted, and fond and worthy ambitions are destroyed, and those we trusted prove untrue, and those we love are summoned away leaving us to tread life's pilgrimage without them, and our sins arise against us so many in number, so enormous in guilt, and God seems to have forsaken us, or to be smiting us in His wrath,—who shall describe the anguish of such experiences? Yet good men sometimes pass through them.

2. *His troubles were many.* "My soul is *full* of troubles." He enumerates some of the many troubles with which his soul was full. His acquaintances were removed from him, he was afflicted and ready to die, and God was pursuing him as with the breakers of an angry sea. He was satiated with sorrows. The utmost limit of his endurance he seemed to have reached. The cup of his distresses would not contain one drop more.

3. *His troubles were bringing him speedily to death.* He uses various expressions setting forth this idea. "My life draweth nigh unto the grave," unto *Sheol*, the abode of the dead. He felt that unless he obtained speedy relief he must die. "I am counted with them that go down unto the pit. I am as a man that hath no strength." He was so near death, his case seemed so hopeless, that men reckoned him among the dead. And his strength had departed from him. "Free among the dead, like the slain that lie in the grave, whom Thou rememberest no more." There is a passage in Job (iii. 17-19) which will help us to elucidate the first clause. "There the wicked cease from troubling; and there the weary be at rest; there the prisoners rest together; they hear not the voice of the oppressor; the small and great are there; and the servant is free from his master." The dead are emancipated from the cares and sorrows, the toils and burdens of life. "The comparison with *the dead* is followed by that with the *slain*, because the Psalmist was threatened with *violent* deprivation of life. 'To be cut off *from the hand of God*,' His helping and protecting hand is to be made away with in a violent manner." . . . The idea which lies at the foundation of the whole verse is this, "that the *dead* are no longer the objects of the loving care of God." Life and immortality were not brought to light in the days of the Psalmist as they are in the Gospel. Men shuddered at, and shrank from, that "land of darkness as darkness itself; and of the shadow of death without any order, and where the light is darkness." "Thou hast laid me in the lowest pit, in darkness, in the deeps." "The lowest pit" is Sheol, deep under the earth. All these expressions are intended to set forth the idea that the Psalmist was on the very verge of the grave, that he was already as one dead, and that hope had almost or altogether forsaken him. Or, if it be held that the language is to be figuratively understood, then we have before us a good man in the most appalling trouble; the darkness which envelops his spirit is like that of the grave itself, his anguish is unsupportable, his griefs are overwhelming, and he is brought to the last extremity.

4. *His troubles isolated him from human society.* "Thou hast put away mine acquaintance far from me; Thou hast made me an abomination unto them: I am shut up, and I cannot come forth." In time of suffering and sorrow the presence and sympathy of a friend are very precious and helpful. But the poet in his great affliction was forsaken by his friends. Such desertions are among the sharpest sorrows of life. It would seem as though the Psalmist was either suffering from some infectious or defiling disease, or from the attacks of slander. Men shrank from him with loathing. In the Hebrew the word which is translated "abomination" is in the plural. Men regarded

him as though he were an assemblage of abominations, or one great mass of abominations. Hengstenberg interprets "I am shut up, and I cannot come forth," as "shut up by public reproach, which keeps me in the house like a prisoner, I do not go out, I stir not from the door." Slander has been truly called "the foulest whelp of sin." And "the worthiest people are the most injured by slander, as we usually find that to be the best fruit which the birds have been pecking at." Human friendships, or the things which so often degrade the high and holy name, are most unreliable and unsatisfactory things. True friendships are as rare as they are precious. Prosperity attracts to us a large number of so-called friends, but adversity tests them, and sometimes all fail in the trial, as did those of the Psalmist. His acquaintance all forsook him, and regarded him with abhorrence or loathing.

5. *His trouble was from the hand of God.* It seemed to the Psalmist that all his distresses came to him from the hand of God. "Thou hast laid me in the lowest pit," &c. "Thou hast afflicted," &c. "Thou hast put away," &c. When faith is in lively exercise it is a relief in trouble to know that the trouble comes from God. Then the tried saint softly sings,

"It is Thy hand, my God;
 My sorrow comes from Thee:
I bow beneath Thy chastening rod,
 Tis love that bruises me.
My God, Thy name is love,
 A Father's hand is Thine;
With tearful eyes I look above,
 And cry,—Thy will be mine!
I know Thy will is right,
 Though it may seem severe;
Thy path is still unsullied light,
 Though dark it may appear."—*Darby.*

But not thus did the matter present itself to the mind of the Psalmist. That his troubles were from the hand of God seemed to him a sore aggravation of those troubles. Evil from so good a hand appeared quite intolerable to him. So deep was his depression, that while feeling acutely the adversity, he could not perceive any of its "sweet uses." The bitterness of his draught he realised completely; its medicinal properties he entirely lost sight of. Everything seemed to aggravate his misery.

6. *His trouble was an expression of the wrath of God.* "Thy wrath lieth hard upon me, and Thou hast afflicted me with all Thy waves." So far was the Psalmist from regarding his distresses as coming from the chastening hand of a Father, that he looked upon them as punishments from the hand of an angry God. Like a huge and insupportable burden, God's wrath was crushing him to the earth; and as the breakers of the stormy ocean dash in thunder and fury upon the shore, so God in anger seemed to be afflicting the Psalmist. We have, indeed, a great depth of affliction here. The deep darkness of this picture of distress has not often been equalled in the history of suffering humanity. Before leaving this part of our subject we shall do well to lay to heart two facts. (1) *That the best of men in this life are exposed to severe sufferings and trials.* Suffering is not necessarily a sign of the Divine displeasure. "Whom the Lord loveth He chasteneth," &c. (2) *That the best of men in this life are liable to misinterpret the meaning of suffering.* Under the burden of severe distresses "even the children of God's love may sometimes apprehend themselves children of wrath, and no outward trouble can lie so hard upon them as that apprehension."

II. **A great urgency of prayer.** "O Lord God of my salvation, I have cried," &c. His prayer was—

1. *Directed to God.* "I have cried day and night before Thee: let my prayer come before Thee," &c. With steady aim he directed his complaints and petitions to God. His appeal was intended to reach the ear, and move the heart, of God. The notice or approbation of men the Psalmist neither sought nor wanted; but his heart was set on obtaining the regard of God. He is the Hearer and Answerer of prayer. "He is, and He is a rewarder of them that diligently seek Him." Moreover, the Psalmist sought the Lord as the God of his salvation. There is a tone of confidence in the address. Bad as things are with him, he is not without hope. He looks for salvation, and he looks for it to God. This is the only cheerful beam which shines in the Psalm.

2. *Earnest.* "I have cried," &c. "I have stretched out my hands unto Thee." The Psalmist's application to God was not a half-hearted, listless thing. He uttered an earnest "cry" for help, and "stretched out his hands" in fervent prayer. Jeremy Taylor says: "When, in order to your hopes of obtaining a great blessing, you reckon up your prayers with which you have solicited your suit in the court of heaven, you must reckon, not by the number of the collects, but by your sighs and passions, by the vehemence of your desires and the fervour of your spirit, the apprehension of your need and the consequent prosecution of your supply."

3. *Unceasing.* "I have cried day and night before Thee. I have called daily upon Thee." Without intermission he sought the Lord in prayer. His afflictions prevented him from resting, and in his unrest he constantly sought God in supplication. "Men ought always to pray, and not to faint." "Praying always with all prayer," &c. "Pray without ceasing." Such importunity, as the expression of earnest desire, is well-pleasing to God. Yet the author of this Psalm was like the Psalmist David in this respect, that for a time there seemed to be "neither voice nor any to answer, nor any that regarded;" and he might have adopted his words, "O my God, I cry in the day time, and Thou hearest not; and in the night season, and am not silent." For a time no answer came to his earnest and unceasing cry. Yet God will speedily "avenge His own elect, who cry day and night unto Him, though He bear long with them."

CONCLUSION. Let the distressed child of God be encouraged to persevere in prayer. In His own wise and good time the Lord will appear for thee, and "turn the shadow of death into morning," and change thy mournful complaint into a joyful Psalm.

EXPOSTULATION FROM THE DEPTH OF MISERY.

(*Verses* 10–18.)

From complaint and prayer the Psalmist proceeds to very forcible expostulation with the Lord God. And in this expostulation he reveals—

I. **His extreme distress.** He speaks of himself as,

1. *Cast off by God.* "Lord, why castest Thou off my soul? Why hidest Thou Thy face from me?" Through suffering and sorrow he was unable to see the face of God. The tears of his distress had for the time blinded his eyes, so that he was unable to recognise the gracious presence of God. But He had not cast off his soul. "For the Lord will not cast off His people, neither will He forsake His inheritance." The mists and clouds which obscure the sun, and give to us dark and cheerless November days arise from the earth. The sun shines ever. And the hiding of God's face from His people is by reason of their sins, and sorrows, and sufferings. His faithfulness and love are unchangeable. Nevertheless, when His people feel abandoned by Him, unspeakably sore is their suffering.

2. *Almost deprived of reason.* "I am distracted." Pain and sorrow, doubt and fear, had so wrought upon him that he was unable to think or reason calmly. His suffering and anxiety and grief seemed to have disturbed the balance of his mind. Calmness he could not command. He was trembling on the brink of madness. As we know, there have been instances in which extreme suffering has led to insanity, and great spiritual depression and anxieties have issued in mental derangement. The Psalmist felt himself to be in danger of this.

3. *Terrified by the wrath of God.* "I suffer Thy terrors," &c. The idea that God was pursuing him in wrath with His plagues is a deep conviction with him. That wrath seems to burn fiercely against him, and he cannot escape from it. Or, like an angry sea, it surrounds him, and its wild billows course over and beat upon him. Alas! for the child of God passing through experiences like unto these! Yet the Psalmist is not the only one who has travelled through this dark, distressing, dangerous valley. We rejoice, however, to know that One, whose "form is like the Son of God," walketh

with them, though they see Him not. While He is with them no real evil shall befall them.

II. His misconception of God. "Thy fierce wrath goeth over me; Thy terrors have cut me off." What he regarded as the "fierce wrath" of God, was the loving though severe discipline of a wise and kind Father. When he thought that God had cast off his soul, God was educating and enriching his soul by means of suffering. When to him all things appeared sadly and sternly against him, God was causing all things to work together for his good. A sense of sin, and much and severe suffering, led him to misconceive the character and dealings of God. He spake hastily and unadvisedly as to God's "fierce wrath." God does not pour forth His fury upon His people. If He chasten us sorely, it is not in anger, but in love that He does so. It is the consciousness of sin and unscriptural theological notions that lead us in suffering to behold an angry God.

III. His nearness to death. "Wilt Thou show wonders to the dead? shall the dead arise and praise Thee?" &c. "I am afflicted and ready to die from my youth up." In these verses, the Psalmist speaks of himself as almost dead, as on the very brink of the grave, as swiftly passing into the land of darkness and forgetfulness. He does this as a reason why God should speedily appear for his help. If deliverance came not quickly, he would be beyond the reach of it. (On his nearness to death, see our remarks in the preceding sketch.)

IV. His belief that there are duties and privileges, the discharge and enjoyment of which are limited to the present life. "Wilt Thou show wonders to the dead?" &c. (vers. 10–12). These verses have a despondent if not a despairing accent. Yet it would be rash to affirm that the Poet had no faith in a future life, or that he regarded death as the extinction of being. But to him Sheol was a dark and gloomy realm, where God's wonders were not made known, where His praise was not celebrated, where remembrance had ceased, and where destruction seemed supreme. Such seem to have been the ideas which he then entertained of the state of the dead. In that day life and immortality were not revealed as they now are in the Gospel. The great truth for us to seize is this, that there are duties to be done now which cannot be done beyond this life, and privileges to be enjoyed now which probably cannot be enjoyed when we have passed hence and are no more seen. This is true,

1. *Of our own salvation.* "Behold, now is the accepted time; behold, now is the day of salvation." There is nothing in the Scriptures to warrant the belief that God will show the wonders of His saving power to the dead—

"There are no acts of pardon past
In the cold grave to which we haste;"

wherefore, "seek ye the Lord while He may be found," &c.

2. *Of many ministries to others.* It is our privilege now to lead the lost to the Saviour, to reclaim the wanderer, and raise the fallen, to comfort the sorrowful, and succour the distressed. Such Christ-like ministries are probably confined to this present world and life. Wherefore, "whatsoever thy hand findeth to do, do it with thy might; for," &c.

V. His faith in God. This is manifest—

1. *In His expostulations,* and especially in that of the fourteenth verse, "Lord, why castest Thou off my soul? why hidest Thou Thy face from me?" In these and in his other inquiries the Psalmist manifests his faith in (1) *the faithfulness,* and (2) *the righteousness of God.* Was He not a covenant-keeping God? Was He not righteous in all His ways? "Shall not the Judge of all the earth do right?"

2. *In his prayers.* The Psalmist would not have cried to God in prayer, and resolved to have anticipated Him in the morning with his supplications, if he had not believed in—(1) *The accessibility of God.* Though on the brink of the grave, he knew that he could draw near to the mercy-seat of God. (2) *The power of God to save him.* Extreme as his case was, he knew that the God of his salvation was able to meet and master it. He is "mighty to save." He saves "unto the uttermost." (3) *The mercy of God.* Though it

seemed that His fierce wrath was going over him, yet he knew that there was mercy in the Divine heart, or he would not have cried unto Him. Sad as was the case of the Psalmist, it might have been worse; for his faith had not utterly failed him. He still turned in prayer to the Lord as the God of his salvation.

CONCLUSION.—Let great sufferers and despondent souls take encouragement even from this most pensive of all the pensive Psalms. It teaches us that in the deepest distress and the greatest extremity—1. *The Lord is still the God of our salvation.* 2. *The way is still open to the throne of grace.* 3. *While faith and prayer are not utterly extinguished our case may be extreme, but it is not desperate.* From above, the Lord saith, "I have prayed for thee, that thy faith fail not."

PSALM LXXXIX.

INTRODUCTION.

Superscription.—"*Maschil*," an instruction, a didactic poem. "*Of Ethan the Ezrahite*," "one of the four sons of Mahol, whose wisdom was excelled by Solomon (1 Kings iv. 31). There is little doubt that this is the same person who, in 1 Chron. ii. 6, is mentioned—with the same brothers as before—as a son of Zerah, the son of Judah." See on "Heman the Ezrahite" in the Introduction to Psalm lxxxviii. "There can be little doubt," says Perowne, "that this Psalm was written in the latter days of the Jewish monarchy, when the throne of David had fallen or was already tottering to its fall, and when the prospect for the future was so dark that it seemed as if God had forgotten His covenant and His promise. . . . The Psalm opens by a reference to the Promise given to David (2 Sam. vii. 8, &c). This Promise, and the attributes of God on which the Promise rests, and which are the great pledge of its fulfilment, form the subject of the Poet's grateful acknowledgment, before he passes to the mournful contrast presented by the ruin of the house of David, and the blighting of his people's hopes. He turns to the glorious past, that by its aid he may rise out of the grief and discouragement of the present. He takes the Promise, and turns it into a song. He dwells upon it, and lingers over it. He dwells on that which is the ground and pillar of the Promise—the faithfulness of God—and then he first lifts his loud lament over the disasters which have befallen his king and people, speaking out his disappointment, till his words sound like a reproach; and next pleads earnestly with God that He would not suffer his enemies to triumph."

A NOBLE CELEBRATION OF THE FAITHFULNESS AND MERCY OF THE LORD.

(*Verses* 1-4.)

In this paragraph the Psalmist announces his determination to praise God eternally because of His mercy and faithfulness, which were promised to David and to his seed for ever. Looking at this announcement as indicating, in brief, the praise itself, we take as our subject, *A noble celebration of the faithfulness and mercy of the Lord.* The nobility of this celebration appears,

I. **In the view of these attributes which is presented.** Two prominent features are set forth by the Poet.

1. *Perpetuity.* "Mercy shall be built up for ever: Thy faithfulness shalt Thou establish in the very heavens." The mercy and faithfulness of God are thus presented to us as abiding things. Look at the heavens and the heavenly bodies,—how stable and enduring, how orderly and regular they are ! The sun with unvarying regularity and absolutely perfect punctuality sets forth on his course and runs his race ; from the creation to the present hour the moon has held on her appointed way and performed her appointed rounds without a shadow of turning, and with the most perfect accuracy ; the stars pursue their appointed orbits with undeviating precision, and with the utmost exactness keep their appointed seasons. The heavens and the heavenly hosts appear now as they did in the beginning of the world ; they present no signs of weariness or decay or change ; they are a fit emblem of the eternal and unchangeable. The Psalmist pictures the faithfulness of God as a part of the very heavens in order graphically to set forth its perpetuity and perfection. But God's faithfulness shall outlast the heavens themselves. "Heaven and earth shall

pass away, but My words shall not pass away." "God is not a man, that He should lie," &c. (Num. xxiii. 19). In reference to His covenant with David, the Lord said, by Jeremiah, "If ye can break My covenant of the day," &c. (Jer. xxxiii. 20, 21). God's faithfulness is perfect and eternal. "With Him is no variableness, neither shadow of turning." "The word of our God shall stand for ever." His mercy also is perpetual. "The mercy of the Lord is from everlasting to everlasting," &c.

2. *Increase*, or growth. "Mercy shall be built up for ever." "Mercy appears here," says Hengstenberg, "under the figure of a building in continual *progression*, in opposition to one which, when still unfinished, falls into ruins." And John Howe well says: "Former mercies are fundamental to later ones. The mercies that we enjoy this day are founded on the mercies of former days, such as we ought joyfully and thankfully to recount with delight and praise; remembering the years of the right hand of the Most High." And we may carry the idea further. The mercies that we enjoy this day will become the foundation for the mercies of future days, and so onward in endless progression. The purposes of God concerning our race are advancing to perfect and splendid completion. The edifice which was founded in mercy shall in mercy be gloriously finished. Thus "the multitude of His mercies" is ever growing more multitudinous. Every hour, ay, every minute, new mercies are being added to the unspeakable and countless mercies of former days.

II. **In the way in which they are celebrated.**

1. *Confidently.* "I have said." By these words he indicates that the statement he is about to make is his clear and fixed opinion. He believes; and therefore speaks. There is the unmistakable accent of conviction in his utterance.

2. *Publicly.* Not in his heart merely does he celebrate the mercy and faithfulness of God, but "with his mouth" he "sings" them. He will sing to others and for others; in words which others may use as their own. He cannot speak their praise; for prose is all too hard and cold for such a theme. He will "sing" them; and even poetry and music seem poor for this rich and glorious theme.

3. *Perpetually.* "To all generations." When his voice was silent in death he would still celebrate the Divine mercy and faithfulness. He would make a record of his praise; he would write his Psalm, so that the Church should continue the strain through all ages. Surely this is a worthy spirit in which to celebrate the Divine praises. There is a heartiness, a confidence, and an enthusiasm in the utterance of the Psalmist which are well worthy of admiration and imitation.

III. **In the basis on which the celebration rests.** The praise of the Psalmist springs from his faith in the covenant of God. The faithfulness of God is both the ground and the object of his praise. His faith is rooted in that faithfulness, and his praise celebrates it. His praise rests on the word of God as its basis. The Lord is the speaker in verses 3 and 4. Consider:

1. *The covenant itself.* "I have made a covenant," &c. This covenant is recorded in 2 Sam. vii. 10-17. Its grand feature was the perpetuation of David's family and kingdom. "Thine house and thy kingdom shall be established for ever before thee: thy throne shall be established for ever." The family, the kingdom, the throne should be established eternally. The throne would be built up, *i.e.*, the sovereignty would be stable and increasing to all generations. We know that this covenant did not receive a material and temporal fulfilment. The material crown has long passed from the house of David; the temporal kingdom has long ceased to be. Yet the covenant abides, and is being splendidly fulfilled. "Jesus Christ, our Lord, was made of the seed of David, according to the flesh." "Of this man's seed hath God, according to promise, raised unto Israel a Saviour, Jesus." He is at once "the Root and the Offspring of David;" David's Son, and David's Lord. In Him and in His kingdom the promise is being accomplished, the covenant is being fulfilled.

Of the increase of His government and peace there shall be no end." His kingdom is ever extending and increasing. His spiritual seed ever grows more numerous.

2. *The origin of the covenant.* It originated in the sovereign favour of God. David was His "*chosen.*" How completely was David's elevation to the throne a thing of Divine sovereignty! David was the youngest son of Jesse; and Jesse's was not the senior house of the tribe of Judah (Ruth iv. 18–22; 1 Chron. ii. 5–12), and Judah was not the eldest son of Jacob; yet God chose the king from the tribe of Judah, from the house of Jesse, and the youngest son of that house. "He chose David also His servant, and took him from the sheepfolds," &c. (Psa. lxxviii. 70, 71). In like manner our Lord is spoken of as the chosen Servant of God. "Behold, my Servant, whom I uphold; Mine Elect, in whom My soul delighteth." The gift of Christ to our race was entirely of the sovereign mercy of God. We may well praise God for His spiritual covenant, for the gift of His Son Jesus Christ to save and reign over men, for the promise to Him of universal dominion, and for the way in which that promise is being fulfilled.

IV. **In the circumstances under which the celebration is made.** When the poet chanted this Psalm one might have thought, judging from its first and greater portion, that the kingdom was prosperous, the throne firm and unmenaced, the royal house numerous and united, the future bright and full of promise. But widely different was the case, as we may see by reading verses 38–45. The covenant seemed to be on the very verge of failure; the country was invaded, their armies were beaten in battle, the crown was profaned, the throne was cast down to the ground, ruin was imminent. Yet at such a time the Poet sang this bright, confident, triumphant celebration of the faithfulness and mercy of the Lord. Brave, trustful Poet! Let us catch his spirit, and imitate his example. When sense is silent in consternation, let faith be songful in the Lord. To the believing soul, "God gives songs in the night." Even the mourner's heart when turned to Him He tunes to music. When all things appear to deny the faithfulness and mercy of God, let us still believe them, and, believing them, let us sing them. Let us walk by faith, and we shall find matter for praise, and a heart to praise even in the midst of outward trouble. "As sorrowful, yet always rejoicing."

Conclusion. Let the character and covenant of God inspire us with confidence, even in the most trying circumstances. Believe in Him, praise Him. Trust and sing.

THE INCOMPARABLENESS OF GOD.

(*Verses 5–7.*)

Hengstenberg heads these verses thus: "The omnipotence and faithfulness of God are devoutly praised even by the angels, His heavenly congregation." The incomparableness of God manifested by the relation of the heavenly hosts to Him. We shall endeavour to set forth the ideas of the Poet on this subject in the following manner:—

I. **Heavenly beings are mighty.** "The sons of the mighty." In another Psalm we read, "Bless the Lord, ye His angels, that excel in strength." The angels are always represented in the Scriptures as "far superior to us, as possessing powers to which, as it regards their extent, we can make no pretensions, and as able to perform operations which may well fill us with astonishment, and which are far above the reach of our ability." For illustrations of the great power of angelic beings, see Exod. xxxiii. 2, where God promises to send an angel before the Israelites to drive out the seven nations of Canaan; 2 Sam. xxiv. and 1 Chron. xxi., where an angel is represented as smiting to death by means of pestilence seventy thousand men, and as having power to destroy Jerusalem; 2 Kings xix. 35, where an angel is said to have destroyed an hundred and eighty-five thousand Assyrians in one night. (See also Psa. xxxiv. 7; Dan. vi. 22; Acts. v. 19, xii. 7–10; Rev. xviii. 1; and xxii. 8.) "They are said to 'excel in strength;' and it is evident that the Psalmist has in view chiefly intellectual and moral strength, which qualifies them for the service of God; for 'they do His commandments, hearkening unto the voice of His Word;' though it does not exclude what is equivalent to physical energy, or power over matter, to mould, and influence, and render it subservient to their will. They are also denominated "*mighty* angels," 2 Thess. i. 7, where the Apostle has in view an occasion on which their might will be put in requisition and manifested in the most striking manner; for the great probability is, that they will be employed to effect many of the changes that will take place, and to exhibit many of the wonderful scenes that will be manifested at the second coming of the Lord Jesus Christ; and we are assured that, at the end of the world, 'The reapers are the angels,' and that, 'the angels shall come forth, and shall sever the wicked from among the just' (Matt. xiii. 39, 49). And it is evident from all the accounts which are given us of them in the Bible, that they excel in wisdom as much as in strength; or, rather that their strength is principally the power of wisdom and knowledge; and that in these they are far superior to men is plainly implied in the language of the Saviour (Matt. xxiv. 36). The same fact is evident from Psa. civ. 4, and Heb. i. 7."—*Walter Scott.*

II. **Heavenly beings are holy.** They are here spoken of as "saints." They are designated by way of eminence "holy angels" (Matt. xxv. 31). They are entirely free from sin, have never known sin. All their thoughts are true, all their sympathies are pure, all their principles are righteous, all their activities are blessed, all their services are sacred, all their being is God's. "We are sure that their moral purity must be *complete*, without the least imperfection or stain, for they dwell in the immediate blissful presence of God, they are the constant inhabitants of those glorious regions into which nothing that defileth can possibly enter. Some of them may have been for millions of ages employed in contemplating the glories of God, and in realising intellectual improvement; and still eternity is before them." "The dignity, the powers, of these celestial beings are also plainly implied in the names and epithets which are given to them in the Scriptures. They are denominated not only angels, or messengers, by way of eminence, but also cherubim and seraphim, thrones, authorities, dominions, principalities, and powers." Yet great and glorious, mighty and holy as they are, these

III. **Heavenly beings worship God.** "The heavens shall praise Thy wonders, O Lord," &c. These holy angels—

1. *Stand in awe of God.* "God is greatly feared" by them. Hengstenberg: "God is very terrible in the confidence of the holy ones." And he gives, what we regard as the true explanation of the clause: "'The *confidence* of the holy ones' denotes the confidential community to whom God vouchsafes to entrust His secrets (Job i. 6, ii. 1); though not His deepest ones (1 Pet. i. 12). Notwithstanding this, there always remains an infinite distance between Him and them (comp. Job iv. 18, xv. 15). God does not cease to be even to His holy ones the object of *fear*." Any one who approaches God thoughtfully must be awed in so doing. We cannot rightly contemplate Him without very solemn thought. The expressions of familiarity and endearment which some men use in their approaches to God in worship stand condemned by the reverence of the Holy angels. The seraphim worship with veiled faces, crying, "Holy, holy, holy, is the Lord of hosts; the whole earth is full of His glory." "God is very terrible in the confidence of the holy ones, and dreadful for all who are round about Him." If such are the regards which are paid to Him by these high and holy beings, surely unholy men should regard Him with humble awe and solemn reverence! These holy angels—

2. *Praise God.* "The heavens praise Thy wonders, O Lord; Thy faithfulness also in the congregation of the saints." (1) They praise Him *for the wonders of His power.* They are deeply interested in His mighty works. They sang the anthem which celebrated the *creation* of the world. "When the morning stars sang together, and all the sons of God

shouted for joy." They are represented in Scripture as being deeply interested in God's work in *Providence*, and as taking part in carrying out its great scheme. They are devoutly and admiringly interested in God's great work in *human redemption*. At the time of the Saviour's advent, there appeared "a multitude of the heavenly host praising God," &c. After the conflict between the Saviour and the seducer of men in the wilderness, angels ministered to the triumphant Saviour. During the agony in Gethsemane, "there appeared an angel unto Him from heaven, strengthening Him." Angels are represented as taking part in the resurrection of our Lord. They are represented by St. Peter as "desiring to look into" the things of human salvation. Our Lord Himself says, "There is joy in the presence of the angels of God over one sinner that repenteth." Yes, angels praise God for His wondrous works. They are acquainted with His mighty and glorious deeds, they admire them, they celebrate them in the worship which they pay to Him. (2) They praise Him *for the truth of His Word*. "Thy faithfulness also," &c. The idea of the Psalmist is that the angels would praise God for the fulfilment of His promises made unto David. Doubtless, by the heavenly host God is constantly and heartily praised for His truth and faithfulness. There are times when it seems to us as though God's faithfulness were about to fail; but even at its best our vision is dim, while the angels see clearly; our range of vision is extremely small, while that of the angels is so vast as to admit of no comparison with ours; and they, with their clear vision and wide range, praise God for His faithfulness. "He keepeth covenant and mercy with His servants." "He keepeth truth for ever."

CONCLUSION.—1. *How great is God!* The most ancient and most mighty of angels cannot be brought into comparison with Him. Angels are great, holy, glorious, yet "the first-born sons of light" pay to Him profoundest homage, worship Him with deepest humility. 2. *How reverently should we regard Him.* All our thought of Him should be humble and reverent. We should never speak of Him except with profound veneration. We should worship Him with holy awe.

"The more THY glories strike mine eyes
The humbler I shall lie."

GOD INCOMPARABLE.

(*Verse* 6.)

"Who in heaven can be compared unto the Lord?" Mark—

I. **The doctrine to which these words point.** God incomparable; and He is so—

1. *In the glory He possesses.* There is in Him a glory of wisdom (Eph. iii. 10), power (Gen. xvii. 1), love (Rom. v. 8), majesty (Psa. civ. 1), and grace (2 Cor. ix. 8, 11), before which every created glory sinks into obscurity.

2. *In the dominion He exercises.* Created beings have only a limited and confined sway, but God's kingdom ruleth over all, and extends itself over the most distant places as well as the most exalted personages.

3. *In the blessings He bestows.* The obedient believer has a peace that passeth all understanding (Phil. iv. 7), his faith is accompanied with joy unspeakable (1 Pet. i. 8), he abounds in hope (Rom. xv. 13), and the glory reserved for him is unrevealed (1 John iii. 2).

II. **The sentiments it should excite in us.** If God be incomparable, so that none is like Him, a holy *reverential fear* becomes us in His presence (ver. 7). With this reverential fear we should also feel in our hearts, and express in every possible way, a *fervent attachment* to Him (Psa. xviii. 1). *Trust*, too, must be confidently reposed in Him, whatever difficulties we have to encounter, and though the dangers which encompass us are great and imminent (Psa. xlvi. 1–7).
—*W. Sleigh.*

THE HIGHEST WORSHIP.

(*Verse* 7.)

"God is greatly to be feared in the assembly," &c.

I. **The highest worship is offered to God.** Not unto saints, or angels, or the Virgin Mary, but unto God. He is Supreme. "There is one God."

II. **The highest worship is offered by saints.** Angels are called saints in the text. The redeemed in heaven are also called saints (1 Thess. iii. 13). The term is frequently applied to the people of God upon earth. When so applied it indicates those who are, 1. *Spiritually regenerated.* 2. *Consecrated to God.* 3. *Imitators of Christ.*

III. **The highest worship is reverent in spirit.** "God is greatly to be feared, . . . and to be had in reverence." This reverence is opposed, 1. To all *thoughtlessness* in worship (Eccles. v. 1, 2). 2. To all *formality* in worship (John iv. 23, 24). 3. To all *unbecoming familiarity* in worship. In the prayers and praises which are recorded in the Holy Book we find no trace of that irreverent and gushing manner of addressing God, which is so prevalent with some sentimental religionists of to-day.

IV. **In the highest worship the presence of God is consciously realised.** The worshippers feel that they are "about Him." They realise the fact that God is present to accept the worship and bless the worshippers who worship Him in spirit and in truth. 1. *God is present everywhere.* 2. *His presence is realised only by those who are spiritual and reverent.* 3. *He is specially present, and His presence is specially realised in the gatherings of saints for worship* (Exod. xx. 24; Matt. xviii. 20).

THE STRENGTH OF GOD AN ENCOURAGEMENT TO HIS PEOPLE TO TRUST IN HIM.

(*Verses* 8-14.)

The Psalmist does not in these verses lose sight of the faithfulness or truth of God in respect to His covenant; but he gives the greater prominence to the might of God. He is not only a God of truth, but also a God of power. He is able as well as willing to keep His covenant. The text teaches us that,—

I. **The Strength of God is manifested in His complete control over nature.** "Thou rulest the raging," &c.

1. *God rules over the sea.* There are times when the sea seems utterly beyond control. Yet when it foams and thunders in anger, when its waves, mountains high, chase each other with awful rapidity and fury, and destroy everything that is at their mercy, when it breaks with terrific violence upon the shore, and when it seems to mock at and spurn all control; God can subdue its angry ragings into calmness and repose at once. Our Lord when He stilled the tempest gave to us an illustration of the Divine sovereignty over the sea. "He arose, and rebuked the winds and the sea; and there was a great calm." The Psalmist seems to have regarded the tempestuous sea as a symbol of the powerful foes who were arrayed against them. David in one of his Psalms speaks of "the floods of ungodly men." God has complete control over the most proud and angry people. He maketh the wrath of man to praise Him, and the remainder of wrath He restrains. To the mightiest and most furious of peoples or nations God can impose limits, saying, "Hitherto shalt thou come, but no further: and here shall thy proud waves be stayed."

2. *God rules over the heavens and the earth.* "The heavens are Thine, the earth also is Thine," &c. God is here set forth as the Creator and Sustainer of the heavens and the earth. "All things were made by Him." "By Him all things subsist." Therefore the

heavens and the earth are His. Creatorship gives the most indefeasible right to possession. If any person can create anything, it is of all things preeminently his own property. "The highest conception of *property* is that which is derived from creation." The idea in the mind of the Psalmist seems to be that as the Creator, Sustainer, and Proprietor of all things, God has the power and the right to control all things. "He doeth according to His will in the army of heaven and among the inhabitants of earth: and none can stay His hand, or say unto Him, What doest Thou?" And therefore He was able to keep His covenant which He made with David and his seed. Notice the *completeness* of God's rule over nature. The Psalmist mentions "the sea, the heavens, the earth, the world." Then he mentions "the north and the south, Tabor and Hermon." Tabor lying on the western side of Jordan, and Hermon on the eastern, are representative of east and west. God rules over all nature in heaven above and on the earth beneath, from east to west, and from north to south. There is no province of nature which is not under His control. God's sovereignty over nature is *frequently asserted in the Bible.* He is at work in all its departments. He is the Force of all its forces. (See Psa. lxv. 8-11; civ. 1-30; Isa. xl. 26.) The doctrine of God's sovereignty over and agency in nature is *philosophic.* It is unsatisfactory to explain the changes in the phenomena of nature by "laws of nature," "nature's forces," "attraction," "gravitation." Such explanations do not satisfy my reason. A law of nature is simply a "generalisation of phenomena." When such a generalisation has been made and named we have frequently gained little more than a resting-place for ignorance rather than a large increase of knowledge. What are "nature's forces"? What is the secret of her forces? By naming a process or a phenomenon you do not remove the mystery of the thing, even though the name applied be ever so polysyllabic and obscure. But when I am told that the changing phenomena of nature are the result of the agency of the omnipotent Creator and Sustainer of nature, working through the wondrous arrangements and means which He has ordained, my reason accepts the statement as intelligent and satisfactory. Moreover, this recognition of God's agency in and sovereignty over nature is *religious.* The intelligent and devout man sees the signs of the Divine presence and working in every department and object of nature. "The heavens declare the glory of God," &c.

II. **The strength of God is manifested in His subjugation of His foes.** "Thou hast broken Rahab in pieces as one that is slain; Thou hast scattered Thine enemies with Thy strong arm." The name Rahab is used to set forth Egypt the ancient foe of Israel. The reference is to the emancipation of Israel from bondage, and the plaguing and destruction of their oppressors. On that occasion, God's sovereignty of the sea was employed to secure the safety of His people and the destruction of their foes. When God makes bare His arm, the proudest and mightiest nations fall before Him. The remembrance of what He had done to Egypt on behalf of His people would be especially encouraging to the poet and the people at this time. His arm had lost none of its ancient might. He was able at this time to break their enemies in pieces as one that is slain, or to scatter them, and so destroy their power. God is supreme over the proudest and mightiest nations. "His kingdom ruleth over all."

III. **The strength of God is ever exercised in harmony with righteousness, mercy, and truth.** "Justice and judgment are the habitation of Thy throne: mercy and truth shall go before Thy face." Justice and judgment are the ground on which the throne of God stands. The Divine government is founded on righteousness. As its basis, it rests neither on force nor on fraud, but on truth and on right. "Even omnipotent power could not maintain permanently a throne founded on injustice and wrong. Such an administration would sooner or later make its own destruction sure." But God's power is never employed for unrighteous ends. His justice is as great as His strength. The exercise of God's great power is also in keeping with His "*mercy.*" Even when it is employed in destroying violent oppressors such as Rahab, it is employed in mercy. Such destructions are a kindness not simply to the oppressed who are set free, but to mankind at large, who are thereby delivered from a tyrant and a curse. God's great power is acting beneficially, mercifully. It is also exercised in harmony with His "*truth.*" What His Word promises His power performs. He is strong to execute His threatenings, and to make good His promises. God's power and righteousness, mercy and faithfulness, are all exercised in beautiful harmony and beneficence, so that an afflicted people looking to Him for help may take encouragement from them.

IV. **The strength of God thus exercised is an encouragement to trust Him.** So the Psalmist evidently thought as he celebrated its praise in connection with the faithfulness of God. We cannot intelligently trust in God without including His "power as a concurrent foundation with His truth. It is the mainground of trust, and so set forth in the prophet (Isa. xxvi. 4) : 'Trust ye in the Lord for ever, for in the Lord Jehovah is everlasting strength.'... How could His mercy succour us without His arm, or His wisdom guide us without His hand, or His truth perform promises to us without His strength? ... Though we value the kindness men may express to us in our distresses, yet we make them not the objects of our confidence, unless they have an ability to act what they express. There can be no trust in God without an eye to His power." So said Charnock in one of his great discourses; and so the Psalmist seems to have thought as he penned this portion of the Psalm; and as he called to mind God's great power in ruling the raging of the sea and subduing the foes of His people, he must have felt confident that He had power to keep His covenant with His people.

CONCLUSION.—1. *Let the ungodly take warning.* You may resist His grace and the order of His laws; but when He makes bare His arm for judgment, you will find that you cannot resist His power. "Acquaint now thyself with Him and be at peace: thereby good shall come unto thee." 2. *Let the anxious Christian be encouraged.* Our evils can never be so great to distress us, as His power is great to deliver us. He is able to perform all the great and gracious things which He has promised. 3. *Let all men fear God.* As Charnock says : "How should we adore that power which can preserve us, when devils and men conspire to destroy us! How should we stand in awe of that power which can destroy us, though angels and men should combine to preserve us !"

THE BLESSEDNESS OF THE PEOPLE OF GOD.

(*Verses* 15-18.)

In the preceding portion of the Psalm the Poet has celebrated the faithfulness, almightiness, and righteousness of the Lord. And now he celebrates the blessedness of the people who had such a God; for He would surely deliver and save them. He sets forth the blessedness of the people of God as found in their relations to Him, and mentions several of these relations. He speaks of them —

I. **As worshippers of God.** "Blessed is the people that know the joyful sound." We believe that by "the joyful sound" we are to understand the call to the religious festivals. In celebrating the great festivals trumpets were joyously blown, and there was great rejoicing (Lev. xxiii. 24; Num. x. 10; xxix. 1). To know the joyful sound is to know and esteem the worship of God. So the meaning of this clause appears to us to be—" Happy is that people whose God is the Lord." They who are the worshippers of the only living and true God are indeed blessed.

1. *Their confidence in Him shall be honoured and rewarded.* A man's god is that in which his supreme affection and trust are reposed. Idolatry is really rife amongst us to-day. Men worship possessions and property, position and power, honour and fame, relatives and friends. Now any of these or all of them must inevitably fail those who trust in them. They are insecure and transient: they are inadequate to meet the needs of the soul. There is but one Being in whom we may safely place unbounded confidence. "He that believeth in Him shall not be confounded." "O Lord of hosts, blessed is the man that trusteth in Thee." He will make good His every promise. He is sufficient to help us in all the needs of life. In Him the soul may find satisfaction for its deepest longings and its highest aspirations. Trust in Him will be amply rewarded.

2. *Their worship of Him is in itself blessed.* Much of the worship of heathen deities was debasing and corrupting. Many of the idolatries of our own age are degrading the noblest powers of our nature, dwarfing our manhood, ruining souls. But the worship of God is the worship of supreme and infinite Perfection. His worship is *joyous*. We do not approach Him with terror, but with humble confidence; not with mourning and dirges, but with gladness and psalms. "Let us come into His presence with thanksgiving," &c. His worship is *transforming*. As we worship Him in spirit and in truth we become like Him, we "are changed into the same image from glory to glory as by the Lord the Spirit." Blessed indeed are they whose God is the Lord.

II. **As conscious of His favour.** "They shall walk, O Lord, in the light of Thy countenance." They possess the favour of God, and they know it, and rejoice in it. The lovingkindness of God they realise as their portion. The figure is a beautiful one. Who does not know the joy of looking into the face of one whom we love when no cloud of anxiety or sorrow or anger darkens it, but when it beams with affection for us? So the people of God live in His smile. "In His favour is life." His "lovingkindness is better than life." They who walk in the light of His countenance enjoy His favour; their life is crowned with His lovingkindness. Their life is marked by *activity and progress.* The consciousness of His favour does not produce indolence, but it leads to exertion; it does not lull the soul into slothful security, but stimulates it to diligent activity. "They shall *walk,* O Lord," &c. Walking is progressive motion from place to place. So the godly soul advances in the Divine life. "They go from strength to strength," from conquest to conquest, from grace to grace, from glory to glory. They "press toward the mark," &c.

III. **As rejoicing in Him.** "In Thy name shall they rejoice all the day."

1. *Their joy is religious.* They rejoice in God's name, *i.e.,* in Himself as made known to them. The good man has ample reason for joy in the being and perfections of God and His relation to him. When we reflect upon His wisdom, and goodness, and power, and holiness, and truth, and love, and upon the fact that they are "all engaged to make us blessed,"—have we not reason for joy? When we call to mind our privileges in the present, and our prospects for the future, have we not cause for rejoicing? "Now are we the sons of God, and it doth not yet appear what we shall be," &c. Let no one regard a godly life as gloomy and sad. Men may be gloomy for want of religion, but not because of it. A truly godly life is a bright and joyous thing.

2. *Their joy is constant.* "All the day." There is no reason why the people of God may not rejoice continually in God. Circumstances may be changeful, trial may overtake us, sorrow may be our portion, and happiness may abandon us; but even then we may have a deep and holy *joy* in God. He is unchangeable. His promises cannot fail. Having Him for our portion it is both our *privilege* and our *duty* to rejoice in Him always. "Rejoice in the Lord alway: again I say, Rejoice."

IV. **As exalted by Him.** "In Thy righteousness shall they be exalted." "The righteousness of God," says Hengstenberg, "is here that property by which He gives to every one his own, salvation to His people." We regard the clause as intended by the Poet to set forth the idea that under the righteous government of God they would find salvation and honour. He would deliver them from their enemies and their dangers. He would exalt them to honour. It certainly is true that the people of God are exalted by Him. *They are exalted now in their character and relations.* "Now are we the sons of God." They are like God in character. They will be exalted *hereafter to heavenly glory and dignity.* "To him that overcometh will I grant to sit with Me in My throne," &c. "Before the throne of God, and serve Him day and night in His temple." "Kings and priests unto God."

V. **As strengthened by Him.** "Thou art the glory of their strength: and in Thy favour our horn shall be exalted." The glory of the strength of the people of God is here set forth as consisting in the fact that it is derived from God. The "horn" is a symbol of power. To exalt the horn is to display the power. The meaning of the verse is, that they derived all their strength from God.

1. *The strength of God is all-sufficient.* "I can do all things through Christ which strengtheneth me." It is sufficient to support us under the heaviest trial; and to empower us for the most arduous duty.

2. *The strength of God is always available.* Whenever we ask for it sincerely and believingly it will be given to us.

3. *The strength of God is our only sufficient support.* No one else is adequate to sustain us in life's trials, and strengthen us for life's duties. The wise, the great, the powerful, the loving amongst men are not sufficient to our need. "Apart from me," said Christ, "ye can do nothing." If we draw our strength from Him, we shall not fail in life's duties, or faint beneath its burdens. "As thy days so shall thy strength be."

VI. **As governed and protected by God.** "For the Lord is our defence; and the Holy One of Israel is our King." The marginal reading is, "For our shield is of the Lord, and our King is of the Holy One of Israel." "The true construction of this verse," says Barnes, "is, 'For to Jehovah (belongs) our shield, and to the Holy One of Israel our King.' That is, all that they had, and all that they relied on as a defence, belonged to God, or was of God; in other words, their very protectors were themselves protected by Jehovah." Undoubtedly, the main idea of the verse is, that they were protected by God. He was their shield and defender. He was their sovereign, and would therefore guard their interests. We have three ideas involved here—

1. *The people of God are exposed to danger.* Their "adversary, the devil, as a roaring lion, walketh about, seeking whom he may devour." They are also in danger from "fleshly lusts, which war against the soul." And by reason of temptation from the world.

2. *The people of God are not able to protect themselves from danger.* They are not, of themselves, wise enough to baffle the deep designs of their enemies; neither are they strong enough to successfully resist their power.

3. *The people of God are securely protected by Him from all danger.* (See Psa. xci., cxxi., cxxv. 1, 2; 1 Pet. i. 5.) They are inviolably and eternally secure.

CONCLUSION.—1. *How great, then, is the blessedness of the people of God!* "There is none like unto the God of Jeshurun," &c. (Deut. xxxiii. 26–29). 2. *How important that we should be found among them!* Are we of the people of God? If so, let us rejoice in our privileges. If not, in the strength of Divine grace "first give your own selves to the Lord," and thus seek union with His people.

BLESSEDNESS OF KNOWING THE JOYFUL SOUND.

(*Verses 15, 16.*)

"Blessed are the people, &c. Whatever these words in their literal sense refer to, they have undoubtedly an ultimate reference to the gospel; and there are three particulars for our consideration respecting it.

I. **What it is.** It is a joyful sound. And why is it so? Because it proclaims—

1. *Pardon to the condemned.* And this pardon is *complete*, reaching to all past offences, however aggravated or multiplied they may be. It is *free*—free of all obligation to and of all price from the creature.

2. *Freedom to the enslaved.* Man by nature is in a state of vassalage; he is far removed from his original condition; bound with the chains of his sins, and yields to the requirements of Satan (2 Tim. ii. 26). In this state he was born; but the sound of liberty has not ceased to be heard since it first saluted the ears of Adam and Eve.

3. *Victory to the oppressed.* The sorrows of man are many; but the gospel offers to rescue him, bringing to him a full and sufficient remedy for them, so that he may have peace within; the reality, and not the shadow merely.

II. **What it demands.** We must "know the joyful sound." What is implied in this? It includes three things—

1. *A proper apprehension of it.* Many content themselves with hearing it; but its import must be understood.

2. *A sense of being personally interested in it.* We know it not aright, if we do not know it experimentally and savingly.

3. *A life and conversation suited to it.* Before we conclude too confidently that we know the joyful sound, we should ask ourselves: how our knowledge operates? To possess knowledge will be of little avail unless it produce a practical effect (1 John i. 6, 7).

III. **What it ensures.** Blessedness. The Psalmist's testimony respecting this is delightful, and shows how peculiar and distinguished the felicity of such people as know the gospel is.

1. *They possess tranquillity of mind.* In their journey heavenward, they have the light of God's countenance to encourage them in their distresses and difficulties.

2. *They have continual joy.* "In Thy name shall they rejoice all the day." His name comprehends those infinite perfections by which He has revealed Himself to us in His works, and in His Word. These being all theirs, on their side, united for their advantages, cannot but afford them unspeakable enjoyment.

3. *They are greatly dignified.* "In Thy righteousness shall they be exalted." By relying on the atonement, made by the death of God's only Son, they are arrayed in His righteousness, and are consequently justified and accepted.

Have we a saving knowledge of the Gospel? If so, how exalted is our privilege. But those who are strangers to the heavenly message, whether they be more or less wicked in respect of gross sins, are in a truly awful state.—*W. Sleigh.*

GOD'S COVENANT WITH DAVID.

(*Verses 19-28.*)

"There follows," says Hengstenberg, "in prosecution of the subject entered on in verses 3 and 4, a more full development in two sections, of the glorious promise made to the anointed, and in him to the people (vers. 19-38).

First (in vers. 19-28), it is represented that God had promised perpetual deliverance to the people in him, perpetual victory over its enemies," and "perpetual dominion." The covenant undoubtedly looks beyond David to the Anointed Saviour and King of men, as will be seen as we proceed with our exposition.

The leading teachings of the paragraph may be indicated under two main "heads."

I. **The Election of David.** The word "*then*" with which the paragraph begins connects it with verses 3 and 4. In those verses the covenant is mentioned; in this paragraph it is more fully stated. We prefer the reading, "*Thy holy ones*" in verse 19 to "Thy holy one." "All the old translators, many MSS. and editions," have "thy holy ones." "The singular," says Hengstenberg, "owes its existence, as in Psa. xvi. 10, to an exegetical incapacity. It was felt to be impossible to reconcile the plural with the application to David or Nathan; and to one or other of these, all interpreters, without exception, down even to modern times, have applied the expression, without observing that in the following part of the Psalm it is the *people* that complain that God does not appear to be keeping His promise, and that it is the *people* that pray that He *would* fulfil His promise. . . . The address cannot be made to David, for he is never addressed throughout the remaining portion of the Psalm." And it is incorrect to say that Nathan is referred to as the "holy one," for historically the address was not directed to him, but to David through him. The promises, though originally directed to David, are intended for all the people of Israel. They are the "holy ones."

But respecting the election of David we are taught—

1. *That he was elected from the people.* "Chosen out of the people." David had not descended from great kings or heroic warriors; he was not of exalted rank; he had grown up in humble life among the people, and had lived in lowliness and obscurity. Our Lord Jesus Christ also was "chosen out of the people." He was "in all things made like unto His brethren." He, too, was born into humble circumstances, and so far as this world is concerned He lived a lowly life of labour. He was bone of our bone, and flesh of our flesh. He had true human sympathies. He endured most really severe human sufferings. He was and is a true man.

2. *That he was elected to sovereignty.* "I have exalted one chosen out of the people. I have found David my servant," &c. David was thrice anointed king. Once by Samuel in his father's house at Bethlehem; once at Hebron as king over Judah; and once again, after seven years, as king over all Israel. God called him from the sheepfolds to the throne. Our Lord is called to universal sovereignty. He is "King of kings, and Lord of lords." "On His head are many crowns." "He made Himself of no reputation, and took upon Him the form of a servant, and was made in the likeness of men," &c. (Phil. ii. 7–11).

3. *That he was elected to service.* "I have laid help upon one that is mighty." David was chosen by God for a great work. God had invested him with power that he might deliver Israel out of the hand of her enemies. Hengstenberg translates, "I have laid help upon a man of war." And Alexander says that the word "*chosen*" has "allusion to its specific use as signifying a young warrior." David was elected of God as the champion of Israel to lead her armies to battle and to victory. We know how successful he was in this respect. At the beginning of his career the people cried, "Saul hath slain his thousands, but David his tens of thousands." And at the close of his career Israel was victorious over all her enemies, and was at peace. So Jesus Christ was elected by God to save mankind. He is the mighty One upon whom our help is laid. He is "mighty to save." "He is able to save them to the uttermost that come unto God by Him."

4. *That he was elected by God.* "I have laid help, . . . I have exalted, . . . I have found, . . . I have anointed." In the fullest and strictest sense David was chosen by God for his high position and his great work. This accounts for his pre-eminent fitness for his place and mission. God knew his great qualifications, his courage, strength, wisdom, faith, piety; and chose him to fill the throne and subdue the foes of Israel. David was indeed "king by the grace

of God." Our Lord was chosen by God for His great work. "Behold my servant, whom I uphold; mine elect, in whom my soul delighteth." He is the Anointed, the Christ of God.

II. **The promises made to David.** Here is a promise of

1. *Constant support.* "With whom My hand shall be established: Mine arm also shall strengthen him." De Wette translates the first clause, "With him My hand shall be continually." The idea of the verse is that God would grant unto David constant support. His hand would be ever present to aid him, and His strong arm would be ever outstretched to strengthen him. This promise was remarkably fulfilled in the case of David. Many were the trials of his life, yet in all of them he was supported by God. Many and arduous were his undertakings, yet he was enabled to bring them to a successful issue. The people now plead this promise for themselves. In their prostrate and perilous condition they plead for a fulfilment of this promise of the covenant. The promise was also fulfilled in the Saviour. He was ever upheld by God. The Father was ever with Him in fellowship, and ever with Him to aid Him. He overcame all His difficulties, He meekly and triumphantly bore all His trials, because God was ever present with Him. The great want of the Christian Church to-day is spiritual power. Here we have the covenant promise of the constant help of God. Let us plead it in faith, and the life and power that we need shall be given unto us.

2. *Victory over His foes.* This promise is twofold. (1) *His foes should be restrained.* "The enemy shall not exact upon him, nor the son of wickedness afflict him." The allusion, in the first clause, is to a harsh and unjust creditor, who, regardless of the ability of his debtor, exacts not only the just debt, but an exaggerated demand. The second clause is taken literally from the words of the covenant as recorded in 2 Sam. vii. 10. For some time David suffered much from the persecutions of Saul. Notwithstanding his oft-repeated manifestations of affection and loyalty, Saul was never satisfied. But those persecutions came to an end, those exactions all ceased. For many years after the making of the covenant, the enemies of Israel did not dare attempt to oppress or exact upon them in any way. (2) *His foes should be vanquished.* "I will beat down his foes before his face, and plague them that hate him." Here is complete victory from the hand of God promised to David and to the people. We know how it was fulfilled. The reign of David closed in peace, and that of Solomon was peaceful. These promises were fulfilled in our Lord. The malice and power of men and devils against Him were curbed by God. Satan could only bruise the heel of the Saviour, while his head was bruised by the Saviour. What Christ said to Pilate was true of all His enemies, "Thou couldest have no power against me, except it were given thee from above." All the enemies of our Lord shall be destroyed. Ignorance, sin, suffering, death, and the grave, shall all be destroyed. His victory will be complete and glorious. Every child of God may claim these promises as his own. Our foes are restrained. God ever imposes upon Satan His, "Thus far shalt thou go, but no further." (See Job i. 12 and ii. 6.) And He will vanquish all our foes for us. Through faith in Him we shall come out of life's battle "more than conquerors." Here is a promise of—

3. *Conspicuous power through the faithfulness and mercy of God.* "My faithfulness and my mercy shall be with him, and in My name shall his horn be exalted." In the commencement of the Psalm the poet celebrated the mercy and faithfulness of God, and here he recurs again to them. They were clearly displayed in the covenant, and now that the covenant seems about to fail, the hope of the Psalmist and the people is in them. Mercy and faithfulness were granted to David, and to his seed; and though, by reason of their sin, the temporal sovereignty passed away and the kingdom was destroyed, yet the line of David continued in un-

broken succession until Christ came, and the spiritual and eternal kingdom was established in Him. Through God's blessing the power of the kingdom was conspicuous in the time of David, and it was especially so in the time of Solomon. But the power of the kingdom of our Lord is growing more and more conspicuous daily. "The stone that was cut out of the mountain without hands" is fast filling the whole earth. Here is a promise of—

4. *Enlarged dominion.* "I will set His hand also in the sea, and His right hand in the rivers." The sea which is here mentioned is the Mediterranean, and the rivers are the Tigris and the Euphrates. These were the boundaries of the promised land as stated to Abram (Gen. xv. 18). The kingdom of David was of this extent. The promise made to Abram was fulfilled in his time and in the time of Solomon. But "David's greater Son" "shall have dominion from sea to sea, and from the river unto the ends of the earth." His kingdom is ever increasing, and ever shall increase, until the whole world bows to His sway. Here is a promise of—

5. *Intimate and exalted relationship.* "He shall cry unto Me, Thou art my Father, my God, and the rock of my salvation. Also I will make Him My firstborn, higher than the kings of the earth." David looked to God as "the rock of his salvation," but we have no evidence to show that he regarded God as a "*Father.*" Mr. Molyneux justly inquires, "When did David call God his Father? It is striking that we do not find anywhere in the Old Testament that the patriarchs or prophets called God their Father. They did not know Him as such. This verse is unintelligible in reference to David, but in regard to the True David it is exactly what He did say—'My Father, and your Father; my God, and your God.' Never until Christ uttered these words, never until He appeared on earth in humanity as the Son of God, did any man or any child of humanity address God in this endearing character." The 27th verse was partly fulfilled in David, but only in a very small degree. It is true that he is pre-eminent among kings "alike in his own personal character and his reign; in his relation to God; and in the fact that he was the ancestor of the Messiah." Yet it was only a feeble type of the fulfilment of this promise that was witnessed in David. Our Lord Jesus Christ is "the firstborn of every creature." He is "appointed heir of all things." "All kings shall fall down before Him: all nations shall serve Him." He "is on the right hand of God, angels and authorities and powers being made subject unto Him." But it is the privilege of every member of the seed of Christ to address God as "My Father, my God, and the rock of my salvation." If by faith "we are made partakers of Christ," then is God our Father, and we may with confidence draw near to Him, and rest in Him.

6. *Perpetual establishment of the covenant.* "My mercy will I keep for him for evermore, and My covenant shall stand fast with him." This promise also looks onward to the Christ. In Him the covenant is sure and lasting. But in what way can God be said to keep His mercy for Christ for evermore? Excellently Matthew Henry elucidates the point. "*My mercy will I keep for Him,* to be disposed of by Him, *for evermore:* in the channel of Christ's mediation all the streams of Divine goodness will for ever run. Therefore it is the mercy of our Lord Jesus Christ which we look for unto eternal life. And as the mercy of God flows to us through Him, so the promise of God is, through Him, firm to us: *My covenant shall stand fast with Him,* both the covenant of redemption made with Him, and the covenant of grace made with us in Him." His covenant made with Christ and His seed cannot fail. His word abideth for ever. The treasures of His grace are inexhaustible. He will fulfil His promises to Christ. And His mercy and grace toward us shall be more richly imparted and more conspicuously displayed to all eternity.

CONCLUSION.—1. *Let all who by faith in Christ are interested in this covenant rejoice in the rich blessings it secures unto them.* "All things are ours, and we are

Christ's, and Christ is God's." 2. Let all who are not by faith savingly interested in this covenant believe in Christ, and so share its blessings. "Incline your ear, and come unto Me," saith the Lord; "hear, and your soul shall live; and I will make an everlasting covenant with you, even the sure mercies of David."

THE MIGHTY HELPER OF MAN.

(*Verse* 19.)

This assurance points first to David, afterwards to Jesus Christ. In Him on whom God hath "laid help" for the restoration of humanity it receives its complete fulfilment. The text expresses this truth, that *man's great need as a sinner is met by Christ's great power as a Saviour.* Consider,

I. Man's Great Need as a Sinner. The text teaches by implication that none but a mighty Saviour was equal to the work of human redemption; that man had fallen so low and sunk so deeply in sin and misery that no arm but that of the mighty One was able to raise him. That we may obtain a clear and correct impression of the greatness of man's necessity as a fallen being, let us consider—

1. *The greatness of the being that fell.* Much has been written and spoken of the physical majesty of man when contrasted with other animals. There is much of both truth and beauty in the well-known words of our greatest dramatist: "What a piece of work is man! how noble in reason! how infinite in faculties! in form and moving, how express and admirable! in action, how like an angel! in apprehension, how like a god! the beauty of the world! the paragon of animals!" And a more ancient poet exclaimed, "I will praise Thee; for I am fearfully and wonderfully made." But the physical is not the man, it is but the "earthly house," the costume of the spiritual. "There is a spirit in man, and the inspiration of the Almighty giveth them understanding." This spirit is the man; and as the inhabitant is greater than the house, as the jewel is more precious than the casket, so the soul is incomparably greater and more precious than the body. . . . Think of the greatness of man's mind, as seen in its astonishing achievements. Mention briefly the wondrous triumphs of the human mind. . . . Now if man has done all this, and much more than this, in his fallen degenerate state, what could he not have done had he not fallen? What could he not have done had his arm never been paralysed by sin, his mental vision never been beclouded, and his constant access to the Great Source of wisdom and power never been interrupted? Moreover, if man has done all this when he is but in his infancy, in the mere "bud of being," what will he not be capable of accomplishing when he is freed entirely from the impediments of sin and in the unfolding of powers much more mature? The exceeding majesty of the human mind in heaven far surpasses our conceptions. "It doth not yet appear what we shall be." When we think of man as an *immortal intelligence*, we are struck into amazement at his greatness. He is capable of companionship with angels and communion with the Father of spirits, and is destined for perpetual growth in all that is true, holy, and beautiful.

2. *The greatness of the Fall.* Man's greatness made his fall the more disastrous and terrible. The fall of man was not as the wreck of some small boat which is quickly destroyed and lost sight of, but as the wreck of a great and majestic vessel,—so great that even now the vast ocean is strewed with its shattered fragments. A once glorious angel fell from his high position, and with him multitudes of high and holy ones rebelled, and lost their purity, their happiness, their God; and now the world is led captive at his will. Man, who was made only "a little lower than the angels," fell from his God-given sphere, and with him fell all the race, and the power which should have been

exercised for the true and good is arrayed in antagonism against them. And, when all the powers of man's being are thus exercised for evil, who can measure the extent and enormity of their evil-doing? St. Paul has graphically depicted the enormities wrought by the mighty but sadly perverted powers of man (Rom. iii. 13-18). Man's greatness has aggravated the terrible character of his fall. His mind is mighty to devise evil, and his arm to execute it. And this state of things is not partial but race-wide (Rom. iii. 10-12). Wherever upon earth you find man you find sin, and wherever you find sin you find misery and death (Rom. v. 12). We may picture man as a once splendid temple now lying in ruins. Who shall restore him? shall education? shall science? shall schemes of social re-organisation? shall systems of political economy? These have been tried and found lamentably deficient. None but God can restore man. Rejoice, for God hath "laid help upon One that is mighty," &c.

II. **Christ's great power as a Saviour.** "I have laid help upon One that is mighty," &c. Notice—

1. *Christ's identification with humanity.* "Chosen out of the people"—one of ourselves. Christ was a true man, although not a mere man. "God manifest in the flesh." "God was in Christ reconciling the world unto Himself." While bowing reverently before His Godhood, we remember gratefully His manhood. As a man we see in Him our *Example.* "Learn of Me," He saith to us. (1 Pet. ii. 21). Our sympathetic *Friend* and *Brother.* (Heb. ii. 11, 14-18; iv. 15, 16).

2. *Christ's exaltation above humanity.* "I have exalted One." Mention the spiritual exaltation of the whole earthly life of Christ. Even while His feet trod this earth He was "the Son of man which is in heaven." There was the sublime exaltation of the cross. In that voluntary self-sacrifice we have the most glorious manifestation of the Godlike in human life that the world has ever seen. But the exaltation referred to in the Messianic application of the text is probably that of *His resurrection, and His ascension to heaven.* In His resurrection we have Divine honour conferred upon Him, and the attestation of His Messianic claims. In His ascension He resumed the glory which He had with the Father before the world was, and also entered upon the glories of Mediator. "For the joy that was set before Him," &c. (Heb. xii. 2; Phil. ii. 8-12).

3. *Christ's power to save humanity.* "I have laid help upon One that is mighty." Because Jesus was "chosen out of the people" He possesses that sympathy with us which is requisite to render His help efficient, and to assure us that it will be imparted. And the exaltation of His miracles, resurrection, and ascension declare Him to be "the Son of God with power" to save man. His manhood is evidence of His willingness to save man; His Godhood is evidence of His power to save man. "The Son of man hath power on earth to forgive sins." He is "mighty to save." "He is able to save them to the uttermost that come unto God by Him," &c.

CONCLUSION.—1. If you have availed yourself of the help of the Mighty One, cleave to Him until you are entirely freed from sin, and all your being is holy to the Lord. 2. If you have not availed yourself of the help of the great Redeemer, do so at once. He waits to save you. Trust His almighty power and infinite love, and so rise to holiness and God.

THE COVENANT OF GOD AND THE SINS OF MEN.

(*Verses* 29-37.)

May the covenant of God be made of none effect by the sin of man? Shall God's covenant with David and his seed be nullified by reason of their transgression? May man frustrate the purpose of God? This question is answered in the paragraph before us.

I. **The sins of men are opposed to**

the covenant of God. All the arrangements of God are utterly opposed to sin. 1. *His laws are against it.* The laws of the material universe are against it. "Whoso breaketh an hedge a serpent shall bite him." God has annexed inevitable and stern penalties to every breach of His laws in the material realm. The laws of the moral universe are all against sin. On all the dreary region of evil the Divine "Thou shalt not" is inscribed in letters of flame. And on all the sunny realm of righteousness the Divine "Thou shalt" is clearly written. 2. *His judgments are against it.* Think of the stern judgments recorded in the Bible which were inflicted by reason of sin: the expulsion of our first parents from Eden, the deluge in the days of Noah, the destruction of Sodom and Gomorrah by fire, the plague of the fiery flying serpents in the wilderness, the terrible overthrow of Jerusalem. 3. *His redemption is against it.* "For this purpose the Son of God was manifested that He might destroy the works of the devil." "He appeared to put away sin by the sacrifice of Himself." His great mission is "to save sinners." The covenant of God has no complicity with evil. The goodness and mercy of God are an encouragement to penitence, but they are hostile to sin. God regards sin with unutterable abhorrence. "Oh, do not this abominable thing that I hate." His ideas, His feelings, His purposes, His arrangements, His operations, are all against it.

II. **Yet men who in the covenant of God are richly blessed may sin grievously against Him.** "If his children forsake My law, and walk not in My judgments; if they break My statutes, and keep not My commandments." Here are sins of *commission.* "If his children forsake My law, . . . if they break," or profane, "My statutes." Here are sins of *omission.* "Walk not in My judgments, keep not My commandments." These sins may be committed by men who are enjoying many blessings of the Divine covenant.

1. *Such was the case with the Jews.* Ancient Israel sadly forsook God and wickedly rebelled against Him. Some members even of the seed of David sinned grievously against Him. 2. *Such is the case with many who are in the enjoyment of Gospel privileges.* What multitudes in this land of religious light and liberty and abounding spiritual privileges, are living in utter disregard of the Will of God! 3. *Such is the case even with true Christians.* Even after we have tasted that God is gracious, we may sadly sin against Him. Nay, who is there of us that is not sensible of frequent sins both of omission and commission, and especially of the former? "Sins of commission may not, perhaps, shock the retrospect of conscience. Large and obtrusive to view, we have confessed, mourned, repented of them. Sins of omission, so veiled amidst our hourly emotions—blent, confused, unseen in the conventional routine of existence;—alas! could these suddenly emerge from their shadow, group together in serried mass and accusing order, would not the best of us then start in dismay, and would not the proudest humble himself at the throne of mercy?" The fact that even good men may and do thus sin against God—

(1.) *Reveals man's moral freedom.* Saint and sinner are alike morally free. God will not compel any one to obey Him.

(2.) *The importance of watchfulness.* "Watch and pray that ye enter not into temptation."

(3.) *The necessity of trust in God.* "Hold up my goings in Thy paths, that my footsteps slip not." "Hold Thou me up, and I shall be safe."

III. **The sins of men will be punished by God.** "I will visit their transgression with the rod and their iniquity with stripes." If the people of God sin against Him, they will be most surely punished by Him.

1. *The rod is used for their correction, not for their destruction.* God sometimes inflicts upon His people pain of body, or losses in business, or family afflictions, or distressing bereavements, as a chastisement for their sins. He would thereby impress them with the heinousness of evil, that they may fear to sin. The Divine hatred of evil is too

intense for sin to go unpunished. God's love of His people is too great for Him to allow them to sin and not chastise them for it. He visits them with the rod of correction that He may reclaim them from their evil ways, and establish their goings in holiness.

2. *The correction is administered by God.* "I will visit their transgressions," &c. "Visitation implies oversight and paternal care. The metaphor is taken from those who undertake to watch over the sick, or train up children, or tend sheep." God, who is wise and gracious, bears the rod and inflicts the chastisement; we may, therefore, rest assured that He will inflict that only which is for our good.

IV. The sins of men cannot frustrate the covenant of God. "Nevertheless My lovingkindness will I not utterly take from him," &c., verses 33-37. Human sin cannot defeat the Divine purposes. This is evident, for—

1. *They are the purposes of an omniscient Being.* No circumstance can arise to disarrange them which has not been foreseen and provided for by Him. His plans are formed with a perfect knowledge of all events in all worlds and in all ages.

2. *They are the purposes of an omnipotent Being.* Man's purposes may be defeated, or he may fail to carry them out for want of power, but God is almighty. He can subdue all opposition. He can accomplish all that He may please. "With God all things are possible."

3. *They are the purposes of an immutable Being.* In Himself He is unchangeable. Man varies, as life advances, and he grows in knowledge and wisdom and holiness; his views of things often change, and he may alter his plans or his methods of action. But it is not so with God. His purposes are eternal and immutable, and He, being immutable, omnipotent, and omniscient, we may justly conclude that His covenant arrangements cannot be made void by man's sin. But let us ascertain the teaching of the text on this point. Hengstenberg's note on the 37th verse appears to us excellent. "The alleviating limitation is here first given in verse 33, as it is in the fundamental passage in verse 15. The alleviation, however, is not to be misunderstood, as if it referred to *individuals* contrary to the nature of the thing, and contrary to the history, according to which annihilating judgments did descend upon the rebellious members of the family of David; but the opposition is of the punishment of sin in the individual, and of grace continually remaining to the *family*. We must not fail to notice that in verse 33 it is not said: I will not withdraw My mercy from *them*, the sinners, but from *him*, the family as such. Now that the kingdom has passed from the *sinful* to the *holy* seed of David, the direct application of this paragraph has ceased. The case provided for in the promise cannot again occur. Still there exists between Christ and His Church a case analogous to that between David and his seed. As David's family was chosen in him (Comp. 1 Kings xi. 36; 2 Kings viii. 19; Isa. xxxvii. 35), so that it always remained in possession of the favour of God, notwithstanding the fall and rejection of many of its individual members, in like manner the Church is chosen in Christ, and the sins of its members may hurt *themselves* but cannot injure *it*. Notwithstanding the fall of a whole generation, it always flourishes again; and under the most inexorable judgments which are not removed by the appearance of Christ, but rendered more severe, compassionate grace is always concealed." Individual members of David's family transgressed, and were visited with the rod, but the mercy was not removed from the family. Individual Christians may fall into sin and forsake God and be visited with stripes, but "the new covenant" shall not fail; the kingdom of Christ shall flourish and increase. Man's sin shall not frustrate God's purposes. "If," saith the Lord, "they profane My statutes, nevertheless My covenant will I not profane." Two things more remain to be noticed. 1. God is again represented as declaring *the stability and perpetuity of the covenant*. The sun and moon are stable, orderly. Generations of men come and go, but they remain. Incessant and

sometimes great changes take place upon earth, but the ordinances of heaven remain unchanged, the sun and moon are the same. So they are used as symbols of the unchangeable and permanent. And so the covenant of God is immutable and eternal. (See remarks on verses 1-4.) 2. *The solemn declaration of the perpetuity of the covenant.* "One thing have I sworn by My holiness, that I will not lie unto David." God, as it were, pledges His own holiness for the fulfilment of the word which He spake unto David. That attribute which seems most precious to Him He here stakes on the fulfilment of His promise to them. This one thing, that He will keep His word to His servant David, He thus solemnly asseverates. "He abideth faithful: He cannot deny Himself."

CONCLUSION. — Our subject urges, 1. *Confidence as to God's covenant.* Neither the unfaithfulness and sin of man, nor the malice and rage of hell, can frustrate the glorious purposes of God. 2. *Caution as to our conduct.* "If his children forsake My law," &c. Though "you cannot break God's covenant you may violate your own interest therein." "Take heed lest there be in any of you an evil heart of unbelief, in departing from the living God." "Grieve not the Holy Spirit of God, whereby ye are sealed unto the day of redemption."

LAMENTATION AND EXPOSTULATION BY REASON OF THE APPARENT FAILURE OF THE COVENANT OF GOD.

(*Verses* 38-51.)

Confident proclamation of the firmness of the covenant is here succeeded by bitter lamentation of its seeming failure, and upon the lamentation an earnest expostulation with God is founded. Consider,

I. **The lamentation.** The general complaint of the Psalmist is that the covenant has failed. "Thou hast made void the covenant of Thy servant." In his complaint the Psalmist mentions several particulars in which it seemed to be failing, or to have already failed. Let us briefly glance at them:—

1. *The king was dethroned.* "Thou hast profaned his crown to the ground; ... and cast his throne down to the ground." Complaints like these show that, if the king was not actually dethroned, his sovereignty was mutilated, his throne tottering to its fall. The crown, which had always been regarded as sacred, the poet represents as having been treated as though it were an unclean or despised thing to be contemptuously cast to the ground. And the kingdom had come, or was speedily and painfully coming, to a ruinous end.

2. *Their defences were destroyed.* "Thou hast broken down all his hedges; Thou hast brought his strongholds to ruin." In the former clause the king and people are compared to a vineyard, the fences of which were thrown down, and which was open to the ravages of wild beasts and to the depredations of every intrusive passer-by. In the latter clause, they are compared to a city whose fortifications were destroyed. The idea is, that they were left defenceless and helpless, and were completely powerless before their enemies.

3. *They were made the prey and reproach of their neighbours.* "All that pass by the way spoil him; he is a reproach to his neighbours." By the "passers-by," the Psalmist probably meant "the nations of the Asiatic kings who visited Judah in marching through against the king of Egypt;" and by "the 'neighbours,' the surrounding nations who, on a former occasion, approached David and Solomon with reverence and paid tribute (comp. 2 Sam. viii. 2; 1 Kings v. 1). Now they despise the anointed of the Lord in his disgracefully degraded condition (comp. Psa. lxxx. 6; lxxxviii. 8)."

4. *They were defeated in battle and their enemies exulted over them.* "Thou hast set up the right hand of his ad-

versaries," &c. (vers. 42, 43.) Their sword seemed to have lost its ancient sharpness, as though its edge were turned. Their weapons failed them in the day of battle. And, which was much worse, their spirit failed them in the day of battle. They did "not stand in the battle." A courageous spirit will achieve victories even with a blunt sword; but a coward spirit will "not stand in the battle" even though his weapons be of the finest. They had been driven before their enemies like craven-hearted weaklings; while those enemies had by their victories over them increased and made firmer their own power, and exulted proudly in their triumphs. "O Lord, what shall I say, when Israel turneth their backs before their enemies?"

5. *Their vigour and glory had ceased.* "The days of his youth hast Thou shortened." Youth is the season of strength. Old age is marked by feebleness and decay. So the period of their prosperity and power had been brought to an unexpected and early close. Premature old age had come upon them. Troubles, calamities, reverses, and, above all, their sins, had cut off their youthful successes and triumphs, and left them weak and decrepit. Their glory had ceased; they were covered with shame. The glory of their sovereign was gone; their splendour and might as a nation had passed away; their circumstances and condition were such as put them to shame. If the Poet and the people contrasted their present state with their state under David, and yet more under Solomon, they must have bitterly felt the change, and may well have bitterly bewailed it. What a difference there was between the *then* and the *now!* and all to the disadvantage of the now.

6. *They attributed their sad condition entirely to their angry rejection by God.* " Thou hast cast off and abhorred, Thou hast been wroth with Thine anointed." They attribute all their calamities to Him. He had wrought all their evils. In His anger He had rejected both his king and the people, as if they had been regarded by Him with contempt or loathing. Now, is this feature of the lamentation true and right? It is true that their calamities came not without the permission of God. He had withdrawn His protection from them, or their enemies would have been powerless against them, and their own power and glory would have remained unimpaired. So far, at least, the Psalmist is right. But why did God withdraw His protection from them? Was it not because they had "forsaken His law and walked not in His judgments, had profaned His statutes, and kept not His commandments?" Their calamities were the natural result of their crimes. They had sown the seed of sin, and were reaping a harvest of shame and suffering. Yet in their complaint there is no confession. They bewail their sufferings, not their sins. Herein they were wrong. Their sins had landed them in their present miseries. And, in complaining to God, they should have humbly confessed and repented of their sins. As it is, there is too much reason for the remark : "The complainings of the saints are so exaggerated, that carnal feeling makes itself more apparent in them than faith." Is there not a lesson here for Christian believers and churches? Are there not churches today in a reduced, feeble, inglorious condition, which are bewailing their depressed state, as though it were entirely of the Lord's doing? Let such churches search for the sins, of omission or commission, which is the root of their failure and misery. Let them put forth every accursed thing from amongst them, and God will invigorate them with power, enrich them with success, and crown them with honour; and if any Christian finds feebleness and failure coming upon him as an individual, let him not blame God, but examine his own life, and renounce the secret sin or the questionable practice, or take up the neglected duty, which has caused the spiritual loss and decline.

II. **The Expostulation.** "How long, Lord? wilt Thou hide Thyself for ever? shall Thy wrath burn like fire?" &c. In his expostulation with God the Psalmist takes up several things and turns them into effective pleas.

1. *The duration of their distresses.* "How long, Lord?" This verse teaches— (1) *That their distresses were very great.* The gracious presence of God was quite hidden from them. All was darkness; and His wrath seemed to be consuming them. (2) *Their distresses had long continued.* So long had God's countenance been hidden from them, that the Poet inquires if it is always to be so. It seemed as though their night would never be succeeded by morning; their winter never pass into spring. (3) *Their distresses threatened their utter extinction.* It seemed to them as though God's wrath, like fire, would burn on until they were utterly consumed; that their miseries would continue until their national existence was clean gone. But the main thought in the mind of the Poet in this verse seems to be the long duration of their distresses. For some time they had pressed heavily upon them. No sign of relief for them could they discover anywhere.

2. *The brevity of their life.* "Remember how short my time is." The brevity of life is frequently stated in the Sacred Scriptures. Human life upon earth is compared to a flower, to grass, to a shadow, to "a vapour which appeareth for a little time and then vanisheth away." The Psalmist here brings in the brevity of life as an argument for the speedy interposition of God. If the distresses were not speedily removed life itself would be gone. If the Divine mercy were to be manifested, it must be manifested speedily, or it would be too late for them. Must their brief life be all spent in misery? We may surely derive a hint from the Psalmist here. If life be so brief, let us seek the favour of God at once. If life be so brief, let us discharge its duties as they arise. If life be so brief, let us improve its opportunities and privileges as they arise.

3. *The vanity of their life.* "Wherefore hast Thou made all men in vain?" The idea in the mind of the Psalmist seems to be, that if their distresses were continued their life itself would be vain. He seems to have had no clear idea of a blessed life beyond death. That was not clearly revealed until our Lord Jesus Christ poured a flood of light upon it. And, in his present troubled mood, the Psalmist was not able to make the most of the light which he possessed upon the subject, and so the future appears dark and cheerless to him. In fact, he writes as if he knew no future; as if all his hopes were bounded by the grave. So man seems to him to have been made in vain. Life seemed altogether shadowy, unreal, worthless. He urges this characteristic of life as a reason why God should grant them speedy relief. His plea seems to amount to this: Consider how worthless the life of man is, and relieve its darkness and vanity by sending us prosperity, and by sending it quickly.

4. *The certainty of death.* "What man is he that liveth, and shall not see death? shall he deliver his soul from the hand of the grave?" "There is no man that hath power over the spirit to retain the spirit; neither hath he power in the day of death; and there is no discharge in that war." Death is no respecter of persons or of characters. The rich and the poor, the distinguished and the unknown, the strong and the weak, the beautiful and the deformed, the wise and the foolish, the holy and the sinful, the useful and the baneful are alike swept away by death. The argument of the Psalmist seems to be this: As all men, even the strongest, even the king himself, must die, deliver us speedily from the miseries which now oppress us, and grant us prosperity before we pass into dark Sheol.

5. *The lovingkindness promised by God.* "Lord, where are Thy former lovingkindnesses which Thou swarest unto David in Thy truth?" The former lovingkindnesses are those which God had granted in earlier and prosperous times, and which were regarded as pledges of future mercies. And God had promised to David a continuance of these mercies to his seed. The Psalmist asks God: Where are Thy promises? Art Thou not the Unchangeable? Wilt Thou not make good that which Thou hast spoken? Thus may we in our distresses plead the former mercies and the promises of God, and we shall never plead them in vain.

What God has done, He will do again. What He has promised, He will perform.

6. *The reproaches which fell upon them.* "Remember, Lord, the reproach of Thy servants," &c. (vers. 50, 51). Their enemies mocked them because of their sore distresses; and they pray God to end their distresses, and so remove their reproach. The Psalmist pleads powerfully in these two verses. They were His "*servants*" who were reproached, and they were reproached for trusting and serving Him; and would He not roll back the reproach from them? This reproach was a great sorrow to the Psalmist, and to all who were concerned for the welfare of the people and the honour of God. The reproach of all the people, their troubles, their complaints, the scoffs of their enemies, all pressed upon the heart of the Psalmist as a burden of deep grief. Should he feel these things so deeply, and would God be unmindful of them? Would not God remove the reproaches, and so relieve the heart of His servant? The reproaches came from the "*enemies*" of God. They were not only foes and mockers of the covenant people, they were enemies of the covenant God, would He not remember and silence them? They reproached the "*anointed*" of God. "They have reproached the footsteps of Thine anointed." They, as it were, followed the king, and wherever he went and whatever he did they reproached him. Would the Most High allow His enemies thus to deride the anointed king of His own people? Thus the Psalmist amidst the national distresses, when the covenant seemed on the very eve of utter failure, pleads with God for His saving interposition. His pleading is not perfect. As we have already indicated, there is no recognition of the fact that their distresses arose from their sins; there is no confession of the gross violation of the covenant on the part of the people. It was their sufferings and not their sins that they bewailed before God. Yet we may learn some useful lessons from the pleadings of the Psalmist. In present distresses we shall do well to plead (1) *Our weakness and the shortness of our life.* God is strong and merciful, and will help and pity us. (2) *We should take encouragement from and plead God's former mercies.* He is unchangeable. Past deliverances are reasons for hope and confidence in present distresses. (3) *We should plead His faithfulness.* By relying upon His word we honour Him. (4) *We should plead our relation to Him.* We are His servants. His enemies are also ours. Will He not protect and save His own?

CONCLUSION.—1. *Learn the exceeding sinfulness of sin.* It was sin that had profaned the crown to the ground, &c. Let suffering deter from sin. 2. *Learn not to judge by appearances.* "Things are not what they seem." The covenant seemed to be utterly failing, yet God was all the time fulfilling it, carrying it forward to deeper, diviner, more glorious issues than the people imagined when this Psalm was written. God's word cannot fail. His promises cannot be broken. He may fulfil them in ways unexpected by and strange to us; but He will fulfil them gloriously. Christ and His seed shall be eternally blessed. "His seed shall endure for ever, and His throne as the sun before Me."

THE VANITY OF MAN APART FROM HIS IMMORTALITY.

(*Verse* 47.)

I purpose to show that, considered merely in this present state, apart from any reference to eternity and the prospect disclosed by revelation, man is made in vain.

I. The first thing that strikes us in such a survey of our being is **the shortness of its duration.** "Remember how short my time is." The transient nature of his existence stamps an inexpressible meanness on man, if we confine our view to the present life; and forces us to confess that, laying aside the hope of immortality, "Every man at his best estate is altogether vanity."

II. The same reflection must have

occurred to most persons of a thoughtful character, when they have contemplated **the general state of that world** in which we are placed : the mischief and misery that pervade it; the disorder and desolation which the unruly passions of men perpetually introduce ; the wantonness with which they rush to deeds of violence and injustice; the almost incessant national contentions, in which the destruction of one part of the human race seems to become the business and sport of the other. . . . Viewed, therefore, merely as they are here, and excluding the supposition of a future state, all men will appear to be made in vain.

III. When we recollect how many thousands of our species are born the **subjects of some inherent, incurable disease, or imperfection of body,** such as may be said to render their life a protracted malady,—when we call to mind how many are constitutionally the victims of dejected spirits and a morbid melancholy, such as cast a gloom over every surrounding object, and dim their perceptions to the fairest scenes of life and nature, we are compelled to acknowledge, of the multitude so circumstanced, that—if we consider them merely as existing in that hypothetical state which terminates with death—they also are made in vain.

IV. When we take into the account those millions of mankind who are condemned, through the whole of life, to **manual and mechanical labours;** whose day after day is consumed in a constant round of the same unvaried employment, . . . who that limits his view of man to this sublunary scene can forbear to sympathise with the desponding Psalmist in the text? In labours like these millions of beings are employed, who are created with a mind capable of looking backward and forward with endless activity of thought, capable of comprehending truth and advancing in knowledge, capable of enjoying a happiness commensurate with its own vast desires. The inheritors of such faculties are employed in labours in which the mind is altogether passive and dormant, nor is any exercise afforded to the reason or the affections. . . . . . .

Without blaming the existing organization of society, I ask whether, if men are condemned to terminate their existence in these pursuits, and are not reserved for another and higher state of being, the great majority of mankind are not made in vain?

V. But there are those, it may be said, who do not fall under this melancholy representation ; **men of wealth,** whose circumstances seem to be formed by their will, and who appropriate whatever they desire. Surely, you will say, such "men of this world, *have* their portion in *this* life ;" surely an existence like theirs, even if we suppose it confined to earth, apart from any ulterior consideration, has a sufficient end in itself ; and, though their existence is short, they are exempt from a charge of having been made in vain. Now there is a delusion in this view ; and if we examine the advantages which men of wealth possess over others, we shall find that nearly all the pleasures peculiar to superfluous opulence are reducible to two classes ; the class of *sensual gratifications* and that of *ambitious distinctions.*

1. How little the *gratifications of sense* which the rich have at their command, can be said to redeem their possessors from the lot of a vain existence, will appear by the following considerations—(1) The pleasures of sense can never be proposed as an adequate end of our creation ; because, in pursuing them, we always regard them as subordinate to something of superior importance, our regard to which is allowed to be the just rule of sensual indulgence. A wise man advises a proper abstinence from such pleasures for the sake of *health ;* a good man for the sake of *virtue ;* either of which is justly regarded as an object superior to that which it ought to regulate. But the true end of existence must be something beyond which nothing can be proposed of superior magnitude, &c. (2) The pleasures of sense pursued beyond a certain limit, so far from tending to create happiness, tend to destroy it, by the very construction of those organs which are the instruments of sensual

enjoyment. That craving after happiness which every bosom feels, and the satisfaction of which involves the perfection of our existence, cannot be supposed to attain its proper object in any of those animal pleasures, of which the pursuit (unless kept in continual check) leads to the extinction of happiness and existence itself. (3) The enjoyment of the senses cannot present to *human* beings the appropriate and distinguishing end of their extinction, because they are only enjoyed by man in common with the lower animals. *That*, whatever it be, which forms the true end of *human* existence, must be something which is adapted to the great peculiarities of our nature as *rational* and *moral* beings; but sensual fruition is received in an equal, perhaps a greater, degree, by the brutes. . . . He who should abandon himself, in the gratification of animal propensities, to the neglect of every higher aim, would be universally allowed to have lived "in vain."

2. But there is another class of pleasures with the command of which wealth supplies us—the *pleasures of ambition* — the respect and homage which are paid to high station and splendid circumstances. Now, on an examination of these pleasures, it will be found that they are unreal and imaginary; that they consist of nothing more than a fiction of the imagination by which we may be said to *identify* ourselves, or to be identified by others, with all those varied instruments of pleasure which affluence commands, by which we *diffuse* ourselves as it were over the whole sphere in which we preside. . . . *Men of wealth* are not, more than others, exempt from the mournful charge of the Psalmist.

VI. Neither can we exempt from the same condition **men of knowledge,** who pass life in the cultivation of intellect and the pursuit of truth, an object better suited to the nature, and better proportioned to the dignity of man as a rational being than those before-mentioned. That the pleasures of knowledge and intellect are noble in their nature, exquisite in their degree, and permanent in their continuance, will not be denied by those who are competent to estimate them.

1. But to how *few* are these pleasures confined? Not one person in a thousand has either the abilities or the opportunities requisite to their high enjoyment; while to the rest, to the great bulk of mankind, they are the hidden treasures of a sealed book. And can *that* be supposed the final object of our being, which can be enjoyed but by a small proportion of those who inherit that being?

2. Of the few who make knowledge the aim of their engagements, none can secure himself from the intrusion of disturbing passions or distressing accidents. The lights of philosophy are liable to be broken by the waves of adversity and darkened by the clouds of grief, &c.

3. We have it, on the testimony of one of the greatest proficients in knowledge that ever appeared among men, that "increase of knowledge," far from being increase of happiness, is "increase of sorrow." Certain is it that the mere *knowledge* of things is something extremely different from the *enjoyment* of things. Knowledge has its abode in the *understanding*, while happiness is seated in the *heart*. Knowledge cannot be supposed to constitute that proper happiness of man without which he is "made in vain."

VII. There yet remains another and a yet more elevated order of men, who place the grand object of their being in **religion**; who think of God, trust in God, and, on all occasions, devote themselves to do the will of God, &c. . . . What shall we say of such men? If this were the only state of being ordained for man, *they*, like others, would be made in vain. "Verily, they have cleansed their hearts in vain," &c. "If in *this* life only they have hope, they are of all men *most* miserable," *most* worthy to be commiserated. For, according to this supposition, they are the *only* persons who are utterly disappointed in their object; the only persons who (by a fatal and irreparable mistake), expecting an imaginary happiness in an imaginary world, lose their only opportunity of enjoying those present pleasures of which others avail themselves. . . .

But that supposition is *not*, for a moment, to be believed: these men are *not* thus deluded; they are *not* thus to be disappointed; it is impossible to conceive that they are. The perplexity, the inconsistency, the palpable absurdity into which *those* are driven who argue upon the non-existence of immortality, the falsehood of revelation, proves, as far as proof can be expected, that *theirs* is a false hypothesis! Upon *their* hypothesis, man is the greatest enigma in the universe; that universe itself is a problem not to be solved: all is mystery, confusion, and despair. Bring in the light of revelation and immortality, the clouds and thick darkness in which the scene was enveloped disperse, and all is clear and harmonious. We learn at once the cause and the cure of that vanity, in subjection to which "the whole creation groans," together with man. The origin of our misery and death, the recovery of life and immortality, are alike brought to light.

To attain a share in this salvation, to recover the true end and perfection of our existence, in the resemblance and the favour of "*the only happy God;*" this is the great object of desire and pursuit to those whose eyes are opened to their real situation, and whose hearts are awakened to a sense of their real want. And "remembering how short their time is," they are the more in earnest that, by a glorious reverse of their naturally ruined state, they may prove at last to have *not* been "made in vain."

I infer the extreme folly and misery of those who persist in the neglect of this salvation, this immortality. What must be our emotion should we discover, at the last judgment, that we have lived *in vain;* that, so far as our own interest is concerned, we have been made *in vain;* that we have received the grace of God *in vain;* that, having neglected the one salvation, we are *lost*, lost in the scale of being; immortal creatures, *lost* to the great purpose for which our Maker gave us existence; *lost* to happiness; irrecoverably and for ever *lost!* . . . "Now is the accepted time," &c.—*Robert Hall. Abridged.*

DOXOLOGY.

(*Verse* 52.)

This verse, says Hengstenberg, "does not at all belong to the Psalm, but contains the doxology which concludes the third book."

I. **God is blessed in Himself.** All distracting and distressing elements are entirely absent from His nature. Man suffers much from guilt, from uncontrolled passions, and from dark forebodings. Conscience accuses and condemns him, evil passions lash his soul into fury, the dread of suffering, and death, and hell afflicts him. All these things are utterly alien from the Divine nature; while all those things which contribute to the blessedness of spiritual being are found in Him in infinite perfection. Truth, holiness, and love essentially inhere in Him in full perfection and infinite degree. In terms such as these He is represented to us in the Scriptures:— "God is light," "God is good," "God is love," "A God of truth and without iniquity, just and right is He," "the God of peace," "the God of hope," &c. Such a Being must be blessed by virtue of His own character. God is an infinite ocean of life, love, and blessedness. "God blessed for ever." "The God and Father of our Lord Jesus Christ is blessed for evermore."

II. **God is blessed by His creatures.** God blesses man by the impartation of benefits; man blesses God by the ascription of praise.

1. *God is praised by His works.* "All Thy works shall praise Thee, O Lord." Nature in her beauty and bounty praises Him. The birds and beasts also, when unoppressed by man, seem in many ways to praise God. Moreover, as God's works answer the beneficent ends for which they were created, they speak forth the praise of His wisdom, power, and goodness.

2. *God is praised by His people upon earth.* They praise Him *for what He is in Himself;* for His truth, purity, power, mercy, love, spiritual beauty. They praise Him for *what He has done, and is ever doing for them* (Psa. ciii. 1–12). But we must remember that this doxology belongs to every Psalm of this third book. And in this book there are Psalms of the doubting and of the distressed as well as of the believing and rejoicing; there are cries of misery and complaints of suffering as well as songs of gladness and hymns of praise. Thus the people of God would praise Him in the varying scenes and circumstances of life. In all circumstances He is good. Even in times of darkness and distress faith will enable the godly man to say, " Blessed be the Lord for evermore." " The Lord gave, and the Lord hath taken away; blessed be the name of the Lord." *The godly soul is earnestly resolved thus to bless God.* The seal of faith is added twice to this doxology, " Amen and Amen." " Here is a double *Amen,*" says Matthew Henry, " according to the double signification. *Amen*—*so it is,* God is blessed for ever. *Amen*—*be it so,* let God be blessed for ever."

3. *God is praised by redeemed men and angels in heaven.* By angels (Isa. vi. 1–3; Rev. vii. 11, 12). By the redeemed in heaven (Rev. v. 9, 10; vii. 9, 10; *et al.*)

4. *God is praised by all His creatures everywhere* (Rev. v. 9–14).

III. **God is blessed for ever.** "For evermore." His worship will occupy His creatures through all eternity. In heaven all our work will be worship, and all our life praise, and all will be perpetual.

PSALM XC.

INTRODUCTION.

Superscription.—"*A prayer of Moses the man of God.*" " The Psalm is described in the title," says Hengstenberg, " as a *prayer.* This description shows, as Amyraldus saw, that the kernel of the Psalm is the *second* part, and that the design of the first is to prepare the way for the second, and lay down a basis on which it may rest. For תפלה denotes only prayer in the proper sense, supplicatory prayer." On תפלה as used here Fuerst says : " תפלה is a peculiar kind of song in the Psalter. Its primary meaning he gives as *prayer.* And on its use in Psalm lxxii. 20, he says : " The first two books of the Psalter are termed in the subscription תפלות probably because they contain *supplications* for the most part." Certainly the word *prayer* better represents the character of this Psalm than the word *Psalm,* or *hymn.*

"*Of Moses.*" " The correctness of the title which ascribes the Psalm to Moses," says Professor Alexander, " is confirmed by its unique simplicity and grandeur; its appropriateness to his trials and circumstances ; its resemblance to the law in urging the connection between sin and death; its similarity of diction to the poetical portions of the Pentateuch, without the slightest trace of imitation or quotation ; its marked unlikeness to the Psalms of David, and still more to those of later date ; and finally, the proved impossibility of plausibly assigning it to any other age or author." And Amyraldus says : " But as this ode is most ancient, so it bears strong marks of the genius and character of antiquity. It is grave, full of majesty and authority, adorned with various comparisons, splendid with figures, but these rare and little used, and for the understanding of which there is needed extraordinary attention of mind." The late Dr. James Hamilton points out that " it is one of the oldest poems in the world. Compared with it Homer and Pindar are, so to speak, modern, and even King David is of recent date. That is to say, compared with this ancient hymn the other Psalms are as much more modern as Tennyson and Longfellow are more modern than Chaucer. In either case there are nearly five centuries between."

"*The man of God.*" Moses is thus described also in Deut. xxxiii. 1 ; Josh. xiv. 6 ; and Ezra iii. 2. The term is very appropriately applied to him because of his singularly noble character, his distinguished rank, and the great part which he played in carrying out the purposes of God concerning our race. " Moses was faithful in all his house, as a servant." Luther points out that the words " the man of God " give additional weight to the Psalm. He says : " As one who has such a duty assigned to him by God, so that we should believe in him and in his instructions no less than in God Himself."

Occasion. It is impossible to decide upon what occasion the Psalm was composed; but the probability is, that it was written towards the close of the forty years wandering in the wilderness. "It was written," says F. W. Robertson, "evidently in the wilderness, after years of apparently fruitless wandering; its tone is that of deep sadness—retrospective; its images are borrowed from the circumstances of the pilgrimage—the mountain flood, the grass, the night watch of an army on the march."

Divisions. The Psalm consists of a Meditation (vers. 1–11), and a Prayer (vers. 12–17).

HUMAN FRAILTY AND DIVINE GREATNESS.
(*Verses 1–6.*)

In these verses, the Psalmist brings before us—

I. The greatness of God. "Before the mountains were brought forth, or ever Thou hadst formed the earth and the world, even from everlasting to everlasting Thou art God."

1. *He existed before the world.* The word "*earth*" is used by the Psalmist to denote our world as distinguished from the heavens; and the word "*world*" signifies an inhabited fruitful land, or a land fitted for habitation. The "*mountains*" are mentioned first, because of all created things they appear most ancient, stable, and enduring. Upon all the generations that have ever trod this planet, with all their anxieties and cares, all their strifes and commotions, the old hills have cast their calm and silent shadows. They seem as though they had ever been where they are and as they are, and that they would for ever continue so. They are most impressive symbols of the unchangeable and the eternal. In the poetic diction of the Bible they are spoken of as eternal. Jacob spake of "the everlasting hills." And Moses, "of the ancient mountains, and of the lasting hills." And Habakkuk, of "the everlasting mountains, and the perpetual hills." Yet they had a beginning. There was a time when they were not. However ancient the earth may be, it has not been from everlasting. The world is not eternal. God existed before the mountains were brought forth, before the world was created.

2. *He created the world.* He is said by the Psalmist to have "formed the earth and the world." As God's existence before the world proclaims the fact that it is not eternal, so His creation of the world proclaims the fact that it is not the product of chance. The sublime mountains were not upreared, the smiling valleys were not laid by any "fortuitous concourse of atoms." "God created the heaven and the earth." "He spake, and it was done; He commanded, and it stood fast."

3. *He is eternal.* "From everlasting to everlasting Thou art, O God." To understand eternity is difficult; to explain it is more difficult; to comprehend it is impossible to all except the Eternal. We are acquainted with creatures which have a beginning, live for a few hours, or days, or months, or years, and then cease to be. We are also acquainted with creatures who have been called into existence and will never pass out of existence. Such are we, and probably such are the angels. A little while ago, and we were not. Now we are called into being, and shall continue to be for ever. Our bodies shall change and pass away, our memory shall cease from amongst men upon the earth. But *we* shall never cease to be. To everlasting Thou art, O man! But God has never had a beginning, and will never have an end. (1) *He is without beginning.* "From everlasting." "Time," says Charnock, "began with the foundation of the world; but God, being before time, could have no beginning in time. Before the beginning of the creation and the beginning of time there could be nothing but eternity; nothing but what was uncreated,—that is, nothing but what was without beginning. To be in time is to have a beginning; to be before all time is never to have a beginning, but always to be; for, as between the Creator and creatures there is no medium, so between time and eternity there is no medium. It is as easily deduced that He that was before all creatures is eternal, as He that made all creatures is God. If He

had a beginning, He must have it from another, or from Himself; if from another, that from whom He received His being would be better than He,—so more a God than He. He cannot be God that is not supreme; he cannot be supreme that owes his being to the power of another. He would not be said only to have immortality as He is (1 Tim. vi. 16), if He had it dependent upon another; nor could He have a beginning from Himself; if He had given beginning to Himself, then He was once nothing; there was a time when He was not. If He was not, how could He be the cause of Himself?" H● is without beginning of days. He is "from everlasting." (2) *He is without end.* "To everlasting." "The reason that anything decays is either its own native weakness, or a superior power of something contrary to it. There is no weakness in the nature of God that can introduce any corruption, because He is infinitely simple without any mixture, nor can He be overpowered by anything else. A weaker cannot hurt Him, and a stronger than He there cannot be; nor can He be outwitted or circumvented, because of His infinite wisdom. As He received His being from none, so He cannot be deprived of it by any: as He doth necessarily exist, so He doth necessarily always exist." He is the SELF-EXISTENT—the "I AM." "The Father," said Christ, "hath life in Himself." The idea of omnipotence is associated with His eternity in the mind of the Psalmist,—His omnipotence to guard His people. Luther says, "If we look at it" (His eternity) "in a right way, it includes all the properties of the Godhead. For, inasmuch as He is eternal, it follows that He is immortal, omnipotent, blessed, and wise." And Schleiermacher: " The eternity of God is to be understood only as the omnipotent eternity, as that in God which conditionates time itself, as well as all that is temporal." How incomprehensibly great is God! When imagination has done her utmost to picture His eternity, it has failed in the attempt. We may add ages to ages, and multiply them by the leaves of the forest in "the leafy month of June," and multiply them again by the blades of grass upon the face of the earth, and again by the grains of sand upon the seashore, and again by the particles of dust on the earth, and we shall be as far as ever from the measurement of the ages of eternity. "Great God, how infinite art Thou!"

II. **The frailty of man.** In the verses in which the Psalmist sets this forth there are three things which call for notice—

1. *The extreme brevity of man's life upon earth.* This is variously represented. *How short is human life in the sight of God!* "A thousand years in Thy sight are but as yesterday when it is past, and as a watch in the night." A day when it is past and gone appears to us but a very short time. To God a thousand years are as brief as one past day is to us. Nay, to Him a thousand years are as brief as a watch in the night is to us. The Jews divided the night into watches, each watch representing the time during which a sentinel remained on duty. Among the ancient Hebrews there were three such watches; the first, or "the beginning of the watches" (Lam. ii. 19); the second, or "the middle watch" (Judg. vii. 19); and the third, or "the morning watch" (Exod. xiv. 24). These would last respectively from sunset to 10 p.m., from 10 p.m. to 2 a.m., and from 2 a.m. to sunrise. A thousand years appear to God as brief as a night watch to the Israelites. Man lives not a thousand years: "The days of our years are threescore years and ten." How short, then, must man's life upon earth appear to God! To man a life of seventy years, especially when it is in prospect, appears very long. To God, who sees all things clearly and truly, man's life, even if it should stretch to a thousand years, would appear brief as a night watch does to us. The Psalmist also speaks of human life as "*carried away as with a flood.*" We have seen the river swollen with heavy rain rushing rapidly and irresistibly onward to the ocean. So the human family is carried away. Generation after generation is hurried from time into the vast ocean of eternity as by an

impetuous and roaring torrent. "The man of God" goes on to say that human life is like "*a sleep in the morning.*" Barnes suggests that the words "in the morning" should be attached to the middle clause of the verse, and expounds the clause thus—" They are as sleep appears to us in the morning, when we wake from it—rapid, unreal, full of empty dreams." Martin Luther says: "We know that sleep is such a thing that it ceases ere we can perceive it or mark it; for, before we are aware that we have slept, sleep is gone and ended. Wherefore truly our life is nothing else than a sleep and a dream, for before we are rightly conscious of being alive, we cease to live." There is much of unreality in human life upon earth.

"We are such stuff as dreams are made of,
And our little life is rounded by a sleep."

Moses also compares our life to the "*grass.*" The last clause in the fifth verse is rendered in the margin—"like grass which is changed." Hengstenberg translates, "It vanishes like grass." Barnes—"Like grass, it passeth away." The sixth verse Hengstenberg renders— " In the morning he blooms and—perishes; in the evening he is cut down and withers." The idea is clear: like the grass or flower which in the morning is green or blossoming in beauty, and in the evening is cut down and withered by the sun, is man's life upon earth. "As for man, his days are as grass; as a flower of the field so he flourisheth; for the wind passeth over it and it is gone, and the place thereof shall know it no more." How frail is human life, and how uncertain! Every day many go forth in the morning in apparent health and vigour, and before night they are cut down by disease or accident. And even at its longest our life cannot be compared to the cedar or even to the oak, but to the frail grass of the field.

2. *The mournful end of man's life upon earth.* " Thou turnest man to destruction, and sayest, Return, ye children of men." Perowne: " Thou turnest frail man to dust." There is without doubt a reference here to the curse pronounced upon our race, " Dust thou art, and unto dust shalt thou return." The human body must return to dust, however noble or beautiful it may be. Kings and the meanest of their subjects, millionaires and paupers, the learned and the ignorant, the beautiful and the deformed, the saint and the sinner, must all alike, as regards their bodies, return to the earth. Let the remembrance of the fact humble us. Let those who are proud of their stateliness or beauty remember that in a little time they will have no pre-eminence over the most deformed and repulsive-looking of their fellow-mortals. Let the rich, who look down with contempt and scorn upon the poor, remember that, though after death their bodies may be carried with pomp and laid in some splendid mausoleum, yet in this respect they have no advantage over those who are buried in a parish coffin and a pauper's grave—the bodies of all alike must return to dust.

3. *The great sovereign of man's life upon earth.* The Psalmist regards human life as entirely under the control of God. "THOU turnest man to destruction," &c. " THOU carriest them away," &c. It is not disease or chance that removes men from this world. Man returns to the dust not because of the decree of fate, or the operation of some inevitable or irresistible law, but because God wills it. He has the keys of death and hades. Man's "days are determined, the number of his months are with Thee, Thou hast appointed his bounds that he cannot pass." "All the days of my appointed time will I wait, till my change come." In the Lord's " hand is the soul of every living thing, and the breath of all mankind." " Thou changest man's countenance and sendest him away." The *time*, the *place*, and the *circumstances* of our death are all determined by God. He is the great sovereign of our life upon earth.

III. **The relation between the great God and frail man.** "Lord, Thou hast been our dwelling-place in all generations." When Moses penned this Psalm the Israelites were homeless wanderers. Indeed, up to this time they never could be said to have had any settled home. Their father Abraham after his call from his own country lived a wandering life, a stranger in a strange land. Isaac and Jacob also had no settled dwelling-place, but dwelt in tents, and confessed that they were "strangers and pilgrims on the earth." Then the people "went down into Egypt to sojourn there," and it was not long before their lives were made miserable by the oppressions of the Egyptians. And after their emancipation from Egypt there followed their long, tedious, homeless, and apparently fruitless wandering in the wilderness. It was probably this unsettled, homeless condition that led them to estimate highly the worth of a habitation, and which suggested the employment of the figure in the first verse. In their defenceless, homeless state God Himself had been their home and defence. By His providence He had preserved them in existence as a people, had supplied their wants, and protected them from harm. Homeless wanderers they were, yet they found their home in God. "Here we have no continuing city." By many and earnest voices God is calling to us—"Arise ye and depart, for this is not your rest." We crave a dwelling-place, a lasting home, a permanent rest for the soul; but we cannot find it here. Here fairest things soonest fade, brightest prospects soon are lost in darkness, the most exquisite pleasures are speedily succeeded by the most painful trials. The home of the soul is not here. The heart seeks rest and home in the love of dear relatives and friends; but these may fail us in our time of need, or may be summoned from us by death. The best and truest of relatives or friends cannot meet all the soul's cravings for protection, and rest, and home. The home of the soul is not in the creature. The home of the soul is in God.

1. *We are weak, and rest in His omnipotence.* The difficulties and dangers which we encounter on our pilgrimage overmatch us, but by the strength of the Lord we are enabled to surmount them. The soul that finds its home in Him is inviolably secure.

2. *We are short-lived and rest in His eternity.* "We are but of yesterday and know nothing, because our days on the earth are as a shadow."

"Like clouds that rake the mountain summits,
Or waves that own no curbing hand;"

so generation follows generation "into the land of the great departed." We are hastening after the great multitude who have passed from earth for ever. Nothing rests here. Here nothing abides. Change, decay, death are stamped upon all earthly things. Yet we crave the permanent and the immutable. Oh, for some rock amid this surging sea! Oh, for some thing or being in which these restless, craving hearts may find satisfaction and repose! God is that Being. "Lord, Thou hast been our dwelling-place in all generations," &c. He lives through all generations. He is the Sovereign of all generations. He is the same through all generations. Here we find rest. Our permanent home is in Him. He is supremely, unchangeably, eternally great and good. In Him let us confide. The generations that have passed away have gone at His bidding. He is the God of our life. Our age, our time of residence here, our departure from here, are all regulated by Him. And when we pass hence He is still our home, our refuge, and our rest. Then we need not mourn the brevity of life or the changes of time. We rest in the eternal and unchangeable God.

THE HOME OF THE SOUL.

(*Verse* 1.)

I. **The soul of man needs a home.** I argue this from—

1. *Our sense of weariness and longing for rest.* The heart often aches in loneliness, droops by reason of exhaustion, and yearns unspeakably for repose. Like worn and weary pilgrims we long for rest.

2. *Our sense of peril and longing for protection.* Like Israel in the wilder-

ness we are exposed to danger, and need some strong defence. We crave the shelter and the security of a home.

3. *Our shrinking from death and longing for immortality.* The soul recoils from the idea of going forth from this life unclothed and alone into the unknown. What is there beyond the mystery which we call death? Is there anything? If there is, what is it that is there? The mere thought of ceasing to be is painful. We long deeply for immortality. In the awful loneliness and dread mystery of death where shall we find a refuge and a home?

II. **The soul of man may find a home in God.** He has been the dwelling-place of His people in all generations.

1. *In Him alone can the soul find the rest it craves.* We want rest from the accusations of conscience and the burden of guilt. He alone can pardon. The rest of satisfied affections; the rest of harmony and progress of being; rest from the dread of death;—He alone can impart this full and blessed rest.

2. *In Him alone can the soul find the security it craves.* He is our only sure defence against spiritual perils; and in the sorrows and trials of life He is the only adequate support. Storms are sure to fall; He only can shelter us from their fury. He can even bring strength and joy to us out of our griefs and trials. His power, wisdom, and love are the pledge of our security.

3. *In Him alone can the soul find the permanence it craves.* "He only hath immortality." The continuance in being and blessedness for which we long He, and He alone, can impart. "A perpetuity of bliss is bliss." He gives "eternal life." At His "right hand there are pleasures for ever more." "So shall we ever be with the Lord."

We enter this home through Christ. By Him we rise into fellowship and union with God. "No man cometh unto the Father, but by Me."

GOD'S ABSOLUTE CONTROL OVER MAN'S LIFE.

(*Verse 3.*)

We pass away at the command of God. Not chance, not disease, not accident, not war, but "*Thou* turnest man to destruction!" "*Thou* carriest them away as with a flood!" We are a family whose members are separated and summoned away only by the word and hand of the great Lord of the house. We regard this great power of God over us as—

I. **A reason for acknowledging Him.** As His power over us is irresistible and righteous, we should bow to His will. It is madness to resist Him. "Hast thou an arm like God? or canst thou thunder with a voice like Him?" "He is wise in heart, and mighty in strength: who hath hardened himself against Him, and prospered?" His rule is a fact. He is moving onward to the most complete and universal supremacy. Let us loyally acknowledge Him as our King and our God. Let us move in the line of His purposes.

II. **A reason for seeking His favour.** His power over us being so absolute it is surely our interest to seek friendship with Him. He is condescending and gracious, He is kind and merciful; we may obtain His favour. He calls us to friendship with Himself. Through Christ we may attain unto assured confidence in His favour and friendship,—may know Him not simply as the absolute Sovereign of our life, but also as our supreme Friend.

III. **A consolation in bereavement.** It is consolatory to know that our loved ones who have passed from us were not the victims of chance. Their departure was in all respects ordered by a God of infinite wisdom and kindness. They left us by the appointment of His will, which is ever good. He doeth all things well.

IV. **An encouragement to labour.** Do not fear to attempt great things in life. Let not the dread of death unnerve your spirit and paralyse your arm. You are immortal till your work is done. Until your education in these sublunary scenes is completed, your life is invulnerable against the shafts of death.

V. An antidote against the fear of death. If through Christ we are brought into friendship with God, when the body returns to dust, the spirit will pass into the immediate presence of God. To the good man death is the voice of the Father summoning His child home to Himself. Why should we fear such a voice or such a summons?

CONCLUSION. Let us be thankful that our times are in His hand. Let us tread the path of life with trustful and fearless hearts, for we are safe in the hands of the eternal God.

HUMAN FRAILTY THE RESULT OF HUMAN SIN.

(Verses 7-11.)

In this section of the Psalm Moses represents the brevity of the life of the Israelites in the wilderness as the result of the Divine anger with them by reason of their sin. Their apparently fruitless lives and their death in the wilderness were the punishment of their sin. By reason of some heinous or aggravated offence many were suddenly cut off by God. See Num. xi. 31-35; xvi. 41-50; xxi. 4-6. Moreover all those, from twenty years old and upward, who went forth from Egypt were cut down in the wilderness because of their unbelieving hearts and murmuring tongues, save Caleb and Joshua. There they were doomed to wander till the unbelieving generation had passed away. Little or nothing is recorded of them from the second year of their departure from Egypt until the fortieth year. The only end of their wanderings during those years seems to have been the consumption of the faithless generation. Well does Mr. Spurgeon say: "Moses saw men dying all around him; he lived among funerals, and was overwhelmed at the terrible results of the Divine displeasure." The Psalm has "a solemn and affecting interest, as a penitential confession of the sins which had entailed such melancholy consequences on the Hebrew nation; and as a humble deprecation of God's wrath; and as a funeral dirge upon those whose death had been pre-announced by the awful voice of God." So far all is clear. Concerning those of whom Moses wrote it is literally true that their frailty was the result of their sin. They perished in the wilderness because of their unbelief and ingratitude and rebellion. But is it true of mankind as a whole that *human frailty is the result of human sin?* Is death the penalty of sin? Some passages of the Holy Word say, Yes. The evidence of geology and other sciences says, No. We firmly believe that both are correct. In what way, then, and to what extent, is death the penalty of sin? This is the subject suggested by this portion of the Psalm, and upon which we shall offer some suggestions.

"What is death?" "Death," says one, "is simply another name for discontinuance." "Death," says another, "is the dissolution of the body." But the word is used to express quite distinct and different things. In the Bible the word has at least three uses; indeed it has more, but let us look at these. It is used to denote *physical dissolution.* (See Gen. xxi. 16; xxvii. 7, 10; Deut. xxxiii. 1; and many others.) It is used to denote *the moral condition of unrenewed men.* (See John v. 24; Ephes. ii. 1; 1 John iii. 14; et al.) It is also used to denote *the future punishment of the wicked.* (See Rev. ii. 11; xx. 14; xxi. 8.) No one will dispute that many of the passages which speak of death as the penalty of sin speak of spiritual death, not of physical dissolution. Thus: "In the day that thou eatest thereof thou shalt surely die," cannot fairly be applied to our first parents in regard to corporeal death; for, according to the record in Genesis, Adam lived for centuries after his disobedience, and "begat sons and daughters." And if the words of St. Paul to the Romans, "The wages of sin is death," be applied to physical dissolution, then saint and sinner pay the penalty alike, nay, in some cases, the physical dissolution of the saint may be more painful than that of thousands of most hardened and corrupt sinners. Still there are passages of scripture in which corporeal death seems to be represented as the result of sin. In the punishment pronounced upon Adam for his disobedience, it is said, "In the sweat of thy face shalt thou eat bread, till thou return unto the ground, for out of it wast thou taken: for dust thou art, and unto dust shalt thou return." St. Paul, in writing to the Romans, says, "By one man sin entered into the world, and death by sin; and so death passed upon all men, for that all have sinned." But here we may not limit the meaning of death to physical dissolution. It signifies, says Alford, "primarily, but not *only*, physical death: as ἁμαρτία, so θάνατος, is *general*, including the lesser in the greater, *i.e.*, spiritual and eternal *death.*" (See also Stuart's commentary *in loco.*) In no instance, we believe, where the word *death* is used to express the penalty of sin should its meaning be limited to the dissolution of the body. For the dissolution of the body is natural, and would have taken place even if man had not sinned. We conclude thus—

1. *Because of the testimony of geology.* "We are confronted," says Mr. Froude, "with evidence that death has reigned through all creation from the earliest period, of which the stratified rocks preserve the record." The world had been familiar with death for ages before the creation of man.

2. *Because of the nature of the physical constitution of man.* "Birth, growth, and arriving at maturity, as completely imply decay and death as the source of a river implies the termination of it, or as spring and summer imply corn-fields and reaping. Hence, whatever the vigour and the powers of repair that may pertain to any given structure, whatever resistance it may offer to the shocks of ages, Time, sooner or later, dissolves it; careful, however, to renew whatever it takes away, and to convert, invariably, every end into a new beginning. There is not a grave in the whole circuit of nature that is not at the same moment a cradle."

3. *Because of the limited accommodation which the world affords as a home for man.* "The command given both to animals and man, to 'be fruitful and multiply,' implies the removal of successive races by death; otherwise the world would long since have been overstocked; plants, for their part, are described as created 'yielding seed,' which carries with it the same inevitable consequence. The produce of so minute a creature as a fly would, if unchecked, soon darken the air, and render whole regions desolate; the number of seeds ripened by a single poppy, were they all to grow and be fruitful in their turn, would in a few years suffice to clothe a continent."

4. *Because the material body is a hindrance to man's complete spiritual freedom and perfection.* The human body as it is in this world seems to us to imprison and impede the soul's action and growth. We have faculties which cannot be fully developed here and under our present conditions. "We that are in this tabernacle do groan being burdened," &c. (See 2 Cor. v. 1-4.)

For these and other reasons which may be adduced, we hold that *in itself* the dissolution of the body is not the result of sin. How, then, are we to regard death as the penalty of sin? In what way is human frailty the result of human sin? We reply: in the sufferings with which death is associated.

I. **Death is associated with physical sufferings, and these are the result of sin.** It is true that there are some who die without any physical suffering. But in the great majority of instances the death of man is a thing of strange and severe suffering. The diseases of which men die are most of them very painful, and death itself is a mysterious and probably a painful thing. But the sufferings are the result of sin. If man had not sinned, death would probably have resembled sinking into an easy and gentle slumber, and have been as sweet as sleep is to the weary; it would have been that *euthanasia* to all men which Augustus Cæsar used so passionately to desire, and which is predicated of the

Christian in a well-known and beautiful hymn—

"How blest the righteous when he dies!
When sinks a weary soul to rest,
How mildly beam the closing eyes,
How gently heaves the expiring breast!
So fades a summer cloud away,
So sinks the gale when storms are o'er,
So gently shuts the eye of day,
So dies a wave along the shore!"
—*Barbauld.*

Had it not been for sin, the probability is that no one would have died from disease; dissolution would have been entirely freed from physical sufferings, and would have been as "a gentle wafting to immortal life."

II. Death is associated with mental sufferings, and these are the result of sin. These sufferings arise from—

1. *The dread of death.* In the Epistle to the Hebrews Christ is represented as dying to "deliver them who through fear of death were all their lifetime subject to bondage." We are travellers in "the valley of the shadow of death." That shadow projects itself over life's fairest scenes. And the dread of death seizes us sometimes even in our brightest hours. (1) This dread arises partly from *the mystery of death.* Who knows what strange anguish of body there may be in death? What mental sufferings utterly unknown to us may await us in dying? In the separation of the soul from the body may there not be an awful sorrow? Millions have passed through this experience; but not one has returned to tell us of the mysteries through which they passed. And those that were raised from death by our Lord uttered no word as to its nature. They removed none of the mystery. Each man must solve the mystery for himself. This mystery is distressing. But had it not been for sin it would probably not have existed. Man would probably have had a clear knowledge of the nature and meaning of the transition. And even if the mystery had existed it would certainly not have been distressing, for man would have had such firm and large faith in God as would have enabled him to rise above anxiety and fear. (2) This dread is partly *the dread of non-existence.* Man shrinks from extinction. The thought of passing into utter nothingness, of *not* being, is full of pain to him. But is there life after death? Is not death the end of man? What is there but darkness, oblivion, nothingness, beyond this present and manifest life? Who has not sympathised with the afflicted patriarch in his meditations and questionings? "There is hope of a tree if it be cut down, that it will sprout again," &c. (Job xiv. 7-14). Is there anything after death but "a long, unconscious, never-ending sleep"?

"When shall spring visit the mouldering urn?
Oh, when shall it dawn on the night of the grave?"

But this dread of non-existence is one of the results of sin. Had man not sinned he would have known that death was but transition; nay, that it was the birth of his spirit into a higher state of being. (3) This dread is partly *the dread of a miserable existence.* The consciousness of guilt leads man to dread a future of misery and endless woe. The guilty conscience arrays God in aspects of terror, and pictures a future of terrible suffering as the punishment of sin. But had man not sinned, the future would have been to him bright, beautiful, and inviting, rich in enjoyment and rich in promise.

2. *The sorrows of bereavement.* In the case of those who are called to die, the greatest anguish which they suffer frequently arises from having to leave those whom they love as their own soul. Inconceivable must be the anguish of the loving mother when summoned away from her tender, helpless babe. And who can conceive the deep and silent grief of the kind husband and father who is leaving his wife and children, widowed and orphaned, to fight life's battle without the aid of his strong arm, or wise head, or loving heart? The sorrow of the bereaved is also very great. Tennyson has given utterance to the feeling of thousands of bereaved mourners:

"For this alone on Death I wreak
The wrath that garners in my heart;
He put our lives so far apart,
We cannot hear each other speak."

Oh, the hearts that are almost breaking in loneliness and unutterable distress because of the bereavements of death! But all this distress is the result of sin. If man had not sinned the dying mother would confidently leave her cherished babe, and the dying husband and father his wife and children, to the wise and loving and all-sufficient care of the Heavenly Father. If man had not sinned we should not mourn the departure of our loved ones. With clear perceptions of the spiritual universe, we should see that the separation was more apparent than real, we should know that they are in the enjoyment of a higher, fuller life, a life of blessedness, and that we should soon join them in their high spheres and Divine services. Oh, it is sin that makes bereavement painful! "The sting of death is sin." Take away sin, and though death remain, its repulsiveness and painfulness would be entirely gone. Sin has made dissolution physically painful; sin has shortened men's lives by diseases and crimes; sin has robed death in mystery; sin has made man to shrink from death lest it should lead to non-existence or miserable existence; sin has caused all the anguish of bereavements, all and everything that is painful in death is the result of sin.

CONCLUSION. 1. *Brothers, let us hate sin.* Let us have nothing to do with sin except to resist it, oppose it, save men from it. 2. *Let us be thankful for the Gospel.* Christ is the conqueror of death. He has taken away its sting. He is the Saviour from sin. Those who believe on Him shall become holy and heavenly. To them death is no longer a foe, but the kind messenger of the loving Father.

SIN ESTIMATED BY THE LIGHT OF HEAVEN.

(*Verse 8.*)

The appearance of objects, and the ideas which we form of them, are very much affected by the situation in which they are placed with respect to us, and by the light in which they are seen. . . . No two persons will form precisely the same idea of any object, unless they view it in the same light, or are placed with respect to it in the same situation. . . . God sees all objects just as they are; but we see them through a deceitful medium, which ignorance, prejudice, and self-love place between them and us. Apply these remarks to the case before us. "Thou hast set our iniquities," &c. That is, our iniquities or open transgressions, and our secret sins, the sins of our hearts, are placed, as it were, full before God's face; and He sees them in the pure, clear, all-disclosing light of His own holiness and glory. Now, if we would see our sins as they appear to Him, that is, as they really are; if we would see their number, blackness, and criminality, and the malignity and desert of every sin, we must place ourselves as nearly as possible in His situation, and look at sin as it were through His eyes. Recollect, that the God in whose presence you are, is the Being who forbids sin, the Being, of whose eternal law sin is the transgression, and against whom every sin is committed. Keeping this in mind, let us—

1. Bring forward what the Psalmist, in our text, calls *our iniquities*, that is, our more gross and open sins, and see how they appear in the light of God's countenance. Have any of you been guilty of impious, profane, passionate, or indecent, corrupting language? How does such language sound in heaven? in the ears of angels, in the ears of that God, who gave us our tongues for noble purposes? . . . Is this fit language for God to hear? Let every one inquire whether he has ever violated the third commandment, by using the name of God in a profane or irreverent manner. If he has, let him bring forward his transgressions of this kind, and see how they appear in the light of God's presence. . . . Have any of you been guilty of uttering what is untrue? If so, bring forward all the falsehoods, all the deceitful expressions, which you

have ever uttered, and see how they appear in the presence of the God of truth; of that God, who has declared, that He abhors a lying tongue, and that all liars shall have their portion in the burning lake. Oh, what is it to stand convicted of falsehood before such a God as this! After the above manner treat the sins of *perjury*, *Sabbath-breaking*, *adultery*, *fraud*, *injustice* or *dishonesty*, and *intemperance*.

While attending to the preceding remarks, probably many of my hearers may have felt as if they were not personally concerned in them, as if they were guilty of none of those gross iniquities. I would indeed hope that of some of them, at least, none of you are guilty. But these are by no means the only iniquities of which God takes notice; for our text further informs us, that He has set our *secret* sins, the *sins of our hearts*, in the light of His countenance. Let us then—

II. Bring our hearts into heaven, and there, laying them open to view, see how they will appear in that world of unclouded light and unsullied purity.

What a disclosure is made, when, with the dissecting knife of a spiritual anatomist, we lay open the human heart, with all its dark recesses and intricate windings, and expose the lurking abominations, which it conceals, not to the light of day, but to the light of heaven! Even in this sinful world, the spectacle which such a disclosure would exhibit could not be borne. The man whose heart should thus be laid open to public view would be banished from society; nay, he would himself fly from it, overwhelmed with shame and confusion. Of this every man is sensible, and therefore conceals his heart from all eyes with jealous care. . . . And if the heart laid open to view would appear thus black in this dark, sinful world, who can describe, or conceive of the blackness which it must exhibit, when surrounded by the dazzling whiteness of heaven, and seen in the light of God's presence, the light of His holiness and love? How do proud, self-exalting thoughts appear, when viewed in the presence of Him, before whom all the nations of the earth are less than nothing, and vanity? Speak of *self-will*, *impatience*, *discontent; angry*, *envious*, *revengeful feelings ;* and *wanton*, *impure thoughts*. If all the evil thoughts and wrong feelings which have passed in countless numbers through either of our hearts were poured out in heaven, angels would stand aghast at the sight, &c. To the omniscient God alone would the sight not be surprising. He alone knows what is in the heart of man ; and what He knows of it He has described in brief but terribly expressive terms. "The heart is deceitful above all things, and desperately wicked," &c.

III. Let us take a similar view of our sins of omission. Our sins of omission are by far the most numerous, and by no means the least criminal offences of which we are guilty. Speak of God's perfections, His glory, His goodness to us, and of our obligations to Him. Does He not deserve to be loved, and feared, and served with all the heart, and soul, and mind, and strength? Yet from Him we have all withheld our affections and services. Our whole lives present one unbroken series of duties neglected, of favours not acknowledged. And, oh, how do they appear when we review them in the light of God's countenance! . . .

While God's law requires us to love Him with all the heart, it also requires us to love our neighbour as ourselves. And this general command virtually includes a great number of subordinate precepts, precepts which prescribe the duties of the various relations that subsist between us and our fellow-creatures. How far have we obeyed these precepts? . . . Oh, how much more might we have done, than we actually have done, to promote the temporal and eternal happiness of all with whom we are connected!

Nor do our sins of omission end here. There is another Being whom we are under infinite obligations to love, and praise, and serve with supreme affection. This Being is the Lord Jesus Christ, considered as our Redeemer and Saviour, who has bought us with His blood. We are required to feel that we are not our own, but His; to prefer Him to every earthly object, to rely upon Him with implicit confidence, to live, not to ourselves, but to Him, and to honour Him even as we honour the Father. Every moment, then, in which we neglected to obey these commands, we were guilty of a new sin of omission. . . . How grossly have we failed in performing this part of our duty! How must the manner in which we have treated the beloved Son appear in the sight of God!

A day is approaching in which you will be constrained to see your sins as they appear in the light of God's countenance. When that day arrives, His eternal Son, the appointed Judge, will be seen coming in the clouds of heaven, &c. . . . Be persuaded now to come to the light, that your deeds may be reproved, and set in order before you; exercise such feelings respecting them, and so judge yourselves, that you may not be condemned of the Lord on that day.—*E. Payson, D.D. Abridged.*

LIFE AN EXCLAMATION.

(*Verse* 9.)

"We spend our years as a tale that is told."

The word translated "*tale*" occurs twice: in Job xxxvii. 2, "Hear attentively the noise of His voice, and *the sound* that goeth out of His mouth;" and Ezek. ii. 10, "And there was written therein lamentations, and *mourning*, and woe." In the first passage the reference is to the thunder, which is the voice, the utterance, the grand soliloquy of God. In the second passage the word describes the broken accents of grief, the abrupt and incomplete exclamation of deep and overwhelming sorrow. So when life is described in the text, the meaning is that it is a brief and broken exclamation, a hurried voice, a short and startling sound which is soon lost in the silence of eternity.

I. The main idea of the text is *the transientness of life:* it has the brevity of a cry. And does not this accord with fact? The utterances may be of different lengths, but life is always short. Some lives have only one word, some several, yet is each an exclamation. Some have the completeness of finished sentences; some fail in the midst; some have only a beginning, rather intimate that there is something to be said than say it. Then is life short, indeed, when man dies, not because he has exhausted a force so much as because he has met with an obstruction. And yet how often is this the case! The days are "cut off:" "the sun goes down while it is yet day:" "the flower fadeth." Why did they live at all? What was the reason of their being?

And then, also, is life short when, though its voice fails not at the commencement of its utterance, it is broken off in the midst, and gives no complete expression to the deep meaning with which it is charged. And yet how often is it as an unfinished cry! How often do men pass away before they have half revealed the significance of their being!

But the brevity assigned to life in the text belongs to all life, and not to any lives in particular. It is brevity which marks it as a whole, marks it in its longest term. . . .

Things are long and short in comparison. The sense of duration is not absolute. The insect that lives but a day has, or might have, the feelings with which we regard seventy years. . . . And what those transient creatures are to us, that should we be to others proportionably longer-lived than we. Suppose a being to live two millions of years, he would look down on our existence of seventy years with the same feelings as those with which we regard the creature of a day. It is only eternity that is really long — absolutely long. Compared with that, all time is short. Whatever can cease is as nothing to that which never ceases; it is simply impossible to compare them. . . . Life may seem long while it is going on, &c. But what is life when put against interminable years! We may appropriate both terms, the transient and the endless. We may connect together the life that is but as a broken exclamation, and the life that is as an everlasting voice. I said we may connect them together, but the solemn truth is, that they are connected together independently of our act or thought. That besides which life is vanity will take its character from life. Eternity makes life nothing, and yet everything; sinks it to utter insignificance, and yet invests it with inconceivable importance. Consider the two as contrasted, and life vanishes in the presence of eternity. Consider the two as related, and life partakes of the augustness and awfulness of eternity.

II. If life is transient as a cry, it is a cry *full of meaning.* The importance of utterances does not depend on their length; it is not how long it takes to express a thing, but the nature of the thing expressed, which decides the greatness of the expression. A few words may reveal a world of meaning. . . . It is the fulness of the heart which seeks relief in cries, and that which makes them short makes them significant. Then do fewest words suffice when many words are felt to be too few. Life is a cry, but what does it not reveal? The broken speech of our earthly days is the voice of souls. It shows what we are as souls; our principles, habits, &c. . . . And, showing what we are, it shows also what we shall be, what we shall be for ever. And it does more than show what we shall be, it helps to make us it.

This is the view of life I wish you to take. . . . Regarded alone, we may despise it; we may be angry with it; we may say, "Let us eat and drink, for to-morrow we die;" we may give way to despondency and depression; but, regarded along with what it indicates and prepares for, it will excite us to holy diligence, gird up our loins for hope and service. Thus regarded, its very vanity will only make it more precious, and we shall tremble to neglect the brief period which is the seedtime of eternity. . . .

I ask you, whose life is so evanescent, yet so significant, what are you saying? what is the meaning of that living word which issues forth, consciously or unconsciously, from your hearts? Many different cries proceed from our common nature. Life in some is a cry of *wonder,* an expression of amazement at this mysterious universe, and their own mysterious being. Life in some is a cry of *pain,* . . . grief from physical suffering, grief from adversities of lot, grief from social pressure on the heart's affections. Life in some is a cry of *joy,* the rapid, incoherent speech of ecstatic feeling. I do not ask which of these your life is, nor does it much signify in relation to the most important of all matters. Be it the expression of wonder, pain, or joy, it may be sad or glorious; it may be the wonder of a believing or a sceptical spirit; it may be the pain of a patient or angry spirit; it may be the joy of a spirit whose portion is the world, or whose portion is the Lord. But I do ask you, what is the temper and the form of your life? With many, it is but an *oath;* a revelation of enmity against God and godliness; a forgetfulness of all that should be remembered, a neglect of all that should be cared for, a dislike of all that should be loved, a disobedience of all that should be submitted to. But there are many with whom life is a *prayer;* its exclamations are like ejaculatory supplications; the pouring out of the heart in adoration, petition, praise; the expression of dependence, desire, devotion, &c.

Let me ask you, what are you and what are you likely to be in that eternity which is so speedily to succeed the days which are as a shadow? . . . Life must be sinful if your heart be not renewed by the Holy Ghost; must be wretched if you be not reconciled to God by the death of His Son. Time, which is so short, is the season for conversion, salvation; and without these, when it is passed, you will find yourselves in an eternity for which no preparation has been made. Everlasting life dates from regeneration, not from death; we cannot have the life immortal if we be not born again. Dying in sin, your destiny must be destruction; without God now, you will be without God for ever. Oh! if you have not yet yielded your soul to the Gospel, . . . let me entreat you to awaken to the transient nature of this probationary period. This evanescent life is big with the fortunes of eternity, and you are deciding what they shall be. Be wise, repent, accept the atonement, go in the way of life, &c.—*A. J. Morris. Abridged.*

HUMAN FRAILTY AN INCENTIVE TO SEEK THE DIVINE BLESSING.

(*Verses* 12–17.)

The Psalmist passes from meditation to supplication. Having meditated upon the eternity of God and the transientness and misery of man's life upon earth, and traced man's sufferings to his sins, he here proceeds to implore the blessings of the eternal and unchangeable God upon His frail creature—man. He asks from God—

I. **Help in forming a correct estimate of life.** "So teach us to number our days, that we may apply our hearts unto wisdom."

It would have been reasonable to have concluded, that since man's life is so short and sad he would form a true estimate of it. Yet this he does not. "All men count all men mortal but themselves." Though life is so uncertain, yet every man acts as though he had a certain future guaranteed unto him. Though life is so brief, yet each man acts as though he had a long earthly future before him. A correct estimate of life must include two things—

1. *That it is brief.* "Behold, Thou hast made my days as an handbreadth; and mine age is as nothing before Thee: verily every man at his best state is altogether vanity." (See remarks on "the extreme brevity of man's life upon earth," verses 1–6.)

2. *That it is preparatory.* This world is a great school, and our life in it is educational. We are here to prepare characters for eternity; primarily and pre-eminently, but not exclusively, our own; and to help others in the formation and development of noble characters. What a vast and important work of preparation for eternity has to be done in this brief life! How much have we to do *in and for ourselves!* In us there are angry passions to be quelled, evil habits whose power must be broken, besetting sins to be conquered. And we have so much to acquire: our deficiencies and imperfections are so numerous, our moral power is so feeble, our spiritual aspirations are so irregular and weak. Verily, our preparation for eternity is advanced only a little way. We have much to do before our spiritual education will be anything like complete. Then we have much to do *for others.* The parent has many plans which he wants to see carried out concerning his children. The Christian minister feels that in the exposition and application of Divine truth, and in the oversight of the souls committed to his charge, he has a vast and unspeakably important work yet to do. Every man who takes an interest in his fellow-man must feel that he has much to do in helping to remove the ignorance and sin and suffering of men, by helping them to acquire knowledge, and by leading them to the Saviour from sin and the Healer of suffering. When life is thus estimated men will "apply their hearts unto wisdom."

" 'Tis not for man to trifle! Life is brief,
    And sin is here.
Our age is but the falling of a leaf,
    A dropping tear.
We have no time to sport away the hours,
    All must be earnest in a world like ours.

" Not *many* lives, but only *one* have we—
    One, only one;
How sacred should that one life ever be—
    That narrow span!
Day after day filled up with blessed toil,
Hour after hour still bringing in new spoil."
    —*Bonar.*

The Psalmist supplicates—

II. **The mercy of God in life.** He

prays that God would exercise His mercy towards them—

1. *In the removal of His anger.* "Return, O Lord, how long? and let it repent Thee concerning Thy servants." The Israelites in the wilderness were visited with some severe expressions of the wrath of God by reason of their sin. Their long, and mournful, and apparently fruitless wanderings in the wilderness were a punishment from God because of sin. For a long time they had been bearing the heavy judgments of the Lord; so they cry unto Him, "How long?" How long shall Thy wrath lie heavily upon us? The petition of this verse is very similar to a petition in a former prayer of Moses: "Turn from Thy fierce wrath, and repent of this evil against Thy people." "According to the usual phraseology of Scripture," says Calvin, "God is said to repent, when, after dissipating sadness, and giving again occasions for joy, He appears as if He had changed." Yet really there is no change in God. Repentance is impossible to Him. But when man turns to Him in repentance, He turns to man in mercy. When He withdraws His anger it is not because a change has taken place in Him; but because man has changed, and taken a different position in relation to His law and government. So Moses prays that God would turn in mercy to them, and bring His judgments upon them to an end.

2. *In the communication of satisfaction to them.* "O satisfy us early with Thy mercy." Literally, "Satisfy us in the morning with Thy mercy." In the Scripture suffering and distress are frequently set forth by the emblem of night. Morning is an emblem of salvation and joy. (Comp. Job xi. 17; Ps. xxx. 5.) If God in mercy appeared to the Israelites, that appearance would be to them as the dawn of a joyous morning. They pray for satisfaction in the mercy of God. Under the displeasure of God there can be no satisfaction. If any soul is satisfied out of God, that soul is dead. In His favour is life. Only in God can the human soul, with its unutterable yearnings, its quench- less aspirations, and its profound cravings, find satisfaction and repose.

3. *In granting gladness to them.* In the petitions for gladness three things demand our attention. (1) They seek gladness *as a result of mercy.* "Satisfy us early with Thy mercy; That we may rejoice and be glad." The night of their mourning would end, and the day of their joy would dawn, when God satisfied them with His mercy. From the conscious possession of God's favour the deepest, highest, purest, divinest joy springs. (2) They seek gladness *as a life-long experience.* "All our days." Much of sin, gloom, and suffering had been in their past life; they desire that in all their future life there may be the Divine mercy and holy joy. It is the privilege of the child of God "to rejoice evermore." "Your joy no man taketh from you." (3) They seek gladness *in proportion to their afflictions.* "Make us glad according to the days wherein Thou hast afflicted us, and the years wherein we have seen evil." It is a principle of God's providential dealings that light and darkness, happiness and distress, in human life shall bear some proportion to each other. "In the day of prosperity be joyful, but in the day of adversity consider: God also hath set the one over against the other." He balances the varying experiences of our lives. The Israelites in the wilderness had many days of His displeasure; they entreat as many days of His favour. They had passed through years of mournful wandering; they pray for a corresponding number of years of peace and joy. The Psalmist entreats—

III. **The manifestation of God's power and grace in life.** "Let Thy work appear unto Thy servants, and Thy glory unto their children. And let the beauty of the Lord our God be upon us." Here is a prayer—

1. *That God would work manifestly on their behalf.* "Show to Thy servants Thy doing," is really a prayer for the interposition of God on their behalf; that He would display His great power in introducing them to prosperity. Moses knew how mighty in working Jehovah

is, and so he prays that He would work for them and for their salvation.

2. *That God would grant unto them of His grace.* "Show Thy glory unto their children. And let the beauty of the Lord our God be upon us." God's glory consists of His goodness. When Moses prayed, "I beseech Thee, show me Thy glory," the Lord answered, "I will make all My goodness pass before thee." He is "glorious in holiness," glorious in grace. It is probable that they prayed that God's glory may be manifested to their children, because God had promised to lead their children into the land into which by reason of sin they entered not. That the glory of Divine grace and strength may be displayed to their children, even though themselves may not see it, they earnestly desire. It has been well pointed out "that this prayer was answered. Though the first generation fell in the wilderness, yet the labours of Moses and his companions were blessed to the second. These were the most devoted to God of any generation that Israel ever saw. It was of them that the Lord said, 'I remember thee, the kindness of thy youth, the love of thine espousals, when thou wentest after Me in the wilderness, in a land that was not sown. Israel was holiness unto the Lord, and the first fruits of His increase.' It was then that Balaam could not curse, but, though desirous of the wages of unrighteousness, was compelled to forego them, and his curse was turned into a blessing." "And let the beauty of the Lord our God be upon us" is also a petition for the favour of God; that the beauty of the Divine character may be revealed in them, and be revealed by them to others. If the grace of God dwell richly in us, it will radiate from us in lives of spiritual beauty and power. The Psalmist prays for—

IV. **The establishment of human work in life.** "Establish Thou the work of our hands upon us; yea, the work of our hands establish Thou it." This petition, in its relation to Moses, has a very touching significance. He was to die without seeing the result of the great work of his life. The millions whom he led from Egyptian slavery remained slaves in spirit throughout life; and, because they were slaves and not men, they were not permitted to enter the promised land. Moses himself may see it, but must not enter therein. To a superficial observer his work must have appeared useless, and his life a failure of most magnificent faculties. But his life was no failure; his work was not in vain. That which he had commenced was carried forward to glorious completion. Dr. James Hamilton has truly remarked, that "for forty years it had been the business of Moses to bring Israel into a right state politically, morally, religiously; *that* had been *his* work. And yet, in so far as it was to have any success or enduringness, it must be God's work. 'The work of our hands' do Thou establish; and this God does when, in answer to prayer, He adopts the work of His servants, and makes it His own 'work,'. His own 'glory,' His own 'beauty.'" Human efforts in a good cause, when they are made earnestly and in humble dependence upon the blessing of God for success, cannot be in vain. God will establish them.

CONCLUSION.—"If man be ephemeral, God is eternal." And through Christ man may dwell in God, and be made a partaker of His character and blessedness. In ourselves we are insignificant, vain, worthless—bewildering and mournful enigmas; but in God we rise into harmony, holiness, power, usefulness; life grows deep in significance, brilliant in prospect, and divine in destiny. Through our Lord Jesus Christ let every man seek to become one with God.

AN ALL-IMPORTANT NUMERATION.

(*Verse* 12.)

I. **The Teacher.** The eternal Lord God.

1. *He thoroughly understands the subject.* "Our days," their number, their importance, &c., He knoweth perfectly.

2. *He is thoroughly acquainted with the pupils.* Our circumstances, temperament, aptitude or inaptitude as learners, He knoweth right well.

3. *He has great influence over the pupils.* He can influence our understanding, direct our judgment, work conviction in us.

II. **The pupils.** Frail men. Strange that we should need teaching on this subject. The remarkable frailty and the unspeakable importance of human life is constantly proclaimed by—

1. *The voice of history.* All the generations of the past have gone "the way to dusty death."

2. *The scenes and circumstances of life.* Crowded cemeteries, funeral processions, bereaved families.

3. *Our own experience.* Infirmities, pains, diseases, announce our frailty. Yet we need that God should teach us in this matter. This need indicates disorder in our moral judgment, disinclination to receive the fact of our frailty, &c.

III. **The lesson.** "To number our days." "It is to take the measure of our days as compared with the work to be performed, with the provision to be laid up for eternity, with the preparation to be made for death, with the precaution to be taken against judgment. It is to estimate human life by the purposes to which it should be applied, by the eternity to which it must conduct, and in which it shall at last be absorbed." He numbers his days well who—

1. *Mourns the time past which has been misspent.*

2. *Diligently uses time present.*

3. *Trusts the time future entirely to God.*

IV. **The end.** "That we may apply our hearts unto wisdom." This wisdom is not speculative, but practical; not intellectual, but moral.

1. *True religion is wisdom.*

2. *True religion requires application of heart.*

3. *The remembrance of life's transientness is calculated to promote this application.*

"Therefore, "So teach us to number our days," &c.

(See a fine sermon on this verse, by F. W. Robertson. Sermons, vol. iv.)

THE MERCY OF GOD SOLICITED.

(*Verse* 14.)

On these words the following observations may be founded:—

I. All men have sinned against God, and therefore need mercy.

II. The consideration that life is short and uncertain, has a remarkable tendency to impress this important truth upon the mind.

III. It is the duty of every one to implore the mercy of God by fervent prayer.

IV. The mercy of God is the only satisfying portion.

V. We ought not only to desire that this mercy may be granted, but should pray that it may be imparted "early."

VI. The possessor of God's mercy is qualified to rejoice and be glad all his days.—"*The Young Minister's Companion.*"

THE THREE PETITIONS.

(*Verses* 16, 17.)

Here are three petitions. Let us look at them in their logical order of thought, rather than their poetic expression.

I. The first petition asks for some *visible results* from the work attempted. "Let Thy work *appear.*" Is not this a most natural and lawful petition? The worker longs to see some fruit of his work, some positive testimony that he has not toiled in vain. Do not most men ardently desire this, no matter what the nature of their work? The statesman wishes it, the merchant, the farmer, the teacher, and why not the Christian?

But the Christian is sometimes tempted to carry his desire too far. God may, therefore, think fit to withhold from his sight no small portion of the actual result, lest the servant forget whose the work really is, and what is his true relation to it. He so deals with us that our patience may take root and grow. He disappoints our desire for visible results to draw us nearer to Himself, to deepen our trust, &c. He helps us to understand what we are so slow to learn, that, from the very character of our work, we never can see in this world more than a few conspicuous ears. Yet "the work of our hands"—all of it—will hereafter "appear," not a grain of it lost, not a single product of that grain hidden or obscured. We may, therefore, still continue to offer the petition to the Lord of the harvest, for some visible results of our sowing; but do not let us be discouraged if, for reasons best known to Him, our prayer is not answered here and now.

II. The second petition asks for the *stability* of the work. And is not this as natural as the desire that the work should "appear"? No one wishes that the thing upon which he has bestowed his deepest thought, his severest and most conscientious labour, should be scattered and lost. It depends, humanly speaking, upon the character of the work, how long it will endure. It is so in material works.... Good honest work, even if it be not of the highest type, is the only durable work. But what work can compare in value with "turning men to righteousness?" Many Christian workers, however, tremble for the future of their work. Losing faith in the power of its living energy, they have, as they thought, "established" it, lest it should die out and be no more seen; with what results a hundred damaging facts patent to our eyes declare. The work, in its root of life, is not man's but God's; hence the appropriateness of the second petition, "Establish Thou the work of our hands," &c. The repetition of the prayer is for the sake of emphasis. He began the good work; He alone can make it constant and firm. "Establish Thou it," set it up, as a throne is set up, as a city is founded, as an altar is reared, &c.

III. The third petition asks for the *succession* and *expansion* of the work, for its widest possible influence. The beauty and glory have come upon us Thy servants. Let them also descend upon our children. This is the parent's wish and continual prayer. We pray "that our sons may be as plants grown up in their youth," &c. The sons of Christians are the hope of the Church. The children of Christians are the best workers in the Church to-day; in the home, in the school, in the sanctuary, in the mission-field.

But the petition is for our descendants, near or remote; for all who shall follow us in that grand and never-broken procession through the ages of living men. Nothing less than this expresses the fulness of the prayer, "Thy kingdom come; Thy will be done as in heaven so in earth."

Two cautions we shall all do well to heed — 1. Prayer without work is mockery. 2. Work without prayer is vain.—*J. Jackson Goadby. Abridged from "The Evangelical Magazine."*

PSALM XCI.

INTRODUCTION.

There is no title prefixed to this Psalm. We know not who is the author of it. The conjecture, which has been made by some, that it was written by Moses, is very inadequately sustained. Neither do we know the time or occasion of its composition. The Psalm is general in its character, and applies to the whole Church.

A remarkable feature of the Psalm is the frequent change of persons, from which some have inferred that it was composed for singing by alternate choirs. The explanation of Hengstenberg seems to us more reasonable: "That the Psalmist speaks at one time from his own person to the soul of the righteous one who is in danger, and revives its courage, while at another time he expresses confidence from the soul of the righteous man; and thus in that pleasant alternation which forms the characteristic peculiarity of the Psalm, he employs at one time the *thou* in the character of *teacher*, and at another time the *I* in the character of *scholar*. .... The call of instruction in Scripture (this is the meaning of the alternation), ought always to be responded to by the acknowledgment of the hearer."

For our homiletical purpose we shall divide the Psalm thus :—*The safe hiding-place of the godly* (verses 1 and 2), *The inviolable security of the godly* (verses 3-10), *The angelic ministers of the godly* (verses 11-13), *The glorious privileges of the godly* (verses 14-16).

THE SAFE HIDING-PLACE OF THE GODLY.

(*Verses* 1, 2.)

Into these two verses is condensed the contents of the whole Psalm. The statement of the first verse expresses in brief what is afterwards set forth with some particularity,—the safety of him who places his trust in God. And in the second verse the Poet expresses his own firm assurance of his safety in Jehovah his God. We have in the text—

I. **An implication of danger.** That the Psalmist was sensible of danger is clear from the fact that he regarded God as a "refuge" and a "fortress." The godly are in peril by reason of—

1. *The trials of life.* Bodily pains, mental perplexities, spiritual sorrows and struggles, involve danger to those who pass through them. The very nature of trial, *i.e.*, testing, involves the idea of possible failure. Bodily pain may result in petulance or bitterness of spirit, mental perplexities may lead to a paralysing unbelief, spiritual conflicts may issue in loss, and even in defeat. The godly soul is in danger and needs a "*refuge.*"

2. *Spiritual adversaries.* The good man has to contend with foes. His "adversary the devil as a roaring lion goeth about, seeking whom he may devour." He is hated by the world. Its spirit and principles, many of its practices, many of its amusements, and much of its literature, are opposed to the interests and even the life of the godly soul. Temptation to evil is a great and sad fact in this world. Moreover, the good man finds that in himself there are "fleshly lusts which war against the soul." His life is a great moral battle. Numerous and powerful forces are arrayed against him. Seductive influences also are brought to bear upon him to lead him astray. His life is one of peril. He needs a "*fortress*" from which he may hurl defiance at his foes.

II. **An assurance of safety.** "He that dwelleth in the secret place of the Most High shall abide under the shadow of the Almighty. Notice here:

1. *The condition.* To realise this safety the godly man must "dwell in the secret place of the Most High." סֵתֶר, which is here translated "*the secret place*," signifies primarily *a veil, a covering,* then, *what is secret,* then, *a hiding-place, protection.* The latter we take to be the meaning in this place. The godly soul dwells in the hiding-place, *i.e.*, in the protection of the Most High. His trust he reposes in God. He looks to Him for protection from the fiery darts of the wicked, and for support and shelter in the storms of life. To assure his safety the good man must "*dwell*" in the hiding-place of the Most High. The literal rendering is, "He that sitteth in the," &c. He dwells in quietude, he finds rest there, he is settled there. "God's children should not come to God's secret place as guests to an inn, but as inhabitants to their own dwellings." Speaking without any figure, the condition of spiritual safety is constant trust in God as our Protector. "They that trust in the Lord shall be as mount Zion, which cannot be removed, but abideth for ever."

2. *The promise.* "Shall abide under the shadow of the Almighty." The rendering in the margin is "*shall lodge.*" Hengstenberg translates: "*spends the night.*" The idea is, that that is his home, the place where he passes his nights. Under the shadow is explained by some by the bird who hides her

young ones under her wings for their protection. Others explain it as indicating the great nearness of God to His people, and their consequent safety. We must be and continue very close to a person for his shadow to fall constantly upon us. Thus to abide under His shadow is to realise His constant presence, and to be always secure in His protection. The names of God which are here used set forth the ground upon which this assurance of the godly man is based: "the Most High," "the Almighty." What power can harm the man who is protected by the constant presence of the Supreme and Omnipotent Being? In the time of temptation, affliction, and darkness, we shall pass the night under His shadow. And in the toil and battle of the day, with its heat and burden, we shall rest secure beneath the Almighty's shade. In His nearness to us our safety lies. While we are under His shadow no evil can befall us. Distance from Him means danger. Closeness to Him means entire security.

III. **An expression of confidence.** "I will say of the Lord, He is my refuge and my fortress; my God; in Him will I trust." Consider here—

1. *The aspects in which God is regarded.* He is spoken of as a "*Refuge.*" God is the refuge of His people from the storms of life. In times of suffering and trial they find safety and comfort in Him. He is also a "*fortress.*" The idea of this word is different from that of a refuge. The refuge was a quiet and secure hiding-place; the fortress is a place of defence against foes, which is strong to resist the attacks of opposing forces. In life's warfare God is the stronghold of His people; He is their shield. "O God the Lord, the strength of my salvation, Thou hast covered my head in the day of battle." Having His protection we are invulnerable. In life's storms He is the safe and quiet shelter of His people. "My soul trusteth in Thee: yea, in the shadow of Thy wings will I make my refuge, until these calamities be overpast." The Psalmist also speaks of the Lord as his "*God;*" the object of His worship; One who is worthy of all obedience and affection, all reverence and confidence, all praise and glory. Jehovah was to the Psalmist all that a man expects in his God.

2. *The confidence which is expressed in Him.* The Psalmist's confidence in God is manifest (1) *In his resolve to trust Him.* "In Him will I trust." The Psalmist confidently leaves His interests in the hands of God. Believing in His power, goodness, and faithfulness, he trusts Him—confides in Him. (2) *In the appropriating nature of his faith.* He says, "*My refuge, my fortress, my God.*" There is little or no strength or encouragement to be drawn from believing in the Lord as a refuge and a fortress unless we realise our interest in Him. But when faith is in vigorous exercise and we claim God as our own, then are we inspired and strengthened. Can we look to God and say, "*My refuge, my fortress, my God*"? (3) *In the declaration of his confidence.* "I will say of the Lord," &c. He was determined to proclaim his confidence in God. He believes, and, therefore, he speaks. Men are ready enough now-a-days to speak of their doubts. But he is the noble man and the useful man who can intelligently and reverently speak of his faith; who says, "I know whom I have believed," &c.; and who is "ready always to give an answer to every man that asketh him a reason for the hope that is in him with meekness and fear." Great was the confidence of the Psalmist in God, and his great confidence he declares unto others.

CONCLUSION.—We also are exposed to trials and dangers, and need a refuge and a defence. Our safety is in God alone. Having Him for our God we are beyond the reach of any real harm. We secure His protection by trusting in Him. By faith we dwell in the secret place of the Most High, and are ever secure under His shadow. Do not fear or hesitate to trust God fully and for ever. Commit yourself with confidence into His hands, and you shall dwell safely by Him for ever.

The Inviolable Security of the Godly.

(*Verses* 3–10.)

In these verses the Poet sets forth with a measure of particularity what he has already expressed briefly and generally. He expresses in joyous song his strong confidence that he is safe from dangers of every kind, because he is protected by God. *The inviolable security of the godly* is here represented—

I. As effected by God. "Surely *He* shall deliver thee from the snare of the fowler, and from the noisome pestilence. *He* shall cover thee with *His* feathers, and under *His* wings shalt thou trust: *His* truth shall be thy shield and buckler." The Psalmist felt that he had for protector no less a being than God Himself. Two features of the Divine protection are here brought into view.

1. *Its tenderness.* "He shall cover thee with His feathers, and under His wings shalt thou trust." The young birds under the wing of their mother are tenderly guarded. (See our notes on Psalm lvii. 1, and lxiii. 7.) Gotthold tells how that during a fire at Delft, in Holland, certain storks, finding it impossible to preserve their brood, placed themselves upon the nest, spread over them their wings, and so perished with them in the flames. "Under these wings," says Bernard, "four blessings are conferred upon us. For under these wings we are *concealed*: under these we are *protected* from the attacks of the hawks and kites, which are the powers of the air: under these a salubrious shade *refreshes* us, and wards off the overpowering heat of the sun: under these also we are nourished and cherished."

2. *Its effectiveness.* Wings and feathers indicate the tender and loving character of the Divine protection. Yet wings and feathers are weak and may be easily broken. But the Divine protection is as strong as it is tender, as efficient as it is gracious. "His truth shall be thy shield and buckler." God's word, and His faithfulness to His word, are as armour to His people, preserving them from the onslaughts of their enemies.

In such a protector we do well to trust and rejoice. He is wise to baffle the crafty designs of the cunning fowler; tender to shelter us from the storm and tempest; and strong to defend us in the day of battle.

II. As gloriously complete. The Psalmist labours to set forth the completeness of the safety of the godly man. He represents him as being—

1. *Safe from all perils.* It is perhaps impossible to assert with certainty what the Psalmist meant by each of the phrases and figures he employed. "*The snare of the fowler*" indicates danger arising from the craft and cunning of enemies. The great enemy of God and man is especially signified. The Lord delivers His people from "the wiles of the devil." "*The noisome pestilence.*" There is a difference in both the translations and the interpretations of this clause. Perowne translates—"The devouring pestilence." Barnes—"The *fatal* pestilence; the pestilence that spreads death in its march." Hengstenberg—"The pestilence of wickedness." And Matthew Henry says—"The contagion of sin is the noisome pestilence." We think the latter view the correct one. The first clause of the verse (ver. 3) we regard as representing the subtle temptations of Satan, and the second the ruinous contagion of sin. God delivers from both all who trust in Him. Hengstenberg, as we think with great probability, interprets verse 5 as setting forth the safety of the godly from the attacks of men, and verse 6 as setting forth their safety from sickness. Perowne, on verse 5, says—"*Terror by night* (comp. Song of Sol. iii. 8, Prov. iii. 23–26), in allusion, probably, to night attacks like those of Gideon (Judg. vii.), a favourite artifice of Oriental warfare; or perhaps to a destruction like that of Sennacherib." And it has been pointed out on verse 6, that "the diseases of all hot climates, and especially where vegetation is highly

luxuriant, and marshes and miry swamps are abundant, proceed from the accumulating vapours of the *night*, or from the violence of the sun's rays at *mid-day*. The beriberi of Ceylon, the spasmodic cholera and jungle-fever of India, and the greater part of the fevers of intertropical climates, especially that called the yellow-fever, chiefly originate from the first of these—'the *pestilence* that walketh in darkness;' while sunstrokes, apoplexies, inflammations of the brain, and liver complaints of most kinds, proceed from the second, 'the *destruction* that wasteth at noonday.' And it is in allusion to this double source of mischief that the Psalmist exclaims most beautifully on another occasion (Ps. cxxi. 6), 'The sun shall not smite thee by day, nor the moon by night.'" The seventh verse seems to refer to warlike relations, and to express the security of the godly in battle. And in verse 10, where the plague is mentioned as not coming nigh the dwelling of the righteous, there is, perhaps, an allusion to the exemption of the Israelites from the plagues of Egypt. But, leaving the examination of details, let us take hold of the main idea of the Poet, that the godly are safe from perils of all kinds and from all perils. "The variety of figures employed shows that the Psalmist is thinking of peril of every kind, coming from whatever source, and that he paints all dangers and fears vividly to the eye of his mind, in order to express the more joyfully his confidence that none of these things can move him, that over all he is more than conqueror. It is St. Paul's fervid exclamation, 'If God be for us, who can be against us?' expressed in rich poetry." From all the assaults of Satan, from the fatal contagion of moral evil, from the attacks of enemies both by night and by day, from hurtful diseases, from every plague, from all evil, the godly man is preserved.

2. *Safe at all times.* "By night, by day; in darkness," and "at noonday" the Divine protection is alike exercised. "He that keepeth thee will not slumber. Behold, He that keepeth Israel shall neither slumber nor sleep. . . . The sun shall not smite thee by day, nor the moon by night. . . . The Lord shall preserve thy going out and thy coming in from this time forth, and even for evermore." The guardianship of God is unremitting, constant, and unchangeable. They who trust in Him are at all times safe in His keeping.

3. *Raised above the fear of danger.* "Thou shalt not be afraid for the terror by night; nor for the arrow that flieth by day; nor for the pestilence that walketh in darkness; nor for the destruction that wasteth at noonday." A stout heart may well be excused if it were afraid of perils such as these, and especially when they approach us in darkness and at night. In the darkness of night evil is apt to assume an exaggerated character. Imagination increases its terrors. If we could clearly see the perils which threaten us they would lose much of their terror-inspiring power. But the godly man, trusting in the Lord, shall not be afraid of the terrors of the night or the perils of the day. In the midst of dangers he shall walk calmly because of his trust in the all-sufficient protection of God.

But is all this true? Is it not a fact that pestilence seizes the saint as well as the sinner? Does not the plague enter the dwelling of the good man as well as that of the evil? It is unquestionable that the godly are not exempt from "the ills that flesh is heir to." Loss, sickness, suffering, death, fall to their lot even as to others. What, then, does the Psalmist mean in these verses? How are we to understand them?

We must bear in mind that we are interpreting poetry, not prose. The sacred poets of the Hebrews, like all other poets, used figurative and rhetorical language. And to interpret their poems in the same way as we interpret an historical document, or a logical treatise, or an apostolic letter, would be utterly misleading. The plain truth expressed in these verses is, that God is the Protector of His people, and that they are secure who put their trust in Him. Nor is it difficult to show that in times of pestilence and peril the position of the godly man is far superior to that of the ungodly. We may mention at least three things in which this is clearly manifest. (1) *Faith in God is a great safeguard against disease and danger.* Stier states that some years ago a distinguished physician in St. Petersburg recommended this Psalm as the best defence against the cholera. And Tholuck admirably says—"As the general who carries within him the conviction that he is called to a great work, whilst the bullets fall thick as hail about him, stands with calm eye and firm foot, and says: I know that the bullet is not yet cast which can strike me, so stands the man of prophetic faith in the hour of danger, with the conviction that the thunderbolt will turn aside from his head, and the torrent dry up at his feet, and the arrows fall blunted from his breast, *because the Lord wills it.*" Faith in God is the great condition of calmness and courage in time of danger. (2) *The godly man observes the laws of health.* Pestilence and disease find their victims chiefly amongst the intemperate and licentious, who by their sinful habits are predisposed to their attacks, and unable to resist their power. But the godly man, by reason of his life of virtue, temperance, and cleanliness, often escapes the most deadly diseases without any attack, or if attacked frequently recovers. (3) *Suffering and death wear a different aspect to the godly man from that which they present to the wicked.* He knows that suffering is educational; "that tribulation worketh patience;" that out of affliction and conflict the saints often bring great spoil of spiritual treasures; that "these light afflictions, which are but for a moment, are working for him a far more exceeding and eternal weight of glory." He has gracious support in all his trials and afflictions; and, being sanctified by God, great blessings accrue to him by means of them. And to the godly men of this Christian age death is not an evil; it signifies not loss, but gain; it is the gate of life; it is birth into a higher and diviner form of life. It is true, then, that no real evil can befall the godly soul who is trusting in the Lord. And if suffering and sorrow and loss should be his portion, God will educe from them blessings of transcendent and perpetual value. "We know that all things work together for good to them that love God."

III. **As conditionated by trust in God.** The godly man is thus secure because he has made the Lord his refuge, and the Most High his habitation. (See notes on the condition of safety in the preceding homily.) This verse (the 9th) is in substance a repetition of the first verse. If we would secure the protection of God we must trust Him fully and constantly.

CONCLUSION.—1. *Let the godly ever trust and rejoice in their Protector.* 2. *Sinner, seek and secure this protection while you may.* "Let the wicked forsake his way," &c.

THE REWARD OF THE WICKED.

(Verse 8.)

These words suggest—

I. **That there is a difference between the sufferings of the righteous and the wicked.** The same external afflictions and trials may befall them; but to the righteous they are *educational*, to the wicked they are *punitive*—"the reward," &c.

II. **That the Divine rule in this world is righteous.** Under it the godly are protected by God, while the wicked are punished.

III. **That the righteousness of the Divine rule is not always manifest in this world.** If the present were our only state of being, there are many things which we could not reconcile with the fact that God reigns in righteousness.

IV. **That the righteousness of the Divine rule will ultimately be clearly manifest to all.** The godly with their eyes "shall see the reward of the wicked." There is a state where all the apparent inequalities of the moral government of our world will be clearly rectified. "Woe unto the wicked! it shall be ill with him; for the reward of his hands shall be given him."

V. **The weak and fearful believer, notwithstanding his fears, shall not** perish with the wicked. "Only with his eyes shall he see the reward of the wicked," while he himself shall enjoy the glorious inheritance of the good.

THE ANGELIC MINISTERS OF THE GODLY.

(*Verses* 11-13.)

In pursuance of the main topic the Poet here speaks of angels as charged by God to help and defend His people. Literally the word angel signifies a messenger, and may be used personally or impersonally. It is used in the Scriptures to designate ordinary messengers, prophets, Christian ministers, &c. In this place it denotes superhuman spirits—angels, as the word is commonly understood at present. From the representations of the holy Word it is clear that the angels rank high in the scale of being. They are said to possess great power. "Angels that excel in strength." "Mighty angels." And most astonishing achievements of *power* are attributed to them. They also possess great *intelligence*. This is plainly implied in the words of the Lord—"But of that day and hour knoweth no man, no, not the angels of heaven, but My Father only." It is also implied in the statement that they are "full of eyes before and behind," and "full of eyes within." The amazing power that they wield is chiefly the power of intelligence and wisdom. They also possess complete *moral purity*. They are spoken of in the Bible as "saints," "holy ones," and "holy angels." Dwelling in that world where not even the shadow of moral defilement can enter, and standing in the immediate presence of God, they must be entirely free from even the smallest moral stain or imperfection. Their power, intelligence, purity, differ from ours in this, that they are perfect in kind. They differ from those of God in this, that they are imperfect in degree. There is before the angels a career of constant progress, both moral and intellectual, through all eternity. Moreover, they are represented as interested in the affairs of this world, and as actively employed by God in connection with those affairs. "They are represented as being, in the widest sense, agents of God's providence, natural and supernatural, to the body and to the soul. Thus the operations of nature are spoken of as under angelic guidance fulfilling the will of God. . . . More particularly, however, angels are spoken of as ministers of what is commonly called the 'supernatural,' or perhaps more correctly the 'spiritual' Providence of God; as agents in the great scheme of the spiritual redemption and sanctification of man." "The angel of the Lord" is said to "encamp round about them that fear Him, and to deliver them." They are represented as watching over Christ's little ones; as rejoicing over a penitent sinner; as bearing the spirits of the redeemed into Paradise; and as "ministering spirits" for the spiritual guidance and help of the heirs of salvation. And in the text they are said to be charged by God to uphold and aid His people. That they should thus minister to the godly is in the highest degree reasonable. (1) From the interest which they take in man (Luke xv. 10; 1 Pet i. 12). (2) Inasmuch as a fallen angel led man to his ruin, and still by malign influences seeks our destruction, does it not seem appropriate and reasonable that holy angels should aid us in every virtuous and worthy effort? (3) It is the law of God's universe that His creatures should minister to each other. All things and all beings are made for service. The higher order of beings are made to minister to the lower—the strong to help the weak, the enlightened to instruct the ignorant, &c. Our Lord "came not to be ministered unto, but to minister." "I am among you," He said, "as He that serveth." God is the Great Minister of all His creatures. How reasonable then that angels should minister to men! If we are asked in what way angels minister to men? or, how they serve us? we may with strict fairness decline to reply. We may accept a fact without being able to explain its mode. All men, indeed, do so in many things. So we accept as true the statement that angelic beings aid men, though we are unable to explain by what method they do so. But may it not be that they aid us by suggesting to our mind thoughts, reasons, and motives to action, and by awakening emotions in our souls? &c. Any way, we thankfully accept and rejoice in their ministry as a precious reality.

"Oh! th' exceeding grace
Of highest God that loves His creatures so,
And all His works with mercy doth embrace,
That blessed angels He sends to and fro,
To serve to wicked men, to serve His wicked foe.

"How oft do they their silver bowers leave,
To come to succour us that succour want!
How oft do they with golden pinions cleave
The flitting skies, like flying pursuivant,
Against foul fiends to aid us militant!
They for us fight, they watch and duly ward,
And their bright squadrons round about us plant;
And all for love, and nothing for reward.
Oh! why should heavenly God to men have such regard!"—*Spenser.*

In the text the angelic ministers of the good are said to be—

I. **Commissioned by God.** "He shall give His angels charge over thee."

1. *They are "His angels."* He called them into being. He sustains them. The most mighty and glorious of their number is dependent upon Him. He is sovereign over them all. Loyally and reverently they acknowledge His sovereign right over them.

2. *They are commissioned by Him.* He allots to them their respective duties. They "do His commandments, hearkening unto the voice of His word." They are "His hosts, ministers of His that do His pleasure." The "charge" which in the text they are said to receive is more than a mere direction or order; it is a solemn command. All the angelic ministers of the godly obey His behests; they serve under Him,—they are carrying out His purposes.

This angelic ministry is—

II. **Exercised for the godly as individuals.** "He shall give His angels charge over *thee.*" God is profoundly solicitous for the well-being of each one of His people. He does not overlook the individual in the multitude. He cares for every godly soul with a care as complete and constant as though He had no other soul to care for. So in the ministry of His angels unto men He gives them charge not simply of His Church or of the communities which compose it, but of every individual member who trusts in Him. So that every true believer may say, "In my lonely labour, and sorrow, and conflict, when far removed from human help and fellowship, my angelic helpers still have me in their charge, and are still near to help me." Thus an angel ministered to Elijah (1 Kings xix. 4-8); to Daniel (Dan. vi. 22); to Peter (Acts xii. 7-10).

This angelic ministry is—

III. **Exercised for the godly only when they are in their true path.** "To keep thee in all thy ways." It is significant that when Satan quoted this verse in the temptation of our Lord, he omitted this clause. Had he quoted the whole verse, his temptation would have refuted itself. "The 'ways' spoken of in the Psalm are the 'ways' of obedience and duty, not the 'ways' of presumption or self-seeking." In the ways which God has prescribed for us to walk in we shall find safety and support even when the way is roughest and we are feeblest. But if we step out of the way, we forfeit the help of the angel ministers. If we are out of the way, their business is not to help us but to oppose us, if haply their opposition may lead us to retrace our steps and re-enter our true path. So long as we are in our way we are sure of the Divine help and protection, for His angels will not fail in their charge; but if we are out of our way, we are exposed to dangers from every quarter. The path of duty is the path of safety.

The angelic ministry is—

IV. **Exercised for the godly always when they are in their true path.** "To keep thee in *all* thy ways." God calls men to tread different ways. He also calls the same person to tread different ways at different times. There are the ways of arduous duty, and of severe trial, and of peaceful progress, &c. God's way for one man is the way of patient endurance, He calls him to suffer; His way for another man is the way of constant and perhaps difficult service, He calls him to work; His way for vast numbers is that of quietly and faithfully discharging "the daily round and common tasks" of life, He calls them to diligence and faithfulness. In all the paths of life which He calls us to tread our angelic ministers are near for our help. When our path lies by the rippling waters of gentle streams, beneath azure skies, amid beauteous scenes and with genial breezes, they keep us in our way. And when we travel the steep and rugged way, beneath heavy clouds and amid furious storms, they bear us up on their hands lest we dash our foot against a stone. In the thronged and dusty way of life's busy scenes, and in the retired and peaceful paths of quiet service, they keep us. "To keep thee in *all* thy ways."

V. **By means of the exercise of this angelic ministry the godly are enabled to surmount all the hindrances and conquer all the foes that beset their way.** "They shall bear thee up on their hands, lest thou dash thy foot against a stone. Thou shalt tread upon the lion and adder; the young lion and the dragon shalt thou trample under foot." "By the 'lion and adder,'" says Perowne, "there is no need to understand exclusively, or chiefly, the powers of darkness, the evil spirits. As by 'a stone' all hindrances, so by 'the lion and dragon' all hostile powers are denoted." By means of this angelic ministry the godly are—

1. *Preserved from falling.* "They shall bear thee up on their hands, lest thou dash thy foot against a stone." One great object of the ministry of angels is to guard the good lest they stumble and fall into sin. They aid us to overcome the hindrances of life. "If we cannot have the way smoothed, it answers every purpose if we have angels to bear us up on their hands."

2. *Enabled to conquer the most powerful foes.* "The lion" and "the young lion" represent enemies of great strength and violence. Satan is said to go about "as a roaring lion seeking whom he may devour." The most powerful enemies of the good cannot cope with one of the angels of God. One angel of the Lord in one night smote one hundred and eighty-five thousand Assyrians. The man who trusts in the Lord, looking upon the most numerous and most powerful enemies, in full assurance of victory may say, "Fear not; for they that be with us are more than they that be with them." Our helpers are more numerous and more powerful than our enemies.

3. *Enabled to conquer the most cunning foes.* "The adder" and "the dragon" represent enemies of great secrecy and cunning. Satan is designated a serpent and a dragon. "And the great dragon was cast out, that old serpent, called the Devil, and Satan, which deceiveth the whole world." St. Paul speaks of the "wiles of the devil." Many of the foes against which the godly have to contend in society to-day seek to gain their victory not by strength but by subtlety, not by force but by fraud. But our angelic helpers aid us in this respect also. We have assurance of complete victory over both "the roaring lion" and the "old serpent." Triumphantly we shall tread our foes under our feet. Over both the might of opposition and the cunning of temptation we shall be more than conquerors.

CONCLUSION. 1. *Our subject affords encouragement to trust in God.* How numerous and efficient are the agencies He employs to save us! 2. *Our subject reveals the dignity of the godly man.* Angels, the highest beings in creation, the holy, the glorious, the powerful, are employed by God to serve him. Child of God, realise thy dignity, walk worthily of it. 3. *Our subject calls us to the service of others.* Angels serve us, Christ serves us now in heaven, the Holy Ghost serves, the Heavenly Father serves, God is the great servant of all. To serve God by ministering to our fellow-creatures is our duty and privilege. Let us secure the blessedness of unselfish and hearty service.

THE FOES AND VICTORY OF THE GOOD.

(*Verse* 13.)

I. **The foes of the good.** These are—
1. *Numerous.* "The lion and adder, the young lion and the dragon."

> "Angels your march oppose,
> Who still in strength excel,
> Your secret, sworn, eternal foes,
> Countless, invisible."
> —*C. Wesley.*

The enemies of the good in human society, in commerce, in amusements, in literature, are very many. And to these and the countless evil spirits must be added the "fleshly lusts which war against the soul."

2. *Various.* "The lion," whose strength, courage, and ferocity are proverbial. The word which is translated "adder" signifies "a poisonous snake." "The young lion" is mentioned as particularly fierce and violent. And the word which is translated "the dragon," signifies here a "land serpent of a powerful and deadly kind." Thus varied are the foes of the godly man. The world, the flesh, and the devil are all arrayed against him. He has to battle with the syren enticements of temptation and the fierce attacks of persecution, &c.

3. *Terrible.* "The lion, adder, young lion, and dragon" are very terrible foes to the traveller. If once they have him in their power, they will destroy him. The foes of the godly soul are to be dreaded for their malignity, subtlety, and power. He is a fool who thinks lightly of the forces of evil which are working and fighting in this world.

II. **The victory of the good.** This is—

1. *Complete.* (1) *Over all foes.* "The lion and adder, the young lion and the dragon" shall all be vanquished. The world, the flesh, and the devil, persecutions and seductions, inward foes and outward, shall all be overcome by the man who trusts in God. (2) *Over all foes completely.* "Thou shalt tread upon the lion and adder, the young lion and the dragon shalt thou trample under feet." "His meaning is, thou shalt intentionally tread upon them like a conqueror, thou shalt tread upon them to testify thy dominion over them. You shall have power to overcome whatsoever may annoy you." "The God of peace shall bruise Satan under your feet shortly." The Christian will come out of life's conflicts "more than a conqueror" through Christ.

2. *Certain.* (1) *Because angels aid us against our foes.* They are intelligent, powerful, swift, glorious allies. (2) *Because God guarantees it.* "Thou shalt tread," &c. Here is no perhaps, but a certain promise from Him who is the truth. Take courage then, brother, in life's battles. Trust and fight, and a glorious victory will be yours.

THE GLORIOUS PRIVILEGES OF THE GODLY.

(*Verses* 14–16.)

The inspired poet in these verses represents God Himself as declaring the high privileges of His servants. We have here—

I. **Some features in the character of the godly.**

1. *Love to God.* "Because he hath set his love upon me." The good man loves God with the love of *gratitude*—loves Him because of what He has done and is still doing for him. "We love Him because He first loved us." When we reflect upon the evils from which He delivers us, and the blessings He bestows

upon us, and the glory which awaits us in the future, our heart glows with gratitude and affection to Him. The good man loves God with the love of *esteem* also,—loves Him because of what He is in Himself. The love which springs from gratitude is first in order of time in the spiritual history of most men; but the love which springs from esteem is first in order of excellence. To love Him because of the divine beauty of His character and life, is a far higher thing than to love Him because of the benefits which we have received from Him, or which He has promised to bestow upon us.

"My God, I love Thee, not because
 I hope for heaven thereby;
Nor because they who love Thee not
 Are lost eternally.

"Not with the hope of gaining aught,
 Nor seeking a reward,
But, as Thyself hast lovèd me,
 O ever-loving Lord.

"So would I love Thee, blessed Lord,
 And in Thy praise will sing,
Because Thou art my loving God,
 And my redeeming King."
—*Xavier.*

The expression, "*Set* His love upon me," indicates *fixedness* of affection. God requires from us an intense single-hearted love. "Thou shalt love the Lord thy God with all thy heart, and with all thy soul, and with all thy strength, and with all thy mind." Our supreme love must be fixed upon God. There is encouragement for us in this verse. "It is not because of *perfect* love that God will deliver. It is to the will to love and serve—it is to the *setting* the heart that the promise is made—to the full purpose of heart, that is set to cleave unto the Lord." Do we love God supremely?

2. *Knowledge of God.* "He hath known my name." Knowledge of God and love to God are closely connected. We must have some knowledge of God before we can love Him. A true knowledge of God leads to trust in Him. "They that know Thy name will put their trust in Thee." To know God's name is to know Himself. Proficiency in this knowledge is attainable only to the man who loves God. As we must have some knowledge of God before we can love Him, so we must love Him before we can know much of Him. "Every one that loveth is born of God, and knoweth God. He that loveth not knoweth not God; for God is love." We can know the heart of God only as we love Him. Where the keen intellect fails to discover any trace of God, He is clearly and preciously manifest to the pure and loving heart.

3. *Prayer to God.* "He shall call upon Me." The godly soul cannot live without prayer. In times of need he calls upon God for grace to help him. In the enjoyment of blessing He calls upon God in grateful praise. At all times he acknowledges his dependence upon God. And there are seasons when prayer grows into holy and blessed communion, in which there are no petitions, but an intense and blessed realisation of the presence of God, and adoration of Him, which humbles and purifies and strengthens the spirit.

II. **Some of the glorious privileges of the godly.**

1. *Deliverance from danger.* The assurance is twice given, "I will deliver him." The good man has enemies to contend with, but God will deliver him out of their hands, and give him the victory over them. The good man is exposed to dangers, but God delivers him safely out of them all.

2. *Exaltation and consequent safety.* "I will set him on high." I will place him out of the reach of danger. God raises those who trust Him above the stormy sea of this life, places them on an immovable rock, where the threatening and thundering waves cannot reach them. "He shall dwell on high; his place of defence shall be the munitions of rocks." God thus exalts His people above the perils of life, because they know His name and confide in Him.

3. *Answers to prayer.* "I will answer him." The answer to prayer is not necessarily the granting of our requests. "It may be a refusal, an explanation, a promise, a conditional grant." Excellently says Matthew Henry, "I will answer by promises (lxxxv. 8), answer by providences, bringing in seasonable relief, and answer

by graces, strengthening them with strength in their souls; thus He answered Paul with grace sufficient." True prayer is always answered by God, and answered in infinite wisdom and love.

4. *The presence of God in trouble.* "I will be with him in trouble." The good man is not exempted from trouble, but supported in the midst of trouble. The celebrated William Dawson says, "At other times God will leave them in the hands of angels: 'He shall give His angels charge over thee to keep thee,' &c. But when they are in trouble, I will say to the angels, 'Stand aside, I will take care of them Myself. I will be with them in trouble.'" So He speaks to His people: 'When thou passest through the waters, I will be with thee,' &c. When languishing in sickness, He will make His bed and his pillow; when travelling through the valley of the shadow of death, the Lord will be with him, and enable him to sing, 'I will fear no evil; for Thou art with me,' &c. Thus He is with them as their physician and nurse, in pain and sickness; as their strength in weakness; as their guide in difficulty; their ease in pain; and their life in death."

5. *The conference of distinguished honour.* "I will honour him." God honours His people in this life by delivering them from danger and trial, by sustaining them in suffering and sorrow, and by raising them into the most exalted relationships. "Now are we the sons of God." In the life that is to come God will honour them by raising them to the highest dignities, the most delightful fellowships, the most glorious service, and to His own immediate presence. "To him that overcometh I will give to sit with Me in My throne," &c. "We know that when He shall appear we shall be like Him," &c.

6. *Satisfaction with the duration of their life upon earth.* "With long life will I satisfy him." "The special promise of long life at the close," says Perowne, "as a temporal blessing, in accordance with the general character of the Old Testament. Still it is possible that men like the Psalmist, full of faith in God, attached a deeper and more spiritual meaning to promises and hopes like these, than was attached to them by the majority of their countrymen." Matthew Henry's exposition seems to us admirable. "(1) They shall live long enough; they shall be continued in this world till they have done the work they were sent into this world for, and are ready for heaven, and that is long enough. Who would wish to live a day longer than God has some work to do, either by him or upon him? (2) They shall think it long enough; for God by His grace shall wean them from the world and make them willing to leave it. A man may die young, and yet die full of days, *satur dierum*—satisfied with living. A wicked worldly man is not satisfied, no, not with long life; he still cries, *Give, give*. But he that has his treasure and heart in another world has soon enough of this; he would not live always." The good man's life upon earth is a completed thing, whether he die young or live to become a centenarian. He knows that his life is ordered by infinite Wisdom, and whenever it ends he is satisfied.

7. *Full salvation.* "And show him My salvation." When the good man's life upon earth is ended, God will admit him to the enjoyment of His complete, glorious, and everlasting salvation in heaven. Here we catch glimpses of His salvation; there we shall see it fully and clearly revealed. Here we know its power and blessedness in part; hereafter we shall know them in their completeness. Here we conquer and have to battle again; there the warfare is all over, and the victory is glorious and endless. Here we partake of His salvation in the kingdom of grace; there in the kingdom of glory.

CONCLUSION. 1. *Have we these distinguishing characteristics of the godly?* Do we love, know, and pray to God? 2. *Do you who have them, value and rejoice in your exalted privileges?* 3. *And you who do not bear the marks of the godly man, what is your hope?* Through Jesus Christ every man may attain to this supreme love to God, this blessed knowledge of Him, and this hallowed communion with Him.

LONG LIFE.
(Verse 16.)

"With long life will I satisfy him." The present life is not a vain thing, but a thing of solemn reality; not a trifling thing, but a thing of stupendous importance; it ought not to be a mean thing, but a thing of sublimity and honour.

I. Long life is desirable.

1. *Because of the obedience which we may render to God.* In this world we obey God in the face of many difficulties and much temptation. In heaven all influences combine to aid its inhabitants in their joyous obedience and service. But here, alas! it is very different. Yet obedience in a state like the present develops some of the noblest elements of character, and is specially well-pleasing to God.

2. *Because of the service we may render to our race.* In heaven holiness is universal and supreme. In hell evil holds undisputed sway. Upon earth good and evil are present, and in conflict. Here we may labour for the cause of righteousness and truth as we cannot in any other state of being.

"Awake, my zeal; awake, my love,
To serve my Saviour here below,
In works which perfect saints above,
And holy angels cannot do.
Awake, my charity, to feed
The hungry soul, and clothe the poor;
In heaven are found no sons of need;
There all these duties are no more."
—*Watts.*

3. *Because of the reward which we may obtain.* Obedience and service rendered in this life will be appropriately and proportionately rewarded in the life to come. Therefore it is natural and right to desire to live long that we may obey long, and serve long, and reap a rich reward.

II. The tendency of true religion is to promote long life. "Keep My commandments; for length of days, and long life, and peace shall they add to thee. Length of days is in her (Wisdom's) right hand." The truly religious man lives virtuously, temperately, cultivates cleanliness, and avoids all violent passions, and such a life contributes incalculably to the prolongation of life.

III. A true estimate of the length of life is not formed by simply numbering its months and years. "They only," said Sheridan, "have lived long who have lived virtuously." "He lives long," said Fuller, "that lives well; and time misspent is not lived, but lost."

"We live in deeds, not years; in thoughts, not breaths;
In feelings, not in figures on a dial.
We should count time by heart-throbs. He most lives
Who thinks most, feels the noblest, acts the best."—*Bailey.*

"He liveth long who liveth well!
All other life is short and vain;
He liveth longest who can tell
Of living most for heavenly gain.

"He liveth long who liveth well!
All else is being flung away;
He liveth longest who can tell
Of true things truly done each day."
—*Bonar.*

IV. A truly godly man at the close of life will be satisfied with its length as determined by God, whatever that length may be. "My times are in Thy hand." Our days are determined, the number of our months is with Him; and He orders all things well. "In short measures life may perfect be."

Conclusion.—Let us see to it that, by the help of God, we live well and earnestly; and thankfully leave the length of our life with Him.

PSALM XCII.

INTRODUCTION.

Superscription.—"*A Psalm or Song for the Sabbath-day.*" It so far combines the properties of both a psalm and a song that either name may be applied to it. This psalm was appointed for use in the temple service on the Sabbath-day. By reason of its contents it is well adapted for use in the public worship of God. "It celebrates," says Perowne, "in joyful strain the greatness of God's works, and especially His righteous government of the world, as manifested in the overthrow of the wicked, and the prosperity and final triumph of the righteous. The apparent success of the ungodly for a time is admitted, but this is a mystery which worldly men, whose understanding has become darkened, cannot penetrate (ver. 6).

The Psalm, therefore, touches upon the same great principles of the Divine government which are laid down in such Psalms as the first, the thirty-seventh, the forty-ninth, and the seventy-third. But here there is no struggle with doubt and perplexity, as in the seventy-third; the Poet is, beyond all doubt, above all perplexity; he has not fallen down to the low level of the brutish man (comp. lxxiii. 22 with ver. 6 of this Psalm); he is rejoicing in the full and perfect conviction of the righteousness of God."

But the author of the Psalm and the occasion of its composition are unknown.

For our Homiletical purpose we shall divide the psalm thus :—*The good man's celebration of the praise of God*, vers. 1-7 ; and, *The rejoicing of the good man in the government of God*, vers. 8-15.

THE GOOD MAN'S CELEBRATION OF THE PRAISE OF GOD.

(*Verses* 1-7.)

In these verses the Poet brings before us the celebration of the praise of God, and presents for our consideration several of the principal features of this celebration. We have—

I. **The ground of this exercise.** " For Thou, Lord, hast made me glad through Thy works : I will triumph in the works of Thy hands. O Lord, how great are Thy works ! and Thy thoughts are very deep." The works of which the Psalmist is speaking are not God's works in creation, but His moral government of the world; those doings by which He brought salvation to His people, and destroyed His and their foes. God's works in creation are great, and His thoughts which are embodied therein are very deep; but these are not the works of which the Psalmist here speaks. " What kind of *works* and *thoughts* the Psalmist means," says Hengstenberg, " is particularly intimated in verse 7, which should be distinguished from verses 5 and 6 as by inverted commas. It is the works and counsels of God for the deliverance of His people, a deliverance which is secured by the destruction of the wicked, their enemies." Now concerning these works the Psalmist says that they are—

1. *Great in themselves.* "O Lord, how great are Thy works !" The Psalmist, as he contemplated God's doings in the moral government of the world, was overwhelmed with a sense of their vastness, and greatness, and depth of significance. The greatness of the works of God in providence appears from considerations such as these : (1) *The extent of the sphere in which He works.* His operations are not limited to any country or countries, or to any particular race or class of men. His moral government of our world extends over the whole world and the entire human race. (2) *The duration of the time through which He works.* He began this work with the beginning of time, He has continued it through all the ages and through all the vicissitudes of human history, and He will continue it for ever. To us, who " are but of yesterday and know nothing, because our days upon earth are as a shadow," how incomprehensibly great are works which are wrought in so extensive a sphere and through so vast a period ! (3) *The grandeur of the objects for which He works.* His aim is the eradication of evil, the extinction of sin and suffering, the universal reign of truth, righteousness, and love. Glorious object ! (4) *The wonderful methods He employs in His works.* Out of evil He adduces good. He maketh the wrath of man to praise Him. He overrules the evil designs and doings of rebellious angels and men for the accomplishment of His own gracious and sublime purposes. By means of suffering and sacrifice He enriches the race with divine and inestimably precious blessings. He saves mankind by means of the Cross of our Lord Jesus Christ. When we consider God's moral government of the world in the way we have so very briefly indicated, we speedily receive overwhelming impressions of its greatness; we grow lost in wonder; we can but exclaim : How vast and wonderful and Divine are Thy works! The Psalmist represents these works as—

2. *Embodiments of profound thoughts.* " Thy thoughts are very deep." God

governs the world by a wise and benevolent design. All His works existed first as thoughts in His own infinite mind. Creation, with its innumerable wonders, and its glory and grandeur, is an embodiment of ideas of the Divine mind. And the moral government of the world is an expression of the thoughts of His mind and the determinations of His will. "God's counsels as much exceed the contrivances of our wisdom as His works do the efforts of our power." "There is no sea so deep as these thoughts of God." He "is wonderful in counsel and excellent in working." "As the heavens are higher than the earth, so are My ways higher than your ways, and My thoughts than your thoughts." "O the depth of the riches both of the wisdom and knowledge of God!" &c. Our puny minds are speedily baffled in the attempt to comprehend the thoughts of God. God's works are regarded by the Psalmist as—

3. *An expression of His loving-kindness and faithfulness.* "To show forth Thy loving-kindness in the morning, and Thy faithfulness every night." These attributes of the Divine Being are conspicuously displayed in His moral government of the world. He manifests His *loving-kindness* in delivering His people from oppression and danger, in leading them during their earthly pilgrimage, in making all things work together for their good, and in crowning their life with His love. His mercy is manifest also in His treatment of the wicked, in His expostulations with them, in His great patience with them, in His provision for their salvation, and in His desire to save them. He manifests His truth or *faithfulness* in fulfilling His engagements, in keeping His promises. This He does in the government of the world. There have been times when, to the limited view of man, His promises seemed to fail, but in His own wise time He has made good His word. We cannot take a comprehensive survey of His work without discovering abundant illustrations of both His mercy and His truth. And it is fitting that we should make mention of them in our praises. The Poet represents God's works as—

4. *Not understood by the wicked.* "A brutish man knoweth not; neither doth a fool understand this." The term "brutish man" (literally, a man-brute) indicates a terrible degradation of human nature. A man, as having been created in God's image; a brutish man, because he has debased himself to brutehood. Man must either soar or sink. Possibilities of unutterable degradation and possibilities of unspeakable glory are within each one of us. As man degrades himself into brutality, his power of recognising the Divine becomes ever less and less, until he is utterly incapable of understanding the ways and works of God. The wicked man is spoken of here as "a fool." Sin is folly. Neither the "brutish man" nor the "fool" can understand the moral government of God. "Were God's thoughts less deep and glorious, did He repay the wicked at every particular transgression immediately with His punishment, and did He bestow salvation immediately upon the righteous according to the canon which Job's friends with their limited views lay down, the government of the world would become plain even to the dark eye of ungodliness. But its depth makes it a *secret*, the understanding of which very often in times of conflict is withheld even from the pious, as is manifest from the example of Job and the author of the seventy-third Psalm, and in which there is always much that may be learned." The Psalmist speaks of God's works as—

5. *A source of gladness to the good.* "Thou, Lord, hast made me glad through Thy work; I will triumph in the works of Thy hands." The godly man rejoices in the moral government of God. It appears to him in aspects of righteousness and benevolence and wisdom, which the brutish man and the fool are totally unable to perceive. Many a glorious chapter in the history of God's providential dealings with our race fills the heart of His people with gladness; and they exult in his sovereignty, and in His mighty and gracious deeds.

II. **The manner of this exercise.**

"'To give thanks unto the Lord, and to sing praises unto Thy name, O Most High . . . upon an instrument of ten strings, and upon the psaltery; upon the harp with a solemn sound." The Most High was praised in holy song with accompaniment of instrumental music. There are persons who are so prejudiced (as it appears to us) that they would exclude all instrumental music from the public worship of God. They allege that it is mechanical, not spiritual; and, therefore, is not to be used in the worship of Him who is a Spirit, and who requires spiritual worship. But may not the mechanical assist the spiritual? To us it seems that instrumental music, when it does not supersede, but supplements vocal music; when it is not a substitute for spiritual worship, but a minister to it, is of great service. It is certain that in the temple-service of the Jews, the details of which were of Divine appointment, instrumental music was used. And in the prophetic and symbolic descriptions of the worship of heaven contained in the Apocalypse, instrumental music is introduced. Instrumental music unquestionably aids us in our attempts to give vocal musical utterance to our praise; and there is no reason whatever, in the nature of things, why it should in the smallest degree diminish the spirituality of our praise.

III. **The seasons for this exercise.**

1. *The Lord's Day.* This Psalm is entitled "a Psalm or Song for the Sabbath-day." The day of rest is a season eminently suited to meditation upon the great and glorious works of God in providence, and to praise Him because of them. In its quiet, in our freedom from the demands and duties of business, in its high and holy associations and enjoyments, in these and other characteristics of the day, we see how eminently suited it is for the celebration of the praise of God.

2. *The morning.* "To show forth Thy loving-kindness in the morning." There is no season more favourable to worship than the morning. The air is fresh and invigorating, and the spirit is refreshed by the repose and sleep of the night. Praise should be the natural expression of the heart every morning, because of God's loving-kindness. We read of our Lord that "in the morning, rising up a great while before day, He went out, and departed into a solitary place, and there prayed."

3. *The evening.* "To show forth Thy faithfulness in the evening." As we praise Him in the morning for the mercies of the night, so in the evening we should praise Him for His faithfulness during the day. When the work of the day is done, and we have retired from life's strain and toil, it is fitting that we should recollect the mercy and truth of God to us, and praise Him for them. Evening, with its quiet and repose, is well suited for meditation, and meditation should lead to grateful praise.

IV. **The excellence of this exercise.** "It is a good thing to give thanks unto the Lord," &c.

1. *Because it is right.* Our praise is due to God. He has a right to our worship. He is supremely great, and therefore we should reverence Him; supremely gracious, and therefore we should be grateful to Him; supremely excellent, therefore we should love Him; supremely glorious, therefore we should adore Him. Not to praise Him indicates the basest ingratitude on our part, and defrauds Him of His right.

2. *Because it tends to lessen life's cares and sorrows.* The man who is mindful of the mercies he receives in life, and notes thankfully the truth of God to him, will ever find matter for praise. In every life, not excepting the most tried and sorrowful, there are many things to be thankful for. This will be obvious in the case of the healthful and prosperous. But look at the case of the afflicted and sorrowful, and even here there are matters for thankfulness,—in the recollection of seasons of health and joy, in the hope of that state in which pain and grief are unknown, in the presence of friends and the support of God in affliction, and in the blessings of salvation. To remember these things with gratitude and praise, will lighten life's burdens and soothe life's sorrows.

3. *Because it elevates the spirit of the worshipper.* Gratitude is strengthened by expressing it. If our praise of the mercy and truth of God be sincere, by the expression of it we ourselves shall in a measure become like Him in these respects. Worship is transforming. We become like the object or being whom we truly worship. Thus by the worship of God we are being changed into His image. "It is a good thing to give thanks unto the Lord," for it purifies, enriches, and exalts our being.

4. *Because it is acceptable unto God.* When our praise is sincere and spiritual, the Lord takes pleasure in it. He loves to be worshipped by His intelligent creatures; not from any delight in self-aggrandisement, nor for any other selfish reason, but because such worship calls into exercise the noblest faculties of His creatures, and exalts and blesses them. In this way our worship gratifies the Divine Being. The Most High is pleased to accept the praise of thankful hearts.

CONCLUSION.— Is God's moral government of the world to us a ground of praise? There are many who, in their short-sightedness and unbelief, perceive little but inequalities and anomalies in it, and criticise and complain of its administration. They forget the vastness of the sphere in which it operates, and the long ages through which it operates, and their own incompetence to comprehend the work of the great God; and so when "the workers of iniquity do flourish" they are offended, or at least sorely tried and perplexed. But to the devout believer this government presents a very different aspect. The flourishing of the wicked he perceives to be only brief, very brief, and to be followed by destruction. God's works are so great, and His thoughts so profound, as to fill him with humble and reverent wonder; and His mercy and truth are so conspicuous as to enkindle his gratitude and praise. Is this the case with us? He doeth all things well. Let us trust Him, praise Him.

ENCOURAGEMENTS TO HOLY SONG.

(*Verse* 1.)

"It is a good thing to sing praises unto Thy name, O Most High."

I. **Singing is the music of nature.** Isa. xliv. 23; Psa. lxv. 13; 1 Chron. xvi. 33. The air is the bird's music-room, where they chant their musical notes.

II. **Singing is the music of ordinances.** The Rabbis tell us that the Jews, after the feast of the passover was celebrated, sang Psalm cxl. and the five following Psalms; and our Saviour and His apostles "sang an hymn" immediately after the blessed Supper (Matt. xxvi. 30).

III. **Singing is the music of saints.**
1. They have performed this duty *in their greatest numbers* (Psa. cxlix. 1).
2. In their *greatest straits* (Isa. xxvi. 19).

3. In their *greatest flight* (Isa. xlii. 10 and 11).
4. In their *greatest deliverances* (Isa. lxv. 14).
5. In their *greatest plenties.* In all these changes singing hath been their stated duty and delight.

IV. **Singing is the music of angels.** (Job. xxxviii. 7; Luke ii. 13; Rev. v. 11, 12).

V. **Singing is the music of heaven.** (Rev. xv. 3). Here the saints laboured with drowsy hearts and faltering tongues; but in glory these impediments are removed, and nothing is left to jar their joyous celebration.—JOHN WELLS, abridged from *The Treasury of David.*

THE SUBJECTS AND SEASONS OF PRAISE.

(*Verse* 2.)

The Poet here sets before us,—
I. **The subjects of praise.**

1. *The "loving-kindness" of God.*
The loving-kindness or mercy of God to

man is manifest in His forbearance with sinners, in His forgiveness of sinners, in His compassion towards the sorrowful, and in the rich provision He has made for us in nature, providence, and redemption.

2. The *"faithfulness"* of God. The faithfulness or truth of God is seen in His performing the promises which He has made, in keeping His covenant with His people. We may observe its manifestations in the operations of nature, in the administration of His moral government, and in the salvation of souls.

These subjects of praise are *inexhaustible.* The loving-kindness and truth of God are infinite. We are ever receiving additional illustrations and expressions of them. These subjects of praise are *elevating in their influence upon us.* We cannot sincerely praise God for His loving-kindness and truth without growing ourselves in truthfulness and love.

II. The seasons of praise.

1. *"In the morning."* Because (1) *The state of the mind is favourable.* By the mercy of God we have been preserved through the night, and should therefore be grateful to Him. The mind has been refreshed by the sleep of the night, and is therefore fitted to praise God with freshness and spirit. (2) *The time of the day is suitable.* There is a freshness in the morning air which stimulates us to worship. In the morning, before we are immersed in the business of the day, we can praise God with freedom from interruption. (3) *It is needful as a preparation for the engagements of the day.* We may have difficulties to encounter, temptations to battle with, disappointments to endure, and we need the calmness and strength which accrue from worship to enable us to meet these things.

2. *In the evening.* "Every night." Because (1) *It is helpful to the mind and heart after the toils and trials of the day.* (2) *Because the time is favourable.* Evening, with its shade, and stillness, and rest, is a favourable season for reflection. (3) *The blessings of the day and the needs of the night incite to it.* There is much in every day which ought to be recollected at night with gratitude; and such recollection will help us to rest calmly in the protection of God. And this we should do *"every night."* New illustrations of faithfulness should be followed by new songs of praise. "As thou wouldst have God prosper thy labour in the day and sweeten thy rest in the night, clasp them both together with thy morning and evening devotions. He that takes no care to set forth God's portion of time in the morning, doth not only rob God of His due, but is a thief to himself all the day after, by losing the blessing which a faithful prayer might bring from heaven on his undertakings. And he that closeth his eyes at night without prayer, lies down before his bed is made."

There are some who interpret the "morning" as signifying prosperity and joy, and the "night," adversity and grief. And we shall do well in the brightness of prosperity gratefully to recognise and praise the loving-kindness of God; and in the night of adversity the thankful recollection of the faithfulness of God will encourage and strengthen us.

"Praise ye the Lord; for it is good to sing praises unto our God; for it is pleasant; and praise is comely."

RELIGIOUS GLADNESS.

(*Verse 4.*)

I. Gladness as the gift of God. "Thou, Lord, hast made me glad." All true joy proceeds from the ever blessed God. The gladness which comes not from Him is illusory, short-lived, and often leaves dissatisfaction and pain.

II. Gladness as arising from the contemplation of God's works. "Through Thy work." God's work is eminently calculated to inspire gladness by reason of the power, wisdom, goodness, and delight in beauty which it reveals.

This is true of creation, providence, redemption.

III. **Gladness finding expression in devout song.** "I will triumph in the works of Thy hands." "I will sing for joy, because," &c. Perowne: "I will rejoice in giving praise, for," &c. If God has given us joy, it is meet that we should give Him praise.

THE TEMPORAL PROSPERITY OF THE WICKED.

(*Verse 7.*)

I. **Temporal prosperity is not a criterion of character.** Rich man and Lazarus the beggar. The prosperous "fool."

II. **Temporal prosperity is not an evidence of the Divine favour.**

III. **Temporal prosperity is of uncertain duration.** "Spring as the grass," which speedily perishes.

IV. **The temporal prosperity of the wicked is followed by eternal ruin.** "That they shall be destroyed for ever." "The prosperity of fools shall destroy them."

THE REJOICING OF THE GOOD MAN IN THE GOVERNMENT OF GOD.

(*Verses 8–15.*)

The Poet, having celebrated the praise of God because of His doings in the moral government of the world, proceeds to show what these doings are in relation to the righteous and the wicked. In His just rule God destroys the wicked and blesses the righteous, and this to the Psalmist affords matter for rejoicing. There are two leading ideas here:

I. **God is the Supreme Ruler.** "But Thou, Lord, art Most High for evermore." Perowne: "And Thou, O Jehovah, art (throned) on high for evermore." "This verse, consisting of but one line, expresses the great central fact on which all the doctrine of the Psalm rests. This is the great pillar of the universe and of our faith." God is supreme, because—

1. *He is the greatest Being.* How unspeakably great is God! We have no words or symbols adequate to set forth His greatness and glory. The prophet Isaiah, in language of wondrous sublimity, endeavours to set it forth (Isa. xl. 12–31).

2. *He is the best Being.* He is not only supremely great, but supremely good. In every moral attribute He is perfect. "God is good." "God is light." "God is love."

3. *He is the Creator and Sustainer.* "It is He that hath made us, and not we ourselves." And He who created still sustains His creations. "By Him were all things created; and He is before all things, and by Him all things consist." Here, then, we have the reason of His supremacy. It is real, a thing of being and character and doing. He is the Supreme Ruler because He is supremely great and good, and because as Creator and Sustainer He has the most absolute right over His creatures. "His kingdom ruleth over all."

II. **God's supreme rule is unchangeably righteous.** To the Psalmist this was a deep conviction. "The Lord is upright; my Rock in whom there is no unrighteousness." *His rule is righteous.* Though for a while the wicked may flourish and the righteous be in adversity, yet God's great plan of government and its administration are true and righteous altogether. "A God of truth, without iniquity, just and right is He." His rule is *unchangeably righteous.* The Psalmist says, He is "my rock." As a rock He is firm, abiding, immutable. "God can no more be moved or removed from doing righteously than a rock can be removed out of its place." This unchanging righteousness of God's moral government the Psalmist exhibits as manifest in—

1. *The destruction of the wicked.* "For, lo, Thine enemies, O Lord, for,

lo, Thine enemies shall perish; all the workers of iniquity shall be scattered. Mine eye also shall see my desire on mine enemies, and mine ears shall hear my desire of the wicked that rise up against me." Matthew Henry very properly points out concerning the eleventh verse that "in the Hebrew it is no more than this, *My eye shall look on my enemies, and my ears shall hear of the wicked.* He does not say what he shall see, or what he shall hear, but he shall see and hear that in which God will be glorified, and in which he will therefore be satisfied." Concerning the wicked and their destruction let us note—(1) *The enormity of their character.* They are "enemies" of God and "workers of iniquity." To be an enemy of God is to be hostile to truth, righteousness, love; to oppose our highest Benefactor. It implies extreme moral depravity. The term "workers of iniquity" implies terrible activity in evil. (2) *The unity of their efforts.* It is implied that the wicked have banded themselves together in their hostility to the Lord. So Milton represents fallen angels—

"Devil with devil damned firm concord holds."

And the Psalmist says, "The rulers take counsel together against the Lord," &c. (3) *The utter dissolution of their unity.* "All the workers of iniquity shall be scattered." The cohesion of the wicked in the pursuit of any object is not of long continuance. When God arises against them they shall be scattered like chaff before the tempest, or like a demoralised and rabble army before a mighty and disciplined host. (4) *Their certain destruction.* "For, lo, Thine enemies, O Lord, for, lo, Thine enemies shall perish." The repetition of the word "lo" is emphatic, and indicates the certainty of their destruction. Men must either loyally submit themselves to God or be crushed by Him.

2. *The salvation of the righteous.* The Poet evidently dwells with delight and triumph upon this part of his theme, and gives to us several particulars of the salvation and blessedness of the righteous. (1) *Their strength and honour.* "My horn shalt Thou exalt like the horn of an unicorn." The horn is the symbol of power. The righteous are blessed with true strength. They "walk in the strength of the Lord God." He upholds them and honours them. (2) *Their refreshment and comfort.* "I shall be anointed with fresh oil." "Fresh oil," or green oil, is the best oil. God by His grace will refresh His people when they are weary, and comfort and cheer them when they are depressed and sorrowful. Our Lord gives "the oil of joy for mourning." The godly may be sorely tried for a time, but in due season they shall be visited by choicest refreshment and joy. (3) *Their Divine planting.* They are "planted in the house of the Lord." "To be planted in the house of the Lord is to be fixed and rooted in the grace communicated by the ordinances of Divine worship. Unless we are planted in the house of the Lord we cannot flourish in His courts." Hengstenberg's note is excellent: "By the house of the Lord we can only understand the external sanctuary; in it, however, the servants of God dwell *spiritually* with him, and are cared for by Him with paternal love. There lies at the bottom an abbreviated comparison: these spiritual trees flourish in the house of God as the natural trees when they are planted in a rich soil (Isa. v. 1), or by rivers of water (Ps. i. 3)." They draw their supplies from God. They live by Him and in Him. (4) *Their flourishing growth.* "The righteous shall flourish like the palm tree," &c. (verses 12-14). "The date-palm and the cedar are selected as the loveliest images of verdure, fruitfulness, undecaying vigour and perpetuity." They flourish *perennially.* "Throughout the year, in the winter's cold as in the summer's heat, the palm continues green." The growth of the godly soul is a continuous thing. "He shall be as a tree planted by the waters, and that spreadeth out her roots by the river, and shall not see when heat cometh, but her leaf shall be green; and shall not be careful in the year of drought, neither shall cease from yielding fruit." They flourish *notwithstanding oppression.* "It has been said of the palm tree, *Sub*

pondere crescit—*The more it is pressed down the more it grows:* so the righteous flourish under their burdens,—the more they are afflicted the more they multiply." "We glory in tribulations also, knowing that tribulation worketh patience," &c. They grow *eternally.* The growth of the cedar must be counted not by years, but by centuries. The godly soul will continue to grow for ever. God will ever have more of Himself to reveal unto us. And we shall ever continue to grow in likeness to Him. The soul has unlimited capacities for growth. (5) *Their continued fruitfulness.* "They shall still bring forth fruit in old age." The palm-tree yields about three hundred pounds' weight of dates annually. It has been known to produce even six hundred pounds' weight. Age makes other things decay, but the godly soul flourishes and is fruitful in age. "They have their fruit unto holiness." Their last days are rich in the results of a long experience, and their efforts to do good are wise, and are sustained by a deep faith in God. Both in their life and in their work they are fruitful.

CONCLUSION.—1. *Let us not waver in our faith in the wise and righteous and beneficent moral government of God.* Under it evil men may flourish for a time in temporal prosperity, but God will destroy all workers of iniquity. Good men for a time may be sorely afflicted, but God will sustain them in their afflictions, make their afflictions the occasion of blessing, and crown them with everlasting joy. 2. *What is our relation to this government?* Are we enemies or loyal subjects? Let those who are enemies submit to Jehovah at once, and let His subjects rejoice in His gracious rule.

THE PALM TREE AN ANALOGUE OF THE RIGHTEOUS.

(*Verse* 12.)

"The righteous shall flourish like the palm tree."

The palm is an analogue of the righteous—

I. **In its resolute upward growth.** It is tall, slender, and *erect.* Dr. Thomson says that "neither heavy weights which men place upon its head, nor the importunate urgency of the wind, can sway it aside from perfect uprightness." It seeks to rise as far as possible from earth and as near as possible to heaven. The good man's affections are set "on things above;" his "citizenship is in heaven." While He was yet in this world our Lord spake of Himself as "the Son of Man which is in heaven." And His followers are not of this world even as He was not of the world.

"A man on earth devoted to the skies,
Like ships on seas, while in, above, the world."

II. **In its growth despite of hindrances.** It flourishes where other trees would wither and die. "On the northern borders of the Great Desert, at the foot of the Atlas Mountains, the groves of date palms form the great feature of that parched region, and few trees besides can maintain an existence. The excessive dryness of this arid tract, where rain seldom falls, is such that wheat refuses to grow, and even barley, maize, and Caffre corn afford the husbandman only a scanty and uncertain crop. The hot blasts from the south are scarcely supportable even by the native himself, and yet here forests of date palms flourish." The palm "does not rejoice overmuch in winter's copious rain, nor does it droop under the drought and the burning sun of summer." It will grow, and grow upwards, even if heavy weights are placed upon its head. A picture this of the godly soul. The influences that try him and threaten to crush him are powerless to do so. By the grace of God they even promote his growth. He grows rich by loss, strong by trial, patient by tribulation, joyous by suffering.

III. **In its perennial verdure.** It is an evergreen. The godly soul shall grow and flourish without intermission. Progress is the rule of its life. The goal attained to-day will be the start ing-point of to-morrow (Psa. i. 3; Jer. xvii. 8).

IV. In its fruitfulness. On an average the palm yields from three to four hundred pounds' weight of dates annually, and has been known to produce six hundred pounds' weight. The godly soul produces the fruits of obedience, purity, charity, and helpfulness to others. "Fruit unto holiness." "Herein is My Father glorified, that ye bear much fruit." "They shall still bring forth fruit in old age."

"*But how to secure the realisation of this promise?* 1. *Who is the righteous?* (1 John iii. 7). Righteousness does not consist in profession (Matt. vii. 21); nor is righteousness a state of opinion; nor is it a state of feeling. It is a state of character. The righteous man is marked by this, that his settled principles, his customary desire, is to do, not what is pleasant, not what is advantageous to self, but what is right.

2. "*But how are we to attain this habit of mind and life?* Not inherent righteousness, but the possession of the Holy Ghost indwelling; this puts us into a condition to receive the blessing (Rom. viii. 14; Gal. v. 16).

3. "*But how to obtain the possession of this Divine indwelling power of becoming righteous?* Is there not an obstacle at the very threshold? What are we to say to our past sin? How can that be removed? It may have been committed long ago; but the guilt of sin remains after the sin has been committed. That guilt can only be removed by free pardon. It is only as 'freely justified by grace' that we can enter upon the path of spiritual blessing. So we are brought to the foot of the cross."

THE CEDAR AN ANALOGUE OF SOUL GROWTH.

(*Verse* 12.)

"He shall grow like a cedar in Lebanon."

Trees are a precious gift of God to us. How *useful!* They yield food, shade, fuel, material for furniture, building, &c. How *beautiful!* What symmetry, sublimity, variety, we see in them! They also present many *spiritual analogies.* Here the cedar is used as an emblem of the progress of the soul.

I. The cedar grows not by repression, but by development. By developing its forces the cedar grows from the little germ. Everything that aids that development aids its growth. So with the soul. We cannot grow by attempting to crush our nature, our desires, affections, &c., but by their right development. Not by self-mortification and fighting against the evil, but by the cultivation of the good. In ourselves we are to "overcome evil with good." Wisely and harmoniously developing our powers, we grow.

II. The cedar grows by the appropriation and subordination of the outward elements. Rain, dew, sunlight, gases, minerals, all are appropriated by the cedar, and used to promote its growth: it assimilates them to its own substance. It subordinates the outward elements. Stormy wind and hail and rain and frost all help its growth. The storm that threatened to sweep it away leaves it more firmly rooted and more majestically spread than it found it. The hurricane that tests it promotes its stability and strength. So with the godly soul,—to its own character it assimilates thoughts, impressions, beauties, &c. It makes all things help its progress. *Gentle influences* help its growth. The ministry of prosperity,—success, friendship, health, joy—promotes its progress. *Trying influences* also help its growth and strength. The ministry of adversity,—failure, desertion, sickness, grief—promotes its firmness, strength, and heroism. "Tribulation worketh patience," &c. We may make the most adverse circumstances, by the grace of God, aid us in the true development of our souls.

III. The cedar grows slowly. We may form some idea of the slowness of its growth from the fact that it continues to grow for centuries. Many generations come and go, but it grows on. The processes of the Divine economy seem slow to us. The preparation of the world for man; of the race of men for the Saviour; and now of the race for glory,—all seem so slow. The greatest and best of things mature very gradually. So with the soul. Proneness to impatience is a mark of imperfection. How impatiently the child awaits the promised pleasure! Much less is the impatience of the man. The wise and good man is truly patient. Patience with thyself, my brother; thy growth is not like that of the gourd, but that of the cedar,—very gradual.

"We have not wings, we cannot soar;
But we have feet to scale and climb,
By slow degrees, by more and more,
The cloudy summits of our time.

"The heights by great men reached and kept
Were not attained by sudden flight;
But they, while their companions slept,
Were toiling upward in the night."
—*Longfellow.*

IV. The cedar grows by ceaseless activities. The sap, which is the life of the tree, is ever active: from the roots it passes through the trunk and through every branch, leaf, and fibre; then from the leaves it returns through branches and trunk to the roots, bearing nourishment, strength, &c. So with the soul. By earnest thought, devout feeling, divine worship, holy activity, &c., we grow.

V. The cedar grows to immense size and magnificence. Very great and grand they are. The soul is destined to grow into great strength and beauty. What great and glorious beings John and Peter and Paul must have grown into! How great and glorious are Isaiah and David and Abraham and Enoch by this time! And yet they have not reached the goal. "It doth not yet appear what they shall be." "Perfect as our Father in heaven is perfect,"—that is the end of our progress. We shall grow into spiritual might, nobility, beauty, and glory. Cedars are most royal trees: under the smile of God we shall grow into royal beings.

VI. The cedar grows during long ages. There are cedars growing now that have been growing while scores of generations of men have come and gone from the earth. While they live they grow. So with the soul. Long as it lives it grows. But the cedars are not everlasting; their life and growth must end. But there is no end to the growth of the soul! We shall live and grow for ever. To advance from grace to grace, from strength to strength, from glory to glory for evermore,—that is our destiny.

THE OLD AGE OF PIETY.

(*Verse* 14.)

"They shall still bring forth fruit in old age."

The subject to which the text invites us is, *the old age of piety, as distinguished from the old age of the worldling.*

I. The old age of the Christian is the old age of a life of faith and communion with God. Amid the infirmities of decaying nature the good man's judgment may begin to fail, his active energy for one work and another may fail, but his faith fails not, and the charity—the holy love—which is communion with God, "never faileth."

II. The old age of the Christian, as distinguished from the old age of the ungodly, is characterised by hope. To him, indeed, as to others, old age is the evening of life, its dim light still fading into darkness. But to him faith opens a vista through which the soul looks forth in hope beyond the deepening shadows around him.

III. The old age of the Christian is one of cheerfulness. How beautiful is an unrepining, bright, cheerful old age! How doubly beautiful when that calm, bright cheerfulness, lighting up the evening of life, is caught from heaven, and is none other than the cheerfulness of a mind at peace with God, and in communion with His boundless blessedness!

IV. **The old age of the Christian, as distinguished from that of the ungodly, is characterised by affection.** The old man's sympathies with those around him are less easily awakened than they once were; and, as he grows older, he feels less and less interest in any of his friends, save those who happen to be essential to his comfort. The Christian in his old age is not exempted from this tendency. But in his case there is a counteracting power. His faith and hope, the habitual cheerfulness of his spirit, and the communion of his soul with the infinite love of God, are like a constant cordial to his nature, that keeps his mind elastic and quickens his better sympathies.

V. **The old age of the Christian is characterised to the last by usefulness.** How many ways does God find to make His children, amid the infirmities of declining age, useful to others! They shall bring forth fruit in old age, to show that God is faithful to them that trust in Him. How persuasive is the testimony which they give for God and for godliness out of their long experience! How winning are their words of counsel and invitation!

LESSONS.—1. *The consideration of the beauty and happiness of piety in old age is an argument to the young to remember their Creator in the days of their youth.* 2. *Our subject addresses itself powerfully to those who are old, or are growing old, without piety.* What a night is that which is gathering around you! 3. *The subject should lead us all to a grateful acknowledgment of the grace of God in the examples which we are permitted to see of aged and venerable piety.*—*L. Bacon, D.D.*, Abridged.

PSALM XCIII.

INTRODUCTION.

The author of this Psalm and the occasion on which it was written are unknown.

"The sum and substance of this Psalm," says Perowne, "is contained in the eighth verse of the preceding Psalm. It celebrates the majesty of Jehovah as Ruler of the world. He is Creator of the world, who has been its King from everlasting: it rests upon Him and is stayed by His might. All the powers of nature obey Him, however lawless they may seem, as all the swelling and rage of men, of which those are but a figure, must obey Him. But His majesty and His glory are seen, not only in controlling the powers of nature and whatsoever exalteth and opposeth itself against Him, but in the faithfulness of His word, and in the holiness of His house."

As to the date of the composition it appears from verse 5 that it was composed after the building of the Temple, and probably before its destruction by the Chaldeans.

JEHOVAH THE KING.

The opening words of the Psalm, as Hengstenberg has pointed out, do not refer to the constant government of God, but to a new and glorious manifestation of His dominion. "The Lord reigneth" is a similar form of expression to that which the Jews used to announce the ascent to the throne of a new sovereign (2 Sam. xv. 10; 2 Kings ix. 13). It refers to the coming of the Lord in His kingdom; and might have been used with great propriety at the destruction of Babylon and the emancipation of Israel. But when His glory and sovereignty shall be fully displayed and acknowledged, the expression shall be used with an emphasis and fulness of meaning unknown before. (See Rev. xi. 15, 17; xix. 6.) The Poet sets before us—

I. **The majesty of the King.** "The Lord reigneth, He is clothed with majesty." The glory with which Jehovah clothes Himself forms the opposition to the pomp and pride of earthly kings, and is an antidote against the fear of them. The glory of earthly sovereigns is as nothing in comparison with His. His is the majesty of meekness, the glory of grace, the beauty of holiness. He reigns in righteousness and love to bless and save men. Yet He is terrible to His foes. Let not His loyal subjects fear the pomp and glory of their enemies; for He has but to manifest His majesty, and theirs shall vanish.

II. The might of the King. "The Lord is clothed with strength," &c. Perowne: "'Jehovah hath clothed, He hath girded Himself with strength.' In the second number of the verse, the verb is rythmically repeated, and the noun 'strength' really belongs to both verbs." The strength of the king is manifested—

1. *In the stability of the world.* "The world also is established that it cannot be moved." The stability of the world is regarded as the effect of the Divine rule and power. The same power which created the world sustains it in its regularity and stability. The "sure and firm set earth" is an emblem of the moral government of God in its firmness and security. So in the time of peril and opposition the people of God need not fear, for no violence can shake His throne. "That there is any stability, either in the world or in the Church, is the Lord's doings, and He is to be adored for it."

2. *In the subjugation of His enemies.* "The floods have lifted up, O Lord, the floods have lifted up their voice," &c. (vers. 3 and 4). We have here (1) *The tumultuous opposers of His reign.* "The floods" are introduced as the symbol of the tumultuous nations and peoples which lift themselves up against the government of God. Like angry waves of the sea men have raged against the anointed King. As the breakers roar in thunder and dash in fury against the shore, so devils and men have hurled defiance at the throne of God. The heathen still rage against the Lord and against His Anointed and against His Church. (2) *The calm Sovereign.* "The Lord on high is mightier than the noise of many waters, yea, than the mighty waves of the sea." The construction of the fourth verse is not very clear. Perowne has a valuable critical note on it. The translation which he adopts is: "More than the voices of many waters, the glorious breakers of the sea, Jehovah on high is glorious."

Hengstenberg: "Than the voice of many waters, than the glorious waves of the sea, more glorious in the height is the Lord." However we construe the verse the main idea is the same. As the furious waves dash against the rocky shore and fall back spent, while the shore remains calm and unmoved, so Jehovah is unmoved by all the fierce opposition of all the rebels against His government. He is greater, stronger, more glorious than all the powers arrayed against Him and His Church. The Lord is calm *in His assured right to reign.* He has no misgivings as to the authority by which He governs. Earthly sovereigns may doubt the validity of their authority, but Jehovah never can do so. The Lord is calm *in His assured power to reign.* With infinite ease He can control and, if He see fit, entirely quell every storm in His universe. Let not the Church, then, fear the might of the world. High over it all, ruling it as He pleases, is the Lord omnipotent and all-glorious.

III. The eternity of the King and of His kingdom. "Thy throne is established of old; Thou art from everlasting." Margin: "Thy throne is established from then." Hengstenberg: "The throne of wickedness has no 'then'; it is of yesterday, like a mushroom sprung out of the earth." God's throne is eternal. In earthly kingdoms and empires the throne is frequently shaken to its base. By the death of kings, or of their wise advisers, or because of the attacks of foes, earthly governments and dynasties are sometimes overthrown. But the throne of God is from everlasting to everlasting. The King also is eternal. "Thou art from everlasting." This eternity includes omnipotence. He who is "from everlasting" is also "to everlasting." When human crowns and thrones have crumbled into dust He shall reign in glory. (See remark on Ps. xc. 2.)

IV. The truth of His testimonies. "Thy testimonies are very sure." Perowne: "The transition is abrupt, from the majesty of God as seen in His dominion in the world of nature, to His revelation of Himself in His Word.

At the same time there is a connection between the two, as in Ps. xix. God who rules the world, He whose are the kingdom, and the power, and the glory for ever, has given His testimonies to His people, a sure and faithful word." His testimonies in this place are especially His promises of salvation and victory to His people. The promises of so majestic and mighty a Sovereign cannot fail. "The testimony of the Lord is sure." The truth of His testimonies is
1. *A rebuke to the unbelief of His subjects.*
2. *An encouragement to their faith.*
3. *A warning to rebels against His government.*

V. **The purity of His court.** "Holiness becometh Thine house, O Lord, for ever." The King has Himself come to dwell among His people, making them and His house holy. The Church of God should be cleansed from all sin and fully consecrated to Him. In His heavenly court the purity is perfect and perpetual; and ultimately the earthly court will be absorbed into the heavenly, which will abide for ever.

CONCLUSION.—1. *Let the people of God trust and rejoice in their King.* He reigns securely, gloriously, eternally, for their salvation. 2. *Let His enemies submit themselves to Him.* "Kiss the Son, lest He be angry," &c.

PSALM XCIV.

INTRODUCTION.

"There is no superscription to this Psalm. There is no indication of its authorship, of the period at which it was written, or of the circumstances to which it refers. There are many of these anonymous hymns in God's Book, nameless utterances, voices of the night of weeping, shouts from the mountain tops of thought, prayers unto the God of Life, which belong to no individual, can be fathered on no solitary period, but descend as an heirloom to successive ages, and enrich every generation. As the circumstances, the victories, the shortcomings, and the possibilities of man are continually being repeated, so the religious experiences of the Church do often reappear in its history, and we may receive the inspired utterances of them in one age as almost equally appropriate to the sorrows and joys of another age."—*Dr. H. R. Reynolds.*

"This Psalm, as may be easily apprehended, is a prayer of all the pious children of God, and of spiritual people, against all their persecutors, so that it may be used by all pious godly people from the beginning till the end of the world."—*Luther.*

A CRY FOR JUDGMENT.

(*Verses 1-7.*)

Consider—
I. **The complaint of the Church.** "Lord, how long shall the wicked, how long shall the wicked triumph?" &c. (vers. 3-7). The poet complains to the Lord of the enemies of the Church, and makes mention of—
1. *Their general character.* "The wicked . . . the workers of iniquity." They are depraved in character, and diabolic in conduct. "Mark the terrible energy implied in the designation, '*workers* of iniquity.' Reference is not made to men who make a *pastime* of iniquity, or who *occasionally* commit themselves to its service, but to those who toil at it as a business. As the merchant man is industrious in commerce, as the philosopher is assiduous in study, as the artist is indefatigable in elaboration, so those slaves of iniquity toil in their diabolic pursuits with an ardour which the most powerful remonstrance seldom abates. They are always ready to serve their master."—*Parker.*

2. *Their arrogant triumph* (vers. 3, 4.) "How long shall the wicked triumph? They belch out, they speak arrogant things; all the workers of iniquity carry themselves proudly."—*Perowne's trans.* In the first line of verse 4, the two verbs have one noun as the object—they pour forth hard, or, proud speeches. The enemies of the people of God were triumphant over them, and were proud and insolent in

73

their triumph. It is not seldom that the wicked in their prosperity and power have arrogantly lorded it over the righteous. Prosperity, apart from Divine grace, engenders presumption, and fancied self-sufficiency, and self-boasting.

3. *Their oppression and cruelty* (vers. 5, 6.) The word which in the A.V. is translated, "they break in pieces," Perowne and Hengstenberg translate, "they crush." The wicked oppressed the people and heritage of the Lord. How frequently was this the case in the history of the chosen people! How frequently has it been so in the history of the Christian Church! The Psalmist complains of cruelty as well as oppression. "They slay the widow," &c. "The widow and the fatherless are mentioned, as often, as particular instances of those whose misery ought to excite compassion, but whose defencelessness makes them the easy prey of the wicked."—*Perowne*. This is invariably represented in Scripture as a crime of great enormity, and especially abhorrent to God. See Exod. xxii. 21-24.

4. *Their practical Atheism.* "Yet they say the Lord shall not see, neither shall the God of Jacob regard it." "The Divine names," says Alexander, "are, as usual, significant. That the self-existent and eternal God should not see, is a palpable absurdity; and scarcely less so, that the God of Israel should suffer His own people to be slaughtered without even observing it." We need not suppose that they uttered this blasphemy in words, but it was expressed in their conduct. Their atheism was not theoretical, but practical. This practical atheism is very prevalent and pernicious at the present time. Immense numbers utter "the Apostles' Creed" regularly, who exclude God from almost every province of their life. In the formation of their plans, in the management of their business, in their relations to society, &c., God is not in all their thoughts.

II. **The appeal of the Church.** "O Lord God, to whom vengeance belongeth," &c. (vers. 1-3). Let it be noted at once and closely that the appeal is for justice, not for revenge. "I do not think that we sufficiently attend to the distinction that exists between revenge and vengeance. 'Revenge,' says Dr. Johnson, 'is an act of passion, vengeance of justice, injuries are revenged, crimes avenged.' . . . The call which the Psalmist here makes on God, as a God to whom vengeance belongeth, is no other than if he had said, 'O God, to whom justice belongeth!' Vengeance indeed is not for man, because with man's failings and propensities it would ever degenerate into revenge. 'I will be even with him,' says nature; 'I will be above him,' says grace!"—*Bouchier*.

1. *Judgment is the prerogative of God alone.* "O Lord God, to whom vengeance belongeth." The two names of the Divine Being which the Psalmist uses, *El* and *Jehovah*, recognise God as almighty, self-existent, and alone entitled to take vengeance. Literally it is, "God of vengeances," the plural indicating that there is in God a fulness of vengeance for His persecuted people; and the repetition of the appeal denotes the earnestness with which it is made. "To Me belongeth vengeance and recompense." "Avenge not yourselves, but rather give place unto wrath; for it is written, Vengeance is Mine; I will repay, saith the Lord." The vindication of His people and the punishment of their enemies is His sole prerogative. He will render righteous judgment to the wicked. He alone has the right to do so.

2. *Judgment is sometimes apparently long delayed.* "Lord, how long shall the wicked, how long shall the wicked triumph?" The persecution seems to the Psalmist to have been of long continuance. He would fain know when it would end. Our time of suffering and trial always seems long and wearisome. In the night of weeping and waiting, wearily drag the hours, and we cry, "How long?" In due season God will appear, &c.

3. *Judgment is earnestly invoked.* Here is a cry for *the manifestation of God*. "Show Thyself." Margin, as in

Heb., "Shine forth." It is an appeal to God to manifest Himself as a God of righteous retributions. Here is a cry for *the judgment of God*. "Lift up Thyself, thou judge," &c. God is conceived as sitting at ease, and entreated to arise and execute judgment, and to give a just recompense to those enemies of His people who, having got the upper hand, exulted proudly over them. Here is a cry for *His speedy interposition*, "Lord, how long?" &c.

CONCLUSION.—Deep in the heart of man is the sense of justice, the conviction that there is a judge of all the earth who will do right. Oppressed humanity in all ages and in all lands has cried to heaven for judgment. That cry will certainly, sooner or later, meet with a full response.

"The sun of justice may withdraw his beams
Awhile from earthy ken, and sit concealed
In dark recess, pavilioned round with clouds:
Yet let not guilt presumptuous rear her crest,
Nor virtue droop despondent: soon these clouds,
Seeming eclipse, will brighten into day,
And in majestic splendour He will rise,
With healing and with terror on His wings."
—*G. Bally.*

THE FOLLY OF PRACTICAL ATHEISM.

(*Verses* 8-11.)

The Psalmist addresses not the theoretical, but practical atheists. He speaks to men who acknowledged the existence of God, and His creatorship, and His government of the world; but who thought that He did not see and would not recompense their conduct. This is the atheism which is the most prevalent and perilous in the present day. The folly of such atheists is seen—

I. In supposing that God does not observe their conduct. "He that planted the ear, shall He not hear? He that formed the eye, shall He not see?" The principle upon which this interrogation is based is this, that an effect cannot be greater than its cause. The picture with the beauty of which we are charmed is not greater than the conceptive and executive power of the artist who produced it. He saw it mentally long before we saw it visually. "This argument," says R. Watson, "is as easy as it is conclusive, obliging all who acknowledge a first cause, to admit His perfect intelligence, or to take refuge in atheism itself. It fetches not the proof from a distance, but refers us to our bosoms for the constant demonstration that the Lord is a God of knowledge, and that by Him actions are weighed." And Tillotson : "We find in ourselves such qualities as thought and intelligence, power and freedom, &c., for which we have the evidence of consciousness as much as for our own existence. Indeed, it is only by our consciousness of these, that our existence is known to ourselves. We know, likewise, that these are perfections, and that to have them is better than to be without them. We find also that they have not been in us from eternity. They must, therefore, have had a beginning, and consequently some cause. Now this cause, as it must be superior to its effect, must have those perfections in a superior degree; and if it be the First Cause, it must have them in an infinite or unlimited degree, since bounds or limitations, without a limiter, would be an effect without a cause." If we see and hear and know, then God does so in a much greater, indeed, in an infinite degree. His knowledge is clear and distinct, ours is dim and confused; His is intimate and thorough, ours is partial and superficial ; His is universal and infallible, ours uncertain and limited. "The Lord knoweth the thoughts of man." How foolish, then, to imagine that God does not hear the arrogant speech, or see the oppressive deed, or note the wickedness of men!

II. In supposing that God will not recompense their conduct. "He that chastiseth the heathen, shall not He correct?" "There is," says Perowne, "a change in the argument. Before it was from the physical constitution of man ; now it is from the moral government of the world." The idea seems to be that even the heathen are governed by God. He has revealed to them by means of creation "His eternal power and Godhead;" His law He has "written in their hearts; their conscience also bears witness" for Him. They are subject to His control. He visits them in mercy; and He reproves them with judgment. Is it not folly then to suppose that He will overlook the injuries inflicted upon His own people by those who have a clearer and fuller revelation than the heathen? Every additional illustration of the judgment of God imparts increased force to the already conclusive evidence, that God will correct those who break His law and oppress His people.

The Psalmist mentions two things which considerably strengthen his argument.

1. *That the evil complained of was of long continuance.* "Ye fools, when will ye be wise?" The inquiry implies that their folly had existed for a long period. During that period they had been "treasuring up unto themselves wrath against the day of wrath and revelation of the righteous judgment of God." If they repent not, that accumulated wrath will surely burst upon them.

2. *That God knows not only words and actions, but thoughts and purposes also.* "The Lord knoweth the thoughts of man, that they are vanity." He has set "our secret sins in the light of His countenance." The thoughts that He would not see and judge for these sins He knew. All thoughts of arrogance and oppression He knew. Let them not imagine that He did "not see" or "regard" their conduct; for even their hearts were known unto Him. "Thoughts are words to God, and vain thoughts are provocations."

CONCLUSION.—1. *Here is warning to practical atheists.* You are acting as though God had nothing to do with some departments of your life and conduct. You do things in business, or in politics, or in pleasure, which will not bear His scrutiny. You say in practice, "The Lord shall not see, neither shall God regard it." But He does see; and "know thou, that for all these things God will bring thee into judgment." Your practical atheism is utter folly. 2. *Here is encouragement to the oppressed righteous.* You cannot pass beyond the region of God's knowledge. He is acquainted with all your afflictions. His love and power are as great as His knowledge. He will sustain you in all your afflictions; and when He ariseth for judgment He will triumphantly vindicate you.

THE BLESSEDNESS OF THE DIVINELY-INSTRUCTED MAN.

(*Verses* 12-15.)

The Psalmist, having complained of the enemies of the Church and appealed to God for judgment, and having warned the enemies of the folly of their conduct, proceeds in these verses to speak of the blessedness of the people of God, even in the midst of the oppressions to which they were subjected. "Blessed is the man," &c. The good man is here represented as blessed,—

I. **Because of the instruction which he receives.** "Blessed is the man whom Thou chastenest, O Lord, &c." (vers. 12, 13). The word which is here rendered "chastenest" does not mean to afflict or punish; but to instruct, to admonish, &c. Perowne renders it, "instructest;" and Hengstenberg, "admonishest." He says, "Those who allow themselves to be admonished and taught by the Lord stand in opposition to the *foolish* among the people, who go to school with the blind ungodly *heathen.*"

1. *The Teacher.* "Thou instructest, O Lord." As a Teacher, the Lord is incomparable, supreme, perfect. (1) *In the extent of His attainments.* All things are known to Him. His resources are inexhaustible. "His understanding is infinite." (2) *In His method of instruction.* His knowledge of each pupil is perfect. He knows the faculties, capacities, attainments, &c., of each

one; and adapts His communications and methods of instruction to each one. The Lord is an infallible, perfect Teacher.

2. *The Text-book.* "Out of Thy law." By means of His Word, God teaches His people the great principles of His government. "The *law* appears here," says Hengstenberg, "as the means which God uses in this instruction, the fountain out of which He draws it, and then satisfies with it by His Spirit the thirsty soul. It comes into notice in connection with *its doctrine of recompense,* and *its rich consolatory promises* for the people of the Lord, whose end is always salvation." The Word of God is the best expositor of His Providence.

3. *The end of the instruction.* "That Thou mayest give him rest," &c. Perowne, as we think, expounds truly: "This is the end of God's teaching, that His servant may wait in patience, unmoved by, safe FROM THE DAYS OF EVIL (comp. xlix. 5), seeing the evil all round him lifting itself up, but seeing also the secret, mysterious retribution, slowly but surely accomplishing itself. In this sense the 'rest' is the rest of a calm, self-possessed spirit, as Isa. vii. 4; xxx. 15; xxxii. 17." The Divinely-instructed man has such views of the Divine administration as inspire him with confidence and calmness, even when the wicked arrogantly triumph over him. God has taught him out of His law that the pit is being digged, into which, if he repent not, the wicked will fall and perish. So the good man has inward rest in the midst of outward affliction and persecution. He is not the creature, but the conqueror of circumstances. His enemies may oppress him, but they cannot invade his peace, &c.

II. **Because of the faithfulness of God.** "For the Lord will not cast off His people," &c. The Divinely-instructed man is in covenant relation with God, by virtue of which he is both secure and blessed. He is blessed, for God will never forsake him. "The Lord may perhaps forsake His people *for a time* (comp. Jud. vi. 13; Isa. ii. 6), as a righteous punishment for forsaking *Him,* Deut. xxxii. 15, but *not for ever.*"—*Hengstenberg.* The righteous are God's "inheritance," and He will not give up His title to it, nor suffer it to be wrested from Him. "For a small moment have I forsaken thee; but with great mercies will I gather thee," &c., Isa. liv. 7, 8. Blessed, indeed, is the man who has the assurance that whatever may befall him, God will not forsake him. Being sure of his interest in God, he will want no good thing.

III. **Because of the righteousness of His judgments.** "But judgment shall return unto righteousness," &c. There are times when judgment seems turned aside from righteousness, such as, when the wicked triumph and the good are oppressed. But at the proper time these apparent perversions will be seen in their true light, and righteousness will be seen to be supreme. Even in appearance, judgment and justice cannot always fail. It must sooner or later appear in its true character as perfect righteousness. In the judgment of the great day this manifestation of the righteousness of the Divine rule will be on a grand scale. This manifestation of the righteousness of God's judgments will be viewed with satisfaction by the righteous. "All the upright in heart shall follow it." They will *approve of it,* avow their attachment to it. They will *rejoice in it.* They shall follow it with joyous hearts and triumphant songs.

CONCLUSION.—Blessed, indeed, is the Divinely-instructed man; for he has rest in the midst of trouble, an everlasting interest in God, and a glorious prospect in the judgment.

A DECLARATION OF CONFIDENCE IN GOD.

(*Verses* 16-23.)

The Psalmist now applies the general doctrine of the Psalm to his own case, and the result is this clear declaration of sublime trust in God. Here is—

I. **Confidence in the midst of formidable enemies.** It is an easy matter to declare a triumphant trust when we are free from trial and danger. But the Poet was threatened and afflicted by unscrupulous and powerful enemies when he uttered these trustful and brave words.

1. *His enemies were evil in character.* "The evil doers, . . . the workers of iniquity." See remarks on verse 4.

2. *His enemies were in positions of authority.* They occupied "the throne" or judgment seat. They were "not common assassins or thieves, but tyrants who, under a false pretext of justice, oppressed the Church. The throne of the king, the seat of the judge, which is consecrated to God, they stained or defiled with their crimes."—*Perowne.* The people of God have often had wicked kings, and corrupt and cruel judges for their enemies.

3. *His enemies acted legally.* "Which frameth mischief by a law." They enacted wicked laws, or propounded wicked interpretations of the law. Iniquity is never so daring as when it is supported by the sanctions of law. A thing may be right legally, yet utterly wrong morally, and right morally, yet wrong legally. We have a notable example of this in the life of Daniel (Dan. vi. 7).

4. *His enemies were confederate in council and action.* "They gather themselves together," &c. The enemies of Daniel afford an illustration, Dan. vi. 6, 11, 15. Surely the enemies of the Psalmist were sufficiently formidable to have aroused his fears. Yet he unfalteringly declares his confidence.

II. **Confidence in the midst of many and anxious thoughts.** The Psalmist speaks of "the multitude of his thoughts within him." Perowne: "In the multitude of my anxious thoughts within me." "Anxious thoughts, or 'perplexities,' lit. '*divided* or *branching* thoughts,' whether doubts or cares." He was fully alive to the dangers of his position. His thoughts were *anxious* and perplexed. They were also *multitudinous.* Luther: "He speaks of the many thoughts which one has in such a state of despair, how he could or might come out of it. Then he thinks this way and that way, and visits all holes and corners, but finds none." Yet faith triumphs over these anxious thoughts. Notwithstanding his deep solicitude, he expresses his firm confidence in God and His Providence. He is anxious, yet victorious.

III. **Confidence in the Divine support.** "Unless the Lord had been my help, my soul had soon dwelt in silence," &c. (vers. 17, 18). Notice here—

1. *The danger, and the need of help.* (1) He was in *danger of death.* His soul was nearly dwelling in silence. The grave is represented as a place of silence. He was near to "the gates of death." (2) He was also in *danger of falling.* He felt his feet slipping. When the soul is painfully exercised as to the Divine administration of human affairs, there is danger of falling into unbelief and rebellion, or of sinking into despair. (3) The danger was *imminent.* His soul was already near to the land of darkness and silence, and his feet were slipping.

2. *The failure of human help.* "Unless the Lord had been my help," &c. There are times when human help fails for want of faithfulness; and times when it fails for want of ability. There are experiences in life in which the truest and most devoted of human helpers are powerless to sympathise with or aid us.

3. *The sufficiency of the Divine help.* The Lord was the Helper of the Psalmist, and His mercy held him up. The help of the Lord was (1) *sufficient.* It saved him from falling and from death. (2) *Seasonable.* It was afforded when he was near "the silent land," when his feet were slipping. (3) *Gracious.* It was the expression of His mercy. He saves us in His lovingkindness. So the Psalmist proclaims his confidence in God, &c.

IV. **Confidence in the Divine protection.** "The Lord is my defence; and my God is the Rock of my refuge." Perowne: "Jehovah hath been a high tower for me." The Psalmist is confident of—

1. *The Security of the Divine Protection.* Jehovah was his "high tower." In Him he would be raised far above the reach of danger. He was "the Rock of his refuge," in the clefts of which he may safely hide.

2. *The Stability of the Divine Protection.* "The Rock" is firm, strong, immovable. It stands securely and calmly amid the driving winds, and pelting storms, and surging, thundering seas. The soul that trusts in Jehovah may exult, for she is inviolably and eternally safe.

V. **Confidence in the Divine retribution.** "Shall the throne of iniquity have fellowship with Thee? . . . . He shall bring upon them their own iniquity," &c. Here is a threefold assurance :—

1. *God has no fellowship with the wicked.* He will have no alliance with injustice, even when it is sanctioned by human laws. He has no complicity with evil. All His arrangements are utterly hostile to it.

2. *God will cut off the persistently wicked.* "He shall cut them off in their own wickedness," &c. A terrible retribution awaits the workers of iniquity.

3. *God will cut off the persistently wicked by means of their own wickedness.* "He shall bring upon them their own iniquity." "It is an ill work wicked ones are about; they make fetters for their own feet, and build houses for to fall upon their own heads; so mischievous is the nature of sin that it damnifies and destroys the parents of it."—*Greenhill.* " A man cannot be more miserable than his own wickedness will make him if God visit it upon him."—*M. Henry.*

VI. **Confidence in the Lord a source of joy, even in the midst of dangers and anxieties.** We have reserved this consideration to the last, because it seems to us the crowning triumph and glory of confidence. Even in the midst of oppression, peril, and multitudinous anxieties, the trust of the Psalmist brought joy to his soul. "Thy comforts delight my soul." Meditation on the perfections of God, trust in His promises, and the realisation of His presence, are Divine comforts which exceedingly rejoice the soul. "They not only *pacify* the mind, but they *joy* it ; they do not only *satisfy* it, but *ravish* it ; they not only *quiet*, but *delight* it. They not only take away the present grief, but likewise put in the room and place of it most unspeakable comfort and consolation, as the *sun* does not only dispel darkness, but likewise brings in a glorious light in the stead of it."—*T. Horton.* Thus, by faith in God, the soul is "more than conqueror" over all hostile powers without, and anxious thoughts and fears within. Let us cultivate such faith. For such faith let us pray. "Lord, increase our faith."

THE SUMMONS TO HOLY WORK.

(*Verse* 16.)

We may regard these words as parallel at least to those of the Judges and Lawgivers of Israel, who when the very existence of Israel as a nation was trembling in the balance, and when devotedness and loyalty were demanded by the circumstances of the case, called with trumpet-voice to the brave and truehearted among them to be "on the Lord's side," and "cursed bitterly" those who would not come "to the help of the Lord against the mighty."

I. **Let us review a few characteristics of the evildoers.**

1. Look at the *number* of the evildoers. Not more than one-seventh of the human race is even nominally Christian ; and among these Christians are reckoned all the populations of Austria, France, Russia, America, and Spain ; the Greeks, the Copts, and the Armenians; the priest-ridden inhabitants of Brazil and Mexico, and all the crowds of our English cities; the Sabbath-breakers, the despisers of God's love, the haters of God's law, the drunkard, the harlot, the miser, the dotard, and the fool. . . . Turn to the six-sevenths of this world's

population.... We are passing out of Goshen into Egyptian darkness.

2. The *variety* of the evildoers. In one place there is subtle speculation, in another gross vice; here utter indifference, there wild fanaticism; in one tribe crushing ignorance, in another daring philosophy and luxuriant imagination.... The regiments of the prince of this world wear various uniforms; the mutineers in God's army are widespread and bear divers colours: they speak a hundred dialects or tongues, and are scattered over the whole world.

3. They are *closely organised*. There are subtle links of faith that bind the millions of the East, and move them in vast masses. In China ... there is abundant organisation, and much coincidence of action. In India, with all the varieties of faith that prevail, there are great and startling signs of combination against God and His Christ.

4. The *depravity* of these evildoers. It is not the mere ignorance which heathendom reveals which constitutes their chief danger or our main responsibility, but it is the fearful corruption of man under these various forms of Christless, Godless life. In these lands of which we are speaking there is no public opinion against sins of the foulest, most unmentionable kinds.

II. **Consider the course which God has taken with these evildoers, and also what is involved in the appeal here uttered.** "Who will rise up for Me against the evildoers?" "Who is on the Lord's side?" By these appeals God seems to tell us that He is not going to crush, or destroy, or convert, or save these evildoers by any fiat of omnipotence, by any touch of His imperial sceptre. His method has always been to teach men by men; to uproot error by truth; to conquer darkness by light; to drive out hatred by love. Nature has unveiled her charms, &c., to men first, and afterwards to nations.

God's greatest acts of revelation have been made through human minds. When He intends to reach the hearts and conquer the wills of men by His love, He calls the sons of men to His help against the mighty. It is not, however, that God is weak and needs our help, but that for infinitely perfect reasons He chooses thus to conquer His enemies, &c. "Who will rise up for Me against the evildoers?" The evildoing is done against Him.

III. **Examine the response which is made to this appeal.** Nature is ready to rise up for God against the evildoers. Tremendous ocean once heaved from his rocky bed, and in the roaring of his billows said, "I will sweep the accursed race of man from the face of the earth." ... And the lust of rule, the spirit of conquest, the demon of war, have come up before Him. And they have said one to another, "We will go and make inroads on these hoary superstitions; we will bring the civilisation of distant tribes together," &c. ... The enemies of the Lord have fought against each other, and the wrath of man has been made to praise Him. But He needs other and nobler service. Led by Death himself, Cholera, Plague, Famine, and Madness have often risen up against the evildoers.... And now a peaceful group come smiling on, confident in their strength, instinct with hope and promise—they are Science and Commerce, Civilisation and Law.... But powers like these cannot reach the root of the evil. In the Gospel of Christ there is the only stay of human corruption, the only rival to the world's fascinations, the only power which is merciful to the sinner while it is just to his sin. It is God's method to overwhelm and subdue the heart of man, to change the evildoer, not by His threats, but by His amnesty—not by the thunder of law, but by the sovereign pleading of love. How shall we obey the summons of the text?—Abridged from "*Notes of the Christian Life*," by Dr. Reynolds.

A Common Incident of the Journey.

(*Verse* 18.)

"My foot slippeth."
The whole verse is, "When I said, My foot slippeth; Thy mercy, O Lord, held me up." Here we have one of the simplest forms of prayer, the bare statement of danger. The child's cry, without introduction or finis. The soul in peril can seldom say much, but that which is said is generally expressive. Take, for example, these words: they imply faith in the *presence of One able to help—abhorrence of the sin to which he is tempted—and confidence in His willingness to save.*

This experience is a common one. All of us are, at some time, found in slippery places. They are of various kinds, more or less dangerous. There are many things incident to ourselves which render them the more perilous. And we have the same method for preservation the Psalmist enjoyed. Let us notice each of these points.

I. **Some slippery places.** We are the more exposed to falling when we are brought into circumstances of—

1. *Poverty and want.* Christ was tempted when He hungered.

2. *Of annoyance and vexation.* Moses smote the rock in anger.

3. *Of dejection and perplexity.* Ps. lxxiii. 2, 3.

4. *Of sore bereavement and trial.* Job.

II. **Some things concerning the traveller, rendering these the more perilous.**

1. *The absence of the staff, or negligence in its use.* Learn the promises and use them.

2. *The foot ill-shod.*

3. *Drowsiness.* "Watch and pray, that," &c.

4. *Carelessness.*

5. *The lantern untrimmed or insecure,* so that it goes out or burns dimly.

III. **The sure means for preservation.** We have simply to cry to the Deliverer. How absurd would it be for a traveller to wait a moment before he cried for help, or took means to extricate himself from peril! Yet some are content merely to cry, "Lead us not into temptation," when the Sabbath service is performed.

The secret of a secure and blessed life is constant ejaculatory prayer. The moment danger is even anticipated, to ask for timely assistance. — *R. A. Griffin.*

The Comforts of Christians under either Worldly or Spiritual Trials.

(*Verse* 19.)

Consider—

I. **Some of the distressing thoughts which are apt to oppress the mind of a good man.** They may be considered as relating to—

1. *The state of the world.* When a good man surveys the general prevalence of irreligion and impiety, when he considers how few there are, comparatively, who seek after God, or are moved by any impression of a serious nature, he cannot but be affected. "I beheld the transgressors, and was grieved," &c. (Ps. cxix. 158, 53). When, again, he considers whither such a course must tend, and in what it will possibly issue, the prospect is still more alarming. "Wide is the gate," &c. (Matt. vii. 13).

2. *The state of the Church.* The palpable inconsistency between the lives of numerous professors of religion, and the real import of that profession, is the subject of much distressing reflection to the sincere follower of Christ. "Many walk of whom I have told you often," &c. (Phil. iii. 18, 19).

3. *His state as an individual.* "The heart knoweth his own bitterness," &c. We may advert to—

(1) *Trials of a worldly nature.* Under these religion neither demands nor boasts a perfect insensibility. The Psalmist

displayed great vicissitude of feeling, arising from this quarter; he mourned under the calumny and oppression of his enemies, and gave utterance to cries and tears under his affliction. Ps. xlii. 9, 10. Job is another example.

(2) *Trials of a spiritual nature.* When we consider our low attainments in religion, compared with our opportunities, our latent corruption, and our frequent miscarriages and failures, we are often tempted to call in question the reality of our religion, and to fear that, after all, we are only "almost Christians."

Under the hidings of God's countenance how many painful thoughts arise!

In the prospect before him; in the contemplation of the dangers and temptations which still await him; while he feels himself nothing but frailty and weakness, how apt is he to apprehend some fatal overthrow! He is ready to cry, "I shall never see the King in His beauty, nor behold the land which is so far off."

II. The consolations of God opposed to these uneasy thoughts.

1. *Such as arise from the disordered state of the world.* On this subject great consolation springs from the conviction that the Lord reigneth. There sit at the helm infinite power, wisdom, and goodness. They are in perpetual operation; and, in the final result, they will appear with ineffable splendour and beauty.

2. *Under painful apprehensions respecting the state of the Church, the comforts of God are neither few nor small.* Reflect: it is incomparably more His care than ours. As the Saviour bought it with His blood, He will not fail to guide and govern it in the best manner possible. His interpositions in its favour afford a pledge of what He will still accomplish. Isa. xliii. 3, 4; Matt. xvi. 18. Afflictions are designed to purify the Church.

3. *Under the distressing thoughts arising from the state of a Christian, as an individual, the Divine comforts are proposed.* Affliction and privations are all ordered in infinite wisdom, and proceed from the purest benignity; they will issue in our advantage, and they will be but of short duration. "Weeping may endure for a night, but joy cometh in the morning."—*Robert Hall.—Abridged.*

PSALM XCV.

INTRODUCTION.

"This Psalm is one of a series intended for the Temple worship, and possibly composed for some festal occasion. Both the joyfulness of its opening verses, and its general character, in which it resembles the 81st Psalm, would render it suitable for some of the great national feasts.

"As to the date of its composition nothing certain can be said. The LXX call it a Psalm of David; and the writer of the Epistle to the Hebrews, in making a quotation from the Psalm, uses the expression 'in David,' but this is evidently only equivalent to saying 'in the Psalms.' In the Hebrew it has no inscription.

"It consists of two very distinct parts:—

"I. The first is an invitation to a joyful public acknowledgment of God's mercies. Vers. 1-7.

"II. The second (beginning with the last member of verse 7 to the end) is a warning to the people against the unbelief and disobedience through which their fathers had perished in the wilderness."—*Perowne.*

AN INVITATION TO WORSHIP.

(*Verses* 1-7.)

The Psalmist, in this invitation to worship, brings before us—

I. **The method of worship.** "O come, let us sing unto the Lord," &c., vers. 1, 2, 6. We are exhorted to worship—

1. *Joyfully.* "Let us make a joyful

noise." "Spiritual joy is the heart and soul of thankful praise." In drawing near to God in worship we have many and forcible reasons for rejoicing in Him. By holy delight in His worship we honour Him, and commend His service to others.

2. *Readily.* "Let us come before His presence." Margin, as in Heb., "Let us prevent His face." Hengstenberg: "Let us anticipate His presence." Perowne: "Let us go to meet His face." He says, "Such is the proper and strict rendering of the word. 'Come before' does not sufficiently express the forwardness, the ready alacrity, which are really denoted by the verb." The exhortation of the Psalmist presupposes unreadiness to worship, and implies that worship should be offered with pleasure and zeal.

3. *Gratefully.* "With thanksgiving." In worship we should gratefully recognise God's gracious dealings with us. For all the blessings which God in His mercy bestows upon us, He expects and requires to be thanked. He bestows them freely and generously for our good, and He would have us give the glory to Him. Thankfulness of heart is one of the great impulses to worship.

4. *Reverently.* "Let us worship and bow down; let us kneel before the Lord our Maker." "All the expressions here employed denote a posture of profound reverence in worship, and the passage is a standing rebuke of all irreverent postures in prayer."—*Barnes.* Reverence of feeling should be expressed in reverent attitudes. If we are duly sensible of the immeasurable distance between us and God, humility and sacred reverence will fill our hearts and be expressed in our words and attitude in worshipping Him. In the worship of God joy should be wedded to seriousness, gratitude to humility, confidence to reverence, and zeal to holy awe.

II. **The motives of worship.** "For the Lord is a great God," &c. The Psalmist invites to worship—

1. *Because Jehovah is Supreme.* "The Lord is a great God, and a great King above all Gods." The word "gods" is sometimes applied to angels, sometimes to judges, and sometimes to heathen deities. It is used in this place to designate the latter. We are not to suppose that the Psalmist credited these heathen deities with any real existence or power. "For all the gods of the nations are idols." "He is merely contrasting heathen objects of worship, clothed in the imagination of their worshippers with certain attributes, and the one true supreme Object of worship, who *is* really all, and more than all, which the heathen think their gods to be." — *Perowne.* Probably the surrounding idolatrous nations regarded Jehovah as some small local deity, far inferior to their "gods." The Psalmist here declares that in His perfections He is exalted far above the highest position ascribed to the gods of the heathen. Let us worship Him because He is supreme over all, the Ruler over all.

2. *Because He is the Creator and Proprietor of all things.* "In His hand are the deep places of the earth," &c. The second clause of verse 4 is variously rendered. Alexander says, "The word translated '*strength*' is plural in Hebrew, and seems properly to mean fatiguing exertions, from which some derive the idea of strength, others that of extreme height, which can only be reached by exhausting effort." Margin : "The height of the hills are His." Perowne: "The heights of the mountains are His." So also Hengstenberg. "The exertions," or "heights of the mountains" is parallel with "the searchings," or "deep places of the earth;" and it "is a poetical expression for the highest summits of the mountains, which can be reached only by exertion." Here are two ideas (1) *Jehovah is Creator of all things.* Mountain summits and cavern depths, sea and land, all were made by Him. (2) *He is the Proprietor and Sovereign of all things.* Creatorship affords the highest and most valid claim to Proprietorship and Sovereignty. By indisputable right Jehovah is the absolute Owner and Ruler of all things. "However deep man may penetrate into the depths, or however high he may ascend into the heights, he is still within the dominions of God, and never comes beyond His boundaries."

3. *Because of His relations to His*

people. (1) *He is their Creator.* "Jehovah our Maker." He has made us capable of worship, and to Him alone our worship should be offered. (2) *He is the Source of their salvation.* "The Rock of our salvation." "God is called the *Rock of salvation* as being its unchangeable foundation and faithful author." Our salvation is entirely owing to Him. Its origin, its outworking, &c., are all due to Him. Therefore gratitude urges us to worship Him. (3) *He is in covenant relation with them.* "He is our God, and we are the people of His pasture." God had covenanted with them that they should obey Him, and promised them, saying, "I will walk among you, and will be your God, and ye shall be My people." We who have "made a covenant with Him by sacrifice" are under special obligations to worship Him. We have special manifestations of His presence, special communications of His lovingkindness, &c. We have made promises of consecration and service, &c. (4) *He exercises the most watchful care over them.* They are "the people of His pasture, and the sheep of His hand." He is their Shepherd,—a relation involving *guidance, government, protection,* and *provision.* (See an outline on Ps. lxx. 20.)

CONCLUSION. Worship such as this—spontaneous, joyous, grateful, reverent—is not only our duty, but our precious and exalted privilege. It calls into exercise the noblest faculties of our being; it engages the thoughts and affections upon the most sublime themes; it brings the spirit into the presence of the Supremely Great and Good; and it transforms it into the Divine image. Therefore, "O come, let us worship and bow down," &c.

A WARNING AGAINST UNBELIEF.

(*Verses* 7 (last clause) to 11.)

The Psalmist, speaking by the Holy Ghost, here holds up the unbelief and disobedience of the Israelites in the wilderness as a warning to their descendants in his day. Consider—

I. **The ensample of human sin.** "Your fathers tempted Me," &c. Notice,

1. *The sin itself.* The root-sin of which Israel was guilty in the wilderness was unbelief. This is distinctly stated by the writer of the Epistle to the Hebrews. (Heb. iii. 18, 19.) Here it is spoken of as (1) *Tempting God.* Two instances of this are mentioned in verse 8. "Harden not your heart, as at Meribah, as in the day of Massah (trial) in the wilderness." "*Meribah,* 'striving' or 'provocation;' *Massah,* 'temptation,' or 'trial.' From Exod. xvii. 1-7 it would appear that *both* names were given to the same locality. But according to Num. xx. 1-13, the names were given to two different places on different occasions. Comp. also Deut. xxxiii. 8."—*Perowne.* (See Alford on Heb. iii. 8.) "*Your fathers tempted by way of trial*—'tempted (Me) in trying' or 'proving (Me.)'"—*Alford.* "Unbelief of every kind and every degree may be said to tempt God. For not to believe on the evidence which He has seen fit to give, is to provoke Him to give more, offering our possible assent if proof were increased as an inducement to Him to go beyond what His wisdom has prescribed. And if in this, and the like sense, God may be tempted, what can be more truly said of the Israelites, than that they tempted God in Massah?"—*H. Melville.* And Spurgeon: "Not to acquiesce in the will of God is virtually to tempt Him to alter His plans to suit our imperfect views of how the universe should be governed." "They tempted the Lord, saying, Is the Lord among us, or not?" (2) *Disobedience of God.* "They have not known My ways." God's ways are the ways which He prescribed for them to walk in. In matters of practical religion, not to know the ways of God implies the not walking in them. The Israelites were guilty not only of disobedience, but of oft-repeated acts of rebellion in the wilderness. Unbelief is the parent of disobedience.

2. *Their persistency in sin.* "It is a people that do err in their heart." Heb.: "A people of wanderers in heart." "I understand χαρδία here," says Stuart, "as used according to the Hebrew idiom (in which it is often pleonastic, at least it seems so to us), so that the phrase imports simply, *They always err, i.e.,* they are continually departing from the right way." Or, if it be taken to mean that their sins were deep-rooted, not mere errors of judgment, but the utterances of a heart far estranged from God, still their persistency in evil comes into view. Disobedience and rebellious murmurings were not exceptional in their case. Strong, indeed, were their proclivities to evil. Nor are we aware of any improvement, until the adult population that came out of Egypt had passed away by death.

3. *The aggravation of their sin.* "Saw My work." They had seen His wonders in Egypt and His marvellous doings for them at the Red Sea. In the miraculous supply of manna, and in the stream from the rock that followed them, they had incontestable proofs of God's powerful and gracious presence with them, and yet in their unbelief "they tempted the Lord, saying, Is the Lord among us, or not?" The works of the Lord which they had seen should have inspired them with an all-conquering faith. But through their perversity His works aggravated their sin, increased their guilt. (Num. xiv. 22, 23.)

II. **The ensample of Divine judgment.** The Lord was not unmindful of their sin. He saw and was grieved. "Forty years long was I grieved with this generation." The word rendered "grieved" is expressive of loathing and disgust. Hengstenberg renders it "disgusted." For forty years their conduct was such that the Lord could not but regard them with displeasure and aversion. And in His anger He sware that they should not enter into the promised land. In God's wrath there is nothing revengeful, passionate, or stormy. It is a calm, just, holy anger against sin. Their rebellions had been many and heinous. All the means used for their moral improvement had grievously failed. Warnings and entreaties, the richest mercies and the most startling and solemn judgments, had produced no lasting impression for good. So Jehovah solemnly resolves and declares that they shall not enter into His rest. (Num. xiv. 21-23, 28-35; Deut. i. 34, 35.) Meditate on this judgment. Think of the wondrous works wrought on their behalf, the design of which they entirely frustrated, so far as that generation was concerned; the years wasted in apparently fruitless wanderings; the expectations which perished; the rest which they forfeited; rest from slavery and from wandering, rest as a free people in a goodly land, &c.

III. **The improvement to be made of these ensamples.** "To-day if ye will hear His voice," &c. Consider—

1. *The import of hearing His voice.* It is not mere hearing; but hearing with attention, faith, and obedience. Hearing is of no avail without believing, and faith which is not followed by action in harmony therewith is unreal, dead. Attend to, believe, and obey His voice. The Holy Ghost, by the Psalmist, indicates one sin as particularly incompatible with proper attention to the Divine voice. "Harden not your heart." In this case, to harden the heart, is to disregard the Divine precepts and warnings, to neglect the Divine voice, and persist in disobedience. "An old man, one day taking a child on his knee, entreated him to seek God *now*—to pray to Him, and to love Him; when the child, looking up at him, asked, 'But why do not *you* seek God?' The old man, deeply affected, answered, 'I would, child; but my heart is *hard*—my heart is hard.'"—*Arvine.* "The pirate Gibbs, whose name for many years was a terror to commerce, was finally captured, and executed in the city of New York. He acknowledged before his death, that, when he committed the first murder, his conscience made a hell within his bosom; but, after he had sailed for years under the black flag, his conscience became so blunted, he could rob a vessel, murder all its crew, and then lie down as peacefully to rest as an infant in its cradle."—*Dict. of Illus.*

2. *The time for hearing His voice.* "To-day." Now. This day of grace, which may be lost. "If we put off repentance another day, we have a day more to repent of, and a day less to repent in."—*Mason.* "He that hath promised pardon on our repentance hath not promised life till we repent."—*Quarles.* "You cannot repent too soon, because you know not how soon it may be too late."—*Fuller.*

3. *The arguments for hearing His voice.* (1) *Inattention to God's voice excludes from His rest.* A glorious rest is provided for the people of God. Rest from guilt, sin, sorrow, suffering, anxiety, wearisome toil. The rest of holiness, love, delightful activities, satisfied affections, &c. Heaven. Unbelief excludes from this rest. "There can be no rest to an unbelieving heart." Heb. iii. 12, 18, 19. (2) *God is deeply solicitous that we should attend to His voice.* He says, "To-day, oh that ye would hear His voice!" He knows the worth of the soul, the blessedness and glory of the rest, the loss and sin and woe involved in exclusion from it; and hence His solicitude that we should hear His voice, &c.

CONCLUSION.—1. Let the people of God beware that they provoke Him not by their unbelief or ingratitude, &c. 2. Let the unbeliever hear God's voice, believe, and be saved to-day, now.

SINNERS ENTREATED TO HEAR GOD'S VOICE.

Verses 7, 8. "To-day, if ye will hear His voice, harden not your heart."

I would press the importance, the necessity, of immediately becoming religious:—

I. Because of the shortness and uncertainty of life. You are *mortal;* it is appointed to all men once to die. You are *frail*, and may die soon and suddenly. Those who enjoy the most vigorous health are most exposed to many of those diseases which arrest their victims by surprise, and cut short the thread of life as in a moment. See the risk of delay. You stake your soul without any equivalent; for if life should be spared you gain nothing; but should it be cut short, you lose all, you are ruined for eternity.

II. Because you cannot properly, or even lawfully, promise to give what is not your own. To-morrow is not yours; and it is yet uncertain whether it ever will be. To-day is the only time which you can properly give to God.

III. Because if you defer the commencement of a religious life, though but till to-morrow, you must harden your hearts against the voice of God. God commands and exhorts you to commence a religious life immediately. If you do not comply, you must refuse, for there is no medium. And this act of disobedience to God's commands tends most powerfully to harden the heart; for after we have once disobeyed, it becomes more easy to repeat the disobedience. If you disobey, you must assign some excuse to justify your disobedience, or your consciences will reproach you and render you uneasy; if no plausible excuse occurs, you will seek one; if none can readily be found, you will invent one. . . . . This tends most powerfully to harden the heart.

IV. If you do not commence a religious life to-day, there is great reason to fear that you will never commence it. The very causes which induce you to defer its commencement, render it highly improbable that you will ever become religious. You allege, perhaps, that you are not able to become religious, or that you cannot give your minds to it, or you know not how to begin. Now, all these causes will operate with equal force another day. . . . . Every day's delay will render it more difficult.

V. Because, after a time, God ceases to strive with sinners and to afford them the assistance of His grace. He gives them up to a blinded mind, a seared conscience, and a hard heart. Thus He dealt with the old world; the wicked sons of Eli; the Jews in the time of Isaiah (vi. 9, 10); and the inhabitants of Jerusalem in our Saviour's time (Luke xix. 41, 42).

VI. Because you are, while you delay, constantly making work for repentance; you are doing what you mean to be sorry for; you are building up to-day what you mean to throw down to-morrow. How irrational and absurd is this! I will not now hear God's voice, but I mean to mourn, to be grieved for it hereafter. Could you say this to your fellow-creatures without blushing?

VII. Because it is the express command of God. "God now commandeth all men everywhere to repent." And the Holy Ghost saith, Obey God's command, hear His voice to-day, and do not harden your hearts against it. Dare any of you trample on a known command of God?

CONCLUSION.—What, after all, is there so very irksome, or disagreeable, in a religious life, that you should wish to defer its commencement? If you must begin some time, why not begin to-day?—*Dr. E. Payson.—Abridged.*

PSALM XCVI.

INTRODUCTION.

This Psalm has no superscription in the Hebrew. But in the Septuagint and in the Vulgate it has the following, " When the house was built after the captivity. An ode by David." There is a great similarity between this Psalm and the great festal hymn which "David delivered, to thank the Lord, into the hand of Asaph and his brethren" on the day when the ark was brought into the sanctuary in Zion. It indeed almost exactly corresponds to that portion of the Psalm, on the placing of the ark in Zion, which is contained in 1 Chron. xvi. 23-33. It is probable that the original Psalm was composed by David, for use on the occasion mentioned above, and that it is recorded in 1 Chron. xvi. 8-36, and that this Psalm was selected from it for use at the dedication of the second temple.

We regard the Psalm as setting before us a picture of—

THE WORLD'S MOST JOYOUS DAY.

We have here a picture of a day of blessing and glory for our world such as never yet has dawned upon it, but most assuredly will dawn in God's own appointed time. The Poet portrays two grand features of the world's most joyous day. It will be—

I. A day when the relations of the Lord to the world shall be rightly apprehended. What are those relations?

1. *He alone is God of the world.* This is clear from (1) *The nothingness of heathen deities and the reality and power of Jehovah.* "All the gods of the nations are idols, but the Lord made the heavens." The heathen deities were nonentities, nothings. They had no real existence. They existed only in the imaginations of their worshippers (Isa. xli. 23, 24.) Even when the objects of the worship of the heathen have a real existence, such as the heavenly bodies, yet they have no existence as gods, no existence which renders them fit objects of homage. But the Lord is real and living and powerful. He "made the heavens." In their creation He has manifested His power and glory to all the world, and given proof that He is the true God and entitled to the worship of His creatures. (2) *The greatness of Jehovah.* "The Lord is great, and greatly to be praised." God is great in His thoughts and purposes, in power and action, in glory and dominion. His greatness is so pre-eminent that Masillon well said, "God alone is great." (3) *The glory of Jehovah.* "Honour and majesty are before Him, strength and beauty are in His sanctuary." Wherever He pleases to manifest Himself there true glory is displayed. All that is really mighty and majestic, glorious and beautiful, is found in Him in full perfection, and flows from Him. Holiness and wisdom, truth and love constitute His strength, beauty,

and majesty. He has displayed His glory in the heavens which He created; but it shines most brightly "in His sanctuary," in the Church militant and in the Church triumphant. In the world's most joyous day the Lord shall be recognised throughout the world as the only true God, incomprehensibly great and glorious.

2. *His salvation is for all the world.* "Show forth His salvation from day to day. Declare His glory among the heathen, His wonders among all people." In the bright day which is drawing near, His salvation will be published amongst all nations and all peoples. "Salvation" from the night of heathen darkness, from sin and all its terrible consequences. "Salvation" to holiness, love, life immortal, into the image of God, and to the vision of God. "Salvation" for all the world as opposed (1) *to the restrictions of Judaism.* "Go ye into all the world," &c. (Mark xvi. 15, 16). "God is no respecter of persons," &c. (Acts x. 34, 35). (2) *To the limitations of human creeds.* Our narrow systems of theology cannot restrict the fulness of the grace of God. The river of the water of life refuses to be pent in the limited channels which men have scooped out for it. It flows in streams broad and deep, for the life and refreshment of all men. Salvation is free for all men. "Ho, every one that thirsteth," &c. (Isa. lv. 1, 2). "Whosoever believeth," &c. "The Spirit and the Bride say, Come," &c. (Rev. xxii. 17). In the glorious day approaching, the freedom and universality of salvation will be recognised, &c.

3. *He is the King of all the world.* "Say among the heathen that the Lord reigneth," &c. "'Jehovah is King,' lit. 'hath become King,' hath taken to Himself His great power and reigned."

"He shall reign from pole to pole
With illimitable sway."

Under His reign the earth will become calm and stable. Agitated and shaken by the sins and strifes of men, it shall become peaceful and orderly under the sway of Jehovah. In the joyous day of which our Poet sings, the reign of the Lord shall be proclaimed in all the world, recognised in all the world, and its blessings enjoyed in all the world.

4. *He is the Judge of all the world.* "He shall judge the people righteously. He cometh, He cometh to judge the earth," &c. Judging is probably used here for ruling. Two prominent features of the Divine rule and judgment are here specified—(1) *Righteousness.* The laws of His kingdom and their administration harmonise with eternal truth and equity. (2) *Faithfulness.* His administration will accord with the truth of His own character, and the declarations of His will. "It is a judgment which is to issue in salvation." "It is not a retributive, but a *gracious* judging, by which controversies are adjusted and prevented, and the law of love is introduced into the lives of the people." In the world's most joyous day the Lord will be heartily recognised as the gracious Ruler and Judge of all men.

II. **A day when the relations of the Lord to the world shall be duly celebrated.** In the day portrayed by the Psalmist the gracious relations of Jehovah to all men will not only be understood, but appreciated and praised.

1. He will be *universally* worshipped. "All the earth" shall sing unto Him. "All flesh shall come to worship before Me, saith the Lord." "From the rising of the sun, even unto the going down of the same, My name shall be great among the Gentiles," &c. (Mal. i. 11). "As I live, saith the Lord, every knee shall bow to Me, and every tongue shall confess to God."

2. He will be *enthusiastically* worshipped. Three times the Poet calls upon the people to "Sing unto the Lord," and three times to "Give unto the Lord glory." The repetition indicates urgency and zeal. The whole soul of the Poet is in the exhortation. In the grand coronation day the Lord the King shall be worshipped with entire heartiness, and with intensest enthusiasm.

3. He will be *joyously* worshipped. "O sing unto the Lord a new song," &c. The "new song" is "one which

shall be the fit expression of all the thoughts and hopes and triumphs of the new and glorious age which is about to dawn. It is the glad welcome given to the King when He enters His kingdom." So great is the joy of the world that even the inanimate creation is represented as sharing in it. "Let the heavens rejoice," &c. (vers. 11, 12). "With the coming of Jehovah and the setting up of His kingdom, all the broken harmonies of creation shall be restored. Not 'the sons of God' only, but the whole creation, is still looking forward to the great consummation (Rom. viii. 21)."—*Perowne.*

4. *He will be reverently worshipped.* "O worship the Lord in the beauty of holiness, fear before Him, all the earth." "'Bow yourselves before Jehovah in holy pomp, tremble before Him all the earth.' 'Pomp,' or 'array,' but the word denotes *all* that lent solemnity and impressiveness to the service."—*Perowne.* In the glorious day which the Psalmist foresaw, the Lord will be worshipped with all that is expressive of admiration and veneration. There will be nothing unbecoming in the worship offered unto Him. All the earth will approach and pay homage to Him in the beauty of pure, loving, adoring spirits.

CONCLUSION.—1. Here is a word of *Exhortation.* For the advent of this most joyous day for the world, let us be untiring both in work and in prayer. 2. Here is a word of *Inspiration.* This bright day will surely dawn. The world advances not to the darkness of night, but to the splendours of a glorious and unfading noontide. Therefore, take heart, ye faithful watchers, and brave workers, and earnest suppliants. The cause to which you are devoted must triumph. The mountain tops are already bathed in glory; and soon the whole world will be flooded with radiance, and break forth into the tremendous and exultant shout, "Hallelujah, the Lord reigneth."

THE OBJECT, OBLIGATION, AND EXPRESSION OF WORSHIP.

(*Verse* 8.)

Consider—

I. **The grand Object of worship.** "The Lord." He is the Creator and Sustainer of all things. "The Lord made the heavens." He is the true and rightful Proprietor of all things and beings. He has a *claim* upon our worship. We *ought* to worship Him. He is supremely great and glorious. His glory consists of His goodness. His worship should be *attractive, delightful.* He is the *only true* Object of worship. He alone is perfect. Worshipping any other object our being will not be developed, or will be developed injuriously. His worship is quickening, purifying, exalting, &c.

II. **The solemn obligation of worship.** "The glory due unto His name." "*Due*" is supplied by our translators. But, if we omit it and read, "The glory of His name," the text still sets forth the obligatoriness of worship. Worship is not optional, but binding.

1. It is due to Him because of *what He is.* He is supremely great, and should, therefore, be reverenced; supremely gracious, and should, therefore, be loved; supremely glorious, and should, therefore, be humbly adored, &c. Think of what He is, and then ask yourself, How much is due unto Him?

2. It is due to Him because of *what He does.* His is the glory of *creation, providence, redemption.* How much He has done for us! How much of gratitude, &c., we owe to Him! "On His head are many crowns."

III. **The appropriate expression of worship.** "Bring an offering," &c. "'Bring presents.' 'Presents' (the collective sing. for the plural), in allusion to the Oriental custom which required gifts to be brought by all who would be admitted to the presence of a king."—*Perowne.* Hengstenberg: "The 'bring offerings' is used of the bringing of gifts of allegiance to earthly sovereigns." The derivation and usage of the word *minchah*—" offering "—point to that

idea of sacrifice, which represents it as a Eucharistic gift to God our King. Let us express our worship in offerings of—
1. *Grateful praise.* " Whoso offereth praise glorifieth Me."
2. *Generous contributions.* (Prov. xi. 24, 25 ; 1 Cor. ix. 6-11.)

3. *Devoted service.* (Acts xx. 24 ; Phil. ii. 30.)
The great Sin-Offering has been made. Our obligations to the Lord are immense. Let us heartily bring our thank-offerings to Him.

PSALM XCVII.

INTRODUCTION.

This is another of the series of Psalms which celebrate the advent of Jehovah as King. There are seven in the series, the ninety-third being the first, and the hundredth the last. The ninety-fourth is not one of the series. We know neither the author by whom, nor the occasion on which, this Psalm was composed. The series may "have been composed with reference to the same occasion, and may have been designed to be used together. They are similar in their contents and structure ; and they refer to the same thing—the sovereignty or the supremacy of God." This one may be taken as presenting two themes for Homiletic treatment,—The Features and Effects of the King's Advent, verses 1-9 ; and The Character, Privileges, and Duties of the King's Subjects, verses 10-12.

THE FEATURES AND EFFECTS OF THE KING'S ADVENT.

(*Verses* 1-9.)

Let us notice—

I. **The features of the King's advent.** The description of the coming of the King is full of poetic grandeur. It represents His advent as characterised by—

1. *Awful Majesty.* " Clouds and darkness are round about Him. A fire goeth before Him," &c., verses 2-5. The images in these verses are suggested by the theophany at the giving of the law on Sinai. God is often represented in the Holy Word as coming with clouds and fire, and inspiring the world with awe and dread. Ps. xviii. 7-15 ; l. 1-6 ; Hab. iii. 3-16. The object of these representations is to set forth the greatness, and sublimity, and glory of God. Moreover, the awful phenomena which accompanied the giving of the law were designed to deeply impress the people with the august and glorious presence of the Divine Lawgiver and Judge. So the coming of the Lord to reign and judge in the world will be with such majesty and glory, that the most exalted amongst men will be as nothing in His presence, and holy awe or unspeakable fear will fill men's hearts.

2. *Widest conspicuousness.* " All the people see His glory." The glory of the Lord here is the revelation of His being and character through His works of righteousness and grace. " The glory of the Lord shall be revealed, and all flesh shall see it together."

3. *Perfect righteousness.* "Righteousness and judgment are the habitation of His throne . . . . The heavens declare His righteousness." Righteousness is here represented (1) *As the basis of His government.* It is the " establishment," or " foundation of His throne." This affords a guarantee of the stability and permanence of His rule. (See remarks on Ps. lxxxix. 14.) (2) *As clearly manifested.* " The heavens declare " it. " It is as conspicuous and illustrious as the heavens themselves." (See remarks on Ps. l. 6.) The advent of the King will be in righteousness, with the utmost conspicuousness, and with awful majesty.

" The Lord shall come ! the earth shall quake ;
The mountains to their centre shake ;
And, withering from the vault of night,
The stars withdraw their feeble light.
The Lord shall come ! a glorious form,
With wreath of flame and robe of storm,
On cherub wings, and wings of wind,
Appointed Judge of all mankind."—*Heber.*

II. **The effects of the King's advent.** " The Lord reigneth, let the earth rejoice," &c. The effects of the reign of Jehovah differ in different classes of character.

1. *It should occasion joy to all.* "Let the earth rejoice, let the multitude of the isles be glad." It should be a source of inexpressible gladness to all men that the world is not anarchic; that it is not ruled by Satan, or by heartless fate, or by blind physical forces and laws, but by the Lord. He rules all things in perfect righteousness and wisdom and goodness. Rejoice; for the Supremely Good is the Supreme King.

2. *It does occasion* (1) *Destruction to His foes.* "A fire goeth before Him, and burneth up His enemies round about." When He comes to judge and reign He will destroy all His foes. He will put down all opposition. Men must either bow to His sceptre, or be slain by His sword. (2) *Confusion to idolaters.* "Confounded be all they that serve graven images," &c. Perowne and Hengstenberg translate,—"Ashamed." "It is a shame," says the former, "arising from the discovery of the utter vanity and nothingness of the objects of their trust." They boast in nonentities and serve mere images; and when the Lord cometh to judge and reign in the earth, they will discover to their shame and confusion the utter powerlessness and worthlessness of these idols. In that solemn day, many will find their gods—those things on which their hearts are set—to be mere idols, shams, and mockeries. (3) *Gladness to His people.* "Zion heard, and was glad," &c. The people of God rejoice, because of the utter abolition of idols, and the supremacy of Jehovah. Some expositors think that "the daughters of Judah" are introduced here, because of "a custom familiar in Judea, of forming choral bands of maidens after a victory or some happy circumstance." (See Exod. xv. 20, 21; 1 Sam. xviii. 6, 7.) But the designation seems to us to denote the smaller cities of Judah, that surrounded Jerusalem as the mother city. So that "Zion and the daughters of Judah" represent the whole of Judah. All the people of the Lord rejoice in His coming to reign. Two reasons are assigned for their joy. *His judgments.* "Rejoiced because of Thy judgments." (See remarks on Ps. xlviii. 11.) *His supremacy.* "For Thou, Lord, art high above all the earth," &c. (See remarks on Ps. xcv. 3.)

CONCLUSION.—What to us will be the effect of the coming of the Lord as King and Judge?

"When Thou, my righteous Judge, shalt come,
To fetch Thy ransomed people home,
Shall I among them stand?"

THE REIGN OF GOD.

Ver. 1. "The Lord reigneth; let the earth rejoice."

The text calls us to consider—

I. **The subjects of the Divine government.** Everything that God has made is subject to His government. The universe of matter; and all the beings, rational and animal, which He has caused to inhabit it. . . . This great work of sustaining and directing all nature is called His *natural* government. By virtue of this government the powers of nature are made instruments in the conduct of His moral government, for the reward or punishment of His creatures.

The *moral* government of God is that which is principally contemplated in the text; and by this is meant the direction and control which He exercises over moral agents, over every rational being. The circumstances of trial in which He places them, the assistance He affords them, and the rewards or punishments He assigns them, are all comprehended in this. *Angels* are under this government. . . . The earth is the great theatre of their exertions, they are put under Christ, and are employed both in judgment and mercy. *Devils* are under the moral government of God. They are not finally judged, but suffered to mix with human kind. Heaven and hell struggle for the soul of man. Between these orders of beings is *man*, to whom the

Divine government seems to stand in a special relation; and principally for this reason, that he is the subject of redemption. The earth is the great theatre chosen for the display of the Divine perfections in a course of moral government. Here the grand struggle of adverse powers and principles takes place, &c. The human race, as subject to the Divine government, are to be considered as distributed into nations, and as individuals. *Nations* are under a peculiar kind of government. They are considered as having a kind of unity as collective bodies. They have their rewards and punishments in this life. The sins of one generation are visited upon another. Yet nations are not governed by a rigid law of works; for Christ is an intercessor for them. The good pray and prevail in behalf of the wicked. *Individuals* are also under the Divine government. "Every man must give an account of himself to God." Offers of mercy are made to him. Rules of conduct assigned. Retribution annexed to conduct. (Rom. ii. 6-11.) Men are under direction and influence, as well as control.

II. **Certain characters which mark His administration.**

1. *It is sovereign and uncontrolled.* Dan. iv. 35; v. 21. This gives certainty to the Divine government, and makes it the hope and joy of good men.

2. *It interferes not with human liberty.* We are so free from constraint, that our actions are properly our own. We have the freedom of moral agents. We feel that we are free.

3. *It is a mediatorial government.* It is in the hands of Jesus, the Mediator between God and man; and it is exercised specially with reference to the great end of His mediatorial office, the redemption of man, and the reconciling of the world to Himself.

III. **The demand which is made upon our grateful joy.**

"Let the earth be glad."

1. As Christians, we shall rejoice *with holy joy*, not with vain mirth. God will be sanctified in His worshippers.

2. We should rejoice, too, *with trembling*. Much is given to us, and much is required.

3. *If we are individually interested in Him that reigneth, we may well rejoice; for all the perfections of the Godhead are engaged in our behalf.—R. Watson. —Abridged.*

GOD'S WAYS, THOUGH OFTEN INSCRUTABLE, ARE RIGHTEOUS AND JUST.

(*Verse 2.*)

Two propositions are contained in this text.

I. "**Clouds and darkness are round about God.**" The appearances of God to the saints in old times are the origin of the figure in the text. These appearances were all accompanied with clouds and darkness. Exod. xiv. 19, 20; xix. 16, 18, 20; 1 Kings viii. 10, 11; Matt. xvii. 5; 2 Pet. i. 17. Clouds are emblems of obscurity; darkness of distress. The works of God's providence are often obscure and productive of distress to mankind, though "righteousness and judgment are," &c. In the affairs of nations we see the interference of Divine Providence; yet it is surrounded with "clouds and darkness." So it is also in instances of a smaller kind; it is thus in the removal of the most eminent, holy, and useful characters, that while we acknowledge the hand of God, we say "clouds and darkness are round about Him." If we look into the book of history we shall perceive much disorder in earthly scenes, much confusion in the affairs of men; and was this to be expected from a God of order and wisdom? Again, look at Christianity. How little has been done by it compared with what might have been anticipated from its Divine principles, the character of its Author, and from the interest it possesses in the heart of God! Paganism yet strikes deep its roots in various lands. Even in Christendom, how little have the known and blessed effects of the Gospel been manifested! Where genuine Christianity is taught, how small, how slow, has been its progress; how few converted to God! &c. And persons of real piety give way to prejudice and party zeal, which prevent, in a great measure, the operation and effect of pure Christianity. A great part of the world is no better than if Christ had never come to save mankind, and the Gospel had never been proclaimed. "Clouds and darkness are round about Him."

II. **Righteousness and Judgment are the habitation of His throne.** Righteousness is an essential perfection of the Divine Being. If there had been no creatures for Him to govern, He would have had an unchangeable and invincible love of rectitude. Judgment is the application of the principle of righteousness in His government of His creatures and their actions; it is a development of His rectitude in the management of the affairs of His great empire. The throne of God is built and stands firm upon these principles; they are the place, the basis, and the foundation of His throne. Though much obscurity must necessarily envelope the government of an infinite mind, yet some considerations may be suggested, which will serve to quell all our anxieties, and afford us repose under all the darkness, beneath His protecting power, His all-directing wisdom, and His paternal goodness.

1. *The dispensations of God towards man are regulated by the consideration of his being a fallen and disordered creature.* This must be kept in view to account for the severities in the Divine dealings with him. Yet, notwithstanding the severities of God, there are mixtures of mercy which we have reason to admire.

2. *The Divine Being was not bound in justice, either to prevent the disordered state of man, or to correct it when it had taken place.* From what we know of the nature of God and of man, it may be safely affirmed that it cannot be required of the Divine Governor to secure the obedience of His creatures any further than the law, as a motive, is calculated to have an effect upon rational minds.

3. *The whole of those evils that form clouds and darkness round about God, are either the penal or natural effect of moral evil.*

4. *Those that receive the grace of Jesus Christ are still in such a situation as renders a great part of their trials and miseries necessary.* Many of the evils of a depraved nature still remain, and need to be subdued and removed. Besides, the virtues and excellencies must be perfected in the same way in which the Captain of our salvation was perfected: he must be conformed to Christ, and have fellowship with Him in His sufferings.

5. *The moral evils of man, and the depravity of human nature, are often, in a great measure, corrected and subdued by the natural evils of life, which thus are made the means of conducting to repentance, reformation, and happiness.* "Our light affliction" may work for us "a far more exceeding and eternal weight of glory; while we look," &c. (2 Cor. iv. 17, 18).

6. *The light of prophecy dispels many of those clouds which would otherwise obscure, for the present, the government and the throne of the Deity.*—*R. Hall.* —*Abridged.*

THE KINGDOM OF CHRIST.

(*Verses 6–9.*)

From the Epistle to the Hebrews we find that this Psalm is a prophetical description of the Messiah; and from that application of it we deduce two important truths concerning the Christ; one, respecting the dignity of His person, "the first begotten;" the other, His glorious exaltation as Messiah. It is to this latter truth that we shall now confine our attention.

I. **The interesting fact to which the prophecy refers.**

The Psalm is introduced with a celebration of the government of Jehovah.

93

"The Lord reigneth." The Psalmist refers to the government of Him who is God manifest in the flesh, and who is received up into glory. His appearing in our world was a veiling of His glory. . . . . His resurrection was a reappearing in glory; in His ascension He exhibited the dignity of His Godhead; and on entering heaven He sat down on the throne of His Father, to administer the affairs of that kingdom which He had now established, the duration of which is to have no end.

1. *In the exaltation of Christ we have abundant proof of the acceptance of His sacrifice, and that it answered all the important purposes for which it was designed.* His death was sacrificial; that sacrifice was expiatory in its nature, and was accepted by the Father. He is exalted, but it is as a sacrifice—as High Priest—as Mediator—as a Prince and a Saviour, to give repentance and remission of sins.

2. *Christ by His exaltation is invested with mediatorial power and dominion.* In Phil. ii. 6-11, you have a proper view of the dominion of Christ. It is mediatorial dominion. All things are put under Him; there is not a creature in the whole range of being who does not yield a willing or an unwilling, a conscious or an unconscious, homage to Him. He employs all things to accomplish the purposes of His mercy. To the salvation of men He subordinates everything, human affairs, opposition of devils, ministry of angels, the whole universe!

II. **The important events flowing from the accomplishment of this prophecy.**

1. *The Revelation of Messiah's righteousness.* The heavens literally attested Christ's righteousness in the voice from heaven at His baptism, and when He appealed to His Father, saying, "Father, glorify Thy Son." The Gospel, which is from heaven, displays the righteousness of Christ.

2. *The manifestation of His glory; mercy and truth here meet together.* To Christ belongs the glory of revealing the Father to the world; of opening a new way of access to God; of peopling heaven with new and holy inhabitants.

3. *The conversion of idolaters.* "Confounded be all they," &c. This is not a malediction, but a prediction of the overthrow of idolatry by the Gospel. Let this light be diffused, and darkness cannot remain.

4. *The presentation of universal homage.* "Worship Him all ye gods." The apostle quotes from the LXX., "Let all the angels of God worship Him." Christ shall receive the homage of adoring multitudes. Rev. vii. 9-12.

5. *The joyous exultation of the Church.* "Zion heard, and was glad," &c. The triumphs of Christ are the glory and the joy of the Church. When He shall have subdued the nations, then the whole host of the redeemed, with all the ranks of angels, will burst forth in one loud, prolonged, eternal song: "Hallelujah! the Lord God omnipotent reigneth."—L. *Abridged from "Sketches of Sermons."*

THE CHARACTER, PRIVILEGES, AND DUTY OF THE KING'S SUBJECTS.

(*Verses* 10-12.)

The Poet here brings into view—

I. The Character of the King's subjects.

1. *They are sincere and upright.* "The righteous, ... the upright in heart." "There is not a just man upon earth, that doeth good, and sinneth not." "There is none righteous." The Psalmist clearly means the upright, the sincere and single-hearted. Not the upright in profession, but "the upright in heart."

2. *They are devout.* "His saints." The idea of the word is not holiness, but piety. "The pious, God-worshipping." The subjects of the Lord add piety to sincerity. They are devout as well as true.

3. *They "love the Lord."* Love to God is with them not obedience to a command; but a holy privilege, a deep and divine joy. They are loyal-hearted subjects of Jehovah. They obey the

King because they love Him. Are these features of character found in us?

II. The privileges of the King's subjects.

1. *Preservation from evil.* "He preserveth the souls of His saints." He guards their lives. They are immortal till their work be done, and His plan in their life be fully developed. He preserves them also from sin, from apostacy, and from despair even under the severest trials.

2. *Deliverance from enemies.* "He delivereth them out of the hand of the wicked." The Lord frequently baffles the designs of evil men against His people. He will not allow their enemies to do them any real harm; and ultimately He will triumphantly deliver them out of their power.

3. *Bestowal of gladness.* "Light is sown for the righteous, and gladness for the upright in heart." "Light" is synonymous with joy. "To be 'sown' is to be scattered abroad, the point of the comparison being only the richness of the gift."—*Hengstenberg*. So Perowne takes "the verb 'sown' in the sense of 'scattered,' 'diffused.'" And Venema: "Light is said to be scattered when the rising sun spreads his rays in every direction."

"Now morn, her rosy steps in th' eastern clime
Advancing, sow'd the earth with orient pearl."—*Milton*.

"Sometimes through secular instruments," says Beecher, "God makes us joyful, for He employs the whole world to work out His purposes; but sometimes, by simply breathing upon the spirit of His people, He makes them joyful. You cannot tell why you are so musical at times. On some days you are full of music. There are some hours that seem radiant above all other hours, when you are lifted up above the ordinary pattern of joy. And when these appear among God's people, it is not an unfair thing to infer that they are signs and manifestations of Christ's presence with them." Again: "There are joys which long to be ours. God sends ten thousand truths, which come about us like birds seeking inlet; but we are shut up to them, and so they bring us nothing, but sit and sing awhile upon the roof, and then flee away." Let us open hand and heart for the reception and enjoyment of our privileges.

III. The duty of the King's subjects.

1. *To "hate evil."* "Ye that love the Lord, hate evil." Love to God must be manifested in holiness of life and hatred of evil. Love to God and the love of sin, or even tolerance of sin, are incompatible. Sin is the "abominable thing which He hates."

2. *To thankfully "rejoice in the Lord."* "Rejoice in the Lord, ye righteous," &c. We have here: (1) *Rejoicing in the Lord.* Not in gaiety, riches, honours, &c.; but in the Lord, —in His grace, in His friendship, in His perfections, in Himself. He is the wisest, the holiest, the most generous of beings. (2) *Rejoicing thankfully.* "Give thanks at the remembrance of His holiness." Hengstenberg: "Praise His holy memorial." Perowne: "Give thanks to His holy name." The holiness of the Divine Being should command our adoring and grateful praise. (3) *Rejoicing as a duty.* Phil. iii. 1; iv. 4. "Joy in the Holy Ghost" is one of the "fruits of the Spirit." By our rejoicing we honour God, and commend His religion to men. Let us regard this devout rejoicing as both our duty and our privilege.

THE CHARACTER AND PORTION OF GOD'S PEOPLE.

(*Verses* 10, 11.)

Walk through the Old Testament with the light of the New. This whole Psalm is a prophecy of Christ. The excellency and glory of His kingdom—the character and blessedness of His people.

I. The character or description of God's people.

1. *They are "the righteous."* A general term, a righteous God will have a righteous people. Equally true in the

sense of perfection and sinlessness, that "there is none righteous, no, not one;" but as contrasted with the wicked, they are righteous, and to be thus distinguished.

2. *They are "His saints."* His sanctified ones, set apart, dedicated to Him. A term of reproach in the world, to be "a saint" is to be a hypocrite, in the cant of fashion, but it is "the highest style of man." "His saints," His own chosen ones, "loved from the foundation of the world," called, converted, &c. Made holy, sanctified by the Spirit, &c. "Saint" is a term not peculiar to the servants of God of the Old and New Testament, but a definition of every one who is in a state of salvation.

3. *They are "upright in heart."* Christian integrity, how excellent! The world affects it, talks much of honour, virtue, justice, high-mindedness — a shallow blustering spirit ;—and one of their own has said, "Every man has his price." But the Christian is "upright in heart," in his inner man, simplicity, self-denying integrity, which seek's not man's applause, resisting temptation, strong in the grace of God.

4. *They "love the Lord."* Love, glowing, tender, pure, as the love of God—whence it springs—casting out fear, terror, and everything that separates from a loving Father, this is the love of believers. (Matt. xxii. 36-38; Rom. xiii. 10.) They love God, and therefore love His people, His house, His Sabbath, His Word, and all His ordinances.

5. *They "hate evil."* This follows of moral necessity, they who love must hate; if they love God they must hate evil, because they cannot serve two masters so different from each other (Matt. vi. 24). In proportion as they love the one they will hate the other (Rom. xii. 9). Sin is the enemy which disturbs their peace, stops their mouth in prayer (Ps. lxvi. 18), separates from God; so they must ever hate it.

II. **The blessed portion of such people.** This is indicated by their very titles. But there are special blessings here.

1. *"He preserveth the souls of His saints."* Not to the exclusion of their bodies, which are His care in this world, "the temples of His Spirit," and in death they sleep in hope of His resurrection and final glory; but, because the soul is the nobler part, "He preserveth them."

This implies danger, many perils here to the soul. *It implies that they cannot preserve their own souls* with all care, vigilance, prayer, faith, love—the soul is a helpless thing without God.

Many precious promises to this effect. (See Ps. xxiii. 3; John xvii. 11; 2 Tim. i. 12; iv. 17, 18; 1 Peter i. 5.)

2. *"He delivereth them out of the hand of the wicked."* This implies that they are surrounded by the wicked, and as it were in their hands—and so they are. Satan, as a roaring lion, seeks to devour them, desires "to have them and sift them," or he ensnares them with his "wiles" and "devices," he puts evil into their hearts, and leads them astray. His people, too, "the children of the wicked one," do his work on earth by persecuting His people, tempting them to sin, "putting the bottle to them," and suggesting pollution, and then, if they succeed, they mock them as the devils do!

"He delivereth them out of their hands." That is enough. God looks on, He sees all, He restrains the wrath of the wicked, He makes a way by which His people escape. (See Ps. cxxiv.)

3. *Their final blessedness:* "*Light is sown for the righteous, and gladness for the upright in heart.*" Beautiful figure! this life is often a time of darkness, but it is the seed-time of light. When the believer is sowing dark tears, sighs, sorrows, trials, temptations, all is cheerless; but these are seeds of light. "Light is sown for him," it will come up, it will shine forth by and by, it may be a long winter, and a backward spring, and even harvest time may be cheerless, but it will come at last! (See Ps. xxx. 5, and John xvi. 20-22.)

If you would have the believer's "*portion,*" you must bear the believer's "*character.*" Study these definitions of the people of the Lord, rest not until you can appropriate them, and then "all things are yours."—*F. Close, D.D.*

PSALM XCVIII.

INTRODUCTION.

"This Psalm is little more than an echo of Psalm xcvi. Its subject is the last great revelation, the final victory of God, when His salvation and His righteousness, the revelation of which He has promised to the house of Israel, shall be manifested both to His own people, and to all the nations of the earth. The inscription of the Psalm in the Hebrew is only the single word *Mizmor*, 'Psalm.' Both the beginning and end of the Psalm are taken from Psalm xcvi. The rest of it is drawn chiefly from the latter portion of Isaiah."—*Perowne*. "In the first strophe, verses 1–3, after a short exhortation to praise the Lord, the object of the praise is given—the Lord has redeemed His people in a wonderful manner. The second strophe, verses 4–6, shows how this praise is to be rendered: all means which, in every place, are within reach, ought to be employed for the purpose. The third stanza says by whom the praise should be given: by the whole earth."—*Hengstenberg*.

AN EXULTANT HYMN.

We have here—
I. Exultation for the most excellent reasons. Regarding the Psalm as a prophecy of the Messiah and His glorious salvation, we have here an exhortation to praise Him because—
1. His works are *wonderful.* "He hath done marvellous things." The life and work of our Lord upon earth were marked by the most wonderful features. His *life* was marvellous in its spiritual beauty and power. His character had no flaw in it, it was perfect. His *words* were marvellous. "Never man spake like this man." His *works* were marvellous. Nature in her wildest moods obeyed His word. At the expression of His will diseases fled. At the utterance of His command the dead started into life again. How marvellous were His death, resurrection, and ascension! And the *salvation* which He has wrought, in its design, in its accomplishment, and in its results, is gloriously wonderful. "His name shall be called Wonderful."
2. The Lord's works are *benevolent.* His works are designed not to surprise and startle men, but to save them. "The Lord hath made known His salvation, His righteousness hath He openly showed in the sight of the heathen." "'Righteousness,' parallel with 'salvation,' as so frequently in the latter portion of Isaiah."—*Perowne*. "For the people of the Lord, 'salvation' is the expression of 'His righteousness,' which gives to every one His own: He has promised them salvation."—*Hengstenberg*. The great object of our Lord's mission was to save men from sin. "The Son of Man is come to seek and to save that which was lost." "Christ Jesus came into the world to save sinners." He imparts pardon to the guilty, peace to the troubled, holiness to the sinful, life to the dead, joy to the miserable. He is the Saviour. He "hath made known His salvation" and "openly showed His righteousness." Not only has He proclaimed His salvation, but gloriously displayed it. He has proved Himself "mighty to save." The triumphs of the Gospel are countless in number, gracious in character, surprising in their magnitude, and ever growing in extent.
3. The Lord's works are *accomplished by Himself alone.* "His right hand and His holy arm hath gotten Him the victory." Literally: "Hath wrought salvation for Him." Hengstenberg: "Have helped Him." Perowne: "'Hath gotten Him salvation,' or 'the victory,' as in E. V. (Comp. xliv. 4; Isa. lix. 16; lxiii. 5.) I have preferred here the former rendering, because in the next verse the noun occurs from the same root, and there the rendering 'salvation' is, I think, preferable to 'victory.'" Christ Jesus our Lord alone accomplished salvation for us. He alone effected the atonement. He alone saves the sinner. In the pursuit of holiness He supplies the motive and imparts the power. From beginning to end salva-

tion is His sole work ; and to Him alone be all the praise.

4. The Lord's works are accomplished *in accordance with His covenant.* " He hath remembered His mercy and His truth toward the house of Israel." "'Loving - kindness . . . faithfulness,' the two attributes expressive of God's covenant *relation* to His people."— *Perowne.* The salvation wrought by the Lord is in fulfilment of His gracious purposes and promises. His word cannot fail. His promises are gloriously reliable. He promises to save " whosoever believeth," and He will do so. He has covenanted "to save them to the uttermost that come unto God by Him," and He will keep His covenant for ever.

5. The Lord's works are accomplished *for the good of the whole human race.* " All the ends of the earth have seen the salvation of our God." Not for the Jews alone is salvation wrought, but for all peoples. Christ "died for all." Salvation is suited to the needs of all men ; our Lord commissioned His Church to proclaim it to all ; and it is free for all. Salvation is for man as man, without distinction of nationality or race, &c.

Here, then, we have surely the most excellent reasons for exultation.

II. **Exultation with the fullest expression.** Verses 4-6. The expression should be—

1. *Joyful.* " Make a joyful noise unto the Lord, and rejoice." Salvation is a source of joy, and should be celebrated in glad songs.

2. *Hearty.* " Make a loud noise." " The word here used is expressive of irrepressible joy." Our praise for salvation should be the full-toned utterance of thankful and rejoicing hearts.

3. *Religious.* " Sing praise, sing unto the Lord . . . with the voice of a Psalm . . . before the Lord, the King." The praise is to God ; the exultation is because of His wondrous works ; the song is sacred as well as triumphant, reverent as well as loud.

4. *With all suitable aids.* " With the harp, with trumpets and sound of cornet." " Trumpets," *Chatzotzeroth,* the straight trumpets used by the priests for giving signals (Num. x. 2-10 ; 1 Chron. xv. 24-28). " Cornet," *shophar,* a loud sounding instrument, made of the horn of a ram or of a chamois (sometimes of an ox), and used by the Jews for announcing the Jubilee (Lev. xxv. 9), for proclaiming the new year, for the purposes of war (Jer. iv. 5-19), and for the sentinels at the watch towers to give notice of the approach of an enemy (Ezek. xxxiii. 4, 5). The joy of salvation is so great that words and human voices are inadequate to express it, and so various musical instruments were used as aids in its expression. Our celebration of the great things which the Lord hath done for us should be with such intense and ardent affection that all means will seem inadequate duly to express that affection.

III. **Exultation in the widest extent.** Verses 7-9. In verses 7 and 8 the Psalmist calls for universal praise ; and in verse 9 he gives the reason for it. (See remarks on Ps. xcvi. 11-13). "As the whole creation, both animate and inanimate, has groaned beneath the weight of the curse, so shall the whole creation partake of the great deliverance," and unite in the exultant celebration. " The Psalm," says Barnes, " calls for universal praise. The very *reading* of the Psalm, so joyous, so jubilant, so animated, so exalting, is fitted to awaken the mind to praise ; to rouse it to thankfulness ; to fill it with joy. One cannot read the Psalm without being a happier man ; without being lifted above the world ; without lofty views of God ; without a feeling that He is worthy of this universal praise; without recognising that we are in a world where the mind should be joyful ; that we are under the dominion of a God whose reign should fill the mind with gladness."

CONCLUSION.—1. *Are we by faith personally interested in the salvation which Christ has wrought ?* Do we know Him as our Saviour ? 2. *Are we* REJOICING *in His salvation ?* Salvation should fill our hearts with music and our mouths with song. 3. *Are we doing all in our power to diffuse throughout the world the knowledge of the Lord Christ and His salvation ?* Let us never cease from our evangelistic efforts till "all the ends of the earth have seen the salvation of our God."

PSALM XCIX.

INTRODUCTION.

This Psalm is one of the series of Psalms which celebrate the Kingship of Jehovah. "All these Psalms," says Perowne, "alike tell of the setting up of a Divine kingdom upon earth. All alike anticipate the event with joy. One universal anthem bursts from the whole wide world to greet the advent of the righteous King. Not Zion only and the daughters of Judah are glad, but the dwellers in far-off islands and the ends of the earth. Even inanimate nature sympathises with the joy; the sea thunders her welcome, the rivers clap their hands, the trees of the wood break forth into singing before the Lord. In all these Psalms alike the joy springs from the same source, from the thought that on this earth, where might has so long triumphed over right, a *righteous* King shall reign, a kingdom shall be set up which shall be a kingdom of *righteousness*, and judgment, and truth.

"In this Psalm, not only the righteous sway of the King, but His awful holiness, forms the subject of praise, and the true character of His worshippers as consecrated priests, holy, set apart for His service, is illustrated by the examples of holy men of old, like Moses, Aaron, and Samuel."

THE SUPREMACY OF THE LORD IN THE CHURCH AND THE STATE.

(Verses 1–5.)

The Psalmist celebrates—

I. **The supremacy of the Lord in the Church.** Verses 1–3.

1. *The Lord dwells in the Church.* "He sitteth throned upon the cherubim." The sitting implies rest and permanence; that Jehovah is not a transient guest, but an abiding resident there. "The Lord hath chosen Zion, he hath desired it for His habitation. This is My rest for ever; here will I dwell, for I have desired it." In a special manner the Lord dwells in the Church. He specially manifested Himself in the Holy of Holies in the Jewish Temple. "The Temple was the royal palace, and the Holy of Holies was the presence-chamber." And in the Christian Church He is specially present. Here He manifests the perfections and glory of His character more fully than elsewhere—(1) *In the salvation of sinners.* (2) *In the communications of His grace which He makes to His people.* (See remarks on Ps. lxxvi. 2; lxxx. 1; and lxxxvii.)

2. *The Lord is Supreme in the Church.* "The Lord reigneth; He sitteth throned upon the cherubim; the Lord is great in Zion, and He is high above all the people." The Lord rules in His Church. He is sovereign there. His will is loyally obeyed there. And He is supreme in the hearts of His people. He has manifested His greatness in the Church,—the greatness of His power, wisdom, righteousness, and grace. And He who rules in Zion rules in all the nations of the earth. He is exalted above all the peoples. The Psalmist speaks of His "great and terrible name," or, "great and fearful name." The Lord's name is equivalent to the Lord himself in His revealed holiness. His name is "terrible" to His enemies, "holy" to His people, "great" to both, and should be held in awe and reverence by all men. Let the Church of this age ask herself two questions.

First. *Does the Lord dwell in her midst?* Are the tokens of His presence manifest? Are sinners converted to Him? Do her members live as members of a society in constant communication with and in the constant presence of the Lord and King?

Second. *Is the Lord supreme in her?* In some Churches Acts of Parliament are supreme, in others rigid creeds and formulæ, in others respectability and fashion, in others sacraments and ceremonies. Oh, for the day when the Lord Jesus Christ, in His spirit and principles, shall be supreme in every community of His professed followers!

II. **The supremacy of the Lord in**

the state. Verses 4, 5. Two prominent features of this supremacy are mentioned by the Poet—

1. *Power.* "The King's strength." "This verse, as regards construction, is entirely dependent upon the preceding one."—*Hengstenberg.* Perowne says: "Others carry on the construction from the last verse, taking the words 'He (or, it) is holy,' as parenthetical, thus: 'They shall praise Thy great and fearful Name (it is holy), and the might of the King who (or, which) loveth righteousness.' It must be confessed that, but for the words of the refrain, which it is awkward to take thus parenthetically, the sense and the construction are better preserved by this rendering." Christ is an almighty King both in Himself, and in and for all who believe in Him.

2. *Righteousness.* This is the great thing. His strength is mentioned, because it is perfectly righteous. His omnipotence expresses itself only in righteousness. We have here — (1) Righteousness *in the heart of the King.* "Loveth judgment." "He loveth righteousness and judgment." "The Lord loveth judgment, and forsaketh not His saints." (2) Righteousness *in His legislation.* "Thou dost establish equity." He has established rectitude as the great eternal law of His government. "The law is holy." (3) Righteousness *in His administration.* "Thou executest judgment and righteousness in Jacob." Under the reign of Jehovah the executive is as just as the legislative. All the laws and all the administration tend to the establishment of righteousness.

Learn here the Divine idea of religion in the state. The government of a country is religious when the king rules in righteousness, when Parliament strives to abolish all unrighteous laws and to enact righteous ones, when magistrates and judges seek to administer the laws justly, and when venality and corruption are swept from all its departments and offices.

There is one feature in the relation of the King both to the Church and to the State which is brought into prominence, viz., *His Holiness.* "He is holy." Charnock well says: "As His holiness seems to challenge an excellency above all His other perfections, so it is the glory of all the rest; as it is the glory of the Godhead, so it is the glory of every perfection in the Godhead; as His power is the strength of them, so His holiness is the beauty of them.... As sincerity is the lustre of every grace in a Christian, so is purity the splendour of every attribute in the Godhead. His justice is a holy justice, His wisdom a holy wisdom, His arm of power a 'holy arm,' His truth or promise a 'holy promise.' 'Holy and true' go hand in hand. 'His name,' which signifies all His attributes in conjunction, is holy.'"

III. **The holy supremacy of the Lord as a reason for worship.** "Let them praise Thy name; for it is holy. Exalt ye the Lord our God, and worship at His footstool; for He is holy." Holiness is the summation of all moral perfections; therefore we should worship the Lord. He is supreme not only in position, but in character; therefore we should adore Him. We should exalt Him—

1. *With reverent fear.* "Let the people tremble; let the earth be moved." Amyraldus points out that the fear which proceeds from simple reverence, as well as that which arises from apprehension of evil, produces trembling. So the first verse may apply to the Church as well as to the world. With awe approach THE HOLY ONE.

2. *With profound humility.* "Worship at His footstool." As weak and dependent creatures, and especially as sinful creatures, it behoveth us to draw near to Him with deep self-abasement.

EXAMPLES OF THE HOLY SOVEREIGNTY OF GOD AND THE BECOMING WORSHIP OF HIS PEOPLE.

(*Verses* 6-9.)

The connection of these verses with the foregoing is not very clear. It is not easy to trace with certainty the continuity or the relation of thought. The relation suggested by Perowne seems to us the most probable with which we are acquainted. "The great subject of the Psalmist's praise is the *holiness* of God. It is a *holy* God whom he calls upon all men to worship. It is 'a holy footstool,' 'a holy mountain,' before which they bow down; it is therefore a holy worship which they must render. Such was the worship of His saints of old: and then likewise Jehovah manifested His holiness both in 'forgiving' and in 'taking vengeance.'" Consider—

I. **The examples of the becoming worship of man.** "Moses and Aaron among His priests, and Samuel," &c. Of these Aaron only was a priest in the usual acceptation of the term. But Moses discharged the priestly duties before Aaron entered upon his office (Exod. xl. 22-27), and he consecrated Aaron and his sons. Samuel also exercised priestly functions (1 Sam. ix. 12, 13; and vii. 9). But the feature of the priestly office which is here brought into view is intercession, calling upon God. "Among them that call upon His name," is an explanation of "among His priests." Examples of this calling upon God in intercession by Moses are recorded in Exod. xvii. 11, 12; xxxii. 30-32; Ps. cvi. 23; and by Samuel, 1 Sam. vii. 8, 9; xii. 16-19, 23. And a signal example of the efficacy of Aaron's intercession is recorded in Num. xvi. 47, 48. These distinguished saints worshipped God—

1. *In earnest prayer.* Intercessions and pleadings such as theirs—so bold, yet so reverent; so confident, yet so humble — greatly honour the Lord. Their living faith in Himself and their sincere and deep trust in His mercy were well-pleasing to Him. "He that cometh to God must believe that He is, and that He is a rewarder of them that diligently seek Him."

2. *In holy lives.* "They kept His testimonies and the ordinances that He gave them." They gave to God the praise not only of the lip, but of the life. "Thanksgiving is good, but thanks-living is better." A holy life is the true expression of a reverent heart. The worship of a holy life excels the purest and most reverent worship of prayer and praise; because (1) it is *constant*, and (2) it is *more influential*.

Let us imitate these high examples of worship.

II. **The examples of the holy sovereignty of God.** "He answered them. He spake unto them in the cloudy pillar. Thou answeredst them, O Lord our God," &c. The Lord's holy sovereignty was manifest in His answers to the prayers of His servants. He answered them—

1. *By His communications unto them.* "He spake unto them in the cloudy pillar." These words are strictly applicable only to Moses and Aaron. But the cloudy pillar may be taken as a figurative expression denoting Divine revelation generally, taken from one of its original forms. The Lord frequently communicated with Moses (Exod. xvi. 10-12; xxiv. 15-18, *et al*); and with Aaron (Num. xii. 5-8). Moreover the Lord often spoke to Samuel. Even in childhood the voice of the Lord was addressed to him; and He continued to communicate with him through a long life. In thus responding to the worship of His servants the Lord manifested His gracious condescension, &c.

2. *By granting the forgiveness for which they pleaded.* "Thou wast a God that forgavest them." These ancient saints interceded with the Lord on behalf of the sinful people, when His wrath was kindled against them (Exod. xxxii. 11-14, 31, 32; Num. xvi. 47, 48; 1 Sam. vii. 9), and in answer to their

prayers He forgave the sins of the people. In their own personal history there are no remarkable examples of the forgiving mercy of the Lord; but there are in their intercessions for the people. The Divine supremacy is merciful and gracious. The King has "no pleasure in the death of the wicked; but that the wicked turn from his way and live."

3. *By inflicting judgment on their evil doings.* "Thou tookest vengeance of their inventions," or "doings." There is perhaps an allusion here to the punishment of the whole adult population of Israel for their murmurings and rebellions. In that portion of their history we see the intercession (Num. xiv. 13-19), the forgiveness (20, 21), and the judgment (22, 23). Thus God manifested His grace in hearing prayer, His mercy to the offenders, His anger against sin, and His holiness in all.

CONCLUSION.—1. *How holy are all the doings of God!* Holiness has been defined "the symmetry of the soul;" and all the attributes and operations of God are gloriously symmetrical, they harmonise; the harmony is holiness.

2. *How great is the power of prayer!* "Prayer is the slender nerve that moveth the muscles of Omnipotence."

PARDON WITH PUNISHMENT.

(*Verse* 8.)

"Thou wast a God that forgavest them, though Thou tookest vengeance of their inventions."

A very great and grave mistake about the whole relations of forgiveness and retribution, and about the whole character of that Divine nature from which they both flow, is implied and concentrated, as it were, in that little word "though." It is no part of the original Psalm, and the rendering is a case of interpretation, rather than of translation. What the Psalm says is this: "Thou wast a God that forgavest them, *and* Thou tookest vengeance of their inventions." There is no apparent antagonism here even hinted at between pardon, forgiveness, and punishment, but they are both regarded as parts of one great whole, and as flowing from the holy love of God, which the whole Psalm celebrates.

"Vengeance"! The modern notion attached to revenge is by no means to be found in the word which is here employed. What the Old Testament meant by vengeance is precisely that public justice to which the modern notion of revenge is diametrically opposed.

Notice,—

I. **That forgiveness is, at bottom, the undisturbed communication of the love of God to sinful man.** We are far too apt to think that God pardons men in the fashion in which the sovereign pardons a culprit who has been sentenced to be hanged. Such pardon implies nothing as to the feelings of either the criminal or the monarch. There need neither be pity on the one side nor penitence on the other. The true idea of forgiveness is to be found not in the region of law only, but in the region of love and Fatherhood. The forgiveness of God is over and over again set forth in Scripture as being—a *father's* forgiveness. "Your heavenly *Father* will forgive you your trespasses." Let us remember our own childhood, our children, and how we do with them. . . . . Not putting up the rod, but taking your child to your heart, is your forgiveness. The blessing of forgiveness is not fully comprehended when it is thought of as shutting up some outward hell, or the quenching of its flames. It goes much deeper than this, and means the untroubled communion of love and delight between the reconciled father and the repentant child. The slave may dread the rod, but the child dreads the father's closed heart. And pardon is the open heart of God, full of love, unaverted by any consequences of my sin, unclosed by any of my departures from Him.

II. **That such pardon does necessarily sweep away the one true penalty of sin.** I have been maintaining that the proper notion of pardon is not the removal of penalty, and that is absolutely true if you think of penalty only as being external and arbitrarily inflicted. But it is not true when we come into the spiritual region. What is the penalty of sin? "The wages of sin is death." What is "death"? The wrenching away of a dependent soul from God. How is that penalty ended? When the soul is united to God in the threefold bond of trust, love, and obedience. The communication of the love *is* the barring of the hell. The one true penalty of sin is to be torn asunder from God by our own evil desires, and therefore the outflow of His love to us sinners is really the cancelling of the sorest penalty and true wages of unrighteousness. The real penalty passes away where the love is welcomed and received.

III. **That the pardoning mercy of God leaves many penalties unremoved.** "Thou forgavest them, and Thou tookest vengeance of their inventions." Forgiveness and punishment are both parts of one process, they both come from one source, the One heart which is all holiness and all love. Let me remind you of historical illustrations that may help to bring this idea out a little more clearly. Aaron, see Num. xx. 24; Moses, see Deut. xxxii. 48-51; David, see 2 Sam. xii. 7-14. The old statement, "Whatsoever a man soweth that shall he also reap," is absolutely true, universally true. God loves us too well, not to punish His children when they sin, and He loves us too well to annihilate, were it possible, the *secondary* consequences of our transgressions. The wo sides of the one truth must both be recognised—that the deepest and the *primary* penalties of our evil, which are separation from God, and the painful consciousness of guilt, are swept away —and, also, that other results are allowed to remain, which, being allowed, may be blessed and salutary for the transgressors. If you waste your youth, no repentance will send the shadow back upon the dial, or recover the ground lost by idleness, or restore the constitution shattered by dissipation, or give again the resources wasted upon vice, or bring back the fleeting opportunities.

IV. **That pardoning love so modifies the punishment that it becomes an occasion for solemn thankfulness.** Whatever painful consequences of past sin may still linger about our lives, or haunt our hearts, we may be sure of two things about them all—that they come *from* Forgiving Mercy, that they come *for* our profit. It is no harsh,—no, nor even only a righteous Judge who deals with us. We are chastened by a Father's hand. "When we are judged, we are chastened of the Lord, that we should not be condemned." The stroke of condemnation will never fall upon our pardoned hearts. That it may not, the loving strokes of His discipline must needs accompany the embrace of His forgiveness. And so the pains change their character, and become things to be desired, to be humbly welcomed, to be patiently borne and used, and even to be woven into our hymns of praise.

Brethren! you know where and how the pardon is to be found. In Christ is all the Divine forgiveness treasured. Trust in Him, and there is no condemnation for you.

You have before you an alternative—*either* you will be separated from your sins by God's pardon in Christ and God's chastisement of love; *or*, clutching your sins, refusing to let Him cast them all away, you will be separated by them utterly from God, and so fall into the death which is the wages and punishment of sin.—*A. Maclaren, D.D.*

PSALM C.

INTRODUCTION.

This Psalm completes the series of Royal Psalms, and "may be regarded as the Doxology which closes the strain. We find lingering in it notes of the same great harmony. It breathes the same gladness; it is filled with the same hope, that all nations shall bow down before Jehovah, and confess that He is God."—*Perowne.*

Of all the Psalms in the collection this rises to the highest pitch of gladness; it breathes the broadest spirit of charity, and expresses the highest mood of devout joy. On the ground of our common humanity as the children of the one Creator-Father, all men are summoned to the exultant worship of the Lord.

The superscription to the Psalm is מִזְמוֹר לְתוֹדָה, "A Psalm of praise." Luther: "A Psalm of thanksgiving." Perowne: "A Psalm for the thank-offering." . . . "To denote that the Psalm was to be sung during the offering of thank-offerings."

A PSALM OF UNIVERSAL PRAISE.

We have here—

I. **The reasons of praise to the Lord.** These are of two classes—

1. *Because of what He is in Himself.* "The Lord He is God," is the grand reason. The gods of the nations were idols, vanities, nonentities. Jehovah is God, supremely great, supremely good; the self-existent, the fountain of being and well-being, the infinitely perfect and ever-blessed God. Therefore He should be praised. It is right and seemly that mental and moral greatness should be reverenced, that goodness should be loved, &c. But the Poet states some particulars of His character.

(1.) *He is good.* "The Lord is good." "He is benevolent."—*Barnes.* "Gracious, kind."—*Perowne.* "The word never means *kind;* and this sense is expressly excluded here by the circumstance that it is not only the mercy of the Lord; but also His faithfulness towards those who have received His promises, that appears here as the expression of His goodness. For the last two propositions are merely the development of the first."—*Hengstenberg.* Fuerst gives the primary meaning of טוֹב, as καλός, *pulcher,* beautiful. It seems to us that the Poet intends to include in this word "good" all the meanings given above. The Lord is gracious and righteous, just and merciful, faithful and almighty. Infinite perfection and beauty are His. "To say that God is in Himself a compacted universe of sweetnesses, beauties, and splendours, is to speak very unworthily, for endless universes lie hidden in the bosom of the Infinite nature. The heavens must improve, and the creatures must mature, in wisdom and holiness, yet for ages of ages, before they will be capable of reflecting the higher, not to say the highest, beauties of 'the Father of lights.' Beauty is the robe of holiness: the more holiness the more beauty. To all eternity we can imagine the first and loveliest of all God's creatures praying: 'Let the beauty of the Lord our God be upon us.'" A being of such spiritual excellence should receive the heartiest, holiest praise of all creatures.

(2.) *He is merciful.* "His mercy is everlasting." This is included in His goodness. God's goodness in forgiving offenders and relieving sufferers we denominate His mercy. God's mercy is His goodness in relation to sinners. This mercy is everlasting. The glorious results of it will be enjoyed for ever. Being sinners we should praise Him for His mercy.

(3.) *He is faithful.* "His truth endureth to all generations." *He is true in Himself.* "A God of truth, and without iniquity, just and right is He." *He is true in His dealings with others.* He fulfils all His promises. And He will be true for ever. No changes, however great, can produce any change in Him. Here then we have another reason for praise.

2. *Because of what He is in relation to others.* "He hath made us, and not we ourselves," &c. (1) *He made us His people.* He is our Creator. He called us into being. But the Psalmist means more than that, as will be seen if we read the verse without the words interpolated by the translators: "He hath made us, and not we ourselves, His people." Not merely has He created us, but He has made us what we are, viz., His people. "By grace are ye saved through faith; and that not of yourselves: it is the gift of God: not of works, lest any man should boast. For we are His workmanship, created in Christ Jesus unto good works." (2) *He shepherds us as His people.* "The

sheep of His pasture." "The Lord is my shepherd." As a shepherd He *rules, guides, protects,* and *provides for* His people. It is theirs to *trust, follow,* and *obey* Him. (See outlines on Ps. lxxvii. 20; lxxx. 1.) Here we have most sufficient reasons for praise. He has made us what we are; and He will not forget the work of His own hands, or forsake His people. He knows us intimately, and cares for us, and provides for us, as the shepherd for his sheep. And He is supremely good, and merciful, and true; and He is so through all ages and through all changes. Surely then it becomes us to praise Him with glad and grateful hearts.

II. **The extent of praise to the Lord.** " All ye lands." Literally, as in the margin : " All the earth." Not simply the Jew, but all people. The Lord is the Creator and Sustainer of all men ; the bountiful Benefactor of all men ; therefore all should praise Him. He is the Redeemer of all men. " He died for all ; " therefore by all should His praise be celebrated. The glorious day draws near when

"Earth, with her ten thousand tongues,
Shall fill His courts with sounding praise."

III. **The character of praise to the Lord.** It should be—
1. *Joyous.* " Make a joyful noise unto the Lord." Hengstenberg : " Shout for joy to the Lord." Perowne : " ' Shout aloud unto Jehovah : ' used of the welcome given to a king who enters his capital, or takes possession of the throne, as in xcviii. 4-6 ; lxvi. 1." " Serve the Lord with gladness, come before His presence with singing." Our worship of the Lord should be cheerful and songful, the utterance of rejoicing hearts. He is honoured by our joyous praise. " Cheerfulness credits religion."
2. *Grateful.* " Enter into His gates with thanksgiving, and into His courts with praise ; be thankful unto Him, and bless His name." The previous verse contains abundant reasons for grateful praise. And in this verse all nations are invited to share in those glorious privileges. " Bless the Lord, O my soul ; and forget not all His benefits."
3. *Practical.* " Serve the Lord with gladness." " By *serving* Him here we are not to understand merely the *worship* of God." We serve Him by loyally obeying His commands, &c. Such service we should render spontaneously, heartily, joyously. " Thy statutes have been my song," &c.

CONCLUSION.—" The great lesson of the Psalm is this," says Mr. S. Cox, " Be unselfish and catholic towards man, trustful and reverent towards God, and pure, deep, religious joy will be yours."

THE SIN AND FOLLY OF BEING UNHAPPY.

(*Verse 2.*)

"Serve the Lord with gladness."

Let us consider the sin and folly of being unhappy, especially of rendering unhappy service to God. His yoke is easy, and His burden light.

I. **God is happy.** He is the blessed God, in whom are the fountains of all gladness. Hence that expression, " the joy of God," is one denoting the joy that is *in God*, even more than the joy He gives. Christ was a man of sorrows during His earthly life, because He was bearing our sins. But He sorrowed that we might not sorrow, but rejoice. He served the Father in sorrow, that we might serve Him with gladness.

II. **The angels are happy.** They are the blessed angels. They only know what sorrow is by seeing it in us when they come to minister to us. They drink always of the rivers of pleasures, which are at the right hand of God. Sometimes their joy rises higher, as when they shouted for joy over the new-made world, or as when they are called on to join in the joy of God over one sinner that repenteth. They serve the Lord with gladness.

III. **Forgiven men are happy.** This is David's testimony : " Blessed is the man whose transgression is forgiven." These are a twofold class—(1) those who have departed and are with Christ; (2) those who are still here. Of that latter section of redeemed men we say they are happy, though imperfect, because they are forgiven. They are in an evil world, and have much evil within them — many trials, sore warfare, great feebleness,—yet they are happy. Why? Because forgiven. The favour of God rests on them. They know it, and find that in His favour is life. Being forgiven, and knowing this, they serve the Lord with gladness.

It would appear, then, not only that there is happiness in heaven with God and the holy angels, but that there is happiness here on earth, and that we may be partakers of it. The basis and the beginning of that happiness must be the forgiveness of sins and the favour of God. These are attainable; they are presented to us as free gifts; we are besought to accept them; we cannot reject them without sinning. Let me notice then—

I. **We can only be unhappy by refusing pardon.** The pardon is provided, and it is preached to the sons of men— (1) It is a *free* pardon; (2) a *righteous* pardon; (3) a *present* pardon; (4) a *comprehensive* pardon, covering all sin; (5) it is to be had in *simply believing* what God has told us about the propitiation of His Son. . . . Then must not the absence of this pardon be the fruit of our own rejection of it; and not God's sovereignty or unwillingness? We are unhappy, not simply because we are sinful and foolish, but because we are resolutely indulging in the sin and folly of rejecting God's gift, and so of refusing to be happy.

II. **We can only be unhappy by refusing Christ.** It is not Christ refusing us (He never did so), but it is our refusing Christ, that keeps us unhappy. He is God's free gift to us; a gift which we are not merely at liberty to accept, but which we refuse at our peril. Persistence in the rejection of Christ is the true cause of all the unhappiness of earth.

III. **We can only be unhappy by determining not to turn.** God says, "Turn ye, turn ye; why will ye die?" turn and live. It is vain for us to throw the blame off ourselves, and say, "I want to turn, but I cannot, and God will not help me." This is not true. "I am most willing to be converted, but God will not convert me," is just as if the drunkard were to say, "I am most willing to give up drinking, but God will not help me to be sober;" or the swearer, "I am most anxious to cease swearing, but I cannot, and God will not give me the power." Whatever, then, the solemn truth of God's sovereignty may be (and He would not be God were He not Sovereign), it is not that sovereignty that is hindering you from turning, but your own determination not to do so. Your not turning is the cause of your unhappiness; you cannot be happy till you turn.

In like manner it is with all of us. We might be always happy, were we always receiving the gifts which Christ presents to us; crediting the Divine testimony as to the sufficiency of the great sacrifice, and the freeness of the great love.

Unhappiness thus is wilful. "Ye *will* not come to Me." It profiteth nothing. It does not liberate, or strengthen, or sanctify, or comfort. To be unhappy is our folly and our sin. When happy, no toil is irksome, no trouble or annoyance is felt. Be happy then in God, &c.—*H. Bonar, D.D.—Abridged from "Light and Truth."*

THE ETERNAL TRUTH OF GOD.

(*Verse 5, last clause.*)

I. **God is true.**
He is true in His very nature. There is no deceit, falsehood, nor error in the essential nature of God. Whatever makes men untruthful, nothing of the kind can operate with God.

He is true to His nature. We are not always true to ourselves. I have known a generous man who, in a pet, has acted very ungenerously. But the Lord is always true to Himself.

He is true in action. He has been

true to *the making of the eternal covenant.*
He has been true to all His purposes. Whatever God resolved to do He has done. " Hath He said it, and shall He not do it ? "
He is true to His promises. There is not a promise which God has made, but what either He has kept it, or else, being dated for the future, He will keep it when the time appointed comes.
He is true to all His published Word, which He has made known to us in Holy Scripture.
He is true in every relation that He sustains. As a King, a Judge, a Father, a Friend, et al.
He is true to every man, to every woman, in the world.

II. **God is true in all generations.**
He has been true in the past. The whole of history, sacred and profane, goes to prove that.
He is true still—true to-night.
He will be true.
Since God is true, ye children of God, why do ye mistrust Him? Ye sinners, why do you belie Him by your unbelief?
—*C. H. Spurgeon.—Abridged.*

PSALM CI.

INTRODUCTION.

According to the superscription, this Psalm was composed by David. Three different times in his life have been suggested as the occasion to which the Psalm refers. First, when, upon the death of Saul, David began to reign in Hebron over Judah ; second, when he began to reign "in Jerusalem over all Israel and Judah ; " and third, when he brought up the ark of the Lord from the house of Obed-edom into the city of David. It is impossible to determine which, or whether either of these suggestions, is correct. Perowne thinks that the Psalm was written in the early part of David's reign, whilst the ark was in the house of Obed-edom. The Psalm has been entitled, " The godly purposes and resolves of a king ; " and " *Speculum Regis,*" a mirror for kings. Matthew Henry calls it " The Householder's Psalm." In it David gives us the rules which he laid down for the regulation of his household and court. In this aspect the Psalm has a universal application ; for the principles which are good in a palace are good also in a cottage, and the virtues which adorn a peasant's humble household will increase the lustre of a king's brilliant court.

A PICTURE OF A PIOUS HOME.

In this picture of a pious household the Poet gives prominence to three of its main features.

I. **Its worship.** "I will sing of mercy and judgment," &c.

1. *Praise for the Divine providence.* "I will sing of mercy and judgment," &c. Here are two ideas—(1) *God's providence is varied in its dispensations.* He visits us with both mercies and judgments. He makes us acquainted with "the dark and stormy day ;" and "He maketh us to lie down in green pastures, and leadeth us beside the still waters." (2) *God's providence is benevolent in its character.* Both " mercy and judgment," rightly understood, are themes for praise. "What," inquires Stowell, "is judgment itself but mercy with a sterner aspect? And what are the chidings of judgment but the sterner tones of the voice of a Father's love? For even judgment is one of the 'all things' that 'work together for good to them that love God.'"

2. *Prayer for the Divine presence.* "Oh when wilt Thou come unto me ? " David longs for the presence and help of God. "The question bursts forth from the heart, moved and stirred to its inmost centre, as it thinks of all the height and depth of that resolve to 'walk in a perfect way.' How shall a frail son of man keep his integrity? The task is too great for his own strength, honest and sincere as the resolution is, and therefore he cries, ' When wilt Thou come unto me ? '—come to be my abiding guest—come not only to dwell in Zion, in Thy tabernacle, but with me Thy servant, in my house and in my heart, giving me the strength

and the grace that I need."—*Perowne.* Great and blessed is the influence of family worship. Thrice blessed is the home in which the presence of God is graciously realised.

II. Its head. The head of the family, as sketched by the Poet, manifests—

1. *Circumspectness of conduct.* "I will behave myself wisely in a perfect way." "And David behaved himself wisely in all his ways; and the Lord was with him." He resolves to exercise "prudence, not sapience; not wise contemplation, but wise action. It is not wise thoughts, or wise speaking, or wise writing, or wise gesture and countenance, will serve the turn, but wise behaviour: the former are graceful, but the other needful." It behoves heads of families to "walk circumspectly."

2. *Integrity of heart.* "I will walk within my house with a perfect heart." Literally: "In the perfectness, or integrity, of my heart." Again he says: "A froward heart shall depart from Me." עִקֵּשׁ = perverse, perverted; with לֵבָב (as here) = a corrupt heart.—*Fuerst.* The heart in this place is the centre of moral life. The Psalmist resolves not to tolerate corruption in his heart; but to walk within his house with an upright heart, "in the blamelessness of his heart." He who would order his household wisely should cultivate purity in his feelings, intentions, motives.

3. *Righteousness of aim.* "I will set no wicked thing before mine eyes." Margin: "Thing of Belial." Perowne: "*Vile thing*, lit. 'thing of villany.' The noun is that which is wrongly rendered in the A. V. of the historical books, 'Belial,' as if it were a proper name. It is really a compound noun meaning 'that which profiteth not.'" The head of the pious home will not entertain evil projects, or follow wicked aims, or imitate morally worthless examples. When the aims of the head of a household are righteous and noble, and are worthily followed, his influence in this respect is unspeakably and immeasurably good.

4. *Hatred of evil.* "I hate the work of them that turn aside; it shall not cleave to me." Perowne: "I hate the sin of unfaithfulness." The idea of the words, and also of, "I will not know a wicked person," is hatred of evil. Sin he abhors. "Hatred of sin is a good sentinel for the door of virtue." The Psalmist knew that he might be tempted, but resolved that he would not yield to temptation. Evil might be presented to him, but it should not cleave unto him. He refuses to listen to the suggestions of the tempter, and frees himself from his hold. Such are the outlines of the portrait of the head of a pious home. This is how he appears in his own family. "How fares it with your family? Do you sing in the choir and sin in the chamber? Are you a saint abroad and a devil at home? For shame! What we are at home, that we are indeed. He cannot be a true saint whose habitation is a scene of strife, nor he a faithful minister whose household dreads his appearance at the fireside."—*Spurgeon.*

III. Its servants. Verses 5-7. We have here—

1. *The rejected.* These comprehend three classes. (1) *The Slanderer.* "Whoso privily slandereth his neighbour, him will I cut off." "In order to constitute slander," says Robertson, "it is not necessary that the word spoken should be false—half truths are often more calumnious than whole falsehoods. It is not even necessary that a word should be distinctly uttered; a dropped lip, an arched eyebrow, a shrugged shoulder, a significant look, an incredulous expression of countenance, nay, even an emphatic silence, may do the work; and when the light and trifling thing which has done the mischief has fluttered off, the venom is left behind, to work and rankle, to inflame hearts, to fever human existence, and to poison human society at the fountain springs of life." The wise householder will keep the slanderer out of his family. The *cowardice, malice,* and *terribly pernicious influence* of slander are potent reasons for doing so. (2) *The proud.* "Him that hath an high look and a proud heart will not I suffer." Literally: "Whoso is wide of

heart," *i.e.*, inflated with pride, haughty, arrogant. A man of overbearing conceit and "vaulting ambition" is *foolish;* he is ignorant, unreal, blown out with empty pretensions. *He is wicked.* Pride is sin as well as folly. "Every one that is proud in heart is an abomination to the Lord." He is *mischievous.* "Only by pride cometh contention." Therefore the haughty and ambitious are excluded from the pious home. Humility is essential both to piety and to peace. (3) *The deceiver.* "He that worketh deceit shall not dwell within my house, he that telleth lies shall not tarry in my sight." Hebrew, as in margin : "Shall not be established." Hengstenberg : "Shall not continue beside me." "Liars," says Epictetus, "are the cause of all the sins and crimes in the world." From the pious home deceivers must be excluded, whether they deceive by telling lies or by acting lies, whether simulators or dissimulators, all insincere persons must be kept without the sacred precincts of the godly family.

2. *The accepted.* "Mine eyes shall be upon the faithful of the land, that they may dwell with Me : he that walketh in a perfect way, he shall serve Me." The servants of the pious home, as described by David, are characterised by (1) *Fidelity.* "The' faithful of the land ;" the true and trustworthy. It is implied here that those who are faithful to God will be faithful to man. David says, "His eyes shall be upon them." "There is an eye of *search*, and an eye of *favour:* the one is for the seeking and finding them out, that they may serve ; the other for countenancing of their persons, and rewarding of their service." (2) *Integrity.* "He that walketh in a perfect way." This does not signify a sinless or perfect man, but one who is sincere and upright. There is an obvious reference to the second verse. The Psalmist would have for his servants those who were actuated by the same pure motives, and pursued the same upright course as himself. "A godly servant," says Gurnall, "is a greater blessing than we think on. He can work, and set God on work also, for his master's good (Gen. xxiv. 12), 'O Lord God of my master Abraham, I pray Thee, send me good speed this day, and show kindness unto my master.' And sure he did his master as much service by his prayer as by his prudence in that journey."

IV. **He who is the head of a pious home will do his utmost to banish wickedness from the world.** This we may fairly infer from the last verse. Piety begins in the heart, extends to the home, then goes out to bless the world. "I will early destroy," says the Psalmist, "all the wicked of the land," &c. Perowne : "Every morning will I destroy," &c. There is here probably an allusion to the Eastern custom of holding courts of justice in the morning. (2 Sam. xv. 2 ; Jer. xxi. 12 ; Zeph. iii. 5.) The "every morning" indicates the persistency of the efforts of the Poet-King to uproot evil from society. With unwearied zeal he would seek to purge the land of its iniquities.

CONCLUSION.—The Psalmist in this Psalm sets us an example we shall do well to imitate. 1. *In his intolerance.* The Psalm "is full of a stern exclusiveness, of a noble intolerance, not against theological error, not against uncourtly manners, not against political insubordination, but against the proud heart, the high look, the secret slanderer, the deceitful worker, the teller of lies. These are the outlaws from king David's court ; these are the rebels and heretics whom he would not suffer to dwell in his house or tarry in his sight."—*Dean Stanley.* Let us copy him in this respect. 2. *In his piety.* His was piety in the heart, in the home, in the world. His religion was sincere and thorough. Let us imitate him in this, especially in showing piety at home. "To Adam," says Hare, "paradise was home. To the good among his descendants, home is paradise."

PSALM CII.

INTRODUCTION.

It is impossible to determine on what occasion and by whom this Psalm was composed. Prof. Alexander and Hengstenberg regard it as a composition of David. But from internal evidence, especially in verses 13–22, we should conclude that it was written during the Babylonian exile, and probably near its close, when the faithful were animated by hopes of returning shortly to their own land. It has been attributed to Nehemiah, Jeremiah, Daniel, and others of the prophets of the period of the captivity. But attempts to determine the authorship of the Psalm are vain. Perowne points out that the "Psalm is clearly individual, not national, and must have been intended for private rather than liturgical use, as the inscription seems designed to inform us. This inscription is peculiar; it stands quite alone among the titles prefixed to the Psalms, and marks the circumstances under which it should be used. In all other instances the inscriptions are either musical or historical." In the Epistle to the Hebrews, verses 25–27 of this Psalm are quoted as addressed to the Messiah.

THE AFFLICTIONS OF LIFE AND THE RESOURCE OF THE GODLY.

The Superscription.

The superscription to this Psalm suggests the following observations,—

I. **Human life is characterised by great afflictions.** The text speaks of "the afflicted, when he is overwhelmed." We are sometimes sorely distressed—

1. *In ourselves*, by reason of physical disease and suffering, mental depression and conflict, &c.

2. *In our families*, by the sinful lives of some of its members, *e.g.*, the prodigal son; by sorely straitened circumstances, by the bereavements of death, &c.

3. *In our social circle*, by the unfaithfulness of professed friends, &c.

4. *In the Church*, when its vitality and power seem to decline, &c.

5. *In the nation*, by reason of national sins, or calamities, or judgments, *e.g.*, the Jews in Babylon.

We do not speak of ordinary or trifling afflictions, but of exceptional and severe ones. The Psalmist speaks of himself as "overwhelmed." He was, as it were, "covered with darkness, affliction, grief. His soul was enshrouded in gloom and sorrow." From such sufferings the true and good are not exempt. Job, David, Paul, *et al.*, are examples.

II. **Great afflictions are characterised by great needs.** The Psalmist in his sufferings felt a great need of *utterance of his trouble.* He indicates this by the words: "poureth out his complaint." His soul was full of affliction, like "a vessel overcharged with new wine or strong liquor, that bursts for vent." Great sorrows must find expression, or the brain would reel into madness, and the heart would break or sink into despair. The prayer of the Poet was the cry of a bursting heart. In great affliction we have need of patience, of trust in God, of sustaining grace, &c. We obtain these by prayer.

" My ending is despair,
Unless I be relieved by prayer;
Which pierces so, that it assaults
Mercy itself, and frees all faults."
—*Shakespeare.*

III. **In great afflictions the godly man has a great resource.** He pours out his complaint before the Lord in prayer.

1. *The Lord hears the complaint of His people* (Ps. iv. 3; xxxiv. 4).

2. *The Lord hears the complaint of His people sympathetically.* "The Lord is very pitiful and of tender mercy."

3. *The Lord graciously responds to the complaint of His people.* "Call upon Me in the day of trouble: I will deliver thee," &c. His ear is ever open; His heart always sympathetic; His grace always all-sufficient. Therefore, "Trust in Him at all times; ye people, pour out your heart before Him; God is a refuge for us."

The Lament of a Distressed Patriot.
(*Verses 1–11.*)

In these verses we have the wail of a sadly troubled soul. Let us consider the miseries of the Poet as they are expressed in this bitter cry to the Lord.

I. His distress was very great. This appears throughout the whole of the lamentation. Every feature of the distress makes manifest its intensity. The more prominent of these features we shall call attention to. In the superscription he speaks of himself as "overwhelmed" with trouble, and in verse 9, he says, "I have eaten ashes like bread, and mingled my drink with weeping." He is smitten down to the ground by the greatness of his grief, or, like Job in his sore afflictions, he prostrates himself in dust and ashes by reason of his great distress, and as an expression of that distress. Persons in great grief are frequently represented as seated or prostrate on the ground.

> "My grief's so great,
> That no supporter but the huge firm earth
> Can hold it up: here I and sorrow sit."
> —*Shakespeare.*

He uses another figure to express the intensity of his misery. So full was his heart of sorrow that his tears fell copiously and constantly, so that they were mingled with his drink. By his posture and his tears he expresses the depth of his distress.

II. His distress was absorbing. "I forget to eat my bread." Many are the recorded instances of persons in great grief being altogether oblivious of mealtime or of hunger. Grief takes away the appetite for food. But that is not the meaning of the Psalmist here. He was so absorbed in grief, his distress so completely engrossed his attention, that everything else was forgotten (1 Sam. i. 7, 8; xx. 34; Job. xxxiii. 20; Ps. cvii. 18; Dan. vi. 18). His "sorrow is so intentive to that it sorrows for, that it cannot intend to think anything else." Great sorrows are so absorbing as to cause those who are experiencing them to be forgetful even of the needs of life.

III. His distress was consuming. The Psalmist expresses this by several figures. "My days are consumed like smoke, and my bones are burned as an hearth." Hengstenberg and Perowne: "As a firebrand." "The point of comparison with the *smoke* is the fleeing past, the disappearing." The bones are mentioned as the most substantial part of the body, and they were being consumed as the brand is when placed on the fire. "My heart is smitten and withered like grass." Adam Clarke: "The metaphor here is taken from grass cut down in the meadow. It is first '*smitten*' with the *scythe*, and then '*withered*' by the sun. Thus the Jews were smitten with the judgments of God; and they are now withered under the fire of the *Chaldeans*." "By reason of the voice of my groaning, my bones cleave to my skin." Hengstenberg and Perowne, literally: "My bone cleaveth to my flesh." The expression describes a state of weakness and relaxation of the bones, brought on by severe pain, in which they lose their force and power of vigorous motion (Job xix. 20). The Psalmist uses one other expression to set forth the consuming nature of his distress. "My days are like a shadow that declineth." His time of life seemed to him like the lengthening shades of evening, which show the near approach of night. The figure beautifully and pathetically suggests the nearness of advancing death. To the Poet it seemed that life was fast passing away under his heavy afflictions.

IV. His distress was isolating. "I am like a pelican of the wilderness, I am like an owl of the desert," &c. (verses 6, 7). The pelican is a bird which dwells in solitude far from the habitations of men; it is most sombre and austere in disposition, and is a most expressive illustration of solitude and melancholy. The "owl of the ruins" is also a striking emblem of desolation.

> "From yonder ivy-mantled tower,
> The moping owl does to the moon complain
> Of such as, wand'ring near her secret bower,
> Molest her ancient solitary reign."—*Gray.*

"Sparrow" is not in this place a good rendering of צִפּוֹר. The sparrow is not a solitary melancholy bird. Naturalists state that the *Blue Thrush* is the particular צִפּוֹר, which sits alone on the house-top. This bird is of a dark blue colour. More than a pair of them are scarcely ever seen together. It is fond of sitting alone upon the house-top, uttering its note, which to a human ear is monotonous and melancholy. Thus the Poet represents the isolating power of his miseries. Deep-rooted sorrow is naturally reserved. "A small grievance makes us beside ourselves; a great sorrow makes us retire within ourselves."—*Richter*.

V. **His distress occasioned reproaches from his enemies.** "Mine enemies reproach me all the day," &c. On the reproaches of the enemies, see remarks on Ps. xlii. 3. Perowne: "'*Made their oaths by me*,' *i.e.*, when they curse, choose me as an example of misery, and imprecate upon themselves or others my misfortunes—say, 'God do to me, to thee, as He has done to this man.'" And Hengstenberg: "'*They swear by me,*' inasmuch as they say, 'May God let it go with you as it does with that miserable man'" (comp. Num. v. 21–27; Jer. xxix. 22; Isa. lxv. 15; Ps. xliv. 14). The distresses of the godly are greatly aggravated when they are made the occasion of revilings from their foes.

VI. **His distress was regarded as an expression of the Divine anger.** "Because of Thine indignation and Thy wrath; for Thou hast lifted me up and cast me down." The figure of the second clause is taken from a storm of wind, which seizes and carries upward its object, and then hurls it to the ground. So God in wrath seemed to have seized the Psalmist, borne him aloft, and then dashed him down. In the opinion of the Psalmist, it is sin which has thus provoked the Lord to anger. It is noteworthy, as Delitzsch points out, that the two nouns "indignation" and "wrath" are in the Hebrew the strongest which the language possesses. It is true that the Chaldean captivity was permitted by God, because His people by their heinous and oft-repeated sins had provoked Him to anger. The Chaldeans were unconsciously the instruments by which He effected His purpose to chastise His faithless people. But we are not to suppose that in *individual* cases the measure of suffering indicates the measure of sin and ill-desert. The bitterest ingredient in the miseries of the Poet arose from his impression that those miseries were the expression of the Divine anger.

VII. **His distress was not hopeless.** He lifted his troubled soul to God in prayer (verses 1, 2). He prays for,—
1. *Divine audience.* "Hear my prayer, O Lord, and let my cry come unto Thee. . . . Incline Thine ear unto me." (See remarks on Ps. lxxxviii. 2.)
2. *Divine acceptance.* "Hide not Thy face from me." (See remarks on Ps. xxvii. 9; lxix. 17.) It is a request that God would look favourably upon him, and regard his supplications.
3. *Divine and speedy answer.* "In the day when I call answer me speedily." The Psalmist believed in answers to prayer, and immediate ones too. Such urgency of prayer, when united with humility and patience, is well pleasing to God.

The patriotic Poet was sore troubled and distressed; but he was neither destroyed nor despairing. The night was dark, but the stars were not all quenched.

VIII. **His distress was patriotic.** If we understand the Psalm aright, the Psalmist does not lament his own woes merely, but the woes of his people, the desolation of his country, and the ruins of their temple.

"Fallen is thy throne, O Israel!
    Silence is o'er thy plains;
Thy dwellings all lie desolate,
    Thy children weep in chains!
Where are the dews that fed thee
    On Etham's barren shore?
That fire from heaven which led thee
    Now lights thy path no more.

"Lord! Thou didst love Jerusalem—
    Once she was all Thy own;
Her love Thy fairest heritage
    Her power Thy glory's throne,

Till evil came and blighted
Thy long-loved olive-tree;
And Salem's shrines were lighted
For other gods than Thee."—*Moore.*

These were the woes which distressed the Psalmist. His was no selfish grief; but the sorrow of a patriotic, philanthropic, and godly soul.

CONCLUSION.—While God continues to hear and answer prayer, we may hope for deliverance even from the deepest distresses.

THE HOPE OF A DISTRESSED PATRIOT.

(*Verses* 12-22.)

Consider—

I. **The object of his hope.** What is it that the troubled and patriotic Poet hopes for?

1. *For the rebuilding of the Temple.* "Thou shalt arise, and have mercy upon Zion. When the Lord shall build up Zion, He shall appear in His glory." The Temple which had stood upon Zion was now in ruins. To the pious and patriotic Jew, of all places in his Fatherland, Jerusalem was the most highly esteemed, and of all places in Jerusalem the Temple upon Zion was the holiest and dearest. Hence the great longing for the rebuilding of the Temple and the restoration of its services.

2. *For the emancipation of the captives.* "To hear the groaning of the prisoner; to loose those that are appointed unto death." By "the prisoner" we understand the whole nation, whose captivity is looked upon as an imprisonment. "Those that are appointed unto death," or "the sons of death," "may mean either those who were sentenced to death; those who were sick and ready to die; or those who, in their captivity, were in such a state of privation and suffering that death appeared inevitable."—*Barnes.* The verse clearly points out the emancipation of the captives as one of the great objects desired and hoped for.

3. *The restoration of the people to their own land and worship.* They longed to "declare the name of the Lord in Zion, and His praise in Jerusalem," and to "gather together to serve the Lord." The pious Jews longed to assemble again in the city of their fathers, and there celebrate the worship of the Lord their God as in former days.

To the truly religious man the loss of national independence is great, subjection to foreign rule is a galling yoke; but the loss of religious privileges is felt to be far greater, and the desire for their recovery will be more intense than for the recovery of national independence.

II. **The ground of his hope.** In whom does the troubled and patriotic Poet hope? Has he a good reason for his hope?

1. *It is directed to God.* Verses 12, 13, 16, 19. He hopes that God will interpose on behalf of His captive and afflicted people. For a long time it had seemed as though God regarded them not, but the Psalmist is confident that He is now interested in their welfare. From His holy height He was intently viewing them; and speedily He would arise and have mercy upon them. When our hope in all others fail, we may yet hope in God.

2. *It rests in His character and perfections.* (1) *In His eternal and unchangeable sovereignty.* "Thou, O Lord, shalt endure for ever; and Thy remembrance unto all generations." Hengstenberg: "Thou, O Lord, art enthroned for ever, and Thy memorial from generation to generation." "The *sitting,*" he says, "is no empty *remaining,* but a sitting as king, a sitting on a *throne*" (comp. Ps. ix. 7; xxix. 10). And Perowne: "Thou, O Jehovah, sittest throned for ever, and Thy memorial is to all generations." In this thought the Psalmist found his great consolation. His own life might pass away, generations of men might pass away; but the Lord would never pass away. Man and his fortunes may change, and all earthly things may appear unstable; but the Lord changes not, and His throne is stable and per-

manent. He is eternally and unchangeably supreme, and the covenanted God and helper of His people. (2) *In His mercy.* "Thou shalt arise, and have mercy upon Zion; for it is time to favour her." The hope of deliverance is built upon the grace of God. The misery of their condition would move the mercy of His disposition. (3) *In His regard for prayer.* "He will regard the prayer of the destitute, and not despise their prayer." Perowne: "He hath turned to the prayer of the poor-destitute." He adopts the rendering of the P. B. V., "poor-destitute," "because the word expresses utter nakedness and destitution." The Psalmist represents himself and others as entirely destitute of all human means of help, and expresses his confidence that God would graciously attend to the prayer of such suppliants. "Whomsoever God neglects, He will listen to the cry of those who are forsaken and destitute." He will not only "not despise their prayer," He will favourably receive and answer it. In all these respects the confident hope of the Psalmist was certainly well founded. He who thus trusts in the Lord shall never be put to shame.

III. The strength of his hope. He speaks of the interposition of the Lord on their behalf in accents of steady confidence. The strength of his hope is manifest in—

1. *His assured declarations of Divine favour toward them.* "Thou shalt arise and have mercy," &c. He utters no perchance or peradventure.

2. *His declaration of the nearness of that favour.* "The time to favour her, yea, the set time, is come." There may be a reference here to the seventy years of captivity prophesied by Jeremiah. The Psalmist himself states one reason upon which his conclusion, that the set time for the manifestation of the Divine favour had come, was based, viz., the deep interest manifested by the people in the state of Zion. "Thy servants take pleasure in her stones, and favour the dust thereof." Even the ruins of the Temple were dear to them, and its very dust was sacred. This affectionate interest the Psalmist regarded as a token that the time of deliverance and restoration was at hand. "There are usually some previous intimations or indications of what God is about to do. 'Coming events cast their shadows before.' Even the Divine purposes are accomplished usually in connection with human agency, and in the regular course of events; and it is frequently possible to anticipate that God is about to appear for the fulfilment of His promises. So it was in the coming of the Saviour. So it was in the destruction of Jerusalem by the Romans."—*Barnes.*

(3.) *His declaration of it as even then present.* Verses 16, 17. "'Shall build,' 'shall appear,' 'will regard,' 'and will not despise.' These futures, in the original, are all present; 'buildeth, appeareth, regardeth, and despiseth not.' The Psalmist, in his confidence of the event, speaks of it as doing."—*Horsley.* His confidence is so great as to annihilate time and make the future present to him, and coming events accomplished realities.

IV. The results anticipated from the fulfilment of his hope.

1. *Grateful joy to His people.* Their reverence and love for the holy city and Temple, manifested by their interest even in its ruins, would be gratified, and they would "declare the name of the Lord in Zion, and His praise in Jerusalem." "When the Lord turned again the captivity of Zion . . . our mouth was filled with laughter, and our tongue with singing . . . The Lord hath done great things for us; we are glad."

2. *Fear to the nations.* "So the heathen shall fear the name of the Lord, and all the kings of the earth Thy glory." "When the Lord turned again the captivity of Zion . . . then said they among the heathen, The Lord hath done great things for them."

3. *Instruction and encouragement to posterity.* "This shall be written for the generation to come; and the people which shall be created shall praise the Lord." The Divine deliverance and blessing should be recorded, and future ages should derive instruction therefrom.

The manifestations of the faithfulness and mercy of God in our age are helpful to the faith of all succeeding ages. As the evidence to His truth and grace grows more voluminous and irresistibly conclusive, His praise also should grow in fulness and resonance and heartiness.

4. *Glory to God.* In the restoration of His people His glory would be manifest to all,—both to His people and to all the nations,—observed by all, respected by all, and celebrated by His people. The restoration of His people and the re-building of His Temple would be the glorifying of His name.

CONCLUSION.—1. *When the Church is in the lowest condition, it may be revived by the Lord.* 2. *When the Church is in a low condition, the faithful should care for her the more solicitously, and pray for her the more earnestly.* Verses 14–17. 3. *When the faithful are thus solicitous and prayerful, the Lord will speedily arise for the revival of His Church.* Verses 13, 14. 4. *The revival of the Church will be followed by the most blessed results.*

A REVIVAL OF THE CHURCH, AND SYMPTOMS WHICH PRECEDE IT.

(*Verses* 13, 14.)

By unanimous consent, Zion is considered a type of the Christian Church, which is a body of Christly men; and if we take these words as the Psalmist's statement with regard to the revival of the Christian Church, we propose to make two statements.

I. **There is a favourable time to promote the revival of the Church.** The revival of religion, important at all times, is especially so at this period:

1. *The source to which the Church must look for a revival.* " *Thou* shalt arise, and have mercy upon Zion." At a suitable time, and in a wonderful manner, God did arise and deliver His people. "The Lord," said they, "hath done great things for us." The teachings of the Bible, which relate to this theme, are regular and uninterrupted in setting forth this grand principle, that the Lord alone can revive the Church, and add to her such as shall be saved. (Ps. lxxx. 1–3; lxxxv. 6; Isa. li. 3; Hab. iii. 2; Zech. iv. 6).

2. *The nature of that revival which the Church may expect.* The words "mercy" and "favour" suggest—

(1) *Deliverance.* Though the character of the Church is of such transcendent excellence that it ought to win the admiration of every beholder, yet, alas! such is the depravity of the heart, that opposition, violence, and blood, have marked her progress; but to the present the Almighty hath been her helper.

(2) *Union.* There may be unity of effort with a great variety of *name*, *method*, and *form*. The union of which God is the Author is frequently spoken of in the Bible (Ps. cxxxiii.; John xiii. 34, 35; xvii. 21).

(3) *Prosperity.* The conversion of sinners. That Church is happy which is favoured with deliverance, union, and prosperity.

3. *The time when the revival of the Church may be expected.* The text speaks of a set or appointed season for the salvation of Zion. "The time to favour her, yea, the set time, is come." The deliverance of the Jews from their captivity was foretold (Isa. xlv. 1, 2; Jer. xxv. 11, 12; xxxii. 36–39). How wonderfully Jehovah brought about the deliverance of His people from Babylon at the set time! He influenced Cyrus and Darius, heathen princes, to forward it. He raised up Ezra and Nehemiah, &c.

II. **That the revival of the Church is always preceded by certain infallible signs.** "For Thy servants take pleasure in her stones, and favour the dust thereof."

1. *Solemn humiliation before God.* Before the Jews were delivered from the Babylonish captivity, they were humbled before God on account of their transgressions. The nation was ashamed and cured of its idolatry, and never since then has it bent its knees at an idol's shrine (Ezra ix. 6, 7; x. 1,

Dan. ix. 7-11). Is there this spirit of humiliation before God in modern churches?

2. *Special, importunate, believing prayer.* What beautiful instructions and examples we have in the Bible of the value of such prayer (Isa. lxii. 1; Ezek. xxxvi. 37; Luke xi. 5-10).

3. *Affection for the ordinances of God's House.* The principal evidence we have that the Almighty was about to visit His people in Babylon was the deep interest they had in Zion. They loved the very stones, and even the dust of their beloved, though dilapidated Zion (Ps. cxxxvii. 5, 6). So it is in a revival of religion. When God is about to visit His people in mercy, everything in regard to the Church is loved.

4. *Activity and self-denying efforts in God's cause.* The Jews showed their love to Jerusalem in a practical manner. (Neh. iv. 6.) They work despite the scorn of their foes.

Let these signs exist in any church, and the fruit will soon appear. She shall increase in purity and influence. "Instead of the thorn shall come up the fir tree," &c. (Isa. lv. 13).—*J. Wileman, in " The Study."*

A SUNDAY SCHOOL SERMON—OUR RESPONSIBILITY TOWARDS THE YOUNG.

(*Verse* 18.)

"This shall be written for the generations to come."

The antecedent to the word "this" are the truths contained in the verses from 1 to 13.

1. That the Lord will have mercy upon Zion.
2. That the heathen shall fear the name of the Lord.
3. That He will build up Zion.
4. That He will regard the prayer of the destitute.

These were the promises that were to be written for the generations to come. Why written? That they might be preserved and handed down.

Tradition is uncertain, imperfect, &c. The New Testament declares that these things were written for our instruction. We have the fulfilment of this text to-day. Nearly nine hundred years before the coming of Christ an Assyrian monarch conceived the idea of a national library of books or tablets of burnt clay. Hundreds of years afterward the library was destroyed. Recently a London newspaper, three thousand years after the establishment of the library, and many centuries after its destruction, has explorations made, and many tablets, and fragments of tablets, are recovered and translated, and in them the Book of Genesis has corroboration. That which is written is permanent. Had those past ages known of our paper and ink, what a wonderful preservation of knowledge we would have had!

I. **What has been written?**

1. *Observe the nature of this knowledge of God which was written.* It concerns God's faithfulness and ability in the performance of all He has promised. We cannot bear testimony to faithfulness until we have tested it. When we have tested God, we can bear testimony. Faithfulness implies obligation. He who makes a promise comes under obligation. In this God differs from man. He was under no obligation to come under obligation; but having promised, He has come under obligation, and Christians everywhere bear testimony to His faithfulness and His ability to perform fully all He has freely promised.

2. *What God has promised.* The great thing is the salvation worked out through atonement; the establishment of a Church; that this salvation should be made known unto the ends of the world; that the heathen people should come to know Him. Salvation can be wrought out only through this atonement. It is loose thinking that makes men imagine that education, culture, political economy, can lift up the world. The fear of the Lord lifts up man. Christ made little or nothing of the culture of

the Pharisee, but much of righteousness, and peace, and joy in the Holy Ghost. He builds up His Zion even as He has promised.

II. **Our duty.**

What shall we, who have received so much, do for the generations to come— for the generation now coming? Fathers, members of Churches, what record are you making for the generation coming? The special work of the Sunday-school is to take care of the children of the nation.

1. Let us be faithful to *our own children*. They are the jewels of the Church. We draw the children into Sabbath-school, not to render needless the home instruction, but to supplement this instruction, by bringing the weight of the personal influence of others upon your children.

2. We want to take care of the *children grown up into youth*. The most critical period in the life of man is when he is breaking away from home. How many of the children at this age become *vagrants* among the churches, wandering here and there, receiving but little benefit and giving none. The class most largely reached are the children of believing parents.

3. We have a great work to do among the *children near us*, those who are to be our fellow-citizens. There is enough of ignorance and criminality around us. These evils must be restrained by knowledge, by virtue, or social ruin is inevitable.

4. We must do all possible for the *children of the entire country*. If we would have the nation Christian, we must work and bear the burdens. *We have the opportunity.*

One practical additional word. How many of you who are giving your money, year by year, to the cause of Christ, are giving *yourselves*, your *love*, your *time?* You who are young, I beseech you dedicate the energies of your youth to this service. When you are passing from earth, what then will be of value save what Christ is to you?—*John Hall, D.D.*

A GREAT CONTRAST AND CONSOLATION.

(*Verses* 23-28.)

We have in this section of the Psalm—

I. **A great contrast.** On the one hand, we have the weakness and shortness of human life upon earth, and the changefulness and transitoriness of nature itself; and on the other, we have the eternity and immutability of God.

First : *Let us look at man and nature.* And—

1. *At man's life upon earth.* It is here represented as—(1) *Weak.* " He weakened my strength in the way." In the journey of life the strength even of the most robust in course of time is diminished until it is superseded by weakness. While others by reason of afflictions are speedily brought low. Probably the Psalmist speaks here in the name of the chosen people. God had weakened their strength, had reduced them by afflictions, &c. How frail is human life upon earth ! (2) *Brief.* " He shortened my days." It seemed to the Poet that God was about to cut off his life speedily. (On the brevity of human life upon earth, see Homily on Ps. xc. 1-6.)

2. *Let us look at nature.* (1) *It is changeful.* " Thou shalt change them, and they shall be changed." The heavens and the earth seem unchangeable and permanent. Sometimes they are so represented in Scripture. " He hath also stablished them for ever." " The everlasting mountains and the perpetual hills." Yet from the testimony of geology and astronomy we know that they change. And as compared with the Lord, the most unchangeable and abiding things are changeable and transient. In the future a stupendous change awaits the entire material creation. (2) *It is transitory.* " They shall perish." (Comp. 2 Pet. iii. 10.)

"Melted into air, into thin air :
And, like the baseless fabric of this vision,
The cloud-capp'd towers, the gorgeous palaces,

117

The solemn temples, the great globe itself,
Yea, all which it inherit, shall dissolve;
And, like this insubstantial pageant faded,
Leave not a rack behind."—*Shakespeare.*

Second: *Let us look at the Divine Being.*

1. *He existed before the world.* This is clearly implied in verse 25.

2. *He created the world.* "Of old hast Thou laid the foundation of the earth, and the heavens are the work of Thy hands."

3. *He is eternal.* "Thou shalt endure." "This" (says Stuart, on Heb. i. 12) "would be true, if it was spoken merely with reference to the future, and should be construed as having respect only to eternity *a parte post*, as it is technically called, *i.e.*, eternity to come. But as it stands here, in connection with having created the heavens and the earth κατ' ἀρχὰς, it can hardly be understood to mean less than absolute eternity, or eternity *a parte ante et a parte post.*" (On each of these points concerning "the Divine Being," see Homily on Ps. xc. 1-6.)

4. *He is unchangeable.* "Thou art the same." From everlasting to everlasting there is no variation in God. His vesture, that in which He manifests Himself, may be changed by Him, but He changes not. "Thou art the same in essence and nature, the same in will and purpose, Thou dost change all other things as Thou pleasest: but Thou art immutable in every respect, and receivest no shadow of change, though never so light and small."—*Charnock.* Here, then, is a tremendous contrast—

"Great God, how infinite art Thou!
What worthless worms are we!"

II. **A great consolation.**

1. *As regards himself.* "O my God, take me not away in the midst of my days; Thy years are throughout all generations." It is the lot of the wicked to be cut off in the midst of their days. "Bloody and deceitful men shall not live out half their days." With such men the Poet desired to have no part either living or dying. He seems also to long to be spared to witness the restoration of his people. And he finds consolation in the eternity of God, which he pleads. That eternity is introduced "here for two reasons: (1) *As a ground of consolation*, that God was ever the same; that whatever might happen to men, to the Psalmist himself, or to any other man, God was unchanged, and that His great plans would be carried forward and accomplished. (2) *As a reason for the prayer.* God was eternal. He could not die. He knew in its perfection the blessedness of *life*—life as such; life continued; life unending. The Psalmist appeals to what God Himself enjoyed as a reason why life—so great a blessing—should be granted to him a little longer. By all that there was of blessedness in the life of God, the Psalmist prays that that which was in itself—even in the case of God—so valuable, might yet a little longer be continued to him."—*Barnes.*

2. *As regards the Church.* "The children of Thy servants shall continue, and their seed shall be established before Thee." Because God is unchangeable and eternal His purposes cannot be frustrated, and His Church shall abide, the witness and the monument of His love. "From the eternity of the Head we may infer the perpetuity of the body." The stability and welfare of the Church are guaranteed by the eternity and immutability of the Lord. So the Poet finds strength in his weakness; he rests in the Everlasting Arms.

CONCLUSION.—1. *To us personally let the greatness of God be both awe-inspiring and trust-inspiring.* Let us not only fear, but hope in Him. 2. *Let us rejoice in the security of the Church of Christ.* "Because I live ye shall live also."

GOD IN NATURE.

(*Verses 25–27.*)

This passage directly opposes two popular errors:—

First: *That matter is self-originated.* "Thou,"—all material forms are traced to a spiritual creative agency.

Second: *That matter is eternal.* "They

shall perish." The destruction of the material universe is placed as the antithesis of the Divine duration—" but Thou remainest;" as surely, therefore, as God shall continue to "remain," the heavens and the earth shall perish.

This passage I regard as presenting the Divine Being in four sublime and impressive aspects—

I. The Divine Being as intimately acquainted with all portions of the universe. I take the words "foundation" and "heavens" as representative terms. The lowest depth and the loftiest height are signified. There is not a shadow in the caverns of solitude which He has not projected, nor is there a curve in the heavens which owes not its gracefulness to His touch. Not only is God acquainted with *places*, but with the most subtle *laws* which operate in the minutest fibres of the stupendous fabric.

God's perfect acquaintance with the universe supplies :—

First: *A guarantee of the perfect safety of the good.* They can never pass beyond the sweep of His beneficent influence. He knows how every change will affect them, and they know that all agencies will be controlled with a view to their final security and happiness. (Ps. xci. 5-7.)

Second : *An unutterable terror to the evil.* They can never pass beyond the scrutiny of God's blazing eye.

The great practical deduction of the argument is this, viz. :—*The supreme importance of being* RIGHT *with this dread Spirit.* You cannot escape Him. If you are to spend eternity with *any* being, mutual *sympathy* is essential to enjoyment. You must spend eternity under the eye of God, &c.

II. The Divine Being as the sovereign Proprietor of the universe. He who created has a right to the possession. Four deductions are obvious :—

First: *That our possession is a mere stewardship.* Yours is a representative ownership.

Second : *That our possession involves corresponding responsibility.* Our five talents are bestowed that they may be self-multiplied.

Third : *That our possession forms no ground of arrogance.* " What hast thou that thou hast not received ? "

Fourth : *That our possession should awaken earnest solicitude.* " Why hast God trusted me with so much ? " should be the rich man's anxious inquiry.

Seeing, therefore, that God is the one Proprietor of all things, we should remember two great facts :—

First : *That we are only tenants-at-will.* We have no lease of life or property.

Second : *That God may justly remind man of the Divine claim.* Can you wonder that the true Proprietor should occasionally assert His right by sending the hail-storm or the lightning to smite the earth ? Were the Divine Being never to assert His claim, man might indulge the thought that he was the terminating centre of all things.

III. God as the all-transforming Spirit of the universe. " As a vesture shalt Thou change them, and they shall be changed." You have marked the spring as it has unfolded its mantle, and hung it gracefully on the shoulders of the hills, and spread its gift of flowers on the lap of the grateful earth ; *that* is a manifestation of God's all-transforming power ! You have marked the blustering winter, as it has torn off that verdant robe, and blown out the floral lights ; *that*, too, is a display of God's all-changing power. This same Spirit is also the *heart*-transforming agent. He who garnishes the heavens beautifies the soul. . . . As no human skill could beautify the earth with the treasures of spring, so no mortal power could have provided the robe of righteousness with which every soul must be clad ere it enter heaven.

IV. The Divine Being as the all-surviving Spirit of the universe. " They shall perish, but Thou shalt endure ; Thou art the same, and Thy years shall have no end."

From this assurance we may draw two lessons—

First : *That matter is not a necessary condition of spiritual existence.* All we know of spirit now is associated with matter. If we speak of the " divinity stirring within us," it stirs within a

119

tenement of clay. If we speak of God, it is in connection with the material forms of the outer universe; but the plain meaning of our text is that spirit may exist independent of such expression. Matter is dependent on spirit, but spirit may survive the total annihilation of the heavens and the earth.

Second: *That the Divine existence is incapable of change.* "Thou art the same." Simple words these, and yet there is only *one* Being in the universe to whom they are applicable. To GOD alone can we truthfully say, "THOU ART THE SAME!" Other beings are not the same in *knowledge;* you are continually increasing your information, but to the Divine knowledge no contribution can be added. Other beings are not the same in *affection;* your affection deepens or withdraws according to the current of circumstances, but the Divine love knows no mutation. Other beings are not the same in *enjoyment;* your joys are fickle as an April day, but the ever-blessed God can know neither increase nor diminution of felicity.

He who made the atonement for human guilt is the Being of whom our text speaks: CHRIST is the all-renewing and all-surviving Spirit!

Have I those before me who profess to worship God in nature? Let me assure you that *admiration of nature will not atone for the neglect of Christ.* God knows those only who have a living faith in the merits of the Saviour's sacrifice —*Joseph Parker, D.D. Abridged from the "Cavendish Pulpit."*

PSALM CIII.

INTRODUCTION.

This, as appears from the superscription, is one of David's Psalms. It is a Psalm of great beauty and preciousness, and has been a great favourite of devout souls in all ages. The fulness of the mercy of God in the forgiveness of sins and the enrichment of the soul, and His tender, fatherly pity for His frail and dying children, are here gracefully and gratefully celebrated. It must have been composed at a time when the Poet's soul was filled with precious and grateful recollections of Divine benefits, and with strong and tender confidence in God.

GOD BLESSING MAN AND MAN BLESSING GOD.

(*Verses* 1–5.)

I. **God blessing man.** Verses 3–5. The Psalmist mentions a number of blessings which he has received from God.

1. *Forgiveness.* "Who forgiveth all thine iniquities." "Thine iniquities," says John Pulsford, "are in-equities. There is nothing just or right in thee. Thy very nature is an in-equity, bringing forth nothing but in-equities. In-equities towards thy God, in-equities towards thy neighbour, and in-equities towards thyself, make up the whole of thy life. Thou art a bad tree, and a bad tree cannot bring forth good fruit." Notice the *completeness* of His forgiveness. Our iniquities are more than can be remembered, and are very heinous, but He forgiveth them *all.* The *continuousness* of His forgiveness. "He forgiveth." Within us are tendencies to sin and around us are temptations. Our life is sadly marred by transgressions and shortcomings, we need repeated forgivenesses, multiplied pardons; and God bestows them. He continues to forgive.

2. *Healing.* "Who healeth all thy diseases." The primary reference is to bodily sicknesses. (Comp. Exod. xv. 26; Deut. xxix. 22). But we cannot regard that as the exclusive reference. "Corruption and disease have a spiritual origin. All material corruption was preceded by spiritual corruption. All diseases were, and are, spiritual to begin with. Disease is a state of in-equity in the body, but it is only the in-equity that pre-existed in spirit, fulfilling itself in matter. The *Divine* art of healing therefore lies in the forgiveness of the

soul's iniquities. Remove the iniquities of the soul, and universal healing comes in. Christ healeth *all* thy diseases, by forgiving *all* thy iniquities."—*Pulsford*. Bodily diseases are analogues of spiritual disorders and infirmities. He heals all these.

3. *Redemption.* "Who redeemeth thy life from destruction." Hengstenberg: "From the grave." Perowne: "'*From the pit*,' including death, the grave, Hades." David had many marvellous deliverances from danger and death which were worthy of celebration. The Lord redeems the soul from sin, and from the penalty of sin, spiritual and eternal death. He will ransom His people from the power of the grave, and endow them with endless and blessed life.

4. *Coronation.* "Who crowneth thee with loving-kindness and tender mercies." "The love of God not only delivers from sin, disease, and death : He makes His children kings, and weaves their crown out of His own glorious attributes of loving-kindness and tender mercies."—*Perowne*. "He heaps upon redeemed sinners untold riches from His full heart; and shows to them the softest ways of His love. Mercies are the softnesses of eternal love, but *tender* mercies are unutterable endearments from the heart of hearts."—*Pulsford*.

5. *Satisfaction.* "Who satisfieth thy mouth with good things." There is diversity of opinion as to how עֶדְיֵךְ—which is rendered "mouth" in the A. V. and in the P. B. V.—should be rendered. See Perowne's critical note, and Barnes *in loco*. But there is no dispute as to the meaning of the clause. God satisfieth the souls of His servants. He, and He alone, can satisfy the deep needs, and respond to the boundless desires of the soul. Out of God the wants of man's great and awful soul can never be satisfied. By His presence and grace He fills it with delightful satisfaction. "He satisfieth the longing soul, and filleth the hungry soul with goodness." (Comp. Ps. lxiii. 5; Isa. lv. 1, 2; lviii. 11.)

6 *Invigoration.* "So that thy youth is renewed like the eagle's." There is no reference here to the fable of the eagle renewing its youth in old age. There is perhaps an allusion to the moulting of its plumage periodically, whereby its strength and activity are increased. As the Christian derives his life from Christ, that life can never become feeble or old. Living in Christ, he will flourish in immortal youth. His eternal life will be an eternal progression towards the perfection of youthful vigour and beauty.

Such are the great and inestimable blessings which the Lord confers upon His servants. It is important that we should notice that these blessings—

1. *Are adapted to man's deepest needs.* Forgiveness, satisfaction, redemption.

2. *Tend to promote his perfection and blessedness*, which can be found only in connection with the loving-kindness and tender mercy of the Lord.

II. **Man blessing God.** (Vers. 1, 2.) God blesses man with gifts; man blesses God with praise. The Psalmist blesses the Lord—

1. *With his soul.* "Bless the Lord, O my soul." Not merely with the tongue or pen, but with the heart and soul.

2. *With his entire spiritual being.* "And all that is within me, bless His holy name." David "would enlist every thought, faculty, power, the heart with all its affections, the will, the conscience, the reason, in a word, the whole spiritual being, all in man that is best and highest, in the same heavenly service."—*Perowne*.

3. *With recollection of His benefits.* "Forget not all His benefits." The Psalmist thoughtfully recalls the blessings he has received from God, and is thereby the more urgently incited to praise Him. We are sadly prone to cherish the memory of injuries, and to neglect the memory of benefits. Let us, like the Psalmist, strive to recollect the blessings we have received of the Lord, that thereby our praise might be more grateful and hearty.

4. *With reverent admiration of His character.* "Bless His holy name." God's holiness consists of all the perfections of His character in harmonious and beautiful union. David praised the Lord not merely because of the benefits he had received from Him, but

because of His own glorious perfections. He praised His beneficence, and adored His holiness.

CONCLUSION.—Let us learn from this subject—

1. *The motives of Divine praise.* Why should I bless the Lord ? (1) Because of what He does for me—"benefits." (2) Because of what He is—"holy."

2. *The model of Divine praise.* How shall I bless the Lord? (1) Heartily. (2) With all my powers and affections.

3. *The means of Divine praise.* By what means can I thus bless the Lord? Recall His benefits, and the heart will grow warm with gratitude, &c.

4. *The blessedness of Divine praise.* It brings holy cheer to the troubled spirit. It is a foretaste of heaven. To the man whose soul is filled with praise this world is a "scene of Divine manifestation, a temple filled with heavenly voices and traces of the feet of God."

MAN'S REMEMBRANCE OF THE LORD'S BENEFITS.

(*Verse 2.* "Forget not all His benefits.")

Consider—

I. **The benefits of God.** Who can enumerate them ? He gives us *physical* benefits ; *e.g.*, food, raiment, health, &c. *Social* benefits, *e.g.*, friends, &c. *Intellectual* benefits, *e.g.*, His own revelation in nature, history, and the Bible, books, &c. *Spiritual* benefits, *e.g.*, pardon, help, &c. His gifts are innumerable. They are also very rich. He gives not only kindness and mercy, but "loving-kindness and tender mercies." "The difference between mere kindness and 'loving-kindness,' between mere mercy and 'tender mercy,' is the difference between a flower without fragrance and a flower that is fragrant."—*Parker.*

Rightly viewed the benefits of God must call forth our *wonder, admiration, gratitude.*

II. **The benefits of God may be forgotten.** In what sense? Not absolutely. Memory treasures all things, loses nothing. Like the records made with invisible ink, not seen under ordinary circumstances, invisible perhaps for years, yet when brought under the influence of heat appearing distinctly ; so with memory, &c. But we treasure that in our memory in which we are most interested. The miser remembers anything that will assist him in accumulating money. The grateful heart remembers benefits. But in depraved human nature there is a sad tendency to forget benefits. Too frequently injuries are treasured, benefits are forgotten. A thankless heart receives benefits, and does not recognise them as such, acknowledges no obligation, &c. All are prone to fail somewhat in treasuring and keeping in view the Divine benefits.

III. **The benefits of God should not be forgotten.**

1. *Because of the gratitude we owe to God for them.* Hengstenberg : "He who has been blessed and refuses to bless has sunk from the state of a man to that of a beast." Has he not sunk lower than some beasts? Every blessing involves the obligation to gratitude and praise.

2. *Because of the confidence they are calculated to inspire.* Every benefit we receive increases our obligation and encouragement to trust in the Lord. Parker : "The atheism of *anticipation* should be corrected by the gratitude of *retrospection.* He who reviews the past thankfully may advance to the future hopefully."

SPIRITUAL DISEASES HEALED.

(*Verse 3.*)

I. **Why sin is called a disease.**

1. *As it destroys the moral beauty of the creature.* (Gen. i. 31, and vi. 5, compared ; Job xlii. 1–6 ; Psa. xxxviii. 3–8.)

2. *As it excites pain.* (Psa. li. 8; Acts ii. 37; 1 Cor. xv. 56.)
3. *As it disables from duty.* (Isa. i. 5; Rom. vii. 19.) To God. To man.
4. *As it deprives men of good sound reason.* (Isa. v. 20.) It stupifies the faculties.
5. *As it is infectious.*
6. *As it leads to death.* (Rom. v. 12, 21; vi. 16, 23.)

II. **The variety of sinful diseases to which we are subject.** "All thine iniquities, all thy diseases." (Mark vii. 21-23; Rom. i. 29-31; Gal. v. 19-21.) Almost as many as the bodily diseases mentioned in the bills of mortality.

III. **The remedy by which God heals these diseases.**

1. *His pardoning mercy through the redemption of Christ.* (See text. Isa. liii. 5; Rom. iii. 23-26.)
2. *The sanctifying influences of grace.* (Ezek. xxxvi. 25-27; Heb. x. 16.)
3. *The means of grace.* (Ephes. iv. 11-13.)
4. *The resurrection of the body.* (1 Thess. iv. 16, 17; Phil. iii. 10, 11.)
5. *The case of an ignorant, insensible sinner is very deplorable.*
6. *The case of a real Christian is very hopeful.* His sinful disease is radically healed. The completion of his cure is certain.
7. *The glory of Christ, as the physician of souls, is great indeed.* (Rev. i. 5, 6).
—F. . . . R, in "*Skeletons of Sermons.*"

THE INFINITY, EXPRESSIONS, AND OBJECTS OF THE DIVINE MERCY.

(*Verses* 6-14.)

The Poet having celebrated the mercy of God to himself, proceeds in these verses to celebrate His mercy to Israel. Consider—

I. **The Infinity of the Divine mercy.** "As the heaven is high above the earth, so great is His mercy toward them that fear Him." The Psalmist uses a figure of the greatest extent which the world affords in order to set forth the immensity of the mercy of God. It is, like Himself, infinite. As we imagine nothing higher or vaster than the heavens, so the favour of God exceeds our highest thoughts, and surpasses our most extensive and expressive figures. All the measures of the universe are inadequate to set forth the infinite love of God. (Compare Ps. xxxvi. 5; lvii. 10). He is "plenteous in mercy." "Above the mountains of our sins the floods of His mercy rise. All the world tastes of His sparing mercy, those who hear the Gospel partake of His inviting mercy, the saints live by His saving mercy, are preserved by His upholding mercy, are cheered by His consoling mercy, and will enter heaven through His infinite and everlasting mercy."—*Spurgeon.*

II. **The expressions of the Divine mercy.** It is manifest—

1. *In His vindication of the oppressed.* "The Lord executeth righteousness and judgment for all that are oppressed." We have here (1) *The sufferings of the Church.* The people of God have often been grievously oppressed and persecuted. (2) *The champion of the Church.* The Lord defends the cause of His people, interposes for their deliverance. He humbles the pride of the oppressor, and exalts the oppressed into safety and honour.

2. *In His general dealings with His people.* "He hath not dealt with us after our sins; nor rewarded us according to our iniquities."—See Homiletic sketch on this verse.

3. *In the long delay of His anger.* "Slow to anger." The Lord has long patience even with the most provoking sinners. He restrains His wrath that the wicked may have longer time and more frequent opportunities for repentance. Though His anger ever burns against sin, yet in mercy to the sinner He bears much, and bears long with him, that he might yet be saved.

4. *In the transient duration of His anger.* "He will not always chide, neither will He keep His anger for ever." "I will not contend for ever, neither will I be always wroth," &c. (Isa. lvii. 16). "The second clause,"

says Hengstenberg, "depends upon Lev. xix. 18, 'Thou shalt not avenge, nor bear any grudge against the children of thy people.' Nahum i. 2 again depends upon the passage before us: 'The Lord will take vengeance on His adversaries, and He keepeth wrath' (not assuredly for His people, of whom the declaration of the Psalmist holds true, but still) 'for His enemies.'" God will manifest His displeasure towards His people if they sin against Him, and will punish them for their sins; but when chastisement has accomplished its mission, He will again manifest His loving-kindness. His "anger is so slow to rise, so ready to abate."

5. *In the forgiveness of sins.* "As far as the east is from the west, so far hath He removed our transgressions from us." The great point here is the *completeness* of the forgiveness of sin by God. On this point see remarks o Ps. lxxxv. 2. "When sin is pardoned," says Charnock, "it is never charged again; the guilt of it can no more return than east can become west, or west become east."

6. *In His fatherly compassion.* "Like as a father pitieth his children, so the Lord pitieth them that fear Him." Matthew Henry well says: "The father pities his children that are weak in knowledge and instructs them, pities them when they are froward and bears with them, pities them when they are sick and comforts them (Isa. lxvi. 13), pities them when they have fallen and helps them up again, pities them when they have offended, and, upon their submission, forgives them, pities them when they are wronged and gives them redress; thus 'the Lord pities them that fear Him.'" Nay, much more than "thus;" "for He is the 'Father of all mercies,' and the Father of all the fatherhoods in heaven and earth."

7. *In His fatherly consideration.* "He knoweth our frame, He remembereth that we are dust." He is acquainted with "our fashioning;" the manner in which we are formed, and the materials of which we are made; He knows how weak we are, and exercises a kindly consideration towards us. He is not exacting in His demands upon us, but is pitiful to our weakness.

8. *In the revelation which He made to His people.* "He made known His ways unto Moses, His acts unto the children of Israel." This verse refers to Exod. xxxiii. 13, where Moses says to the Lord, "I pray Thee, if I have found grace in Thy sight, show me now Thy way, that I may know Thee, that I may find grace in Thy sight; and consider that this nation is. Thy people. And He said, My presence shall go with thee, and I will give thee rest." God made Himself known in the guidance and protection of His people, and in the many mighty acts which He wrought on their behalf. The children of Israel saw His acts, His marvellous doings for them. But Moses saw the principles underlying those acts, and the methods of the Divine administration. This revelation the Psalmist rightly regards as an expression of God's mercy. Varied and countless are the manifestations of His mercy to us.

III. **The objects of the Divine mercy.** To all men upon earth the mercy of God extends. Holy angels need not the Divine mercy, apostate angels need it, but receive it not. Man both needs and receives it. Of *all* men upon earth we may say,—"The Lord is slow to anger, and plenteous in mercy. He hath not dealt with us after our sins, nor rewarded us according to our iniquities." But in this Psalm the people of God are specially mentioned as the objects of His mercy. Thrice His mercy is said to be upon "them that fear Him." And the Psalmist in the eighteenth verse gives a further description of them: "To such as keep His covenant, and to those that remember His commandments to do them." Holy fear is expressed in obedience. Excellently says Perowne on verse 17: "For the third time God's mercy and loving-kindness is said to be upon 'them that fear Him,' as if to remind us that there is a love within a love, a love which they only know who have tasted that the Lord is gracious, who fear Him and walk in His ways, as well as a love which 'maketh the sun to shine, and sendeth rain upon the just and the unjust.' In the next verse there is the same limitation, 'To such as keep His covenant,' and to those who not only know but '*do*' His will. The blessings of the covenant are no inalienable right; *mancipio nulli datur;* children's children can only inherit its blessings by cleaving to it."

CONCLUSION.—Are we of those who are thus designated? Do we reverently "fear Him"? Let those who do rejoice in the manifold expressions of His mercy toward them. Let those who do not, accept the offer of pardoning mercy, trust His grace, &c.

THE MERCY OF GOD IN THE AFFLICTIONS OF MAN.

(*Verse* 10.)

Consider—

I. The views which this declaration presents to us of the Divine covenant.

1. *He has not dealt with us as our sins deserve.* Do they not deserve banishment from God, the forfeiture of His parental relation to us, the execution of His righteous sentence upon us? When is it that afflictions appear heavy? When sin is felt lightly. When is it that afflictions appear light? When sin is felt to be heavy. . . . We know the light we have resisted, the convictions we have disregarded, the mercies we have received and forgotten, and the impressions against which we have rebelled. . . . And then in proportion to our actual knowledge of God, our experience of the Divine mercy, our acquaintance with the Divine goodness, is the aggravation of our guiltiness.

2. *He has not dealt with us as He has dealt with others.* Look at the conduct of a righteous and holy God towards fallen angels; . . . the antediluvian world; . . . the cities of the plain; . . . the ancient Israelites for their backslidings. Look at others for the purpose of deepening your gratitude and raising your admiration of the Divine mercy towards you.

3. *His dealings towards us have always been mingled with mercy even in the severest dispensations.* Had He "rewarded us according to our iniquities," there would have been no mercy and no hope—no termination, no diminution, no alleviation of suffering. When we think of the mercy, mingled with all His judgments and chastenings, have we not reason to adopt the language of the Psalmist in the text?

4. *There is mercy in the support we have under affliction.* He does not allow us to suffer alone. . . . What consolation is mingled in the cup of suffering placed in our hands! what promises! what supports! what precious, everlasting consolation and good hope through grace!

5. *There is mercy in the removal of affliction.* How often do we find the God of grace and of providence wondrously interposing to remove affliction by unexpected means, by unthought-of alleviations, by circumstances of which we had not the least conception, &c.

6. *The mercy which is displayed in the results of His dispensations.* He intends, by blighting the gourd, to bring us to the shadow of the tree of life—by cutting off the stream, to bring us nearer to the fountain of living waters—by putting the taint of bitterness in our earthly comforts, to bring us to taste that He is gracious. It is the end of His dispensations to make us more humble, more watchful, more spiritual, more holy, more alive to God and eternity. In the school of trial God prepares His children for their inheritance.

II. The practical uses we should make of this declaration.

1. *It should lead us faithfully to inquire what has been the effect of chastening and trial on us?* When the rod is upon you, what is the course you pursue? Where do you get rid of your troubles? Are you brought to God's throne? Are you brought to humility, to self-abasement, to penitential sorrow?

Are you brought to feel there is no mystery in the rod, that all the mystery is in the mercy towards you?

2. *It should excite adoring gratitude for the love, the patience, the wisdom, and the faithfulness of our Father in heaven.*

3. *It should teach us to cherish humble confidence.* "All things work together for good to them that love God." "All His paths are mercy and goodness." "I will trust in Him, and not be afraid."

4. *It should lead us to exercise unreserved submission.* The submission of patience, the submission of obedience, ought to be the result of these views of the Divine character.

5. *Let there be practical imitation of the Divine conduct* in our temper towards others—in patience, forbearance, forgiveness. "Be ye imitators of God, as dear children, and walk in love, as Christ also hath loved us."—*Dr. Fletcher.—Abridged from "The Preacher."*

GOD'S MERCY AND MAN'S FRAILTY—A CONTRAST.

(Verses 15-18.)

The contrast between man's frailty and transitoriness and God's unchangeableness and eternity, which we found in Ps. xc. 1-6, is here repeated. The similarity of thought and expression is so great that Hengstenberg says, "That David without doubt drew it from Moses." As most of the ideas occurring in this passage were considered in our Homily on Ps. xc. 1-6, it will be sufficient to present the outline of our subject here, and refer the reader to that homily. The chief points of the contrast seem to be these—

I. **The frailty of man's life upon earth, and the mercy of God.** How frail is human life here! As the hot and burning east wind destroys the grass and the flower, so sickness, sorrow, suffering speedily cut short man's career. The flower with its beauty and fragrance soon fades and dies, and man in his glory of corporeal beauty, mental ability, geniality of temper, and holiness of heart and life, soon passes away. But the mercy of the Lord is not a weak, perishable thing. It is great, glorious, abiding. Here is consolation and strength and inspiration for man. He is frail; but he may take refuge in the rich and all-sufficient mercy of God.

II. **The brevity of man's life upon earth, and the eternity of the mercy of God.** As for the life of man, "the wind passeth over it, and it is gone. But the mercy of the Lord is from everlasting to everlasting." The loving-kindness of the Lord is eternal as His own Being. Man, saddened with the transciency of human strength and beauty and life, here is rest for thee in the eternal mercy of God! Here is what we, as sinners, need; and it is here in inexhaustible and unchangeable fulness and freeness.

III. **The final departure of man from the earth, and the eternal mercy of God present with him wherever he may be.** "It is gone, and the place thereof shall know it no more." Man goes hence to

"The undiscover'd country, from whose bourne
No traveller returns."

It is a saddening and a solemn consideration that at death we leave this world never to return to it. The farm, the shop, the office, the study, the home, the Sunday school, the Church will "know us no more" when we have trod "the way to dusty death." We shall have gone from earth for ever. But gone *where?* Ay, where? How shall we fare when we have taken the last, the lonely, the irretraceable journey? These considerations would be insupportably mysterious and painful, but for this fact: *Wherever we may be, the loving-kindness of the Lord will be present with us.* "The mercy of the Lord is from everlasting to everlasting upon them that fear Him." We do not leave that behind us. We do not travel into any region where it ceases to be present and operative. Having that upon us, all must be well, &c.

IV. **The final departure of good men from the earth, and the eternal mercy of God resting upon their descendants.**

Good men pass away for ever, but the loving-kindness of the Lord is continued to their posterity. Church members die, but the Church remains. God's "righteousness is unto children's children." The covenant of mercy extends from generation to generation, provided that they do not violate their interest in it. For here is the limiting condition: "To such as keep His covenant, and to those that remember His commandments to do them."

God will not forget or fail in His part of the covenant; let man also remember and keep his; and then he may take to himself the consolation, and inspiration, and strength of the contrast we have been considering.

THE GLORIOUS REIGN AND PRAISE OF THE LORD.

(*Verses* 19-22.)

I. **The glorious reign of the Lord.** "The Lord hath prepared His throne in the heavens, and His kingdom ruleth over all." Here are three ideas—

1. *The stability of His reign.* "The Lord hath prepared His throne." Perowne: "Jehovah hath established His throne." His throne is firm and stable. All the rage and rebellion of earth and hell cannot shake it. "His dominion is an everlasting dominion."

2. *The majesty of His reign.* "His throne in the heavens." The heavens are the most vast and sublime portion of the universe. In them the glory of the Lord is most conspicuously and splendidly displayed. His throne is said to be established there to indicate its loftiness and majesty.

3. *The universality of His reign.* "His kingdom ruleth over all." He rules in all *places*. The heavens, the earth, and the seas are subject to His sway. The regularity and order of the universe proclaim His sovereignty. He rules over all *creatures*. He is the Creator, Sustainer, and Sovereign of all creatures. He rules over all *persons*. Holy angels delight to do His will. He is supreme in the world of men. And devils cannot sever their connection with His authority. He controls Satan himself.

II. **The glorious praise of the Lord.** The Poet began the Psalm by calling upon His soul to bless the Lord for His benefits; he proceeded to celebrate His goodness to all "them that fear Him"; now he summons the entire universe to unite in ascribing blessing to Him; and he concludes by calling upon his own soul to join in the praise. The praise of the Lord is celebrated by—

1. *Holy angels.* "Bless the Lord, ye His angels," &c. (verses 20, 21). In speaking of these angelic beings, the Psalmist brings into view—(1) *Their great power.* They "excel in strength." Margin and Perowne: "Mighty in strength." Hengstenberg: "Strong warriors." The deeds ascribed to them in Scripture indicate their amazing might. But in our text the strength which is spoken of is clearly intellectual and moral chiefly. They are mighty to do the will of God, and grow stronger by doing it. (2) *Their ready obedience.* They "do His commandments, hearkening unto the voice of His word." They wait and listen for the intimations of His will, and then hasten to carry them out. They are prompt in obedience to Him, and eager to "do His pleasure." (3) *Their immense numbers.* "All His hosts." God's angels are multitudinous. There are vast armies of them. (4) *Their Divine service.* "Ministers of His, that do His pleasure." They are His, for He made and sustains them; His, for He employs them in His service; His, for they are reverently and lovingly loyal to Him. These glorious beings bless the Lord by reverently celebrating His perfections and joyfully obeying His behests. They praise Him both by song and by service.

2. *The unintelligent creation.* "Bless the Lord all His works, in all places of His dominion." All His works praise Him as they answer the end for which they were created. Sun, moon, and stars by diffusing light and heat, and by

unfolding their beauty and glory, praise Him. The earth by its verdure, fruitfulness, &c., praises Him. All His works throughout the universe unite to bless Him.

3. *Redeemed men.* "Bless the Lord, O my soul." The Poet ends the Psalm as he began it by calling upon his own soul to bless the Lord. We who know His redeeming love have the most moving and mighty reasons for celebrating His praise.

CONCLUSION.—While the universe is songful in praise of the Lord, shall my tongue be silent? While others are glowing with enthusiasm, shall my heart be cold? "Bless the Lord, O my soul." While others gladly obey and serve Him, shall my service be wanting? Shall I praise Him in words and not in deeds? Rather let my ears be attentive to hear His commands, and my feet swift and my hands dexterous to obey them. Let us all praise Him, both in song and in service, with lips and with lives.

PSALM CIV.

INTRODUCTION.

"This Psalm," says Calvin, "differs from the last, in that it neither treats of God's special mercies bestowed on His Church, nor lifts us to the hope of a heavenly life; but painting for us in the frame of the world, and the order of nature, the living image of God's wisdom, power, and goodness, exhorts us to praise Him, because in this our frail mortal life He manifests Himself to us as a Father." In the former Psalm God is praised as the God of grace, in this as the God of nature—the Creator and Sustainer of the universe.

"In its main outline the poem follows the story of creation contained in the first chapter of Genesis. There manifestly is the source whence the Psalmist drew. Meditating on that sublime description, itself a poem, he finds in it his subject and his inspiration. And yet the Psalm is not a mere copy of the original. Breathing the same lofty spirit, it has a force and an originality of its own. In some respects the Psalm, even more strikingly than the early record, exhibits the infinite greatness, the order, the life of the universe. But the creation of Genesis is a creation of the past; the creation of the Psalm is a creation of the present. The one portrays the beginning of the eternal order, the other its perpetual, living spectacle. Hence, too, the Ode has far more animation than the Record. The latter is a picture of still life; the former is crowded with figures full of stir and movement." . . . In the Psalm "we have a picture which for truth and depth of colouring, for animation, tenderness, and beauty, has never been surpassed."—*Perowne.*

In the Hebrew the Psalm has no superscription; and there are no means for determining by whom or when the Psalm was composed.

THE MAJESTY OF GOD IN CREATION.

(*Verses 1-5.*)

The Psalmist expresses his thoughts and feelings in a strain of poetry of unsurpassed sublimity. Underlying the glorious imagery of these verses is the brilliant display in which Eastern princes delighted, in their robes and equipages and attendants. The majesty of the appearance of the Divine King, Jehovah, far exceeds their most gorgeous displays. The Poet sets before us—

I. **The glorious vesture of the Lord.** "Thou coverest Thyself with light as with a garment." St. Paul represents the Lord as "dwelling in the light." And Milton—

"Hail, holy light, offspring of heaven firstborn;
Or of th' Eternal co-eternal beam,
May I express thee, unblamed? Since God is light,
And never but in unapproached light,
Dwelt from eternity, dwelt then in thee,
Bright effluence of bright essence increate."

But the reference in the text is not to the unapproachable, the concealing light, but to the revealing light. In the light which daily shines upon us God unfolds to us glimpses of His glory. He apparels Himself with light. There is nothing in the universe so fitted to be the robe of God as light.

1. *Light is an emblem of His own nature.* "God is light." "Light unites in itself purity and clearness, and beauty and glory, as no other material object does: it is the condition of all material life, and growth, and joy; and the application to God of such a predicative requires no transference. He is Light, and the Fountain of light material and light ethical. In the one world, darkness is the absence of light; in the other, darkness, untruthfulness, deceit, falsehood, is the absence of God."—*Alford.*

2. *Light is essential to life and growth.* Without it the earth would speedily become one vast sepulchre.

3. *Light is pure and purifying.* Milton: "Light ethereal, first of things, quintessence pure."

4. *Light is joy-inspiring.*

"Prime cheerer, light!
Of all material beings, first and best!"
—*Thomson.*

How fitting, then, for to be the robe of Deity.

II. **The splendid palace of the Lord.** "Thou spreadest out the heavens like a curtain," &c. (verses 2 and 3). The heavens are the expanse or firmament which God has spread to divide the waters which are under it from the waters which are above it. And in the waters which are above it God is represented as laying the beams of His chambers, the floor of His palace. His palace He has built above the expanse in the lofty and glorious heavens. He has fixed His abode in the most exalted and brilliant place in the universe. The most stately and magnificent of earthly palaces is mean in comparison of this.

III. **The sublime chariot of the Lord.** "Who maketh the clouds His chariot, who walketh upon the wings of the wind." "The clouds appear as the chariot of God, because He drives them about at His pleasure, as a king his car."—*Hengstenberg.* Jehovah came "in a thick cloud" at Sinai. God appeared in "a bright cloud" upon Hermon at the Transfiguration. In the last day He will "come with clouds." On the sublime aspects of clouds, and their fitness to inspire reverence towards God, see a fine passage in Ruskin's "*Modern Painters*" (I. Pt. ii. sec. 3, ch. iv. § 35–38). He "walketh upon the wings of the wind," controlling and directing them as He will, and they obey Him as horses do an earthly king, except that the winds never contest His authority or deviate from His will.

IV. **The wonderful messengers of the Lord.** Verse four is of disputed interpretation. Some of the ablest commentators renders it: "Who maketh the winds His messengers, the flaming fire His ministers." But in this rendering the order of the words is inverted. Perowne: "The natural order in Hebrew, as in English, is verb, object, predicate, and no instance has as yet been alleged in which the predicate stands after the verb before the object. Unless the grammatical difficulty can be removed, we must render, 'He maketh His messengers winds, His ministers a flaming fire;' *i.e.*, 'He clothes His messengers with the might, the swiftness, the all-pervading subtilty of wind and fire.'" Alford advocates this view. See Perowne's "Critical Note" *in loco*, and Alford on Heb. i. 7. The Lord has countless messengers. He can use any of His creatures as His servants; and He can clothe His messengers with the attributes of wind and fire. His attendants are characterised by *power* and *celerity*, like the "wind;" by *purity*, like the "fire;" and by *pervasiveness*, like both "wind" and "fire." The most numerous and splendid retinue of earthly princes, or all their retinues combined, are as nothing when compared with the countless and wonderful messengers of the Lord.

V. **The firm footstool of the Lord.** "He laid the foundations of the earth, that it should not be removed for ever." Margin: "He hath founded the earth upon her bases." "The earth is held as firm by the omnipotence of God, without a foundation, as if it had one; He has given to the earth, which is propped up by nothing, a firm existence, like a building which rests on a solid foundation."—*Hengstenberg.* Job: "He hangeth the earth upon nothing." Milton: "And earth self-balanced from her centre hung." Ovid: "*Ponderibus* *librata suis,"*—poised by its own weight. Yet it is immovably firm and secure. How unsearchable is His wisdom, and how unlimited His power, who thus wonderfully sustains the world! And how glorious is His majesty as manifested in the heavens and the earth!

Our text warrants the following remarks:—

First: *The universe is a Divine creation.* It is not eternal, not self-originated, not the product of chance or fate; but it is the creation of the Almighty.

Second: *The creative energy of the Lord is in continual exercise.* The participles denote continued action, and teach us to regard the exercise of the creative energy of the Lord as a present thing. Every morning God, as it were, arrays Himself anew in His robe of light, &c. The Supreme Worker is ever working. Creation is a continuous process.

Third: *That the Divine creations are effected with consummate ease.* With the same ease with which a man spreads out a tent curtain, God spreads the expanse of heaven—nay, with far greater ease: "He spake, and it was done," &c.

Fourth: *The universe is invested with profound significance.* To the devout student it is a revelation of infinite wisdom, almighty power, Divine beneficence, &c.

Fifth: *The universe is invested with Divine sanctity.* It is the garment of the great God—a scene of Divine manifestation. Rightly understood the earth is a temple, instinct with the presence and resounding with the voice of God. Therefore, "Bless the Lord, O my soul. O Lord, my God, Thou art very great; Thou art clothed with honour and majesty."

THE PRAISE OF THE LORD.

(*Verse* 1.)

I. **The Lord should be praised with the soul.** "Bless the Lord, O my soul." "The Lord looketh at the heart."

II. **The Lord should be praised because of His attributes.** "O Lord, my God, Thou art very great." We should honour Him not only from motives of gratitude, but from motives of esteem. In Himself He is worthy of all homage.

III. **The Lord should be praised because of His work in creation.** This is a great hymn of creation. His works in nature are worthy of praise. We should regard them with admiration and reverence for the Great Worker. We do well to celebrate the glories of redemption, but not to the exclusion of the glories of creation.

IV. **The Lord should be praised both for what He reveals and what He conceals of Himself.** "Thou art clothed with honour and majesty." Creation is the vesture of Deity. "Nature half reveals and half conceals the SOUL within." We should be thankful for both the hiding and the disclosing. Both are merciful.

V. **That man is best qualified for this service "whose God is the Lord."** "O Lord, my God." He who trusts in and communes with God will find praise a natural and joyous service.

CREATION A REVELATION OF THE LORD.

(*Verses* 6-18.)

These verses suggest the following observations:—

I. **The work of the Lord in creation displays His absolute power.** This is manifest—

1. *Over the waters.* "At Thy rebuke they fled, at the voice of Thy thunder they hasted away," &c. (verses 7-10). His control over the waters is seen (1) *in setting boundaries for them.* The Psalmist represents the earth as completely enveloped in water. "Thou

coverest it with the deep as with a garment; the waters stood above the mountains." And Milton—

"The earth was formed, but in the womb as yet
Of waters, embryon immature involved,
Appeared not : over all the face of earth
Main ocean flowed."

At the command of God the water finds its appointed place and is confined there. This is very poetically represented as "the effect of the Divine rebuke and thunder: thrown into a state of tumultuous excitement, the waters quickly again ascend the mountains, their high abode, from which the rebuke of God had brought them down; but unable to keep themselves there they go down to the valleys, until they find themselves in their proper situation, and enter into the place where God designs them to be."—*Hengstenberg.* And there God imprisons them. "Thou hast set a bound that they may not pass over, that they turn not again to cover the earth." Though the waters of the sea are higher than the earth, yet is it confined in its "decreed place" by the command of God. He says, "Hitherto shalt thou come, but no further; and here shall thy proud waves be stayed." The Lord's control over the waters is seen (2) *in distributing them.* "He sendeth the springs into the valleys, which run among the hills. God has wisely and wonderfully distributed the waters, and in so doing has provided for the watering of the earth and the creatures that dwell thereon." The way in which this is done is among the most wonderful and most benevolent in nature,—by that power derived from heat, by which the waters of the ocean, contrary to the natural law of gravitation, are lifted up in small particles—in. vapour—and carried by the clouds where they are needed, and let fall upon the earth to water the plants, and to form fountains, rivulets, and streams—and borne thus to the highest mountains, to be filtered through the ground to form springs and streams below."—*Barnes.*

2. *Over the earth.* "He causeth the grass to grow for the cattle, and herb for the service of man." The fruitfulness of the earth is an effect of the Divine power. The earth, with its mountains and valleys, barren rocks and fruitful fields; the seas and lakes, the rivers and streams; and the heavens, with its wind-driven clouds and its glorious orbs, all display the almighty power of the Creator.

II. **The work of the Lord in creation displays His delight in beauty.** In this poem of creation the Psalmist brings into view the mountains and valleys, the seas and rivers, the fountains and streams, the herbs and trees, the beasts and birds; and all these contribute to the beauty of the world. That God delights in the beautiful in form and in colour is clearly manifested in His works. It is possible to conceive a world in which utility alone was aimed at, and beauty entirely ignored. But such a world would form a complete contrast to the creations of God. To take only one feature, think of the wonderful beauty and sublimity of the mountains. "Loveliness of colour, perfectness of form, endlessness of change, wonderfulness of structure, are precious to all undiseased human minds; and the superiority of the mountains in all these things to the lowlands is as measurable as the riches of a painted window matched with a white one, or the wealth of a museum compared with that of a simply furnished chamber. They seem to have been built for the human race, as at once their schools and cathedrals; full of treasures of illuminated manuscript for the scholar, kindly in simple lessons to the worker, quiet in pale cloisters for the thinker, glorious in holiness for the worshipper. These great cathedrals of the earth, with their gates of rock, pavement of cloud, choirs of stream and stone, altars of snow, and vaults of purple, traversed by the continual stars!" (See the whole passage, of which the foregoing is only a fragment, in Ruskin's "*Modern Painters,*" IV. pt. V. ch. XX. § 3, 4, 5, 9). The beauty of creation (1) *increases our obligations to the Creator;* (2) *should incite to holiness,* which is spiritual beauty. God's delight in spiritual beauty is greater than His delight in material beauty.

III. **The work of the Lord in creation displays His great law of service.** Everything which He has made has its uses. Everything has relations, is dependent, and is designed to be ministrant. The sea is made to serve man by supplying the air with ozone, man with food, &c. Fountains and streams water the earth, and quench the thirst of men and animals. The earth produces food in abundance for man and beast, and wine for the rejoicing of man's heart. And birds, trees, mountains, rocks, all have their uses. Usefulness as well as beauty characterises all the creations of the Divine Hand.

"Oh! not in vain doth He create
Aught from His affluent love proceeding;
The meanest hath appointed state,
If only for the mightiest's heeding.
The meteor and the thunder-stone
Have use and mission of their own."
—*Punshon.*

Man is no exception to this rule. We are created by God to serve others. A useless man is a self-perversion of the idea of the Creator. He frustrates the Divine idea of his life. Are we fulfilling our part in the universal law of service?

IV. **The work of the Lord in creation displays His regard for all His creatures.** Verses 11-18. There is no uncared-for creature. The wild asses, the fowls of the heaven, the cattle, the wild goats, the conies, all are provided for by God. The earth produces the endless varieties and the immense quantities of food required for the creatures that dwell upon it. And in trees, rocks, mountains, &c., they find suitable homes. "Behold the fowls of the air: for they sow not," &c. (Matt. vi. 26.)

V. **The work of the Lord in creation displays His supreme regard for man.** "And wine that maketh glad," &c. God gives to man not only the necessaries but the luxuries of life.

Here is "bread" for his sustenance. Here is "wine" for his enjoyment. "Here is wine," says Matthew Henry, "that makes glad the heart, refreshes the spirits, and exhilarates them, when it is soberly and moderately used, that we may not only go through our business, but go through it cheerfully. It is a pity that that should be abused to overcharge the heart, and unfit men for their duty, which was given to revive their heart and quicken them in their duty." Here is "oil" expressive of gladness. On festive occasions they were accustomed to anoint their heads with oil. The face is said to shine because the radiancy of joy is seen there. The face shines not because of the "oil," but because the heart is glad. God gives to man not only support in life, but joy. He manifests special regard for man's interests. At the Creation He gave him dominion over the earth with all its tenants and all its productions. In Christ He has displayed His interest in human well-being in a still clearer and more conclusive manner.

CONCLUSION. — The subject supplies—

1. *An argument for humility.* We are dependent creatures. We have no resources but such as are in God.

2. *An argument for obedience.* We are parts of a great and orderly system, having intimate relations and dependencies, and designed for mutual service. Let us not violate the order and harmony; let us fulfil our service, &c.

3. *An argument for gratitude.* The Divine regards claim suitable and proportionate acknowledgment.

4. *An argument for trust.* The Lord cares for "the wild asses"; will He not much more care for man who was made in His own image?—for man, redeemed by the precious blood of His Son Jesus Christ?

THE USES OF THE SEASONS.

(*Verses* 19-23.)

The Psalmist here refers to the work of creation on the fourth day, as stated in the Mosaic record. The sun and moon were appointed not only to give light, but for the measurement and division of time, and the indication of seasons. Of these, two—night and day—are mentioned, and their uses pointed out.

I. The uses of day.

1. *The day is the season of work for man.* "Man goeth forth unto his work and to his labour." Labour is a Divine institution, and the day is the fitting time for engaging in it. (1) *Man is urged to work by his necessities.* He needs food, raiment, a dwelling; and to obtain these he must work. He has to encounter difficulties, he requires knowledge and skill; and to acquire these he must work. He needs pardon, moral purity, and power; and for these also he must work. (2.) *Man is fitted for work by his faculties.* He has arms and hands admirably adapted for labour, brain for mental exertion, and the soul with its wondrous faculties for spiritual effort. (3) *Man is commanded to work by his Maker.* Unfallen man was placed in a garden "to dress it and to keep it." "Six days shalt thou labour" is a Divine command. "This we commanded you, that if any man would not work neither should he eat." God Himself is the Supreme Worker. "MY FATHER worketh hitherto and I work." "The law of nature is," says Ruskin, "that a certain quantity of work is necessary to produce a certain quantity of good, of any kind whatever. If you want knowledge, you must toil for it; if food, you must toil for it; and if pleasure, you must toil for it. But men do not acknowledge this law, or strive to evade it, hoping to get their knowledge, and food, and pleasure for nothing; and in this effort they either fail of getting them, and remain ignorant and miserable, or they obtain them by making other men work for their benefit; and then they are tyrants and robbers." And Carlyle: "All true work is sacred; in all true work, were it but true hand-labour, there is something of divineness. Labour, wide as the earth, has its summit in heaven." Again—"The modern majesty consists in work. What a man can do is his greatest ornament, and he always consults his dignity by doing it."

The day is the season for work. Our Lord recognised this fact in His pregnant utterance, "I must work the works of Him that sent me while it is day: the night cometh, when no man can work."

2. *The day is the season of retirement for wild beasts.* "The sun ariseth, they gather themselves together, and lay them down in their dens." We see in this (1) *An evidence of man's original sovereignty* "over every living thing that moveth upon the earth."* The wild beasts still have some dread of him, and hide themselves in their dens during the hours of the day when he is most abroad. (2) *An arrangement for man's safety.* The sluggard cannot excuse himself from daily labour by saying, "There is a lion in the way."

II. The uses of night.

1. *Night is the season of rest for man.* "Labour until the evening." Man was not fitted for incessant toil. He needs frequent rest. And night is the season marked out by God for this. Its shade is a relief after the brightness, and its cool after the heat of the day. These conduce to sleep; and so man is invigorated for further toil.

> "Night is the time for rest;
> How sweet when labours close,
> To gather round an aching heart
> The curtain of repose,
> Stretch the tired limbs, and lay the head
> Upon our own delightful bed."
> —*J. Montgomery.*

2. *Night is the season of activity for wild beasts.* "It is night, wherein all the beasts of the forest do creep forth. The young lions roar after their prey, and seek their meat from God." Observe: (1) *Their dependence upon God.* They seek their food from Him. "The roaring of the young lions, like the crying of the young ravens, is interpreted *asking their meat of God.*" "The natural cries of the distressed creatures are in substance nature's prayer to its Maker for relief and help." Here we have *a hint on prayer.* If God so interprets the cries of the young lions, shall He not much more regard favourably the broken cries of His children? (2) *God's provision for them.* He makes the darkness in which they go forth in

quest of food, and He provides the food for them; otherwise they would go forth in vain. Here is *a hint on Providence.* Shall the Lord provide for the beasts of the forest, and shall He not much more supply all the needs of His people who trust in Him?

III. **The moral uses of the seasons.** By them He teaches us—

1. *The measurement of time.* "He has made the very universe to be the clock of the universe, and admonish every mortal heart of the sure and constant passage of time. We are not left to our inward judgments. Time has its measures without, in the most palpable and impressive visitations of the senses. Every twilight tells us that a day is gone, and that by a sign as impressive as the blotting out of the sun! . . . One season tells us that another is gone; and, when the whole circle of seasons is completed and returned into itself, the new year tells us that the old is gone. And a certain number of these years, we know, is the utmost bound of life."

2. *The preciousness of time.* He appointed the sun and moon for signs and for seasons to "declare to every creature, in every world, the certain flight of time, and signify its sacred value. The gems He has buried in the sands of His rivers; on the gold He has piled His mountains of rock; the pearls He has hid in the depth of the sea; but time,—time is out on the front of all created magnificence." Thus He silently proclaims to us constantly "that time is the most precious of His gifts."

3. *The fitness of certain times for certain duties.* "The tradesman observes the seasons. The husbandman watches them for his life. Whatever we do, must be done in its time. You cannot plant in the winter, nor gather fruit in the spring. God's times are set, and the seasons of His mercy all ordained from the beginning. There is no time of salvation but the time of God!" *

THE LORD AND HIS UNIVERSE.

(Verses 24–30.)

In these verses there is allusion to the work of the fifth day of creation; and an expression of devout admiration of the number of the works of the Lord, and the wisdom displayed therein. The Poet very clearly sets forth certain aspects of the relation of the Lord to the universe.

I. **The Lord as the Creator of all things.** "O Lord, how manifold are Thy works!" &c. The Divine creations are here represented as characterised by—

1. *Their multitudinousness.* "O Lord, how manifold are Thy works! . . . This great and wide sea wherein are things creeping innumerable, both small and great beasts." The earth, the air, and the sea all teem with life, in endless variety. The sea with its life is specially mentioned here. In its depths there is abundant life "of things small and great, a life of the coral insect, as well as of the whale, and also a life on its surface, where 'go the ships' carrying the thoughts and the passions, the skill and the enterprise of human hearts."

2. *Their wisdom.* "In wisdom hast Thou made them all." Every creature which God has made, in its adaptations to the ends of its existence, presents the most admirable indications of the wisdom of its Creator. How immeasurably great the wisdom represented in the whole of His countless and infinitely varied productions!

3. *Their greatness.* "This great and wide sea." To us the earth seems vast, the sea vaster. But when the astronomer discourses to us, we are overwhelmed with the vastness of the heavens, and the earth and sea shrink into comparative littleness and obscurity.

4. *Their usefulness.* To some persons the sea seems a great waste. It is really far otherwise. It is the great highway of the world, and from its waters man draws a great portion of his food. In

---

* See a very suggestive and striking Sermon by Dr. Bushnell on "The Great Time-Keeper." Gen. i. 14.

all the creations of God there is no useless creature, no useless thing.

5. *Their continuity.* "Thou sendest forth Thy Spirit, they are created; and Thou renewest the face of the earth." The miracle of creation is constantly going on in the world. Men die, but man remains. "Generation passeth away, and generation cometh." Life succeeds death. Out of the grave of winter ariseth the bright and blooming spring.

II. **The Lord as the Proprietor of all things.** "The earth is full of Thy riches"—literally, "Thy possessions." All things in earth, air, and sea belong unto the Lord. The fact of creatorship establishes the most indefeasible claim to proprietorship. The fact of the Lord's proprietorship of all things should—

1. *Inspire us with gratitude.* How bountifully has He enriched us out of His storehouse!

2. *Teach us humility.* Our utter dependence upon the Divine resources should strip us of every vestige of pride.

3. *Encourage our confidence.* The resources of the Lord are inexhaustible. Depending upon Him we can never lack support.

III. **The Lord as the Sustainer of all things.** "These wait all upon Thee, that Thou mayest give them their meat in due season." All creatures are dependent upon His bounty. He supplieth the wants of all creatures. The Divine support of the universe is marked by three things:

1. *Regularity.* "He gives them their meat in due season." As want returns the Divine provision is bestowed.

2. *Ease.* "Thou openest Thine hand, they are filled with good." The sustenance of the entire universe imposes not the slightest strain upon His resources. He has but to "open His hand," and the needy millions are satisfied.

3. *Plenteousness.* "They are filled with good." In the dispensation of His gifts the Lord is bounteous. He giveth to all His creatures liberally, and they are satisfied.

IV. **The Lord is the absolute Sovereign of all things.**

1. *In His hand are joy and trouble.* He opens His hand, and His creatures are satisfied. "In His favour is life," and joy. He hides His "face, they are troubled." Let Him avert His face and withdraw the tokens of His favour, and His creatures are terrified; they are filled with consternation, as of one in the presence of inevitable and utter ruin. His smile is the joy and beauty of the universe; His frown would blast and terrify it into death.

2. *In His hand are life and death.* "Thou takest away their breath, they die, and return to their dust. Thou sendest forth Thy Spirit, they are created." When God withdraws His support from any of His creatures, death instantly supervenes. He is "the God of the spirits of all flesh." All life has its origin in Him, and is in His hand. "In Him we live, and move, and have our being." Over the birth and death of individuals, over the coming and going of generations, He presides in infinite wisdom and goodness.

CONCLUSION.—What is our acquaintance with this great Being? To know Him simply as Creator, Sustainer, and Sovereign, is not enough for us. We have violated the order of the Creator, abused the bounty of the Sustainer, and defied the authority of the Sovereign. But blessed be His name, He who is the Creator of all things is also the Saviour of men. Do we know Him as such? Our most urgent necessity and imperative duty is first to approach the Redeemer by faith; and then, without any faltering of the tongue or misgiving of the heart, we may join in this Hymn of Creation.

VOICES OF CREATION.

(*Verses* 24, 27, 28.)

There are three preliminary points—
First: *That this world is not unfavourable to moral culture.* The Psalmist is holy on a planet which has been cursed.

and even through the darkness of the Divine frown can see gleamings and blazings of true glory.

Second: *That all agencies are under the control of an Infinite Intelligence.* All forces are under the management of Divine wisdom and paternal love. Our Father knows every tempest that sweeps through the air—notes every dew-drop that quivers on the opening flower—and is acquainted with every breeze that stirs the atmosphere.

Third: *That the Divine resources are equal to every exigency.* The necessities of nature are endless. In all parts of the universe there are mouths opened, eyes upturned, and hands outstretched to a central Being. And what is His reply to this million-tongued appeal? "Thou openest Thine hand, they are filled with good." Note the sublime *ease* which is here indicated. Compare it with the anxiety and fretfulness of man when besieged with numerous appeals. The Divine Benefactor simply "*opens His hand*," and the universe is satisfied.

The Psalm suggests—

I. **That the Divine existence is to constitute the central fact in all our contemplations of the universe.** God was the central fact in the Psalmist's contemplations. This fact serves three purposes—

First: *It disproves the speculations of Pantheism.* Pantheism teaches the *identity* of God and nature; but in this Psalm we have more than fifty references, by noun or pronoun, to the existence and attributes of a *personal* agent. The Psalmist distinctly teaches the existence of a Being who is infinitely above the powers and glories of nature, and for whose pleasure they are and were created.

Second: *It undermines the materialistic theory.* This theory teaches the non-existence of mind. What we call mind, it denominates a refinement of *matter*. The entire Psalm, however, proclaims and celebrates the presence of Infinite Mind.

Third: *It invests the universe with a mystic sanctity.* Everywhere we behold the Divine handiwork. As the architect embodies his genius in the stupendous temple or noble mansion, so has God materialised His wisdom and power in the physical creation. To me the wind becomes sacred, as I remember that it is written, "HE WALKETH UPON THE WINGS OF THE WIND."

II. **That the principle of dependence is everywhere developed in the universe.** "These all wait upon Thee," &c. The Psalmist ignores the presence of "chance," or "accident;" in his view God is enthroned, and the Divine dominion is over all! We infer, then—

First: *The existence of an absolutely self-dependent power.* Finite conception is totally unequal to the comprehension of such an existence... Our want of comprehension, however, does not affect the sublime doctrine of God's infinite independence.

Second: *The special mission of each part of the universe.* The Psalmist in his wide excursion and minute observation detects nothing that is wanting in purpose.

Third: *The profound humility by which every intelligence should be characterised.* Seeing that we are dependent on God for "life, and breath, and all things," it becometh us to dwell in the dust of humility. *Men of genius! Men of money!* What have you that ye have not received?

III. **That a devout contemplation of the universe is calculated to increase man's hatred of sin.** Having beheld the symmetry, the adaptation, and the unity of the Divine works, the Psalmist directs his gaze to the moral world, and, beholding its hideous deformity and loathsomeness, he exclaims, "Let the sinners be consumed out of the earth, and let the wicked be no more;" as though he had said, "There is one foul blot on this glorious picture; one discordant note in this enrapturing anthem. Let this spot be removed, and the picture will be perfect; bring this note into harmony, and the melody will be soul-enthralling"... I would consume the sinner by consuming his wickedness. Christ came to consume the sinner by taking away the sin of the world.

CONCLUSION.—First : *God must be the central fact in your being.* Second : *What is the highest relationship you sustain to the Creator ?* You must sustain one relationship to God, viz., that of a *dependant.* The worm beneath your feet, if gifted with utterance, would say, " I, too, am a dependant." I call you to be the sons and daughters of the Lord Almighty. Third : *This beneficent Creator also reveals Himself as man's Saviour.* You revere the God of nature ; I ask you to accept Him as the God of salvation. Fourth : *The extinction of sin should be the good man's supreme object.* " He who converteth the sinner from the error of his way shall save," &c. "They that turn many to righteousness shall shine as the stars for ever and ever."—*Joseph Parker, D.D.—Abridged from " The Cavendish Pulpit."*

THE RENEWAL OF THE FACE OF THE EARTH AN ILLUSTRATION OF THE RENEWAL OF THE SOUL.

(*Verse* 30. " Thou renewest the face of the earth.")

The renewal of the face of the earth which takes place every spring speaks to us (1) Of *the presence of God.* He effects the great and beautiful change. " *Thou* renewest." (2) Of *the faithfulness of God.* (Gen. viii. 22.) Every returning spring is an additional witness to the Divine constancy. (3) Of *the tenderness of God.* How tender are the young leaf, the primrose, and the violet ! Faintly, yet truly, they mirror forth the tenderness of God. "The Lord is very pitiful and of tender mercy." " Thy gentleness hath made me great." (4) Of *the Divine delight in beauty.* All the beauty of the season is an outflow of the Divine beauty ; it tells us that God loves beauty, that " God is beauty and love itself." We regard the renewal of the face of the earth as an illustration of the renewal of the soul.

I. **The renewal of the face of the earth succeeds to the dreary and seemingly dead state of nature in winter.** Black, bleak, barren, and lifeless is the aspect of the earth in winter. The unrenewed soul is "dead in trespasses and sins." Apart from the renewing influence of the Divine Spirit there is no beauty, no love, no life in the human soul.

II. **The renewal of the face of the earth is marked by life and freshness.** Buds, leaves, blossoms, grass, all are fresh and new in spring. The man who has passed from the winter of sin and death into the spring of life and grace is " a new creation, old things have passed away, all things have become new." He is " created in Christ Jesus unto good works ; " he enters upon a new career, having new sympathies, new purposes, new delights, new fellowships, new conduct.

III. **The renewal of the face of the earth is very gradual.** Only by slow degrees does spring vanquish winter, and cover the earth with the proofs of her gracious reign. So is it with the renewal of the soul. Though the soul is quickened into divine life, yet the full beauty and promise of the spiritual spring will not be manifest until many a battle has been waged with the sinful tendencies and habits that formerly ruled in us. The work of God both in nature and in grace is very gradual.

IV. **The renewal of the face of the earth is irresistible.** However reluctant winter may be to relinquish his reign in favour of spring, relinquish it he must. So with the renewed soul. Its progress may be very gradual, but it is certain. If the life of grace is in the soul, it will produce the flowers and fruits of grace.

V. **The renewal of the face of the earth is initiatory to a glorious season of maturity.** Spring prepares the way for the bright and beauteous summer, and the bounteous and beneficent autumn. This is the spring-time of our spiritual life. And God will lead us on into the summer and autumn, into the beauty and perfection of our life. Only we must use the spring-time and its opportunities well. If we would reap bountifully we must sow bountifully.

The most glorious of all renewals is yet in the future. The spring-time of the world is not yet, but it comes on apace. (Isa. lxi. 11; Ps. lxxxv. 11.) The whole world shall be arrayed in the freshness and beauty of spiritual and divine life.

THE HARMONY OF CREATION RESTORED.

(*Verses* 31-35.)

The Poet brings the Psalm to a close with the expression of the desire that the glory of God may be universal and perpetual. In so doing he presents for our consideration—

I. **The glory of the Lord in His works.** "The glory of the Lord shall endure for ever," &c.

1. *He manifests His great power in His works.* "He looketh on the earth, and it trembleth; He toucheth the hills, and they smoke." When the Lord came down upon Sinai "the smoke ascended as the smoke of a furnace, and the whole mountain quaked greatly." So great are His majesty and power that He has, as it were, merely to look upon the earth, and it is awed and fearful before Him; He has but to touch the mountains, and they smoke as with His wrath. By His omnipotence He sustains the universe, and in a moment He could blot it out of existence.

2. *He realises joy in His works.* "The Lord shall rejoice in His works." When He created the world, He looked upon His works with complacency, and pronounced them "very good." He still rejoices in the order, beneficence, and beauty of His creations. In His redemptive works also He realises great joy.

3. *He is praised by His intelligent and loyal creatures.* "I will sing unto the Lord as long as I live; I will sing praise to my God while I have my being." With joy the godly man resolves—

" I'll praise Him while He lends me breath;
And when my voice is lost in death,
 Praise shall employ my nobler powers :
My days of praise shall ne'er be past,
While life and thought and being last,
 And immortality endures."—*Watts.*

4. *This glory is perpetual.* "The glory of the Lord shall endure for ever." The glory of man and of his works passeth away, but the glory of the Lord shall continue and increase for ever.

II. **The joy of the righteous in the Lord.** "My meditation of Him shall be sweet; I will be glad in the Lord." Hengstenberg: "May my meditation be acceptable unto Him." Perowne: "Let my meditation be sweet unto Him." The desire of the Psalmist is that his meditation on the works of the Lord may be an acceptable offering unto Him. He rejoiced in the Lord. All his joys centred in the Lord. Such joys are *pure.* They are one of the fruits of the Holy Spirit. (Gal. v. 22.) *Strengthening.* "The joy of the Lord is your strength." *Constant.* "That My joy might remain in you, and your joy might be full." "Your joy no man taketh from you." *Perpetual.* "In Thy presence is fulness of joy; at Thy right hand there are pleasures for evermore." "This is the truest, highest harmony of creation; God finding pleasure in His creatures, His reasonable creatures finding their joy in Him."

III. **The desire of the righteous concerning the wicked.** "Let the sinners be consumed out of the earth, and let the wicked be no more." The glorious harmony of creation "has been rudely broken; the sweet notes of the vast instrument of the universe are 'jangled out of tune.' Sin is the discord of the world. Sin has changed the order (κόσμος) into disorder. Hence the prophetic hope that sinners shall be consumed, that the wicked shall be no more, that thus the earth shall be purified, the harmony be restored, and God once more, as at the first, pronounce His creation 'very good.'"—*Perowne.* The eradication of evil should be the earnest desire of every good man. (See the remarks of Dr. Parker on this point in his sermon on "Voices of Creation," on a preceding page.)

CONCLUSION. Here is a glorious prospect. The broken harmonies of creation shall be restored. The "Very good" of ancient time shall again be heard; and heard over a world never more to be marred by sin. For the realisation of this prospect let us *pray* and *labour*.

PSALM CV.

INTRODUCTION.

"This Psalm," says Perowne, "like the 78th and the 106th, has for its theme the early history of Israel, and God's wonders wrought on behalf of the nation; but it differs from both those Psalms in the *intention* with which it pursues this theme. The 78th Psalm is didactic: its object is to teach a lesson; it recalls the past as conveying instruction and warning for the present. The 106th Psalm is a psalm of penitential confession. The history of the past appears in it only as a history of Israel's sin. In this Psalm, on the other hand, the mighty acts of Jehovah for His people, from the first dawn of their national existence, are recounted as a fitting subject for thankfulness, and as a ground for future obedience. Those interpositions of God are specially dwelt upon which have a reference to the fulfilment of His promise, which exhibit most clearly His faithfulness to His covenant. Hence the series begins with the covenant made with Abraham, tracing all the steps in its fulfilment to the occupation of the promised land." Neither the author of the Psalm nor the occasion on which it was composed is known.

THE WORKS AND WORSHIP OF THE LORD.

(Verses 1–7.)

Let us consider—

I. **The worship of the Divine Being.** The Psalmist calls upon Israel to celebrate the worship of Jehovah, in—

1. *Thankful praise.* "Oh give thanks unto the Lord, call upon His name. Sing unto Him, sing psalms unto Him. Glory ye in His holy name." The reasons for this praise are the Lord's glorious deeds, afterwards mentioned in the Psalm, and His holiness. God should be thankfully and joyfully praised because of His perfections and works.

2. *Trustful prayer.* Here is prayer for Divine *strength:* "Seek the Lord and His strength." Only as we are strengthened by the Lord are we able to perform the duties and endure the trials of life. For Divine *favour:* "Seek His face evermore;" *i.e.,* Seek His favour. (See a sketch on Ps. lxxx. 3.) Here is *perpetual* prayer: "Evermore." The godly soul will seek the favour of the Lord through all time and all eternity, and will progress in the enjoyment of that favour evermore. Here is prayer *with gladness of heart.* "Let the heart of them rejoice that seek the Lord." Barnes: "Let their heart rejoice, (*a*) because they are *permitted* to seek Him, (*b*) because they are *inclined* to seek Him, (*c*) because they have *such* a God to come to,—one so mighty, so holy, so good, so gracious." And, may we not add? because of the *encouragement* which His former deeds afford us in seeking Him.

II. **The character of the Divine works.** The deeds to which the Psalmist refers are those wrought on behalf of His people. He represents them as—

1. *Marvellous.* "His wondrous works, . . . marvellous works that He hath done." The deeds mentioned in this Psalm (verses 27–41) were fitted to excite wonder and admiration.

2. *Significant.* In verse 5, Perowne does not translate "His wonders," as in the A.V., but "His tokens." The miracles which He wrought were not only surprising but instructive. His doings in the past were a foundation on which to base a joyful hope for the future. They abounded in encouragement and in warning.

3. *Judicial.* "The judgments of

His mouth." "The wonders of God in Egypt were exactly so many judicial decisions of God in the case of Israel against the Egyptians, or of the Church of God against the world."

III. **The treatment of the Divine works.** The Poet calls upon the people to—

1. *Remember them.* "Remember His marvellous works." The doings of God on behalf of His people, both providential and redemptive, should never be forgotten by them. To forget them would involve (1) *base ingratitude to God;* (2) *foolish disregard of the advantage of remembering them.* The recollection of them would tend to strengthen faith, promote obedience, &c.

2. *Ponder them.* "Talk of all His wondrous works." Both Hengstenberg and Perowne translate, "Meditate," &c. Reflection must follow recollection. (See a sketch on Ps. lxxvii. 11, 12.)

3. *Publish them.* "Make known His deeds among the people." Declaration should follow reflection. (See on Ps. lxxvii. 11, 12.)

IV. **The people of the Divine choice.** "Ye seed of Abraham His servant, ye children of Jacob His chosen. He is the Lord our God." "*His chosen,* plural, referring to the people, not to Jacob. It is on this ground, because they are Jacob's children, heritors of the covenant and the promises, that they are bound beyond all others to 'remember' what God had done for them."—*Perowne.* As the chosen people of God, they were the heirs of His promises, and so His mighty deeds in the past were pledges of His omnipotent help in the future. Being the people of God, theirs was the *privilege* of His protection and support and salvation. And theirs was the *duty* of praising His name, publishing His deeds, and performing His commands.

Let the people of God, in this age of Gospel grace, be mindful of both their privileges and their responsibilities.

SPIRITUAL JOYS.

(*Verse 3.* "Let the heart of them rejoice that seek the Lord.")

Here is *a generic term* for God's people—"*they seek the Lord,*"—definite, yet comprehensive; it may be applied to the awakened sinner — he "*seeks the Lord,*"—to the professing Christian—all his life he is "*seeking the Lord,*"—and the matured, departing believer can do no more; he dies, "*seeking the Lord,*" nor will he fully find Him until he sees Him as He is in glory,—"I shall be satisfied when I awake with Thy likeness." To such persons it is that the Psalmist addresses the exhortation of the text: "Let the heart of them rejoice," &c. Observe—

I. **That it is God's will that His people should be happy.** We might show that, notwithstanding all the disturbing causes, the goodness of God in desiring His creatures' happiness appears in the animate world and among men in general, but the text limits it to His own people.

1. *Consider what God has done to promote and secure the happiness of His people.* He has redeemed them from sin, guilt, and corruption by the death, and passion, and glorification of His dear Son. That Son lives to intercede for them, and supplies them with all grace out of His fulness in glory. To comfort, cheer, animate, as well as to sanctify them, His Holy Spirit dwells in them. "All things are theirs." They have abounding consolation and Divine joys, and "peace which passeth all understanding." See Ps. lxxxiv. 11.

2. *The exhortations to joy and peace abound in Holy Scripture.* It is a duty, as well as a privilege, for believers to be happy. See Ps. xxxiii. 1; John xvi. 22; 2 Cor. ii. 14; Eph. iv. 4.

II. **Still in all ages God's people have been for the most part a sad and sorrowing people.**

It is often assumed that their portion in this world is usually a sorrowful one. Large portions of sadness were administered to Jacob, to Joseph, to Moses, to

David, Elijah, Jeremiah—to say nothing of Job himself. See Acts xiv. 22. *And of modern Christians it is constantly alleged that they are gloomy and melancholy,*—and there is much in them to justify the world's accusation, as happy and rejoicing believers are rather the exception than the rule among persons of piety.

III. **How is this to be accounted for?** God has made a rich provision for His people's happiness, but they are not happy,—why is this?

May it not be accounted for by their trials, temptations, afflictions? Certainly not! because God sends corresponding help and grace; all persons of experience would attest that the happiest and most rejoicing Christians are to be found among those who are most deeply afflicted. See 2 Cor. i. 5.

Does not God sometimes withhold spiritual consolations from His faithful and consistent people? He does so. See Isa. l. 10. But such cases are rare, and the time of shadows short, and speedily lead to stronger exercises of faith and surer joys. The absence of religious joy and peace is chiefly to be accounted for—

1. *In some instances by the hollowness of religious profession.* The heart is not true and right with God,—some secret passion, appetite, lust, desire, is allowed or indulged in. There can be no real happiness in religion while an idol is in the heart. See Matt. vi. 24; 1 John iii. 21.

2. *Where there is not direct heart treachery nor self-deception there may be an unsuccessful conflict with indwelling sin.* See Rom. vii.; 2 Cor. v. 4; Gal. v. 17. Natural character, impure or sceptical, or vain, passionate, and revengeful—and the workings of these destroy peace of mind.

3. *Defective views of God's all-sufficient grace;*—labour as slaves, as hirelings,

as legalists—forgetting that He who purchased forgiveness secured grace. See John xv. 4; Rom. vii. 25; 2 Cor. xii. 8, 9.

4. *Errors as to the ground and source of a believer's rejoicing.* Our joy, peace, comfort, &c., must spring not from our growth in grace, nor from anything in us nor done by us, but in and out of Christ alone—and all our sorrows are intended to drive us to this. (Ps. v. 11, 12; Isa. xii. 1-3; lxi. 10, 11; Hab. iii. 18.) So in the New Testament. (Phil. iv. 4.) God in Christ is the only abiding source of happiness to His people.

1. *Let all sincere Christians believe that a sorrowful experience is a defective and imperfect condition of soul.* Better be sad than indifferent, slumbering, &c. But a melancholy, gloomy, downcast, doubting state is not the normal condition of a believer.

2. *Let all search and see whether any allowed sin, or inconsistency, or idol, remain in their hearts.* There can be no peace, no success, no joy, till this Achan is stoned and burnt.

3. *Let no one be satisfied until he is both happy and holy. Both within your reach.*

Are you afflicted?—no matter from what source, rejoice. "Suffer affliction with people of God," &c.

Consolation withheld? Wait, and watch, and pray—and look for the Spirit, and search for Christ until you find Him.

Corruptions? "Nothing too hard for the Lord." Union with Christ by His Spirit alone subdues them.

Confused ideas? perplexed views? doubt? See Isa. liv. 13. Pray for light, &c.

Happiness, present now, immediate, in store for you. "My soul doth magnify the Lord, and my spirit rejoiceth in God my Saviour."—*F. Close, D.D.*

The Faithful Promiser.

(*Verses* 8-15.)

The Poet here sings of the covenant of the Lord with His ancient people, and the early stages of its fulfilment. In doing this he brings out several truths of universal application as to God and His engagements with man, on which we may profitably reflect.

I. **The Lord's remembrance of His promises.** "He hath remembered His covenant for ever." God cannot forget anything. All the things which He hath promised He will perform, though tedious ages may intervene between the giving of the promise and its fulfilment. If God were to forget His engagements He would cease to be God. "If God were to forget for one moment," says Macdonald, "the universe would grow black—vanish—rush out again from the realm of law and order into chaos and night." His *infinite intelligence*, His *unchangeableness* and His *past doings* afford ample guarantees of the Lord's unfailing remembrance of His promises.

II. **The perpetuity of His promises.** "The word which He commanded to a thousand generations." Hengstenberg translates: "The word which He ordained." &c. Perowne: "The word which He confirmed," &c. "A thousand generations" means innumerable generations, always. As the Psalmist says, the covenant is "an everlasting covenant." "For the gifts and calling of God are without repentance." "Heaven and earth shall pass away, but My words shall not pass away." The promises of God are to all generations. This is a glorious truth. Promises of pardon, sufficient grace, eternal and blessed life to every believer in the Lord, are for man in all ages and in all lands.

III. **The confirmation of His promises.** "The covenant which He made with Abraham, and His oath unto Isaac, and confirmed the same unto Jacob for a law, and to Israel for an everlasting covenant." For the confirmation to Isaac, see Gen. xxvi. 3–5; and to Jacob, Gen. xxviii. 13–15; and to Israel, Gen. xxxv. 9–12. In the experience of every generation God confirms the truth of His promises. Every age, as it passes away from this world, leaves behind it an additional volume testifying most conclusively to the faithfulness of God.

IV. **The recipients of His promises.** Concerning these the Psalmist indicates three characteristics. They are—

1. *Believers of the Divine Word.* Abraham, Isaac, and Jacob were eminent for faith. (Heb. xi. 8, 9, 17–21.) God required the Israelites to believe His word and obey His commands. The blessings of salvation are promised to those who believe.

2. *Consecrated to the Divine service.* "Mine anointed." The patriarchs were not anointed; but the Poet uses the language of his own day to set forth the idea that they were called and consecrated to the service of God. Those who truly believe the word of God, and accept the offers of His grace, devote themselves to His service. To them the promises of protection, sanctification, and the heavenly inheritance are made.

3. *Recipients of Divine communications.* "My prophets." "A good instance," says Perowne, "of the wide signification of this word. It is derived from a root signifying *to boil, to bubble up*. The prophet is one in whose soul there rises a spring, a rushing stream of Divine inspiration. In the later language he not only receives the Divine word, but he is made the *utterer of it*, the organ of its communication to others. But in the earlier instances, as in that of Abraham, his official character does not distinctly appear, though doubtless, like Noah, he was 'a preacher of righteousness,' and taught his own family (and through them ultimately the whole world) the way of the Lord. See Gen. xviii. 19. Here the prophet means little more than one to whom God speaks, one with whom He holds converse, whether by word, or vision, or dream, or inner voice. (Comp. Num. xii. 6–8.) We approach nearest to what is meant by styling the patriarchs prophets when we read such passages as Gen. xviii. 17: 'And Jehovah said, Shall I hide from Abraham that thing which I do?' or again, the pleading of Abraham for Sodom, in verses 23–33 of the same chapter. It is, indeed, as pleading with God *in intercession* that Abraham is termed a prophet in Gen. xx. 7. The title is thus very similar to that of the 'Friend of God' (Isa. xli. 8; 2 Chron. xx. 7; James ii. 23)." The people of God, in whose experience His

gracious promises are fulfilled, are in communication with Him. He speaks to them by His Word and by His Spirit. They have fellowship with Him. Such are three of the characteristics of the recipients of the promises of the Lord.

V. The fulfilment of His promises.

1. *God's promises will be fulfilled however great the apparent improbability.* When God promised the land of Canaan to the patriarchs, the fulfilment of the promise seemed utterly improbable. At that time they were (1) *very "few in number."* Was it likely that they would ever be able to take possession of the land? or that their seed would ever be "as the stars of the heaven" for multitude? (2) They were *strangers in that land.* They did not unite themselves with the people of the land, or acquire property there. (3) They were *wanderers.* "They went from one nation to another, from one kingdom to another people." They had no fixed residence. They were exposed to frequent dangers. How improbable that the land promised to them should ever be theirs! Yet the Lord fulfils His promise, and gives them the land. The things which appear to man improbable, or even impossible, God accomplishes, if He has promised to do so. Apply this to the *perfection of individual character*, to the *future triumphs of Christianity* in the world, &c.

2. *God's promises will be fulfilled though their fulfilment may necessitate the control of the greatest powers.* "He suffered no man to do them wrong; yea, He reproved kings for their sakes." See Gen. xii. 10-20; xx. 1-7. The Lord controls the mightiest as well as the meanest powers, for the protection of His people and the fulfilment of His promises.

CONCLUSION. 1. *Warning to the wicked.* God will inflict the punishment which He has denounced against sin. 2. *Encouragement* (1) *to the repentant sinner.* The promises of forgiveness and grace are gloriously reliable. (2) *To the people of God.* However improbable, apparently, not one good thing of all that He hath promised shall fail.

HISTORICAL SURPRISES.

(Verses 16-24.)

From the 16th verse to the 38th verse the Psalmist gives an outline of the history of Israel in Egypt, exhibiting in it the fulfilment of the Divine purposes and the working of the Divine power. In the verses under consideration at present we have several surprises of the Divine providence.

I. A famine driving the people from the land promised to them, yet contributing to their possession of it. "He called for a famine upon the land; He brake the whole staff of bread." The famine referred to is that which occurred in the time of Jacob, and which occasioned his migration into Egypt. This famine was no chance occurrence; it came not merely by the operation of material laws; God called for it; He ordered it. By reason of it "Israel also came into Egypt, and Jacob sojourned in the land of Ham." Thus they departed from the promised land; and so the fulfilment of the promise was rendered apparently more unlikely than ever. Yet in the providence of God their absence from the land of Canaan contributed to their ultimate possession of it. While in Egypt they increased in number, in power, in intelligence, &c.

II. A slave becomes the saviour of a country and of the chosen people. Notice here—

1. *The sin of man.* "Joseph was sold for a servant," or slave. Joseph's position as a slave in Egypt was brought about by the envy and jealousy, the hatred and cruelty, of his brethren.

2. *The providence of God.* "He sent a man before them." God so ordered events that Joseph was taken into Egypt, and there wondrously enabled to preserve the people of that land from perishing by famine, and to arrange for the reception and support of Israel and his family. Joseph's position in Egypt

was not an accident or a freak of fortune. "Be not grieved, nor angry that ye sold me hither; for God did send me before you to preserve life. Ye thought evil against me; but God meant it unto good, to bring to pass, as it is this day, to save much people alive." The brethren of Joseph were free in their wickedness in selling him; they were guilty, in the sight of God, of jealousy, hatred, cruelty. God's overruling of man's sin does not extenuate his guilt. "Surely the wrath of man shall praise Thee," &c. In the providence of God, the detested slave became the honoured saviour of nations.

III. **A prisoner is made the ruler over the land.**

1. *Imprisonment as the result of the wickedness of another.* Joseph was imprisoned despite his own virtue, and by reason of the sins of his master's wife. (Gen. xxxix. 7-20.)

2. *Imprisonment painful to the sufferer.* "Whose feet they hurt with fetters; he was laid in iron." Margin, as in the Heb.: "His soul came into iron." P. B. V.: "The iron entered into his soul" is a very expressive rendering, but it is incorrect. Perowne points out that in this verse we have a picture of an imprisonment much more severe "than that given in Gen. xxxix. 20-23, xl. 4. But it may refer to the earlier stage of the imprisonment, before he had won the confidence of his gaoler, or it may be tinged with the colouring of poetry." But even, under the least unfavourable circumstances, imprisonment is painful to an upright man. It is one of the most severe trials to the soul of such a man. Moreover, in the case of Joseph, imprisonment was a trial of his faith. "The word of the Lord tried him." God had promised to the family of which he was a member the possession of Canaan; and to him, in his dreams, exaltation and honour had been promised. So the saying or promise of God is said to try him, because during the years of his suffering and imprisonment it tested his faith and patience. Would God make good His word and raise him to honour? was an inquiry which often pressed itself upon Joseph.

3. *Imprisonment Divinely overruled.* Joseph's imprisonment was overruled by God to promote the accomplishment of purposes the most important and benevolent. The Psalmist mentions (1) *The means by which his release was brought about.* "Until the time that his word came." The "word" is the word of Joseph by which he interpreted to the servants of Pharaoh their dreams in the prison. The verification of his interpretation of the dreams and his release from prison are regarded as cause and effect. (2) *The wisdom which he displayed.* Joseph manifested such wisdom in interpreting the dreams of Pharaoh, and advising him as to the measures to be adopted to provide for the people during the years of famine, that the elders of Egypt were instructed by him. "To teach his senators wisdom," is not to be interpreted that he literally instructed them in the art of politics. He displayed a wisdom superior to theirs, by which they were instructed. (3) *The power with which he was invested.* As a result of the wisdom which he manifested, Pharaoh "made him lord of his house and ruler of all his substance," &c. The administration of the affairs of the kingdom was placed entirely under his control. The most complete authority was given unto him. (Gen. xli. 44.) Wonderful are the changes brought about in the providence of God, and wonderful the means by which they are brought about!

IV. **A subject people growing stronger than a sovereign people.** "He increased His people greatly, and made them stronger than their enemies." (Exod. i. 7-9.) This increase in number and power the Poet attributes to God. The virtues of a godly character promote the growth and progress of a people. We have an illustration in the growth of the Christian provinces of Turkey in Europe, while the dominant Mahommedans are decaying.

CONCLUSION. From these surprises in the outworking of the Divine Providence, let us learn to TRUST GOD amid its mysteries. 1. *Let those who are condemned and suffer wrongfully trust Him.* In due time He will vindicate them, even as He did Joseph. 2. *When the current of events seem opposed to His avowed purposes and promises, let us trust Him.* He oft moves in a way that is mysterious to us. But He will accomplish His purposes and fulfil His promises.

A CRUEL PERSECUTION AND A GLORIOUS EMANCIPATION.

(*Verses 25-38.*)

In these verses the Psalmist gives us a glimpse of—

I. **Israel persecuted in Egypt.** We see here

1. *The root of the persecution.* "He turned their heart to hate His people." The hostility of the Egyptians to the Israelites is here ascribed to God. Now we know that God is not in any sense the author of moral evil. "God is light." Hence the statement of the Psalmist has occasioned much difficulty. The difficulty is of the same kind as when it is said that the Lord hardened the heart of Pharaoh. (See *Homiletic Commentary,* Critical Note, on Exodus vii. 3.) We shall do well to bear in mind three facts. (1) Pharaoh and his people were free in what they did to the Israelites. (2) The Lord manifested His disapprobation of their conduct. (3) Yet, "nothing—not even the human will, free as it is—is independent of God; and not even the worst passions of men are *outside of His plan,* or independent in such a sense that He does not afford the opportunity for their development and display." God so ordered events that the Egyptians became the enemies of His people, and rendered their removal to another land necessary. The goodness of the Lord to the Israelites exasperated the Egyptians against them. "Though God is not the author of the sins of men, yet He serves His own purposes by them." The root of the persecution was the hatred of the Egyptians. The growing number and power of the Israelites aroused the jealousy, suspicion, and hatred of the Egyptians. Hatred is incipient murder.

2. *The manner of the persecution.* "To deal subtilly with his servants." The word which is here rendered "to deal subtilly," in Gen. xxxvii. 18, is rendered "they conspired against." There is a reference to Exod. i. 10: "Come on, let us deal wisely with them, lest they multiply," &c. So, with diabolic cunning and cruelty, the male children were ordered to be slain as soon as they were born, and the burdens of the people were grievously increased. "Malice is crafty to destroy: Satan has the serpent's subtlety with his venom."

II. **Israel emancipated from Egypt.** God listened to the cries of His oppressed people and delivered them. Their emancipation was effected by the Lord God—

1. *By human instruments.* He employed Moses and Aaron to accomplish this great work. They were (1) *Divinely commissioned.* "He sent Moses His servant, Aaron whom He had chosen." They were not popular agitators, but men of distinguished abilities, called of God to a great work. (2) *Divinely authenticated.* "They showed His signs among them, and wonders in the land of Ham." (Comp. Exod. iv. 28, 30; x. 2; Psalm lxxviii. 43.) (3) *Obedient to the Divine commission.* "They rebelled not against His words." At first Moses was unwilling to undertake the mission; but afterwards he and Aaron shrank not from the task, but faithfully performed the bidding of the Lord. Unmoved by fear of Pharaoh, or by pity for his people, they did the work which the Lord committed to them.

2. *By overcoming the most persistent resistance on the part of Pharaoh.* Pharaoh would not obey the Divine command until the Lord had visited him and his people and country with terrible plagues. Verses 28-36. (See *Homiletic Commentary* on Psalm lxxviii. 42-53, and Exod. vii.-xii.)

3. *In circumstances favourable to His people.* They were brought out of Egypt with (1) *Wealth.* "He brought them forth with silver and gold." In Exodus xii. 35 it is said, "They borrowed of the Egyptians jewels of silver and jewels of gold." "Borrowed" is an unhappy rendering, as the word— שָׁאַל—signifies *to penetrate, to ask pressingly, to require, to request, to beg,* &c. (2) *Health.* "There was not one feeble person among their tribes." Perowne: "There was none among their tribes that stumbled." Notwithstanding their afflictions, the people were healthy and hardy when they left Egypt. (3) *Respect.* "Egypt was glad when they departed; for the fear of them fell upon them." The Lord had so pleaded their cause that they were regarded by the Egyptians as under the special protection of God. The Egyptians were afraid of them, and realised a great feeling of relief when they had gone out from amongst them. (4) *Joy.* "He brought forth His people with joy, His chosen with gladness" (verse 43). God exchanged their cry by reason of their burdens, for glad songs by reason of their deliverance.

CONCLUSION. Our subject speaks—
1. *Encouragement to the oppressed.*
2. *Warning to the oppressor.*
3. *Hope for the future of the race.* "The Lord reigneth."

DIVINE BLESSINGS IN HUMAN PILGRIMAGE.

(*Verses* 39–45.)

In these verses the Psalmist briefly refers to the goodness of God to the Israelites in the wilderness, and their inheritance of Canaan, and states the reason why He had so dealt with them, and His purpose in His dealings with them. This portion of the poem may be used as illustrating *the blessings of God in the pilgrimage of human life.* These blessings are—

I. **Adapted to human needs.** The needs of Israel in the wilderness represent the needs of human life. The Divine blessings were adapted to those needs.

1. *Direction.* "He spread a cloud for a covering, and fire to give light in the night." "In the daytime He led them with a cloud, and all the night with a light of fire." See Exodus xiii. 21. "The way of man is not in himself; it is not in man that walketh to direct his steps." "In all thy ways acknowledge Him, and He shall direct thy paths." He does so —(1) *by the teachings of His Word;* (2) *by the influences of His Spirit;* (3) *by the indications of circumstances.*

2. *Protection.* In the burning wilderness the cloud was a protection to the people against the heat of the sun by day; and by night the fire shielded them from the attacks of wild beasts. God is the sure defence of His people. "Who is he that will harm you, if ye be followers of that which is good?"

3. *Provision.* "They asked, and He brought quails, and satisfied them with the bread of heaven. He opened the rock, and the waters gushed out; they ran in the dry places like a river." (On verse 40, see *Homiletic Commentary* on Ps. lxxviii. 24–29; and on verse 41, see *Homiletic Commentary* on Ps. lxxviii. 15, 16.) God provides for His people all needful things for *the body.* Of the righteous the Lord says, "Bread shall be given him, his waters shall be sure." "No good will He withhold from them that walk uprightly." (Matt. vi. 30–32). *Spiritually* His provisions are adapted to all our needs. "As thy days, so shall thy strength be." "My grace is sufficient for thee; for My strength is made perfect in weakness."

4. *Possession.* "He gave them the lands of the heathen, and they inherited the labour of the people." (See *Homiletic Commentary* on Ps. lxxviii. 55.) During the wanderings in the wilderness the Israelites looked forward to the possession of Canaan as the end of their wanderings, their rest and home. A glorious inheritance awaits the good at the end of their pilgrimage,—"an

inheritance incorruptible, and undefiled, and that fadeth not away, is reserved in heaven" for them. This is an inspiration during the pilgrimage, &c.

II. **Adequate to human needs.** "He satisfied them." "The waters ran in the dry places like a river." The Divine provision for the Israelites in the wilderness was abundant. No one lacked anything. Having the Lord with them, they had all-sufficiency. So in the pilgrimage of human life the Divine provisions are adequate to every need. "God shall supply all your need according to His riches in glory by Christ Jesus." "God is able to make all grace abound toward you, that ye, always having all-sufficiency in all things, may abound to every good work." "He is able to do exceeding abundantly above all that we ask or think." His wisdom is adequate to our direction; His wisdom and power to our protection; His resources for our provision, &c.

III. **Guaranteed by Divine faithfulness.** "For He remembered His holy promise, and Abraham His servant." It is said of Israel in Egypt: "And God heard their groaning, and God remembered His covenant with Abraham," &c. (Exodus ii. 24, 25). "Because the Lord loved you, and because He would keep the oath which He had sworn unto your fathers, hath the Lord brought you out with a mighty hand," &c. They were unworthy and unfaithful, but God did these great things for them because of His word to their fathers. The faithful promises of God guarantee to us the blessings we need during our pilgrimage. Harvest may be blighted; fountains may be dried up; all finite resources may fail.

"If this fail,
The pillar'd firmament is rottenness,
And earth's base built on stubble."

IV. **Bestowed for the most worthy purpose.** The end of all God's dealings with the Israelites was "that they might observe His statutes, and keep His laws." His design was that Israel should be a holy nation, representing Him in the world, and claiming the world for Him as His own. The final cause of all the blessings He confers upon His people now is their conformity to His will. We are redeemed, called, guided, guarded, sustained, and animated with hopes of heaven, all with a view to our holiness.

The blessings of God in the pilgrimage of life—

V. **Call for devout praise.** "Praise ye the Lord." He has done, and is ever doing, great things for us; and to Him let us ascribe the praise. Hallelujah!

PSALM CVI.

INTRODUCTION.

"This is the first of a series of Hallelujah Psalms: Psalms of which the word Hallelujah is, as it were, the inscription (cvi., cxi.-cxiii., cxvii., cxxxv., cxlvi.-cl.). As in the last Psalm, so here the history of Israel is recapitulated. In that it was turned into a thanksgiving; in this it forms the burden of a confession. There God's mighty acts for His people were celebrated with joy; here His people's sin is humbly and sorrowfully acknowledged. Nothing is more remarkable in these great historical Psalms than the utter absence of any word or sentiment tending to feed the national vanity. All the glory of Israel's history is confessed to be due, not to her heroes, her priests, her prophets, but to God; all the failures which are written upon that history, all discomfitures, losses, reverses, the sword, famine, exile, are recognised as the righteous chastisement which the sin of the nation has provoked. This is the strain of such Psalms as the 78th, the 105th, the 106th. This is invariably the tone assumed by all the divinely-instructed teachers of the people, by the prophets in their great sermons, by the poets in their contributions to the national liturgy.

"From verse 47 it may be fairly inferred that the Psalm is of the date of the Exile, or was written shortly after the return of the first company of exiles."—*Perowne*.

Hengstenberg: "The situation is described exactly in verses 46 and 47;" and "is that towards the end of the captivity."

The author of the Psalm is not known.

CHARACTERISTICS OF THE BLESSED PEOPLE.

(*Verses* 1-5.)

"The first five verses," says Perowne, "seem to stand alone, and to have little or no direct connection with the rest of the Psalm. . . . The first verse, no doubt, is of the nature of a doxological formula, such as we find in some other of these later Psalms. But the second and third verses have an immediate bearing on what follows. What so fitting to introduce the confession of a nation's sin and ingratitude as the rehearsal of God's goodness manifested to it, and the acknowledgment of the blessedness of those who, instead of despising that goodness, as Israel had done, walked in the ways of the Lord, keeping judgment and doing righteousness (verse 3)? Or, again, what more natural than that the sense of the national privilege, the claim of a personal share in that privilege, should spring in the heart and rise to the lips of one who felt most deeply the national sin and ingratitude?"

We regard these verses as presenting to us certain characteristics of the blessed people.

I. **They are a worshipping people.**

1. *They have exalted views of the Divine greatness and glory.* "Who can utter the mighty acts of the Lord? who can show forth all His praise?" The acts of the Lord are so *many*, so *great*, so *marvellous*, and so *glorious*, that man is unable adequately to celebrate them. "The transcendent greatness of the deeds of God ought not to keep us back from praising Him, but contains in it the strongest motive to praise; the farther off the goal is, the more earnestly must we strive."—*Hengstenberg.*

2. *They appreciate the Divine benefits.* "He is good, His mercy endureth for ever." The goodness here mentioned is not so much the excellence of His own nature, as His gracious dealings with man. The manifestations of His mercy and generosity were so numerous, so constant, so glorious, that the Poet was moved by admiration, and desired to give God the honour of them.

3. *They praise the Divine Being.* "Praise ye the Lord. O give thanks unto the Lord." Worship—the adoration of the Divine excellence, and beneficence, and beauty—is an essential element of the highest blessedness. The true worship of the true God is the heaven of the soul.

II. **They are a righteous people.**

"Blessed are they that keep judgment, and he that doeth righteousness at all times." For moral beings there can be no blessedness except that which is based upon righteousness of principle and of practice. Conscience will not admit of blessedness on any other condition. The Psalmist speaks of *habitual* righteousness. If we would be truly blessed, righteousness must be not an occasional but a constant disposition of heart and rule of conduct. The blessed man is one who "doeth righteousness at all times." Barnes points out that "the Psalm is designed to illustrate *by contrast;* that is, by showing, in the conduct of the Hebrew people, the consequences of *disobedience*, and thus implying what would have been, and what always must be, the consequences of the opposite course."

III. **They are the Lord's people.**

We cannot be truly blessed without a hearty recognition of our true relation to God. When by faith and consecration we are His people, great is our blessedness. Concerning the people of God and their blessedness the Poet indicates—

1. *The source of all their blessings.* "Remember me, O Lord, with the favour of Thy people." All our blessings flow from the unmerited and free "favour" of the Lord.

2. *The sum of all their blessings.* "Oh visit me with Thy salvation." "Salvation" includes pardon for past sin, "grace to help in time of need," and eternal and blessed life.

3. *The result of all their blessings.* (1.) *Gladness to man.* "That I may rejoice in the gladness of Thy nation." The favour of God is joy-inspiring. (2.) *Glory to God.* "That I may glory with Thine inheritance." The people of God

glory not in their wisdom, wealth, or power, but in their relation to Him. In Him they make their boast. To Him they ascribe their praise.

CONCLUSION.—1. *God has a people who are in a special manner His.* 2. *To these people He imparts special blessings.* 3. *Are we of the number of these people?*

THE FAVOUR OF GOD DESIRED.

Verse 4. "Remember me, O Lord, with the favour of Thy people."

I. **That the Lord has a people, who in a different way from others are His.** They are so by adopting love, Rom. ix. 25; by renewing grace, Eph. ii. 10; by voluntary consent, 2 Cor. vii. 5; by public avowal, Isa. xliv. 5; by inward testimony, 1 John v. 19, Rom. viii. 16; by divine appropriation, Zech. xiii. 9, and by open evidence, 2 Cor. iii. 2, 3.

II. **That to these He bears a peculiar and distinguished favour.** While others are the recipients of common mercies, they have blessings of a peculiar and pre-eminent description, so that the congratulation given by Moses to the Israelites is applicable to the Lord's people in every age and place. (Deut. xxxiii. 29.)

III. **That to be remembered of God with this favour is infinitely desirable.** And why is this the case? Because it sweetens the comforts of life; because it quickens us in the performance of duty; because it yields relief in scenes of sorrow and suffering; and because it is the ground of all our hope.

IV. **That those who would have the Divine favour must pray for it.** "God is ready to bestow His favour upon us (1 John iv. 10, Rom. viii. 32), but application on our part must be made (Ezek. xxxvi. 37); and the reasonableness of the duty leaves without excuse those persons who refuse to comply with it. Let us never despise a favour so freely offered, so greatly needed; a favour which may be obtained on terms so easy."—*W. Sleigh.*

THE LORD'S GOODNESS AND MAN'S SIN.

(*Verses 6-12.*)

In these verses the Psalmist begins the confession of the sin of the Israelites as manifested in their history. Let us notice—

I. **Man's sin notwithstanding the Lord's goodness.** Verses 6-8. We have here—

1. *The sins acknowledged.* (1) *Thoughtlessness.* "Our fathers understood not Thy wonders in Egypt." Perowne: "Our fathers in Egypt considered nót," &c. The marvellous and glorious deeds of the Lord in their behalf they saw but did not consider, and therefore did not understand them. "They thought the plagues of Egypt were intended for their deliverance, whereas they were intended also for their instruction and conviction, not only to force them out of their Egyptian slavery, but to cure them of their inclination to Egyptian idolatry, by evidencing the sovereign power and dominion of the God of Israel above all gods, and His particular concern for them."—*M. Henry.* Want of consideration is a sin frequently charged against Israel, and to which men are painfully prone in our own day. We see the Divine wonders, receive the Divine benefits, but do not reflect on their significance, &c. (2) *Forgetfulness.* "They remembered not the multitude of Thy mercies." Although the wonders in Egypt were so many and great, yet they made so small an impression upon the people on whose behalf they were wrought that they were speedily forgotten by them. "Eaten bread is soon forgotten." (3) *Rebellion.* "But provoked Him at the sea, at the Red Sea. Hengstenberg and Perowne translate: "rebelled at the sea." (See Exod. xiv. 10-12.) Notwithstand-

149

ing all the mighty works that had been wrought for their deliverance from Egypt, on the first approach of danger they distrusted the Lord, and, like craven-hearted slaves, they murmured against the servant of the Lord. They distrusted the power, mercy, and faithfulness of God. Observe the *gradation* and *connection* of their sins. Want of reflection upon the mercies of God leads to forgetfulness of those mercies, and forgetfulness of His mercies leads to distrust, &c. Evil is terribly progressive.

2. *The aggravation of their sins.* Many were the "wonders" wrought on their behalf, yet they failed to consider them. The Lord bestowed upon them a "multitude of mercies;" it is sinful to forget one of His loving-kindnesses; yet they forgot a "multitude" of them. The sin of their rebellion also was aggravated by the place in which they were guilty of it. It was "at the Red Sea," directly after their emancipation from Egypt, when the wonders of power and grace which God had wrought for them should have been fresh in their minds, and a powerful inspiration to faith.

3. *The confession of their sins.* "We have sinned with our fathers, we have committed iniquity, we have done wickedly." Here is (1) *A deep sense of great and manifold transgressions.* This is impressively indicated by the three verbs. (2) *A sad successiveness of sin.* "We have sinned with our fathers." The sins of the fathers had been reproduced in the children, generation after generation; so that the nation as a whole was regarded by the Psalmist as guilty before God.

In most of the points which we have touched upon the sins of the Israelites, notwithstanding the goodness of the Lord, represent the sins of the men of our age and country. (Show this, and urge confession).

II. The Lord's goodness notwithstanding man's sin. Verses 8-12. Though the sins of Israel were so aggravated, yet the Lord continued to manifest His mercy to them.

1. *His goodness was displayed in their salvation.* The deliverance here referred to was a very remarkable one. It was (1) A deliverance *from extreme danger*. They were shut in by the mountains, the sea, and the Egyptians. There seemed to be no way of escape. (2) A deliverance *marvellously effected*. A path was opened through the sea, whose waters stood as guardian-walls on either hand of them. (3) A deliverance *effected with the utmost ease*. The Poet represents the sea as "dried up" at the "rebuke" of the Lord. Nature is thoroughly loyal to the Divine will. (4) A deliverance *gloriously complete*. Israel not only crossed over in safety, but "the waters covered their enemies, there was not one of them left."

2. *His goodness was displayed for His own glory.* "He saved them for His Name's sake, that He might make His mighty power to be known." Notwithstanding their offences He saved them because of what He is in Himself, —a being of unchanging truth and mercy; and that the glory of His power might be manifested.

3. *The display of His goodness awoke them to a transient exercise of faith and praise.* "Then believed they His words; they sang His praise." (See Exod. xiv. 31; xv. 1.) For a time distrust gave place to faith, and murmuring to praise. But it was only for a little time; for "both the faith and the song are mentioned, not in praise of their conduct, but only as still further proof that whatever impressions were produced, whether by God's judgments or His mercies, were but temporary and on the surface. The goodness of Israel was like the dew, early gone."— *Perowne.*

CONCLUSION.—This scene from Hebrew history presents to us (1) *Admonition.* Let us not sin against that Being who is ever manifesting so much goodness to us. (2) *Encouragement.* God does not "deal with us after our sins," &c.

Sin in its Root, Expressions, and Punishments.

(Verses 13–23.)

We now come to the confession of the transgressions of the Israelites in the wilderness ; and in the verses now before us three of their offences are mentioned. As the Homiletic suggestions arising out of these sins and their punishments will be brought out in treating of their history as recorded in Exodus and Numbers, we shall simply deal with the points suggested by the Psalmist.

I. Sin in its root. "They soon forgat His works . . . They forgat God their Saviour, which had done great things in Egypt ; wondrous things in the land of Ham ; terrible things by the Red Sea." (See our remarks on verse 7, and on Ps. lxxviii. 11, 12.) The small impression which the greatest mercies and most marvellous deliverances made upon them is astonishing. Bad as men are, it is not often that favours so extraordinary are forgotten so quickly. "They made haste, they forgat His works." They, as it were, manifested impatience to rid themselves of the recollection of His glorious deeds wrought for them. Even the mighty miracles in Egypt and at the Red Sea passed away from them as tales that were told. Had they retained in their mind the great things which God had done for them, they would have had in these things such a revelation of His character as would have precluded the committal of their offences against Him. Forgetfulness of deeds of marvellous mercy and power wrought on their behalf, and of Him who wrought them, was the root from which their base rebellion sprang.

II. Sin in its expressions. From the root of forgetfulness of God there sprang up some base and pernicious branches. Here are three heinous sins—

1. *Their sin as regards the Divine provision.* "They waited not for His counsel ; but lusted exceedingly in the wilderness," &c. "They were not content," says Perowne, "to exercise a patient dependence upon God, leaving it to Him to fulfil His own purposes in His own way, but would rather rule Him than submit themselves to His rule." (See *Homiletic Commentary* on Ps. lxxviii. 17, 18.)

2. *Their sin as regards the Divinely-appointed leaders.* "They envied Moses also in the camp, and Aaron the saint of the Lord." (Num. xvi. 1–3.) The reference in this place is rather to the rebellion which resulted from the envy, than to the envy itself. Aaron is denominated "the saint," or "the holy one of Jehovah," because of his priestly office. It is an official, not a personal designation. The leaders of the insurrection claimed that the whole congregation was "holy," that they were all set apart and consecrated, and were therefore on an equality with Moses and Aaron. Rebellion against the Divinely-appointed leaders was equivalent to rebellion against Him who appointed them.

3. *Their sin as regards the Divine Person.* "They made a calf in Horeb, and worshipped the molten image. Thus they changed their glory into the similitude of an ox that eateth grass." (Exod. xxxii.) "*They made*—contrary to the prohibition in Exod. xx. 4, 5—*a calf*, intended to represent an ox (comp. verse 20). They would gladly have made an ox, but they were not able to get this length, so contemptible was the whole undertaking. The name 'calf' is everywhere used in contempt; the worshippers without doubt called it a bull; according to Philo they made 'a golden bull.'"—*Hengstenberg.* "Their glory" was the Lord God, and they changed Him for the likeness "of an ox that eateth grass." (Comp. Rom. i. 23.) The intention of the people was to worship God under the symbol of the calf, but as this symbolising was utterly incompatible with the nature of Jehovah, and opposed to His express command, it was regarded by God as bartering Him for the image, the renunciation of Jehovah for the model of a calf. Miserable and terribly

sinful absurdity to exchange the Lord of heaven and earth for a calf-like model of a grass-eating ox! The sin which began in forgetfulness of God ended in idolatry. The development of evil is from bad to worse, and is sometimes fearfully rapid.

II. Sin in its punishments. We have here—

1. *Punishment corresponding with sin.* (On the punishment of those who lusted for flesh in the wilderness see *Homiletic Commentary* on Ps. lxxviii. 30, 31). "He gave them their request, but sent leanness into their soul." The "soul" here means the animal soul, the physical life. The Lord gratified their sinful desire, and in so doing and by the same means punished their sin; for they ate until there came on a wasting sickness which led to alarming mortality. But although the "soul" is here used with its physical meaning, "the figurative sense is equally true, and equally pertinent. The very heart and spirit of a man, when bent only or supremely on the satisfaction of its earthly desires and appetites, is always dried up and withered. It becomes a lean, shrunk, miserable thing, always craving more food, yet drawing thence no nourishment, '*magnas inter opes inops.*'"—*Perowne.*

"Heaven is most just, and of our pleasant vices
Makes instruments to scourge us."
—*Shakespeare.*

In the rebellion against Moses and Aaron we note a correspondence between the sin and its punishment. In the rebellion against Moses, who was the ruler in all affairs of state, "Dathan and Abiram, as princes of the tribe of Reuben, Jacob's eldest son, would claim to be chief magistrates, by the so-much-admired right of primogeniture." And for rebelling against "the civil authority they were punished by *the earth,* which *opened and swallowed them up,* as not fit to go upon God's ground, because they would not submit to God's government."—*M. Henry.* In the rebellion against Aaron, which took place among the Levites and was headed by Korah, "a fire was kindled in their company, a flame burnt up the wicked." "These had *sinned* by fire and were *punished* by fire like the sons of Aaron" (Lev. x. 2). (Comp. Num. xvi. 1–35.)

2. *Punishment averted by intercession.* When the people made and worshipped the golden calf, God "said that He would destroy them, had not Moses His chosen stood before Him in the breach, to turn away His wrath, lest He should destroy them." Moses is here compared to a brave soldier who, when a breach has been made in the walls of the fortress which he is defending, plants himself in the breach, and so keeps back the invaders. (Comp. Exod. xxxii. 11–14.) God would have destroyed the people, if Moses had not interposed and interceded for them. See here—

1. *The power of prayer.*
2. *The greatness of the Divine mercy.*
3. *An illustration of the intercession of Christ for our race.*

FORGETFULNESS OF THE DIVINE WORKS.

(*Verse 13.*—"But they soon forgot His works.")

I. That the works of God are supremely worthy of an attentive review, and a thankful remembrance.

1. *What did they forget?* His works. Review all their variety—the creation, the appointment of a salvation, the work of redemption, the works of Providence; they are to be considered in their peculiar aspect, whether prosperous or adverse. Review their multitude; they are to be considered in their meaning. Providence is our daily preacher.

2. *What sort of recollection should it be?* Not a mere notional recollection—a recollection accompanied with suitable emotions—astonishment, gratitude, love, and heartfelt consideration. It must be a devotional and practical recollection.

3. *Why are these works to be remembered?* Because they are God's works; because they are all-important; because

the least of them is the purchase of infinite price.

II. **That there is in human nature a strange tendency to forget the works of God.**
This is no calumny on human nature. It is the express statement of Scripture, and is confirmed by daily experience. It arises from—
1. *The injury the memory has sustained by the Fall :* it retains what is impure, but not what is holy.
2. *The bias of our mind is directed to earthly things.*
3. *The secret disinclination to contemplate a subject in which God is intimately concerned.*

III. **The sinfulness and danger of thus forgetting the works of God.**
1. *It arises out of a sinful state of mind, and it is culpable forgetfulness.*
2. *It is an actual transgression of God's Word.* (Deut. iv. 9 ; 1 Chron. xvi. 12.)
3. *It involves in it the commission of other sins*—inconsideration and ingratitude.
4. *They who forget their mercies forfeit them.*

5. *God has denounced fearful judgments on such.* (Ps. ix. 17.)

IV. **What are the best means of preserving in our minds a grateful sense of the Divine goodness ?**
1. *Seek that you be renewed and sanctified.*
2. *Attention will much assist in the recollection of mercies.* (Prov. iv. 20.)
3. *Meditation* cannot be done in a crowd ; then *seek solitude.*
4. *Order and arrangement* are like cells in which our mercies may be deposited and called out in order.
5. *Strive to maintain lively affections towards God ;* for what we love we do not easily forget.

LESSONS : 1. How mistaken are those who suppose that forgetfulness is not a sin !
2. Here a wide field is opened for the exercise of repentance.
3. Reprove those who have a good memory for their calamities and a bad one for their mercies.
4. Address those who will not recollect. God will not forget.—*George Clayton.*—From " *The Homiletic Quarterly.*"

THE GRANTING OF SELFISH DESIRES AN INJURY TO THE SOUL.

(*Verse* 15.)

The history of the event referred to is given in Num. xi.

I. **Many things which are good in themselves may not be good for us individually.** Material wealth is good ; but upon attaining it some men have become spiritually bankrupt. (Luke xii. 15-21.) Popularity may be a good thing ; but, having gained it, many a man has lost his integrity, independence, heroism. *How this view of things corrects the prevalent notion of success in life ! " Success in life," says the world, " is getting on in business, making money quickly, living well " (by which is meant eating and drinking luxuriously), " mixing in good society." How shallow, false, ruinous ! These things may not only consist with spiritual poverty, imbecility, and ruin, but very frequently lead to them.

II. **Many things may be good for us at one time and under certain circumstances which may not be good for us at another time and under other circumstances.** The flesh which the Israelites desired would have been good for them when they arrived in Canaan ; but in the wilderness, where they should have been satisfied with the Divinely-provided manna, it proved a terrible curse.

III. **The most fervent prayers are not always most acceptable.** The motive and the character of the fervour must be taken into consideration. Fervent prayers are sometimes only the passionate cries of selfish hearts—the determined pursuit of an object of selfish desire.

IV. **God may grant the passionate desire of a selfish heart with terrible**

153

results. He may give the fancied good which is so eagerly demanded, and it may prove to be a direful injury. It was so in the case before us. Instances are numerous in which unsubmissive requests have been granted with most painful results.

V. **God may refuse to grant the request of even a good man, and the refusal may be a blessing.** It was in love that the Lord refused the repeated request of St. Paul for the removal of the "thorn in the flesh." That torturing thorn was the means of preventing the spiritual pride which might otherwise have effected his overthrow. (1 Cor. xii. 7-9.)

"We, ignorant of ourselves,
Beg often our own harms, which the wise powers
Deny us for our good; so find we profit
By losing of our prayers."—*Shakespeare.*

VI. **The wisest, holiest, most acceptable prayer is for conformity with the will of God.** "Not my will, but Thine be done," expresses the true spirit of acceptable prayer.

"Covet earnestly the best gifts." Seek those things which are pure blessings for all persons, at all times and under all circumstances.

A SAD PICTURE OF HUMAN PERVERSITY.

(*Verses* 24-27.)

The sinful perversity of the Israelites appears here in several mournful aspects.

I. **Despising the choicest inheritance.** "They despised the pleasant land." Margin: "A land of desire." Perowne: "They rejected the desirable land." (Deut. viii. 7-9; xi. 9.) The Israelites frequently manifested a desire to return to Egypt. The good land before them had few attractions for them. God calls men to holiness, communion with Himself, heaven. All who do not heartily respond to His call despise the most glorious inheritance.

II. **Disbelieving the best authenticated word.** "They believed not His word." They had proved the reliableness of the word of God; yet they did not believe it as regards the land which He had promised to them. They preferred to accept the testimony of the unbelieving and cowardly spies. (Num. xiv. 1-6, 10.) We have here—

1. *Unbelief dishonouring God.*
2. *Unbelief excluding man from his inheritance.* Man's unbelief has kept him out of many "a good land."

III. **Murmuring against the arrangements of the wisest and kindest of beings.** They "murmured in their tents." This they did repeatedly. (Num. xiv. 2, 3, 27.) "They complained of Moses, of their food, of the hardships of their journey, of God. They did this when 'in their tents;' when they had a comfortable home; when safe; when provided for; when under the direct Divine protection and care. So men often complain; perhaps oftener when they have *many* comforts than when they have *few.*"—*Barnes.*

IV. **Disobeying the commands of the most sovereign authority.** "They hearkened not unto the voice of the Lord." Unbelief of God's word speedily leads to refusal to listen to His voice and disregard of His commands. They disobeyed their Creator, Sustainer, Sovereign, and generous Benefactor — not only the greatest, but the best being. His will is supremely binding. Yet they disobeyed it.

V. **Receiving deserved punishment.** "Therefore He lifted up His hand against them, to overthrow them in the wilderness." The lifting up of the hand is the gesture of swearing. "Ye shall not come into the land which I lifted up My hand to make you dwell therein" (Num. xiv. 30). "I lifted up My hand also to them in the wilderness," &c. (Ezek. xx. 23). "I sware in My wrath, They shall not enter into My rest." It is fitting that they who despise their inheritance shall not enter upon it.

VI. **Entailing misery upon their posterity.** "He lifted up His hand to overthrow their seed also among the nations, and to scatter them in the lands." "The result of their rebellion and murmuring would not terminate with them. It would extend to their posterity, and the rebellion of the fathers would be remembered in distant generations. The overthrow of the nation, and its captivity in Babylon, was thus one of the remote consequences of their rebellion in the wilderness."—*Barnes.*

CONCLUSION. 1. *Shun sin; for by committing it you may hand down to your descendants a heritage of woe.* 2. " *Take heed, brethren, lest there be in any of you an evil heart of unbelief,*" &c. (Heb. iii. 12; iv. 1 and 11).

PASSAGES FROM THE HISTORY OF A REBELLIOUS PEOPLE.

(*Verses* 28-33.)

The heart grows weary and sad as we follow this narrative with its abounding unbelief, ingratitude, meanness, and rebellion. The picture which the Poet draws of Israel is painfully sombre, yet it is true. In no portion of it has he inserted too much shadow. We have in these verses—

I. An incorrigibly rebellious people.

1. *Here is idolatry.* "They joined themselves also unto Baal-Peor, and ate the sacrifices of the dead." "Baal was the name of an idol; Peor was the name of a mountain in Moab where the idol was worshipped." "The sacrifices of the dead" are the sacrifices offered to idols, in contradistinction from the living God (Num. xxv. 1-3).

2. *Here is adultery.* The worship of Baal-Peor was connected with licentious rites. Fuerst: "*Baal of the shame uncovering,* in whose honour virgins yielded up their innocence." (Num. xxv. 1-6.)

3. *Here is rebellious murmuring.* "They angered Him also at the Waters of Strife" (Num. xx. 1-5, 13). Here in the fortieth year of their wandering they are still an unbelieving, complaining, rebellious people.

II. A brave man acting as minister of justice in a critical time. "Then stood up Phinehas and executed judgment, and so the plague was stayed" (Num. xxv. 5-8).

1. *Here is a brave act of justice.* Moses had commanded the judges of Israel to stay the idolaters; but they seemed to have been deficient in the strength and courage necessary to enable them to obey the command; they only stand and weep. At this critical moment, with zeal and courage and energy, Phinehas rose up and slew two of the offenders of the first rank.

2. *A brave act of justice staying the Divine vengeance.* "And so the plague was stayed." This act of justice was propitiatory; it appeased and turned away the wrath of God. "National justice prevents national judgments."

3. *A brave act of justice recognised and rewarded by God.* "And that was counted unto him for righteousness unto all generations for evermore" (Num. xxv. 10-13). Perowne says: "It was looked upon as a righteous act, and rewarded accordingly. . . . This verse has given occasion to whole disquisitions on the subject of justification, with which it really has nothing to do, though at least the language is in perfect accordance with that of St. James (ii. 20-26). The reward of this righteousness was the perpetual continuance of the priesthood in the family." Hereafter the position of Phinehas and his posterity was one of marked distinction and honour.

III. A holy man sinning and suffering by reason of the sin of others. "It went ill with Moses for their sakes; because they provoked his spirit, so that he spake unadvisedly with his lips." Through the sin of the people Moses lost his self-control, was betrayed into the utterance of unbecoming and rash words, and to undue assumption of power; and in consequence was not permitted to enter the promised land. (Num. xx. 7-12.)

1. *Their provocation of Moses agravated the guilt of the rebellious people.*

2. *Their provocation does not exonerate*

Moses from guilt. Provocation is not compulsion.

3. *God punishes sin even in the best of men, in whom it is a great exception.*

IV. The great God contending against human sin.

1. *By the plague, because of the idolatry and licentiousness of the people.* "The plague brake in upon them." "Those that died in the plague were twenty and four thousand."

2. *By the exclusion of Moses from the promised land.* God is the determined antagonist of moral evil. The arrangements of the material universe, the workings of Providence, and the grand aim of redemption, are all utterly hostile to sin. The voice of God to man concerning sin in all history is, "Oh, do not this abominable thing which I hate!" From the cross of the Lord Jesus Christ He utters this entreaty in a manner that ought to arrest the attention and secure the compliance of all men. Let us listen to His voice, and heartily strive to comply with His entreaty.

SIN IN ITS PROGRESS, POLLUTION, AND PUNISHMENT.
(Verses 34-43.)

In these verses we have—

I. Sin in its progress. Here is—

1. *Disobedience.* "They did not destroy the nations concerning whom the Lord commanded them." (For the command and its reasons see *Homiletic Commentary* on Exod. xxiii. 27-33; xxxiv. 11-16; Num. xxxiii. 50-56.) Though the command was express, solemn, and repeatedly proclaimed, yet they did not obey it by driving out or destroying the Canaanites.

2. *Evil associations.* They "were mingled among the heathen and learned their works." By intermarriage and commerce they became mixed up among the Canaanites, and conformed to their evil customs and practices. Had they not first been guilty of disobedience, they could not have been guilty of entering into these prohibited and evil associations.

3. *Idolatry.* "They served their idols, which were a snare unto them" (Judg. ii. 11-13). God had warned them that, if they did not drive out the Canaanites, they would be snared by them and drawn into their idolatrous customs. And this result very speedily appeared.

4. *Offering human sacrifices.* "Yea, they sacrificed their sons and their daughters unto devils, and shed innocent blood," &c. Hengstenberg: "And offered their sons and their daughters to the lords." Perowne: "And they sacrificed their sons and their daughters to false gods." Heb. שֵׁדִים = lords; it is here used to designate the gods of the Canaanites. God had strictly prohibited the offering of these sacrifices (Deut. xii. 29-32; xviii. 10). Yet they offered them, thus adding to their idolatry the most unnatural and horrible murder. Now, mark their *progress* in evil. "The way of sin," says Matthew Henry, "is down hill; omissions make way for commissions; when they neglect to destroy the heathen, the next news we hear is, 'They were mingled among the heathen, made leagues with them, and contracted an intimacy with them, so that they learned their works.' . . . The beginning of idolatry and superstition, like that of strife, is as the letting forth of water, and there is no villany which those that venture upon it can be sure they shall stop short of, for God justly gives them up to a reprobate mind." Avoid the first step in evil courses.

These sins are still flourishing in different forms. The professed people of God are still guilty of disobedience in many things, and of conformity to the world in many customs that are questionable, and in some which are unmistakably evil; they are often found bowing at the shrines of mammon and fashion, and still they sacrifice their sons and daughters to idols. "Among us such sacrifices take place by careless bringing up of children, when parents encourage them, for example, in pride and other sins, offer them to the god of the world, carefully inculcate the maxims of the world, and fill them with love of vanity and show."—*Berleb.*

II. Sin in its pollution. "The land was polluted with blood. Thus were they defiled with their own works, and went a whoring after their own inventions." The very soil itself is here represented as polluted and accursed by reason of the sin of the people. The religious practices which they had adopted became a source of terrible contamination and corruption to their nature. Their very worship was spiritual whoredom. This corrupting tendency of sin is one of its most fearful characteristics. It effects a terrible deterioration in man's moral and religious nature.

III. Sin in its punishment. Verses 40-43.

1. *Their punishment was long delayed.* "Many times did He deliver them." The reference is to the deliverances effected on their behalf during the time of the judges, and afterwards during the time of the kings. Judges ii. 11-19 furnishes a clear exposition of verse 43. The Lord was loath to leave them in the hands of their enemies, or to send them into captivity. He is "slow to anger, and plenteous in mercy. He hath not dealt with us after our sins, nor rewarded us according to our iniquities."

2. *Their punishment was an expression of Divine anger.* "Therefore was the wrath of the Lord kindled against His people, insomuch that He abhorred His own inheritance." God's anger burns against sin and against the workers of iniquity. God pities the sinner as a man, and seeks to save him, but as a worker of iniquity He abhors him. Sin persisted in renders the people of God an offence and abomination unto Him. Nothing shows the enormity of sin more than this, that it renders those who were once well-pleasing in His sight loathsome unto Him.

3. *Their punishment corresponded with their sin.* "He gave them into the hand of the heathen," &c. (verses 41, 42). This punishment the Lord had threatened them with if they failed to drive out the Canaanites. (Num. xxxiii. 55, 56.) And it came to pass according to His word. Their punishment grew out of their sin, and was its natural result. In opposition to the will of God, they intermingled with the heathen and adopted their worst customs; and, after long forbearance and many deliverances, God at length abandoned them to the heathen, who led them into captivity, and tyrannically lorded it over them. They had forsaken the Lord, and given their hearts to heathen customs, and after "long patience" the Lord forsook them, leaving them to the heathens, whose ways they so much admired. "Sinners often see themselves ruined by those by whom they have suffered themselves to be debauched. Satan, who is a tempter, will be a tormentor. The heathen 'hated them.' Apostates lose all the love on God's side, and get none on Satan's." Thus a man's punishment is not a something tacked on to his sin, but ever grows out of his sin. The wicked man collects the fuel for his own hell-fire.

CONCLUSION. The chief Lessons of our subject are:—(1) *Do not enter upon an evil course.* (2) *If any one find himself already in the way of evil, let him retrace his steps at once.* "Let the wicked forsake his way," &c. (3) *The surest means of guarding against evil courses is to walk diligently in the way prescribed by God.* He will give us wisdom and strength so to do, if we ask Him.

STAGES FROM MISERY TO EXULTATION.

(*Verses 44-47.*)

The Poet now presents to us another aspect of the dealings of the Lord with His people. He visited them in anger, because of their ungodly counsels and iniquitous practices. But He never forgets His loving-kindness and His truth concerning them. Soon as their sufferings led them to cry unto Him, He sent them relief. The Psalmist indicates the stages from misery to exultation.

I. **Misery leading to a cry for mercy.** "He heard their cry." In their prosperity they had forgotten the Lord, had forsaken Him for idols. In their misery they cried to Him for relief. This is common. Sometimes the cry is the utterance of mere *selfishness*. In this case, when the suffering is removed, men pursue their old course of ingratitude and rebellion. Sometimes the cry is the utterance of *penitence*. In this case the sin which caused the suffering is felt more keenly than any outward affliction. Reformation of life is the result. In the former case the cry is worthless and mean; in the latter it indicates that suffering has led to gracious results.

II. **A cry for mercy securing the Divine regard.** "He regarded their affliction when He heard their cry."

1. *God heard their cry.* The cry of distress, the sigh of unutterable sorrow, the whispered longing of the heart, the reverent prayer of devout worship, all are heard by God. This is a fact fraught with consolation, inspiration, and strength.

2. *God graciously regarded their cry.* "He remembered for them His covenant, and repented according to the multitude of His mercies." Perowne: "And pitied them according to the greatness of His loving-kindness." "God's repentance is not a change of His will, but of His work. Repentance with man is the changing of his will; repentance with God is the willing of a change. *Mutatio rei, non Dei; effectus, non affectus; facti, non consilii.*" In answer to their cry the Lord turned to them in mercy. Man may forget Him, but He never forgets His covenant. Great is the sin of man; but the mercy of God is incomparably greater. The reason of His loving-kindness to the Jews, and to all men, is to be found in the perfections of His own nature.

III. **The Divine regard securing relief from trouble.** "He made them also to be pitied of all those that carried them captive." Notice here—

1. *The power of God over all men.* He made the hearts of the oppressors of His people to relent towards them, so that they treated them with kindness. "The king's heart is in the hand of the Lord, as the rivers of water: He turneth it whithersoever He will." Even so can He turn the hearts of all men.

2. *The kindness of God to His people.* He influenced the hearts of their oppressors in their favour. He employs His power to promote the interests of His Church.

IV. **Relief from trouble awakening prayer for complete salvation.** "Save us, O Lord our God, and gather us from among the heathen," &c. "The grace of God, already shown to His people," says Perowne, "leads to the prayer of this verse—a supplication for which the whole Psalm has prepared the way. The language would seem to indicate that the Psalm was written in exile, though the same prayer might also have been uttered by one of those who returned in the first caravan, on behalf of his brethren who were still dispersed."

1. *The beginning of the work of Divine grace is an encouragement to expect and pray for full salvation.*

2. *The Divine praise should ever be regarded as the grand end of salvation.* The glory of redemption is due wholly and solely to God in Christ.

DOXOLOGY.

(*Verse* 48.)

This Doxology marks the close of the fourth book of the Psalms. For its Homiletic suggestions see a Sketch on the Doxology to the first book, Psalm xli. 13; on that to the second book, Psalm lxxii. 18–20; and on that to the third book, Psalm lxxxix. 52.

PSALM CVII.

INTRODUCTION.

Many expositors are of opinion that this Psalm was written to celebrate the return of the Jews from the Babylonian exile. This opinion is based chiefly on verses 2 and 3. But the Psalm as a whole does not seem to us to favour such a conclusion. Perowne says: "It is obvious that this Psalm is not historical. It describes various incidents of human life, it tells of the perils which befall men, and the goodness of God in delivering them, and calls upon all who have experienced His care and protection gratefully to acknowledge them; and it is perfectly general in its character. The four or five groups, or pictures, are so many samples taken from the broad and varied record of human experience. Such a Psalm would have been admirably adapted to be sung in the Temple-worship, at the offering of the thank-offerings.

"But, whatever may have been the circumstances under which the Psalm was written, or the particular occasion for which it was intended, there can be no doubt as to the great lesson which it inculcates. It teaches us not only that God's Providence watches over men, but that His ear is open to their prayer. It teaches us that prayer may be put up for temporal deliverance, and that such prayer is answered. It teaches us that it is right to acknowledge with thanksgiving such answers to our petitions. This was the simple faith of the Hebrew Poet."

The author of the Psalm is not known.

DISTRESSED TRAVELLERS AND THEIR DIVINE HELPER.

(*Verses* 1-9.)

It is probable, as Perowne suggests, that the first three verses are "a liturgical addition, framed with particular reference to the return from Babylon, and prefixed to a poem originally designed to have a wider scope." The Psalm begins with the same liturgical formula as the preceding; and the Poet proceeds to represent the people of God as—

1. *Redeemed by Him.* "Let the redeemed of the Lord say so, whom He hath redeemed from the hand of the enemy." The allusion is probably to the deliverance of the Jews from the captivity in Babylon. The people of God now are redeemed from sin by the precious blood of Christ. They have had precious experiences of the goodness of the Lord, and are under special obligations to praise Him.

2. *Gathered by Him.* "Gathered them out of the lands from the east, and from the west, from the north, and from the south." The Lord gathered the exiles out of all the lands into which they had been driven in the day of their distress. He gathers men now into His Church. And He is gathering His people to their home in heaven. From all lands they are being assembled in our Father's home on high.

Then the Poet proceeds to represent the people as distressed travellers, relieved by Divine goodness, and calls upon them to praise the Lord. Consider—

I. **The distressed travellers.** "They wandered in the wilderness," &c.

1. *They were travellers through a pathless desert.* "They wandered in the wilderness in a solitary way." "A solitary way" is not a correct translation. Perowne: "In a pathless waste." Hengstenberg: "The pathless desert." A wilderness is a scene of dreary desolation; and in this case the travellers are represented as having no path along which to travel through this dreary desert. The track is lost, perhaps obliterated by some violent sand-storm.

2. *They were travellers through a homeless desert.* "They found no city to dwell in." There were no habitable places in the wilderness through which they journeyed.

3. *They were travellers through an inhospitable desert.* "Hungry and thirsty, their soul fainted in them." Their life was faint and exhausted by reason of hunger and thirst. We have here a picture of the pilgrimage of life. Apart from Divine guidance, man is a traveller who has lost his way; the track is clean gone; he is perplexed, bewildered. In this world there is no place of settled residence for man.

"Here we have no continuing city, but we seek one to come." And unless man look to God for support, he will find in this world nothing to sustain his spiritual nature, nothing to satisfy the hunger and thirst of the soul.

II. **The all-sufficient Helper.** The Lord interposed in their need, and delivered them from all their distresses.

1. *The Divine help was granted in answer to prayer.* "Then they cried unto the Lord in their trouble, and He delivered them out of their distresses." Perowne: "So it ever is: only the pressure of a great need forces men to seek God. Prayer is not only the resource of good men, but of all men in trouble. It is a natural instinct even of wicked men to turn to God at such times." The fact that all men thus cry to God in their distresses implies—Faith (1) in the *existence* of God; "that He is." (2) In His *power to help* His creatures; that He is able to relieve the distressed. (3) In His *regard* for His creatures; that He is interested in their welfare. (4) In His *accessibleness* to His creatures; that they may approach Him in prayer; "that He is a Rewarder of them that diligently seek Him." Prayer is a great and glorious reality. There is ONE who hears and answers prayer.

2. *The Divine help was adequate to their need.* They were in a "pathless desert," and He granted to them *direction,* guidance. "He led them forth by the right way." They were in a homeless desert, and He *directed them homeward.* "He led them forth by the right way, that they might go to a city of habitation." They were fainting in an inhospitable desert, and He gave them *abundant provision.* "For He satisfieth the longing soul, and filleth the hungry soul with goodness." Both the hunger and the thirst He effectually relieves. And still for all who seek Him there is all-sufficient help in Him. He is the infallible Guide through life. His smile transforms a barren wilderness into a richly provided banqueting house. And he has prepared for us a home, peaceful and permanent, beautiful and blessed.

III. **The manifest obligation.** "Oh that men would praise the Lord for His goodness, and for His wonderful works to the children of men."

1. *God's gracious doings for man are wonderful.* "His goodness, and His wonderful works to the children of men." They are wonderful *in themselves,* and in *their object.* "The children of men" are unworthy of the least of His favours. Yet He guides them, sustains them, &c.

2. *Men are prone to overlook the gracious doings of God for them.* His mercies often "lie

> Forgotten in unthankfulness,
> And without praises die."

Men have to be urged to the celebration of the praise of their Divine Benefactor. "Oh that men would," &c.

3. *Men are under the most sacred obligation to celebrate the gracious doings of God for them.* God rightly expects that those who receive His mercy will celebrate His praise. He requires this. Gratitude urges to this. Not to thank Him is to manifest extreme baseness.

> "The stall-fed ox, that is grown fat, will know
> His careless feeder, and acknowledge too;
> The generous spaniel loves his master's eye,
> And licks his fingers though no meat be by;
> But man, ungrateful man, that's born and bred
> By Heaven's immediate power; maintained and fed
> By His providing hand; observed, attended,
> By His indulgent grace; preserved, defended
> By His prevailing arm: this man, I say,
> Is more ungrateful, more obdure than they.
> Man, O most ungrateful man, can ever
> Enjoy Thy gift, but never mind the Giver;
> And like the swine, though pampered with enough,
> His eyes are never higher than the trough!"
> —*F. Quarles.*

THE WAY OF THE REDEEMED.

(*Verse* 7. "He led them forth by the right way.")

I. **The way of the redeemed.** 1. Long. 2. Difficult. 3. Lonely. 4. A desert way.

II. **The rectitude of the way.** It is the "right way." Consider—1. That *it is the Divine way.* "He led them forth" as a shepherd his flock. 2. *To what it leads.* "The city of habitation." *Two lessons.* 1. Take an enlarged view of the Divine conduct. Think of the goal, as well as of the way which leads to it. The way is painful; but consider why you are called to tread it. Remember the *end* of it all. 2. Ever seek the Divine guidance. God goes before; follow, trust Him.—W. M., in *The Pulpit Analyst.*

THE AFFLICTED CAPTIVES AND THEIR GLORIOUS EMANCIPATOR.

(*Verses* 10–16.)

We have in these verses—

I. **The picture of a painful captivity.** "Such as sit in darkness and in the shadow of death, being bound in affliction and iron." The Poet represents the captivity as characterised by—

1. *Distress.* They "sit in darkness." The dark prison-house is an emblem of misery. To the patriotic and pious Jews the Babylonian Captivity was a source of much trouble and distress.

2. *Apprehension.* "In the shadow of death." Death seemed to stand fully disclosed to their view, and to cast his chilling and fearful shadow upon them. The captives, in their distress, were as men constantly menaced by death.

3. *Painful restriction.* "Bound in affliction and iron." The captives were not literally bound thus; but their distress seemed to them like that of the man who is held in iron fetters.

The most terrible captivity is moral—the bondage of sin. The wicked man is in darkness; the beauties of the spiritual universe—of truth, righteousness, love,—he sees not. "The second death" projects its dread shadow over him. He is the slave of sinful appetites, habits, and passions; is "holden with the cords of his sins." Physical captivity is a calamity; moral captivity is a crime. Death will terminate the former; it has no power to affect the latter. The man who dies in sin enters eternity a manacled slave.

II. **The reason of this painful captivity.** "Because they rebelled against the words of God, and contemned the counsel of the Most High." "The words of God" are His commands delivered unto them in His law, and by His servants the prophets. "The counsel of the Most High" is the advice which was given to them by the prophets of the Lord. Their painful captivity was the result of their wilful disobedience. The Poet in this verse exhibits sin in two aspects—

1. *Sin in its guilt.* It is rebellion against the authority of the greatest and holiest Being—the Supreme Being.

2. *Sin in its folly.* It is the rejection of the counsel of the wisest and kindest Being. "God will *command* nothing which He would not *advise*, and which it would not be *wisdom* to obey."

III. **The design of this painful captivity.** "He brought down their heart with labour; they fell down, and there was none to help." Their heart had proudly risen up in rebellion against God and contempt of His counsel, and their captivity was designed by its sufferings to subdue their pride. עָמָל here rendered "labour," signifies also affliction, trouble. God sought to humble them for their sins, to show them their own helplessness, and that their strength and succour were in Him alone. Afflictions are teachers. The man who is not altogether foolish, when visited by them, will strive to ascertain and appropriate the lessons which they have to impart.

IV. **The deliverance from this painful captivity—**

1. *Was effected in answer to prayer.* "Then they cried unto the Lord," &c. (See remarks on ver. 6.)

2. *Was effected by the Lord.* "HE brought them out," &c. "HE hath broken the gates," &c. In the deliverance of the Jews from Babylon, the hand of the Lord was clearly displayed. Our Lord proclaims liberty to the captives of evil, and the opening of the prison to them that are bound by sin. There is no power in the universe, but that of God

in Christ Jesus, that can emancipate the slaves of sin.

3. *Was gloriously complete.* "He brought them out of darkness and the shadow of death, and brake their bands in sunder. He hath broken the gates of brass, and cut the bars of iron in sunder." The delivery was as great as the distress. "'The gates of brass' refer probably to Babylon; and the idea is that their deliverance had been as if the brazen gates of that great city had been broken down to give them free egress from their captivity." (Comp. Isa. xlv. 2.) The Poet mentions three features of their deliverance, which taken together strikingly exhibit its completeness. Their fetters were riven asunder, they were brought out of their cold and gloomy prison, and the city gates were broken down, so that they could go forth entirely from the land of their captivity.

4. *Demanded grateful acknowledgment.* "Oh, that men would praise the Lord," &c. (See remarks on ver. 8.)

CONCLUSION.—This subject has a practical and urgent application to all moral captives, all slaves of sin. Yours is a bondage far more terrible than that of Israel in Babylon. But from bondage such as yours Jesus Christ is the great and glorious Emancipator. From your dark prison-house cry unto Him for deliverance, and you shall speedily walk forth a free man in the bright universe of God.

HUMAN SICKNESS AND DIVINE HEALING.

(*Verses* 17–22.)

Consider—

I. **Human sickness.** It is here set forth—

1. *In its cause.* "Fools because of their transgression, and because of their iniquities, are afflicted." Perowne's translation is better: "Foolish men, because of the way of their transgression and because of their iniquities, bring affliction upon themselves." The chief ideas here are two: (1) *Wickedness is folly.* The transgressor is a "fool." The foolishness is not intellectual, but moral. The wicked are "fools" because of the moral infatuation of their conduct; they despise counsel; they are heedless of warning; they betray their own interests; they will only be brought to reason by chastisement. (2) *Wickedness leads to sickness.* The Psalmist expressively indicates that the suffering was self-produced; the sufferers had brought it upon themselves. Many physical afflictions are the direct result of sin. Gluttony and drunkenness lead to untold sickness and suffering. All suffering results from sin. Abolish moral evil, and physical evil would soon be utterly unknown.

2. *In its effect.* "Their soul abhorreth all manner of meat, and they draw near unto the gates of death." The Psalmist describes the sufferer as loathing food, turning from it in disgust, and drawing near to death. Sheol, the realm of death, he represents as a city which is entered through gates. And the sufferer is solemnly near to those gates; in a little while, unless relief be imparted to him, he will have passed through them for ever.

II. **Divine healing.** This the Poet exhibits as—

1. *Effected in answer to prayer.* "Then they cry unto the Lord in their trouble," &c. (See remarks on ver. 6.) "Prayer is a salve for every sore."

2. *Effected with supreme ease.* "He sent His word and healed them." Perowne detects here "the first glimmering of St. John's doctrine of the agency of the personal Word. The Word by which the heavens were made (xxxiii. 6) is seen to be not merely the expression of God's will, but His messenger mediating between Himself and His creatures." At the command of the Lord diseases flee. He has but to utter His word, and the result is achieved. Doubtless many have been "lifted up from the gates of death" by God in answer to prayer. And in all cases of restoration from sickness to health, "whatever means may be used, the healing power comes from God, and is under His control."

3. *Demanding grateful acknowledgment.* "Oh that men would praise the Lord for His goodness," &c. (See remarks on ver. 8.)

CONCLUSION.—This sketch of human disease and Divine healing may fairly be regarded as *a parable of sin and salvation*. 1. *Sin produces an awful deterioration in human nature, and, " when it is finished, bringeth forth death."* 2. *The Lord is the almighty and all-merciful Saviour from sin.* 3. *Prayer is the condition of deliverance from sin.* "Whosoever shall call on the name of the Lord shall be saved." "Seek ye the Lord while He may be found, call ye upon Him while He is near."

DISTRESSED SEAMEN AND THE SOVEREIGN OF THE SEA.

(*Verses 23-32.*)

This " is the most highly finished, the most thoroughly poetical, of each of the four pictures of human peril and deliverance. It is painted as a landsman would paint it, but yet only as one who had himself been in 'perils of waters' could paint the storm—the waves running mountains high, on which the tiny craft seemed a plaything, the helplessness of human skill, the gladness of the calm, the safe refuge in the haven."—*Perowne.* Notice—

I. **God's sovereignty over the sea.** " He commandeth and raiseth the stormy wind, which lifteth up the waves thereof." Again : " He maketh the storm a calm, so that the waves thereof are still." The force and fury of the storm are not blind, irresponsible, reckless things. They are not merely the outworking of natural laws. Behind the laws there is the Lawgiver. Behind the force of the winds and waves there is the Force of all forces —the great God. The old Hebrew poets and prophets spake literal truth when they represented the ocean as entirely under the sway of Jehovah.

"Who lifts up on high
The ocean's maddening waves, tremendous sight?
Or bids them sleep along the feeble sands?
'Tis God alone."—*Pollok.*

To regard God as the Ruler of the sea is—

1. *Philosophic.* It is unsatisfactory to tell me that certain laws, or forces of Nature, or certain combinations of her elements, are the cause of storms and calms. But it is thoroughly reasonable to attribute them to the Creator and Lord of Nature, a Being of infinite wisdom and almighty power.

2. *Scriptural.* The Bible ascribes all the phenomena of Nature to the agency of the Divine Being.

3. *Assuring.* It is some satisfaction to know that the furious elements are not governed by blind laws or stonyhearted fate, but by the wise and holy God. When the angry ocean engulfs hundreds of human beings, much sorrow and distressing mystery are the result. Yet the sorrow and distress would be far greater if, in the dreadful storm, we beheld only the work of mere laws or relentless fate. But God is wise, and strong, and kind. We know His will is good. We bow reverently before the mystery, and wait for more light. It is assuring to know that our Father rules the winds and waves.

II. **Man's impotency when the sea rebels against him.** "They mount up to the heaven," &c. (verses 26, 27). Man has great power over the sea. He employs it in his service. To a great extent he can control it even in its angry moods. In its depths he hides the medium of communication with far distant lands. He can navigate it in almost all weathers. Yet there are limits to man's power over the sea, and when he attains these limits, his impotence is complete. There is a " Hitherto shalt thou come, but no farther," and when man has reached that boundary, if he attempt to advance beyond, the sea will whelm him.

How great is man ! See how he curbs the elements and employs them in his service.

How insignificant is man ! See how the stormy waves sport with him, buffet him, engulf him. When the ocean speaks in thunder, and surges in might and fury, men's souls are "melted because of trouble. They reel to and fro, and stagger like a drunken man, and are at their wit's end." But even when impotent and defeated by the warring elements, man is greater than they; for he is conscious of his impotence and defeat, while they know not of their triumph.

III. **Man's resource when the sea rebels against him.** "Then they cry unto the Lord in their trouble." In the storm, when Jonah was fleeing from Joppa to Tarshish, "the mariners were afraid, and cried every man unto his god." In the storm on the sea of Galilee, when the disciples of Christ thought they were perishing, they cried, "Lord, save us: we perish." Even the professed atheist ceases the insane boast of atheism and cries to God for mercy in the storm when hope of deliverance by mere human skill is gone. In a heavy storm, when wreck seemed inevitable, the captain of a ship inquired anxiously—"Is there a praying man on board?" But no one responded. He inquired again. And eventually it was found that there was a person on board, who had formerly been a Wesleyan, but who had cast away his confidence. "Can you pray?" said the captain to him. "I could once, sir," he tremblingly replied, "but I have left off praying." "Try again," said the captain. And all the crew bowed down to that Almighty Being

"Who rides upon the stormy sky,
And calms the roaring seas;"

whilst the poor backslider tried to pray, and did pray, fervently, powerfully, and successfully; for the storm subsided and the vessel was preserved.

How affecting, in the wreck of the *London*, to find the people gathering round the Rev. Mr. Draper, and in prayer to God learning how to sink into the deep, not with the wild shriek of despair, or the heartless indifference of stoicism, or the atheistic excitement of epicureanism, but with the calm heroism of Christian faith! Prayer to God is the resource of imperilled mariners. That men thus cry to God in their trouble, as by an instinct of their being, suggests—

1. *The absurdity of atheism.* Atheism is a contradiction of the consciousness of man as man.

2. *The reality of prayer.* The existence of the instinct which leads men to cry unto the Lord in their distresses, suggests that there is some One who hears prayer, that the utterance of petition is not in vain.

But is it only when you are at your wit's end that you cry unto God? Do you ignore Him when "the south wind blows softly," yet cry unto Him when the wild tempest raves? Is such conduct worthy of you? What right have you to expect that He whom you seek only when you are in trouble will answer your selfish cry?

IV. **God's answer to man's cry.** "He bringeth them out of their distresses," &c. Sometimes this is true literally. The heathen mariners on their voyage to Tarshish in the storm, with their dim lights as to religion, cried earnestly to their gods, and the true God directed them as to how they should proceed so as to secure the allaying of the storm. The disciples of the Lord Jesus cried to Him in the tempest, and He hushed it into peace. We could cite numerous instances of modern times, in which earnest prayer in the storm has been followed by a calm. But God does not always literally allay the storm, and save from it those who cry unto Him. He, however, calms the inward tempest, so that the waves of anxiety and terror are still. He did so in those on board the *London*, who sank in the act of worship. If He does not avert the calamity in answer to the prayer of the imperilled, He nerves them for the calamity, in their case takes away the sting and evil of it, and makes it the occasion of blessing to them. In answer to the cry of "those in peril on the sea," God does not always bring the ship into the desired haven; but "He bringeth *them* unto their desired haven,"—that calm haven where no storm raves, but all is peaceful, serene, and blessed.

V. **Man's obligation for God's interposition.** "Oh, that men would praise the Lord for His goodness," &c. (See remarks on ver. 8.)

TERRESTRIAL REVOLUTIONS.

(*Verses* 33-43.)

"The character of the Psalm," says Perowne, "changes at this point. We have no longer distinct pictures as before: the beautiful double refrain is dropped, the language is harsher and more abrupt. Instead of fresh examples of deliverance from peril, and thanksgiving for God's mercies, we have now instances of God's providential government of the world exhibited in two series of contrasts. The first of these is contained in verses 33-39, and expresses a double change—the fruitful well-watered land smitten, like the rich plain of Sodom, with desolation, and changed into a salt-marsh; and anon, the wilderness crowned with cities, like Tadmor (of which Pliny says, *vasto ambitu arenis includit agros*), and made fertile to produce corn and wine. The second is contained in verses 40, 41, and expresses the change in the fortunes of *man* (as the last series did those of *countries*)—viz., how the poor and the humble are raised, and the rich and the proud overthrown."

Here are three chief points for consideration:—

I. **Revolutions in countries.** Verses 33-39. Here is—

1. *A picture of a fertile land reduced to barrenness.* "He turneth rivers into a wilderness," &c. (verses 33, 34). (1) *This change was effected by God.* "HE turneth," &c. He can dry up rivers, and make the fruitful plain a salt waste or sandy desert. (2) This change was effected by God *by reason of the wickedness of its inhabitants.* "For the wickedness of them that dwell therein." There is an allusion here to the destruction of Sodom and Gomorrah, and the change of "the plain well-watered everywhere, as the garden of the Lord," into a salt sea and a salt soil on which nothing grows. "If the land be bad, it is because the inhabitants are so."

2. *A picture of a barren land made fertile.* (Verses 35-38.) The 35th verse is taken from Isa. xli. 18. The arid wilderness is transformed into a well-watered country, the barren desert into a scene of fruitfulness and beauty; where solitude reigned, a populous city is found; and where no life was, both human and animal life increases and multiplies. This transformation is brought about by—(1) *The labour of man.* "They prepare a city for habitation; and sow the fields, and plant vineyards, which may yield fruits of increase." Labour is an eternal and immutable condition of prosperity both for individuals and for communities. (2) *The blessing of God.* The Divine blessing precedes and prepares for human labour. "He turneth the wilderness into a standing water," &c. The Divine blessing succeeds and crowns human labour. "He blesseth them also, so that they are multiplied," &c. Some expositors have connected these verses with certain historical events; but, as Perowne points out, "the language employed is far too general to be limited to one event. It describes what frequently has occurred. The histories of Mexico and of Holland might furnish examples of such a contrast." Matthew Henry says: "The land of Canaan, which was once the glory of all lands for fruitfulness, is said to be at this day a fruitless, useless, worthless spot of ground, as was foretold (Deut. xxix. 23). This land of ours, which formerly was much of it an uncultivated desert, is now full of all good things."

3. *A reminder that the temporal prosperity of communities is inconstant and uncertain.* "Again, they are minished and brought low through oppression, affliction, and sorrow." (1) *The most prosperous communities are not exempt from calamities.* (2) *The most prosperous communities are sometimes brought low by calamities.* Barnes: "God so deals with the race as in the best manner to secure the recognition of Himself;—not always sending prosperity, lest men should regard it as a thing of course, and forget that it comes from Him;—and not making

the course of life uniformly that of disappointment and sorrow, lest they should feel that there is no God presiding over human affairs. He visits now with prosperity, and now with adversity;—now with success and now with reverses, showing that His agency is constant, and that men are wholly dependent on Him." Matthew Henry: "Worldly wealth is an uncertain thing, and often those that are filled with it, ere they are aware, grow so secure and sensual with it that, ere they are aware, they lose it again."

II. **Revolutions in human life.** Here is—

1. *The humiliation of the highest.* "He poureth contempt upon princes, and causeth them to wander in the wilderness where there is no way." If men of exalted rank do evil and dishonour God He will bring them down from their elevation, make them to be scorned of men, and reduce them to helpless embarrassment. "He bringeth the princes to nothing, He maketh the judges of the earth as vanity."

2. *The exaltation of the lowest.* "Yet setteth He the poor on high from affliction, and maketh him families like a flock." God exalts the poor above their enemies, and out of the reach of their troubles. He raises them from suffering and adversity into joy and prosperity. He blesses them with large increase in their families,—"maketh families like a flock," a figure denoting a great multitude. Amongst the Hebrews large families were accounted a blessing. *Over all these revolutions God presides.*

"His kingdom ruleth over all." "God is to be acknowledged," says Matthew Henry, "both in setting up families and in building them up. Let not princes be envied, nor the poor despised, for God has ways of changing the condition of both."

III. **The salutary impression of such revolutions.** The Psalmist represents the result as threefold.

1. *To the righteous, joy.* "The righteous shall see it and rejoice." The manifestation of God's righteous government of the world is a source of gladness to the upright.

2. *To the wicked, silence.* "All iniquity shall stop her mouth." "The Divine dealings shall be manifestly so just, and so worthy of universal approval, that even though the wicked are disposed to complain against God, they will be able to find nothing which will justify them in such complaints."—*Barnes.*

3. *To the thoughtful, increased acquaintance with God.* "Whoso is wise and will observe these things, even they shall understand the loving-kindness of the Lord." (1) *In the revolutions in human history there is a manifestation of the goodness of God.* His rule is beneficent. (2) *This manifestation of the goodness of God is perceived only by the attentive observer of those revolutions.* The significance of God's works and ways cannot be discovered by a glance, or by the superficial observer. But he who will consider them attentively and reverently, shall find in them sufficient reason for intelligent and hearty confidence in Him.

PSALM CVIII.

INTRODUCTION.

"This Psalm consists of portions of two others, the first half of it being taken from the 57th Psalm, verses 7–11, and the latter half from the 60th, verses 5–12. It bears the name of David, because the original passages both occur in psalms ascribed to him as their author. But there is no reason for concluding that these fragments were thus united by David himself. Some later poet probably adapted them to circumstances of his own time; possibly wished thus to commemorate some victory over Edom or Philistia."—*Perowne.*

As the whole of the Psalm has already been expounded in "*The Homiletical Commentary*" on Psalms 57 and 60, it will be sufficient if in this place we suggest a method of developing its main homiletic ideas. The Psalm affords an excellent illustration of—

THE COMPLETE TRIUMPH OF THE CHRISTIAN LIFE.

The Christian life is a warfare. Every spiritually-renewed man has to do battle with fleshly lusts and evil tendencies in his own nature, with corrupt opinions and practices in society, and with the temptations of the devil. The renewed man is assured of ultimate victory in this conflict. And this Psalm very suitably represents the spiritual attitude of the Christian warrior, who, although he has gained many conquests, is not yet completely victorious, but in the strength of God is pressing on to the full and final triumph. The complete triumph of the Christian life is—

I. Promoted by praise to God. The Poet begins his Psalm with praise to God. Observe the main features of his praise. It is—

1. *Praise from a confident heart.* "O God, my heart is fixed." A fixed heart is one which is firm and fearless by reason of its confidence in God. Its praise would be unfaltering and fervent.

2. *Praise with the noblest powers.* "Even with my glory." By his "glory" the Poet means his soul, with all the capacities and faculties which belonged to him as an intelligent being, created in the Divine image. The praise of God should engage the noblest powers of our being. Soulless worship is repugnant to Heaven.

3. *Praise in the most public manner.* "I will praise Thee, O Lord, among the people; and I will sing praises unto Thee among the nations." The peoples of the whole earth alone constitute a sufficient auditory for the praise which the Psalmist would offer.

4. *Praise because of God's covenant relationship.* "For Thy mercy is great above the heavens, and Thy truth reacheth unto the clouds." The mercy and truth of God are the attributes which are celebrated by Hebrew poets and prophets as marking His covenant relationship with His people. These are *conspicuous, exalted, vast* as the heavens.

5. *Praise of universal extent.* "Be Thou exalted, O God, above the heavens, and Thy glory above all the earth." The heart which is fixed to praise God would exalt Him in the highest degree and widest extent. He is worthy the praise of the highest intelligences of heaven, and of all upon earth.

How does this praise promote the complete victory of the Christian life?

First: *It honours God.* "Them that honour Me, I will honour." If we honour Him with sincere praise He will honour us with courage, strength, triumph.

Second: *It strengthens faith.* As we heartily celebrate the Divine mercy and truth, our faith in them will grow stronger. And in moral conflicts nothing nerves the heart with heroism and the arm with power like faith in God. In the warfare of the spiritual life if we would "wax valiant in fight, and turn to flight the armies of the aliens," it must be "through faith."

II. Promoted by consideration of the triumphs already achieved. The Poet calls to mind the victories already won. "I will rejoice, I will divide Shechem and mete out the valley of Succoth. Gilead is mine, Manasseh is mine, Ephraim also is the strength of mine head, Judah is my lawgiver, Moab is my washpot." Shechem on the west of Jordan, and Succoth on the east; Gilead (including the region occupied by the tribes of Gad and Reuben), and Manasseh on the east, and Ephraim and Judah on the west, are mentioned as representing the whole land of Canaan. The powerful tribe of Ephraim is represented as "the strength of his head," *i.e.*, the great protection of the most vital interests in battle. Judah is spoken of as the lawgiver, probably in reference to the ancient prediction, "The sceptre shall not depart from Judah, nor a lawgiver from between his feet until Shiloh come." All this land of Canaan was subdued. Moab also was conquered. "Moab is my washpot" expresses the reduction of the

Moabites to a state of utter servitude. "The Moabites became David's servants, and brought gifts" (2 Sam. viii. 2).

But the victory of Israel was not complete. Edom was still unconquered. But its subjugation is anticipated. "Over Edom will I cast my shoe." In the preceding clause Moab is described as a mean vessel in which the feet are washed, and now Edom is described as a servant of the lowest grade to whom the sandals are thrown to be removed or to be cleaned. Or the figure may mean the placing of the foot upon Edom in token of its complete subjection. The idea undoubtedly is that Edom should be completely vanquished by, and subjected to, Israel.

But how would the consideration of past triumphs promote the complete victory?

First: *Their consideration reveals the fact that many an enemy which seemed too mighty for us has been vanquished by believing effort.* The Israelites had conquered the fierce and strong Canaanites. Could they not also conquer the formidable Idumeans? In the Christian life we look back upon many a difficulty overcome, many a temptation successfully resisted, many a foe slain, and are encouraged to hope and contend for the full and final conquest. Past victories are an earnest of future and entire triumph.

Second: *Their consideration brings into clear and impressive light the faithfulness and sufficiency of God as our Helper.* He had made good His promise to Israel in their past triumphs, which they had achieved by virtue of His help; and, as He changes neither in His faithfulness nor in His power to help, would He not enable them to vanquish the Idumeans? In the past of our individual Christian life He has been our unfailing Helper and Supporter. "Having obtained help of God, we continue unto this day." Our past triumphs are due to His assistance. And as we review them, remembering His unchangeableness, we are encouraged boldly to encounter future difficulties and enemies. John Newton very clearly expresses this thought—

"His love in time past
Forbids me to think," &c.

III. **Assured by God.** We discover this assurance in—

1. *His interest in His people.* David speaks of Israel as His "beloved." "That Thy beloved may be delivered." God loves His people; and that love is a guarantee of their ultimate and complete triumph over all their foes.

2. *His power to give His people the victory.* "Save with Thy right hand. . . . Through God we shall do valiantly; and He shall tread down our enemies." "The right hand of the Lord doeth valiantly." "No weapon that is formed against thee shall prosper." "The God of peace shall bruise Satan under your feet shortly." To those who believingly prosecute this warfare God gives the victory.

3. *His promise to give His people the victory.* "God hath spoken in His holiness." The holiness of God is the pledge that He will perform His promises. He has promised to those who believe on Him the victory over all their foes; and what He has promised He will perform, for His word is both almighty and unchangeable.

CONCLUSION. Here is *encouragement* for the Christian soldier. Ours is not a doubtful battle. The Lord is on our side; therefore we must conquer. Here is *counsel* for the Christian soldier. If we would conquer we must be found in the way of duty. Trust and fight, watch and pray, so shall you come off at last more than conqueror through Christ.

THE GREATNESS OF GOD'S MERCY.

(*Verse 4.*—" Thy mercy is great above the heavens.")

A thing may be radically evil in itself, and yet may by a superior power be made the occasion of good. The entrance of sin into the world was a most evil and painful thing, yet under the glorious government of God it is so overruled as not to prove an unmixed evil. Some of the most glorious representations of the character of God have been occasioned by the sin of mankind. This is true of His mercy. Sin did not originate His mercy, but was the occasion of its display. Mercy is the form which the goodness of God assumes to the sinful and wretched. It is the disposition of God to pardon sinners and to relieve sufferers. Our text sets forth *the greatness of the Mercy of God.* This is seen—

I. **In the blessings of daily life.** The use of the word "mercy" implies suffering and sin on the part of those to whom it is applied. Man is a sinner: sin deserves misery, death. But there is much enjoyment in the world. Every day we receive innumerable blessings. What a proof of His mercy! Life itself is a gift of God's mercy. His mercy crowns the life of hell-deserving rebels with joy! It becomes us to receive every comfort and joy as a proof, not only of God's goodness, but of His mercy. "It is of the Lord's mercies that we are not consumed," &c.

II. **In the grand end for which it is manifested.** Why, when sin entered our world, did mercy also appear? Why does God continue our life here? Why does He in countless ways manifest His mercy to men? In order that man may be delivered from sin, and be established in a state of holiness. Salvation, the restoration of man to God, is the grand purpose of Divine mercy. How transcendently great! How Divine!

III. **In the numerous and glorious means by which it seeks to accomplish this end.** These are—

1. *The incarnation, life, ministry, sufferings, death, resurrection, and intercession of the Son of God.* The great blessing of salvation could not have been obtained apart from Christ. He is the great Gift of mercy, the great Channel of mercy, the great Minister of mercy. This gift transcends that of salvation. That our redemption should be through the blood of Christ is a wonderful display of mercy. Wonderful that mercy should seek our salvation; more wonderful that such means should be employed to secure it. Jesus Christ is the greatest gift of the mercy of God.

2. *The agency of the Holy Ghost.* He strives, calls, convinces, converts, establishes, sanctifies men—all in mercy, and all with a view to their salvation. In this we have a great display of mercy. He is distinguished, glorious, divine; and He is the gift of God's mercy to us.

3. *The ministry of the Gospel preacher.* God hath sent forth ambassadors to beseech men in Christ's stead to be reconciled unto Him. Every true preacher of the Gospel is a gift of Divine mercy to men. Every Gospel sermon is a proof of God's mercy to those who hear it.

4. *The arrangements of Providence.* God's providence is a great institution of mercy, a vast organisation of mercy in constant operation to secure the salvation of men. All the circumstances, scenes, and events of life are ordered or controlled by mercy for the salvation of men.

How various and glorious, then, are the means and agencies which God in His mercy uses to secure the salvation of mankind! These means and agencies are devised by Mercy, bestowed by Mercy, employed by Mercy, for a most merciful end.

IV. **In the vast multitudes to whom it extends.** It extends to all men. God in mercy gave Christ a Saviour for all men. His salvation is *adequate* to the needs of all, *suited* to the needs of all, *offered* to all, and *free for all.* Like the heavens which encompass all, and pour their light and warmth on all and freely, so God's mercy embraces all, and freely offers to all her ample provisions. Countless multitudes have been saved by mercy. The trophies of her saving power are ever passing into the realms of the blessed. This great mercy is equal to all the sin and misery of our sinful and suffering race—nay, it transcends the sin and suffering. It meets the needs of *the worst* sinners. Manasseh, Mary Magdalene, the dying malefactor, Saul the persecutor, found mercy, and through mercy entered heaven. At present it is more than sufficient for the vilest. It is sufficient for *all* sinners that are now and will yet arise, until its grand end is accomplished, the race restored, and God glorified in man. His mercy is infinite. "He delighteth in mercy." He "is rich in mercy." "Oh, give thanks unto the Lord, for He is good, for His mercy endureth for ever." This great mercy increases our obligation to God. Accept this mercy; in sin and weakness trust in it; rejoice in it; praise God for it.

PSALM CIX.

INTRODUCTION.

"This," says Perowne, "is the last of the Psalms of imprecation, and completes the terrible climax. In the awfulness of its anathemas, the Psalm surpasses everything of the kind in the Old Testament. Who the person was who was thus singled out for execration, it is in vain to conjecture. Those who hold, in accordance with the Inscription, that the Psalm was written by David, suppose that Doeg or Cush, Shimei or Ahithophel, is the object of execration.

"In Acts i. 20, St. Peter combines a part of the 8th verse of this Psalm, 'His office let another take,' with words slightly altered from the 25th [Heb. 26th] verse of the 69th Psalm, and applies them to Judas Iscariot. Hence the Psalm has been regarded by the majority of expositors, ancient and modern, as a prophetic and Messianic Psalm. The language has been justified not as the language of David, but as the language of Christ, exercising His office of Judge, or, in so far as He had laid aside that office during His earthly life, calling upon His Father to accomplish the curse. It has been alleged that this is the prophetic foreshadowing of the solemn words, 'Woe unto that man by whom the Son of Man is betrayed; it were good for that man if he had not been born' (Matt. xxvi. 24). The curse, in the words of Chrysostom, 'is a prophecy in form of a curse.'

"The strain which such a view compels us to put on much of the language of the Psalm ought to have led long since to its abandonment. Not even the woes denounced by our Lord against the Pharisees can really be compared to the anathemas which are here strung together. Much less is there any pretence for saying that those words, so full of holy sorrow, addressed to the traitor in the Gospels, are merely another expression of the appalling denunciations of the Psalm. But, terrible as these undoubtedly are—to be accounted for by the spirit of the Old Dispensation, not to be defended by that of the New—still let us learn to estimate them aright. This is the *natural* voice of righteousness persecuted. These are the accents of the martyr, not smarting only with a sense of personal suffering, but feeling acutely, and hating nobly, the triumph of wickedness."

THE PITIABLE, THE COMMENDABLE, AND THE REPREHENSIBLE, IN THE TROUBLED LIFE OF A GODLY MAN.

(*Verses* 1-20.)

I. The pitiable in the troubled life of a godly man. The Psalmist is to be commiserated because of the cruel treatment he received at the hands of unprincipled enemies. He complains of their—

1. *Slander.* "The mouth of the wicked and the mouth of the deceitful are opened against me; they have spoken against me with a lying tongue." (See "Hom. Com." on Ps. xli. 5-8, and ci. 5.)

"No might nor greatness in mortality
Can censure 'scape; back-wounding calumny
The whitest virtue strikes: what king so strong,
Can tie the gall up in the slanderous tongue?"
—*Shakespeare.*

Again—

"Virtue itself 'scapes not calumnious strokes."

And again—

"Be thou as chaste as ice, as pure as snow,
thou shalt not escape calumny."

2. *Malignity.* "They compassed me about also with words of hatred, and fought against me without a cause." Hengstenberg says: "The words of hatred are malignant accusations. The swords with which they fight are their tongues. The language used in the Psalm refers only to false accusations, not to deeds." Their bitter hostility to the Psalmist was unprovoked. He had given them no cause for it. He had done them no wrong.

3. *Ingratitude.* He had done them good, and they injured him in return. "For my love they are my enemies." And they have rewarded me evil for

good, and hatred for my love." This is base and atrocious wickedness, yet David often suffered from such conduct. "At the battle of Alma, in September 1854, a wounded Russian was calling piteously for water. Captain Eddington, whose heart was kind and charitable, ran to him, and, stooping, gave him the much-desired beverage. The wounded man revived. The captain ran forward to join his regiment, when the wretch, who had just been restored by his kindness, fired, and shot him who had been his friend in the time of need."

"Blow, blow, thou winter wind,
Thou art not so unkind
As man's ingratitude;
Thy tooth is not so keen,
Because thou art not seen,
Although thy breath be rude."
—*Shakespeare.*

Kind and godly men are still exposed to the slander, malignity, and base ingratitude of the wicked. When they suffer from these they should be sustained by the sympathy of all true men. A good man smarting under the unmerited assaults of the wicked should be encouraged and defended by all upright men.

II. The commendable in the troubled life of a godly man. The troubled Psalmist is to be commended because he committed his cause to the Lord in prayer. Notice—

1. *The object of his prayer.* He prayed that God would vindicate him from the slanders of his enemies. "Hold not Thy peace." Hengstenberg and Perowne: "Be not silent." The desire of the Psalmist was that God would interpose for his help, and so witness for him against his adversaries.

2. *The intensity of his prayer.* "'But I give myself unto prayer,' lit. 'I (am) prayer,' *i.e.*, one who prays, having recourse to no other means of defence."—*Perowne.* Matthew Henry, Barnes, and others are wrong in representing him as praying continually for his enemies. The spirit which breathes through the Psalm is utterly irreconcilable with such a view. In the most terrible manner he prays *against* his enemies, not for them. He devoted himself entirely to prayer; his supplications were continuous and absorbing.

3. *The ground of his prayer.* "O God of my praise," *i.e.*, the God whom I praise. This title contains the ground of the prayer. In former times the Lord had given the Psalmist reason to praise Him, and He will now interpose for him, and so give him fresh reason for praise. Hengstenberg: "The representation of all that the Lord has already done for us, and the appeal to it, form a sure ground of answer, and a mighty quickening of hope. He cannot be unlike Himself."

For thus committing his cause to God in prayer, the Psalmist is to be commended. His example is well worthy our imitation. Let the good man who is slandered and calumniated by the wicked commit his cause to God, and in due time he shall be amply vindicated.

III. The reprehensible in the troubled life of godly man. Vers. 6–20. Various attempts have been made to free the Psalmist from the charge of revengefulness. Some have said that in these verses he speaks as a prophet, and simply declares what would come upon his enemies, and not what he desired concerning them. Others seek to get rid of the difficulty by regarding the Psalm as Messianic, and Christ as the speaker; others by supposing the words to be merely recorded by him as the words of his enemies. We have met with no satisfactory explanation which seeks to exonerate the Psalmist from blame. To us these laboured and strained attempts to exculpate the Psalmist do not seem very creditable to their authors, or in any way necessary. Religious experiences find utterance in the Psalms which are not commendable. In them the poets express their doubts as well as their confidences, their depressions as well as their exultations. Many things are recorded which are also condemned. The Bible faithfully records the defects and sins of the best men. One of the chief elements of the worth of the Psalms is that in them we have a faithful utterance of the varying religious experiences of imperfect yet unquestionably godly men. But it is essential to bear in mind that it is not just to judge David by the principles and spirit of this Christian dispensation. His utterances must be estimated in the light of the Decalogue, not in that of the Sermon on the Mount. But, after we have made every legitimate allowance tending to mitigate the harshness and bitterness of spirit here manifested, still the Poet appears to us here as a beacon, not as a pattern. His spirit and its expressions are to us things not to be imitated, but to be sedulously avoided. Without entering into a detailed exposition of these verses we would call attention to three considerations which they have suggested to us.

1. *To pray for the wrath of God on any one is* (to say the least) *unbecoming in man*. A due sense of our own sin and demerit ought effectually to repress such petitions. "If Thou, Lord, shouldest mark iniquities, O Lord, who shall stand?"

2. *To pray that even a man's prayer might "become sin" is much worse than unbecoming.* "Let his prayer become sin." Perowne: "*His prayer*, not addressed to the human judge for mitigation of the sentence, but here, as always, prayer to God. The criminal, looking in vain for pity or justice at the hands of man, turns in his extremity to God; but even there, at the very fount of mercy, let mercy fail him, let his prayer aggravate his guilt. The utterance of such a wish is the most awful part of the imprecation. That prayer may thus draw down not forgiveness but wrath, see Isa. i. 15; Prov. xv. 8, xxi. 27, xxviii. 9. But it is one thing to recognise this as a fact in the Divine government of man, it is another thing to imprecate it."

3. *To pray for such curses as are here invoked on the wife and children of an enemy is to us unspeakably dreadful.* We shudder as we read verses 10 and 12, and are reminded of the words of Shakspeare :—

"Oh that the slave had forty thousand lives;
One is too poor, too weak for my revenge!
I would have him nine years a killing."

So unappeasable seems the revenge of the Psalmist. Antoninus well says, "The best sort of revenge is not to be like him who did the injury." But David resembled his enemies in this, that they "fought against him without a cause," and he invokes the most dreadful injuries upon those who had done him no wrong, because they were related to one who had. Let good men as they read this portion of the Psalm take warning. The holiest of men in the present state may be tempted into the manifestation of a most unbecoming and sinful spirit. There is a revenge which is noble and God-like. Let us greet our enemies with it. "If thine enemy hunger, feed him," &c. (Rom. xii. 20, 21).

COMPLAINT, PRAYER, AND CONFIDENCE.

(*Verses 21-31.*)

In this portion of the Psalm we have—

I. **A mournful complaint.** The Poet complains of—

1. *Mental distress.* "I am poor and needy, and my heart is wounded within me." He was miserable and in need of help. His troubles had pierced his heart as with a sword. It is trying to be troubled in our circumstances, or to be afflicted in body, but the sorest trials are those of the heart. "The spirit of a man will sustain his infirmity; but a wounded spirit who can bear?".

2. *Physical exhaustion.* "My knees are weak through fasting, and my flesh faileth of fatness." "Or it may be rendered, *hath fallen away from fat.*"—*Perowne*. The fasting spoken of is probably that of penitence, because of sin; or humiliation, because of suffering. It was a voluntary, not a compulsory fasting. By reason of this the Poet's strength had failed. The knee joints no longer afforded him firm support, and his body was wasting to mere skin and bones.

3. *Approach to death.* "I am gone like the shadow when it declineth; I am tossed up and down as the locust." Henstenberg: "I must go hence like the shadow when it declineth, I am carried away like the locust." Perowne: "As a shadow, when it lengtheneth, am I gone hence, I have been driven away as the locust." As the lengthening shadows of evening show the near approach of night, so the afflictions of the Psalmist seemed to indicate his nearness to death and the grave. The Poet gives special prominence to the *irresistibleness* of his approach to death. He says literally, "I am made to go hence." And as the locusts are seized and carried away by the wind, being powerless against its force, so he was being urged towards the gates of death by a force which he was unable to resist.

4. *The reproach of his enemies.* "I became also a reproach unto them, they looked upon me, they shaked their heads." The wicked reviled the Poet as a bad man, and shook their heads in insult and mockery. Or it may be, as Henstenberg says, that they shook the head to express the desperateness of the Poet, saying by the movement, "It is all over with him."

Such is the mournful complaint of the Psalmist. It is sometimes a relief to express our afflictions and griefs to God. It lightens the burden of the heart, &c. This is especially so when complaint is followed by prayer.

II. An earnest prayer. Consider here—

1. *The objects sought in his prayer.* The Psalmist petitions God for (1) *Salvation from his afflictions.* "Deliver Thou me. Help me, O Lord my God; O save me according to Thy mercy." He seeks support from God in his trouble, and deliverance from his trouble. The Lord can turn the shadow of the darkest night into the light of joyous day. (2) *Vindication from reproach.* "That they may know that this is Thy hand, that Thou, Lord, hast done it." In the view of the Psalmist, if the interposition he sought from God were granted unto him, it would completely silence the reproaches of his enemies. (3) *Confusion for his enemies.* "When they arise, let them be ashamed, let mine adversaries be clothed with shame, and let them cover themselves with their own confusion as with a mantle." Baffle their dark designs, and clothe them with shame from head to foot.

2. *The pleas by which he urges his prayer.* "Do Thou for me, O God the Lord, for Thy name's sake; because Thy mercy is good, deliver Thou me. O save me according to Thy mercy." The grace of God is the grand plea of the Psalmist. He urges his petition not on the ground of his own merit, but of God's mercy. This he sets forth (1) As the *reason* of salvation. "Do Thou for me, for Thy name's sake; because Thy mercy is good," &c. The originating cause of salvation is the infinite generosity of God. (2) As the *measure* of salvation. "Save me according to Thy mercy." The salvation that is measured by the infinite grace of God will be gloriously complete. The pleas urged by the Psalmist (α) Indicate confidence in God. (β) Honour God. (γ) Are mighty with God. We shall do well to imitate them.

III. An encouraging confidence. The Poet expresses—

1. *An assurance of salvation from God.* "For He shall stand at the right hand of the poor, to save him from those that condemn his soul." He shall stand at the right hand of His afflicted people, to plead their cause against those who would unjustly judge them, and to deliver them. Take heart, ye tried and true, ye suffering and godly souls, for your Deliverer is mighty and your salvation sure.

2. *A determination to offer praise to God.* "I will greatly praise the Lord with my mouth, yea, I will praise Him among the multitude." He resolves that he will offer praise, and that it shall be (1) *Hearty.* "I will greatly praise the Lord." (2) *Expressed.* "With my mouth." (3) *Public.* "Among the multitude."

"Awake, my soul! not only passive praise
Thou owest! not alone these swelling tears,
Mute thanks and secret ecstasy! awake,
Voice of sweet song! awake, my heart,
awake!"—*Coleridge.*

A PATTERN PRAYER.

(*Verse* 21. "But do Thou for me, O God the Lord, for Thy name's sake.")

This is a brief yet a model prayer for a good man.

I. It is true in its direction. It is addressed to "God the Lord." There is but One all-sufficient being to whom we can address our prayers. Think what is requisite to be able to answer prayer at all times—infinite intelligence, unlimited goodness, universal sovereignty, &c. The petition of the Psalmist indicates his belief that he was approaching such a being; if he could but secure the help of God, he would leave everything else to Him. He could do so only in approaching a being of whose perfection he had no doubt. Only the Lord God can hear and answer prayer.

II. It is personal in its aim. "Do Thou for me." Man's first business is to secure the blessing of God for himself. We should not keep the vineyard of another and neglect our own. We should not attempt to lead others unto Jesus Christ until we know Him as our own Saviour. Unless we are assured of the Divine blessing, we should seek it first for ourselves, and then for others. This is not selfish, but benevolent. Show this.

III. It is submissive in its spirit. The Psalmist leaves everything to God, only praying that His interposition may be "*for*" him. He leaves the *manner* of the interposition to God. God delivers His people by different methods; sometimes by removal of their afflictions, and sometimes by increase of their strength. He blesses His people by different means; sometimes by adversity, and sometimes by prosperity. The wise and good man leaves the means and the manner of the blessing to God. He leaves the *time* also to God. Now or in the future, early or late, as may seem good unto Him. This submission is both *wise* and *pious*.

IV. It is powerful in its place. "For Thy name's sake." The name represents the character of God. The honour of the Divine name is bound up with His treatment of His people. If any one trusting in God were to perish the glory of His name would be sullied. This is a plea which prevails with God.

This prayer is suitable for all occasions; it is brief and comprehensive. And if it is answered in our experience, we shall "have all, and abound."

PSALM CX.

INTRODUCTION.

I. A Messianic prophecy. 1. From internal evidence. 2. From the unanimous consent of Jewish expositors. 3. From the testimony of Christ (Matt. xxii. 41, &c.; Mark xii. 35). 4. From the silence of the Pharisees (Luke xx. 41). 5. From the witness of the Apostles (Acts ii. 34; 1 Cor. xv. 25; Heb. i. 13). 6. And the Early Church (*Justin Martyr, Tertull., Cyp., Chrys.,* &c.). II. Its Messianic character denied. 1. Ewald refers it to David. 2. Hitzig, &c., to a Maccabean priest. Without foundation, for (1) verse 1 can scarcely be applied to a mere man; (2) verse 4 could certainly not apply to David or any human priesthood. III. Of Davidic authorship. 1. From internal evidence. 2. Almost universal tradition. 3. Our Lord's testimony.

THE SOVEREIGNTY OF CHRIST.

(*Verse* 1 *and last clause of verse* 2.)

Our subject occupies a foremost place in the Old Testament. The first prediction (Gen. iii. 15) asserts it; the promise to Abraham (Gen. xxii. 17) implies it; the destiny of Judah (Gen. xlix. 10) involves it. It all but commences the Psalms (ii.), which indeed teem with it (xlv., lxxii., cx., &c.). Prophecy proper opens with it (Isa. ii. 1–4), and closes with it (Luke i. 33).

Our Lord's ministry was a proclamation of His Kingdom, but He did not reveal His own sovereignty till at the close. Then His sentiments are those of our text (John xvii. 2; Matt. xxv. 31, 32; xxviii. 8). Afterwards the glorious company of the Apostles (Acts ii. 33, 34; Phil. ii. 9; Eph. i. 22, 23), the goodly fellowship of the Prophets (Rev. xix. 16), the noble army of Martyrs (Polycarp: "How can I blaspheme my KING"), and the holy Church throughout all the world (Rev. vii. 9–12), acknowledge Him to be the King of glory.

I. Christ reigns by divine appointment. "The Lord said." The Psalmist is admitted into the council chamber of the Trinity. There God the Father and God the Son occupy one throne (Eastern thrones are extended benches. "Sit on my throne at my right hand"—*Schnurrer*), and are in communion.

1. *God assigns to Christ coequal authority.* "At My *right hand*" (Ps. xlv. 9; Mark xvi. 19; Eph. i. 20, 21).

2. *God assigns to Christ coequal honour.* "Sit" (Ps. xxix. 10; 1 Kings i. 46, ii. 19).

II. Christ reigns by divine right. "My Lord," אֲדֹנִי a divine name.

1. *By an inherent divine fitness.* His attributes of wisdom, justice, power, and goodness, qualify Him for universal monarchy.

2. *By an essential divine prerogative.* He has created all, He preserves and sustains all, He has redeemed all, therefore He has a claim on the obedience and fealty of all.

III. Christ reigns by a devout acknowledgment. "My Lord." Christ's monarchy is not elective, and therefore does not depend on fluctuating human opinions and passions; but, having been divinely established, His authority and fitness to rule have received ample recognition.

1. *Kings in the political world* have been proud to acknowledge their servitude to Him:—David, Constantine, Alfred, &c.

2. *Kings in the world of scholarship and philosophy* have submitted their giant intellects to His sway, and laid their conquests at His feet:—Origen, Bacon, &c.

3. *Kings in the world of science* have employed their genius and implements in widening His domain. Explorers, astronomers, &c.—Livingstone, Newton, Faraday, &c.

4. *Kings in the world of morals,* who have achieved conquests over human souls, have presented to Him their trophies. Philanthropists, missionaries.

5. *Kings in the world of spirits* acknowledge His royalty, and crown Him Lord of all. "Angels, principalities, and powers are made subject to Him." Redeemed and glorified humanity casts its crowns before Him, and sings, 'Worthy is the Lamb that was slain to receive power and riches, and wisdom and strength, and honour and glory and blessing."

IV. Christ reigns over a disputed empire. "Rule Thou in the midst of Thine enemies." There are countless multitudes who revel in the enjoyment of their Lord's bounty, who, alas! deny His crown rights.

1. *Christ reigns in the midst of infidel enemies.* The Atheist, the Materialist, the Socialist, and the Unitarian all say, "We will not have this man to reign over us."

2. *Christ rules in the midst of a heathenism* that is ignorant of or hostile to His claims. All idolatry, whether æsthetic like that of ancient Greece, or absurd and barbarous like the fetish worship of the modern Hottentot, or like the debasing idolatry of *self,* is an usurpation of His rights.

3. *Christ rules in the midst of a devil-ridden and death-stricken world.* Nevertheless, the words stand true (Ps. ii. 1–6). The usurpation of traitors is a standing witness to the rights of kings.

V. Christ reigns by the enforced service of His foes. "Until I make Thy foes Thy footstool." All in His dominions, whether willingly or unwillingly, are constrained to subserve His interests.

1. *Tacitly.* (1.) *Infidelity* serves Him by its inability to satisfy the crav-

ings of the human heart. Man cries out for *God.* Infidelity says, "No God," and drives man to Him who said, "He that hath seen Me hath seen the Father." Man cries out for *immortality.* Infidelity says, "No hereafter," and compels man to go to Him who has "the words of eternal life." Infidelity has no *moral guide,* and thus sends man to Him who has given "an example that we should do as He has done." Infidelity has no *solace* for man's remorse and sorrow, and thus drives man to Him who alone can give peace through purity. *Atheism* serves him by trying to repress man's instincts for God, which effort can only intensify those instincts, and send men to Him who alone can satisfy them. *Pantheism* serves him by its doctrine of the divine presence in the universe, and sends men to Christ, who alone can reveal that presence, and bring man into its conscious fellowship. *Unitarianism* serves him by maintaining the Divine Fatherhood and the perfect humanity, and sends men to Christ's Godhood, which can alone explain the perfection of His humanity, and bring the prodigal back to his Father's arms. (2.) *Idolatry* serves Him, inasmuch as it is the parent of ignorance, vice, and superstition, and creates in the human heart a craving after the wisdom, holiness, and moral light and power, which are derived from Him alone. (3.) *Selfishness and sin* serve Him, because, in spite of their fascinating seductions, men see that underneath them lie debasement, ruin, death. (4.) Yes, even the *devil,* wary though he is, serves Him. His hard service and his fearful wages drive men to Him whose yoke is easy, and whose burden is light, and who gives a hundredfold in this present world, and in the world to come life everlasting. (5.) And *death* serves Him, for it carries into His presence His servants, and removes all impediments to their perfect service.

2. *Explicitly.* Testimonies to Christ's supremacy, from those least disposed to acknowledge it, show that Christ reigns, and that His enemies have become the support of His feet. (1.) *Paganism* sends its testimony through Julian, "O Galilean, thou hast conquered." (2.)

Devils. (Mark i. 23–26.) (3.) *Atheism.* "The most valuable part of the effect on the character which Christianity has produced by holding up, in a divine person, a standard for excellence, and a model for imitation, is available even to the absolute unbeliever, and can never be lost to humanity. It is the God incarnate more than the God of the Jew or of nature, who, being idealised, has taken so *great and salutary* a hold on the human mind. And whatever else may be taken away from us by rational criticism, Christ is still left, a unique figure."—*J. S. Mill.* (4.) *Rationalism,* Kant says He is "the union between the human and the divine." *Strauss* speaks of Him as the "highest object we can possibly imagine with respect to religion, the Being without whose presence in the mind perfect piety is impossible." *Renan* exclaims, "Rest now in thy glory, noble initiator; thy work is completed, thy divinity is established; fear no more to see the edifice of thy efforts crumble through a flaw. . . . For thousands of years the world will extol thee . . . a thousand times more living, a thousand times more loved, since thy death. . . . Thou wilt become to such a degree the corner-stone of humanity, that to tear thy name from this world would be to shake it to its foundations. Between thee and God men will no longer distinguish." *Lecky* says that Christianity has presented "an ideal character which, through all the changes of eighteen centuries, has inspired the hearts of men with an impassioned love, and has shown itself capable of acting on all nations, ages, temperaments, and conditions . . . has done more to regenerate and soften mankind than all the disquisitions of philosophers, and all the exhortations of moralists." (5.) *Pantheism. Spinosa* thought Him "the best and truest symbol of heavenly wisdom, or ideal perfection." (6.) *Selfishness.* Napoleon: "Alexander, Cæsar, and myself, founded great empires; but upon what? Force. Jesus alone founded His empire upon love, and to this day millions would die for Him. I know man; Jesus Christ was more than man."

VI. Christ will reign over an un-

disputed universe. This is the sense of our text. The prophets, without a dissentient voice, predicted this. Christ Himself foreshadowed it. The souls under the altar groan for it. The Universal Church waits for it.

"What successes did the Jews anticipate from their Messiah? The wildest dreams of their rabbis have been far exceeded. Has not Jesus conquered Europe, and changed its name into Christendom? All countries that refuse the Cross wither. ... And the time will come when the vast communities and countless myriads of America and Australia, looking upon Europe as Europe now looks upon Greece, and wondering how small a space could have achieved such mighty deeds, will still find music in the songs of Zion, and still seek solace in the parables of Galilee."—*B. Disraeli.*

THE ROYAL ARMY.

(*Verse 2, clause 1, and verse 3.*)

This is a vivid sketch of the Church and its prerogatives, inserted in the midst of the king's coronation hymn. What is this but a foreshadowing of the union between Christ and His people. In ver. 1, Christ is glorified with "the glory which He had with the Father before the world was." In vers. 2, 3, that glory "He gives them." In ver. 4, He is a priest; in ver. 3, His people are arrayed in sacerdotal robes. The influence of Christ's character on the world is to quicken and refresh it; so here His people are as the dew. Christ's years do not fail; so here His people are endowed with perennial youth, and out of their midst the "rod of His *strength*" goes forth."

I. Church weapons. "The Lord shall send the rod of thy strength out of Zion." The King first equips His chosen ones, and then sends forth to war. The rod of Christ's strength may be any one or all of those points of Zion's panoply catalogued in Eph. vi. The girdle of truth, the breastplate of righteousness, the sandal of peace, the shield of faith, the helmet of salvation, and the sword of the Spirit. In vain does the Church go forth when unprovided with them. Notice these weapons are—1, Of divine manufacture; 2, Of tried temper; 3, Of invincible strength; 4, Of irresistible power.

II. Church character. Threefold—
1. *The Church belongs to Christ.* "Thy people." (1.) *By the terms of the everlasting covenant.* (2.) *By the redemption of the Cross.* (3.) *By His own declaration,* "My Church." (John xvii. 6–10.) (4.) *By its own free consent.* (Rom. xiv. 8.)

2. *The Church is of priestly dignity.* "In the beauties," lit. *robes,* "of holiness." (Chron. xx. 21; Ps. xxix. 2; Exod. xxviii. 2.) The splendid vestments were symbolical of the majesty, purity, and power of sacerdotal service. The fitness of this character is seen from the fact that the Church follows the royal priest. (*Cf.* verse 1 and 4.) (1.) The *quality* of this priesthood is like that of the great high priest, *royal.* (1 Pet. ii. 5; Rev. i. 6.) (2.) The *functions* of this priesthood are—(*a.*) *Sacrificial,* not however expiatory, but eucharistic. (Rom. xii. 1; 1 Pet. ii. 5); and (*b.*) *Intercessory.* (Phil. iv. 6, &c.) (3.) The *appearance* of this priesthood is beautiful. Everything in God's world is beautiful. It is fitting, therefore, that His people should be so. The Church is a bride adorned with her jewels. She is called to cultivate not only purity but grace. And thus here the gorgeous vesture of the Jewish priest is a fit emblem of his beauty and attractiveness who has "put on the Lord Jesus Christ."

3. *The Church is ever youthful.* "Youth" here means young men. Christ's followers possess the secret of perpetual youth. (1.) *Individually.* Time, work, and strife, may age the outer man, but they cannot touch the spirit, that is renewed continually day by day. (Is. xl. 30, 31; 2 Cor. iv. 6.) That continues fresh and vigorous through wrinkles and material decay.

(2.) *Collectively.* The Church was never more mighty in her numbers and in her influence than she is in this the 19th century of her history. Human institutions fail from internal weakness, or for the want of external support, and lose their influence in the lapse of years. Not so with Christ's people. "They flourish in perpetual youth," and "go from strength to strength."

III. **Church spirit.** "My people shall be willing." It is not without significance that נְדָבָה willingness, or free-will offerings, is derived from נָדַב prince, or noble one. Hence the Christian *esprit de corps* is

1. *Unmercenary.* Christ's people are actuated by no sordid motives. The reward before them is splendid if they win, but their all-absorbing aim is to "please Him who called them to be soldiers."

2. *Unconstrained.* Christ's soldiers are volunteers. They are called, but they may disobey. They may enlist, but are at liberty to retire.

3. *Free by a glad surrender of the will.* "If any man *will* come after Me, let him take up his cross and follow Me."

4. *Princely;* and princely because free. The spirit of willing consecration raises these priests into "*kings* unto God." As the servants of kings are noble, and as the suzerainties of emperors are governed by monarchs, so is the follower of the King of kings and Lord of lords a "prince with God."

IV. **Church opportunity.** "In the day of thy power." There are two interpretations of this expression. "The day of thine own might;" and "the day when thou dost muster thy forces and set them in battle array." The text in its present application implies both, for they are both characteristic features of the Gospel dispensation. The spectators of Christ's miracles were amazed at the mighty power of God. (Luke ix. 43.) Christ's promise was that His Church should receive power then, and when He who is the power of God should "ascend far above all principalities and power and might" (Eph. i. 21). Then He strengthened His disciples "according to His glorious power," and made their faith stand "by the power of God." Thus the Church is made strong "in the Lord, and in the power of His might." "The kingdom of God is not in word but in power." What is this but to prove that Church opportunities are ever present. Let her not wait then in indolence for special outpourings of the Spirit, but be faithful to the power she already has. Christ is the same in power "to-day, yesterday, and for ever," and is with the Church alway; and every day is the Church under marching orders for expeditions against her foes.

V. **Church influence.** "From the womb of the morning thou hast the dew of thy youth."

1. *Abundant.* It covers the whole earth. Every nation, rank, and order of intelligence have felt its power.

2. *Marvellous.* The influence of Christianity has never been, and can never be, accounted for by natural hypotheses. Its only explanation is that, like its Divine Author, it "proceeded forth and came from God."

3. *Refreshing.* It pours new life into dead humanity, and culture and civilisation follow in its train. The desert under its influence rejoices and blossoms like the rose, and becomes as the garden of the Lord. Contrast the world eighteen hundred years ago with what it is to-day. Fiji fifty years ago.

4. *Gentle.* Not with the force of arms or pride of learning. Yet before it tyranny, serfdom, and superstition flee.

Concerning its influence as a whole, hear the words of an impartial witness: "By the confession of all parties, the Christian religion was designed to be a religion of philanthropy; and love was represented as the distinctive test or characteristic of its members. As a matter of fact, it has probably done more to quicken the affection of mankind, to promote piety, to create a pure and merciful ideal, than any other influence that has ever acted on the world." (Lecky's "Rationalism," vol. i. p. 358.)

5. All *moral* tyranny (2 Tim. ii. 26).

II. All tyranny is subject to the wrath of Christ.

1. *Because of His own inherent righteousness.* He, the King of men, does not break the bruised reed, &c., and He will not permit them who wield His delegated authority to do so.

2. *Because His government is based upon the freedom of the subject.* All His great blessings are free. The great end of His coming was to make men free. The great legacy He bequeathed to man is the "freedom of sons." His express command is that man should "stand fast in liberty." Any attempt, therefore, to unsettle or overthrow this foundation principle does and must excite His righteous indignation.

3. *Because the well-being of man,* the creature whom He loves and has taken into his own brotherhood, *can only be maintained by political, social, domestic,* and *religious liberty.* Of what value are national institutions unless man as man is free to enjoy them? Of what use are spiritual blessings if enforced on unwilling minds? Where is the benefit of domestic blessings if doled out or enforced by the iron rule of a despot? The only bond which keeps society together is the liberty of its individual members; and moral tyranny destroys the soul. Despotism is the upas blight which has ruined more institutions and more men than any other evil that has ever issued from hell. And therefore does it excite the anger of Christ.

III. All tyranny will be destroyed by Christ.

"Shall strike through kings . . . fill the places with dead bodies. He shall wound the head over many countries."

1. *Christ's policy in the past, is a promise, of what it will be in all time to come.* Every species of despotism has been destroyed by Him. Autocracy in those terrible oriental and western tyrannies which have left behind them but the phantom of a name. Egypt, Assyria, Babylon, Persia, Rome, have all been destroyed by the "stone cut out of the mountain without hands;" Democratic tyranny in the overthrow of the republics of Greece and Rome, and the bloody rule and bloody end of French socialism; *intellectual* despotism in the extirpation of an overweening philosophy and a no less overweening priesthood. Domestic tyranny in those nations where women were but chattels and slaves of less account than beasts. *Moral* slavery in his subjection of "him who has the power of death which is the devil." All these despotisms seek to revive and propagate themselves to-day, but let them be assured that, as sure as Christ lives and reigns, their doom is sealed.

2. *Christ's policy is pursued for the benefit of humanity at large.* All souls are on an equality before Christ. They have all shared a common creation and a common redemption. Heaven is not imposed upon by coronets and thrones. All mankind have crown rights, and woe to those who injure them. Those who do so must and will be removed. The tyrant must be hurled from his throne before the subject can breathe the free air of liberty. Pharaoh must be engulfed, that Israel may pursue her path of progress.

3. *Christ's policy presents an alternative.* Despots *may* cease to be despots, tyrants may cease to oppress. Those guiltless of the crime will not then inherit the curse.

IV. All tyranny will be supplanted by Christ.

Tyranny is better than anarchy. But, having destroyed the tyrant, Christ assumes His sceptre and His throne, and reigns over a divinely-liberated people. "He shall judge among the heathen." "On His head are many crowns." Christ's right and fitness to rule may be judged by what that rule when acknowledged has achieved. 1. *The Christian Sabbath,* the great barrier to the tyranny of toil. 2. *The Bible,* the grand charter of moral freedom. 3. *Liberty for the soul* from Satan's power. 4. *Liberty of thought.* 5. *Liberty, equality, and fraternity for all;* for woman, for the child, and for the slave, for "One is your Master; even Christ, and all ye are brethren.

Men and brethren—(i.) Prize your freedom, and let no man entangle you again in the yoke of bondage. (ii.)

Thank Christ for your freedom. He who has made you free. (iii.) Employ that freedom in Christ's service, that is, in making others free.

CHRIST REFRESHING HIMSELF.

(*Verse 7.*)

The picture is that of the conqueror pursuing his foes, and partaking of momentary refreshment at some wayside brook; then in the strength of that refreshment pursuing his joyful and victorious way. The scene is typical of those encouragements which are His support who is contending for rightful and universal empire.

I. The Divine refreshment. "He shall drink of the brook in the way."

1. Christ is encouraged by *the sense of His Father's approval.* The kingdom for which He fights is His Father's gift (Ps. ii. 8). In fighting for it He always does the things which please Him. In the hottest conflict He is cheered by the voice from heaven: "This is My beloved Son in whom I am well pleased (John x. 17).

2. Christ is encouraged *by the justice of His cause and the beneficence of His work.* Those engaged in selfish projects have to look away from the work for encouragement. Those who know they are working for the bettering of the world can afford to despise obloquy and persecution. Christ knows that His work through crosses and conflicts will end in the regeneration of the world. He "sees of the travail of His soul and is satisfied."

3. Christ is encouraged *by the enthusiasm of His followers.* Around no other name do such affections cluster, and behind no other banner do such earnestness and determination range. "Alexander," remarked the great Napoleon, "Cæsar, and myself have founded empires. But upon what do we rest the creations of our genius? Upon force. Jesus Christ alone founded His empire upon love; and at this moment millions of men would die for Him. I die before my time, and my body will be given back to the earth to become food for worms. Such is the fate of him who has been called the great Napoleon. What an abyss between my deep misery and the eternal kingdom of Christ, which is proclaimed, loved, and adored, and which is extended over the whole earth?"

4. Christ is encouraged *by the conquests He has already achieved, and by the certain triumphs which yet await Him.* Behind is the cross, around is His redeemed and adoring Church, and onward is the millennium. (Heb. xii. 2; Is. xlii. 4.) "I, if I be lifted up, will draw all men unto Me." All His past victories are prophetic of His success in time to come. Witness the trophies of the Cross in the first three centuries. Witness what it is doing in the realms of infidelity and heathenism to-day. On Himself He builds this Church which "triumphs o'er the gates of hell."

II. The consequence of that refreshment. Invigorated and encouraged the conqueror pursues his path to victory. "Therefore shall He lift up His head."

1. *Christ's conquests are progressive.* He does not complete His work at once. His work in the world is gradual and growing. Having achieved one success, He passes on to another, and will do so till "every knee shall bow, and every tongue confess that He is Lord."

2. *Christ's conquests are permanent.* That is to say, no hostile power shall ever win them back again. "They shall never perish." True, His subjects may revolt. They may say, "We will not have this King to reign over us." But they resign the fealty to Christ by their own free-will, and not by any power of the adversary. Then they become Christ's enemies, and, if they will not let Him win them back again, in *their* destruction He displays His glorious power.

3. *Christ's conquests are glorious.* (1.) *Christ lifts up His head over redeemed and consecrated souls.* To conquer inert matter and to sway blind forces were easy work for Omnipotence.

But to convince the intellect, subdue the will, invite the affections and draw out the forces of the life, this is glorious indeed. (2.) *Christ lifts up His head over the defeated and destroyed powers whose energies have been inimical to the interests of heaven and earth.* The joy which was set before Him, and for which He endured the cross and despised the shame, was victory over the devil, sin, the world, and death. These He has vanquished. Sin has no more dominion over His people. They have the faith He gives, and have overcome the world, and through Him they can now say, "O grave, where is thy victory? O death, where is thy sting?" 4. *Christ's conquests will have an end.* The time will come when Christ shall lift up His head over a regenerated universe. When all His enemies shall be subdued under His feet then (Cor. xv. 24–28.)

Learn (i.) That all the sources of the Saviour's encouragement are ours. (ii.) That if we are faithful we shall participate in His final triumph and share His throne.

PSALM CXI.

INTRODUCTION.

1. Authorship unknown, probably late. 2. One of the ten alphabetical Psalms, the clauses beginning with the letters of the Hebrew alphabet in succession. This is no more artificial than the measure, rhyme, or rhythm of other poetry. 3. One of the ten Psalms which begin with *Hallelujah.*

PRAISE.

(*Verse* 1, *Clause* 1.)

"Praise ye the Lord." (Heb. HALLE-LUJAH.) Worship is an universal instinct of humanity. In all places where we find men we find religious exercises. Polytheism, Pantheism, and even Positivism testify to the necessity of gratifying the religious instinct by providing objects for worship. "The man who has nothing else above him has self, that ugliest, most obscene of deities: Belial, and Mammon, and Beelzebub in one. Self is the deity of millions, and its worship is as vile, as brutalising, as ever were the rites of Chemosh, or Milcom, or Ashtoreth. In general, even fallen man has something besides himself above him; even where self presides in the worship, it is rather as priest than idol."—*Dr. Vaughan.* Our text sets before us—

I. **The true object of worship.** "The Lord."

1. *The only rightful object.* (1.) On the grounds of creation and providence. (2.) On the ground of express revelation: "Him *only* shalt thou serve."

2. *The only satisfying object.* (1.) *Idols are nothing in the world.* (2.) *Nature and humanity are only abstractions.* (3.) None but God is *good,* strong, and therefore *willing* and *able* to accept our *worship.*

3. *The only ennobling object.* All other objects, because of their vanity, inability, or degradation, are unworthy of man's adoration, and therefore their worship is debasing. But the worship of God (1) *Elevates the mind.* The imagination and reason are lifted up above the mean or petty considerations of sense and time to the contemplation of the boundless perfections of the infinite and eternal. (2) *It elevates the will* above the debasements of selfishness, to free consecration to the authority of the noblest being and the execution of the noblest purposes. (3) *It lifts the heart above* all ignoble objects of affection, and reposes it on inimitable beauty and eternal loveliness. (4) It exalts the whole man intellectually, morally, socially, and even physically, into an atmosphere of holiness and purity.

183

II. **The true character of worship.** "Praise." All other elements of worship condense themselves into this. *Prayer* is a form of praise, because it tacitly acknowledges that God has answered it before, and is worthy of our grateful homage. *Communion* is a form of praise, inasmuch as it confesses that God is worthy of the time that we snatch from other engagements to consult His will.

1. *Praise implies gratitude.* It expresses thankfulness for past and present mercies.
2. *Praise implies self-forgetfulness.* Self is in oblivion when we contemplate and are thankful for those blessings which have made self possible.
3. *Praise implies an adoring and strong recognition of God's claims upon our practical service*, who has showered those benefits which are the subject of our thanksgivings.
4. *Praise is the result of the combined operation of all our faculties.* The mind contributes its thought, the emotions their rapture, the will its volitions, the spirit its fervour, and the body its activities.

III. **The true spirit of worship.** "Ye."
1. *Personal.* God is no respecter of proxies. Incense, beads, and other ritualistic paraphernalia, and even men of unquestionable piety and spiritual power, can be no substitute for the personal homage of the soul.
2. *Yet not so personal as to exclude all reference to or company with others.* God's blessings are like stones cast into the water. The ripples and influences are felt far and wide. The mercy a parent receives extends more or less to his family, dependants, and connections. Let him, therefore, praise the Lord for those who have felt the influence, and in their company.

IV. **The true medium of worship:** Christ. "No man cometh unto the Father but by Me."

CHURCH AND CONGREGATIONAL WORSHIP.

(*Verse 1.*)

I. **Distinctions in worship.** The expressions, "assembly of the upright" and "congregation," are not synonymous. They express the modern ideas of public and private; church and congregation.
1. *Public worship as against the specious sophistries of Plymouthism, &c., may be defended* (1.) *On the ground of convenience.* No private dwelling can afford the facilities presented by houses set apart exclusively for that purpose. (2.) *On the ground of fraternity.* "The Church in the house" if the *only* Church must necessarily be narrow and exclusive, and be confined in most cases to the family dwelling there, in all cases to the nearest neighbours. (3.) *On the ground of unrepealed law.* Man has not yet outgrown this provision for his spiritual nature provided under the old dispensation, and therefore the laws concerning it are still binding. (4.) *On the ground of Christ's example,* in the use of temple and synagogues. (5.) *On the ground of apostolic precedent.* Paul in the "School of Tyrannus," &c. (6.) *On the ground of universal custom in all ages,* from the churches in the Catacombs till now.
2. *Private worship, as against formalism or latitudinarianism must be provided for and practised by the Church.* (1.) *On the ground of convenience.* In public a certain amount of restraint is necessary. In private the Church is away from critical eyes and ears, and can unbosom herself without fear of being misunderstood. (2.) *On the ground of Christian fraternity.* The Church being a family should have opportunities of family worship. (3.) *On the ground of universal custom.* In all ages the Church within the Church, "The upright," "Those that fear the Lord," have had their separate assemblies. The Jews, our Lord and His disciples; the early Church, Reformers, Puritans, Methodists, &c.

II. **Places of worship.** "In the assembly of the upright and in the congregation." This suggests to us—

1. *That the Church and congregation should not be confounded.* "The upright" is a designation of God's covenant people as such. "Congregation," a general term for all who attend God's ordinances. Gentiles were admitted within certain precincts of the Temple, but the inner enclosures were for Israel alone. A body of people assembling for worship or adhering to the tenets of a given communion may, for convenience sake, be called a church. But, strictly speaking, that term belongs to the mystical body of Christ. And while all are entitled to the privileges of congregational worship, yet there are certain specific privileges which belong to the Church as such alone.

2. *That the Church should strive to make itself conterminous with the congregation.* (1.) *By a willing fraternity.* Let not the member of the Church say directly or by implication to the member of the congregation, "Stand by, for I am holier than thou;" or thank God that he is "not as other men." (2.) *By an earnest and edifying testimony* to the grace of God, and energetic evangelism (1 Cor. xiv. 24, 25). (3.) *By generous invitation and genial encouragement.* But not (1) *By a lax and miscalled charity*, cheapening church privileges and bringing them into contempt. (2) *By mere desires of numerical increase;* or (3) *By the resignation of divinely conferred and responsible rights.* Churches should demand and obtain moral qualifications for membership. It will be an evil day for the Church when she relaxes her discipline, but a happy day when all congregations are churches in the fulfilment of their duties and the blamelessness of their lives.

3. *That Church and congregational duties are alike obligatory.* The members of our congregation have much to be thankful for, and are the heirs of many hopes. Let them praise God for what they enjoy. The members of the Church have every cause for gratitude. Let that gratitude be expressed in the presence of the congregation, publicly and emphatically.

III. **Manner of worship.** "I will praise the Lord with my whole heart." Which suggests—

1. *That praise should be earnest.* Indifference or perfunctoriness is a gross offence to God. Where warmth, fervour, glow are wanting, the very elements of praise are wanting.

2. *That praise should be complete.* "Whole heart." Wandering thoughts must be checked, vagrant affections and interests must be reined in. "Glorify God in your bodies and spirits, which are God's."

3. *That praise should be spontaneous.* It should well up freely and naturally from the thankful heart.

IN CONCLUSION. (i.) Are you a member of the Church of Christ? If not, why? From indifference? Shrinking from public testimony to the power of God? From the lack of moral qualifications? Brethren, the worship of such must be lacking in many elements desirable in the sight of God. (ii.) Are you a member of the Church of Christ? If so, what are you doing for the community to which you belong? Are you enjoying its privileges without contributing to its strength? Are you at ease in Zion? Remember, worship without work is hypocrisy (1 Pet. ii. 9).

THE WORKS OF GOD, THE SUBJECT OF SOUL-SATISFYING SEARCH.

(*Verse 2.*)

These words, summing up God's works in general, and describing our proper attitude towards them, and the fruits of their patient study, suggest—

I. That God's works are **great**. They are great—

1. *In the mystery of their origin.* Like Him who made them they are past finding out. Even if the statements of modern scientists be true, viz., that all life may be traced back to one primordial germ, yet, as Professor Huxley has said,

"The present state of knowledge furnishes us with no link between the living and not living."

2. *In the length of their duration.* Astronomy and geology tell us something of the time which must have elapsed since they first came into being, and the Bible does not attempt to limit it. About their future science can say nothing, and about their *absolute* termination God's Word gives no hint.

3. *In the vastness of their extent.* The most moderate computation of the distance between the sun and other planets, and our earth, to say nothing of realms of matter beyond, loses us in wonder and awe.

4. *In the wisdom of their arrangement.* Subject to unvarying law; exquisitely adapted for their various purposes; regularly serving their appointed ends.

5. *In the beneficence of their intention.* "All things working together for 'the general' good."

II. That God's works **should be the subject of study.** The popular religious outcry against science is (1) unreasonable; (2) contrary to God's Word; (3) condemned by the example of the best spirits in all ages. The psalmists and prophets were profound natural philosophers, and many of their revelations have anticipated the discoveries of modern times. Our Lord revelled in nature, and Paul had a keen eye for its beauties. (4) It is fatal to the interests of truth. But God's works should be studied—

1. *Cautiously.* None but facts should be acknowledged. Probable hypotheses should be considered and respected, but conclusions should only be built upon unquestionable certainties.

2. *Fearlessly.* God cannot deny or contradict Himself. All that He has revealed in nature should be explored; and genuine discoveries, however much they may shock our prejudices or explode our preconceived convictions, should be welcomed and acknowledged.

4. *Reverently.* Nature is the revelation of "the invisible things of God;" explain many of the truths of God's Word, and should be made the handmaid of piety.

III. That God's works are **promotive of soul satisfaction.** "Exquisitely excellent, and fully satisfying all those who delight in them; *i.e.*, excellent, precious, incomparable, in the judgment of those who best understand them—His faithful worshippers" (see Ps. xii. 1). —*Speaker's Comm.*

1. *The believer finds there revelations of his own dignity.* Surveying the magnificent expanse above him, he will say, "I am greater than all that; for that gorgeous canopy has no mind." Contemplating the immense ages which have elapsed since the world came into being, he will say, "All those ages were necessary to fit the world for me." Watching the operation of inexorable laws, he will say, "I am free."

2. *The believer will find there intimations of his relation to God and his immortality.* Man stands alone in the universe. "Communion with nature" is all very well as poetry; but between man's soul and the material universe there is nothing in common, and therefore there can be no communion. He is thus driven to the Author of nature, and with Him man finds that he has some affinity, and can therefore have communion. Again, man lives in the midst of things that are ever changing and passing away. But when man turns within himself he is conscious of something that will "survive the wreck of matter and the crush of worlds."

3. *The believer will there find ample confirmation of all that is revealed in God's Word respecting his Maker's wisdom and power and goodness.* He will there see the truth of the declarations: "Behold, it was very good;" "Thou hast done all things well."

4. *The believer will there find abundant cause for thankful and adoring gratitude.* The more he becomes acquainted with God's works the more he knows of his Father's beneficence towards Him, and will concerning him.

IN CONCLUSION.—(i.) Let nature be the subject of your studious search. (ii.) Let the design of your search be to find harmonies between God's Word and God's works. (iii.) Let the result of your search be thankful praise.

NATURE'S BEAUTY AND THE RIGHTEOUSNESS OF NATURE'S GOD.

(Verse 3.)

The union of the useful and the beautiful in nature is perfect. The two cannot be separated as is the case with the works of man. If you were to deface a Phidian statue, the useful marble would remain. Again, man uses beauty to conceal deformity. Not so nature. Man is the only blot on her fair surface. Nature's beauty and utility are one and the same. The gorgeous tints which decorate the region of the setting sun are but the result of a certain combination of the laws by which we live. The same lines which make up the beauty of the landscape are the measure of distances and the guide of motion. We shall consider the utility of nature further on. Here observe—

I. Nature's beauty. "Honourable and glorious" הוֹד־וְהָדָר. Shining and glittering, majestic and splendid.

1. Nature exhibits herself in *beautiful positions*. The starry heavens, the distant landscape, alternations of mountain and plain, land and water, meadow and garden, forest and plateau.

2. Nature exhibits herself in *beautiful forms*. This is seen by the naked eye in the graceful foliage, the rippling stream, the foaming cataract, the raging sea; in flowers, fruits, herbs, &c. But the telescope and microscope open up the wondrous splendours of a new world.

3. Nature exhibits herself in *beautiful operations*. The march of the seasons, progress of the earth, dawn, meridian, sunset, night.

4. Nature teaches *beautiful lessons* of grace, dignity, generosity, order, dependence on God.

5. Nature is full of *beautiful perfumes and beautiful sounds*.

II. Nature is beautiful, says the Psalmist, **but nature's God is righteous.** Is there any break in the thought? No.

1. *Nature's beauty is but a reflection of that eternal moral beauty which we call the divine righteousness.* Nature is beautiful, because it is the expression of the established will of heaven.

2. *Conversely, nature teaches us that the mind which clothed her in those beautiful forms is beautiful.* No effect can be greater than its cause. No water can rise above the level of its source. Order only can produce order, beauty only can evolve beauty.

3. *Nature exhibits her harmony with her Maker.* This is so complete that certain theologians have identified the two, and have regarded the universe as the splendid robe of deity.

"Thus time's whizzing loom unceasing I ply,
And weave the life-garment of deity."
—*Goethe.*

4. *Nature exhibits by contrast the causes of the moral deformity of man.* Man is out of harmony with the universe, because out of harmony with God. When that harmony is restored man puts on the beautiful garment of holiness, and grows in grace.

III. Nature is beautiful, **as the expression of the everlasting righteousness of nature's God** Then beauty is the permanent order of things, for moral beauty is eternal. Some day nature will put off her splendid vestments, but that will only be preparatory to the creation of the new heaven and the new earth, *wherein dwelleth righteousness.* Those who exhibit themselves in contrast with her now, being then in harmony with her God, will be in harmony with her. It is not without significance that all the visions vouchsafed to man of the life to come are exquisitely beautiful. Beautiful scenes, forms, sounds, fragrance, food; because all righteous (Rev. xxii. 1–6).

THE PURPOSE OF NATURE, AND THE GOODNESS OF NATURE'S GOD.

(*Verse 4.*)

I. **The purpose of nature.** "He hath made His wonderful works *to be remembered.*"

1. *Their wonderfulness adapts them to man's memory.* The "Speaker's Commentary" paraphrases thus: "He has done such wonderful deeds that a remembrance of them abides for ever" (Ps. lxxviii. 3, 4; Num. xvi. 40; Josh. iv. 6, 7). Those things are most easily remembered which strike upon man's sense of wonder. Trivial incidents we forget, great things we call memorable. God's works are wonderfully great, wonderfully mysterious, wonderfully old, wonderfully novel and fresh, wonderfully grand.

2. *The memory stands as the result of the operation of all the faculties of the mind.* We must study, apprehend, reason, and compare, if we would remember. Memory is but the treasure-house of the things we put into it; and we can only store it with the facts of God's universe by the exercise of all the intellectual powers. But memory is fickle, hence the necessity of constantly examining it to see if its contents are still there and in their right places.

3. *The retention of God's marvellous works ennobles memory.*

(1.) *By the exercise which it gives.* Memories enlarge and grow by exercise. Bad memories, as a rule, are idle and unexercised memories.

(2.) *By the love which they impart.* How debasing are the contents of most memories! Recollection of wasted opportunities gives a tone of remorse. Recollection of sins gives a tone of vice. God's works are pure and good, and must give a pure and good tone to that which stores them up.

(3.) *By alien recollections which they expel.* A memory that is full of God's wonderful works must have emptied itself of all base subjects. And as they take hold of the mind they cast out things unworthy of retention.

True, this is a process largely dependent on habit. Let then the habit be cultivated, and all base and unworthy memories will gradually fade.

II. **The purpose of nature is to be remembered**: why? That we may have a perpetual evidence of the goodness of nature's God.

1. *God's works show that He is gracious:*—REMEMBER THEM. All nature shows that God is mindful of man and visits him. Creation is no testimony of a creator distant from and indifferent to its operations. It postulates the presence of One who watches the movements of all its laws and processes, and who continually prevents its going wrong. And what for? The whole universe replies, "For man." All things work together for his good. Natural forces have other ends to serve, but emphatically and pre-eminently they serve him. The sun by day, and the moon and stars by night, afford him light and regulate his time. Birds, beasts, fishes, vegetables, &c., serve him for labour, clothing, or food. All this evidences the fact that God is gracious to man. Above all, there is God's gracious work of Redemption, the operations of the Holy Ghost, the Church, the Word, the Sacraments.

2. *God's works show that He is "full of compassion:"*—REMEMBER THEM. Compassion is the sentiment of a higher and richer to a lower and more needy creature. God's works contemplate the alleviation of human wants. Man suffers from exhaustion: "God giveth His beloved sleep." Man suffers from cold: God has laid up for him a treasury of coal. Man suffers from heat: God has provided healthy and refreshing breezes. Man suffers from disease: God's works are full of healing medicines and curative appliances. Man suffers from sin, and, behold, all heaven is opened and placed at his disposal.

THE BOUNTY AND FAITHFULNESS OF GOD.

(*Verse 5.*)

Old and New Testament alike recognise the Fatherhood of God. In that Fatherhood all the divine perfections inhere. As a Father, God is just and holy as well as merciful and kind. Consequently the results of that Fatherhood do not spring from mere spasms of affection, but are based upon eternal principles. Hence our text recognises the provision for our daily wants as the result of God's fidelity to His covenant engagements.

I. God's bounty. "He has given meat, *i.e., prey*, contemplating a nomadic life, or Israel's wandering in the wilderness.

1. *God's gifts are as varied as man's need.*

(1.) *Man's material blessings are God's gifts, not his own earnings.* The health, strength, and physical force by which he acquires them are loans from God to enable him to acquire them.

(2.) *Man's intellectual blessings are God's gifts.* Information, learning, and all mental wealth necessary for the nourishment and support of the intellect.

(3.) *Man's moral blessings are God's gifts.* Man is entirely destitute of the means of making spiritual provision. God gives the power to repent and believe, and on the exercise of these saving instrumentalities depend all God's mercy by Christ, by the Holy Ghost in regeneration, sanctification, &c.

2. *God's gifts are as plentiful as man's need.*

(1.) *Wherever man exists he is found to be a needy creature, but everywhere his needs are met.* When it is cold, animals are found with skins which afford him suitable clothing and food, which contributes to warm his blood. In hot climates, suitable vegetable and fruits preponderate. In temperate zones both abound as and when he needs them. Political economists borrow from providence their law of supply and demand.

(2.) *Wherever man is found, he is full of need.* Physically, intellectually, and morally, but everywhere the promise holds good: "My God shall supply all your need according to His riches in glory by Christ Jesus."

3. *God's gifts are equal to all the emergencies in which man through need is plunged.* Everywhere "man's extremity is God's opportunity." Illustrations—Marah, water out of rock, quails, &c. In business perplexities, "If any of you lack wisdom let him ask of God." In family worries, "Casting all your care on Him." In painful sickness, "My grace is sufficient for thee."

II. God's bounty is based upon God's faithfulness. "He will be ever mindful of His covenant," which covenant binds Him over to care for His people. The Psalmist wrote this with reference to the Sinaitic covenant alone. Christians base their hope in its frequent repetition. (Jer. xxxi.; Ezek. xi.; 2 Cor. vii.; Rev. xxi. 7.)

1. *God's bounty is not capricious.* Faithful in opposition to fickle.

2. *God's bounty is not administered by favouritism.* Faithful as opposed to unjust.

3. *God's bounty is exactly suited to man's need.* Faithful as opposed to sentimental.

4. *Therefore man's supplies are sure.* Is not this contradicted by facts? No. (1.) We must take ALL *the facts into account.* The poorest Christian has more than the richest worldling. (2.) *We must give God the eternity He demands in which to work out His purposes.* "He will ever be mindful of His covenant." (3.) *If God withholds one gift it is only to give a greater.* (4.) *Men can afford to wait for the "eternal weight of glory."*

III. God's bounty is conditional on man's piety. "Unto them that fear Him," so says our Lord; "Seek ye first," &c. Paul: "Godliness is profitable," &c.

1. *Piety is necessary to secure the whole of God's bounty* — intellectual, material, moral. If a man loves his neighbours better than himself, and promotes their wellbeing to the neglect of that of his family and himself; if, while fervent in spirit, he is slothful in business; if, while devotional and philanthropic, he is neglectful of the laws of health, let not God be charged with the result.

2. *Without piety none of God's blessings will be secured.* The semblance or shell may be, but not the substance. To look at riches, luxury, &c., is to take an inadequate view of the case. In themselves they are unsubstantial, transitory, may be a curse, and are only valuable for results which without piety are never obtained.

3. *True piety is the sure means of securing God's blessings.* (1.) *Love of God.* (2.) *Proper love of self.* (3) *Love of others.* Fidelity to these laws is the basis of everlasting prosperity.

THE PURPOSE OF THE REVELATION OF GOD'S POWER.

(Verse 6.)

While we study God's revelations in the Bible, in nature, and in the course of providence, and read of His goodness there, never let us overlook the fact that they contain records of His glorious power. The thought in the Psalmist's mind was the conquest of Canaan, which (see the narrative) could only have been effected by the miraculous arm of God. Notice—

I. That God's people have acquired the heritage of the heathen.

1. *Materially.* God did not more give Canaan to Israel than He did the Roman Empire to the early Church, than He has done India, &c., to the modern Church. Witness the progress of those nations who have been true to God—England, Scotland, America. Contrast the decay of the great Oriental powers and superstitions, and Italy and Spain.

2. *Intellectually.* Christianity wields the sceptre over the world of mind. She has passed whatever precious metal there was in heathen philosophy through her mint. Whatever revolutions there have been in human thought she has impressed them into her service, and it is a remarkable fact that nothing that has not been received by the Church is acknowledged as unquestionable truth. And for many centuries it is the Church that has given to the world its explorers, scientists, and teachers.

3. *Morally.* The Christian wave moved by the breath of God has swept away many an idolatry, superstition, and vice, and is doing so wherever it rolls. There is much of each form of evil still, but compare the world to-day with the palmiest era of ancient Rome. Contrast the moral deserts with the Christian oases in the midst of them in Africa and Hindostan. What was Fiji a century ago? What is it to-day?

II. That this acquisition is the result of divine power.

1. *From the extreme unlikeliness of the result.* Imagine Nero's smile if Paul had predicted to him the changes which would take place in his empire within three centuries. Imagine Philips' incredulity if he had been told of the probable or even possible destruction of the invincible Armada. Who would have looked for such a development of Scotland's scanty resources, and the progress of the United States? Equally unlikely was it that the sayings and writings of a Nazarene peasant and His disciples should shake the schools of philosophers, and produce such thinkers as Augustine, Aquinas, Bacon, and Newton. Yet the simple preaching of Christ crucified has been the power by which God has changed the face of the world.

2. *From its complete success.* Wherever Christianity has gone, heathenism has receded, and the idols have been given to the moles and the bats; and it still goes on conquering and to conquer.

III. That this acquisition is for the benefit of humanity at large. It is not for the exclusive good of those who make the acquisition in the first instance, but for the good also of those from whom the acquisitions are derived. A good and wise conqueror contemplates the good of the vanquished. And so Christian conquests are achieved that the heathen may also become the children of God.

The Rectitude of God's Works and the Stability of God's Word.
(Verses 7, 8.)

The Bible goes upon the assumption that both nature and itself are the work of the same hand and the revelation of the same being. That being the case there can be no contradictions between them. (See Butler's "Analogy," chap. I.)

I. The characteristics of God's works.

1. *They are true*, "verity." They are real and genuine, and contrast with many of the works of man. In working out an end God employs the right materials. From the star to the grass-blade every means is adapted to its proper end in the best possible way.

2. *They are just*, "judgment." (1.) God uses *right materials in the right way*. He does not trench on the interests of any of His creatures. Everything is found in its proper and therefore best place, and is working out its best and therefore proper destiny. (2.) God uses *right materials to subserve right ends*, and seeks the good of all that He has made.

3. *Therefore God's works endure.* The second member of verse 7 certainly applies to God's Word. The application of verse 8 is uncertain. Perhaps this is intentional, that it may apply to both.

From the analogy of things we gather that what is good will stand. Man's works decay, many of them for the want of rectitude and justice. God's works stand fast for ever; they will be transformed, but not destroyed, because God has made them very good.

II. Characteristics of God's Word.

It is "sure" for the same reason as His works. As Matthew Henry says, it is "straight and therefore steady." It is founded no less upon the justice and truth of God than upon His mercy. "My word shall never pass away."

1. God's COMMANDMENTS *are sure.* There is no repeal for them. "God is not a man that He should repent." Let the wicked tremble.

2. God's PROMISES *are sure.* They are part of the "everlasting covenant." Let the righteous rejoice.

3. God's COUNSEL *is sure.* "Thou shalt guide me with Thy counsel, and afterward receive me to glory." Let all men hope. Learn—(1) *That the qualities of God's works and word are the qualities of its Author.* Truth, rectitude, immovableness. (2) *That these qualities afford an unshakable foundation for faith and hope* (Matt. vii. 24, 25).

Redemption: Its Sure Foundations and its Awful Sanctions.
(Verse 9.)

It is to be feared that the doctrine of redemption is underestimated and undervalued, from an inadequate conception of the majesty of its Author, and of the fulness of its obligation. God's justice had as much to do with it as His love, and its intent is not only to deliver men from hell, but from sin; and not only to privilege, but to duty. The Israelites were redeemed, not only by the visitation of God's compassion, but by His covenant; and not only out of Egypt, but to the promised land; and in that land they were to be a *holy nation.* The Redeemer of man is the "holy one;" and the end of His work is to "separate unto himself a peculiar people, zealous of good works."

I. Redemption. The redemption out of Egypt, to which this undoubtedly refers, was very suggestively typical. Egypt representing human bondage in general; the blood sprinkled on the doorpost, the ransom price; and the promised land in every respect the antithesis of the land of serfdom, the duties and privileges of God's believing people.

II. The sure foundations on which this redemption rests are "His covenants."

1. *God undertakes by virtue of this covenant to redeem all who will be redeemed,* and confirms that covenant with His oath (Heb. vii. 13-20).

2. *Redemption by price is secured for all.* Redemption was made possible for all Israel, but it was open to any to reject the privileges it involved. So Christ has died for all, yet the benefit of that death will be secured only to those who believe in Him.

3. *Redemption by power is only effected in those who fulfil the covenant conditions.* God has fulfilled all the conditions on His side that are possible, and waits to fulfil the rest. Man must fulfil his, and repent, and believe.

4. *To those who fulfil the conditions of that covenant, the covenant is made sure for ever.* "Unbelief may perhaps tear the copies of the covenant which Christ has given you; but He still keeps the original in heaven with Himself. Your doubts and fears are not part of the covenant; neither can they change Christ." —*Rutherford.*

5. *The covenant of God is the ground of the expectation of final and perfect redemption.* "The strong hope of our fastened anchor is the oath and promise of Him who is eternal verity; our salvation is fastened with God's own hand and Christ's own strength to the strong stake of God's unchangeable nature."—*Rutherford.*

III. The awful sanctions by which the duties of the redeemed are enforced. "Holy and *fearful*" is the name of Him who has redeemed us and to whom we owe allegiance. Redemption therefore involves—

1. Our holiness.
2. Our reverence for, as well as our love of God.

IN CONCLUSION. (i.) *Redemption gives God the absolute right to our service.* (ii.) *Selfishness and sin are sacrilegious thefts.*

THE NATURE AND ADVANTAGES OF TRUE PIETY.

(*Verse* 10.)

Both the character and advantages of religion have been sadly misrepresented. This authoritative declaration is therefore appropriate and valuable.

1. *Religion has been misrepresented as a thing of the emotions,* without vigour or intelligence; as that which is fit only for the Sunday exercise of those who have declined or lost the battle of life.

2. *Its advantages have been misrepresented as belonging exclusively to another sphere,* and to belong only to the future life; and therefore

3. *Secularists and others have condemned it as emasculating the human powers and imposing drawbacks on human progress.*

In opposition to this the authoritative document on the question declares—

I. What true piety really is.

1. *It is "the fear of the Lord."* Not slavish terror or alarm, but such respectful reverence as a good son will afford a good parent on his recognition of superior mental and moral qualities. Surely there is nothing degrading in this. On the contrary, it is sublimely elevating inasmuch as it involves (1) *The contemplation and love of infinite wisdom and holiness.* (2) *The careful avoidance of those things which infinite wisdom and holiness have condemned.* (3) *Such studies and practices which will bring man into harmony with infinite wisdom and holiness, and which will secure the approval of them to whom those attributes belong.*

2. *It is "to do His commandments."*

Is there anything degrading in this? (1) *We have nothing to do with those traditions which human folly has elevated to the dignity of divine commands.* Nor (2) *with the unworthy conduct of so-called Christian men.* (3) But *we have to do with the moral law of the Old and New Testaments, which the greatest moralists and statesmen have all but unanimously pronounced perfect.*

II. What the **advantages of true piety** really are.

1. *True piety is "the beginning of wisdom."* Wisdom may be defined as the choice of the best end, and the employment of the best means to secure that end. What is man's best end? Is it not the complete good of his complete nature, and that of his neighbour? What is the best means of gaining it? How can we know in the first instance and *do* in the second? (1.) *By insight?* Insight has never discovered the answer to these questions, as is proved by heathenism. (2.) *By learning?* Witness the moral degradation which preceded the downfall of the wisest nations of antiquity. (3.) *By experience?* History shows that man, except under Christian conditions, has never enjoyed such experiences as could help him to come to a right conclusion. (4.) *How then?* By that temper of mind induced by the fear of God which leads men to "love the Lord their God with all their heart and soul," &c.

2. *True piety, being the beginning of wisdom, grows with its growth and strengthens with its strength.* Having the true wisdom all other wisdom follows in its train. Fearing God (1) *I shall study His character.* That character is infinite. Therefore its study will enlarge my mind, train it for prolonged and patient efforts, for deep and abstruse subjects, secure its balance, safety, and sanctity. (2) *I shall study His works.* Hence follows all *science.* I am forbidden to investigate nothing. But my fear of God will prevent me indulging in unprofitable speculations and pushing my researches beyond desirable limits. (3) *I shall study His ways.* All *history* is open to me; and by regarding it as a development of God's providence I shall have a key to unlock its mysteries which merely human wisdom would not afford me. All *politics* are open to me, all *commercial enterprises*, all *discoveries* and *explorations*.

3. *True piety is the harbinger of success.* שׂכל would appear to mean the success which the exercise of wisdom implies, and the respect which wisdom commands. (1.) Those who fear God and keep His commandments make the best of both worlds. It implies *prudence*, as translated (2 Chron. ii. 12), *sense* (Neh. viii. 8), *knowledge* (2 Chron. xx. 22), *policy* (Dan. viii. 25). (2.) They gain respect and esteem; not the hypocrite, but the truly godly.

Eternal Praise.

(*Verse* 10, *last clause.*)

The occasional glimpses which we get of the service of angelic beings in the past eternity is singularly corroborative of our text. "The morning stars sang together," &c. "When He brought His first-begotten into the world He saith, Let all the angels of God worship Him." The ample revelations of the eternity to come confirm the same. The one theme upon the lips of unfallen beings in the past, and unfallen and redeemed beings in the present and future, is the praise of God. Notice—

I. **The object of praise** is eternal. God in His being and perfections is ever the same.

II. **The subjects for praise** are eternal. Man has always been receiving benefits. These will ever be remembered in grateful song. For *creation*, Rev. iv. 11; *redemption*, Rev. v. 9, 10. For *benefits that will ever accumulate*, Rev. xxi., xxii.

III. The **worshippers** are endowed with "life eternal" (Rev. iii. 2). The mind will be keener than ever for the appreciation of the divine wonders and goodness. The *heart* will be warmer than ever in its gratitude and affection. The *organs of praise* will be clearer and more powerful than ever.

PSALM CXII.

INTRODUCTION.

1. An alphabetical and hallelujah Psalm. 2. Author unknown; ascribed by Vulg. to Haggai and Zachariah after the exile. 3. A hymn on the excellence and reward of piety. 4. The concluding verse of cxi. and the first verse of cxii. form the point of union. "All human righteousness has its root in the righteousness of God. It is not merely man striving to copy God; it is God's gift and God's work. There is a living connection between the righteousness of God and the righteousness of man, and therefore the imperishableness of the one pertains to the other also."—*Perowne.*

THE CHARACTERISTICS AND BLESSEDNESS OF TRUE RELIGION.

(*Verse 1.*)

This verse may be taken as a text of which the Psalm is an exposition. True religion consists of (1) *Love of God's commandments*, (2) *Righteousness*, (3) *Grace*, (4) *Compassion*, (5) *Discretion*, (6) *Firm Trust in God*, (7) *Benevolence*. Its blessedness involves (1) *The superiority of the offspring of the religious man;* their (2) happiness, (3) temporal prosperity, (4) spiritual establishment, (5) everlasting remembrance, (6) confidence. In contrast with all this is the *misery, destruction, and disappointment of the wicked.* To restrict ourselves to the text, notice—

I. **The characteristics of true religion.**

1. *The "fear of the Lord."* "The Old Testament lays great stress on the fear of God. Everywhere it is the cardinal virtue, the corner-stone of the saintly temple—the root of grace out of which, if it be fully planted in a man's heart, all the other graces, all the varied fruits of righteousness, will be sure to grow."—*C. Vince.* This sentiment is peculiar to the godly; for the wicked have "no fear of God before their eyes." It is not a dread of consequences, but a dread of sin as alien to God and to man made in the image of God.

2. *Great delight in God's commandments.* "All that fear God are well pleased that there is a Bible, a revelation of God, of His will, and of the only way to happiness in Him."—*M. Henry.*

(1.) Those COMMANDMENTS *warrant our delight.* They are the revelation of His will who is the subject of man's filial reverence, and are the only means whereby the well-being of man may be secured.

(2.) *The* STUDY *of those commandments should be our delight.* Their wisdom and suggestiveness expands the intellect; their goodness excites the best feelings; they brace the will by their firm and resolute sanctions, they elevate and give a spiritual tone to all the faculties.

(3.) *The* PRACTICE *of those commandments should be our delight.* Their yoke is easy; their duties are pleasures; and in the volume of the book it should be written of the servant as well as of his Lord: "I delight to do Thy will, O my God."

3. *Divine praise.* "Praise ye the Lord." Fear and obedience are worthless without this supreme symptom of love.

II. **The blessedness of true religion.** "The word אֶשֶׁר is properly, in the plural form, blessednesses; or may be considered as an exclamation produced by contemplating the state of the man who has taken God for His portion. 1. *God made man for happiness.* 2. *Every man feels a desire to be happy.*

3. *All human beings abhor misery.* 4. *Happiness is the grand object of pursuit among all men.* 5. *But so perverted is the human heart that it seeks happiness where it cannot be found;* and in things which are naturally and morally unfit to communicate it. 6. *The true way of obtaining it is here laid down."—A. Clarke.* Learn—(1.) *That blessedness is God's gift.* (2.) *That duty is God's path to blessedness.* (3.) *That religion is the truest blessedness, because it involves relationship with God and fulfilment of duty.*

THE POSTHUMOUS RESULTS OF RELIGION.

(*Verse* 2.)

A conspicuous feature of the Old dispensation was that the blessings of the righteous were also the inheritance of their children. And those promises which were conferred on the posterity of the righteous Jew have not only never been recalled, but are among the express provisions of the Christian covenant. The second command is still unrepealed. Isa. xliv. 3 never received its fulfilment till Pentecost; *cf.* also Joel ii. 28–32, Acts ii. 17. Notice—

I. What our text presupposes.

1. *True piety*, which, consisting as it does in true wisdom, fearing God, greatly delighting in His commandments, and praising Him, (1) *will*, by the cultivation of healthy physical, intellectual, and moral qualities, through the well-known law of heredity, *will transmit the same.* (2.) *Will strive to predispose the child to the choice and reception of piety.* A good parent will carefully attend to the circumstances which surround his child, shielding him from temptation, and facilitating his choice of the good, at home, at school, in the selection of a profession, &c. (3.) *Will "train up a child in the way he should go,"* "in the nurture and admonition of the Lord;" will not neglect things spiritual in favour of things temporal; will strive to implant the fear of God, and the love of God's commandments, on the plastic character wisely and well; not making religious exercises burdensome but delightful.

2. *Firm faith that God will help and crown its efforts with success.* (1.) *It leans on the divine power.* It will pray, therefore, for the continual exercise of that power. (2.) *It relies on the divine promises,* which makes it hopeful of the result.

3. *Patience.* (1.) *In training.* A child has naturally a free and wayward will. To mould that will requires time and perseverance. (2.) *In waiting for results.* Seeds do not germinate all at once. The good seed may lie dormant for a considerable time, and the wise parent will not hurry it.

4. *The possibility of failure in certain cases.* "He who would share in the blessings of pious ancestors must follow after their faith."—*Starke.* A child may be proof against all piety and care, in which case the divine promises, which are all conditional, will not be fulfilled.

II. What our text declares.

1. *That "his seed shall be mighty in the earth."* (1.) *He will act upon mighty principles.* He will "seek first the kingdom of God," &c., and will exercise his father's prudence, patience, and piety. (2.) *He will overcome mighty difficulties.* He has God behind him to help him through all his perplexities, over all his impediments, to guide him by His counsel, and assist him with His arm. (3.) *Undaunted, he will achieve mighty successes.* Adopting his father's principles he will win victories on the field of mind; he will rule his own spirit; and be "not slothful in business." (4.) *He will wield a mighty influence.* He will excite confidence. His word will be taken, his opinion respected, his patronage courted, his example followed. Knowing the value and responsibility of his principles he will propagate them in his family, society, country; and neglect no opportunity to get the "Will of God done on earth as it is done in heaven." (5.) *He will leave behind him a mighty name.*

2. *They shall be blessed.* All the virtues are theirs,—Temperance, purity;

that diligence which makes fat; that prosperity which is conducive to spiritual good. All *moral privileges* are theirs,—the love of God, the grace of our Lord Jesus Christ, the indwelling and communion of the Holy Ghost, the means of grace, the hope of glory, and perhaps an early heaven.

III. **What our text implies.**

1. *That parents have a control over the destiny of their offspring.* If parents do not put these revealed laws concerning their children into operation, let them not blame God or fortune for the sad result. The promises still hold good; let parents plead them, and employ the means of securing their fulfilment.

2. *That as the result is in the hands of God, and might and blessedness His gifts,* let not parents be anxious about the result. If the conditions have been fulfilled, the bread cast upon the waters will return, though after many days. The great Augustine is a case in point. (See Confessions, Book III., par. 19-21.)

3. *That children incur grave responsibilities for the blessing of pious parents.* This is one of God's choicest privileges. Therefore children should yield their parents (1) *Love and reverence,* (2) *Obedience.* "Honour thy father and thy mother" is the first commandment with promise. To despise this gift is to forfeit the title to all the rest.

PROSPERITY AND ITS QUALIFICATIONS.

(*Verse 3.*)

It has been said that prosperity is the blessing of the Old Testament and adversity of the New. Nothing could be more untrue. The New Testament never elevates poverty into a virtue. Its poverty is that of spirit. With regard to the injunction addressed to the young ruler, notice—(1) *Provision for his wants would have been made;* (2) *by his poverty many would be enriched.* Warnings are uttered against the *danger of riches.* But there are other ways of avoiding danger than fleeing from it. It is dangerous to embark on the ocean in an open boat. So riches without corresponding protection are dangerous. Both testaments promise this protection. (Matt. vi. 33 ; Tim. iv. 8.)

I. **What is prosperity?** This demands a large definition. The miser is not prosperous, nor the man who amasses wealth and does not know what to do with it, or uses it for his own harm. To be prosperous is to have that which will promote the well-being of man's whole nature and which has that end secured. Material, moral, and intellectual wealth and its results.

II. **What is calculated to produce it?** The Psalmist, our Lord, and St. Paul are at one as to the qualification. "Righteousness." This also demands a large definition. It is not profession, emotion, or devotional exercises. It is the harmony of a man's whole nature with the will of God.

1. *When that is the case, a man is moderate, temperate, observant of natural laws,* and (supposing of course no constitutional ailment) therefore healthy. Thus righteousness affords a physical basis for success.

2. *He holds in check the feverish desire to succeed,* and thus godliness with contentment becomes great gain. Every day affords instances that *making haste to be rich* is but making haste to pauperise the health, the intellect, or the soul.

3. *He holds those passions in check which cloud the understanding and impair the vision.* He avoids all excess, either in self-aggrandisement or self-indulgence; the first of which dries up the sources of prosperity, and the second of which throws them away. Righteousness holds the golden mean.

4. *He respects the rights of others.* Hence, those whose rights you respect, will respect yours. No one cares for him who cares for nobody. While selfishness is everywhere condemned and scouted, those who are generous and helpful will not fail to find the same qualities in others.

5. *He will be frugal of his time, his money, &c.*, in recognition of God's claims upon both, and, as God's steward, will put them out to usury, and strive to be prosperous, that he may advance God's interests in the world.

III. **What objections can be urged against all this?**
1. *That the righteous are not better off than others.* But (1) Do those who are called righteous answer to the law of righteousness *in its entirety?* (2) Without controversy it is all true respecting *communities*. All history proves that they prosper in proportion to their righteousness. Theatres, taverns, houses of ill-fame, never exalted a nation. But that which promotes temperance and industry does, and that is righteousness. (3) It is so by the *common* consent of the world. How often do we hear the expression that such an one is "worth his weight in gold."
2. *That men prosper who violate the laws of righteousness.* But (1) *Are* these men prosperous? (2) Supposing them to have all that heart could wish, "*what shall it profit a man?*" &c. (3) Supposing it true of an individual, *when was it ever true of a nation?* To CONCLUDE.—"A man who is in possession of his whole manhood, so that every part is developed and harmonised and carried up into a beautiful symmetry, a perfect man in Christ Jesus; such a man is better adapted to develop prosperity than any other man in a lower sphere can be. . . . Manhood as contemplated by the Word of God: the Christian character made up of all elements, largeness of soul, wise judgment, reverence for God and His laws, love to man and kindly sympathy, belief in divine providence, hope of immortality, judgment of earthly values by the golden rod of the sanctuary; all these elements form a sure basis for prosperity in the world."—*H. W. Beecher.*

LIGHT: TO WHOM AND WHEN?

(*Verse 4.*)

Light and darkness, as symbols of moral conditions, are of frequent use in Holy Scripture. "God is light, and in Him is no darkness at all." The process of conversion is "from darkness into light." The wicked "love darkness," &c. The righteous "walk in the light," &c. These figures have peculiar force in the East, where the light of day is splendid, and the darkness of night intense. These illustrations are *generally* descriptive. There are breaks in the darkness of the most depraved, or their lot would be hopeless. There are clouds resting on the most pious, or their probation would be at an end. Our text

I. **Characterises those to whom it applies.** Not the perfectly sinless, but the *upright.* The figure is appropriate. Light descends, and those who stand erect are the most likely to catch its rays. The morally upright are those whose posture is straight, elevated towards God and towards heaven. Their attitude, therefore, is most calculated to catch the beams of the Sun of righteousness. 1. *They are upright in heart* (Ps. xcvii. 1). Their desires and emotions are pure. 2. *They are upright in mind;* candid, unprejudiced, welcoming light from all quarters. 3. *They are upright in will;* inflexible, just. 4. *They are upright in life;* examples, models, guides.

II. Implies that those whom it characterises have their **seasons of darkness.**
1. *The character of this darkness.* (1) *Religious perplexity.* Temptation to doubt God's providence, promises, and word. The mysteries of life, duty, and destiny will sometimes press upon the mind and dim the clearness of its vision. (2) *Domestic trials,* bereavements, sicknesses, disaffections, difficulties respecting the education and prospects of children will sometimes cast a gloom upon the heart. (3) *Business anxieties,* duties, failures, (4) the sense of personal sinfulness, and (5) slander, misrepresentation, and persecution will overcast the soul.
2. *The purpose of this darkness.* Being abnormal, and yet of divine ordination, there must be some reason for it. (1.)

It is merciful. Night is a necessary adjunct to day. The eye cannot bear the unclouded lustre of the sun. (2.) *It is disciplinary.* The repose of the eyelids during night prepares for the strain of daylight. (3.) *It is testing.* Darkness is a trial of our faith in God, &c.

III. Declares that, to those it characterises, **light ariseth in the darkness.**

1. *Observe, light ariseth* IN *the darkness.* It was so with our Lord, Luke xxxii. 43; St. Paul, 2 Cor. xii. 8–10. In neither case was the darkness entirely removed. There was *enough* light, but not superabundant.

2. But it is light in the *darkness.* There is the light of innocence in the darkness of slander; the light of forgiveness in the darkness of sin; the light of divine comfort in the darkness of sorrow; the light of revelation in the darkness of perplexity. "They shall be delivered in due time and perhaps when they least expect it; when the night is darkest the day dawns; nay, at evening time, when night was looked for, it shall be light." —*M. Henry.*

IN CONCLUSION. (i.) *The upright have all their darkness here and mitigations even of that, but they travel to a land of perfect light.* (ii.) *The perverse and crooked have darkness too, but enough illumination to lead them to perfect light, neglecting which, it gradually fades into outer darkness.*

THE ATTRIBUTES OF THE UPRIGHT.

(*Verse* 4, *second clause.*)

The upright will be able to bend without breaking. Like true steel, pliant enough to accomplish its purpose without injury to its temper.

I. The upright **bend,**

1. *In graciousness.* They are not distant, cold, haughty, harsh in their judgments, or critical in their estimates. They are ready to consider all cases of need, and in such a spirit as shall not deprive their benevolence of all value. It will be a bending that does not seem to bend; a stooping of genial familiarity, "seeking not its own."

2. *In compassion.* The proud see no misery. The upright stoop that they may see it, and pity as they see. In that position compassion becomes practical and develops into active mercy and benevolent generosity.

II. Yet the upright **maintain their integrity.** They love, but it is the love of dignity and righteousness.

Illustration.

1. When the Queen visited the London Hospital, a poor little Irish girl expressed a wish to see her. Her Majesty went and encouraged the child by words, and smiles, and gifts. Did she lose her dignity by so doing? Far from it, majesty there bent in the right direction.

2. When "God so loved the world" did He drag His justice in the dust? Nay, His justice bent to provide justification for the sinner.

THE GOLDEN MEAN.

(*Verse* 5.)

The golden mean is much needed in those matters which concern justice on the one hand and generosity on the other. How to do good with money, time, influence, &c., without inflicting an injustice on self and injury on others is often perplexing. The Psalmist shows that it is possible to "show favour and lend," and yet "guide one's affairs with discretion." An alternative translation is, "Happy is the man that showeth favour and lendeth, he maintaineth his cause in the judgment," showing that the golden mean is the happy medium and the golden *rule,* and that an upright man will not show such favour, &c., as will bring down upon him the disapprobation of the just. Our text teaches us—

I. **That such circumstances will arise as to need and justify favour and loans.** All are liable to reverses of fortune. The sudden failure of a creditor, the dishonesty of a subordinate, ill health, family bereavement, may put any man in circumstances that require a temporary loan.

II. That that man is happy who so guides his affairs as to be able wisely to afford those favours and loans.

1. *Happiness will spring from the possession of those things which makes this possible.* It presupposes in the lender comfort and affluence, which have been the result of honesty, diligence, and frugality.

2. *Happiness will spring from the disposition to show favour and lend.* "Mercy
is twice blessed,
It blesseth him that gives and him that takes."

III. That that man is happy who can so guide his affairs as to do good and no evil by his favours and loans.

1. *It is no small source of misery all round when a man through a benevolence has done harm.* He is a loser himself, and his self-denial has been used for unworthy ends; and thus good becomes evil spoken of, and charity brought into disrepute.

2. *It is no small cause for satisfaction where beneficence secures good and profitable ends.* It will secure (1) *Individual gratitude;* (2) *The benediction of heaven;* (3) *The approbation of the good.* LEARN (i.) *That generosity should be the outcome of a careful consideration of means.* As God hates robbery for burnt-offering, we may be sure that He is displeased with the charitable use of other people's money. (ii.) *That generosity should be the result of a careful study of the merits of the case.* To encourage the professional beggar or the vicious person were sorry work indeed. (iii.) *That generosity should be exhibited in a discreet and just way.* To entrust money to the needy but improvident or careless, is to waste it. Actual need may be relieved by gifts in kind or the proffer of employment. (iv.) *But let no man screen himself behind the dictum, "just before generous," so as to be neither.* The good man will seek for opportunities. (v.) *Woe unto the man who seeth his brother in need and shutteth up his bowels of compassion against him.*

THE STABILITY AND MEMORY OF THE RIGHTEOUS.

(*Verse 6.*)

Only that which is stable is memorable. Monuments which crumble are soon forgotten. Memorials are built of durable materials. So the good man standing firm on unmovable foundations will be had in everlasting remembrance.

I. The **Stability** of the righteous.

1. *He rests upon immovable foundations.* God and His righteousness, love, and power.

2. *On that foundation he maintains a steady course.* He is not tossed about. He stands "foursquare to every wind that blows."

3. *From that foundation he hurls with steady aim.* He does not sin (ἁμάρτια), and thus miss the mark of his high calling.

II. The **memory** of the righteous. They shall be in everlasting remembrance, because—

1. *They are stable, and therefore endure* (Ps. i. 1-3).

2. *They are made of enduring materials.* Righteousness and goodness, like charity, can "never fail."

3. *They are worth remembering.* "The world has no interest in keeping up the memory of bad men, and, as soon as it can be done, hastens to forget them. Wicked men are remembered only when their deeds are enormous, and then their memory is cherished only to admonish and to warn. The world has no interest in keeping up the memory of Benedict Arnold, or Alexander VI., or Cæsar Borgia, except to warn future generations of the guilt and baseness of treason and profligacy. It has an interest in never suffering the names of Howard, Wilberforce, Henry Martyn to die, for these names excite to noble feelings and to noble efforts wherever they are

known."—*Barnes.* They are held in *grateful* remembrance; in *instructive* remembrance, examples, &c.; in *celestial* remembrance, for in heaven they receive "a crown of glory that shall never fade away."

"But strew his ashes to the wind,
Whose sword or voice has served mankind,
And is he dead, whose glorious mind lifts
  thine on high?
To live in hearts we leave behind is not to
  die."

FEARLESSNESS, FIXEDNESS, AND FAITH.

(*Verse 7.*)

Three great and closely allied qualities, always needed and always the heritage of God's people. The three stand or fall together. Where there is fear there is no fixity; and where there is no fixity there is no faith. But he who has a strong faith in God, will not fear "though mountains be removed," &c. (Ps. xlvi. 1–5).

I. **Fearlessness consists—**
1. *In not being afraid of evil tidings before they come.* The fearless man has no carking care, or harassing anxieties. He will wait patiently and courageously till evils arrive before he pronounces them fearful (Matt. vi. 34).
2. *In not being afraid of evil tidings when they come,* but a manful determination to make the best of them. The fearless man will face them, examine them, and conquer them.
3. *In not being afraid of evil tidings after they have come.* The fearless man does not fear consequences, but carves a new career out of misfortune, and educes good out of evil.

II. **Fearlessness is impossible without fixedness.** Fear is trepidation, wavering, retreat. Fearlessness implies settledness and steadfastness. Fixedness is—

1. *A steady preparation to meet possible fears;* a concentration and consolidation of forces around weak points that may be attacked, a gathering up of solidity and strength. Our *faith* may be attacked: let us examine its evidences, and purge its weaknesses, and fortify ourselves with irrefutable arguments. Our *virtue:* let us surround it with impregnable fortifications. Our *intelligence:* let us brace it by healthful thought and reading. Our *property:* let us by prudence and diligence prepare.

2. *A strong determination to resist the shock of evil when it comes.* "None of these things move me," said Paul. "A man who has not learned to say 'no'—who is not resolved that he *will* take God's way in spite of every dog that can bay or bark at him, in spite of every silvery voice that woos him aside, will be a weak and a wretched man till he dies. . . . Whoever lets himself be shaped and guided by anything lower than an inflexible will, fixed in obedience to God, will in the end be shaped into a deformity and guided to wreck and ruin. . . . We need a wholesome obstinacy in the right, that will be neither bribed, nor coaxed, nor bullied. . . . 'Whom resist steadfast in the faith.' "—*Maclaren.*

III. **No fixedness without faith.** "There is no stability and settled persistency of righteous purpose possible for us, unless we are made strong, because we lay hold of God's strength, and stand firm because we are rooted in Him. Without that hold, we shall be swept away by storms of calamity or gusts of passion. Without that . . . . there will not be solidity enough in our character. . . . To stand amidst . . . earthquakes and storms we must be built upon the rock, and build rocklike upon it. Build thy strength upon God." —*Maclaren.*

This faith is exercised—(1.) In the divine existence, power, goodness, and promise. (2.) In our own God-given strength. (3.) In our ultimate victory (1 John v. 4, 5).

THE NEED, SUCCOUR, AND TRIUMPH OF THE SOUL.

(Verse 8.)

I. The soul in need.

1. The soul needs *support in times of weakness*. It is like the body, debilitated, when out of health. Physical conditions, circumstances, temptations, sometimes engender spiritual weakness, and make the soul cry out for some support.

2. The soul needs *help in times of exhaustion*. Its strenuous efforts against its many foes frequently exhaust it. Those foes are strong, relentless, vigilant. The soul must be recruited by forces outside itself, or it will fail.

3. The soul needs *protection in time of danger*. There are some temptations which we must resist; some against which resistance is unavailing. Our only chance in this latter case is a strong refuge, or a powerful auxiliary.

II. The soul succoured. "He shall not be afraid." Weakness, helplessness, and danger will engender fear. Courage will be stimulated by timely succour. Such succour is afforded by God.

1. *God is the secret of the soul's strength*. When in weakness and debility, let the soul flee to Him. He has promised to "heal our sicknesses." He is the "health of our countenance." "They that wait upon the Lord," &c. And with strength will come fearlessness.

2. *God is the support of the soul in times of exhaustion*. "My flesh and my heart faileth," &c. "Come unto Me, all ye that are weary," &c. "God is a very present help in time of trouble." "Greater is He that is for you," &c. And, conscious of the upholding of Omnipotence, all fear will flee.

3. *God is the refuge of the soul in times of danger*. "The Lord God is a . . . . shield." "The name of the Lord is a strong tower," &c.

III. The soul triumphing. "Until he see his desire upon his enemies."

1. *God has promised not only timely succour, but ultimate victory*. He has promised, "grace to help," that "we shall withstand in the evil day," that we shall "overcome *all*," and to "give us the victory through our Lord Jesus Christ."

2. *That victory shall be complete.* We shall come off "more than querors," and have "an abundant entrance." Difficulties, doubts, sin, Satan, and death shall be beaten down under our feet.

LIBERALITY.

(Verse 9.)

There is a great deal of pseudo-liberality. Reckless almsgiving, needless charity, and benevolences from an unwilling heart, are not genuine liberality. That must have righteousness for its basis, need for its object, and usefulness for its end. The Christian law is based upon this (2 Cor. ix. 6-15).

I. True liberality must have righteousness for its basis, and constant righteousness, *i.e.*, not righteousness and favouritism mixed.

1. *It must proceed from a righteous motive*—not to secure praise, &c., as the hypocrites.

2. *It must be done in the right way*, *i.e*, on a just *principle* of selection, which implies investigation; by a just *method*—loans, when loans would be helpful; money, clothes, employment, food, as the case may require.

II. True liberality must have need for its object.

1. Not (1) *Sloth*, (2) *Drunkenness*, (3) *The misery of vice*. But

2. *Real poverty*. (1.) *The temporarily distressed.* These are frequently the most needy and the most worthy, and require the most righteousness to find out and relieve. (2.) *Widows and orphans*. (3.) *Charitable institu-*

tions. (4.) *Those depending upon us. To neglect them is worse than infidelity.*

III. **True liberality must have usefulness for its end.** "He hath dispersed." St. Paul (2 Cor. ix. 6–15) applies it in the sense of seed-sowing. Liberality contemplates a harvest of usefulness.

1. *God has made us treasurers of His bounty.* He has not given, only entrusted to us for special purposes what we have. A " man has made a sovereign honestly; it is his in point of fair service, by what is called right. If he wills it away, or spends it on himself, or keeps it, he violates no law. . . . Yet he says in effect, 'The money is mine, but I myself am not my own. I have no property in myself. I am God's agent. I have given society an equivalent for this sovereign; but the strength and skill by which I gained it are the gifts of God. I will hold what I have as Christ's. Holding it so, I instantly yield it at His call, saying, "Thine is to right." ' "—*Dr. J. Parker.*

2. *That purpose is useful dispersion.* (1.) A timely gift to a poor man will enable him to weather the storm and start afresh. (2.) A seasonable donation to a charitable society will be a means of boundless usefulness. (3.) Ample provision for those depending upon us will enable them to follow out and multiply our own schemes of usefulness. True liberality will plant roses in the desert, and turn the wilderness into the garden of the Lord. Barren wastes will smile with genial harvests, and solitary places will be made glad.

IV. **True liberality will have success and honour as its reward.** All experience shows generosity to be the best policy. Both have been tried. The miser is not only not really enriched, but positively impoverished. "Horn" is the symbol of power and influence.

1. *The liberal man will be enriched by the blessing of God.* He scatters only to increase. "The very act of scattering breaks up the mastery of selfishness, enlarges the circle of kindly interests, shows that there is something in the world beyond our own personal concerns. It were better therefore for man, better as a discipline, better for his heart, better for every quality that is worth having, that a man should throw some of his money into the river than that he should never give anything away. . . . Even if a man should get nothing back " he always increases in heart volume, in joy, in love, in peace; his cup of comfort is sweetened, he walks on a greener earth, and looks up to God through a bluer sky. Beneficence is its own compensation. Charity empties the heart of one gift that it may make room for a larger. 'Give and it shall be given you, good measure, shaken together, and running over.' 'The liberal soul shall be made fat,' &c." —*Dr. J. Parker.*

2. *His " horn" shall be exalted" in the estimation of mankind.* Who is it that the world delights to honour? The Bonapartes and the Rothschilds, or the Peabodys and the Wilberforces? Learn—

(i.) *That selfishness is a bad policy.* (ii.) *That liberality extends not only to money, but to time, life, influence, and work.*

THE WICKED SPIRIT.

(*Verse* 10.)

Our text is a most admirable exposition of what is termed the "bad" or "wicked" spirit. No tendency meets with more emphatic condemnation than that which sets in the direction of regret and annoyance at the well-being of others. Those who are the subjects of such feelings may well be styled "wicked."

I. **The character of the wicked.** רשׁע would seem to signify one who lies in wait, a mischievous and injurious person, and an oppressor. Hence the main points in his character are craft and cruelty. "Sin" and so the sinner, "like a ravenous beast, as crafty as it is cruel, is crouching outside the door, . . . only waiting for opportunity to be given to spring in and devour."—*Samuel Cox.* (Ps. xxxvii. 12.)

II. **The inspection of the wicked.** "Shall see." רָאָה, to see critically.

1. *The wicked look carefully for everything that is bad.* They would if they could be blind to everything that is good. They are keen hunters for slips, discrepancies, and falls.

2. *The wicked, however, find everything that is good.* They are compelled by their very search for inconsistencies to see the true character of the righteous. When they slander him, plunder him, and do all manner of harm to him, he returns good for evil. These are but so many opportunities for his righteousness, stability, compassion, and trust in God, and so many coals of fire for his enemies' heads.

III. **The disappointment of the wicked.**

1. *It is twofold.* (1.) *At not finding what they wish to find.* (2.) *At finding the exact opposite of what they wish to find. E.g.* Balak.

2. *It is intense.* (1.) *It takes the form of vexation.* Their machinations have been frustrated, and instead of working evil their worst attempts have worked together for good. (2.) *It takes the form of furious but ineffectual wrath.* "Gnash their teeth" (Ps. xxxv. 16, xxxvii. 11).

IV. **The fate of the wicked.** "Shall melt away." Instead of calamity falling on the righteous it falls upon them. The figure is very expressive and is often used.

1. In Ps. lviii. 7, they are described as melting away *as "waters which run continually,"* i.e., running to waste in the sand or evaporated by the sun. So the wicked waste away physically, intellectually, morally.

2. In Ps. lviii. 8, they are like *"the snail which melteth away."* (See Tristram's Natural History, p. 295, for peculiarities of snails in the East.) "The heat often dries them up by a long continued drought, or by the sun's rays penetrating into their holes." So all the resources of the wicked shall be dried up.

3. In Ps. lxviii. 2, they are likened to *"melting wax;"* so they form no real obstacle to the good.

(i.) *A word of warning.* (1.) *"Be vigilant,"* &c. (2.) *Beware lest you give the enemy an occasion for his spirit.* (ii.) *A word of comfort.* "No weapon that is formed against thee shall prosper," &c.

THE DESIRE OF THE WICKED.

(*Verse 10, last clause.*)

The Bible is full of statements and illustrations of the instability of sin. The righteous stand—are held in everlasting remembrance, while the wicked are tossed about, moved from their foundations, and finally melt away. The text points out the perishable character of the desire of the wicked. *That desire perishes—*

I. Because it is **selfish.** It breeds so to speak in and in, and thus first vitiates and then destroys production. This is illustrated by the fate of innumerable cravings. The lust for gain, drink, &c., literally dies out, and becomes a morbid habit which is never satisfied. So the soul that is greedy of the reputation of the righteous shall not be satisfied notwithstanding all it may get.

II. Because it has **nothing to fall back upon in case of disappointment.** The righteous, if disappointed in a given end, have always the desire for duty and God's glory to fall back upon, and thus they have a continual source of satisfaction. On the contrary, the frustration of wicked schemes ends in utter despair.

III. Because it has **no resources on which to rely.** The desire of the righteous is supported by God, conscience, and humanity. That of the wicked only by feeble and unsubstantial self. Their colleagues only afford assistance up to a given point.

IV. Because set on **unsatisfactory objects.** Those objects are sinful, and, as James says, "Desire, when it has conceived, bringeth forth sin; and sin, when it is finished, bringeth forth death."

V. Because the **frown of God is upon it.** Desire can only live under the smile and with the favour of God.

This favour rests upon the desire of the good; but turned away from the wicked their "desires perish."

IN CONCLUSION (Is. xxix. 8).

PSALM CXIII.

INTRODUCTION.

1. Another of the Hallelujah Psalms. 2. Date and authorship unknown. 3. The first of six Psalms in the Jewish liturgy (cxiii.-cxviii.) termed *Hallel*, or the Egyptian Hallel, as distinguished from the great Hallel. "This Psalm continued to be recited while the temple stood, and is still recited in Palestine eighteen times a year, apart from its customary, though not legal use, at the new moon. Outside of Palestine it is now yearly recited twenty-one times. . . . At the family celebration of the Passover Psalms cxiii. and cxiv. were sung before the meal, and indeed before the emptying of the second cup, and the others after the meal, and after the filling of the fourth cup."—*Moll*.

A NOBLE PEOPLE AND A NOBLE SERVICE.

(*Verse* 1.)

Nobility consists in those endowments which render the possessors worthy of honour. Nobility of service consists in the consecration of those endowments to the best being, for the best ends. This is nowhere fully the case except in the service of God.

I. The servants of God are a **noble people.** All God's servants are noblemen. Abraham, Moses, Caleb, Job, Isaiah, Zerubbabel, and the promised Messiah, God speaks of as "My servants." Christ's designation of Himself is, "I am among you as one that serveth." Nebuchadnezzar and Darius saw that Daniel and the three Hebrew youths were "servants of God." Paul, Peter, Timothy, James, and Jude called themselves servants of God. All Israel was such *ideally*; all Christians are so *actually*.

1. *God's servant realises the noblest and most perfect ideal of life.* (1.) *Some men live for pleasure.* (2.) *Some for intellectual effort.* (3.) *Some for moral excellence.* (4.) *But God's servants live for Him.* And here they have what they can never otherwise have, a powerful motive for virtue, full mental culture, and all legitimate enjoyment, for the education and completion of their whole being, hence God's service is the noblest ideal of life.

2. *God's servants have the noblest master.* It ennobles the proudest peer in the land to be in the service of his sovereign.

3. *God's servants yield to the noblest claims.* "I have made thee for Myself." This was not based upon any merit in us, but upon His free love and mercy. And therefore God's claims rest—(1.) *Upon the right of property.* We have rights over the products of our hand and brain. So has God. (2.) *Upon the right of sustenance and preservation.* The basest ingratitude is that which ignores the right of those to whose generosity we owe our all. (3.) *Upon the right of redemption.* Note the *price* by which it was effected, the curse from which it rescues, the *dignities* to which it elevates.

4. *God's servants have the noblest warrant for their service.* (1.) *The warrant of reason.* Their service is a "reasonable service." (2.) *The warrant of conscience.* (3.) *The warrant of love.*

5. *God's servants are promised and enjoy the noblest rewards.* God Himself. "I will be their God." There are many subordinate rewards, but this comprehends and crowns them all.

II. God's service is a **noble service.** "Praise the name of the Lord." This injunction no doubt refers to acts of religious worship as such. But it suggests much more, for all the acts of religious life are worship. "That ye should show forth the praises of Him," &c. "Glorify God in your bodies and spirits which are His."

1. *It is noble in the dignity of its sphere.* It links man with God Himself. Man becomes a "worker together with God," with Christ, who accomplishes His mighty undertakings by human agency; with the Holy Ghost, who uses man as His mouthpiece for conviction of sin, &c.

2. *It is noble in the motive from which it springs.* All life is noble or ignoble according as it is actuated by noble or ignoble aims. God's servants aim at "pleasing God." This motive animated our Lord, John viii. 29; Enoch, Heb. xi. 5; Solomon, 2 Sam. vii. 29.

3. *It is noble in the instruments by which it is accomplished.* All that is morally worthy is pressed into this service; the mind purged from error; the will freed from prejudice; the heart emancipated from irregular passion and sin; the body a temple of the Holy Ghost.

4. *It is noble in the freedom of its consecration.* It is not pressed service, it is purely voluntary under the "royal law of liberty."

5. *It is noble in the uses which it serves.* Doing the "will of God on earth as it is done in heaven."

GRATITUDE.

(*Verse 2.*)

Our text suggests—

I. That there are **grounds for gratitude.** We bless God for blessing us. These grounds are universal. "What hast thou that thou didst not receive?" From Him descends "every good and perfect gift." 1. *Physical.* The body with its organs, senses, members, susceptibilities of pleasure, provision for clothing, shelter, food, &c. 2. *Mental.* Literature, science, art, authors, poets, artists, are gifts from God. 3. *Spiritual.* The Bible, Gospel, means of grace, &c. 4. *Political.* Government, liberty.

II. That these grounds are **often ignored.**

1. *Men lose sight of their benefactor.* This may be (1) *Deliberate.* Men dislike to be under an obligation. The Emperor Basil was saved when hunting by a courtier, and all Constantinople was speculating about the reward, when, to the astonishment of all, the preserver of his sovereign was ordered out to execution on the ground that the debt could never adequately be repaid. So men owe so much to God that the sense of obligation becomes burdensome, and they therefore endeavour to banish Him from their minds. (2) *Careless.* Like the conduct of many children towards their parents. The blessings are so very regular that we forget their source.

2. *Men make light of their blessings.* (1.) Of their *physical* gifts. Sin prostitutes them, and the attendant misery is charged upon God. (2.) Of their mental gifts. The mind has wandered into unprofitable speculations, and is forthwith made responsible for the doubts and errors into which men fall. And men wish themselves dogs, without the power of thought. (3.) *Spiritual* gifts, from their fancied sufficiency. (4.) *Political* gifts, from love of lawlessness.

3. *Men deny the utility of thankfulness.* "If man serves us we repay him, in kind if he needs it; or by gratitude which gratifies his spirit. But what kind of repayment or gratification can God receive?" True, the divine benefactor is not dependent on man's gratitude or gifts; but this overlooks the duty of acknowledging a gift whether it advantages its giver or not.

III. That these grounds should be **acknowledged by present thankfulness.** The obligation commences the moment the gift is conferred, and should therefore be acknowledged forthwith.

1. *Circumstances should not be allowed to interfere.* Those circumstances are God's gifts, and should not be turned

205

into instruments for robbing Him of His rights.

2. *Persons should not be allowed to interfere.* The dearest human relative ought not to be so close as God. Debts incurred to man are not to be compared with those we owe to God.

3. *Inclination should not be allowed to interfere.* They do not interfere with our service to man, nor should they with our duty to God.

IV. That these grounds should be acknowledged by **perpetual thankfulness.** " I have loved thee with an everlasting love." " His mercy endureth for ever," therefore, &c. Learn—

(i.) *The evils of ingratitude.* It narrows the intellect, contracts the heart, restricts the sphere of service, and engenders a cold, hard, barren selfishness.

(ii.) *The advantages of thankfulness.* It secures further blessings from God, enlarges the volume of manhood, and prepares for the service of heaven.

UNIVERSAL WORSHIP.

(*Verse 3.*)

I. **God's name ought to be praised everywhere,** because—

1. *Everywhere He is worthy of praise.* (1.) *God's government is everywhere founded and administered on principles of righteousness.* (2.) *His beneficent provision for His creatures' want—His sun, His showers, His fruits, &c.—is made everywhere.* (3.) *His almighty protection, upholding the universe and protecting His creatures, is afforded everywhere.* (4.) *His offers of mercy extend, without distinction of race or order, everywhere.* His Son died for all, His Spirit strives with all, His Church welcomes all, and His heaven was made for all.

2. *Everywhere He is acknowledged to exist.* Sometimes this belief has been adulterated with error, but the substratum of the truth everywhere remains, and nothing can eradicate it. In all the great civilisations it has universally obtained. It has been said recently that a few savage tribes are without it, which, if true, is very unfortunate for atheism ; for that would prove that unbelief in God is only possible to the most degraded and brutal barbarism. In all ages God has been the trust of mankind.

3. *Everywhere, that is the end of God's providential plan.* " All shall know the Lord from the least even unto the greatest." " All nations shall do Him service." That is the grand destiny of the human race (Mal. i. 11 ; Rev. v. 8–14).

4. *Everywhere, that is the law of man's true dignity.* The history of the world shows that men are elevated and civilised in proportion to their recognition of the Most High. Everywhere it ennobles and sanctifies.

II. **God's name ought to be praised under all circumstances.** Under all the various conditions revealed by the progress of the sun, should man render grateful homage.

1. *In the business of the day,* for He makes it possible.

2. *In the family affairs of the day,* for He controls them.

3. *In the vicissitudes of the day.* In prosperity or adversity, for He is the author of both.

4. *In the transactions of government,* for He is King of kings and Lord of lords.

5. *And, since " He giveth His beloved sleep," in the repose which follows the setting sun.*

III. **God's name ought to be praised at all times.**

1. *In the beneficent march of the seasons,* for they are led by Him.

2. *In the gracious division of day and night,* for it was fixed by Him.

3. " *Early in the morning,*" at noon (Daniel), *at night* (our Lord on Olivet) ; for all departments of the day are ordained by Him.

THE DIVINE GOVERNMENT OF NATIONS.

(Verse 4, clause 1.)

The figure is that of God seated on His throne as King of kings and Lord of lords.

I. The divine government is **personal.** "The Lord is high." Human governments are institutional. But, while God usually works through natural laws, &c., He can work without them, and is always superior to them. "*He* maketh His sun to shine." "*He* doeth according to His will," &c.

II. The divine government is **exalted** "above all nations." Superior in its basis, aims, methods, to the best human government. It is superior in wisdom, comprehensiveness, sympathy, goodness, and resources, because directly administered by supreme wisdom, goodness, and power.

III. The divine government, from its exaltation, is **suitable to the circumstances of all nations.**

1. It is *absolute perfection*. Human legislation is made up of caprices, mistakes, changes. The great task of human governors is to alter, modify, or improve on the legislation of their predecessors, and thus it cannot be suited to all the circumstances of *mankind*. On the contrary, God's laws are unalterable, because incapable of improvement, and because promulgated by the all-perfect mind.

2. It is *founded on the reason of things*, and, therefore, is not arbitrary. It does not contemplate classes, &c.; it is perfect equity, and all nations may expect even-handed justice from the hands of God.

IV. God's government is **benevolent** towards all nations. Many societies are founded on the supposition that men were made for governments, and not governments for men. God rules for the express benefit of nations. They require, and so they receive, His control and care. But is this borne out by facts? Look at the miseries of nations. Answer—

1. *Much of this misery is self-inflicted.* If men will break God's laws they must take the consequences. All nations who are faithful to God are blessed.

2. *These miseries are insignificant compared with their blessings.* Our years of tyranny or depression must be balanced by the years of prosperity and freedom.

3. *These miseries subserve benevolent and righteous ends.* How often have famines been sent to drive a nation to its God. How often has God used a destructive war to expel a tyrant from his throne. Famine brought free trade. The Marian persecution inaugurated the Elizabethan reformation. The American war abolished slavery.

V. The divine government is **administered by Christ.** "The Father hath committed all judgment into His hands." (Daniel vii. 13, 14, Phil. ii. 9.) Christ is qualified for this office. 1. *By a personal acquaintance with His subjects.* (2.) *By a personal relation with His subjects.* He is a true King, not only the "able" but the "kinsman" of the race, born out of the bosom of humanity. (3.) *By an intense sympathy with His subjects.* (4.) *By His accessibility to His subjects.*

IN CONCLUSION. Let men and nations beware how they rebel against this government. Can they produce a better? They rebel against omnipotent goodness when they throw off their allegiance to God.

THE DIVINE GOVERNMENT OF HEAVEN.

(Verse 4, clause 2.)

God rules in heaven; and the difference between His government there and His government here is, that here men break its laws and thwart its beneficent designs; yonder all is harmony and obedience. "The Lord is high above all nations," but His *glory* is above the heavens. Here that glory is but faintly illustrated amidst the partial obedience of the best of His creatures and the rebellion of the rest; there fully. This government is based on the same principles, conducted by the same methods, and contemplates the same ends among glorified spirits as among men, and is acknowledged and obeyed;—

I. **Universally.** Rev. v.
II. **Reverentially.** Is. vi. 2. "With twain he covered his *face*."
III. **Swiftly.** Is. vi. 2. "With twain he did *fly*."
IV. **Comprehensively.** The ends of the divine government are the sole object of their service; they have no *personal* aims to secure, because in doing God's will they secure all.
V. **Continually.** "They rest not day nor night."
VI. **Willingly.** Their wills are in complete harmony with the will of God. Sin does not warp their inclination, and they are under no powerful restraint towards wrong.
VII. **Perfectly.** No sin blears their vision or blights their faculties. They see what is the perfect will of God, and do it with all the completeness of their being.

Let all Christians pray, "Thy will be done on earth as it is done in heaven."

THE ABSOLUTE.

(*Verse 5.*)

Verses 5 and 6 in the original present a parallelism which is not preserved in the English version. As Hebrew poetry they would stand thus:—

Who is like unto Jehovah, our God,
Who sits throned on high,
Who casts looks so low,
In the heavens and in the earth?

The italics of A. V. are of course supplied by the translators to make what appeared to be the best sense. We propose to treat the second and third lines (with Bunsen, Delitzsch, Hengstenberg, &c.) as a parenthesis. Our subject, therefore, is The Absolute; the incomprehensibleness of Deity. "Who is like unto Jehovah, our God, in the heavens and in the earth?" Notice—

I. **That the incomprehensibleness of God is generally acknowledged.** Observe—

1. *How it is presented in the Bible.* (Exod. iii. 14, xv. 11; Deut. iv.; 1 Sam. ii. 2; 1 Kings viii. 12–27; Job v. 9, xi. 7–9, xxxvii. 5, 23; Psalms lxxxix. 6, cxlv. 3; Eccl. xvi. 21; Is. xl., xliii.; Rom. xi. 33, 34.)

2. *How it is presented by philosophy.* Socrates maintained that "he only knew this, that he knew nothing." Plato: "The Maker and Father of the worlds, it is difficult to discover, and when found impossible to make him known to all." The *Eleatic* school held that "we ought not to assert anything concerning the gods, for we have no knowledge of them." So the *Stoics*. *Modern schools* assert the same. Schelling says, "God is that which is in itself and only from itself can be conceived." So indeed Hamilton, Mansel, Spenser, and Matthew Arnold. "A God all known and comprehended is no God. That which I fully know and understand, is below, not above me, for I have mastered it. I have not to worship it, it must bow down to me. That which towers immeasurably above me, which I cannot scale and cannot fathom, before which I am as nothing, *that* and that alone, I fall down to and adore—not ignorance, but knowledge is the mother of devotion. Nevertheless, the sense of ignorance in the created mind, of immeasurable ignorance and infirmity, is preliminary and essential to all true adoration."—*Dr. J. Young.*

3. *How it is presented by heathen religions.* "Seek fellowship with Zeus and Epictetus." Alas! it was the Zeus that was wanting. . . . There was a yearning for God, for personal fellowship with God, for personal likeness to God. . . . 'But who is the Zeus, the god of whom you talk, that I may believe on Him,' was the cry which grew more hopeless and agonising generation by

generation . . . to which religion had no answer."—*Baldwin Brown.*

II. **That men have universally striven to solve the mystery,** by taking up the challenge of our text. Sir W. Hamilton says, "From Xenophanes to Leibnitz the infinite, the absolute, th unconditioned formed the highest principle of speculation." And, as the only way in which man can define anything is by a process of more or less adequate comparison and illustration, he has endeavoured to figure God, and thus much of theology in all ages has been but the projected shadow of human thought.

1. *Much of* **natural theology** *has been constructed in this way.* It assumes that God is, and then undertakes to show what God is like. Man is capable of fashioning and combining existing materials, and directing them to the accomplishment of new results. So he thinks of a God like himself, a creator. He is capable of directing his materials to serve a definite and intelligent end. So he ascribes skill and design to the creator, and by his observation of the adaptation of means to ends in the world, that belief is confirmed. He is a father or king ruling by laws which he enforces by rewards and punishments. So his maker is argued to be his governor, who will bless his obedience and punish his sin.

2. *Much of both* **so-called orthodoxy and heterodoxy** *has been constructed in this way.* Arianism arose out of the transfer of human paternity to the divine nature. Calvinism starts with a sovereignty of God built upon the idea of remorseless human despotism. Many other theories, particularly some prevalent in the present day, proceed upon the assumption that God's thoughts are as our thoughts, and His ways as our ways.

3. *The various* **heathen mythologies** *have been built up in this way.* Very few are disposed to deny that the spiritual unity of God was the primitive belief of mankind. St. Paul shows the process from this to the most debasing forms of idolatry (Rom. i. 18–32). Sin darkened man's understanding and led his reason astray. It is easy to see how the divine attributes might have become dissociated, then made to represent independent divine forces, and then separate divine persons. It is a'so easy to see how these independent persons could be symbolised by natural powers and objects supposed to be most like them; and it is only a step further to manufacture a permanent symbol; and hence idol worship. Thus the progress of symbolism was first downwards from God, then upwards to Him. Nature worship was the earliest form of idolatry. Then human. The gods of nature were endowed with human attributes and forms, and heroes and ancestors were deified. The process went on till not a natural object, beautiful or monstrous, good or malign, and not a single human quality, good or bad, wise or ridiculous, but had its temple, peculiar, and in many cases consistent, worship, and its symbolical form. The difficulty became to distinguish what was *not* divine. What an exposition of "Thou thoughtest I was altogether such an one as thyself"!

4. "*The fundamental position of* **rationalism** *is, that man by his own reason can attain to a right conception of God.*" "Fools, to dream that man can escape from himself, that human reason can draw aught but a human portrait of God! They do but substitute a marred and mutilated humanity for one exalted and entire; they add nothing to their conception of God as He is, but only take away a part of their conception of man."—*Mansel.*

III. **That the Bible gives us a revelation of all that may be known of God in a manner suited to our faculties and saving to our soul.** "The infinite cannot be grasped within our thoughts, nor within any limits, for on all sides it has no limits. To know God *in His infinity* is impossible, but to know much respecting the God who is infinite is quite another thing, and may be grandly possible."—*Dr. J. Young.* The Biblical representations of God are very bold, but they are carefully guarded; and the difference between the symbolism which is the result of human speculation and that of divine revelation is, that the former degrades the Deity, the latter guides the human mind to transcend itself and lifts it up to the idea of infinite perfection. We may see notably in the mystery of the Incarnation, "the light which was manifested, that He the Eternal Son might reveal to men the Father whom no man hath seen or can see. . . . Parable after parable led men from earthly relations to those of the kingdom of heaven . . . the sower, the householder, the bridegroom, the father, the king. . . . But it was much more in Himself. . . . It was through His human nature as the Son of Man that men were to approach to a knowledge of the divine mind. . . . We who believe that the Word was in the beginning with God and was God, became flesh and tabernacled amongst us, . . . can enter into the meaning of the words, 'The only begotten Son which is in the bosom of the Father He hath declared Him,' and listen with awe and adoration to that which, if it were not true, would have been a blasphemy to make us shudder : ' Have I been so long time with you, and yet hast thou not known me, Philip? He that hath seen Me hath seen the Father.' "—*Plumptre.*

IV. **These considerations lead us to the following conclusions.**

1. *That the question of our text must remain unanswered.* God, like every other great truth, is incapable of full definition, whether by words or illustrations. The most perfect painting conveys no adequate idea of the sun. The most perfect model only faintly resembles a flower. The ablest disquisition leaves the mystery of life unsolved.

2. *That God has given us similitudes of what is best and holiest within the grasp of man's feeble intelligence, that* **every one** *may be able to form* some *conception of His character and will.* The hem of the garment was enough for the poor woman in the gospels ; so our notions of power, wisdom, love, &c., are permitted faintly to illustrate the infinite perfections of God.

3. *That God has given us these illustrations to lead us up to Himself.* He tells man *what He is like,* that man may know by spiritual apprehension and indwelling *what He is.*

"One day Martin Luther was catechising some peasants. 'Say thy creed,' he said. 'I believe in God, the Father Almighty.' 'What is it to be almighty?' asked Martin. 'Indeed, I cannot tell,' and Luther, with rugged beautiful honesty, said, 'Neither indeed, can I; and if I were to tell you truly there is not a doctor in all Europe who could tell you what it is to be almighty; but if you will always remember that He is your Father Almighty, high enough to rule you, wise enough to teach you, strong enough to help you, kind enough to love you, it will be well and enough.' "—*Coley.*

THE MAJESTY AND CONDESCENSION OF GOD.

(*Verses* 5, 6.)

The two extremes of God's infinite perfections are exhibited in our text : "Who sits throned on high, who casts looks so low." He is infinite in majesty, and demands our adoration ; yet He is infinite in condescension, thus making our worship possible. The first attribute alone would appal us by its awful grandeur. The second alone would lead us to presume.

I. **The majesty of God.** "Who sits throned on high."

1. *Above the realm of space.* There is nothing more sublime than the idea of infinite space. Of this we can understand little amid the contracted landscapes of our own country. We must stand where the mighty hills rear their cloud-capped pinnacles to heaven. But what is the grandest mountain range compared with the world of which it is but an excrescence ! And what is the world itself but a speck in the system to which it belongs. And what is that system in comparison with those eighty millions of systems in the vast universe. And "these are part of His ways ; but how small a portion is heard of Him."

Draw the line where we will, the immeasurable lies yet beyond, and above that immeasurable God sits throned.

2. *Above all duration.* Equally with the conception of space is that of time sublime. We cannot fix the mind on a continuous succession of periods without a corresponding elevation. (1.) Look at the history of our own nation. We can trace it back till it is lost in hoar antiquity. But compare it with the history of the neighbouring continent. When Britain emerged from obscurity, Rome after a long and splendid history was approaching its fall. When Rome arose, the fortunes of Assyria were beginning to decline, and the monuments of Egypt were worn by the elemental battles of centuries; and before that comes patriarchal history and the years before the flood. Yet what is all this compared with scientifically recorded time? Millions upon millions of years may have elapsed between the creation of the first man and the beginning in which God created the heavens and the earth. And beyond that, "before the mountains were brought forth, or ever Thou hadst formed the earth or the worlds—from everlasting to everlasting Thou art God." (2.) *But this is only half the conception.* How much there is of life remaining to us we know not. But beyond the limits of the longest life possible to us there is a vast ocean of time measurable only by the infinite mind; and beyond that is boundless eternity. "Time reaches not to the steps of the eternal throne. No law of succession narrows in His doings. All things are ever before Him. He is the Everlasting now—past, present, future; time and space, these creatures of His hand, are not, in relation to His infinite perfection."—*Bishop Wilberforce.*

3. *In the sense of exalted spirituality.*
II. The condescension of God, "who casts looks so low." God does not dwell in solitary and indifferent grandeur in the high and lofty place. He is the Governor of the universe; its Father and its Friend.

1. *God condescends to look on physical laws and employs them.*
2. *God condescends to look upon man and visits him.* Adam, Enoch, Noah, Abraham, David, the Jewish nation, and at last through His Incarnate Son.
3. *God condescends to look upon human governments and employs them.* "He doeth according to His will," &c. "By Him kings reign," &c.—

"He sees with equal eye, as God of all,
A hero perish, or a sparrow fall;
Atoms and systems into ruin hurled:
There a bubble burst, and here a world."

Learn (i.) *The danger of antagonism to God;* (ii.) *The blessedness of the Divine condescension.*

HUMAN EXALTATION.

(*Verses 7, 8.*)

1. Verses 7–9 are almost word for word from the song of Hannah. (*Cf.* Song of Mary, Luke i. 46–48.) 2. Human exaltation is the result of the Divine benignity. Had God never noticed our lost race it had remained for ever in misery and degradation. But God's notice was God's redemption. The sentiment of our text may be illustrated—

I. In the various spheres of daily life, the poor have been lifted out of the dust, and have sat with princes.

1. *In the scientific sphere,—Sir Wm. Arkwright,* the inventor of the spinning jenny, was once a barber's apprentice. *Brindley,* the engineer; *Hugh Miller,* the geologist; *John Hunter,* the physician, were day labourers. *Thos. Edwards,* the naturalist, was a shoemaker; *Bewick,* the engraver, a coalminer; *Herschell,* a bandsman; *Faraday,* the son of a poor blacksmith; *Sir Isaac Newton,* the son of a farmer; *Davy,* a country apothecary's assistant. 2. *In the artistic sphere,—Turner,* the painter, was a barber; *Chantrey,* a journeyman carver; *Etty,* a journeyman printer; *Sir Thomas Lawrence,* the

son of a tavern-keeper; *Inigo Jones, John Gibson, Romney,* and *Opie* were labourers. 3. *In the literary sphere,*—*Shakespeare* was the son of a butcher; *John Foster,* a weaver; *Ben Jonson* and *Allan Cunningham,* day labourers; *Drew,* a shoemaker; *Adam Clarke,* the son of a poor schoolmaster; *Elihu Burritt,* a blacksmith; *Dr. Lee,* the great Hebrew scholar, a carpenter. 4. *In the judicial sphere,*—*Lord Tenterden* was once a barber's boy; *Talfourd,* the son of a brewer; *Baron Pollock,* son of a saddler; *Lord Eldon,* the son of a coal-fitter. 5. *In the army and navy,*—*Bonaparte* rose from the ranks; *Sir Cloudesley Shovel* was a shoemaker, and *Warren Hastings* was an East India clerk. 6. *In the Church,*—*Adrian IV.* was a swineherd; *Wolsey,* the son of a butcher; *Thomas à Beckett,* of obscure origin, *Bunyan* a tinker; *Whitfield,* the son of an innkeeper; *Martyn,* the son of a miner; and *Carey* and *Morrison* were shoemakers. 7. *In the field of discovery,*—*Cook* was a day labourer; *Baffin,* a man before the mast; *Livingstone,* a weaver; and *Layard,* a solicitor's clerk. Many more might be adduced in the political, social, and commercial spheres, but these are sufficient to show that God blesses the diligent use of the powers He has given. Would that they all had been employed for Him.

II. **In God's method of Redemption.** All men are by sin sunk in moral degradation. They are lost to self, lost to destiny, lost to God. When God looks upon them He raises them from their fall, and by the regenerating power of His Spirit they become God's heirs, joint-heirs with Jesus Christ, and are anointed kings and priests unto God, and look forward to a crown, a sceptre, and a throne.

III. **In the history of the Christian Church.** Its beginnings were of the humblest possible character. Its Founder was the reputed son of a carpenter; its first officers peasants or fishermen. For the first century, the "wise and noble" were conspicuous by their absence. Its beginnings everywhere are the same. It aims to seek and to save the lost, and it is the lost and degraded that it welcomes. Its beginnings are humble, but its progress is ever mighty. Philosophers and statesmen are proud to partake of its privileges on a level with the peasant and the slave, and kings receive their crowns from its hands.

IV. **In the resurrection of the body.** (1 Cor. xv.)

IN CONCLUSION.—(i.) *All true greatness is the gift of God.* (ii.) *All true greatness commences with the recognition of God.* (iii.) *All greatness fails if it does not secure the consecration of God.*

MOTHERHOOD: ITS BLESSINGS AND RESPONSIBILITIES.

(*Verse 9.*)

There is no sweeter name to a child than mother, and no sweeter name to a mother than her child's. The two greatest curses of mankind are bad mothers and thankless children. Our text suggests—

I. **That children are the subject of fond and prayerful desire.**

1. *This desirableness is in certain quarters denied.* (1.) *By a false political economy.* Children beyond a certain number are said to be the fruitful cause of misery and pauperism. So thought the Hindoos, and till recently the waters of the Ganges and the jaws of the alligator were the all-sufficient "check." So thought the Spartans, and the "check" with them was wholesale infanticide. Not more unnatural and not less vile are the artificial checks of modern civilisation (?). But that civilisation forgets that the miseries of the world proceed not from large families, but from the parental vices which it permits and sanctions. (2.) *By a false sentiment.* Children are said to be a trouble and expense, and men blasphemously treat the advent of children with

humorous resignation, if not with positive chagrin, and feel that society requires that demeanour. What makes children a trouble and expense but the indolence, hardheartedness, or extravagance of parents? 2. This desirableness is recognised by (1) *The nature of things.* "There is nothing addressing itself to nature to which the response is so quick, so universal, and so joyful as the coming of the young into the world. . . . There is almost nothing possessing a spark of intelligence which has not this inward preparation for rejoicing at the birth of offspring. . . . It is a bright day, or should be, in every household, in every neighbourhood, when a child is born, and a member added to society."—*H. W. Beecher.* (2) *By the barren mother* (see 1 Sam. 1, 2). Vain are all well-meant consolations. Tell her that they are but "careful comforts," that she has her husband, and immunity from family cares, and she will tell you that she is willing to bear every anxiety, if she can only be the joyful mother of children. (3) *By a just moral sentiment, and a sound political economy.* The object of existence can be but imperfectly attained without children. A family is a great incentive to industry. How many a wife has saved her husband from drunkenness and crime by the light and joy which children bring! (4) *By the word of God.* Sarah, Rebecca, Rachel, Hannah, Manoah's wife, &c. 3. *This desirableness is ennobling.* Because it is (1) *in harmony with the will of God* (Gen. i. 28). (2) *A desire to live for another.* (3) *An evidence of the paternity of God, and in conformity with it.*

II. That children are a mother's joy. This is now happily, thanks to the Bible, passed into a proverb, and children in all healthy circles are now regarded as a necessary element in the happiness of life. There is—
1. *The joy of expectation.*
2. *The joy of new maternity* (John xvi. 21).

3. *The joy of giving birth to citizens of the kingdom of heaven.* They are the Lord's heritage under both testaments (Ps. cxxvii. 3).
4. *The joy of training.*
5. *The joy of a nature ennobled and enlarged by maternity.*
6. *The joy of a* HOME.

III. That children are a mother's care. "He maketh a barren woman to keep house." He "not only builds up the family, but thereby finds something for the heads to do."—*M. Henry.* That being the case—
1. *Value them.* "Take heed that ye despise not one of these little ones." Their value does not lie altogether in their *charms,* &c., but in the fact that they are rational immortal beings, lent that you may enable them to realise the fact that they are "sons and daughters of the Lord Almighty."
2. *Study them.* Constant watchfulness, careful discrimination. It is not a virtue, but a vice that you are not guilty of to horses or dogs, *to treat them all alike.*
3. *Provide for them* (1 Tim. v. 8) (1) *Sufficient maintenance.* (2) *A good education.* (3) *A bright prospect.*
4. Consecrate them to, and train them up in the nurture and admonition of, the Lord.

IV. That children are divine gifts. "He maketh." Thus are they uniformly regarded in the Bible.

IN CONCLUSION.—"God is on the side of little children, and He is on the side of parents who wish to bring up their children right . . . and with some degree of teaching, and some degree of trust in God, you are adequate to lift your children from the plane of animalism, to the plane of social beings, and from that again to the plane of moral and spiritual beings; and when that is accomplished, the next change is to drop the animal altogether, and rise to the realm above, and be as the angels of God."—*H. W. Beecher.*

PSALM CXIV.

INTRODUCTION.

Date and Authorship unknown; ascribed to the three Hebrew children, Esther and Mordecai.

BONDAGE AND DELIVERANCE.
(*Verse 1.*)

I. The bondage was **degrading.** "Israel," "Egypt." The descendants of the "prince with God" making bricks for Pharaoh. So is the bondage of sin. All men are princes. They have crown rights by virtue of their divine parentage and royal brotherhood. They should occupy thrones. All their faculties are regal. Yet how are they employed? In a bondage that is humiliating because of (1) *The master that is served;* (2) *The nature of the service;* (3) *The wretchedness of the remuneration.*

II. The bondage was **unnatural.** "The house of Jacob."

1. *Once a free and independent tribe,* who previously to this had never been in bondage to any man. So man was once independent and free. No evil forces were permitted to exercise dominion over him. (1.) *His reason was free.* All God's vast domain was open to its scrutiny. (2.) *His will was free.* No power was permitted to tamper with it, and no predestination fettered it. (3.) *His affections were free.* (4.) *His soul was free.* All this shows that the bondage under which he groans is not natural to man.

2. *A family of a long, ancient and honourable lineage.* They were not a people of yesterday, yet they were slaves. Man is a member of a household which dates its origin from before the foundation of the world. The eternal God is his father, and Christ his elder brother. With an ancestry compared with which the oldest dynasty on earth is but of yesterday, man is enslaved. Surely this is the climax of unnaturalness. For the heirs of the Mowbrays, the Bourbons, the Guelphs, the Hohenzollerns, the Hapsburgs, to be in bondage were enough to strike the world dumb with astonishment. Man is a child of God, and yet he is a slave.

III. The bondage was **exasperating.** "From a people of strange language." These are circumstances which mitigate that "execrable sum of all human villanies"—slavery. These obtained largely among the Jews. Often the slave spoke the same language, was protected by the same laws, and was of the same blood as his master. Not so with the poor Egyptian slave.

1. *There was no community of feeling and sentiment.* Hence terrible oppression and thankless service. Between man and his oppressors there is nothing naturally in common. Man knows it. Satan knows it. Hence the terrible burden of sin and woe, and the terrible insurrections of reason and moral sense against the tyranny.

2. *There was no community of language between the Egyptian and the Jew.* Hence misunderstanding and distress. Man does not take altogether naturally to the language of hell. Facility in the understanding and use of that language requires long practice, and that practice never makes perfect. Hence constant misunderstandings. Good is represented by evil; evil by good. Ignorance exchanges places with knowledge, and knowledge with ignorance. Pain is substituted for pleasure, and pleasure for pain. And amidst these conflicting dialects man is bewildered; and it is of that bewilderment that Satan takes advantage.

3. *There is no community of law.* There is a show of one. Liberal terms are offered. Emoluments, honours, rewards, are promised. But there is nothing to make Satan keep his own terms; and, after years of painful and unremunerative toil, the "*wages* of sin is death." All these circumstances combine to make the sinners' bondage most exasperating.

IV. This bondage was **followed by a Divine Redemption.**

1. *That redemption was an historical fact.* "When?" Israel looked back upon it as such. So is the redemption of the world by Christ. The Church can be traced back to it without a missing link. Institutions were connected with it, date from it, and are still commemorative of it. In the one case, the Passover, &c., Scripture references and doctrines. In the other, all evangelical preaching commenced with it and refers to it. One day in the year is set apart for its contemplation, and one rite most impressively sets it forth.

2. *That redemption was not an iniquitous proceeding.* "Went out." They were not driven out or stolen out, but went out, through the divinely supported claim of their national rights. Pharaoh had no claim upon them. His service was robbery. Contrast and analogy.

(1.) *Contrast.* Man is subject to the rightful claims of law on his service. Those claims have been deliberately disregarded, and the law imposes a curse and a penalty. Man is redeemed from the law by Christ bearing that curse and suffering that penalty.

(2.) *Analogy.* Satan has no right to man's service. When that ceases Satan suffers no wrong. When man is released he is not stolen or driven, nor does he flee. He marches forth in honourable triumph, because Satan is overthrown and the law satisfied.

(3.) *That redemption was the beginning of their national life.* "When Israel.... House of Jacob." Before they were merely a tribe; in Egypt merely a caste; when redeemed, a nation. By Christ's redemption those who were not a people became the people of God and a holy nation. Before men were disintegrated members of the human race; afterwards brothers, friends, one in life, one in feeling, one in aim. Let political rulers, social agitators, and moral philanthropists note this. The redemption of Jesus Christ has succeeded in social purification and unity where every other scheme has failed.

IN CONCLUSION.—(i.) *If the Son has made us free, we are free indeed.* (ii.) *Stand fast in that liberty,* &c.

THE TEMPLE AND THE KINGDOM.

(*Verse* 2.)

God dwells among His people in a twofold character: as an object of worship, and as a monarch to rule. Hence in the sanctuary He secures His people's reverence and love. On His throne and over His dominion He secures their obedience and homage. Both the sanctuary and the throne are combined (1) *in the human heart;* (2) *the Christian Church;* (3) *the material universe.*

I. The **Temple.** "Judah was His sanctuary." The name is singularly appropriate. "The praise of Jehovah." In the sanctuary—

1. *God dwells.* His presence makes the temple what it is. "Nature" would be no "temple" if God were absent from it. Christ in the midst makes the Christian Church a temple; and the indwelling of the Holy Ghost the human heart.

2. *God manifests Himself.* In nature (Rom. i. 20). In the Church by the means of grace. In the soul (John xiv. 23).

3. *God communicates His will.* In nature (Rom. i. 19). In the Church, which is the depository of His written word and the organ for its dissemination. In the heart (Heb. viii. 10, 11).

4. *God must be adored.* In nature. "All Thy works praise Thee." In the Church (1 Cor. xiv. 25). "Bless the Lord, O my *soul.*"

II. The **Kingdom.** "Israel His dominion." The term again is appropriate. God is not the despotic master of a number of slaves, but King of *kings* and Lord of *lords.* His people are "princes with God," "a royal priesthood." It is the acknowledgment of His rule that ennobles nature, the Church, and the individual soul.

1. *God reigns in His dominion.* His presence pervades infinite space, and nature's orderly movements betoken the indwelling of nature's King. The Church in its spiritual powers, extension, working out of the divine plans, witnesses to the all-pervading presence of her Lord. The soul, in the provision that is made for its wants, and its power to withstand its foes, bears testimony to the presence of its Master.

2. *God reigns over His dominion.* The forces of nature emanated from Him, and He guides them to the fulfilment of their various destinies. The Church is under His command. It is "Go ye into all the world.". " Ye are My friends, if ye do whatsoever I *command* you." The soul is His, and is subject to His authority.

3. *God reigns for the good of His subjects.* In nature everything serves benevolent ends. Philosophy and legislation have not improved on the laws Christ gave to His Church. Only by keeping God's laws can the benefit of the soul be secured.

4. *God reigns that His dominion may be universally acknowledged.* It is so acknowledged in nature. It will be in the moral world by His Church. Christ "shall reign," &c. God yearns for the homage of each individual heart, and says, " Be ye reconciled to God."

THE REMOVAL OF OBSTACLES.

(*Verses* 3, 4.)

"The sea (the Red Sea) saw the mighty movement—the marshalled hosts —the moving masses—the cattle—the pursuing enemies—the commotion—the agitation on its usually quiet shores. We are to conceive of the usual calmness of the desert—the waste and lonely solitudes of the Red Sea; and then all this suddenly broken in upon by vast hosts of men, women, children, and cattle, fleeing in consternation, followed by the embattled strength of Egypt,—all rolling on tumultuously to the shore. No wonder the sea is represented as astonished at this unusual spectacle, and so fleeing in dismay."—*Barnes.*

I. **Antagonisms are quelled.** " The sea saw it and fled." Wherever the Church has advanced—

1. *Sin and Satan have receded.* Where it has not been so the Church is to blame. The promise depends on the proper spirit and the use of proper means. It is only when she loses her spirituality, or fights with carnal weapons, or depends upon the arm of flesh, that she has failed. When clad in her armour, she encountered the vices and follies of Roman civilisation, she was "fair as the moon, bright as the sun, and terrible as an army with banners."

2. *Idolatry has receded.* Christianity simply annihilated the classical, Druidical, Saxon, Tartar, and Scandinavian mythologies, the bloody rites of the South Seas, and is now doing the same for the debasing superstitions of Africa and the foul abominations of Hindostan. If not Christianity, what has? Not civilisation: it boasts that religion is out of its sphere. Not philosophy: in its palmiest days it gave itself to its exposition and was glad of its alliance. Not legislation: it has been the aim of human governments to protect it on utilitarian and other grounds. Clearly no other theory will account for it.

3. *Infidelity has receded.* For all the ancient philosophies she proved an overmatch. From her infancy she has given birth to giant intellects, who have saved the world from intellectual anarchy. She has vanquished the infidelity of the Renaissance, the French Revolution, the elder Deism, and Tom Paine. Socialism and rationalism have been weakened, and scientific materialism is met by an array of learning and acuteness without a parallel, and it will pass away.

II. **Boundaries are removed.** "Jordan was driven back."

1. *Christianity levels all class distinctions.* To all castes, Jewish, Roman, Indian, &c., it is a formidable foe. " In Christ Jesus there is neither bond nor

free," &c. It reduces all mankind to one common level of crying need, for which but one provision has been made.

2. *Christianity obliterates all physical barriers.* It goes into all the world and preaches the Gospel to every creature. It was not made for home consumption, but is the property of all nations.

3. *Christianity fills up all intellectual chasms.* No greater remove could possibly be than that between the old philosopher and the common people. Christianity appeals to both. Its truths are the food of the scholar and the refreshment of the slave.

III. **Difficulties are overcome.** "The mountains skipped," &c.

1. *All difficulties of nature.* Wherever Christianity has appeared "the valleys have been exalted," &c. Crooked ways have been made straight. No mountain has been too high, no sea too broad, no continent too wide, for the pioneers and missionaries of the faith.

2. *All difficulties of human prejudice.* Armies have been levied to extirpate it. Fires have been kindled to burn it. Learning has been accumulated to refute it, but in vain.

IN CONCLUSION.—This history is prophecy. Fulfilled prophecy in some instances. It holds good through the ages. Let the Church in the strength of it redouble her efforts, brighten her hope, perfect her faith, and go on conquering and to conquer.

WHY OBSTACLES ARE REMOVED.

(*Verses 5–7.*)

I. Because of the **omnipotent presence of the Lord.** "Nothing is too hard for the Lord" in the physical, intellectual, or moral world. He is the Author of nature, and can either suspend her laws or give His people strength to overcome them. He is the Lord of mind. He can bring to naught the understanding of the proud, or give His servants wisdom to expose their sophistries. He is the Lord of soul. He can subdue its sinfulness, or enable His ministers to bring that moral influence and suasion to bear upon it which shall turn it from darkness to light, &c. He has done, does, and will do so (Is. xl., liv. 14–16).

II. Because of the **covenant presence of the Lord.** "The God of Jacob." He has pledged His gracious presence with His people to lead them on to victory (Is. liv. 17 ; Rom. viii.). It was by virtue of the covenant made with Abraham, Isaac, and Jacob, and renewed to them, that Israel overcame their obstacles and inherited the promised land. And by virtue of a new and better covenant, God is on the side of His Church and against her numerous foes, and prepares her rest in heaven when her work is done.

III. Because of the **merciful presence of the Lord.** God rules in mercy as well as in power. It was good for Israel, good for the world then and through all time, that the sea should flee and Jordan should be driven back. The Canaanites were a curse to God's earth. It was in mercy that they were cut off. God established His people in their place, that through them all the nations of the earth might be blessed. This end has been answered, for of them, "as concerning the flesh, Christ came." The same applies to the Church.

IV. Because of the **righteous presence of the Lord.** "Tremble, thou earth," &c. Since God rules in righteousness He holds the power of retribution. The measure of the iniquities of the enemies of His people became full before the judgment fell. Righteousness still characterises God's rule. And because of that nations fall and are swept away when they disrespect His covenant and disobey His law.

TO CONCLUDE.—The Lord Omnipotent, covenant, merciful, and just, is with His Church. Let the Church be encouraged, humbled, energised, brave.

DIVINE PROVISIONS.

(Verses 7, 8.)

Verse 7 is the point of connection between verses 3-6 and verse 8. God's presence enabled His people to overcome their difficulties, and guaranteed a permanent provision for their need. God employs the Church to accomplish His magnificent designs, and His presence in its midst assures it constant blessing. Divine provisions are—

I. The result of the divine presence. God in His *works* is the source of their continual stability and strength. The fountain of their life and fruitfulness is there, and by His supports they flourish. God in His *word* is the source of its continual inspiration and suggestiveness, and because He is there, there is ever more "light to break forth from" it. God in His *Church* is the guarantee that the means of grace shall be efficient, and in consequence of this she grows in strength as she grows in grace. So in the *soul*.

II. Contemplate real need. God does not promise the luxuries or superfluities, but the necessaries of life; not confections or things merely grateful to the palate, but things necessary for refreshment, strength, and life. God does not undertake to pamper His people with worldly grandeur and mere material success; but He does promise that all things necessary for life and godliness shall be secured. Men can dispense with wine, but they cannot dispense with water. And so the Church can dispense with State alliances and popular applause, but cannot dispense with the water of life.

III. Come in unexpected forms. Even the faith of Moses would hardly have looked to the hard granite of Horeb, or the basalt of the desert, for refreshing streams. Yet at the command of God the rock was turned into standing water. And so invariably with the operations of providence and grace. Israel was led out of Egypt and to the promised land under the guidance of a shepherd. By a shepherd she was consolidated into a permanent kingdom. The prophets and apostles, as a rule, were drawn from the lowest stratum, and the foolishness of preaching has silenced the rhetoric of the schools. The good things of the world's redemption came out of Nazareth, and the power that has moved the world emanated from a malefactor's cross. Gain has come out of loss, life out of death, prosperity out of suffering "at the presence of the Lord."

IV. Flow with abounding fulness —"a fountain of waters." Wealth and prodigality characterise the divine gifts. Men minimise and contract them, but not God. The air, light, showers, sun, the magnificence of the heavens, the beauty of the landscape, and the grandeur of the mountains and the sea, all witness to the bounty which is at the disposal of needy man. But "these things are an allegory" of "the riches of His grace." "Ask whatsoever ye will;" "My God shall supply all your need;" &c. "God is able to do exceeding abundantly," &c. God "multiplies to pardon," gives "plenteous redemption," and finally vouchsafes "an abundant entrance into His everlasting kingdom."

V. Are constantly permanent. "Fountain." "Standing water." As God changes not, His bountiful provisions do not change. Man's need is abiding, so is God's gift. Man always needs water—at all times His water is sure. The Church needs a perpetual application of the benefits of Christ's death. His "eternal redemption" supplies the eternal need. The Spirit abides ever in the soul to confirm its faith, soothe its sorrow, and brighten its hope.

FINALLY.—It is to this and other passages (Exod. xvii. 6, 7; Num. xxviii. 11) that the Apostle (1 Cor. x. 4) draws his spiritual inferences respecting the support and refreshment Christ gives to His people. In the wilderness Israel (i.) *Were supplied without money and without price.* So Christ offers the water of life freely. (ii.) *Were indebted* to the cleaving of the rock at the word of Moses. So Christ, the Rock of ages, was cleft for us, and from His riven side flowed those streams which are for the cleansing and refreshment of the world. (iii.) *Now, as then, the blessings are permanent*, to stimulate our courage and confirm our faith.

PSALM CXV.

INTRODUCTION.

1. Date and authorship uncertain. Has been ascribed to the immediate *post exilic* psalmists, and to the poets of the time of the Maccabees. 2. Characteristics. Allusion to or quotation of Isaiah. The iterations (verses 9–13) suggest Temple service. 3. Ewald conjectures that the Psalm was sung while the sacrifice was offered, and that verses 12–15 were spoken by the priest declaring the acceptance of it; verses 1–11 and 16–18 sung by the congregation.

THE SOLE GLORY OF GOD, AND THE ABNEGATION OF MAN.

(*Verse* 1.)

The Bible everywhere gives bold prominence to the glory of God. That glory is said to be the end of all the divine works and ways. "The heavens declare the glory of God." "The whole earth is filled with His glory." Says the Old Testament Psalmist: "Give unto the Lord, ye kindreds of the people, give unto the Lord glory and strength; give unto the Lord the glory due unto His name." Says the New Testament Apostle: "Now unto God and our Father be glory for ever and ever." Notice—

I. That God's glory consists in His own supreme and solitary perfection. "Thy name." שֵׁם denoting internal essence, authority, rank, and dignity. When Moses inquired, "What is Thy name?" the reply was, "I AM THAT I AM." The divine glory consists in God being Himself. There is no glory in imitation. The glory of man consists in his being a man. When he becomes a child or a beast he loses his glory. So God's glory consists in His being what He is and nothing else; perfect and incapable of improvement in dignity, by time or through the homage of His creatures.

II. That God's glory is expressed in the mercy and truthfulness of His works and ways. These two expressions sum up the divine perfections, and illustrate two sides of the divine character. Their harmony in action—forgiving, yet not so as to violate the law of righteousness; truthful, yet not so as to deprive the guilty of hope—is God's glory, revealed to and manifested towards His creatures. This receives its full expression only in Christ, who is the "brightness of His glory," &c., in His ministry and death.

III. That God's glory should be apprehended and acknowledged by man. It must be apprehended before it can be acknowledged. No man can glorify God till he has some sense of His perfections as revealed in Jesus Christ. He must see the King in His beauty before he can admire Him. He must feel, in penitence and faith, that God is "just and the Justifier," "a just God and a Saviour," before he can adore Him. Then the honour due unto God's name will be a thankful and spontaneous tribute, and herein will God "be glorified that we bear much fruit."

IV. That God's glory is not the object of God's solicitude, but man's.

1. *God has no need to seek His own glory.* That comes in the nature of things. Even evil in some mysterious way subserves this end. 2. When God is spoken of as doing this or that for His name's sake or for His glory, it means that *He is not indifferent to what we think of Him*, and that it is only by our right thoughts and actions towards Him that our well-being can be secured. 3. When

man is solicitous to promote God's glory, God's object is secured. 4. Man's blessedness. "The glory which thou gavest Me I have given them," &c. (Rev. vii. 9–12.) V. That God's glory removes all ground of boasting on the part of man. "Not unto us." Boasting is here for ever excluded.... All the good we do is done by the power of His grace, and all the good we have is the gift of His mercy, and therefore He must have all the praise.... All our songs must be sung to this humble tune.... All our crowns must be cast at the feet of Him that sitteth on the throne."—*M. Henry.*

A GODLESS INQUIRY AND A GODLY RESPONSE.

(*Verses* 2, 3.)

This is an everyday question, asked by various people and on various grounds, and should be met every day with its all-sufficient answer. While a Christian man should not court controversy for its own sake, he should be ready to give an answer for the hope that is in him.

I. **The question,** "Where is now their God?"

1. *Why is it asked?* (1.) *Because of the spirituality of God.* God is invisible, and beyond the reach of man's physical sense. (2.) *Because of the fancied independence and power of man.* Pharaoh in his vain pride asked a similar question. So did Sennacherib. Surrounded by marshalled hosts, or protected by material forces, man sees no need of God; hence this question. (3.) *Because of the disinclination of depraved humanity to serve God* (Job. xxi. 14, 15). Man is a sinner, and feels if there be a God that God must have vengeance on his crimes, and that that God has strong claims upon his gratitude and service. (4.) *Because of the folly of the human heart.* If the evidences written on the heavens above and in the earth beneath are not enough, the question of our text must be regarded as the outcome of mental incapacity or moral obliquity. (5.) *Because of the apparent inequalities of God's providential rule.* (See Asaph's mournful wail, Ps. lxxiii.)

2. *By whom is it asked?* By (1) *The Atheist who, as the Antetheist,* dogmatically denies the divine existence; or, as the *Agnostic* and *Positivist,* maintains that God is unknown and unknowable. (2) *The Pantheist,* who denies the divine personality, and if God be impersonal He must be unintelligent and unconscious, and therefore virtually non-existent. (3) The *Deist,* who would acknowledge the existence of God as an hypothesis to account for the universe, but would deny his power to interfere with His works or the laws by which they are controlled. As Sir I. Newton remarked : " A God without dominion, providence, and final causes, is nothing but fate and nature." (4) *Unitarian;* for the only God we know of is He whom Christ reveals. (5) By the *Idolater.* All these sections of modern heathenism are asking the question to-day.

II. To this question there is **an all-sufficient answer** (ver. 3). The answer to the taunt of the heathen, who, seeing no image of Jehovah, mocked at His existence, is " (1) *He is in heaven,* invisible indeed, yet thence ruling the universe; (2) *He doeth what He will,* in fine contrast to the utter impotence of the idols of the heathen. (3) *God's almighty power and absolute freedom.* This, truthfully accepted, does away with all *à priori* objections to miracles."—*Perowne.*

1. *God exists;* as against the non-existence of idols. The world is full of thought and beauty and design which bespeak an intelligent mind and a powerful will. The universe is without a rational explanation on any other theory; and the human heart and mind are vacant without the thought of God.

2. *God exists in the heavens.* That accounts for His spiritual invisibility. God's being is too great to be within the comprehension of our poor faculties, and too holy to be perfectly manifested to our sinfulness. It is irrational to question the unseen because it is unseen.

3. God does according to His pleasure, not according to MAN's. This accounts for (1) *the fact that men question His existence.* He permits it that He may ultimately show its vanity, and confirm His people's faith. "A grand old Methodist preacher, called John Nelson, was obliged to become a soldier, and as he was arrayed, a mocking, bad woman came to him and said, 'Nelson, where is now thy God? Thou didst say at Shent's door that thou hadst no more fear of all His promises failing than thou hadst of falling through the centre of the earth. Where is now thy God?' Nelson, in whom the Word of God dwelt richly, said, 'You will find the answer in Micah vii. 8-10: "Rejoice,"' &c. I have some reason to believe that the answer was literally fulfilled."—*Dr. J. Parker.* (2) *For the apparent inequalities of His providential government.* God bears with tyrants, hoping that their repentance may avert His vengeance (Luke xvii. 1, &c). God permits the suffering of His people as the chastisement for their sin, the trial of their faith, or because His just designs for the *whole* of mankind could not be otherwise fulfilled.

"IDOLS AND THE LIVING AND TRUE GOD."

(*Verses* 3-7.)

The Psalmist having replied to objectors now carries the war into the heart of their camp. Nothing can exceed the contempt which the old Hebrew prophets poured on the various systems of idolatry. (Deut. iv. 28 ; 1 Kings xviii. 27-29; Isa. xxxvii. 19, xl. 19-24, xliv. 9 20; Jer. x. 3-5, &c.) The irony of *Juvenal* is very fine : " Dost thou hear, O Jupiter, these things ? Nor move thy lips when thou oughtest to speak out, whether thou art of marble or of bronze ? Or why do we put the sacred incense on thy altar from the opened paper, and the extracted liver of a calf, and the white caul of a hog? As far as I can discern there is no difference between thy statue and that of Bathyllus." Bathyllus was a fiddler.

I. **Idols vary** in every age and among various nations. **God remains the same.** The inhabitants of the old Pantheon grew in number with the years. First the elements, then deceased heroes, then good things, then evil things, and finally everything. Idolatry still lives on. Men worship themselves, their friends, wealth, pleasure, power, &c. But all fluctuate and die. Only God lives on.

II. **Idols are numerous and conflicting ; God is one and in harmony with Himself.** Olympus was a house divided against itself. The great Jove was supreme only in name. The suggestions of the patrons of all the virtues were met by the counter suggestions of the patrons of all the vices. The decrees of the goddess of wisdom were neutralised by the passions of the god of war ; and so with the idols of modern England. The living and true God, on the other hand, is one, and eternally self-consistent.

III. **Idols are the work of men's hands ; God is eternal and uncreated.** The same power which could make an idol can unmake it. An image can be worshipped one moment, used as a footstool the next, and destroyed the next. The living and true God is untouched by His creatures, and from everlasting to everlasting is God.

IV. **Idols at best can occupy only** "**temples made with hands.**" "**God is in the heavens.**" Men may erect their splendid temples and fashion their golden shrines. They may adorn them with the magnificent conceptions of human genius, with breathing canvas and speaking marble, and celebrate their worship with grand and costly ritual. But all is of the earth, earthy. The living God from His high and holy place looks down with pity and contempt on all.

V. Idols are senseless (5-7) ; **but God is keenly sensitive of the wants of His creatures,** and kindly attentive to their prayers.

" Little children, keep yourselves from idols."

THE MORAL CONSEQUENCES OF IDOLATRY.

(*Verse* 8.)

Men read into nature their own imperfect views of the supernatural, and thus their gods were like themselves; with the same bodies, parts, and passions. The gods again found their reflection in the hearts of their devotees. Both gradually grew worse and worse, till no passion was too vile for a god to feel, and no vice too bestial to be in some measure sanctified (Rom. 1). And now a man's character is formed by the god he worships. "Those that make them, and trust in them, are like unto them:"—

1. **In mental incapacity.** It would be hard to conceive the utter blindness of the idolater to the utter blindness of his god if it were not too sadly true. Wealth, personal appearance, pleasure, &c., are worshipped, in spite of the universal fact that they can of themselves do nothing for man; and yet man continues his mad and stupid idolatry. This worship blinds man to the inevitable result. He goes on till some rude shock wakens his mind into activity, and sometimes that shock comes too late.

II. **In moral insensibility.** The miser is as hard against moral impressions as his gold. The Midas fable is only too true. The self-worshipper is hardened in his conceit. The power-worshipper is encased in an ambition which few things can pierce. This insensibility is not of sudden, but gradual growth. The miser may have been tender at one time, but by degrees his love of gold has destroyed it all. Beware lest any of *you* be hardened by the deceitfulness of sin.

III. **In deep degradation.** All mythologies have deities which are the proper object of execration rather than worship. In the elegant (?) classical mythology the father of the gods was a buffoon and a sensualist, his father devoured his offspring; the god of valour was an example of domestic treason; and the patron of commerce was the special favourite of thieves. The Egyptian and Oriental gods are even worse. Their worship is consistent with their character, and makes their votaries like themselves. What degradation does the worship of Isis, Bacchus, Venus, Vishnu, Baal, and Astarte, &c., reveal. And so with the idols of a mis-called Christian civilisation. Gold and pleasure are hardly less animalising.

IV. **In malign harmfulness.** Idols can of course do nothing of themselves. But the influence of their supposed example can have but one effect. What the effect is heathenism in all ages abundantly shows. Bloody, impure, and implacable deities have produced men who rivalled them in debauchery and crime. And the influence of the lust of power, pleasure, or gain, is to wither the affections, blight the intellect, and blast the soul.

V. **In spiritual death.** Idols having no life cannot nourish or sustain it. The soul goes to them in vain for pardon and purity. The mind finds no base for its operation, no satisfaction for its craving; the life no authoritative rule, no guide in perplexity, no encouragement in duty. Everything upon which this Upas casts its shadow, dies. Learn—

(i.) *The danger of idolatry.* In itself and in the condemnation that rests upon it. "Ephraim is joined to his idols, LET HIM ALONE." (ii.) *The missionary duty of the Churches* towards heathenism abroad and at home.

TRUST IN GOD.

(*Verses* 9–11.)

I. **The nature of trust.** בָּטַח is used in two senses. (1.) To hang upon something, to rely, to trust. (2.) To live secure, careless, and calm.

1. *The believer depends fully on the help and protection which God affords,* and avails himself of them at all times and everywhere. He feels that there is

no other security or strength but in the power and goodness of God.

2. *Consequently he abandons all other refuges*, and fearlessly casts himself on God's care, and lives calmly in the midst of all his foes.

II. The **grounds** of trust. "He is their help and their shield."

1. *The divine help* is omnipotent, and therefore sufficient; wisely made, and therefore to be depended upon; ever present, and therefore available; willingly vouchsafed, and therefore fearlessly accepted. This help is offered when wanted, and therefore never superfluously; in sin, to pardon it; in perplexity, to remove it; in physical distress, to alleviate it; in trials, to safely conduct us through.

2. *The divine protection*. This was specially God's covenant character (Gen. xv. 1, Deut. xxxiii. 29). (1.) *The believer wants provision for his safety in his warfare*, and not simply help. The mightiest warrior is at the mercy of his weakest foe without a shield. So while the Christian wields the "sword of the Spirit," he wears other accoutrements, and "over all" the "shield of faith." (2.) The believer needs protection in time of exhaustion. The strength of the stoutest warrior must give way in time, and woe to him if the fortified camp or citadel is not within reach. So, for the exhausted believer, "the name of the Lord is a strong tower, the righteous runneth into it and is safe."

III. Those who trust. "Israel." "House of Aaron." "Ye that fear the Lord."

1. *The whole body of God's people*. Because (1) they are warranted in their trust. (2) *It is their duty to trust*. (3) *Their trust is necessary to their safety*.

2. *God's ministers*. In whatever sphere, let those who are working for God (1) *Trust in the help of God*, in the study and proclamation of His word; in their contest with infidelity; in their conflict with sin. (2) *Trust in the protection of God* against temptations, spiritual monotony, indolence, doubt, and fear.

IV. The consequences of trust.

1. *The believer is confident*. "He knows whom he has believed," &c.

2. *The believer is* TRUSTY. He is faithful; *full of faith*. Fulness of faith means full reliance on God, which guarantees fulness of sufficiency, hence fidelity.

IN CONCLUSION.—(i.) *A warrant*. "The Lord God is a sun and shield." (ii.) *A command*. "Trust ye in the Lord for ever," &c. (iii.) *A promise*. "Be thou faithful unto death," &c. (iv.) *A prayer*. "Lord, increase our faith."

GOD MINDFUL OF MAN.

(*Verse* 12.)

This is a continuation of the controversy between the believer and the idolater. In answer to the question, "Where is now your God?" the Psalmist replies, "In heaven, where yours is not. Your gods are silver and gold, articles of human manufacture, devoid of both sympathy and sense; but our God has been mindful of us, and will bless us."

This is one of the many proofs that the Hebrew faith was not an abstract monotheism, and that the Incarnation was its logical development. Jehovah was not some grand inaccessible power. He was their Father, brought into familiar contact with them, careful of their wants, and joyful when they were glad. This doctrine is followed by the revelation of Him who is the great expression of the mindfulness of God.

I. Why is God mindful of man? Scepticism scoffs at the idea as it did of old. Religious men sometimes wonder at it. The vastness of the universe, the enormity of man's guilt, the apparent insignificance of his age, size, actions, ever suggest the question, "What is man, that Thou art mindful of him," &c. God is mindful of man—

1. *Because He is God*. (1.) *He is the Father of man*, and naturally solicitous of the interests of His children. (2.) *He is the ruler of men*, and it therefore behoves Him to protect and regulate His subjects. (3.) *He is the creator of man*, and it is but natural that He should care

for that which He was at the trouble to make.

2. *Because of man's dignity.* When He created him He pronounced him to be very good. Alas! it is not so now. Nevertheless, compared with the rest of the universe, he is still " crowned with glory and honour." " There is but one object greater than the soul, and that one is its Creator."—*Augustine.* " Man is a feeble reed trembling in the midst of creation. . . . It does not need the universe to arm for his destruction. A breath of wind, a drop of water, would suffice to kill him. But, though the universe were to fall on man and crush him, he would be greater in his death than the universe in its victory ; for he would be conscious of his defeat, and it would not be conscious of its triumph."—*Pascal.*

3. *Because of man's sinfulness.* Sin is the disturbance of the moral order of the universe. The moral governor cannot be indifferent to this disturbance, and must as such endeavour to restore harmony.

4. *Because of man's needs.* Man comes into existence and continues a creature with wants which Omnipotence only can satisfy.

II. **When and how is God mindful of man ?**

1. *In need.* This indeed covers the whole of his life. From the moment of his birth to that of his death. God provides for helpless infancy by natural love and paternal strength ; for nakedness by the skins of animals, and the flax and cotton of the field ; and for his food, drink, habitation, sickness, &c., all creation seems to have reference.

2. *In sin.* He has come so near to him as to be born of a woman. He has given His Son to be a sacrifice for his guilt; His Spirit to regenerate his heart ; and His means of grace to support and strengthen the new spiritual life, so that he may resist sin and triumph over it.

3. *In His moral capacity.* Man cries out for the living God. God has given a revelation of Himself in His Word. Man needs laws, hopes, guidances, and God's Word is revealed as a lamp unto his feet and a light unto his path.

4. *In trouble.* God has given him the Comforter and the consolations and promises of His Word.

5. *For ever.* "O Lord, Thou hast been our dwelling-place," &c. "This God is our God for ever and for ever," &c.

III. **For what purpose is God mindful of man ?** That man may be mindful of Him. "I have created thee for Myself."

DIVINE BENEDICTIONS.

(*Verses* 12-14.)

The Psalmist, drawing upon past experience, looks forward into the future and sees it luminous with the presence and blessing of God. So may the believer. God has been mindful of him ; he may expect that God will bless him.

I. The **subjects** of the blessing.

1. *His covenant people as a whole.* That is God's part of the covenant. The Church undertakes to fulfil the divine commands, and God undertakes to crown that fulfilment with success and benediction.

2. *His chosen ministers.* Those whom He has called to arduous duty.

3. *The great among His people.* Those distinguished by extraordinary talent may expect that blessing without which all their talents are vain.

4. *The small among His people.* The weak. The lambs of the flock.

II. The **characteristics** of the blessing.

1. *It is a blessing.* The pure, spontaneous gift of God, which can neither be merited, purchased, nor earned.

It is a suitable blessing. Given with exact references to need. *His ministers may expect* blessings which will help them in their work ; enlarged views of truth, deep insight into the Word, power and success in its proclamation, strength in weariness, comfort in depression, and the crown of righteousness at the close. *His people may expect* spiritual enrichment and establishment; power to resist sin, subdue it, and triumph over it. *The great* among His people may expect special consecration for special talents, and special help in putting them to account. The small among His flock may expect help in their weakness; and as for the lambs, did He not "take them up in His arms, and bless them"? He does so still.

3. *It is an increasing blessing.* (1.) It increases those and theirs upon whom it falls. It enlarges every capacity, and widens every sphere of influence and usefulness. (2.) It increases in proportion to the enlargement of their capacity. It is grace upon grace, blessing upon blessing, until the whole nature is filled with the fulness of God.

4. *It is a personal blessing.* "He will bless." All mediatory benedictions, except in His name and declaratory of His promise, are an impertinence. The blessings fall direct from God's hands.

5. *It is an hereditary blessing.* "Your children."

III. The **conditions** of the blessing. "Them that fear Him." The God-fearing man is the God-blessed man, and as long as he fears God, and no longer, is he warranted in expecting the divine blessing.

THE CREATOR, THE CREATION, AND THE CREATURE.

(Verse 15.)

A leading tenet of Jewish belief was the creatorship of God. This, too, is a foundation article of the Christian creed. All the blessings that man has enjoyed under all the dispensations may be traced to this.

I. The **Creator.** "The Lord."

1. *The Creator is One.* The dualistic theory is here answered by anticipation. "God saw everything that He had made, and behold it was very good." The evil that is in the world has been introduced by the creature, and not by an equal or subordinate deity.

2. *The Creator is yet the Divine Trinity.* "Lord, Thou art God which hast made heaven and earth, the sea, and all that therein is." "One Lord Jesus Christ, by whom are all things." "The Spirit of God moved on the face of the waters."

II. The **creation.** "Which made heaven and earth."

1. *Everything,* Himself only excepted (1 Cor. xv. 27; Col. i. 16; Heb. iii. 4; Exod. xxxi. 17, &c.). "Whatsoever hath any being is either made or not made; whatsoever is not made is God; whatsoever is not God is made. One independent, uncreated essence, all others depending on, and created by it; one of eternal and necessary existence; all others indifferent either to be or not to be, and that indifferency determined by the free and voluntary act of the first cause."—*Pearson.*

2. "*The action by which the heaven and the earth were made* was the production of their total being, so that whatsoever entity they had when made, had no real existence before they were so made, a manner of production we usually term *Creation,* as excluding all concurrence of any material cause, and all dependence on any kind of subject, as presupposing no privation, as including no motion, as signifying a production out of nothing."—*Pearson.* (Rom. iv. 17; Heb. xi. 3.)

3. *The manner of creation.* (1.) *Absolute* (Gen. i. 1). (2.) *The adaptation of existing materials to special ends* (Gen. i. 11, 12; ii. 7).

III. **The Creator's benediction on the creature.** "Ye are blessed of the Lord." God's end in creation was the enjoyment of the creature. "The earth hath He made for the children of men." There is no natural gift from which man is debarred, and none but will in some way promote his wellbeing. It is nature's gifts polluted and perverted that are the cause of misery. "To the Christly man nature becomes a wonderful organ, and the opening of every stop can yield some tone of joy. The beauty of the wild flowers, the stars — 'the forget-me-nots of the angels,' the loveliness of the butterfly's wing, the glory of the forest foliage, the music of the bee as it hums, of the birds as they warble, of the wind as it sings among the trees and hills, or of the sea, in 'the everlasting thunder of the long Atlantic swell,' will make him feel that all that beauty, all that music, is the gift and revelation of 'God the Father Almighty, maker of heaven and earth;' and, overborne by emotions utterly unknown to others, he will—

"Lift to heaven an unpresumptuous eye,
And, joyful, say, My Father made them all."
—*Thomas.*

THE DIVINE DWELLING-PLACE.

(*Verse* 16, *clause* 1.)

NOTE.—"The heavens (are) heavens (*i.e.*, a dwelling-place) for the Lord" (Acts xvii. 24).

I. The divine dwelling-place is **exalted**. The exact locality of heaven the Bible has nowhere chosen to reveal. The expressions "high," "lifted up," &c., are probably to be interpreted morally. God dwells at an infinite remove from the constant mutations and moral imperfections of the children of men.

II. The divine dwelling-place is **holy**. It is emphatically the "holy place." Nothing that is defiled can enter there. Those who enter there have either never sinned, or have been purged from sin, and share the holiness of Deity.

III. The divine dwelling-place is to be the **dwelling-place of man**.

1. *Now spiritually.* "Set your affections on things above," &c.
2. *Hereafter perfectly.* "In My Father's house are many mansions," &c. "Father, I will that them which Thou hast given Me be where I am," &c.

THE EARTH: GOD'S GIFT, AND MAN'S INHERITANCE.

(*Verse* 16, *clause* 2.)

The earth is man's inheritance. No one disputes this. But how and why he came by it has been fiercely contested. He did not have it always, and science seems to prophesy a time when it will be no longer his. Why is earth his more than the heavens? And how? Most property has been either purchased or won by conflict. But how did it become theirs who had neither money, strength, nor arms? The Bible affords the only solution. God made man out of the dust of the earth, and therefore earth, and not heaven, became his sphere. God then *gave* him that with which he had so much in common, and told him to replenish and subdue it.

I. The earth, then, is **God's gift to man**.

1. *It is an equitable gift.* Belonging to God by the right of creation, God could do as He chose with His own. In doing this the right of no other creature was invaded. No other creature had the capacity for this possession. Birds and beasts can enjoy the harvests, but they cannot till the soil or sow the seed. Upon man's possession of it, therefore, largely depends the good of the inferior creation.

2. *It is a magnificent gift.* Compared with the largest planet and the universe, the earth may be very small. But with his faculties, it is all that he can enjoy, and God has given him that all. If he cannot enjoy the fruits of other worlds, yet this earth is a platform upon which he can enjoy the warmth and splendour of the sun, the light of the stars, and the influence of the moon, and his mind can be uplifted and enlarged by all that astronomy reveals. But in and of itself it is a magnificent gift. It affords science for his mind, beauty for his taste, trade for his practical instincts, material produce for his material wants; yes, and if he has eyes to see it, religion for his heart.

3. *It is a prepared gift.* "They were necessary those enormous stretches

of time, during which matter was consolidating into worlds; those vast geologic periods of fire and flood, of volcanic fury, of awful convulsion, of slow subsidence, of slow upheaval; those dark mysterious epochs of conflict between the inferior types of life;—in order that at last I might have a clear heaven above my head, a firm earth beneath my feet; that I might have an atmosphere to breathe; that I might have rivers to fish, and fields to plough; that I might have wood and iron for use, and flowers and precious stones for beauty."—*R. W. Dale.*

4. *It is an universal gift.* "To the children of *men.*" Not to the children of the noble, &c. Nowhere more than in this sphere has man been robbed of his natural rights. Sometimes he has robbed himself, and by a succession of degenerate descendants the wide acres which thrift has gained, have been drunk, gambled, or idled away. Sometimes others have plundered him, or outwitted him. But all the inequalities introduced by sin will be re-adjusted in that new *earth* wherein dwelleth *righteousness.*

II. **The earth is God's gift to man for certain definite uses.** Man is not the absolute owner of the earth. True, within certain limits, he may do what he likes with it, but he is morally bound to consider the ends for which it was given. It is let to him on lease. That lease expires with life; and then he will have to render an account of his stewardship.

1. *The world has been given to promote religious ends.* "The invisible things of God are clearly seen," &c, and thus the soil which man treads is holy ground.

2. *The earth has been given for the enlargement and education of his mind.* "The *Astronomer* has learned the thoughts that are written in that starry universe. The *Geologist* goes down and reads many thoughts in the rocky crust of the earth. The *Botanist* unveils the structures of flowers, and explains the actions and peculiarities of living plants; but all these things were written before he examined them. So with the *Anatomist:* he has discovered volumes of thought in this body which is fearfully and wonderfully made; but every thought was there before ever man looked within. . . . This vast universe exhibits thoughts in every leaf and every grain of sand, in every drop of water, in the mountains and in the heavens. Whence came those thoughts?"—*Alex. Stewart.*

3. *The earth has been given for man's use and enjoyment.* The air for his lungs; food to supply his bones with strength and his veins with blood; occupation for his exercise; stones, metals, wood, for the necessities and elegancies of life, &c.

4. *The earth has been given to be evangelised for Christ.* Since the original donation man has become marred by sin. But Christ has died for him, and now He says, "Go ye into all the world," &c.

LIFE AS THE SPHERE OF DIVINE SERVICE.

(*Verses* 17, 18.)

A *part* of this text has been quoted to support the opinion that the Old Testament saints were in the dark on the subject of immortality. The *whole* text goes to prove the very opposite. The Psalmist contemplates man in his material sphere. The earth has been given him; and on that earth it is his duty to serve the only living and true God. *That* ministry is over when he dies. "Nothing is more impressive than the utter *silence* of the grave. Not a voice, not a sound is heard there—of bards or men, of song or conversation, of the roaring of the sea, the sighing of the breeze, the fury of the storm, the tumult of the battle. Perfect stillness reigns there; the first sound that shall be heard will be the archangel's trump."—*Barnes.* The dead, as such, do not praise God. But who are the dead? The physical organs, limbs,

&c. These cannot praise God, because they have no object to praise. "God is not the God of the dead, but of the living." But worship may go in with different organs, and in a different sphere. The Psalmist goes on to say, "But we will praise the Lord *from this time forth and for evermore.*" עֹלָם is a word of very frequent use and has but one meaning, and that meaning is *Eternity.* When our Lord said, "I must work," &c., He did not imply surely that He had no work to do beyond the grave. Notice—

I. The characteristic features of divine service. "Praise." "Bless."

1. *Praise.* הָלַל throws light on the moral character of this service; to be bright, to shine. This splendour is borrowed from Him in whom is no darkness at all. Those who worship "walk in the light as He is in the light," &c. Hence (again true to the original) the Christian *boasts* not of his own excellences, but of the divine excellence which illuminates him (2 Cor. xii. 1–21). Through them his soul makes her boast in God: "God forbid that I should glory," &c. The Piel of our text יְהַלְלוּ means (1) *to diffuse brightness.* The beauty of Christian holiness, and the splendour of Christian life and worship, are so that we may be "lights of the world" and "show forth the praises of Him who hath called us," &c. (2) *Hence a large portion of worship consists in the most beautiful art;* viz., music, the only art as far as is revealed to us in the upper and better world.

2. *Blessing,* נְבָרֵךְ Piel of בָּרַךְ. To bow, to do homage, to utter blessing. (1.) *Our blessing must be based upon our homage.* Religious rhapsody is often profane. To bless God is a very solemn thing. A benediction on the King of kings and Lord of lords should be pronounced with bared head and on bended knee, and should not degenerate into mere ejaculation. (2.) *Our homage should be acknowledged by joyous gratitude.* Solemnity is not inconsistent with joy.

As we acknowledge God's sovereignty we may remember that that sovereignty is the basis of all our blessings.

II. The sphere of divine service. Life. "The dead praise not the Lord." With the occupation of their glorified spirits the Psalmist has here nothing to do. His ministry is for living men, and suggests that the sphere of religious activity is—

1. *The whole of the man.* His living entity. The aim of the Bible is to bring all the faculties of man into subordination to the will of God, and into full consecration to His service (1 Thess. v. 23, Mark xii. 29, &c.). And what is worship but the harmonious action of all man's powers. Music is harmony. One note by itself, or clashing with another note, the treble only, or the bass only, is not perfect music. So intellectual, or ethical, or emotional religion exclusively, is not perfect, much less so when the mental belief clashes with the ethical action.

"Let Knowledge grow from more to more,
But more of reverence in us dwell,
That mind and soul, according well,
May make one music as before."
—*Butvaster.*

2. *The whole of man's time.* Every moment there are reasons and opportunities for service. (1.) "*This time.*" Here and now God supplies our need; here and now the fact should be acknowledged. (2.) *To eternity.*

III. Exceptions to divine service. (Ver. 17.) The exact reference is not to the morally dead, yet the whole Bible is full of the doctrine that spiritual life is necessary to spiritual service. The morally dead are incapable of divine service for ever. Now they lack the motive, the will, and the power. And no new faculties, and no stronger desires, and no brighter opportunities will be vouchsafed beyond the grave. Our text may be used as (i.) *a plea for deliverance,* (ii.) *a call to instant decision,* (iii.) *an expression of full consecration,* (iv.) *an expectation of future blessedness.*

PSALM CXVI.

INTRODUCTION.

"This Psalm is an evidence of the truth and depth of the religious life in individuals after the return from the Exile. . . . It reminds us of earlier Psalms, and especially of the Psalms of David. His words must have laid hold in no common degree of the hearts of those who were heirs of his faith, and have sustained them in times of sorrow and suffering; and nothing would be more natural than that later poets would echo his strains, and mingle his words with their own, when they poured forth their prayers and praises before God."—*Perowne.*

PRAYER: ITS OBJECT AND ITS VALUE.

(*Verse* 1.)

The exact rendering would be, "I love, because the Lord heareth my voice," &c., and brings before us the proper object and the ethical value of prayer.

I. Characteristics of prayer.
1. "*My voice.*" Prayer should, as far as possible, be vocal. The conditions of prayer are hardly fulfilled when it is merely a current of devotional thought passing through the mind. True, there are circumstances under which sighs, unexpressed desires, are acceptable to God; but expression (1) *gives definiteness,* prevents the mind from wandering; (2) *gives completeness;* the sacrifice of the heart is then accompanied by the sacrifice of the lips.
2. "*My supplications.*" Which teaches us that prayer should be (1) *humble.* We are simply beggars at the throne of grace, and are absolutely dependent for every gift on God's free bounty. (2) *Full.* One supplication is not enough. We must multiply our supplications, as showing our need, and our confidence in God's infinite resources. We fail because we do not ask enough, or for enough. (3) *Earnest.* Cold formalities never reach the ear of God.

II. The object of prayer. "The Lord heareth."
1. *God can hear prayer.* "He that planted the ear shall He not hear?" God made man for communion with Himself, which would be impossible unless God could hear when man prays.
2. *God is willing to hear prayer.* (1.) *His commandments prove it.* "Make your requests known unto God." (2.)

His promises prove it. "Call upon Me in the day of trouble," &c. (3.) *Direct revelations to this effect prove it.* (Jer. xxix. 11–14., Zech. xiii. 9.)
3. *God does hear prayer.* (Isaiah xlv. 19.) All the Bible proves it; all Christian experience has proved it. "This poor man cried," &c.

III. The value of prayer.
1. *Prayer secures the object for which it asks.* "The Lord heareth." For God to hear is for God to answer, and His all-comprehending answer is Himself.
2. *In securing this grand object it secures all that it wants.* To answer some petitions would be harmful. The promise is, "My God shall supply all your *need.*"
3. *The effect of prayer* "is to put the affections in motion. Its object is the uncreated love, the eternal beauty; He of whose beauty all that moves love and admiration here is at best a pale reflection. To be in His presence is to be conscious of an expansion of the heart, and of the pleasure which accompanies it, which we feel in another sense, when speaking to an intimate and loved friend or relative. And this movement of the affections is sustained throughout the act of prayer. It is invigorated by the spiritual sight of God; but it is also the original impulse which leads us to draw near to Him. (Matt. xv. 8, 1 John iii. 21, 22.) In true prayer: 'Out of the abundance of the heart,'" &c.—*Liddon.*

IN CONCLUSION.—"How vain and foolish is the talk 'To love God for His benefits is mercenary, and cannot be pure love !' Whether pure or impure, no other love can flow out of the heart of the creature towards its creator. 'We love Him,' said Christ's holiest apostle, ' because He first loved us ;' and the increase of our love and filial obedience is in proportion to the increased sense of our obligation to Him."—*Dr. A. Clarke.*

THE MOTIVE FOR PERSEVERING PRAYER.

(*Verse* 2.)

There can be no reasonable objection to motives as long as they are pure, and so long as they are adequate for the purpose for which they are employed. The motives in God's Word are worthy and sufficient. We have a very beautiful one in the text. God has heard the particular request of the Psalmist, and he takes that as a guarantee of His willingness to hear and answer in all time to come. In the strength of this he vows to pray without ceasing. Notice—

I. **This motive reveals God's condescension and anxiety to hear.** "The Psalmist represents himself as so sick and weak that he could scarcely speak. The Lord is here considered as bowing down His ear to the mouth of the feeble suppliant, that He may catch every word of His prayer."—*Dr. A. Clarke.*

II. **The determination that is based upon this motive,** "I will call," &c.

1. *What?* "I will call," implying (1) *Resolution:* "I will." Prayer requires effort. "No man is likely to do much good in prayer who does not begin by looking upon it in the light of a work, to be prepared for, and to be persevered in with all the earnestness which we bring to bear upon subjects which are, in our opinion, at once most interesting and most necessary."—*Bishop Hamilton.* (2) *Confidence.* Unless there is an expectation of being heard the voice will falter. (3) *Earnestness.* Not a feeble whisper, but a loud cry. (4) *Publicity.*

2. *When?* "As long as I live." Heb. : "In my days." (1.) *Whenever opportunities occur.* These occur constantly. (2.) *As long as life lasts.* Not by fits and starts. (3.) *In the hour of death.* (4.) *In eternity.*

III. **The divine intention that is suggested by the ground of this motive, and the warrant for this determination.** God answers prayer—

1. *That we should believe that He hears and answers it.*

2. *That we may have "boldness of access with confidence."*

3. *That He may surround Himself with a royal priesthood,* who shall " show forth the praises of Him who hath called them," &c. Learn—(i.) *For our encouragement* that God desires our prayers, and is anxious to hear them. (ii.) *For our warning.* Unless we call, God will not hear. A prayerless people are a godless people.

SPECIAL PRAYER.

(*Verses* 3, 4.)

Prayer must be the Christian's atmosphere. As long as there is necessity for prayer we must pray. But there are special seasons which require special prayer. Our text indicates some of them.

I. **The time for special prayer.**

1. *In the pangs of disease,* either hopeless or apparently so. Heb. : "The cords of death encircled me." In the Old Testament death is represented as a hunter with a cord and net. In consumption or any lingering sickness the cord gets tighter and tighter, and the meshes more and more intricate, until all possibility of escape is cut off. One by one hopes fade, and encouraging symptoms disappear. Step by step does the fell malady march to conquest, and then the time comes when there is but a step between man and death. The Psalmist would appear to have been in the death

struggle. Whether the affliction was physical disease, overwhelming trouble, or extreme danger, does not appear, but the expression is suggestive of all.

2. *In the painful anticipation of the future.* Heb. : " The pangs of the underworld discovered me." "As if they had been searching for me, and had found my hiding-place. Those sorrows ever in pursuit of us will soon find us all. We cannot long escape the pursuit. Death tracks us, and is on our heels "—*Barnes.* (1.) *The pain of leaving those we love.* (2.) *The pain of unfinished work.* (3.) *The sorrowful contemplation of sin.* (4.) *For some, the fearful apprehension of wrath to come.*

3. *In bitter disappointment.* "Death found *me,* and *I* found trouble and sorrow. I did not seek it, but in what I was seeking I found *this.* Whatever we fail to 'find' in the pursuits of life, we shall *not* fail to find troubles and sorrows "—*Barnes.*

4. *In any kind of trial.* Whole text.

II. The **subjects** of special prayer. "O Lord, deliver my soul."

1. *The Psalmist's prayer literally was for life.* This value of and desire for life runs through the Old Testament. Not that we are warranted in believing that the Jew held that death was the extinction of the soul's life. But life that was spared was ever viewed in the light of consecration to God. The rest of this Psalm, and the conclusion of the previous, bears this out. He wished for life that he might pay his vows.

2. *The Psalmist's prayer admits of a spiritual interpretation.* Soul deliverance is deliverance from sin. Sin is the soul's death. All other aspects of death are comparatively insignificant. Of all legitimately special subjects this is the sum. If the *soul* is saved from death, physical dissolution can be apprehended calmly.

3. *The Psalmist's prayer suggests that subordinate details should be left in the hands of God.* His subsequent path is a matter of unconcern. If God spares his life, he knows that God will support it. "Is not the life more than meat?" All God's larger blessings include the lesser. (Rom. viii. 32.)

III. The **manner** of special prayer.

1. *Earnestly.* "Called." The case is urgent.

2. *Resignedly.* "I beseech Thee," *i.e.*, if it be Thy will.

IN CONCLUSION.—God sometimes allows His servants to approach extreme peril, that they may experience His extreme nearness, and the extreme efficacy of prayer.

ENCOURAGEMENTS FOR PRAYER.

(*Verse* 5.)

Under certain circumstances prayer would be impossible. If its object were unbending, and therefore incapable of hearing it, it would be useless ; if capricious, or too easily moved, it would be worthless ; if severe and implacable, we should have no heart to pray. The Christian is encouraged by the fact that God is gracious, righteous, and merciful. "He is righteous, He did me no wrong in afflicting me ; He is gracious, and was very kind in supporting and delivering me. Let us speak of God as we have found : and have we ever found Him otherwise ?"—*M. Henry.* "Instead of saying, 'Jehovah answered me,' he magnifies those attributes, which, from the days of His wonderful self-revelation to Moses (Exod. xxxiv. 6) had been the joy of every tried and trusting heart." —*Perowne.*

I. **Pray because God is "the Lord."** Jehovah, the Unchangeable One, who has eternity with its wealth and in its duration, in which and by which to supply all our need.

II. **Pray because the Lord is "our God."** Our dwelling-place, inheritance, and covenant possession. Hence all He is and has is ours. (Rom. viii. 32, 1 Cor. ii. 22, 23.)

III. **Pray because the Lord is "gracious."** חנון

1. *Condescending.* God stoops to hear prayer, and comes down to answer it.

2. *Favourable to prayer.* He has commanded it and promised to bless it. His Son has taught men how to pray, and ever lives to mingle their prayers with His. His Spirit helps men to pray.

3. *Kind to those who pray.* Does not lay upon them heavy burdens. Does not impose heavy penances or long liturgies. Hears the faintest sighings of the broken and contrite heart.

4. *Beneficent is His answers to prayer.* "Ye know the grace of our Lord Jesus Christ," &c.

IV. **Pray because the Lord is "righteous."**

1. *God is just in all His dealings.* Nothing that is right will be withheld; nothing that is wrong, bestowed.

2. *God is truthful in all His words.* His promises can never fail, because "He is not a man that He should lie," &c.

3. *God is reliable in all His ways.* We may depend upon the principles of His government as on an **unshakable** foundation.

4. "*God is faithful and just to forgive us our sins,* and to cleanse us from all unrighteousness."

V. **Pray because "our God is merciful."** רחם.

1. *God interests Himself in our case.* He is perfectly acquainted with it. "He knoweth our frame," &c.

2. *God is tenderly solicitous of our interests.* We are His "inheritance;" the "apple of His eye;" the "sheep of His pasture," &c.

3. *God is compassionate of our sorrows.* "In all our afflictions He was afflicted." Christ is "touched with a feeling of our infirmities."

4. *God is friendly towards our persons.* We are His "children," His "friends," "loved with an everlasting love," and "loved unto the end."

IN CONCLUSION.—Notice (i.) *The crime and folly of unbelieving despondency.* (ii.) *Let the considerations urge you to earnest and believing prayer.*

THE TIMELY HELP OF HELPLESSNESS.

(*Verse 6.*)

I. **Who are the helpless?** "The simple." פתה has three meanings:—

1. *To be open in the sense of being foolish and thus simple.* The immature in experience, the weak in understanding or will. God does not despise the poor imbecile, nor those who, through no fault of their own, are peculiarly open to the craft of those who "lie in wait to deceive."

2. *To be open in the sense of being frank, trustful, and ingenuous.* One who yields readily to truth and duty; without cunning, trickery, or guile. A Nathaniel.

3. *To be open, as in the case of little children,* which is indeed the rendering of nearly all the versions. Such, being members of the Kingdom of Heaven, are under the special care of its King. "Take heed how ye offend," &c.

4. *To be open, as in the weakness of sickness and old age.*

II. **When are they helped?** In their extremity. דלל to wave, to totter, to be loose; to be dried up, drained, to fail; to hang, to swing from side to side, as miners letting themselves down (Job xxviii. 4); *lit.*, they hang, they swing, far from men.

1. *In their insecurity.* The simple of all kinds are open to crafty and unscrupulous foes. How often are the weak of intellect or will outwitted in trade, opportunity, or health! How often does the guileless honesty and unsuspicion of the man who is determined to do right lay him open to intrigue! How often is the trustfulness of little children, and the semi-imbecility of old age, imposed upon! How often is sickness taken advantage of! But let their foes beware; for the Almighty has pledged Himself to be on their side.

2. *In their exhaustion.* (1.) *In the exhaustion of their natural resources.* (2.) *In the failure of their understanding* "God will guide them by His counsel." (3.) *In the abortion of their preventive efforts* the Lord will fly to their

succour. (4) *In the decrepitude of their physical strength,* in the feebleness which harassing anxiety has engendered, and in the failure of power at the hour of death. "His rod and His staff shall comfort" them.

III. **How are they helped?**
1. "*The Lord preserveth.*" שָׁמַר. To pierce, to be wakeful and active as a gatekeeper or shepherd, to protect and to attend to strictly. Then (1) *God keeps a vigilant watch over the weakness of the simple and the strength and subtlety of their foes.* "He that keepeth Israel neither slumbers nor sleeps." (2) *God throws an omnipotent protection round the simple.* "The name of the Lord is a strong tower," &c. "The Lord God is a sun and shield." "Underneath are the everlasting arms." But *are* the weak thus cared for? Notice (1) *Do the weak trust in God, or lean to their own understanding?* (2) *Have the* TRUE *interests of the weak, in so far as they have trusted in God, been permanently assailed?* Have their losses, sufferings, been real? Unsuspecting persons have been robbed of their temporal rights, perhaps, but has not the soul been safe, and is there not treasure in heaven? Children have been slaughtered, but they have passed to their crown without the pain and danger of the conflict.

2. "He helped me" יָשַׁע (1.) *God will* SAVE *the simple in their extremity.* Let them be assured that if they will trust in Him they are safe. (2.) *God will* SUPPORT *them in their weakness.* "My grace is sufficient for thee." (3.) *God will ultimately give them victory* (Eph. vi. 13, Rom. viii. 35–37).

IN CONCLUSION.—(i.) "*Man's extremity is God's opportunity.*" (ii.) *The enemies of the simple are the enemies of God.* (iii.) Is. xl. 27–31.

THE SOUL'S RETURN TO ITS REST.

(*Verse 7.*)

The many afflictions of the Psalmist had agitated his soul and shaken his confidence in God. He had been bound by the cords of death. He had felt the painful straitening of the tomb. Trouble and sorrow were the discovery of his search for good. His enemies had overmatched and exhausted him. In the midst of his affliction miraculous help had been vouchsafed. The Lord saved him, and now he returns to the rest of joyous confidence in God which stills for ever the tumult of his soul.

I. *The soul is commanded to return to its rest.* **Therefore this rest is its rightful heritage.** "Thy rest."

1. *This rest is not* (1) *the rest of mere local habitation.* The soul may be in a state of the greatest disquietude on the most comfortable couches, and in the most splendid dwelling-place. It refuses to be stilled by the tenderest caresses, and by the enchantment of the richest music, and is proof against slumber on beds of the softest down. Heaven itself would afford no repose to a soul in certain moral conditions. (2) *Insensibility.* When the soul ceases to feel it is not at rest, it is diseased or dead. Better the keenest anguish than this. (3) *Inactivity,* if, indeed, that were possible. An inactive soul would be a soul exhausted of its powers.

2. *This rest is, the harmony, health, and tranquil action of all the forces of the soul.* (1.) *The soul's rest consists in pure affection for a worthy object.* The soul was made for love: "Thou shalt love . . . with all thy soul." There can be no rest where there is no love, where that love is impure, or where it is fixed on unlovely objects. Hell is the state where irregular passions rage and clash with one another and cause agony, because there is no love and no object for love. Unholy love is feverish and insatiable lust. Love of the unlovely is the cause of more unrest than all other causes combined. The soul returns to its rest when it sets its regenerated affections on the things above. (2.) *The soul's rest consists in satisfying faith in an all-sufficient power.* Man was made for trust. No man is conscious of independence. He is therefore at unrest

until he finds some one on whom his faith can utterly repose itself. He is at unrest if he is trusting to a broken reed; and when that has given way he trembles to trust again. The doubtful mind (Luke xii. 29, μετεωρίζεσθε) is that which is tossed about in the open and stormy sea. The soul can only be at rest when its anchorage is in God. Only as we can say with Paul when the blast of Euroclydon was on the vessel, "I believe God," can we have peace. (3.) *The soul is at rest when its volitions are in harmony with a will higher than its own, and stronger.* Self-will is the cause of perpetual unrest. It is constantly thwarted and disappointed, and therefore never at peace. Only as far as the soul is in harmony with Him whose will rules the universe, and cheerfully assists in the fulfilment of the counsel of that will, can it be at rest. Its rest is this, "I *delight* to do Thy will," &c. (4.) *The soul is at rest when engaged in that work for which it is divinely fitted.* Ignoble callings, vulgar ambitions, and immoral pleasures, have no affinity with that which is the image of the great Creator. The soul was made to fight the good fight of faith, to work the works of Him that sent it; and only in such occupations can it be at rest. (5.) *Therefore, only as the soul is free from the perturbations of sin can it be at rest.* Sin has destroyed the moral balance of the soul, and introduced discord where all was harmony. That, thank God, can be removed. Peace follows pardon. Purity precedes refreshment. And the soul pardoned and refreshed, with its love fixed on God, its faith reposing on God, its will governed by God, and its work directed by God, it realises the promise to the full : " I will give you rest."

II. The soul is commanded to return to its rest ; **there is hope for weary man, that his lost rest may be regained.** Man *has* lost his rest. Furrowed brows, blasted hopes, ruined fortunes, early graves, all bear witness to this.

"Art thou weary, art thou languid,
Art thou sore distressed ?
Come to Me, saith One, and coming,
Be at rest."

" For the Lord hath dealt bountifully with thee." The details of that bounty are specified in the following verses. Those details may be summed up in one word, GOD. Elsewhere the soul may seek rest, but it will find none. God provides the soul with (1) *a lovely object:* He is "the King in His beauty;" (2) *a trusty object:* " Casting all your cares on Him ;" (3) *a governing will :* so that the soul can say, "Thy will be done;" (4) *an appropriate work;* " Workers together with God ;" (5) purity, harmony, peace.

IN CONCLUSION.—(i.) *Seek the true rest,* God. (ii.) *Seek it in the proper place,* God. (iii.) *Seek it by the best means,* God. " God is the centre to which all immortal spirits tend, and in connection with whom they can find *rest.* Everything separated from its *centre* is in a state of violence ; and if intelligent cannot be happy. All human souls, when separated from God by sin, are in a state of violence, agitation, and misery. From God all spirits come ; to Him all spirits must return, in order to be finally happy."—*A. Clarke.*

DELIVERANCE.

(*Verse* 8.)

I. Of "the soul from death." We are warranted in taking this in its most comprehensive sense. Of the life—

1. *From physical death.* The Psalmist had been brought to death's door and was restored to health and strength. There are few men who cannot say the same. Most have passed through dangerous sicknesses, or just escaped what might have been fatal accidents but for the interposition of a higher power. And, indeed, subtle perils lurk in the atmosphere we breathe, and the circumstances by which we are surrounded every moment, and yet we are spared.

2. *From intellectual death.* How near men are to that let our asylums show. The brain has a limit to its power, and

excess, the anxieties of life, and the grapple with great intellectual problems, sometimes brings us to the very margin which bounds sanity from madness. But God has interposed His "hitherto shalt thou go," &c.

3. *From social death.* How near are many men to ostracism from the friends who love them and the homes that cherish them! Many a man has uplifted a hand, which, had it fallen, he would thenceforth have been an outcast from his fellow-men. Many a man has entertained thoughts, which, had he uttered in the feeblest breath, men would have shunned him as a wild beast. Many a man has spoken five words, which, had they been six, the very wife of his bosom and the children of his heart would have spurned him. There have been men whose emotions have risen fifty degrees, and one degree more the brand of Cain would have been written on their forehead for life. God has saved their soul from death. Some men have committed social suicide, and God has given life to the dead.

4. *From moral death,* the real death of the soul. The soul is now dead in trespasses and sins. Those who live in sin are dead while they live. God can and does raise the soul into newness of life. Sinners, remember that there is a death, which, while it never dies, admits of no resurrection. This is "the second death."

II. Of the "eyes from tears."

1. *God sometimes delivers us from the occasions of sorrow.* Many things which would have caused us helpless grief, God has mercifully checked. Friends have been spared, losses averted, sharp arrows of pain missed their mark.

2. *God sometimes gives us grace to bear our sorrows,* so that we can say with more than resignation, more than acquiescence, with adoring gratitude even through our tears, "The Lord gave, the Lord hath taken away," &c.

3. *God sometimes wipes the tears from our eyes.* He "comforts those who mourn," &c., sends the Comforter, whispers the promises, and assures of the time when there will be no more pain, and when "He will wipe *all* tears from all faces."

III. Of his "feet from falling."

1. *Preservation from snares and pitfalls,* enabling us so to thread our way as to avoid those dangers which, if encountered, would be perilous to the soul.

2. *Firm establishment.* On a rock, so that nothing shall shake us. On a broad basis, so that looking down from the lofty pinnacle we shall not be made giddy, and fall.

3. *Sudden rescue.* The Psalmist's feet, like Asaph's (Ps. lxxii.), may have well-nigh slipped, one foot over and the other going, but God interposed. We have all had times like this.

IN CONCLUSION.—Notice (i.) This deliverance was *personal.* "*Thou,*" "*My.*" Not law, chance, providence. (ii.) This deliverance was *conscious.* It was not a beautiful theory, or a clever speculation. It was a fact. These two ideas, a personal relationship with a personal God, constitute the charm of the Psalms. Let us not break it. Speaking thus the Psalmist speaks for *man.*

WALKING BEFORE GOD.

(*Verse 9.*)

"We mean by men's 'walking' their conduct, the mode in which they carry themselves, and the progress they make as men. All men have 'ways,' all men 'walk' somehow. The difference between men spiritually is not between walking and not walking, but between walking rightly and wrongly; walking to heaven and to hell. Activity, incessant activity, is impressed upon all. It is the universal law. But some walk after the spirit, and others after the flesh; some in darkness, others in light. True religion is walking with God." —*A. J. Morris.*

I. What walking before God implies.

1. *That man is a social being.* Man

was made for companionship. Hence marriage. "It is not good for man to be alone." Man seldom cares for a solitary walk. Hence, in the journey of life, some "walk with the wise," others "go with the evil."

2. *That man was made for social intercourse.* Without this companions are useless or a burden. Man must have fellowship and interchange of thought and feeling. Without this his best life is sapped. His mind will be dwarfed by narrowness. His affections will be consumed in their own fires.

3. *That man's social instincts find their full development in intercourse with God.* Only by this means can the mind be *fully* fitted for man who is made in the image of God. His love for God, whom he has not seen, will qualify him for loving his brother, whom he has seen.

4. *That this bringing of God and man together in social intercourse is the end of providence and grace.* This was man's natural privilege as having affinity with God. By sin he forfeited it. God became offended, and man careless. But in the *fulness of time Emmanuel* came, and through Him God and man are reconciled and made at one.

II. What walking before God means.

1. *Conscious companionship.* Not mere intellectual belief in God's existence, nor a consciousness of God's omnipresence, but the nearness of God experienced and enjoyed.

2. *Spiritual sympathy.* "Two walk together because they are agreed." There must be unity of purpose, of taste, a correspondence of circumstances, and a harmony of will. We can admire a man, converse with him, receive favours from him, confer favours on him, dwell in the same house, exchange the courtesies of life with him, without walking with him. There is a general benevolence or humanity that engenders politeness, *i.e.*, kindness seasonably offered 'in form or reality.' But the man I walk with is my friend. I have proved his character, and I find it sound. I have noted his conversation, and not only approve his opinions, but imbibe his spirit. I have watched the issues of his heart, and I find their counterpart in my own bosom. He may be separate from me, his profession may be opposite to mine, his attainments, rank, look down upon mine, I still walk with him. . . . I doubt whether a man or an angel could commune with so entire a union. Then how are we to conceive of a man walking before God ?" Gen. i. supplies the answer.—*E. E. Jenkins.*

3. *Moral progress.* Going on to that perfection to which God leads.

4. *Careful circumspection.* "As ever in the great Taskmaster's eye."

III. Where walking before God takes place. "In the land of the living."

1. *Not in the other world.*

2. *Not in the contemplative sphere.* Men have considered this as presenting unusual facilities. Alas! they have found as many hindrances as they have escaped. Men now frequently look forward to the time when, retired from the turmoil and business of the world, they will be enabled to walk before God without distraction. But before that time arrives disinclination sets in, powers are demoralised, and walking before God fully becomes next to impossible.

3. *But in the land of the living.* In the midst of the living; in the engagements of the living; consecrating living activities to His services.

In conclusion.—"What a glorious life is this! Who loves not to walk with a dear friend ?—and the more if he be very wise and pure and good. Who that had to travel a doubtful road would not rejoice if that friend were a safe guide as well ? and still more, if there were fear of evil, one of a strong and skilful arm ? And further yet, if, being poor himself, that friend were able to meet all the possible charges of the way ? We 'walk with God,' who can supply 'all our need,' who 'guides us with His eye,' encompasses us with favour as a shield ; and 'we joy in God.'"—*A. J. Morris.*

THE NATURE AND POWER OF FAITH.

(*Verse* 10.)

I. The nature of faith. הֶאֱמַנְתִּי Hiphil preterite of אָמַן. To make fast or strong; to build. Hence, fig., to maintain, foster, bring up. The Hiphil (text) signifies to hold fast, to stand firm, to trust. "Powerful as is the effect of these words (Gen. xv. 6, where same word is used) when we read them in their first untarnished freshness, they gain immensely in their original language, to which neither Greek nor German, much less Latin or English, can furnish any full equivalent. 'He supported himself, he built himself up, he reposed as a child in his mother's arms (such seems the force of the root of the Hebrew word) in the strength of God; in God whom he did not see, more than in the giant empires of earth, and the bright lights of heaven, or the claims of kindred or country which were always before Him.'"—*Dean Stanley.* Hence the Psalmist's faith was not a mere intellectual assent to certain truths; but the conscious experience and actual realisation of certain facts. "The true living Christian faith ... is a sure trust and confidence in God, that through the merits of Christ his sins are forgiven, and he reconciled to the favour of God."—*Wesley.*

II. The power of faith. "I believed, *therefore* have I spoken." Everywhere faith and speech should be inseparable. The man who speaks what he doesn't believe is a hypocrite; the man who does not speak what he believes is a coward.

1. *The power of faith is to find expression for itself.* Hence this Psalm becomes a creed, and from this fact springs the vitality of creeds. The three great confessions of the Christian Church are a witness to the heroic faith of those who composed them. May they long continue the same for those who use them.

2. *The power of faith is to constrain those who believe to confess their belief.* The Psalmist had the burden upon him. He could not help but speak (Acts iv. 20). And so the Christian who is conscious of the great salvation will not only proclaim it, but do so under an irresistible impulse.

3. *The power of faith is to inspire loyalty to the truth we believe.* This saves from (1) *narrowness*, which contracts the truth and conceals part of it. A sound Christian faith holds "all the truth" and proclaims "all the counsel of God." (2) *From latitudinarianism.* The Psalmist's was not only a comprehensive, but a **correct** faith. Latitudinarianism mixes error with truth, or softens its rigour by a spurious charity. A sound Christian faith takes hold of and proclaims "the truth, the whole truth, and nothing but the truth."

4. *The power of faith is to impress us with the necessity of its declaration.* He felt his confession to be not only truth, but the only truth. The Lord, and the Lord alone, helped him; the Lord, and the Lord alone, could help others. Mighty is the obligation which rests on Christian men. Christian faith takes the facts of humanity and of God as they stand. Man sinful and helpless. Christ not one Saviour among many, but alone sufficient. It will brook the presence and pretentions of no rival in the work of man's regeneration, and declares again and again that without its efficacy man must perish. Hence the "woe is me, if I preach not the Gospel" which rests on the Christian man.

5. *Faith is the power of loyalty to the Lord of faith.* The Psalmist believed God, and was thereby strengthened in his submission to God's will. Faith empowered him to declare what God had done for his soul. And if we believe Christ as the Psalmist did God we shall keep that command, "Go ye into all the world," &c., disobedience to which is disloyalty to Christ.

6. *Faith is the power of confidence, and confidence is the power of successful*

enterprise. This faith has moved and still will move the world. Men who have faith in themselves succeed everywhere. What, then, must that faith be which has as it object the Lord God Omnipotent?

CYNICISM.
(*Verse* 11.)

The Cynics were a sect of Greek philosophers founded by Antisthenes, who from his morose and disagreeable proclivities was termed "the dog." He with his more famous disciple, Diogenes, are representatives of a class of men all through the ages who cultivate and exhibit a feeling contemptuous of or hostile towards their fellow-men. All are more or less subject to this, and all should strive against it. The Psalmist fell into it in his trouble, but soon got out of it.

I. The Psalmist's cynicism consisted in a **hasty conclusion** and an **uncharitable verdict**. On the spur of the moment. "I was greatly afflicted, and then I said in my haste," &c. ; somewhat rashly and inconsiderately in my amazement (so some) ; when I was in a consternation—in my flight (so others). Observe the faith of the best of saints is not perfect, nor always alike strong and active. When the Psalmist believed he spoke well ; but now through unbelief he spoke amiss.—*M. Henry.* "The Psalmist, on reflection, felt that he had said this without due thought, and that he was now disposed to think better of men than he did on the day of affliction and trouble. The world is much better than what we think it is when our minds are morbid and our nerves unstrung."—*Barnes.*

II. That the Psalmist's cynicism was **natural under the circumstances**, **although not justifiable**. He had been brought low, near to death, and was greatly afflicted. We may suppose that a great deal of his affliction was the result of treachery and bitter disappointment. The words seem to imply the cry of one who fled from men in ambush. But such a hasty generalisation, although natural, was not justifiable, because not true.

III. That the Psalmist's cynicism was only a **passing mood**. "He does not seem to have cherished this mood ; on the contrary, he seems to have been conscious of its wretchedness. . . . Most of us must have known what it is to have our sympathies and affections temporarily soured in times of vexation and disappointment. . . . The great danger is lest it should pass into a habit—lest we should nurse it until it becomes a chronic attitude of mind, and take a morbid pleasure in indulging it. . . . The fully-developed cynic prides himself on his indifferent tone. Like Iago he is 'nothing if not critical.' It is simply his 'way' to pick faults and sneer. We find the culmination of cynicism in Mephistopheles ; and indeed the word 'devil' means 'accuser,' slanderer of God and man."—*Finlayson.*

IV. That the Psalmist's cynicism was **successfully resisted and overcome**. The spirit of cynicism is abroad, how shall we resist it?
(i.) *By a charitable estimate of human infirmity ;* (ii.) *By a generous recognition of human excellencies ;* (iii.) *By a modest estimate of our own worth.* "Wounded vanity and disappointed ambition and trouble coming on an intense egotism are fruitful sources of cynicism. . . . A humble recognition of our own faults and defects will help to keep us from it ;" (iv.) *By looking at all men through Christ.* "This is the great antidote to the cynical spirit."—*Finlayson.*

SPIRITUAL REQUITAL.
(*Verses* 12, 13.)

The Psalmist is overwhelmed with a sense of the divine benedictions. He asks what return he can make. He feels that no return is so appropriate as acknowledging them in devout and public thanksgiving, and in asking God for more. A later custom of the feast of Tabernacles was to form a grand procession from the Temple to the Pool of Siloam, and for the high priest to hold aloft a golden goblet full of water from that pool, and pour it out as an oblation to God for His goodness. It was on that occasion, and probably in reference to that ceremony, that our Lord said, "If any man thirst," &c. After the Passover the master of the house lifted up the cup of wine, and blessed God for His mercy, and then passed it round. To this the Apostle referred when he said, "The cup of blessing which we bless," &c.; and the Evangelist when he tells us that Christ took the cup which was the cup of the New Testament in His blood; so typifying to us the sacrifice of thanksgiving, which becomes us until, as His guests, we shall sit down with Him in heaven and drink the cup of full salvation, which He, the Master of the house, shall pass round to all who shall be with Him there. Notice—

I. **That God requites His saints for their prayers.** "All His benefits towards me." These benefits were the salvations for which he had prayed (ver. 4), and the answers he had received (vers. 6, 7). This requital is based on

1. *The goodness of God.*
2. *The fidelity of God to His promises.* "Call upon Me in the day of trouble," &c.
3. *God's approbation of the use of divinely-prescribed means* (2 Chron. vii. 14).

II. **That the divine requital is ample and sufficient.** There is not enough in God's benefits to intoxicate; they are not dealt out at random; but they exactly meet, and to the full, the creatures' need.

1. *Temporal benefits.* God has favoured each one of us with that which is sufficient for our good. The sorrowful and suffering are the first and most earnest in their acknowledgments, that, as their necessities have arisen, God's supplies have been adequate.

2. *Spiritual blessings.* These have been full and overflowing. God's gift of Himself, by His Son and through His Spirit; the means of grace, the hope of glory, &c. All are as rare and costly as they are rich and full.

3. *Mitigated sorrows.* "It is good for me that I have been afflicted." They are benefits from the beneficent hand of God. They are mitigated by the fact that they are not penal, but disciplinary; that they are shared by the "Man of Sorrows;" that they are the subjects of the ministry of the precious promises and the consoling Spirit.

4. *Holy joys.* God's benefits are for the purpose of making us happy; they are earnests of our inheritance, and heaven begun below.

III. **That the divine requital of man's prayers should be reciprocated by man's requital of God's love.**

1. *How should man requite God for benefits received?* (1.) *By a cheerful reception of what God has given.* The cup of salvation is of God's filling. We requite that by drinking it. There is nothing more wounding to a generous heart than to slight his gifts. And to refuse to make our own the things which are freely given us of God is to slight and affront His love. And yet, alas! although God spared not His own Son, and that Son spares not His own Spirit, and that Spirit spares not Himself in providence and the means of grace, yet the great mass, not merely of mankind, but of professing Christians, stand stolidly indifferent, and allow divine blessings to run to waste. (2.) *By a correct appreciation of the contents of our cup.* We must recognise that whatever of bitterness there is in it, that it is of God's filling; and that, however nauseating it may be to our depraved palate, its contents are salvations. Let us take care that we know our blessings, or the empty cup will be eloquent of the mercies of which it once was full—

"That which we have we prize not to the worth
Whiles we enjoy it; but being lacked and lost,
Why then we rack the value, then we find
The virtue that possession would not give us
While it was ours."—*Shakespeare.*

(3.) *By a thankful recognition of the fact that all our benefits are from Him.*

"Call upon the name of the Lord." Only he who enjoys life in Him enjoys it at all. This is the true infusion that gives sweetness to the bitter, and more sweetness to the sweet. Without this religion will be but a drudgery, and life an empty void.

2. *Why should we requite God in this way,* viz., by a thankful reception of His gifts? (1.) *Because we are already so much in debt to His mercy.* "One reason why we should never come to a fellow-mortal for a favour is, that we have received so much already. Yet this is the only way in which we can discharge our debts to God; and, strange to tell, every such attempt to discharge the debt only serves to increase it."—*A. Clarke.* (2.) *Because God delights in no recompense, except* "in the payment of a heart won to His love and melted by His mercies. His deep heart is glad when we taste the full cup of His blessings, and as we raise it to our lips and call on the name of the Lord." —*Maclaren.* (3.) *Because this will test the contents of every cup proffered to us in life.* "There is an old legend of a cup full of poison put treacherously into a king's hand. He signed the cross over it, and it shivered in his grasp. Take this name of the Lord as a test. Name Him over many a cup which you are eager to drink, and the poison will be spilled on the ground. What you cannot lift before His pure eyes, and think of Him while you enjoy, is not for you. Friendships, amusements, &c., can you call on the name of the Lord while you put these cups to your lips ! If not, fling them behind you ; for they are full of poison, which, for all its sweetness, at last will bite like a serpent and sting like an adder."—*Maclaren.*

IN CONCLUSION.—There is another cup. "In the hand of the Lord there is a cup, and the wine is red—it is full of mixture, and He poureth out the same ; but the dregs thereof all the wicked of the earth shall wring them out and drink them." Why should you drink of that cup while God offers to you the cup of salvation ?

Verse 14, *see Verse* 16.

GOD'S ESTIMATE OF DEATH.

(*Verse* 15.)

I. **A high estimate.** יָקָר is applied to things of (1) Substantial importance. (2) Considerable dignity or magnitude. (3) Rare and costly value. (4) Majesty, splendour, beauty. (5) To things held dear, beloved, and precious.

II. **An unusual estimate.** This value is placed upon *death.* Death is usually regarded as loss, and with dread. He is called the great robber. It deprives the body of animation.

"Absorbs me quite ;
Steals my senses, shuts my sight,
Drowns my spirit, draws my breath."

Takes ruthlessly that which is most near and dear to the weeping wife, child, husband, friend. Yet, according to our text, "To die is gain."

III. **An unexpected estimate.** "In the sight of the Lord." One would have thought it otherwise. Death is a blast upon God's fair creation, and blights all on whom it falls. It takes the bloom from the pictures which the divine artist has pencilled, withers the majestic tree which the divine gardener has planted, crumbles the monument which the divine architect has reared, and curses him into whom God breathed the breath of life. Yet *God* says, "Death is precious."

IV. **A specific estimate.** Precious is the death of *saints.* Their death is a thing of (1) *Substantial importance* to God, to the final result of the universe, to the deceased himself. (2) *Considerable dignity.* "God took him," "With Christ." (3) *Great value.* It is a release from the uncertainties, cares, and pains of life. (4) *Majesty.* It is the portal of immortality. (5) *To be held dear.* It unites us to our friends and to the noblest of our race for ever. And above

all, "We shall be like Him, for we shall see Him as He is."
IN CONCLUSION.—How precious it is may be *seen*. Ignatius, Polycarp, Huss, Latimer, Jerome of Prague, Baxter, Scott, Wesley, Halyburton, Payson. "Let me die the death of the righteous," &c.

TWO VIEWS OF DEATH.

(*Verse* 15.)

1. The Psalmist had been snatched from the very jaws of death. He therefore may have meant that it was too costly to be given *to the foe*. 2. The Psalmist's life had been lengthened that he might fulfil the Divine purposes: death was too costly a thing to be *given him* till his work was done. Both views are true.

I. Death is very precious, therefore **God spares life.** No weapon can touch God's people till their appointed time has come.

1. *In the family.* The great Father sees how far a parent, a child, a friend are necessary, and the reason why so many are *spared* is because of the preciousness of death.

2. *In the nation.* The great Governor sees how far, and for how long, princes and citizens are necessary, and the reason why He stays His hand is because of the unspeakable value of death.

3. *In the Church.* The great Shepherd and Bishop of souls spares as many of His ministers as can be spared, because of the costliness of their death.

II. Death is very precious, therefore **God gives it.**

1. *It is the fitting reward of a saintly life* (2 Tim. iv. 6).

2. *It is the soul's movement towards perfection.*

3. *It is a stage in the direction of the completion of God's plans in the universe.*

4. *It illustrates the triumphs of redeeming grace* to those who are left behind.

IN CONCLUSION.—These two views are one theory. Death is too precious to be given without deliberation. Death is so precious, that at the appointed time it must not be withheld. It was Paul's theory, "To me to live is Christ, and to die is gain." *There is another.* A precious life makes a precious death, a worthless life a worthless death. If to me to live is self, then death is loss and despair. "Died—as a fool dieth"—is the epitaph on the lost soul.

DIVINE RELATIONSHIPS.

(*Verses* 14, 16–19.)

This is the appropriate conclusion of the Psalm. The Psalmist has all along recognised a relationship between himself and God, by which God has given certain benefits and he rendered certain services. This relationship is so close that its termination is too costly to be lightly entertained. God cannot spare him just yet, but when He does it will be to dismiss him to his reward. This relationship is now fully disclosed. He is God's servant, yet God's friend. God's friend, but His servant still. As His servant God spares his life, as His friend God walks with him. And while he feels that God has loosed his bonds, he feels that he must not relax his service.

I. This relationship is one of **obedience, yet friendship.** "I am thy servant.... Thou hast loosed my bonds."

1. *This relationship is characterised by generous devotion.* We obey God not as a hireling toils for wages, but as a friend gives himself to promote the interest of his friend.

2. *This devotion is based upon an interest in our friend's wishes.* Every word of our text displays the Psalmist's interest in what he was doing. And why?

Because he felt that God had taken an interest in him. Could he fail to see that? Can we?

3. *This interest is based upon love of our friend.* "I will offer Thee the sacrifice of thanksgiving."

II. **This relationship is one of friendship, yet obedience.** Friendship must not degenerate into over familiarity or presumption. Remember—

1. *That this relationship ceases with our obedience.* The moment we forget the special conditions on which this divine friendship is based, that moment God ceases to be our friend.

2. *That this relationship is not merely human choice, but Divine election.* "Thou hast loosed my bonds." We have not gained this liberty by our own might and by our own power. God has freed us from the thraldom of sin, that He might bind us by the loving cords of the royal *law* of liberty.

3. *That the power to fulfil the duties of this relationship comes from God.* "I will call upon the name of the Lord. I will pay my vows unto the Lord." Our divine friend shows Himself friendly in hearing our prayers. He hears them that He may empower us to fulfil our obligations.

III. This relationship must receive a **formal and public acknowledgment.**

1. *In personal consecration.* "*I will pay.*" So august a friendship, and so noble a service, must not be passed by with the informalities of our ordinary life and friendship. And yet if a friend is worth having he is worth marking out before all others; and if our worldly occupations deserve our attention at all, they deserve special attention. Much more God and His service.

2. *In union with His people.* "In the court of the Lord's house." He who is God's friend and servant will associate gladly with God's friends and servants. (1.) *He will gladly unite with them in their public worship.* (2.) *He will let not a little hinder him in showing who and what he is by formal membership.* A Christian, and yet a member of no church, is an anomaly.

3. *Before the world.* "In the midst of thee, O Jerusalem!" He is no true friend whose friendship is for private and home consumption.

IV. This relationship should be **sought and professed at once.** "Now." Every hour's delay is a loss of privilege and a neglect of duty. If not done soon, it will be done never.

PSALM CXVII.

INTRODUCTION.

1. Authorship, &c., unknown. 2. Probably a liturgical introduction to, or dismissal from, a service, either by separate choirs or the whole people. 3. "The lyrical expression of the consciousness of the Old Testament Church, that it was the object of the special and everlasting care of God; that the former proceeded from His mercy, the latter from His truth; and that for this very reason Jehovah is the worthy object of praise for all peoples."—*Moll.* "In Rom. xv. 11, the Apostle developes the idea which is the germ of the Psalm; it calls upon the heathen to praise God for His mercy and truth exhibited to His chosen, in which the heathen will one day share. (Deut. xxxii. 43.) It expresses all the elements of a Messianic Psalm."—*Speaker's Com.*

MAN'S RECOGNITION OF GOD'S GOODNESS.

(*Verses* 1, 2.)

"Some of the Jewish writers confess that this Psalm refers to the Kingdom of the Messiah; . . . that it consists of two verses to signify that then God would be glorified by two sorts of people—by the Jews according to the law of Moses, and by the Gentiles according to the seven precepts of the son of Noah—which should make one Church, as these two verses make one Psalm." Notice—

I. **That God's goodness is manifested to meet man's need.** Men everywhere need mercy and truth. All need is represented here.

1. *Man needs God's mercy.* Jew and Gentile alike need forbearance and redemption; for "all have sinned and come short of the glory of God." God's merciful kindness is *great* (1) *in forbearing to punish;* (2) *in the gift of His Son;* (3) *in the mission of His Spirit;* (4) *in the establishment of His Church;* (5) *in its comprehensiveness;* (6) *in its regenerating and glorifying power.*

2. *Man needs God's truth.* The provision for that is, "His truth endureth for ever." This may mean God's word, or God's fidelity to His word. Both are true. Consider the state of the world without the Bible. Natural religion is only known when Bible light is thrown upon nature. Man needs (1) *the true knowledge of God;* (2) *guidance in his duty;* (3) *comfort in his trouble;* (4) *a revelation of his hereafter.* Nothing supplies that need but God's truth. From that truth God has never swerved. He has never repealed it. He has ever fulfilled it. What was truth to Adam, Abraham, Moses, David, Paul, is truth to us, and will be throughout the ages.

II. **That the divine goodness shall be universally recognised.**

1. *Why?* Because (1) *it deserves to be.* (2) *Because the order of things destines it to be.* It was so at the beginning; it must be so at the end.

2. *By whom?* (1.) *By the Jews.* The Cross is now a stumbling-block because the veil is on their hearts (Rom. xi.). But that veil will be removed, and "all Israel will be saved." (2.) *By the Gentiles,* to many of whom both the Cross and its revelation are foolishness. They shall yet confess it to be the wisdom of God. "At the name of Jesus every knee shall bow," and every tongue shall confess that Christ is "the Light to lighten the Gentiles, and the glory of His people Israel."

3. *How?* By praising God. (1.) *Gratitude.* (2.) *Consecration.*

III. **That universal recognition will characterise the redeemed and glorified Church for ever.** (Rev. vii. 4–12; xix. 5, 6.)

IN CONCLUSION.—(i.) *When is the implied prophecy of our text to be fully realised?* Apart from the speculations of ingenious commentators, and the tabulations of prophetic almanacs, it will be (1) *In God's own time.* (2) *In the right time.* And (3) "*It is not for us to know the times and the seasons,*" &c. (ii.) *How is the prophecy of our text to be fulfilled?* By earnest Christian testimony. The means are *efficient:* "The Gospel is the power of God unto salvation," &c. The means are *consecrated:* "Go ye into all the world," &c. The means are *permanent:* "The everlasting Gospel." We have no warrant for the belief that the presence of the King will effect that for which the power and influence of the crucified and risen Saviour are not equal. Christian men, put on your strength. Vitalise and increase your agencies. Work in faith. "*Jesus shall reign,*" &c.

PSALM CXVIII.

INTRODUCTION.

1. The last of the group (cxiii.–cxviii.) constituting the Hallel. 2. Certainly a temple Psalm, most probably composed for a great occasion. "Some incline to the Davidic authorship, when he was anointed king, when he brought back the ark, or after (2 Sam. xxi. 16). Others to Hezekiah (*cf.* v. 17 with Isaiah xxxviii. 1). Others, after the exile, in celebration either of Feast of Tabernacles (Ezra iii. 1-4), or Founding of the Temple (iii. 8-13),or its Dedication (vi. 15-18), or Feast of Tabernacles (Nehem. viii. 14). 3. Often quoted in New Testament. Many Rabbins interpret the Psalm of Christ; and Jerome says that the ancient Jews so interpreted it, which is borne out by Matt. xxi. 9. This was Luther's favourite Psalm."

THE DIVINE MERCY.

(*Verses 1–4.*)

Our text forms an appropriate introduction to, and is a miniature of, the whole Psalm. It contains the germ of all God's goodness, and the ground for all human gratitude. Next to the phrase, "Praise ye the Lord," the expression of verse 1 is of most frequent use in the Book of Psalms.

I. The nature of divine mercy.
1. *It is divine.* "*His* mercy." It is therefore perfect. It is not liable to the fluctuations and temptations to which human mercy is exposed. The divine character is not only perfect as a whole, but in its parts. The divine perfections characterise each other. The divine mercy is omnipotent and all wise, beneficent, yet just. It always goes far enough, it never goes too far. Man's mercy sometimes stops at the boundary of self-interest, and thus leaves its object unattained; sometimes goes beyond both and defeats its object. Not so with perfect mercy. It ascertains accurately the measure of our need, and powerfully supplies it.

2. *It is the outcome of the divine goodness.* Man's mercy is often the result of weakness. Thus it rests on unworthy objects, encourages sin, and manifests itself in unproper ways. God's mercy is ever governed by sound motives, manifested in good ways, to worthy objects and beneficent results.

3. *It is everlasting.* Man's mercy is frequently a matter of mood, tense, and ability. God is always in a merciful mood, and always powerful to bless.

II. The objects and manifestation of the divine mercy.
1. *Nations :* "Israel." God, as King of kings, cares for national life. Illustrations of this are plentiful in the history of Israel and in the history of England. The divine mercy is seen (1) In the planting of nations, with due regard to wants and peculiarities. The characteristics of a nation *may* be due to the circumstances in which they are placed, but it may also be due in the divine adaptation of circumstances to temperament — *e.g.*, Greece, art and poetry ; England, commerce, &c. (2) *In the growth of nations.* Wars, revolutions, reforms, &c. (3) *The decline of nations.* When a nation has lost its virtue and its vigour it is a mercy to itself and to other nations that it should fall. Israel, Rome, &c.

2. *Ministers :* "House of Aaron." (1.) *In their call* (1 Tim. i. 16 ; Gal. i. 15, 16). (2.) *In their preparation for their work.* (3.) *In their encouragement in the midst of difficulties and dangers.* (4.) *In their spiritual enrichment.* (5.) *In their moral success.* (6.) *In their eternal reward.*

3. *The Church.* "Them that fear the Lord." (1.) *As a whole.* α. In its marvellous preparation ; the gradual consolidation of the world into a political brotherhood by the Persian, Alexandrian, and Roman conquests; the dispersion of the Jews ; the spread of the Greek language and Roman civilisation; the yearning for spiritual life and unity. β. In the merciful gift of Jesus Christ to be its living head, and of the Spirit to guide it into all the truth. γ. In the persecutions which dispersed it, and the blood which watered it. δ. In its marvellous preservation when the whole world was against it. ε. In its enrichment by the stores of learning and art. ζ. In its Pentecostal baptisms in all ages. η. In its continual progress. θ. In the promise of its glorious close. (2) *As individuals ;* in conversion, the means of grace, &c.

III. The recognition of the divine mercy. "Oh, give thanks unto the Lord."

1. *This mercy is often unrecognised.* Nations attribute their blessings to fortunate circumstances, patient perseverance, or martial prowess ; ministers to their learning, eloquence, or zeal ; the Church to its orthodoxy, political alliances, or enthusiasm ; individuals to happy chances, or human sympathy and help.

2. *This recognition is a matter of imperative obligation.* Without this recognition (1) *the evils of selfishness and sin can never be extinguished,* (2) *the mercy will be withdrawn,* and (3) *retribution follow.*

3. *This recognition should take the form of devout, grateful, and earnest praise.*

"Man's Extremity God's Opportunity."

(*Verses 5-7.*)

I. Man in distress. כִּן־הַמֵּצַר "Out of straits." The figure is that of a fortress surrounded by a beleaguering army, or of soldiers hemmed in on every side (see ver. 10), or of a torrent dammed up by the pass through which it rushes; imprisoned, constrained. This applies to—

1. *The Church.* How often is it surrounded and hemmed in by infidelity, ungodliness, superstition, persecution, want of opportunity, political restriction, and popular opinion!

2. *The individual.* In business, family, society, by temptations, hostility of friends, personal weakness, malignity of foes.

II. Man's duty in distress.

1. *Prayer.* Without this we shall always be in distress. Our own resources are soon expended. Friends are often unwilling or helpless. Let us "call upon the Lord." (1.) *It is our duty to God, for He has commanded it.* (2.) *It is our duty to ourselves.* A prayerless man is a moral suicide. "Not sit by thyself, or lie upon thy bench, hanging and shaking thy head, and letting thy thoughts bite and devour thee; but rouse up, thou indolent fellow! fall upon thy knees, raise thy hands and eyes to heaven, and present thy distress before God with tears."
—*Luther.*

2. *Courage.* "I will not fear." Fear blanches the courage, exhausts the strength, and diverts the aim. As long as courage lasts, hope is not extinct; but the moment fear comes in, defeat supervenes.

III. Man's consolations in distress.

1. *The Lord is on his side.* The Lord has pledged Himself (1) *to be with His Church always;* (2) *with His individual children.* What is there then to fear? "Greater is He that is for you" (Isa. xliii. 1, 2).

2. *The Lord consecrates all His confederates for His good* (ver. 4). Whether they be friends or instrumentalities.

IV. Man's deliverance in distress.

1. *Victory over foes.* This has been the realisation of the Church in *all ages.* (Rom. viii. 35, 39).

2. *Perfect liberty.* "The Lord set me in a large place." The misery of the Psalmist was that he was straightened. His deliverance was liberty in a large open plain. This may be applied (1) *to Missionary enterprise.* The Lord is ever opening doors for His Church, loosing her bonds, and enlarging the field of her operations. (2) *To spiritual life.* We are "called unto liberty," freedom, from sin, of thought, of mental and moral cultivation, philanthropy.

COURAGE.

(*Verses 6, 7.*)

Courage is a very complex and difficult subject. We speak of physical courage, mental, moral courage, courage of convictions, &c. Many a man who could walk up to a cannon's mouth could not face a public audience. Many a man who has planted his country's flag in the thick of her foes has betrayed his most cherished convictions. *True* courage is described in our text.

I. In its **source.** "The Lord is on my side." Courage is supposed to spring from self-reliance. That man is counted brave who scorns all allies and dares to face the enemy alone. Hence much of human courage is reckless hardihood. True courage is the courage of trust in God.

II. In its **manifestations.** "I will not fear," &c.

1. *It trusts God to do for it what it cannot do for itself.* It wisely dares to acknowledge that by itself it is unequal to certain enterprises. This of itself re-

quires a great deal of courage, because it requires so much self-abnegation, is so unpopular, and is often apparently not warranted by circumstances.

2. *This trust produces fearlessness of consequences.* Who can fear who has taken this initial and most formidable step of declaring himself on the side of God? Young men, take this initial step; for who can fear who knows that God is on his side.

3. *Fearlessness of consequences produces the true courage of fidelity.* Why is it men are unfaithful? Consequences, unpopularity, poverty, &c. "The fear of man bringeth a snare." "Fear Him, ye saints, and you will then have nothing else to fear."

Trust, Human and Divine.

(*Verses* 8, 9.)

I. **Man must trust.** All experience proves this. Like the creeping parasite, the soul must throw its tendrils round some support.

II. **Whom** should man trust? Some one whose qualities warrant that trust.

1. *He must be all-sufficient*, able to provide for all actual and possible necessities. To trust for wisdom to the foolish, for strength to the weak, &c., nothing but disappointment can follow.

2. *He must be of supreme moral excellence.* If we trust to the suspected or the worthless we shall be in a state of perpetual unrest.

3. *He must be the same at all times.* Trust in the feeble is ruin. Man must have as the object of his trust one whose omnipotent resources and spiritual perfection are beyond the mutation of this world and abide for ever.

III. **Who** warrants that trust?

1. *Do men generally?* No; (1) man is weak in wisdom and material resources; (2) *morally imperfect;* (3) *ever changeful.*

2. *Do princes?* Least of all. They are but men, sometimes the weakest, worst, and most fickle of men. What they have done let the followers of Confucius, Buddha, Mohammed, the Pope, and Priestcraft everywhere tell. One thing: ruin.

IV. **God offers Himself as the object of human trust.** It is better that man should trust Him—

1. *Because He warrants that trust.* "He is able to do exceeding abundantly," &c. He is "glorious in holiness." He is "the same yesterday, to-day," &c.

2. *Because man's confidence can thereby be secured.* That confidence has been sadly shaken. Hence man's distress. In God it will stand firm.

3. *Because of the blessed consequences which will follow.* (1.) salvation; (2.) inward peace; (3.) human brotherhood; (4.) heaven.

Spiritual Warfare.

(*Verses* 10–13.)

I. **Danger.**

1. *A surrounding danger*, "compassed." The foes of the Christian are not all in the front or in the light. They are subtle, and everywhere. A sudden temptation may reveal a weakness hitherto unobserved. They assail us at all points, at home and abroad, at work and at rest, in the Church and in the world.

2. *A formidable danger.* (1.) *In point of numbers*, "like bees." We wrestle with principalities and powers. Countless multitudes are waiting for every weakness, and plotting for every fall. (2.) *In point of pertinacity.* The fourfold repetition of the phrase, "They compassed me," indicates assiduity and perseverance. (3.) *In point of weapons.* The sting of the bee is formidable from its very insignificance. So it is not at first by great temptations, but by small, that we are assailed. The sting of the bee is sharp, so the weapons arrayed

against us can pierce body, affections, temper, intellect, and soul. (4.) *In the point of dexterity.* It is difficult to strike the bee when on the wing. Happy the man who has transfixed the tempter with the sword of the Spirit, and has him under his feet.

3. *A fatal danger.* "They thrust sore at me that I might fall." Their aim is not to weaken, but to destroy. Hence quarter is neither given nor taken. Victory or death is the only issue for either side.

II. **Help.** "The Lord helped me."
1. *By fighting Himself where and when we are helpless.* There are certain antagonists we can never cope with. Sin, Satan, and death have to be encountered by Him first, and their power crippled and themselves chained. In effecting this Christ becomes "the Captain of our salvation."

2. *By animating us with the warlike spirit.* "God has not given to us the spirit of cowardice (δειλείας), but the spirit of power."

3. *By arming us for the conflict.* (Eph. vi. 13-17).

4. *By assurances of victory and reward.*
III. **Victory.** "In the name of the Lord, I will destroy them."
1. *The victory will come swiftly.* Like the dry thorns, they shall consume. It remains very much with the Christian, with his faith, courage, and fidelity, when the victory shall be won.

2. *The victory shall be complete.* "Destroy." "*Sin* shall have no more dominion over you." "The God of peace shall bruise *Satan* under your feet shortly." "*Death* shall be swallowed up in victory."

3. *The glory of the victory shall be given to him to whom it is due.* "In the name of the Lord." Note:—This takes all the malevolence out of this determination. It was a judicial vengeance of which the Psalmist was only the instrument. God takes all the responsibility. Let persecutors see to it that they have God's warrant. We know we have it in our war of extermination against sin. "Not unto us, but to Thy name," &c.

PERSONAL AND FAMILY PIETY.

(*Verses* 14, 15.)

Notice :—
I. **That piety is sadly wanting.** There are men to whom these words are unintelligible. They know nothing of God's strength; they are strangers to His salvation; no song wells up from their thankless hearts. Sad is their condition; sad the condition of their homes. In many homes all is vice, misery, want, and broken-heartedness, as the result of the parent's irreligion. In all houses which are not sanctified by the Word of God and prayer, the deepest wants of the family are unsatisfied.

II. **That the want of piety is supplied.** "The Lord . . . has *become*," &c. Piety consists of three things.
1. *Salvation.* "The *Lord* is become. . . *He* is my salvation." Not simply personal rescue or divine blessing, but indwelling God. This involves every other phase. It drives out sin, rescues from impurity and death, gives heaven.

2. *Salvation employed.* "My strength," for use, of course. Strength unemployed will be strength dissipated. If we do not "work out our salvation," viz., that which God has worked in, "to will and to do of His good pleasure," spiritual loss and death will supervene.

3. *Salvation acknowledged.* "My song." Salvation will and must express itself. The praiseless lip argues the thankless heart, and the thankless heart is the heart from which God has fled.

III. **That piety must be personally appropriated.** "My."
1. *Piety is a matter between the personal soul and its personal Saviour.* There can be no mediation or proxy. No man can either get or keep our religion for us.

2. *The means of its appropriation is personal faith.* "Believe on the Lord Jesus Christ, and thou shalt be saved."
3. *The test of its appropriation is personal experience.* "Is become." The Psalmist's experience was no fiction. He knew that there was a time when he felt nothing of the sort. He knew that now that time was over. He had entered on a new phase in his career, and of that phase he was sensible.

IV. **That piety is appropriated to be diffused.** The sphere of its diffusion here is the home (ver. 15). Piety may be diffused at home by
1. *Personal example.*
2. *Careful self-discipline.*
3. *Intelligent and patient training.*
4. *Interesting and constant worship, &c.*

V. **That piety, and piety alone, will make a home happy.** "The voice of rejoicing . . . is in the tabernacles of *the righteous.*"
1. Some pious homes, it is said, are not *happy.* Does true piety reign there? or cant, laxity, or severity?
2. *True piety must make a happy home,* because it is "alway rejoicing."

VI. **A happy home is a miniature of and a nursery for heaven.**
IN CONCLUSION.—(i.) *Parents, it rests with you whether your home is a heaven or a hell.* (ii.) *Children, value your homes.* The time may come when you will want them. (iii.) *Children of pious parents, make your future home what your past has been.*

THE LORD'S TRIUMPH.

(*Verses* 15, 16.)

These words may be applied (1) to God's sovereignty over the material universe and His power over its laws; (2) to national deliverances, such as Moses, David, elsewhere acknowledged, yes, and such as we ought to acknowledge. But (3) it suggests (and we will consider it as suggesting) the triumphs of Christ and His Gospel in the world.

I. **The personal triumph of Christ.**
1. *Over Satan.* This began in the wilderness, continued without intermission during His life, and ended by the victory of the Cross.
2. *Over the world.* Our Lord confronted the world in all its forms, provincial, metropolitan, social, political, upper, lower. "He measured the world and condemned it. And it fully understood Him. It recognised His aim; it quailed before Him, and it hated Him; and it rested not till it had led Him to His Cross; but He said, 'I have overcome the world.'"—*Liddon.*
3. *Over sin,* by bearing its penalty on Calvary.
4. *Over death,* by His resurrection.
5. *This fourfold triumph condensed into one at His ascension* (Col. i. 15, Eph. iv. 8).

II. **The triumphs of His Gospel in the human heart.**
1. *In its conversion from sin to holiness.* Every other means has been tried and has failed, human efforts, education, moral philosophy. But Christ has subdued the will, cleansed the soul, introduced a powerful motive, and imparted a new life.
2. *In empowering the soul to resist sin,* strenuous opposition, favourable circumstances, human encouragement have been in vain.
3. *In promoting the growth of moral excellence.*
4. *In giving us victory over the world, tribulation, and death.*

III. **The triumphs of His Church in the world.**
1. *Over persecution.* Its early years were years of blood.
2. *Over old heathenism,* supported as it was by poetry, learning, and extensive popularity.
3. *Over heresy, e.g.* (1) *Arianism,* in spite of its wide influence and royal patronage; (2) *Popery,* that giant superstition, still reels under Luther's blow, and will yet fall.
4. *Over religious indifference.* Nothing

ever has, or ever will excite such interest and move so much as the simple preaching of the Gospel. Where are the crowds so numerous as at our churches?

5. *Over human hearts.* Witness Pentecost, the preaching of Luther, Latimer, Wesley, Whitfield, &c. Nor are its triumphs confined to one class. In its early ages the illiterate fisherman, the intelligent publican, and the learned rabbi were charmed and subdued. And the same Gospel has since exerted its influence over Bunyan the tinker and Newton the philosopher.

CHASTISEMENT.

(Verses 17, 18.)

The first of these verses was hung up by Luther in his study, as his favourite verse of his favourite Psalm. "It has come to my aid again and again, and supported me in heavy trials, when Kaiser, king, philosopher, and saint could do nought." Chastisement—

I. Its **nature.** "The Lord hath chastened me sore."

1. *It was the Lord's chastisement,* therefore sovereign, fatherly.

2. *By human instrumentality.* His enemies were permitted to "thrust at him sore."

3. *Thorough.* "Sore." Not too much, not too little, but sufficiently to accomplish the divine purposes (Job. xxx. 11).

II. Its **limits.** "He hath not given me over to death."

1. *Physical death.*
2. *Intellectual death.* Despair.
3. *Moral death.* Destruction.

III. Its **consolations.** "I shall not die, but live."

1. *It was corrective,* remedial, and therefore not simply punitive (Jer. x. 24).

2. *Hopefulness* against the worst. "I shall not die."

3. *Confidence* for the best. "But live" (Acts xxvii. 22-25).

IV. Its **effects.** "And declare the works of the Lord."

1. *Devout gratitude.*
2. *Personal improvement.*
3. *Religious earnestness and testimony.* "No affliction for the present seemeth to be joyous but grievous, but afterward," &c.

THE SACRED ENCLOSURE.

(Verses 19-21.)

I. The **enclosure.**

1. *Literal.* Our text primarily refers to the sacred enclosure that was accessible to true Israelites alone. (Isa. xxvi. 2.) That enclosure was the house of God, where His glory was manifested, His name worshipped, and His people's righteousness confirmed and strengthened. So the Christian Church is where God's presence is felt, His word proclaimed, His worship celebrated, &c.

2. *Moral.* Christian life is a temple of the living God and the sphere of righteousness. A way of holiness where God dwells and walks with His people.

3. *Heavenly* (Ps. xxiv. 7). Heaven is the sanctuary of God, and the dwelling-place of righteousness.

II. The **gates** of that enclosure. "The gates of righteousness." "The gate of the Lord."

1. *The gate which belongs to the Lord.* The Lord keeps the gate; not Peter, not His ministers, but Himself.

2. *The gate is of the Lord's appointment.* All who enter by any other climb over the wall and are thieves and robbers. There is only one way opened. "There is only one name given under heaven," &c.

3. *The gate is the Lord Himself.* "I am the way." "I am the door." Christ alone is the entrance to God's righteousness.

III. The **keys** to that enclosure.

1. *Ardent supplication.* "Open," implying need of entrance, desire to enter. "Ask;" "seek;" "knock, and it shall be opened unto you."

2. *The divine willingness.* "Thou hast heard." God has a sovereign right to admit or exclude all He chooses; but we know that He will be guided by righteousness, and will not select on arbitrary principles.

3. *Salvation.* "Art become my salvation." Nothing that is defiled or maketh a lie can enter. Only "the redeemed shall walk there." They "enter in and find pasture."

IV. The **privileges** and **duties** of that enclosure.

1. *Worship.* "I will praise the Lord."
2. *Righteousness.*

IN CONCLUSION.—(i.) *The outer courts are open to all.* (1.) *Many privileges of the material sanctuary.* But let the Church beware how she throws all her privileges open. (2.) *Opportunities for righteousness.* (3.) *Opportunities for qualifying for heaven.* (ii.) *The inner court is open to all who are qualified to enter.* (1.) *All the means of grace;* (2.) *the fulfilment of all righteousness;* (3.) *all the hopes and fruits of glory.*

CHRIST THE CORNER-STONE.

(*Verses* 22, 23.)

Whatever literal application these verses may have had, that application is now merged into the richer, larger, and undoubted application to the Messiah. No text is more frequently quoted in the New Testament. Six or seven times it is quoted word for word, and in innumerable instances is it unquestionably referred to where Christ is made the one, true, and only foundation of the Church. "Must we, in opposition to the perverted and obstinate exegesis even of believing commentators, begin to prove that this Psalm is Messianic—that the corner-stone is a real prophecy of the Spirit concerning Christ? We frankly confess ourselves to be so often vexed by such contentions with brethren who do not understand the *scripture*, that we lose patience; and, however unscientifically, are inclined rather to rebuke them with Christ (Luke xxiv. 25) until their hearts burn, and their burning *hearts* begin to read in the light of the Pentecostal fire what is written."—*Stier.* Observe—

I. That **Christ is the corner-stone.**

1. *What the corner-stone is not.* (1.) Feelings towards Christ. These are most unsubstantial and shifting. (2.) *Doctrines concerning Christ.* These merely tell us about the corner-stone. (3.) *The example of Christ.* This is simply the character of the corner-stone. (4.) *The Church of Christ.* That is the building reared on the corner-stone.

2. *What the corner-stone is.* "Jesus Christ Himself being the chief corner-stone." This only is solid, constant, and eternal. All else is sand. This is rock. Jesus Christ in His divine-human personality. Incarnate, crucified, risen, glorified, and reigning.

3. *What the corner-stone is for.* (1.) *For beauty.* Corner-stones are the most costly, choice, and adorned. Other stones derive their excellency from them. So the Christian building derives its beauty from Him who is "full of grace and truth." "Of His fulness all we have received, and grace for grace." (2.) *Stability.* They are chosen for firmness, strength, and durability. They uphold and maintain the building which without them would crumble and fall. So Christ supports the individual believer and the collective Church, in weakness, trials, hour of death, day of judgment. (3.) *Unity and compactness.* Take away the corner-stone and the sides of the house become separate buildings. *This unity is not uniformity.* The other stones are of various sizes, value, colour, material. The corner-stone gives harmony. So different men have different capacities, preferences, modes of thought and feeling. Christ binds them into a mighty whole—His Church.

II. That **Christ is the only corner-stone.** There have been many rival corner-stones. They have been tried, but they have failed, and so have those who have built upon them. Paganism, Unbelief, Socialism, Philosophy, Ethics. "Other *foundation* can no man lay than that is laid," &c. He is the only corner-stone by which God and man can be brought together on terms that are at once honourable, amicable, strong, and abiding. He alone can bring the dispensations together into a harmonious whole and make them an enduring basis for faith and morals. He is the only means by which the disintegrated masses of mankind can find their principle of cohesion. "One is your Master, even Christ, and all ye are brethren." He is the only means whereby the disorganised faculties of our nature can be reduced to order and compacted in strength and "so make our new man."

III. That **Christ is the divinely established corner-stone.** "This is the Lord's doings." It is no myth or speculation. It is not the doing of men or angels, but of—

1. *The Holy Trinity.* The Father "sent forth His Son," and consecrated Him. "Him hath God the Father sealed." The Son "came," and by His own power laid " down His life and took it again." The Holy Spirit takes of the things of Christ and imparts them to us.

2. *The divine attributes.* Wisdom devised it; justice instituted it; love gave it; and power laid it.

3. *The divine providence.* (1.) By a wonderful preparation. Moral: the Jews; intellectual: the Greeks; political: the Romans. (2.) In an age which by its peculiar fitness was "the fulness of the times."

IV. That **Christ is the rejected corner-stone.** In all ages since His advent He has been the despised and rejected of men. The Jewish people and the whole heathen world combined at first to resist His claims. He was a stumbling-block to the one, and foolishness to the other. Persecution and controversy since have proved that the human heart is alien to Him. Sin, infidelity, heresy, and worldliness all refuse to build upon Christ.

V. That **Christ is the marvellous corner-stone.**

1. *Marvellous when we consider who is the corner-stone.* (1.) *In its unlikelihood.* The man Christ Jesus, born in a manger; the Man of Sorrows, crucified as a malefactor. (2.) *In its condescension.* The brightness of the Father's glory, creator of the universe, governor of angels, Lord of man.

2. *Marvellous when we consider the means by which He has become the corner-stone.* By the simple preaching of truths alien to natural inclinations, political institutions, moral usages; demanding the resignation of pride of intellect, independence of will, pleasure, profit; by men, weak and unlearned in the world's estimation, whose weapons were not learning or swords, but holiness, suffering, zeal, and prayer.

3. *Marvellous when we consider the numbers and quality of those who have made it their corner-stone.* Countless millions have eschewed beliefs consecrated by the profession of unnumbered ages, have thrown off their allegiance to priesthoods armed with every terror and device, have resisted the fascinations of philosophy, and have left darling vices and besetting sins. These have been from all ranks—monarchs, nobles, warriors, statesmen, poets, &c.

THE LORD'S DAY.

(*Verse 24.*)

I. The **day**—

1. *Of temporal deliverance.* God has made that. By a variety of providential dispensations. *Indirectly,* through men and other instrumentalities, *e.g.,* in sickness, through the physician; in perplexities, by friendly advice and help. *Directly,* by the interposition of His mighty power.

2. *Of salvation.* The whole Christian dispensation is the time accepted by God in which to bless mankind. It is the time acceptable *to man* in which his pressing spiritual wants may be supplied.

3. *Of conversion.* The day when God gives, and we personally take, Jesus Christ to be our chief corner-stone. Let that "happy day" never be forgotten.

4. *The sabbath day*, by Jehovah's rest and Christ's resurrection.

II. **The duties of that day.**

(1.) *Rejoicing.* Implying intense gratitude, cheerful consecration, holy zeal.

(2.) *Gladness.* Let no man say that religion is a thing of gloom. God blesses us that we may be happy. Let the day of rest be the gladdest of all the seven.

BENEDICTIONS.

(*Verses* 25, 26.)

This passage received its fulfilment only in Him who came in the supremest sense in the name of the Lord (Matt. xxi. 9). Here, however, it admits of a human and general interpretation.

I. **The blessing supplicated.**

1. *This supplication is the expression of a want.* "Save." "Send prosperity." "Save," implying moral evil and degradation; "Prosperity," loss and misery.

2. *This supplication was earnest.* "Beseech." Our need is great, so must be our cry. Listless prayer implies unconsciousness of need.

3. *This supplication was urgent.* "Save *now.*" "Send *now.*" Need is always present. Blessings are ever wanted.

II. **The conditions of blessing fulfilled.**

1. *Coming.* (1.) *This is inexorable.* "Come, now, let us reason;" "Seek ye the Lord," &c. (2.) *Can only be fulfilled through Christ.* "No man cometh unto the Father but by Me." (3.) *Is equivalent to Christian faith.* Faith is the soul's approach to God through Christ.

2. *Coming in the name of the Lord.* (1) *Not in our name*, or (2) *by our own merits*, but (3) *in the name of the Lord.* Self-distrust, resignation, confidence.

III. **The blessing vouchsafed.**

1. *Salvation;* from the guilt, power, pollution, and punishment of sin.

2. *Prosperity.* The great gift of God through His Son and Spirit. Regeneration, sanctification, indwelling peace, joy, power, heaven.

IV. **The place of blessing.** "The house of the Lord."

1. *All the means of grace are there concentrated.*

2. *The vast majority of Christians receive their highest blessings there.*

PERSONAL RELIGION.

(*Verses* 27–29.)

I. Personal religion consists in the **acknowledgment of a personal God.** Religion must rest on a dogmatic and theological basis. Whatever definition we give to the term religion, this is primarily involved. If it consists in the bond which unites the soul to the Supreme Being, then we must know who that Supreme Being is. If it consists in duty, then with reference to whom are those duties performed. To resolve God into a "stream or tendency which makes for righteousness" does not avoid theology or dogma.

II. Personal religion consists in the acknowledgment of a personal God **accessible to man.** God is accessible, because He is "good." If He is not good, He is unapproachable, and must be the object of man's fear. God is permanently accessible, because His mercy endureth for ever. Religion must have an object who can be approached through all the vicissitudes of life.

III. Personal religion consists in the **apprehension of a personal God.** "My God." "This is a truth unknown beyond the precincts of revelation. The Almighty and Eternal gives Himself in the fulness of His being to the soul that seeks Him. Heathenism, indeed, in its cultus of domestic and local duties, of its penates, of its θεοὶ ἐπιχώριοι, bare witness to the deep yearning of the human heart for the individualising love of a higher power. To know the true God is to know that such a craving is satisfied."—*Liddon.*

IV. Personal religion consists in the **acknowledgment and enjoyment of a divine revelation** "which hath showed us light." If God is to be approached and apprehended, He must reveal Himself. If man is to receive his Maker's blessing, be united to his Maker's person, and fulfil his Maker's will, he must be told who that Maker is and what He would have him do. God hath showed us light in the Bible and in the revelation of Him who said, "He that hath seen Me hath seen the Father."

V. Personal religion consists in **personal sacrifices** (ver. 27).

VI. Personal religion consists in **devout worship, thanksgiving, and praise** (vers. 28, 29).

PSALM CXIX.

INTRODUCTION.

1. **Date and authorship.** Some ascribe the authorship to "David, before his accession to the kingdom, in exile and peril (vers. 9, 23, 46, 141, 161). Others (of chief authority), from the language and contents, imagine it to be of much later date. Jebb thinks, Daniel; others, Ezra; Dean Stanley says that the rhythm seems to mark the age of Jeremiah; Kay supposes it to depict the mental state of those who have passed through the discipline of the captivity; Hitzig, as usual, refers it to the days of the Maccabees (see Macc. xii. 48)."—*Speaker's Com.*

2. **Character.** There are twenty-two sections in this Psalm, arranged according to the Hebrew alphabet, each consist of eight verses, and every eight begins with the same letter. Thus, there are eight initial Alephs, eight initial Beths, &c. In nearly every verse the divine law is mentioned, and the sacred name of Jehovah is brought in twenty-two times once for each letter. "It contains many repetitions and imitations of earlier Psalms. . . . No part of Scripture is more suggestive of edifying trains of thought, or more saturated with a spirit all but Christian, of humility, trust, devoted love to God, and realisation of His near presence. . . . It is an epitome of all true religion, and must be studied by any one who wishes to fathom the meaning of the law, and the elevation, hope, joy, confidence, felt in presence of kings and princes by pious Jews."—*Speaker's Com.*

3. **Contents.** "There is no *grouping* or *arrangement* of the subjects of this Psalm, and little or no connection between the sentiment of its verses. Much in it is proverbial or aphoristic. . . . It might be possible to make an arrangement under particular heads—such as the following —under the general title of the Word of God :—1. In youth. 2. In trial. 3. In duty. 4. In meditation. 5. At night. 6. In public. 7. In private. 8. In prosperity. 9. In adversity, &c."—*Barnes.*

THE BLESSED LIFE.

(*Verses* 1-3.)

Notice—

I. That all men are not happy. Our text specifies those who are, and implies that all else are unhappy.

1. *All men desire happiness.* The heathens were ever in quest of the chief good. Bad men and worldly men are ever pursuing their vices and follies to this end.

2. *This happiness is not attained*—(1) *Because the end aimed at is only mistaken for happiness.* Riches, honour, pleasures, &c., when secured are frequently found to be misery rather than bliss (Luke xvi. 25). That which makes a man happy must *exactly answer all the cravings of his soul and secure the equilibrium of his being,* so that intellect, conscience, will, &c., shall cry in harmony, "It is enough." Again, that which makes a man happy must be *enduring,* but the things of the world perish in the using (1 Cor. vii. 30, 31), and the pleasures of sin are only "for a season." (2) *Because the means employed are not adequate.* Some are ignorant of the true means, and some dislike them (John vi. 34., *cf.* 66); (3) *and if adequate means* are not employed, and the right end not secured, all becomes "vanity and vexation of spirit."

II. That all men can secure happiness only **by a right state of the heart.** "That seek Him with their whole heart."

253

1. *A right state of the heart contemplates the true end of happiness.* "Him." God alone is the soul's satisfying portion. The completest worldly abundance leaves some craving unsatisfied. When the soul is "filled with all the fulness of God," it can ask no more.

2. *A right state of the heart seeks happiness in the right way.* "With the *whole heart.*" The sensualist seeks physical gratification; the intellectualist, mental; the moralist, ethical. A right state of the heart seeks complete happiness, the satisfaction of *all* its higher cravings, so as to leave none unblessed.

III. That all men can maintain happiness only by **a right state of the life.** The blessed are those who

1. "*Are the undefiled in the way.*" (*Marg.* Sincere; not absolutely perfect men, but men with a clear conscience and an upright intention.)

2. "*Walk in the law of the Lord.*" The inconsistent, the lawless, are unhappy. The law of God is so exactly suited to all our faculties, that only by keeping it can their well-being be secured.

3. "*Do no iniquity.*" "The way of *transgressors* is hard."

IV. That provision is made for man's happiness in the Word of God.

1. *That word indicates what true happiness is.* It tells us that man was originally happy; that angels and the spirits of just men made perfect are happy; that God only can make men happy, and that He does so by the gift of Himself and the "unsearchable riches of Christ."

2. *That word is an infallible guide to true happiness.* There can be no happiness where there is uncertainty as to means or ends. Man left to this world's fluctuating rules of good intention, custom, desire, &c., adopts measures which land him in disappointment. The Bible is the perfect and authoritative counsel of God. Guided by that we shall be received into glory.

3. *That word affords us a powerful help towards true happiness.* It is God's "testimony." It testifies to the facts of God's fatherhood, goodness, and power; to Christ's atonement and intercession; to the Holy Spirit's regenerating, consoling, and sanctifying influences; and to heaven.

LAW, PRAYER, DUTY.

(*Verses* 4-6.)

I. Law. "Thou hast commanded us," &c.

1. *The Bible is based upon the personal authority of God.*" "*Thou.* (1.) *Not man's.* The obligation to attend to its precepts does not rest upon the fact that great and good men wrote it, acknowledged it, and kept it. (2.) *Not its own.* The inherent excellence of its doctrines and morals would be enough if only intellectual or moral assent and admiration were demanded. But (3.) *God's.* This accounts for its moral excellence and commanding influence. But let it be emphasised that primarily it rests upon His sovereign will. There are many things that transcend reason and run counter to merely human interests; but we believe and obey them, because "*God* spake all these words."

2. *The Bible comes to us on the personal authority of God.* "Thou hast commanded." (1.) *The Bible is not a recommendation from God,* which man may or may not accept either as a whole, or on a principle of eclecticism in its parts. The Bible as a whole and in its parts being the charge of sovereign will and the revelation of the only remedy for human sin, therefore man must keep it as a whole. (2.) *The Bible is not the product of man's intellect in a high spiritual mood.* Its philosophy and virtue were not the discovery of good men studying and sympathising with the need of their fellow-men. But (3.) *the Bible is the collection of certain "precepts,"* exhibited in the form of doctrine, history, example, &c., binding on the heart and conscience of men, direct from the counsels of the Most High.

3. *The Bible must be diligently kept.* (1.) *It must be kept. In the mind.* It is necessary first to have it, so "he that

receiveth the word into good ground is he that heareth the word and understandeth it." *By the will,* in assenting to it. *By the heart,* in loving it. *By the life,* in practising it. "If ye know these things, happy are ye if ye do them." (2.) *Comprehensively;* Heb.: *very much, all of them.* In small duties, as well as great, must we exercise ourselves to have a conscience void of offence, &c. *At all times.* "Blessed is he that doeth righteousness at all times." "Blessed are they that sow beside all waters." *With all our powers.* (3.) *Diligently.*

II. **Prayer.** The Psalmist contemplating the exceeding breadth of God's commandments, and his own weakness, implores divine help (ver. 5). This shows us—

1. *The necessity of prayer.* The Heb. particle, "O that!" is an intense sigh, indicative of earnest desire. This necessity is based upon (1) *Our ignorance.* We know not what to do till we are told. Religion does not come to us by instinct. (2) *Our forgetfulness.* Anxiety and self-conceit often drive the most necessary things out of our mind, we therefore need and must pray for what is promised (Isa. xxx. 21). (3). *Our moral weakness and indisposition.* Our hearts are naturally averse and our feet prone to wander from God's statutes. "These people do err in their hearts," &c.

2. *The substance of prayer.* "Were directed." (1.) *Generally* by the Bible, the course of providence, and the example of good men. (2.) *Specifically* by the Spirit, in the various ways which we from time to time have to tread. "The Lord directed his steps." "O Lord, I know that the way of a man is not in himself; it is not in man to direct his steps." (3.) *Literally,* "Thy word is a lamp unto my feet, and a light to my path." "In all thy ways acknowledge Him," &c. (4.) *Effectually* by the Holy Ghost applying to the heart and disposing it. "The Lord direct your hearts into the love of God," &c.

3. *The end of prayer.* "To keep Thy statutes." (1.) It is to be remarked that, of *all the ends desired in this long Psalm, the first is holiness.* (2.) *That end is practical holiness,* not contemplative or ascetic "ways," "statutes." (3.) *That is the best and most desirable end.* "Seek ye first," &c.

III. **Duty.** The Psalmist looks forward to the result of answered prayer, and feels that under divine guidance he will not be ashamed when he has respect unto God's commandments.

1. *Duty contemplates a regard for God's law;* implying (1) *moral susceptibility.* The wicked are callous, their hearts being hardened, and their wills set. (2) *Mental respect.* Unless we respect God's law, we can never acknowledge it. (3) *Practical observance.*

2. *Duty consists in an universal obedience to God's law.* "Unto *all* Thy commandments," whether (1) *its precious promises,* (2) *its elevating precepts,* or (3) *its stern obligations.*

3. *Duty is rewarded by the approbation of God's law.* "Shall not be ashamed," *i.e.,* shall have no reason to be ashamed. (1.) *God's law will approve a clear conscience* (Rom. viii. 1). (2.) *God's law will approve us so that we may dispense with the judgment of man.* "With me it is a very small thing to be judged with man's judgment," for "God will bring forth thy righteousness as the light, and thy judgment as the noon-day." (3.) *God's law will approve us at the great day.* "And now, little children, abide in Him, that when He shall appear we may have confidence and not be ashamed at His coming."

IN CONCLUSION.—(i.) *God's commandments are commandments with promise; if* we keep them we shall not be ashamed. (ii.) *We are unable to keep them without divine help;* let us pray for that help. (iii.) *When that help is vouchsafed let us use it diligently, comprehensively, and perpetually.*

GOOD RESOLUTIONS.

(Verses 7, 8.)

Our text shows—
I. That good resolutions depend on the presence of God for their fulfilment. "O forsake me not utterly." Therefore—

1. *God's presence should be earnestly supplicated.* (1.) *Because of our impotence.* "Without Me, ye can do nothing." (2.) *Because of our instability.* Nothing is more fluctuating than mere resolutions. Peter said, "Though all should forsake Thee," &c. (3.) *Because it is of God to give grace to help,"* &c. (Eph. vi. 10).
2. *God's presence will be vouchsafed.* Not always sensibly, but always effectually. "Lo, I am with you alway." Therefore (1) *Be not discouraged when God seems to be away.* When the bird is away from her young, she is in search of food. When pioneers are away from the army, they are preparing the way for it. So God sometimes fulfils the promise, "I will go before thee, to make crooked places straight." (2) *Be not discouraged when God withdraws His comforts.* We may sometimes lose our *sense* of God's love, as Asaph did. But is God necessarily away? No (Ps. lxxxiii. 23). But (3) *Be encouraged to resolve under the inspiration of the promise,* "Certainly, I will be with thee."
3. *God's presence may be withdrawn.* "My Spirit shall not always strive with man." And nothing will drive Him away more than selfish, conceited, or hypocritical resolutions.

II. That good resolutions have **respect to divine law.** "I will keep Thy statutes." All other resolutions are vain which omit this as their great and commanding aim.
1. *God demands it.*
2. *Our new nature demands it.*
3. *Our desire for blessedness demands it.*

III. That the fulfilment of good resolutions depends on the right state of the heart and life. "With uprightness of heart, when I shall have learned Thy righteous statutes." Good resolutions are easily formed; their fulfilment is a very different matter. God's presence is easily supplicated; but God's power is exerted in the employment of adequate means. There must be—
1. *A right state of the heart.* Before God's statutes can be kept, the heart must be disposed to keep them. The heart naturally inclined from the law of God, must be re-bent and inclined towards it.
2. *A learning of "the judgments of righteousness"* concerning our state, Matt. xvi. 6; thoughts, Heb. iv. 12; actions, Eccl. xii. 14; the way of justification, Rom. iii. 22. We must ascertain the things we ought to resolve, and then trust to God's Spirit to enable us to carry them out.

IV. That the fulfilment of good resolutions should be **followed by gratitude.** "I will *praise* Thee."
1. *Duty binds us to it.* The fulfilment of resolutions that are really good has been by the help of God, and has secured our highest good.
2. *The permanent result depends upon it.*
3. *Fresh resolutions are strengthened by it.*

IN CONCLUSION.—(i.) *Let your life be characterised by strong and noble resolutions.* Don't be discouraged if you fail at first. Resolve, by the grace of God, not rashly, but firmly. (ii.) *Compare your resolutions with the Word of God.* (iii.) *Carry them out at all costs* (Matt. xvi. 24). (iv.) *Crown and glorify them all by profound gratitude.*

A SERIOUS WORD FOR YOUNG MEN.

(*Verse* 9.)

"The case supposed is that of a young man pondering the question how he may be saved from the corruptions of his own heart, and escape the temptations to which he is exposed in early years, and lead a pure and upright life. There can be no more important inquiry for one just entering on the journey of life; there can be found nowhere a more just and comprehensive answer. All the precepts of ancient and modern wisdom, and all the results of the experience of mankind, could furnish nothing in addition to what is here suggested."—*Barnes.*

I. **A serious question asked.**

1. *The importance of a way.* "A way has a direction, and leads some whither. A way is continuous, and if we are in it we are advancing in it. A way differs in its direction from other ways, and diverges more and more from them the farther one travels upon it. There are in our lives no isolated acts, but only ways. Every present has its closely affiliated future. We are moving on in character as in years. The wrong of which you say, 'Only this once,' provokes its own repetition and starts you in its own direction. The violation of truth, &c., involves you in a labyrinth of mole paths. You meant an act, you have found it a way; a precipitous way, too, in which you gain momentum at every step."—*Dr. Peabody.*

2. *The danger of having an impure way.* Our text "is a metaphor which appeals to our experience. What is more disheartening than the necessity of treading muddy streets. There is a consciousness of unfitness for society. There are miry soul paths, miry they are to every eye in their more advanced stages; for there is no evil course that does not tend by sure and generally rapid steps to open shame, squalor, and misery."—*Ibid.*

3. *The special appropriateness of this question.* אֹרַח, "a track, a rut, such as are made by wheels, &c. A young sinner has no broad beaten path; he has his private ways of offence, his secret pollutions; and how shall he be cleansed from these? how can he be saved from what will destroy body and mind and soul?"—*Dr. A. Clarke.* The future, too, depends on the young; upon the pure or impure paths they follow depends the intellectual, social, and political life of the future.

II. **A satisfactory answer given.** "By taking heed thereto according to Thy Word."

1. *God's Word is the only rule of righteousness.* All other rules must, in the long run, lead astray. *Conscience* will never give a wrong direction, but it sometimes fails to give a right. You can't bribe it into falsehood, but you can drug it into silence. When on the judgment seat you can depend on its decisions; but it is not always there. So with sentiments of *honour, self-respect, self-interest,* &c.; there is no security in any of them. Only the Word of God is pure. It alone exhibits the sum of all perfection in the holiness of God and the character of Christ. "I have given you an Example." "Be ye holy, as He who has called you is holy."

2. *The Word of God is the only means by which we can be cleansed.* "Sanctify them by Thy truth," &c. (1.) *It is the only clear revealer of the character of sin.* (2.) *It alone urges upon us the necessity of holiness.* (3.) *It alone encourages us to seek holiness* by its exceeding great and precious promises (2 Cor. vii. 1, 2 Pet. i. 4). (4.) *It alone reveals the all-sufficient remedy for sin.*

3. *The Word of God must be studied and applied.* "By taking heed." (1.) *A careful study of its principles.* (2.) *A careful reference of its precepts to our special requirements.* (3.) *A careful walking according to its rule.*

III. **Sufficient reasons suggested.**

1. *Because God demands it.* (1.) *God should not be long kept out of His rights.* "Remember now thy Creator." The vessel should as soon as possible be made meet for the master's use. God has made everything ready, so there need be no delay. (2.) *God should have our best at its best.* All we enjoy we owe to Him. The Mosaic law recognised this (Lev. ii. 4). Youth is the best time. Health and vigour belong to it. Shall the best be devoted to the devil, and when you are no longer of use to him will you offer God the dregs? (Rom. xii. 1.)

2. *Because reason demands it.* (1.) Youth is the time of special temptations (2 Tim. ii. 22.) Children are of no use to the devil. The aged he has done with. But he loves to get hold of young men (1 Tim. iii. 6.) (2.) *Evil habits grow and strengthen by every indulgence.* A twig may be easily bent, but the branch is fixed; a sapling may be transplanted, an oak never. (3.) *The longer you delay the more useless you are for God and good.*

3. *Because self-interest demands it.* (1.) *Life is uncertain.* Such a momentous question must not be trifled with. Warning is not always given. Nadab

and Abihu were young men. There is but a step between us and death. (2.) *God is provoked to anger by delay*, and retribution accumulates both in this life and the next (Job. xiii. 26). (3.) *Divine blessings are delayed.* It is good for a man to bear this yoke in his youth.

IN CONCLUSION.—You are beginning life, begin it with God. You have great temptations, but you have great help (Job. ii. 28, 29) and bright prospects (Mark x. 14). There are only two ways, the way of life and the way of death—where are you?

ARGUMENT WITH GOD.
(Verse 10.)

God offers to reason with man. He offers to reason with the *sinner*, permits him to state his own case and to "bring forth his strong reasons" in support of it. He offers to reason with the *saints;* and the saint here takes up the challenge. The Psalmist presents before God's notice a *fact.* He then bases an *argument* upon this fact, and then turns the fact and argument into a *prayer.*

I. The **fact**, "With my whole heart have I sought Thee."

1. *What is it to seek God?* (Ps. xxiv. 6). It is an earnest and diligent endeavour to find God in certain definite characters for certain definite purposes. (1) *As our God, Sovereign, Father, Friend;* (2) *as our Guide* by His Word and Spirit; (3) *as our exceeding great reward.*

2. *Where should we seek God?* (1.) *In sinfulness*, notwithstanding Adam's flight from Him and Peter's desire that He should depart. That is the one reason why we should desire God's presence to pardon it, and help us out of it. (2.) *In difficulties.* In doubt for His direction; in weakness for His strength; in sickness for His health; in trouble for His consolation; as Paul (2 Cor. xii. 7-9). (3.) *In our daily life.* The heathen consulted their penates; Laban, his teraphim; Balak, Balaam. Shall God's people be behind these? Seek God's permission, counsel, blessing. (4.) *In personal communion*, not when we are obliged to go, and simply because we are obliged to go, but because we love to go (Ps. xxii. 26).

3. *How should we seek God.* "With the whole heart"—(1.) *Personally.* "*Thee*" with "*my.*" Men sometimes profess to seek God, when they are but seeking their own interests (John vi. 26). When we seek from God other than Himself, or send others with our requests, we fail. We cannot find God by proxy. (2.) *Comprehensively.* "Whole." The combined faculties of the soul. Intelligently by the study of His Word and works; morally, by faith and love. (3.) *Earnestly and uniformly*, not by fits and starts. Such, then, is the fact that the Psalmist lays before God, and which forms the premises of his argument.

II. The **Argumentative value** of the fact.

1. *The Psalmist does not offer it* (1) *Boastfully*—the plea goes side by side with confessions of unworthiness — or (2) *Meritoriously.* No one can argue with God on that basis. "What hast thou that thou didst not receive?" We can only glory that we are in debt to God (1 Cor. i. 31).

2. *The Psalmist does offer it as a reason why God should help him.* (1.) *He wants to find God.* He is using the means. God is implored to bless those means. (2.) *He wants further blessing.* God has already commanded and wrought in him the desire to seek. He now asks that he may find.

III. The **prayer founded on the argument and fact.** This is worthy of special note. He does not ask for temporal advantages, but for steadfastness in God's ways. Notice—

1. *Man's proneness to wander* (Jer. xiv. 10, Isa. liii., Luke xv.).

2. *The saint's sensibility of this proneness to wander.* The more we desire to seek God, and are on the way to find Him, the keener will be our sensibility of error.

3. *The saint's conviction of God's ability to keep him from wandering.* FINALLY.—Those who seek God shall find Him. Those who have arguments to plead will find those arguments valued. Those who pray shall have their prayers answered.

THE WORD OF GOD, ITS SPHERE AND ITS SERVICE.

(*Verse* 11.)

The Word of God is the revelation of His person and will. It is the duty of man to treasure it up where it can be preserved most safely. If it is only on our shelves or in our heads, it may be stolen or forgotten; but if it is in our hearts, cherished by our affections and guarded by our will, and embodied in our spiritual life, it is safe from loss or decay. But once in the heart it is not only kept by the heart, but keeps the heart. "Thou bearest Cæsar and his fortunes." The fortress keeps the granary, but the granary keeps those who man the ramparts.

I. What is done? "Thy Word have I hid in my heart," which implies—

1. *Understanding it.* Thoughts must pass into the heart through the mind (Prov. ii. 10). Not that it is necessary that it should be fully comprehended. Water does not always fill the channel through which it flows. It is enough if it fills the vessel into which it flows. Many mysteries baffle the intellect, but the heart is the proper organ for their comprehension.

2. *Believing it.* Until unbelief is broken down, the Word appeals for entrance in vain. When, however, it is welcomed by the hand of faith, it enters in and dwells there. It did not profit the ancient Jews, because it was not mixed with faith.

3. *Loving it.* The heart is the seat of the affections, and where there is no love the Word cannot enter. "If ye love Me, keep My commandments."

4. *Appropriating it.* There may be understanding faith and even love, and yet no hiding of the Word. These are but means to an end; its reception into our very heart's life, so that we may become a law unto ourselves, walking Bibles, living epistles.

II. How it is done.

1. *By reading it* continuously, constantly, and systematically.

2. *By searching it:* as the miner does for hid treasures, as the workman does for the best materials and the best tools. Superficial work will produce only superficial results.

3. *By meditating upon it.* If we simply read it, we shall forget it. If we merely search, we may treat what we find as subjects of interest or curiosity. But if we meditate, what we have found in our search will become seed-corn in our hearts, to bring forth fruit to the glory of God.

III. The advantages of doing it. In the heart the Word of God is—

1. *Safe* (1) *from the fluctuations of memory;* it has become part of ourselves, and is as unchangeable as our identity. (2) *From the assaults of unbelief.* It has passed out of the region of speculative belief and tentative hypothesis into the region of facts. (3) *From the deprivations of affliction.* We may be unable to hear the Word of God or even to read it, but if it is stored up in the heart we can dispense, if necessity demand it, with external means. (4) *From the hand of the persecutor.* Said that lad of whom Foxe speaks, when the Marian persecutors took his Bible from him, "Thank God, you cannot take away those chapters He has written on my heart."

2. *Ready for every emergency.* The most powerful remedy and the most valuable blessings are nothing worth if not close at hand when required. "Every scribe that is instructed unto the kingdom of heaven bringeth forth out of his treasures things new and old." It is ready (1.) *To comfort in distress.* (2.) *To provide arguments against unbelief.* (3.) *To furnish us with pleas in prayer.* Our prayers are effectual in proportion as the word of Christ dwells in us richly.

(4.) *To make spiritual intercourse more sweet and edifying*, Col. iii. 6. (5.) *To afford instruction, stimulous, sanctity, and diligence in the concerns of daily life.*

IV. **The grand purpose of doing it.** "That I might not sin against Thee." The Word of God hid in the heart safe from attack, but ready to attack will:—

1. *Expel sin.* The heart "abhors a vacuum." It will be filled with something. If not with the Word of God, with sin. But both will not dwell together there. Divine principles, however, will extirpate sin.

2. *Preserve from falling into sin.* "The law of the Lord is in his heart, none of his steps shall slide."

3. *Enable us to overcome sin.* In this great warfare all other weapons but the sword of the Spirit will fail (1 John i. 14).

THE SOURCE AND MEANS OF BLESSEDNESS.

(*Verse* 12.)

I. **God is the source and fountain of all blessedness.** "Blessed art Thou, O God."

1. *God is absolutely blessed in Himself.* He is "the blessed God," "the blessed and only potentate." "Over all, God blessed for ever;" free from all misery, enjoying all good, all-sufficient in Himself, contented with Himself, delighted with Himself, neither needing any good or fearing any evil from the work of His hands (Ps. xvi. 2).

2. *God communicates all blessings from Himself* (P. cxlv. 16, Eph. i. 3). He is the most conspicuous illustration of His own saying, "It is more blessed to give than to receive" (John i. 16).

3. *God appropriates all blessings to Himself* (Ps. cxlv. 10, Rev. v. 13).

II. **Man's blessedness consists in the enjoyment of God.** "Happy is the people whose God is the Lord." God, being absolutely blessed, has enough for Himself, and therefore enough for us. He is "God all-sufficient."

1. *Man misses happiness if he seeks it from any source short of God.* Everything else is (1) *imperfect.* Let the world's contributions be ever so copious they leave some void. Solomon, Ahab, Naboth, &c. (2) *Illusive.* The happiness they bring is only apparent. They cannot quell one unquiet passion, or still or satisfy conscience (Prov. xiv. 3). (3) *Transient.* An immortal soul can only be satisfied with "pleasures for evermore."

2. *Man gains happiness when he seeks it in God.* (1.) *God is "able to supply all our need." "In His presence is fulness of joy."* (2.) *God's blessings are real.* Sin is cleansed, passions subdued, conscience satisfied, soul fed, and the whole man kept in perfect peace. (3.) *God's satisfactions are charged with His own immortality.*

III. **Man's blessedness is secured through instruction in God's statutes.**

1. *They teach us the way to God.*

2. *They teach us how to partake of the blessed nature of God* (2 Peter i. 4).

3. *How we may live the life of God and engage in His blessed work.*

IN CONCLUSION.—Prov. viii. 34, 35.

TESTIMONY.

(*Verse* 13.)

This verse is closely connected with the two preceding. In verse 11 the Word is hid in the heart, now it finds expression on the lips. To express what we do not feel is hypocrisy; and what is really in the heart will find an outflow. In verse 12 God is asked to teach His statutes: the prayer is now answered, and, mentally and morally qualified, the Psalmist teaches others.

I. **The subject of this testimony.** "All the judgments of Thy mouth."

1. *God's judgments are divinely revealed.* Not human discoveries or speculations.

2. *God's judgments are the divine criteria* whereby to decide in all matters affecting truth, duty, and destiny (Isa. viii. 20). Not reason, interest : what man thinks or feels ; but God's infallible *judgment.*

3. *God's judgments are the rule by which He judges the world.* Now (John v. 45, 46). They are not arbitrary and capricious, but fixed, written down. By them He will adjudicate at the last day. (John xii. 48). Notice, then, that what God has said, and said in His sovereign and official character, is the subject of *our* testimony.

II. The **manner** of this testimony.
1. *Clearly.* "Declared."
2. *Fully.* "All the judgments" (Acts xx. 27).
3. *Faithfully.* "All the judgments of Thy mouth." Not our own opinions, speculations, or *doubts* (1 Peter ii. 2). ἄδολον γάλα, unmixed milk. "To mix it with sugar and the luscious strains of human evil disguises it and hides it from a spiritual taste. To mix it with lime (as Jerome says of heretics) makes it baneful and noxious."—*M. Henry.*

III. The **reason** for this testimony.
1. *It is a duty we owe to God.* He gave us the organs of speech (Ps. xii. 4). When we give our bodies a living sacrifice we must not reserve our tongue (Jas. iii. 9).

2. *Because the lips should be in harmony with the character.* "The tongue of the just is as choice silver." The sensualist will talk of his pleasures, the man of business of his trade, the student of his books, and shall the righteous restrain their testimony ? (Matt. xii. 35.)

2. *Because the tongue is the most important member in the propagation of divine truth.* Perhaps example is overvalued. True Christianity is not profession, but life. But how can example influence without a declaration of those judgments upon which it is based ? The preference of life over testimony may perhaps spring from a shrinking from an arduous duty.

IN CONCLUSION.—Let the example of the Psalmist stimulate us to a more perfect fulfilment of this much-neglected or badly-discharged obligation. How much there is of mere speculation and laboured rhetoric in preaching ! How much of foolish talking and jesting, to say no more, in the family and social circle ! Let the preacher prepare himself by the more diligent study of the judgments of God, and let private Christians remember Coloss. iv. 6, and let the Church in its private gatherings remember Heb. iii. 13, and Ps. xxxvii. 30.

GOD'S TESTIMONIES A GROUND OF JOY.

(*Verse* 14.)

I. **What the Psalmist did.** "I have rejoiced in the way of Thy testimonies as much as in all riches." The testimonies themselves are a "way." God's Word is a *progressive* revelation. And the life to which it bears testimony and for which it is a guide is the "*way* of holiness." Thus the Psalmist rejoiced in the study and practice of the Word of God. Looking around him he observed that riches were the main elements in human joy, and that men considered themselves happy in proportion to their wealth. But his conclusion is, that *all* riches could afford him no greater joy than that which he had in the Word of God. He rejoiced in the way of God's testimonies.

1. *As truth,* which was good for his understanding (Prov. xxiv. 13, 14). When any capacity is filled with that which is suitable to it, joy and satisfaction will naturally arise. The mind is disordered by perplexities and errors, but is satisfied with truth.

2. *As the highest and most absolute truth* (Deut. iv. 6, 7). What man calls truth is not always certain truth. The so-called truths of philosophy and science to one generation are often errors to another, and the mind is often bewildered by the dogmatism of its

teachers. What men have taught most certainly has frequently been exploded or revised. Only the truth of God is immutable, and subject to no revision. The mind can, therefore, rest upon it without fear.

3. *As truth which could satisfy the higher cravings of his soul.* All truth is more or less satisfying. More or less, because there are degrees of value even in truth. A truth which shall guide a man to a right destination is of more value to him than a scientific curiosity. Truth which makes a man better and nobler, is of more value than that which tells the number of the stars. God's truth is of the supremest value, because it guides the soul to God and immortality, and "converts the soul."

II. **Why he did it.** The Psalmist rejoiced in God's testimonies as much as in all riches, because—

1. *Of their exact suitability to his need.* Joy is that which inevitably results from the reception of a suitable blessing. Food rejoices the hungry soul, not the full one. The parched ground rejoices after a shower, not the saturated morass. So riches are good in their way, they bring bread to the starving, clothes to the naked, &c. In that way do the testimonies of God "rejoice the soul." There is a class of need which they alone satisfy. They are God's great spiritual treasure-house of food, raiment, &c., which fully meet all the requirements of our nature.

2. *Because the greater covered the less.* Profit and pleasure, the sum of the worldling's store, and the result of his expenditure of his wealth, are these his alone? Nay, verily. God's people have these and a hundredfold beside if they fulfil the conditions (Ps. xix. 10, 11).

The distinction between God's people and others is that the former seeks true riches and true happiness and gets them, the others false riches and false happiness and do not always get them. (1.) *They get the true profit.* True wealth makes not the surroundings but the man more valuable. The value of a picture does not consist in its frame, neither does that of a man in the abundance of the things which he possesses. True wealth relieves in the greatest extremities. Money is of no use in the day of sickness and the hour of death. True wealth purchases things of the highest value. True wealth is that which is so estimated by those who are best capable of judging. The savage may think himself wealthy, and be thought wealthy by his fellow-savages, by his accumulation of shells and beads, but what does civilised man think of him? So true wealth is that which is pronounced so by God (Luke xii. 20, 21). *Knowledge* (Col. ii. 2, iii. 16). *Faith* (James ii. 5). *Good works* (1 Tim. vi. 17, 18). The *favour of God* (Rom. x. 12). (2.) *True pleasures.* The pleasures purchased by wealth are transient; those that lie on the path of God's testimonies are "for evermore." The one by overindulgence leads to sin and death (Luke xii. 19); the other to joy unspeakable and fulness of glory.

IN CONCLUSION.—Seek the way of God's testimonies. Riches and joy are there. It is a calumny to speak of religion as an unprofitable or gloomy thing. Riches even of the baser sort are sanctified, and pleasures so far from being abrogated are perfected. The way of God's testimonies is our way home. Does not that thought generate strength, lighten labour, and ease pain?

A FOURFOLD DETERMINATION.

(*Verses* 15, 16.)

The Psalmist has been mainly speaking of the past; upon that he builds the future. He had sought, hid, declared, rejoiced; now he will meditate, observe, delight, remember. These different determinations suggest to us the refreshing changes of spiritual life.

Rest consists more in the variation than in the cessation of employment. So the Psalmist, while his love for all the departments of his work is the same, yet changes his exercise. Now it is meditation, now observance, now recreation, now the exercise of memory. Observe the twofold order in these verses. The precepts point to the ways, the ways are regulated by the statutes, and the Word covers the whole. Again, meditation on God's precepts results in respect unto God's ways. To have respect unto God's ways is to see the pleasure and profit of God's statutes; and, finally, rejoicing in God's statutes is the best protection against forgetfulness of God's Word.

I. "I will meditate in Thy precepts." Meditation is the contemplation, digestion, and spiritualisation of truth. The heart sanctified by the grace of God is an alembic in which those noble and profitable thoughts are distilled which are necessary to the spiritual life. God has enforced upon us this duty (Josh. i. 8), and promises His approbation and blessing upon it (Ps. i. 2). If we would maintain our spiritual health we must meditate. Without it faith, the evidence of things not seen, becomes weak; things hoped for vanish away; love, forgetful of its true object, consumes itself in its own fires; and prayer, lacking both thought and verbiage, droops and dies.

II. Those that meditate in God's precepts will have respect to God's ways. Meditation will show that God's ways are *right* ways; that God's ways are the *only profitable and useful ways*. Meditation will open up the whole way. It will therefore lead to—

1. *Deliberate choice of God's ways.* He who meditates will not decide to serve God simply because his fathers did so, or because it is the fashion to do so, or for fear of hell, &c., but from intelligent and conscientious conviction.

2. *Avoidance of every other way.* Meditation will show a man the impossibility of walking in God's path and the devil's at one and the same time. He will be able to resist the fascinations of those ways which diverge on both sides from the way of God, and will elect to keep in that way alone.

3. *Firm, steady, and persevering progress in that way.* Meditating on his chart, and communing with his divine companion, he will not pursue his journey by fits and starts, with sudden progresses and equally sudden declensions, but will run with patience and walk without faintness.

III. Respect for God's ways will beget delight in God's statutes. By keeping to those ways alone and by continuous progress in those ways it will be seen—

1. *That God's statutes deserve delight* (1.) *Because of Him who is their Author*, and the substance of what they teach about Him. The further we go the more we shall see of His tender fatherhood, His mighty helpfulness, His beneficence and grace, what He is to us, what He does for us, what He will make of us. (2.) *Because of their own intrinsic excellence.* The further we travel the more we shall know of their elevating doctrines, their interesting history, their precious promises, and their mighty hopes.

2. *That God's statutes must be our delight.* (1.) *They are our charter* (Heb. vi. 18). (2.) *Our infallible directory on the way* (ver. 105). (3.) *Our encouragement and support* (ver. 54). They are God's storehouse of riches for our poverty, comfort for our afflictions, life for our death.

IV. Delight in God's statutes will be helpful to the memory of His Word. The mind most easily fastens on and treasures up that in which it is most delighted. "Where the treasure is," &c. That which is displeasing is gladly forgotten, but it is an increased and increasing delight to be able to remember the delightful. If a student has no delight in his book he will soon forget it; but, taking pleasure in it, his comfort will be promoted by his recollection. There are two ways of forgetting God's Word—(1.) *Forgetfulness of its literal precepts.* (2.) *Forgetfulness to obey those precepts.* Delight in God's statutes is the sure corrective of both.

LIFE: ITS SUSTENANCE AND AIM.

(*Verse 17.*)

Everything depends upon true and adequate views of life. It is perilous to entertain false or one-sided views. The worldling views life as a field for pleasure, the soldier for military prowess, the student for learning, the merchant for wealth, the statesman for politics, the Psalmist as a sphere for divine service.

I. **Life.** The Psalmist's idea of life was *servitude.* He was God's servant. This conception runs through the Bible. The proud distinction of Patriarchs, Psalmists, Prophets, and Apostles was that they were servants of the King of kings. This view implies honourable acceptance, dignified privilege, and exceeding great reward.

II. The **sustenance** of life. God's bounty. Notice that this bounty is—
1. Unmerited. We can lay no natural claim to it.
2. Adequate. By it God is able to supply all our need.
3. Everlasting.

III. The **aim** of life. The Psalmist prays that life thus sustained may keep God's word. This aim is—
1. *The divinely-ordained aim.* God has made man for Himself. It is His will, therefore, that man should keep that which shall enable him to fulfil that design.
2. *The highest, noblest, and truest aim.* It is that which angels consciously reach, and God's inanimate universe unconsciously.
3. *The soul-satisfying aim.* The Word of God is the law of our being, and in the keeping of that there is great reward. Learn—
(i.) *That the life spiritual is of more value than the life natural.* (ii.) *That if the latter is of God's bounty, so is the former.* (iii.) *That the sustenance of both should be supplicated, that the true aim of both may be reached.*

WONDROUS THINGS, AND HOW TO SEE THEM.
(*Verse* 8.)

The law was a very small portion of what is now the Word of God. Yet the Psalmist saw and hoped still to see in that narrow compass vastly more than we do in the large and complete revelation of God's will. This is accounted for from the fact that he made the very best use of what he had, and that God, in answer to his prayer, had enabled him to do so. Notice—

I. **That man by himself cannot see wondrous things.** The Hebrew phrase is, "Unveil mine eyes;" implying—
1. *That man is spiritually blind* (Rev. iii. 17, Job. xi. 12). (1.) *By sin* (Eph. iv. 18). (2.) *By reason of ignorance.* (3.) *By reason of self-conceit* (1 Cor. viii. 1, 2). (4.) *By reason of prejudice and disaffection* (Luke xvi. 14, 2 Cor. iv. 4).
2. *That man is not only thus naturally blind, but lacks that divine light which can alone reveal and illuminate the sacred mysteries.* Man is both blind and in the dark. His therefore is "gross darkness."
3. *That this blindness and darkness are universal.* The Psalmist's case before his prayer was not the exception, but the rule.

II. **That there is a process by means of which man may not only see, but see wondrous things.** The Psalmist did not complain of the inherent obscurity of the law, but of the darkness which rested both on him and it. So he does not ask for another law, nor for a new faculty, just as a blind man would not wish for a new sun, or for new organs. All he asks is that that which was hidden might be brought to the light, and that in that light he might *see* light. This process is—
1. *The unveiling of man's eyes* (2 Cor. iii. 14, 15, Luke xxiv. 45).
2. *The diffusion of spiritual light.*
3. *The employment of the faculty which has been unveiled in the contemplation of that upon which supernatural light has been thrown.* By this means a clear and experimental knowledge of the word of God will be obtained (Heb. viii. 10).

III. **When this process is complete, wondrous things are seen in God's law.**
1. "Wondrous *things.*" The Bible is a register of facts. Myths are wonderful. Prodigies are wonderful. But the plain truths of the Word of God are more wonderful than the strangest fiction.

2. "*Wondrous* things." The things of God's law are (1) *Wondrously beautiful.* No poets have ever had so exquisite a sense of the beauties of nature. No histories are so charming, no examples so sublime, no eloquence so grand. (2) *Wondrously surprising.* The Bible is full of surprises. This is so if we consider the way and the form in which the Bible has at length reached us. Every successive step in its development opens up new wonders, and every book has something fresh to say about the wonderful works of God. Then what a history it has had ! What escapes, what triumphs ! (3) "*Wonderfully mysterious.* Its aim is, all through, to lead us to such subjects as the soul and God, and the eternal world, and sin—the great mystery and root of mysteries—and the marvellous remedy which has been provided for it in the descent of the Divine nature into the human, that great mystery of godliness—" God manifest in the flesh." . . . If the " powers of the world to come " have anything in them to excite wonder and awe, the Bible, beyond all other books, holds them in his hand."—*Ker.* (4) *Wondrously perfect* in its wisdom (Deut. iv. 6), purity (ver. 49), equity (Rom. vii. 12), power (Rom. i. 16), unity.

STRANGERS AND PILGRIMS.

(*Verses* 19, 20.)

" When a child is born into the world it is spoken of as a 'little stranger.' Strangers indeed come from far, out of immensities from the presence and touch and being of God, and go into the immensities again, into and through all the unreckonable ages of duration. But the little stranger takes vigorous root . . . and life goes on deepening and broadening in its flow, . . . and then after elaborate preparations, opening into a great, restful, sunny plain, lo ! the shadows begin to fall . . . and a voice speaks and calls for the 'little stranger' to go through that door men call death ; and the stranger is not ready, the pilgrim's staff is not in hand, and his eye, familiar enough with surrounding things, is not accustomed to the onward and ascending way. . . . Alas ! he has made one grand mistake. He has been looking at the things which are seen and temporal, and not at the things which are not seen and eternal ; and so there is hurry and confusion and distress in the going away, all which may be helped and throughly hindered if a man will but say, ' I am a stranger in the earth.' "—*Dr. Raleigh.*

I. **The stranger.** "A stranger is very well known, not perhaps in the great city where there are always thousands of such, but in a country town or on a country road. See him as he enters the village at nightfall : you can see at once he is not of the place. The dust is on his raiment ; he is footsore and weary ; yet he has no mind to stay—he will be away again before the inhabitants are up. His language is different ; his questions are those of one who has but a superficial and momentary interest in the answer that may be given ; his very look is the life spelling of the word 'onward ;' his home, wherever it may be, is not here."—*Dr. Raleigh.*

1. *All men are strangers.* Good or bad alike, whether they will or not, are fast travelling to " that undiscovered country," &c. " One generation passeth away and another generation cometh, but the earth abideth ever." " The pavement we walk upon, the coals in our grates—how many millenniums old are they ? The pebble you kick with your foot—how many millenniums will it outlast ? Go into a museum and you will see hanging there, little the worse for centuries, notched swords and gaping helmets—ay, but what has become of the bright eyes that once flashed the light of battle through the bars ? what has become of the strong hands that once gripped the hilts ? . . . The money in your purses now will some of it bear the head of a king that died half a century ago ? It is bright and useful —where are all the people that in turn

said they 'owned' it? Other men will live in our houses and preach from this pulpit when you and I are far away."—*Maclaren*.

2. *Specially are the children of God strangers*. Those who are not the children of God would be at home here if they could; but God's children are conscious of being and willing to be strangers, because (1) *Their native country is elsewhere*. Everything tends towards the place of its origin. All men love their native soil. Christians are "born from above." "Jerusalem which is from above is the mother of us all," and therefore we "seek those things which are above." (2) *Their inheritance is elsewhere* (Eph. i. 3). (3) *Their kindred are elsewhere*. Father, elder brother, &c. (Matt. viii. 11; Heb. xi). (4) *All the endowments of their nature point to a fuller and unrestricted exercise elsewhere*.

II. The stranger's **prayer.** "Hide not Thy commandments from me."

1. *God's commandments are man's chart and directory on his way to heaven*.
2. *Those commandments are hidden from the natural man;* their dialect is altogether foreign to him.
3. *Prayer should be offered that these commandments may be made intelligible*.
4. *When made known, they should become a "lamp unto our feet and a light unto our path" till our pilgrimage is o'er*.

III. The stranger's **longing.** "My heart breaketh for the longing that it hath unto Thy judgments at all times."

1. *The more our hearts are bent on the end of our journey, the more shall we desire fully and accurately to know the way*.
2. *The more we know of the way, the more ardent will be our desire to know all about it at all times*.
3. *The more we desire to know of the way, the more diligent and practical will be our study of that which can alone guide us to our destination*.

IN CONCLUSION.—
(i.) *What provision are you making for your journey?*
(ii.) *Are you astray on your pilgrimage?*

PROVIDENTIAL INEQUALITIES READJUSTED.

(*Verses* 21–24.)

The Psalmist here and elsewhere states the standing problem of the apparent prosperity of evil and adversity of good, and solves it. He was seemingly in great misery, while his enemies flourished; but it was not really so. The Psalmist had privileges to which his oppressors had no title. He had God's testimonies as his delights and counsellors; while those who oppressed him were of a debased moral character, and were under the condemnation of God. This solution satisfied him; may it satisfy us.

I. **The problem stated.**
1. *The prosperity of the wicked.* (1.) "*Princes*." The wicked are often in the ascendant as regards power, wealth, position, popular esteem, &c. (2.) "*Proud*." The wicked are always, when they can be, arrogant and self-sufficient.

2. *The adversity of the righteous.* (1.) *They are "reproached" for their conscientious scruples, integrity, endeavours, and aims.* (2.) *They are treated with ridicule and "contempt,"* because of those things that they hold most dear: God's Word, Christian character, hope of heaven. (3.) *They are unjustly judged* (ver. 23), because man cannot estimate the worth of godliness.

II. **The problem solved.**
1. *The adversity of the wicked.* Our real state is what we are in the sight of God. (1.) *They stand rebuked of God*, and are therefore cursed. (2.) *They err from God's commandments*, and thus miss the true end of their being and the full glory and perfection of their life. Can theirs, therefore, be *true* prosperity?

2. *The prosperity of the righteous.* (1.) *Their reproach and contempt is that of man*, and therefore removable,

and will be removed by the justice and compassion of God. (2.) They have a certain and infallible guide. God's testimonies tell them of God's will and how to submit to it with resignation and patience. (3.) They have perennial sources of delight. God's Word testifies of God's presence, God's comfort, God's heaven. Can there be any real adversity with all this?

"TENEO ET TENEOR."

(Verse 22, clause 2, and Verse 24.)

Those who keep God's testimonies shall be kept by them.

I. **How do we keep God's testimonies?**

1. *By remembering them.* To forget is to lose. To have them kept in the memory is to have them ready for every time of need.

2. *By obeying them.* Every act of obedience is an additional stone in the fortress, in which they are kept. Every duty formed strengthens habit and confirms steadfastness.

3. *By propagating them.* Giving is the condition of keeping all through life. The vitality of a tree is conditional upon its yielding fruit and leaves. Material wealth depends on the outlay of money. So unless we give in proportion as it is given unto us of the word of life, even that which we have will be taken away.

II. **How do God's testimonies keep us?**

1. *By ministering to our delight.* God's Word brings that light and gladness which saves the world from suicide. It testifies of God, who is the health of our countenance; of Christ, who cleanses us from the source of all misery; of the Holy Ghost, who comforts us in the day of trial; of the precious promises which buoy us up with hopes of better things to come; of heaven, where all tears are wiped away.

2. *By guiding us with their infallible counsel.* They keep us in the path of truth, guide us in the way of holiness, direct us in the road to heaven, and as we go shield us from all harm.

IN CONCLUSION.—The principle of our text holds good everywhere. Those who hold good or bad principles are kept or lost by them and with them. The man who knows how to keep his temper, his money, &c., will find that they will keep him. Hold, then, the best things, the firmest things, and you will be ever safe.

THE BENEFIT OF GOD'S TESTIMONIES.

(Verse 24.)

The Psalmist in his trouble and distress, under the contempt and reproach of the proud, and under the oppression of princes, turns to God's Word, and there finds direction and joy.

I. "Thy testimonies are **my delights.**" Notice—

1. *That there are joys AND joys.* Worldlings have their joys, but they are unsubstantial and evanescent. The delight engendered by God's testimonies is (1) *Divine and powerful.* It is the "joy of the Lord," and *is* God's people's strength. (2) *Real* (2 Cor. vi. 10). (3) *Great* (1 Pet. i. 8). (4) *Endless.* "Everlasting joy."

2. *That God's people are commanded to rejoice*—(1) *Not merely permitted;* (2) *Not merely suggested on reasonable grounds;* (3) *But enjoined as a necessary duty.* It is not a matter of indifference or choice. We must rejoice (Phil. iv. 4; Matt. v. 12; James i. 2).

3. *That this rejoicing is founded on and derived through the Word of God* (Rom. xv. 4; Heb. xii. 5). Joy is particularly needful in affliction, as in the Psalmist's case. God's testimonies tell us (1) *Who permits it* (John xviii. 11); (2) *The benefit of it* (Isa. xxvii. 19, Heb. xii. 10); (3) *The brevity of it* (Isa. liv. 7, 8); (4) *Helps in it.* Con-

soling help (Rom. v. 3). Effectual help (Ps. cxxxviii. 3, Heb. xiii. 5); (5) Its end (2 Cor. iv. 17).

II. "Thy testimonies are my counsellors." As a divine rule in all matters of faith and practice it is sufficient. Man cannot improve upon it, let him not tinker with it. It is an unerring guide in all perplexities. It will help us to a right decision in all matters of right and wrong. Its counsel is safe for good thinking, good speaking, for the prudent management of our affairs to successful issues (James i. 6), and supporting in all painful or difficult duties (Prov. xvi. 3, Ps. xxxvii. 5).

AFFLICTION AND ITS REMEDY.

(*Verse 25.*)

Our text teaches us—

I. **That God's children are afflicted.** This affliction may be a sorrowful inward experience (Ps. lxxxviii. 3-7 ; lxxvi. 1), or an extreme outward pressure (2 Sam. xii. 16, 17 ; xv. 30). We know that "God does not willingly afflict." Why then do His people's souls sometimes cleave to the dust? (1.) *To humble them* (2 Cor. i. 7-9). (2.) *To correct for past transgressions.* The righteous have their evil things in this life. God punishes them now that it may not be necessary to do so by and by. (3.) *To test* the strength of their character, their faith in the promises, their hope in His mercy, the depth and sincerity of His love. (4.) *To awaken the spirit of prayer* (Ps. cxxx. 1). To show more of the riches of His grace in their recovery (Ps. lxxi. 20, 21).

II. **That affliction should drive us to God for help.** Notice—

1. *The unwisdom of any other course.* Man cannot help us.
2. *The disastrousness of any other course* (Dan. ix. 13). To choke sorrow is to be choked by it, whereas if we go to God the burden can be thrown off. To depend upon the charlatan or to neglect proper means is suicide.
3. *The wisdom and blessedness of this course.* God sends the tempest of affliction after His Jonahs, that out of the depths they may cry to Him to be delivered. Because God is powerful, able, and willing to help. Let us (Heb. iv. 16).

III. **That God undertakes to apply the remedy for affliction,** not according to our merits, or merely according to His compassion, but according to His pledged and covenant "word." The remedy must therefore be adequate, firm, and everlasting.

DIVINE EDUCATION.

(*Verses 26, 27.*)

1. The Psalmist presents himself for **examination.** He puts his whole case, his qualifications and disqualifications, before God, and God hears him.

II. The **result of this examination** is a consciousness and confession of ignorance and error. His prayer to be taught God's statutes, to understand the way of God's precepts, implies ignorance of the one and departure from the other. And he who comes away from the throne of grace with any other consciousness has been there in vain.

III. His ignorance and error leads him to **cry to the great Teacher for instruction.** This instruction was twofold. *Intellectual,* "Teach me Thy statutes;" and *practical,* "Make me to understand *the way* of Thy precepts." First the information, then its correct and proper application. Remember that the instructor is God, not man; and the instruction is not in human guesses and speculations, but in divine truth and holiness.

IV. Upon this instruction being vouchsafed and his education complete, he feels that he will then be in a position to **instruct others**, "So shall I talk of Thy wondrous works." 1. God's works, not his own or man's. 2. God's wondrous works, in revelation, providence, redemption. This in our case is due to God, due to ourselves, due to man.

STRENGTH IN WEAKNESS.

(*Verse* 28.)

I. **The Psalmist's case.** It was one of extreme trouble. His very soul "dropped away." Why so extreme? Just as the sorrows of a man are greater than the sorrows of a beast, from his superior knowledge and keener susceptibility. So the knowledge of the spiritual man is clearer and more accurate, and his susceptibilities keener, than those of the natural man. He knows the character of sin and the claims of God, and his conscience responds to the slightest touch of evil.

II. **The Psalmist's prayer.** Not for the removal of his affliction, but for the strength of grace to bear it. "Strengthen me." This implies a recognition of the need and benefit of this disciplinary and sanctifying affliction, and a desire to be sustained until it should have accomplished its perfect work. We would do foolishly with our afflictions what a child would do with its restraints and the discipline of school or home. Better far to be able to say, "*Thy* grace is sufficient for *me.*"

III. **The Psalmist's plea.** "According to Thy word." Prayer avails in proportion to the power and prevalence of its pleas. No plea is like that of God's own pledged word. And what does God promise? Not to deliver us as we wish, but always either to deliver or to give us that grace and strength which renders deliverance a matter of comparative indifference. What God then has promised let man plead, and if prayer is not answered it is not from indifference or unwillingness on the part of God.

THE TWO WAYS.

(*Verses* 29, 30.)

Our text teaches us—

I. That there are **two ways**, and two ways only, which determine the character and decide the destiny of mankind. The way of lying and the way of truth. The false and the true. There is no third way, and there are no characteristics common to both. A man must either walk in the way of truth or the way of error.

II. That these two ways are **open to man's deliberate preference and choice.** God does not urge us towards the one or the other by the force of a predestined and inexorable necessity. Neither is the force of any circumstance such as to leave man no option but to be untrue to himself and to his God. The practical common sense and experience of man laugh at all metaphysical endeavours to deprive him of the freedom of his will.

III. That the **false way is most natural to man.** The Psalmist felt so, or why his urgent request that it might be removed? All Scripture is emphatic on this point. "They go astray from the womb, speaking lies." This way is very broad, and many elements enter into its composition. Hypocrisy, insincerity, error, false religions, false maxims, false customs, as well as deliberate lying. Experience is as emphatic as Scripture. No evil habit is so strong, so general, so growing, as the habit of untruthfulness. It is the one habit more than another that grows upon the young.

IV. That in order to **walk firmly in the true way divine assistance is indispensable.**

1. God must "*remove the way of lying.*" He alone can break the force of evil habits and check the evil tendency.

2. *God must vouchsafe the chart by whose guidance alone we can walk in the way of truth.* "Grant me Thy law graciously." This God has answered in the case of every man. The heathen have the law written on their heart, and their conscience accuses them when they

do wrong, and excuses them when they do right. For Christians there is the written law and the living law of the life of Christ in addition, and guided by this threefold law the wayfaring man though a fool shall not err therein.

V. **That continuance in the way of truth is conditional on the use of divinely-appointed means.** "Thy judgments have I laid before me." Only by a diligent, careful, and accurate study of the judgments of God can our feet be kept in the way of truth. "As he who learns to write lays his copy before him, that he may write according to it; as the workman lays his model and platform before him, that he may do his work exactly; as we must have the word in our heart by an habitual conformity to it; so we must have it in our eye by an actual regard to it upon all occasions, that we may walk accurately and by rule."—*M. Henry.*

PERSEVERANCE.

(*Verses* 31, 32.)

Having chosen the way of truth, the Psalmist does not regret his choice, but adheres steadfastly to it, and makes steady but rapid progress in it. This was perseverance.

I. **Steady.** "I have stuck." It was not a restless and fitful movement, but a firm and consistent adhesion to fixed principles. The race is not to the swift, but to the steady. The battle is not to the strong, but to the steadfast. "It is hard pounding, gentlemen," said Wellington at Waterloo, "but we shall see who will pound the longest." The man who runs, till he is out of breath, for one hour, and is obliged, panting, to rest for the next, will not win the prize. And so the Christian who is very earnest on set occasions and makes great efforts at certain times, but who tires of service, and is forgetful of his principles on ordinary occasions, is not the man who will take the crown of life. "Run with patience."

II. **Rapid.** "I will run." Steady perseverance is not necessarily slow. It certainly is not slow in the long run. The man who steadfastly runs by rule and with self-restraint, although he may be distanced by him who is careless of rule and impulsive for the moment; time will show who has made the greatest progress. But the perseverance of the Christian life is rapid in its attainment of results, and *ought to be*. Consider how soon the course is traversed, the number of obstacles overcome, the character of the help vouchsafed, the nature of the incentives offered, and how quickly, comparatively speaking, habits are formed and graces developed and strengthened! In view of all this, it is appropriately likened to the swift flight of the eagle, and to the short, eager race for the incorruptible crown.

III. **Shameless.** "O Lord, put me not to shame." There is a perseverance which can only bring shame. Perseverance in an inconsistent, insincere, lying course can only bring contempt on those who run there. The path of truth is the only one in which it is possible to run secure from shame. Circumstances may arise which may prevent us in other paths from so persevering as to win that towards which we reach forth the hand, and thus, for want of success, others are ashamed of us and we are ashamed of ourselves. Here, however, if we are faithful we shall win, and thus be secure from shame.

IV. **Divinely assisted.** "Lit., 'For Thou wilt enlarge my heart.'" Expressing confidence that God *would* do this, so that he would be thus inclined and enabled to keep His commandments. It is an acknowledgment of dependence and confidence. The phrase means, to make the heart *free* from all hindrances to what is right; to fill it with noble and holy purposes; to stimulate and animate it. The heart is contracted by selfishness, pride, vanity, ambition, covetousness; it is made large by charity, love, hope, &c. Sin narrows the soul; religion enlarges it."—*Barnes.*

CHRISTIAN PROGRESS.

(*Verses* 33–35.)

Our text suggests—

I. That the way of Christian progress is **divinely revealed**. "Teach me, O Lord, the *way* of Thy statutes." The way of life is not a path discovered by study, intuition, or speculation. Nor is it a path upon which it is possible to light by happy accident. As it is not human learning, scientific knowledge, or even ethical development, but the knowledge and practise of *God's* statutes, God must make those statutes known.

II. That Christian progress is **possible only under certain definite conditions**. The racer in the old Greek games was not crowned except he had striven according to fixed and stringent rules. So with this and every other path in life worth traversing, the conditions are twofold—

1. *Knowledge of the way.* "Give me understanding." This is the prime condition. Ignorance is the fruitful source of failure everywhere. No man can make progress in business, unless he knows his business; in scholarship, unless he is acquainted with his books; in politics, unless he is conversant with affairs of State. So Christians can make no progress without understanding God's law. Notice—(1) *God gives this understanding.* God reveals not only the entrance of the way, or the panorama of the way as a whole, but the details of the way, its dangers, duties, difficulties, blessings, losses, and rewards. And not only so, but also that spiritual enlightenment without which progress is impossible. With this we "shall not walk in darkness, but have the light of life." But (2) *Man must use the understanding that God gives.* Scholarship is of no value unless turned to practical account. Letters are useless unless employed in the formation of words; words are of no service except they convey thought; thoughts are of no use unless adequately expressed. And so all theoretic knowledge in the way of Christian progress is of no effect unless applied "with the whole heart." Alas! many men know every step of the way to heaven who, from the want of this, fail to get there.

2. *Earnestness in the way.* "I shall observe it with my whole heart." Another universal condition. Unless men give "earnest heed" to the securing of a given object, they "let it slip." This earnestness implies (1) *Love.* The "heart" is the seat of the affections. Unless a man loves his career, he will not be successful in it. So our love must be fixed on ours. There is everything in it to excite affection. Christ is at once the entrance and the goal. To "me to live is Christ," being "built up into Him our living Head, in all things," who is "the fairest among ten thousand, and altogether lovely," is the inspired description of the Christian way. Love to Christ, again, is the motive force of Christian progress. (2) *United effort.* The earnest man is he who gives his "whole heart" to his work. His motto is, "This one thing I do." We say a man is not in earnest when his efforts are desultory or divided; and such men never succeed. Alas! there are many Christian men who, for the same reason, come short of the prize.

3. *Absorbing interest in the way.* "Therein do I delight." Again, no man will succeed who does not delight in his work. If he entertains ignoble views about it, or depreciates it, or shows he can afford to treat it with carelessness, he will never make himself proficient. Those men who have succeeded in politics, learning, &c., have been the men who have counted their callings most worthy of their supreme interest. And shall we depreciate or be careless about "the high calling of God in Christ Jesus," so grand and delightful, and leading to such issues? No, the Christian man, of all men, should take pride in his career; for is it not "ways of pleasantness and paths of peace?"

4. *Constancy in the way.* "I shall keep it unto the end." Most failures are due to the want of this. If a man lacks this one thing needful, in spite of genius and practical ability, he will run in vain and labour in vain. And many well-meaning Christians fail because they make no sustained effort. "He that endures to the end shall be saved." "Wherefore" (1 Cor. xv. 58).

III. That Christian progress is **impossible without divine assistance.** "Make me to go."

1. *God must supply the stimulus.* "Make me to go." A stimulus is needful, for Christianity is not natural to man. No effort can be made without a force behind and an attraction in front. Thank God, these are not wanting. The promises and comforts of God's Spirit are ever near us lest we should be weary and faint in our souls. Heaven is set before us to gain; hell for us to shun. Yea, "The young men shall faint, and be weary," &c. (Isa. xl. 31).

2. *God must supply the qualifications.* "Make me." Not certainly in the sense of compulsion, but in the endowment of the requisite ability. As He gives us the knowledge of the way, so He will supply all its requirements. He will give us the elements of moral earnestness, shed abroad His love in our hearts, supply the principle of cohesion which will enable us to serve Him with our whole heart; make us interested in our work, and enable us to continue steadfast unto the end.

3. *God must supply the fact.* "To go." He must make us Christians, and thus empower us to begin our progress. He must sow the seed of grace before we can grow in it. It is only by "looking unto Jesus" that we can lay aside every weight, &c. At every stage He must guide us by His counsel, go before us, making "crooked places straight," &c., and afford us the support and discipline of His rod and staff in every dark ravine. Man cannot go without this great Leader. But our comfort is that we are continually with Him, &c. (Ps. lxxiii. 23).

Men and brethren, we are all going. Whether we like it or not, we must all go. (1.) *How are we going;* with God, or without Him? (2.) *Where are we going;* to heaven, or to hell?

THE SERVANT OF GOD.

(*Verses* 36–38.)

Notice—

I. **That God qualifies His servants by a special fitness.** "Incline my heart;" which suggests—

1. *That man is naturally disqualified for divine service.* His heart is inclined in the opposite direction. It is warped and twisted from the straight line of God's law. Consequently there is a preference for that which is averse from God.

2. *That man, if qualified at all, must be qualified by God.* No force within a man is capable of doing this, nor any force without, either of example, instruction, or compulsion. But God does so incline the hearts of those who are willing, that, like the great servant of the Lord, they can say, "I delight to do Thy will." God does not break the will; He softens it, and then stretches it back again. He never compels, but draws by the persuasion of His entreaties, the allurement of His promises, by reason and affection; and then when the heart is prepared He moves it back again by His Spirit into conformity with His will and way. And when man's heart is inclined to do the will of God, not for what can be got, but because it is felt to be right and joyous, then is man qualified for divine service.

II. **That those whom God qualifies for, He consecrates to His service.** These two ideas overlap, as indeed do all the Christian doctrines and privileges. Consecration not only implies fitness, but supplies it. It separates from sin, and imparts the power of divine life.

1. *God's servants, by virtue of their consecration, are separate from sin.* (1.) *The eyes are turned away "from beholding vanity."* Sin loses its attractiveness,

and becomes an object of abhorrence. (2.) *The eye turned away, the whole man is turned away.* Men walk in that direction on which their eyes are set. (3.) *The eyes and the whole man turned away from the vanities of sin are glad to look on the realities of God.*

2. *God's servants, by virtue of their consecration, are made instinct with divine life.* "Quicken Thou me in Thy way." This life of consecration is (1) *divine.* God's servants are born of His Spirit, born into His house, born from above. They are not slaves or hirelings, but sons; and their duties those of filial affection. (2) A special gift for a special service: "In *Thy way.*" Not for our spiritual gratification, or for our safety and blessedness merely, but in and for His way. (3) *Progressive.* "In" all departments and stages of "Thy way." We need moment by moment the divine quickening, and that constant quickening continually enlarges, develops, and intensifies all the powers and faculties of our being.

III. Those whom God consecrates He supports by special encouragements. "Stablish Thy word unto Thy servant."

1. *God's servants are the subjects of special promises.* God undertakes to preserve them from evil in the prosecution of their tasks, and empower them to overcome all their difficulties.

2. *God establishes those promises.* He fulfils His undertakings. No servant of His, while trusting in His Master's strength and doing His Master's work, has ever suffered harm or lacked any good thing.

3. *God's promises established afford a basis for future hopefulness.* Since no word of God has failed, man has solid ground to rest upon. Were His word untrustworthy, or His promises broken, nothing but disappointment could result.

IV. Those whom God qualifies, consecrates, and encourages, are expected to exhibit certain traits.

1. *Negatively:* "Not to covetousness." That the servant of God should not be inclined to covetousness is seen from the fact that covetousness (1) *Disposes the soul to occupations that are averse from the service of God.* It is the root of all evil (1 Tim. vi. 10); leads to violent theft and oppression (Micah ii. 2); to treason, as in the case of Judas; dishonour of God; in the case of Gehazi; dishonesty, in that of Achan; murder, in Ahab; apostasy, in Ananias and Sapphira. (2) *It utterly incapacitates for the service of God.* It destroys the principle of obedience, which is love of God (1 John ii. 5), is contrary to all the commands of God (Matt. vi. 14), and it slights all the encouragements of God's grace by seeking other rewards.

2. *Positively.* Devotion to God's fear. (1.) *To fear God is to revere Him and adopt that posture which befits His service.* (2.) *Devotion to that fear saves us from sinning against God, and stimulates us to His service.*

FEAR AND ITS REMEDY.

(*Verses* 39, 40.)

God's people are the subjects of a twofold fear: the fear of God and the fear of sin. The former fear is dealt with in the previous verse, the latter in this. "Guard me from the reproach which (alone) I fear of sinning against Thee; for Thy judgments, *i.e.,* revealed laws, *are good,* and happy is he that keeps them."—*Speaker's Com.* Observe—

I. That the Christian has nothing to fear but sin, and the only reproach he need deprecate is that of having sinned.

1. *Because sin is the only evil.* Nothing is evil except from its alliance with sin. Trial, persecution, sickness, poverty, pain may be good, and under certain circumstances are to be desired rather than deprecated. But sin can only work harm. It saps the foundation of spiritual life, deteriorates the quality and diminishes the volume of true manhood, blinds the intellect, befouls the heart, destroys hope, kills usefulness, and blasts the soul.

2. *Because sin has terrible and eternal consequences.* Sin deliberately rejects

the sources of the soul's life and blessedness, and therefore fixes its own destiny, which is the death and misery of hell. Sin, too, entails a terrible "reproach" which man may well fear. (1.) *The reproach of the good*. (2.) *Self-reproach*. An active conscience will not let the sinner rest, for persisting in his own destruction and wronging his Master and his Friend. (3.) *The reproach of God*. God reproaches in love now. "What iniquity have you or your fathers found in Me?" "Why will ye die?" But, by and by, in anger and judicially will He utter that reproach which shall never be wiped away, and dismiss the sinner to "shame and everlasting contempt."

II. That the only safety from sin and its reproach is the life of righteousness.

1. *There is no other safety*. Watchfulness and resolution may save us from gross and palpable sins; pardon may remove its guilt, but only a quickening in the divine righteousness can save us permanently from its power.

2. *With this we are secure*. God does not simply cease to impute sin, He regenerates. So quickens, that sin has no more dominion over us,—quickens us in a new mould, so that we "live unto righteousness." Thus the cause and the reproach are both rolled away, and God's approbation secured.

III. That the danger and the safety are revealed by the Word of God. "Thy judgments are good." Sin is a vague consciousness, and its consequences a vague dread without the judgments of God; and nowhere but there do we read, "Repent ye, and believe the Gospel."

IV. That the danger is to be deprecated, and the safety sought by prayer. "I have longed after."

SALVATION.

(*Verses* 41, 42.)

The primary object of this prayer was doubtless providential deliverance. The Psalmist was afflicted, God had promised deliverance. He trusted in that promise, yet salvation stayed. Now the enemy began to reproach, "Where is now thy God?" This led to the passionate entreaty of our text. He prayed for salvation that he might give the enemy to see the stability of "the confidence wherein he trusted." Learn that salvation is—

I. The outcome of the divine mercies. "Let Thy mercies . . . even Thy salvation." Man is lost and ruined—has lost and ruined himself—not by chance, but deliberately. To salvation, therefore, he can lay no moral claim. By disobedience and rebellion he has lost all title to the divine regard. He can, therefore, be saved only by an act of mercy. But his sins are so many, and his depravity so deep, that multiplied mercies can alone meet his case. So thought the Psalmist when he said, "Let Thy *mercies*," &c. So thought God when He offered to "multiply to pardon." So we must think when we consider the wealth and variety of divine grace: the Mosaic and prophetic dispensations, the work of Christ, the operation of the Spirit, the Gospel ministry, and the means of grace. So in every individual case, forbearing, prevenient, saving, sanctifying grace. "Not according to our works, but according to His own mercy."

II. Not a human effort, but a divine visitation. "Let Thy mercies come unto me." Salvation is not the effort by which the sinner lifts himself out of one moral atmosphere into another, and loosens his hold of vice, and educates himself into virtue. It is altogether an act of God upon the sinner, and an act which, being essentially supernatural, does not admit of the co-operation of natural agencies. True, these are conditions, but repentance and faith merely put man into a salvable condition. "Mine own arm brought salvation."

III. The subject of divine promise. "According to Thy Word." The promises of salvation in God's word are the

IV. A witness to the steadfastness of the divine word. Professor Tyndall's proposed experiment was manifestly unfair. There may be reasons, however inscrutable, whereby the sovereign of the universe may see fit not to relieve physical affliction, or save from physical death. Great moral purposes may be in the process of evolution, and for their accomplishment individuals may have to be removed to another sphere. But here the challenge may be taken up. God has promised to save on the condition of believing prayer. Let the vicious try it, pleading God's promises, and if reformation does not follow the experiment has failed. But it has been tried, and again and again men have had "wherewith to answer" them that reproached them. Learn—

(i.) *The value of salvation.* The mighty and merciful visitation of God. (ii.) *The necessity of trusting in God's Word for salvation.* (iii.) *The duty of the public exhibition of that salvation for the glory of God, and the refutation of unbelief.*

PREACHING AND PRACTICE.

(*Verses* 43, 44.)

Observe:—

I. The Psalmist's **prayer**. "Take not the word of truth utterly out of my mouth." He regards it both as a *duty* and a *privilege* to declare God's truth. How many, alas, forget this obligation! They have been saved themselves through hearing and obeying this declaration, and that is their only concern. There are others who look upon it merely as a burden to be borne with resignation. God, however, would have us regard the command to testify of His grace as a commandment with promise. We *must* preach if we would be true to our convictions, and fulfil the divine plan for the conversion of the world. But consider the *honour* of being ambassadors from God, the *blessedness* of conveying the tidings of God's love to sinful and sorrowing men, the *glory of the reward*. Let this therefore be every Christian's prayer. If he does not feel called, let him pray God to call him. If circumstances render the practice of this duty and the enjoyment of this privilege difficult, let him ask that the word of truth may not be taken *utterly* out of his mouth.

II. The Psalmist's **purpose**. The Psalmist felt that lip service alone was a mockery. No one would listen to a man whose practice gave the lie to his preaching. Ornate eloquence, profound learning, or subtle logic are useless gifts if the life be wrong. But he felt, too, that living without preaching was but mutilated service; so he wishes to combine the two, and determines to make his preaching not merely subordinate to his practice, but helpful to it. "*So shall I keep Thy law.*" What he preaches to others he will preach to himself. He will water others and himself at the same time. Preaching shall strengthen his own convictions and promote his own growth in grace. This shall be not occasional, but continual and "for ever and ever."

III. The Psalmist's **consolation**. "I have hoped in Thy judgments."

1. *In the strength of this consolation he goes to God in prayer.* He felt that God's judgments were his only hope. He prayed that he might preach them and keep them lest that hope should die.

2. *This consolation is the strength of all powerful preaching.* A man who is not hopeful cannot preach at all. But if a man has a well-founded hope on the power of God's Word, and in the effects of its proclamation, he *must* preach, and his preaching will be intense and successful.

3. *This consolation is the power of holy living.* Unless a man has a strong hope that the basis on which he stands is strong and enduring, and that the

end at which he is aiming is attainable, he will all his lifetime be the subject of anxious fears. But if he hopes in God's judgments he will be sure that he is on a rock, and that success will attend all his efforts.

FREEDOM.

(*Verse* 45.)

Nothing is more precious or desirable than liberty. Yet there is nothing about which men make more mistakes, or enjoy so little. What passes for liberty is frequently the basest servitude. And what men call thraldom is often the finest liberty. Notice—

I. That man's natural condition is one of **bondage**. He has deliberately resigned and rejected his title to liberty by transgressing the terms on which it is based. Scripture everywhere represents the unredeemed man as sold under sin, led captive by the devil, desiring good but unable to reach it. This bondage is painful and degrading in its nature, and terrible in its consequences.

II. That man **walks at liberty when he seeks and finds God's precepts.** God's Word is the charter of man's freedom.

1. *It defines true liberty.* The subordination of the soul to God (James i. 25). The soul is free only when it moves unhampered in that sphere where its true interests lie. Restraints are not laid on the soul, but on those passions and preferences which hinder its full activity. When a command is imposed upon it, it is implied that its breach or negligence would militate against our freedom.

2. *It confers true liberty.* It is the only revelation of the great redemption, and alone shows how through the death of Christ and the work of the Spirit we may enjoy the liberty of the children of God.

III. That man walks **permanently and securely at liberty** only as long as he seeks and finds God's precepts.

1. *They must be sought and found by God's help, for they are God's precepts.*
2. *They must be applied by God's grace.*
3. *Their requirements must be rigidly kept.*

IN CONCLUSION.—(i.) *The exchange of servitude for freedom is an exchange of masters and an exchange of services.* (ij.) *Serve the new Master who has emancipated you from a terrible tyranny with the same diligence as you did your old.*

BIBLE DUTIES.

(*Vers.* 45–48.)

I. **To seek for it.** If we seek for the word of God literally, or for that word which has special reference to us in given circumstances, we shall find it.

II. **To meditate upon** it. Finding it, our first duty is to see what it is, what it means, what it is for, and to make it subserve those circumstances which led to our search for it. Meditation does all these.

III. **To love** it. Meditation will show its infinite beneficence and beauty, its exact suitability to the needs and aspirations of the soul, instruction for the mind, direction for the will, cleansing for the heart, guidance for the life, comfort for affliction, strength for duty, peace for distraction, hope for death, and will beget as it must, love.

IV. **To delight** in it. The heart that loves the Word will delight in it (Ps. i. 2, cxi. 1 ; Rom. vii. 22). Thus the study and practice of God's Word is not a matter of dry duty, but of joy. Who can help rejoicing in that which is the revelation of God's character, will, helpfulness, redemption, heaven ? Let the soul love these revelations and it will delight in them.

V. **Not to be ashamed of it.** Suspicion and dislike are at the root of shame. Those who suspect the authority or dislike the teaching of the Word of God are ashamed of it. But those who delight in it say, "God forbid that I should glory," &c. What are the promises or laws or dignities of earthly monarchs in comparison with it? Even the reproach of Christ is greater riches than the treasures of Egypt. We who delight in God's commandment are not ashamed to stand with Moses before Pharaoh, Daniel in Babylon, Peter and John in the presence of the Sanhedrin, and Paul at Cæsar's bar.

VI. To earnestly practise it. What we are not ashamed of we should "lift up our hands to." It is not enough to seek, find, meditate, love, delight, and glory in God's Word. The servant who knew his lord's will but did it not was beaten with many stripes. "If ye know these things, happy are ye if ye do them" (1 John ii. 4; James i. 22). Everything depends upon this. If we do not practise God's commandment with both hands earnestly, our ardour will cool, our love diminish, our meditation cease, and our Bible be withdrawn. But if we practise it, our weakness and ignorance will drive us to its wisdom and strength, finding which our affections will be stirred and our delight and boasting stimulated.

IN CONCLUSION.—Seek God's Word diligently. While you are musing on it, let the fire burn. That fire will kindle joy. That joy will give us holy boldness before princes and governors, and help us in the prosaic application and practice of it in our daily life.

AFFLICTION: ITS COMFORTS, DUTIES, AND DANGERS.

(*Verses* 49-53.)

Notice—

I. That God's servants are permitted to suffer affliction. This Psalm, the whole Bible, and all experience testifies to this. "They that are godly in the world shall suffer persecution." The glorified "have come out of great tribulation." "Ye shall have tribulation."

1. *These afflictions are aggravated by, or in some cases mainly consist in, the derision of ungodly men* (ver. 51). "They ridiculed him, bantered him, did all they could to expose him to contempt; they laughed at him for praying and called it *cant*, for his seriousness and called it *mopishness*, for his strictness and called it *needless preciseness*. They were the proud who sat in the scorners' seat and valued themselves in so doing.—*M. Henry*.

2. *Whether despised or not, the godly man is always afflicted by the prevalence of sin* (ver. 53). "The LXX. render the word ἀθυμία, by "depression;" Arab. and Syr., "sadness;" Jerome, "horror;" Calvin, "terror." (See Ps. xi. 6.) "Probably a burning wind or simoom is meant, which scorches up and destroys vegetation in a moment; and, metoph., a sharp penetrating pain or horror."—*Speaker's Com.* Other aspects of affliction are as nothing when compared with man's treatment of God and His Word. A sure mark of grace is extreme sensitiveness to the exceeding sinfulness of sin.

II. That God has special comforts for His afflicted servants.

1. *His word is the repertory of exceeding great and precious promises for those who are in affliction.* All our vicissitudes are divinely provided for. "I remember Thy judgments of old." God does not wait for His servants' extremities. The provision for them is antedated by eternity. When the believer goes to the Word of God he finds waiting for him all he wants.

2. *His Word quickens* (ver. 50). The worst feature of affliction is the exhaustion it engenders, and that is intensified sometimes by the thought that it is hopeless. But God tells us that our sickness is not unto death, and thus immortal hope and new life are kindled in the breast.

III. That affliction should lead us to call upon God to fulfil His promises (ver. 49).

1. *We should plead the promise itself.* This is an appeal to God's faithfulness. We must go to God's Word to find what promise meets our case and then plead it. Is our case that of sinners : God's promise is to abundantly pardon. Distress : God has promised peace. Darkness : light. Pain : sufficient grace.

2. *We should plead the hope that the promise has excited.* This is an appeal to the divine justice and goodness. If God could give rise to groundless expectations, all faith in Him would fail. This we know to be impossible.

3. *We should plead God's fulfilled promises and man's answered hopes.* "The Psalmist remembered that the principles of the divine administration were always the same." In the trials of life, &c., it is well for us to think of the unchanging principles which mark the divine dealings. Under such an administration those who trust in God *must* be safe.

IV. That affliction should not lead us to decline from God's law (ver. 51).

1. *Pain should not lead us to doubt God's goodness.* Pain is not an evil in itself. The physician and parent have often to inflict pain.

2. *Adversity should not lead us to swerve from our principles.* Remember the compensations. It is something to suffer for the right. God is always on the side of the right. God will always reward the right.

3. *Derision should not lead us from an open avowal of our piety* (Ps. xliv. 12-22). This is a temptation to which the young are most susceptible. Many a man can face death who quails before sarcasm. Peter. Happy the man in the scoffing world who can say, "I have not declined from Thy law."

IN CONCLUSION.—(James i. 2-5; 1 Peter i. 6, 7; Rom. v. 3, etc.).

THE EARTHLY PILGRIMAGE AND THE HEAVENLY SONGS.

(*Verse* 54.)

"When the Eastern traveller takes shelter from the scorching heat or halts for the night at some caravansary which is for the time the house of his pilgrimage, he soothes his rest with a song—a song it may be of war, romance, or love. But the poet of Israel finds his theme in the statutes of Jehovah. These have been my pastime, with these I have refreshed myself onward through the wearisome journey, and across the scorching deserts of life. Not songs of old tradition, &c., have supported me, but *these* have been the solace of my weary hours and the comfort of my rest."—*Bushnell.*

I. God's people are on a **pilgrimage**.

1. *They have here no continuing city* (Heb. xiii. 14). This life is but the passage of the soul to its eternal inheritance. All things here are fleeting, are partaken of in haste, while the traveller is moving onward. All things change, avocations, pleasures, friends, &c., but this, that we are journeying to the grave.

2. *They have here no home.* They *sojourn* here for a time. Soon they strike their tents for the last time and enter into their *rest.* All the journey is characterised by the discomfort incident to homelessness. There is nothing to give harmony, satisfaction, or repose.

3. *They are ever seeking their country and their home.* This implies patient employment of the means at their disposal ; the temporary rests and refreshments of the way ; the supports and charts of the way ; and the companions of the way.

4. *This being the case they are not ashamed of the character of strangers and pilgrims,* but glory in it. There is nothing here worthy of their inheritance (John xv. 19, 1 Peter iv. 4).

II. **Delightful provisions** are made for God's people on their pilgrimage. "Thy statutes have been my songs." "Multitudes of men have a very different conception of this matter. Divine law, divine obligation, responsibility in any form, authority under any conditions, they feel to be a real annoyance."—*Bushnell.* God's statutes are delightful, nevertheless, because—

1. *They clearly reveal the end of our journey.* While other books give only dim hopes or shrewd guesses, God's Word is most explicit. It is full of assurances of our future home. It tells us of its many mansions, its splendid cities, its wide domain, its freedom from sin, pain, and death; its Fatherly Sovereign; and of the joys which are at His right hand for evermore.

2. *They contain directions how we may reach our journey's end.* It is no small joy amidst the questionable maxims and the halting speculations of the world to have a light shining in a dark place, a chart which maps out every day's march, and indicates every danger, and following which it is impossible to go astray.

3. *They contain the history of our ancestors and fellow-countrymen who have gone the way before us* and have entered into rest, and encourage us to emulate their patience and heroism. (Heb. vi. 12, xii. 1).

4. *They contain the precious promises;* assure of the leadership and companionship of God; provide comfort for the anxiety, and solace for the pain, we meet with by the way.

THE NIGHTLY OCCUPATIONS OF THE GODLY.

(*Verses* 55, 62, 148.)

That God has given the light is a reason why we should dedicate the day to Him and make Him the end of all our active services. But God has also given the night, and that blessing of blessings, sleep. Should not that be recognised, and at its appropriate season? The Psalmist thought so and then meditated on God's Word, remembered God's name, and rose to give thanks to Him.

I. **The duties of the night.**

1. *Meditation on God's Word.* Measuring by that the actions of the day, and composing our thoughts for the night.

2. *Remembrance of God's name;* who has preserved us during the day, and under whose protection we hope to be preserved during the darkness and solitude of the night.

3. *Celebration of God's praise.* Thankfulness for the blessings of both seasons.

II. **How these duties are to be performed.**

1. *With alacrity* (ver. 148).

2. *With self-forgetfulness.* At midnight. Remembering only the gratitude we owe to God.

3. *With joy* (ver. 62).

III. **Why these duties are to be performed.**

1. *Night is most suitable for profitable meditation on the Word of God.* Amidst the distraction of worldly cares the mind is unfitted for the sustained effort that is required.

2. *Night is most suitable for remembering God's name.* The mind is then unoccupied. The bustle of life often drives away thoughts of God.

3. *Night is most suitable for thanksgiving.* The time most suitable to thought is most suitable for gratitude.

IV. **These nightly occupations will prepare us for the exercise of daily duties.**

1. *Nightly meditation will prepare us for daily obedience.* The task learned overnight will be easily repeated on the following day.

2. *Nightly remembrance of God will stimulate daily thoughts about Him.*

3. *Nightly thanksgiving will be a healthy preparation for the recognition of daily mercies.*

THE BLESSINGS OF OBEDIENCE.

(*Verse* 56.)

Some expositors refer the "this" literally to the blessings enumerated in the preceding verses. It is better, perhaps, to view the expression indefinitely. Taking a review of his whole experience, the Psalmist bursts out in the joyful exclamation, "All is mine, because I kept Thy precepts." The evangelical results of obedience are—

I. **Protection** in the further course of obedience (Ps. xxxi. 19, 20; Job i. 10; Zech. ii. 5).

II. As much of **success** in life as God may see good for us (Matt. vi. 33; Ps. lxxxiv. 11).

III. **Gracious manifestations** of God's presence and favour (Ps. xvii. 15; John xiv. 21).

IV. **Growth in grace** (Ps. lxxxiv. 7; Prov. iv. 18; Rom. vi. 19).

V. **Peace.** Verse 165. (Isa. xxxii. 17; Gal. vi. 16; Phil. iv. 8.)

VI. **Joy.** Verse 14. (Rom. v. 2, xiv. 17.)

VII. **Heaven** (Rev. iii.)

THE SOUL'S PORTION.

(*Verses* 57, 58.)

I. **What the soul's portion is.** "Thou art my portion, O Lord." Not His ordinances, or Word, or Church, or anything about Him, or from Him, but **Himself.** Heb., "Jehovah (is) my portion, *i.e.*, mine inheritance more precious than any other." (See Ps. xvi. 5, cxiii. 5; Josh. xvii. 14, xviii. 10.) The soul's portion is—

1. *Accessible* with them who are of a contrite heart.
2. *Ever present.* "Lo, I am with you alway."
3. *Unchanging.* "The same yesterday, to-day, and for ever."
4. *Soul-satisfying.* "In Thy presence is fulness of joy."
5. *Eternal* (Ps. lxxiii. 26).

II. **How the soul's portion is attained.** "I entreated Thy *face* (Heb.) with my whole heart."

1. *Not by bribes of benevolence.* But
2. *By earnest supplication.*
3. *By the undivided aspirations of our whole nature.*
4. *By the effective pleading of the divine promise,* "According to Thy word."

III. **On what grounds the soul's portion is given.** "Be merciful," &c.

1. *Not on the ground of merit.* But
2. *On the ground of the divine mercy.*
3. *On the ground of the divine promise.*

IV. **For what purpose the soul's portion is vouchsafed** (ver. 57).

1. *Consecration,* "I have said."
2. *Obedience,* "I will keep Thy words."

THE HEAVENLY ROAD.

(*Verses* 59–61.)

The author of this Psalm reviews the way in which God had been leading him. He looks back on the time when he was on another road, and contemplates with gratitude the thought which induced him to change his destiny. Having changed the tenor of his ways, he sped with joyful haste along the path of God's commandments and was not driven therefrom by the malice of his foes. These words suggest—

I. That man is naturally in the **wrong way.** "I thought on *my* ways."

1. *The wrong way is a hard way.* "The way of transgressors is hard." Christian men are too prone to complain of the difficulties of God's way. Let them think of the perils they have escaped.

2. *The wrong way is an unsatisfying way.* No sinner can give a reasonable account of himself. To speak of its pleasures or profits is but irony. They are husks which the swine do eat.

3. *It is a ruinous way.* It wears out the spiritual energies, and leads to everlasting destruction.

4. *It is a selfish way.*

5. *It is a way peculiar to the individual transgressor.* "We have turned every one to his own way."

II. **That reflection will lead men into the right way.** "I thought."

Sin is a reckless absence of thought. In order to sin, a man cannot, must not, think. The sinner is beside himself, and, as in the case of the Prodigal, when he comes to himself and contemplates his own misery and degradation, and the comfort and honours of his father's house, he turns his feet in a homeward direction.

III. **That the choice of the right way must be followed by a deliberate change of habit.** "And turned my feet." "He does not say that he *waited* for God to turn him, or that he could not turn of himself. Man is always active in conversion. *He* changes, repents, believes, turns, not *God*. It is indeed by the grace and help of God,—but the effect of that grace is not to make him idly wait; it is to rouse him to *act*."—*Barnes*.

IV. **That the right way is to be pursued with alacrity.** "I made haste."
1. *Much time has been lost.*
2. *Many dangers are pursuing.*
3. *Much has to be done ere we reach the end*, and the day is far spent.

V. **That this alacrity is not to be lessened by the dangers and privations of the road** (ver. 61). The surrounding perils, so far from discouraging us, should hasten us. Does the despoiled traveller sit down and bemoan his losses when he knows his home is in sight? No, he hastens on, lest worse accidents should happen him. So let our losses and dangers drive us nearer to God, and quicken our pace towards that heavenly country "where thieves do not break through nor steal."

THE COMMUNION OF SAINTS.

(*Verse* 63.)

Man is a social creature. God has said, "It is not good for men to be alone" (Eccl. iv. 9–12). For the purposes of mutual help God has set the solitary in families. This being the case for the promotion of spiritual life man should not rush into monasticism, but should seek fellowship with those with whom he has moral affinity (Rom. i. 11, 12). This can be safely neglected by none. Our text suggests—

I. **That religious communion must have a religious basis.** The fear of God and the keeping of His precepts.

1. *The Bible knows of no basis that is not in some sense theological.* The fear of God implies a belief in the person to be feared. We cannot fear an abstraction, or a "stream or tendency which works for righteousness," nor love it, which indeed is included in that fear. To keep God's precepts is to believe in their divine inspiration and authority, or we shall deem keeping them optional. To fear God necessitates fearing Him through the divinely-appointed means, through the grace of Christ and in the power of the Holy Ghost. If we keep God's precepts we must not omit those which demand a full intellectual assent to certain doctrines. It is impossible for the man who believes that the only way to the Father is through Christ, to worship with the Unitarian or the Deist. It is impossible for the man who when he prays believes it is with the help of the Spirit, to pray with the man who believes in no such Spirit. To do so argues either hypocrisy on the one hand, or the suppression of cherished convictions on the other. "What part hath he that believeth with the infidel?"

2. *The Bible knows of no basis that is not practically religious.* Profession without practice is everywhere sternly condemned. There are no words in the whole Bible stronger than those used by St. Paul to the Corinthian Church for its admission of a known profligate to its communion. The original covenant with the Jews was on the condition of their "circumspection" and their separation from the people and customs among whom they lived. *Creed and conduct, therefore, is the broad basis for the communion of saints.*

II. **That religious communion is the spiritual intercourse between spiritual men, and between spiritual men and God, through the divinely-appointed means.** It involves—

1. *The common profession of a common faith and obedience.* Christian faith, salvation, love and service, are common to

all believers, and form the bonds by which Christendom holds together.

2. *Common communion with a common God,* through a common Saviour, by means of the help of a common Spirit.

3. *Participation in a common lot* (Rev. i. 9). In its fullest extent it involves a communion of suffering as well as of fellowship (Rom. xii. 15; Heb. x. 33, xi. 25).

4. *The exercise of a common spiritual help* (Ps. xv. 4, xvi. 2; Rom. i. 12).

III. **That religious communion is reasonable and natural, when on this basis,** *e.g.,*

1. *Religious men are members of the family of God.* They are begotten by the same Father, regenerated by the same Spirit, share the same life, are washed in the same blood, and are travelling to the same heaven.

2. *The inclinations of the members of this family all flow in this direction* (1 Thess. iv. 9; 1 John v. 1).

IN CONCLUSION.—(i.) *Religious communion is necessary to maintain the faith once delivered to the saints.* (ii.) *Religious communion is profitable as promoting the interests of charity and growth in grace.*

GOD'S GOODNESS: ITS NATURE AND ITS RELATION TO PRAYER AND LIFE.

(*Verses* 64, 66, 68.)

I. The nature of the divine goodness.

1. *It is divine.* "Thou art good." God is good in Himself. All the attributes of love, truth, and justice, which go to make up perfect goodness, inhere in Him.

2. *It is operative.* "Thou doest good." It is not a negative or passive goodness; it is positive and active. God is good in (1) *Creation.* "The earth is full of Thy mercy." No perfection is more resplendently exhibited in the universe than this, and the universe teems with its manifestation. The cheering sun, the shining stars, the singing birds, the waving corn all proclaim that the earth is full of the goodness of the Lord. (2) *In human experience.* The course of individual history tells the same tale. His wings have overshadowed us, His arm has upheld us, and into our hearts He has caused to flow the ceaseless benedictions of His grace. Well may we say with the Psalmist, "Thou hast dealt well with Thy servant." (3) *In the Word.* This is the one theme of all the precepts and all the promises. All our wants are there anticipated and fully met. There is light for our understanding, government for our will, cleansing for our conscience, guidance for our life, help for our weakness, comfort for our trouble, God for our portion, and heaven for our home.

II. These views of the divine goodness encourage us to pray.

1. *Without them prayer would be impossible.* To be uncertain about God, or to know Him only as indifferent or implacable, would stifle prayer. Prayer implies confidence, freedom of access, expectation of answer. But we should not be so foolish as to approach one whom we were sure could not or would not hear us, or so courageous if we knew He would frown upon us or spurn us.

2. *But with this assurance we have a sure ground for confidence and expectation, and a mighty plea.* God is good, and does good to the fowls of the air, the grass of the field; shall He not much more be good to us? Plead His goodness, His promise to do good, and you will not plead in vain.

III. Our prayer, based upon such sure warrant and such glad encouragement, should be of the largest kind and for the best things. We cannot ask too much, for our text tells us that God is willing as well as able to supply all our need. "Teach me Thy statutes . . . good judgment and knowledge." The Psalmist felt that instruction was the best thing to be desired, and he prayed to be instructed in the best things.

1. *God's statutes.* The Bible is the best book, because "given by inspiration of God, and profitable," &c. Some books are good, others bad, others in-

different. He prays therefore that the contents of this best book may be expounded to him by their true interpreter.

2. *Good judgment.* This is another of the best things to which all should aspire. To bad judgment may be traced all the evils that are in the world, and to good judgment all that is good. A good judgment will (1) *Accurately distinguish* between truth and error, good and evil (1 Cor. ii. 15, x. 15; Heb. v. 14). (2) *Determine and decide* (Ps. xxxix. 1; Acts xi. 23; 2 Tim. iii. 10).

(3) *Guide in the right direction,* which is indeed its main end and use (Ps. l. 23).

3. *Knowledge.* God's statutes are the sources of true and saving knowledge. Good judgment will guide us to them, and apply them, digest them, and use them. Upon these three things thus hang all spiritual good. Having these all the rest will follow.

IN CONCLUSION.—(i.) *Entertain large views of God's goodness.* (ii.) *Come for the provisions of that goodness with large petitions.*

THE PURPOSE AND BENEFIT OF AFFLICTION.

(*Verses* 67, 71.)

At first sight we are startled by the apparent contradiction, *good* to be *afflicted.* Good to be afflicted because driven to the painstaking study of a book whose revelations humble us and imposes further hardships? Good because driven from having our own way to walking in God's? Even so a storm drives a vessel into harbour when she should be nearing her destination, and the sailors deem that storm a calamity. Not so; they find while in the harbour a leak that would have given them a watery grave, and there they repair the leak, and then proceed on their way. It was good for them to be afflicted. So God tosses us in a sea of trouble to drive us to the harbour of His Word, where our defects may be ascertained and remedied. A traveller bent upon a given destination, through forgetfulness, or self-conceit, or indolence, neglects to consult either wayfarers or charts. He resumes his way, but still blindly pushes on. He meets with an accident, and can go no further for the time. Was that a calamity? No. It brought him to his senses. Now he examines his chart, makes inquiries, and finds that he is on the wrong road, and can never that way reach his journey's end. It was good for him to be afflicted. So a man errs from the way of happiness, the way of truth, the way of his true destiny, the way of God. The Bible is too dry for him, how can he with his sublime genius condescend to examine its tedious details? Ah! that book is the only itinerary to heaven. He goes madly on till he comes to disaster and to ruin. Then he is glad to consult that book, and then he finds how far he has gone wrong and how he may get right. Truly may such use these words, "It is good for me that I have been afflicted. Before that I went astray: but now have I kept Thy word."

CONTRASTS AND COMPENSATIONS.

(*Verses* 69, 70.)

The lesson to be learned here is the old one, "Things are not what they seem." There was a great contrast between the Psalmist and his persecutors, to all appearances in favour of the latter. *They* were in a position which lifted them up with pride; *he* in a position which cast him down in sorrow. But below the surface the contrast is reversed. *Their* heart was as fat as grease, unsusceptible to spiritual impressions, and incapable of spiritual enjoyment. *He* had both the appetite and the privileges, for he delighted in God's law. Again, he had that which enabled him to triumph over their slanderous accusations, the answer of a good conscience towards God.

I. The **contrast**.

1. *Apparent.* Pride and affliction. To his enemies, to the world generally, evil prospered, and goodness played a losing game. So it appears to many now (Ps. lxxiii. 4-12).

2. *Real.* Down below the surface, and in the sight of God, there is a contrast which tells altogether the other way. Hearts as fat as grease—delight in God's law. "Their heart is dull and brutal (Isa. vi. 10 ; Ps. xvii. 10, lxxxiii. 7), so that they understand not Thy statutes, in which I delight; yea, I love them with my whole heart, and above all price." — *Speaker's Com.* "Senseless, secure, and stupid, sensual and voluptuous ; they roll themselves in the pleasures of sense and take up with them as their chief good; and much good may it do them. I would not change conditions with them."— *M. Henry.*

II. The **compensation**.

1. "*The wicked have forged a lie against me.*" Heb., To patch together. "It is applied to accusations made up of shreds and patches,—units, small matters, things having no necessary connection, words dropped here and there which, being artfully woven together, seem to make out a case against a man. Most slanders are formed in this way."—*Barnes.* "All the falsehoods which men *smeared,* or *smeared all at once* over him, making the true nature of things undiscernible by daubing them over with false colours, or pasting on deceit."—*Moll.*

2. *The compensation consisted in the fact that they were lies, and that the Psalmist had and would keep God's precepts with his whole heart.* This, with the consequent sense of God's approbation, supported and cheered him. Learn—

(i.) *To judge accurately and not by appearances.* (ii.) *The needful thing is not to be rich and prosperous, but to be right and good.* (iii.) *Those who are right and good will have abundant consolation in the midst of trial.*

THE BIBLE BETTER THAN RICHES.

(*Verse* 72.)

This, like all great truths, is a most difficult thing to believe. The real value of wealth has been estimated over and over again, yet men cling to it as the best possible if not the best conceivable thing. But the testimony of those who could best judge the relative value of both, pronounces God's Word to be the best conceivable and the best possible thing in the world, *e.g., David* (Ps. xix. 10), *Solomon* (Prov. iii. 14, viii. 11).

I. **What wealth can do the Bible can do better.**

1. *Wealth brings honour.* Mammon has never wanted worshippers. No title is refused, and no door closed, to the millionaire. The magisterial bench is reached by golden stairs, fashion wields a gilded sceptre, and coronets adorn the brow of gold. But the Bible confers higher dignities than these. By it man obtains the peerage of heaven, enjoys the companionship of God, and obtains a crown of glory that shall never fade away.

2. *Wealth can purchase what is supposed to constitute happiness.* It lifts a man above the privations of poverty ; may give magnificent mansions, costly furniture, gorgeous attire, and luxurious diet. All the arts and adornments of life are open to those who can purchase them. But what are these in comparison with what the true riches of the Bible can purchase; the house not made with hands, the robe of righteousness, the wine of the kingdom, the heavenly manna, fulness of joy, and pleasures for evermore?

3. *Wealth may purchase learning,* buy books, found libraries, pay school fees, and open the doors of colleges. But no money can purchase what the Bible offers freely. True wisdom, the saving knowledge of God in Christ,

understanding of the will of God, and immortality. Granted, then, that riches can do much, the Bible can do more, and do it without money and without price.

II. What wealth cannot do the Bible can.

1. *Money cannot purchase pardon for sin.* If it could, many would part with their all for it. It has been tried. Under a debasing superstition it is tried to-day. But no priestly fees, no costly masses, have or can ease the burdened conscience or cleanse its guilty stains—

"Vainly we offer each ample oblation;
Vainly with gifts would His blessing implore."

But the Bible leads us to Him "who is faithful and just to forgive us our sins," &c.

2. *Money cannot purchase a clear and safe guide in the practical paths of life.* It can lead astray, but it cannot lead back again, and cannot train man in the way he should go. Much has been spent in the supposition that it can; but it has been spent on blind guides. The Bible, on the contrary, is "a lamp unto our feet," &c.

3. *Money cannot purchase dignities of character.* It has purchased the opposite. Many a man has been weighted down by it into the lowest abysses of moral degradation. The best it can do is to gild the exterior. But the Bible ennobles man. It endows him with the Spirit of God. It enables him to live the life of Christ. It has trained statesmen, heroes, and philanthropists. It has given scholars their wisdom, martyrs to progress their fortitude, and saints their sanctity.

4. *Money cannot purchase the needful blessing in time of trial.* It straightens no crooked path. It may intensify trouble, but can never remove it; it can wipe no tear from the eye; and in the hour of death man turns to his gilded idol in vain. It can destroy, but it cannot save. And in that land where gold is not the currency the miser has no place. But the Bible gives to the afflicted, the promises; to the poor, the unsearchable riches of Christ; to the dying, the hope and consciousness of heaven. Therefore, "The law of Thy mouth is better," &c.

III. What wealth will do the Bible wont. Wealth must bring anxieties and cares. Every penny brings its additional solicitude. With increased riches comes the disquieting question, What is to be done with them? Increased possessions mean increased oversight and responsibility. With fresh social honours comes fresh and inexorable demands. And all this means gray hairs, brain exhaustion, heart straining, with no adequate return. But the Bible will not fret the heart; it will comfort it. It will not wear the brain; it will soothe it. It will not injure the nerves; it will brace them. It will not impair the moral sense; it will sanctify and invigorate it. Therefore, because what wealth will do the Bible will not, is "the law of God's mouth better," &c.

CREATION A PLEA IN PRAYER.

(*Verse* 73.)

This Psalm is remarkable for its spiritual aspirations, and the pleas by which their fulfilment is urged. The Psalmist is here seeking the highest moral good. He seeks it in the best and shortest way, by praying for understanding that he may learn God's commandments. The argument he employs why his prayer should be answered is simple, practical, powerful—viz., that God had created him, and created him that he might seek and gain the end he now desires to reach. Note then—

I. That man is the creation of God "Thou hast made me." Either the original creation (Gen. i. 26, ii. 7), or the creation of the individual himself (Ps. cxxxix.), or both.

II. That man was created for divine service (Prov. xvi. 4; Isa. xlix. 5; Rom. xi. 36). God has "fashioned" man for that purpose. With mind, that man may apprehend and remember Him; with hearing, that he may listen to Him; with speech, that he may testify of Him; with hands and feet, that he may do His will; with a heart, that he may love Him; and a spirit, that he may enjoy Him. Man is full of marks of design. What is that design? That he may eat, and drink, and sleep? Nay, the animals do that; but that he may know God and enjoy Him for ever.

III. **That man is not now as he was when he was created.** He not only does not fulfil his Maker's design, but is incapable of doing so (Eccl. vii. 29; Rom. iii. 23). By some great injury and loss, and by the infusion of some new principles, he falls short of the divine glory, and is bent on fulfilling precisely opposite ends. All his faculties so exquisitely adapted for divine purposes are prostituted to base and injurious works. His understanding, will, affections, &c., are engaged in warfare against God, the devil's service, and self-destruction.

IV. **Hence the necessity of a new creation.** A new heart, a new understanding that can grasp the wisdom, duty, and necessity of God's commandments, and a new nature that will render the learning and practice of those commandments easy and possible (Deut. v. 29; John vi. 5, 6; Rom. viii. 10, 11; Col. iii. 9, 10).

V. **Desiring this new nature, so that we may answer the divine purposes, no plea is more appropriate and powerful than the fact that we are God's creation.**

1. *It is natural that God should take an interest in His own work;* and if it come to grief, that He should desire to repair and perfect it (Job x. 3, xiv. 15; Isa. lxiv. 8, 9).

2. *The divinely-ordained order is that we should ask God to multiply His blessings* (Ps. cxvi. 12, 13; Matt. vi. 25; Rom. viii. 32). The more God gives, the more He delights to give.

3. *The fact that God has created us is strong ground for the belief that He will not forsake us.* We may reasonably suppose that the same hand which imposes the obligation will help us when we endeavour to discharge it.

4. *This prayer implies a state of the heart which God will own and bless.* It is the expression of a strong and ardent desire to fulfil a divine obligation.

IN CONCLUSION.—Come as creatures to the great and beneficent Creator, and ask Him, your Father, to help you His offspring. (i.) *Let the unconverted come.* Although you cannot call God Father by the spirit of adoption, yet He has created you. Make this your plea, that you should receive that filial spirit which will enable you to learn and obey your Father's will. (ii.) *Let believers under trial come for both reasons.* Plead creation old and new, and you will not plead in vain.

RELIGIOUS FELLOWSHIP.

(*Verses* 74, 79.)

I. **Is possible only to religious persons.** Fellowship implies a common experience, bond, and purpose. There is family fellowship, social fellowship, fellowship between those engaged in trade, science, or art, requiring similarity of nature, taste, and aim. "How can two walk together except they are agreed?" So there can be no religious fellowship except between those who fear God and have known His testimonies. That is, the qualities of sainthood are essential to the communion of saints.

II. **Is to be desired by religious persons.** "Let those that fear thee turn to Me." Man feels as God felt for Him, that it is not good for him to be alone. He is a social being and longs for society. So God has "set the solitary in families." This feeling is developed in fraternities, guilds, trades' unions, &c. So the spiritual man yearns for communion with those who have been baptized into the same spirit. But it is noteworthy how the Psalmist desires this fellowship to be brought about, not by "the selective action of spiritual affinities," but by the providence and grace of God. Verse 79 is not merely the expression of a want, it is a prayer (Jer. xv. 19). This is just the New Testament idea of the Church. It is not merely a congregation of people who for mutual profit, spiritual or otherwise, have left other things for it. It is a company, every member of which God "has called out of darkness into His marvellous light." Christians do not simply gravitate to each other, God calls them to Himself, and then the Church finds its true unity. A shade of thought worthy of note is found in the expression, "Let them that fear thee *turn to Me*," and shadows forth the principle of Christian evangelisation. "Here am I, yearning for fellowship. Let Thy people in their search for lost members of their fold find *me*." What a striking condemnation does the example of this old Jew afford those who shrink from and must be urged to membership in Christ's Church! The Psalmist's absorbing desire and prayer is, that the faithful may find him and take him into fellowship.

III. **Is profitable to religious persons.** "They that fear Thee will be glad when I," &c. We are glad when we find a fellow-countryman on a foreign shore. The scholar is glad of the company of his fellow-scholar, &c. Converse over identical callings is healthful and stimulating.

1. *The Church is glad when it finds one lost member of its body and can bring it back again into union with itself.* There is joy not only in heaven but on earth. The members of the Church have been increased, its territory and spiritual life and power augmented, one more jewel is added to its Redeemer's crown.

2. *The Church is glad when one of its members can testify to God's special grace.* The Psalmist had been afflicted, but God had sanctified his affliction and had delivered him. He felt that those who feared God would be glad when they knew *that*, particularly the sorrowful, whom it would lead to resignation and hope.

3. *The Church is glad when one of its members contributes to the common stock of knowledge.* The Psalmist had prayed for understanding and had been answered. We can imagine the gladness of the God-fearing company as he would open up the new and enlarged views of truth which had been vouchsafed him.

4. *The Church is glad when one of its members can strengthen the common confidences.* "They . . . will be glad because I have hoped in Thy Word." Nothing is more depressing to a society than for one of its members to lose his hope.

IN CONCLUSION.—Why do some religious men shrink from religious fellowship? This question is of vast importance when we consider that the members of our congregations vastly outnumber the members of our churches. There is something wrong, we may depend upon it, when members of a family or class are out of fellowship with each other. If it is natural and healthy for men in their social or professional capacity to meet together, and if *they* have no hesitation in speaking to one another about matters which affect their common interest, much more so should the travellers of Zion meet together and comfort and edify one another by the way. Religious fellowship, it is true, may degenerate into sentimentality and unreal sameness, but a thing is not to be neglected because it is abused. The great want of the world is men and women of the type before us. Pentecost, the Reformation, Puritanism, and Methodism resulted from such.

RESIGNATION: ITS DUTIES AND USEFULNESS.

(*Verses* 75, 79.)

I. The Psalmist expresses his **resignation** to the divine will. This is based on two grounds—

1. *God's judgments are right.* God is holy in His nature, and wise and just in all the acts of His government, and

therefore His judgments are right in general, though there may be in some particular instances difficulties which we cannot easily resolve."—*M. Henry.*

2. *God's judgments are the expression of the divine faithfulness.* They are not arbitrary or cruel, but they are necessary, that the divine and beneficent schemes which God has in hand may be worked out.

II. Resignation does not preclude, but rather **presupposes and includes prayer for comfort and support.** It is impossible without special grace to see and acknowledge the righteousness and faithfulness of God's dispensations. The heart is naturally prone to resist and rebel against all discipline. We must therefore cry for help in our time of need. This is based on three things.

1. *The divine mercy.* "Thy merciful kindness." We may plead that God is too kind to withdraw or not to bestow His help, the thought of which will encourage us under the heaviest trials.

2. *The divine promise.* "According to Thy word." God is not only disposed but bound by covenant promise to help. Plead *that* promise that seems most to suit *your* case.

3. *The divine ownership.* "Thy servant." Despondency, &c., will unfit us for our duties, and we may therefore ask for help because we want to work.

III. **Prayer for life** is not only not incompatible but consistent **with resignation.** "That I may live." Let it be remembered that the Psalmist does not express that desire for life that is common to all men for its own sake. Life may be a blessing or a curse as it gains or fails in gaining the end for which it was given. The prayer here is for a life of holy joy and holy usefulness. "For Thy law is my delight." Yet he would not wish for it except as the expression of the mercy, and therefore by the will, of God.

IV. **Prolonged life is to be desired for the twofold influence that it may wield.**

1. *The conviction of gainsayers.* Life is desired (1) *That imputations of the ungodly may be repelled* (vers. 69, 78); (2) *That their atheistical arguments may be confuted* (cxv. 2), and (3) *Themselves put to shame* (ver. 72).

2. *The comfort and confirmation of God's people* (ver. 29). It will stimulate to (1) *stronger confidence in God,* (2) *resignation,* (3) *hope.* What God can do in one case He can do in all.

ORTHODOXY.

(*Verse* 80.)

I. Orthodoxy **implies** a correct apprehension of the meaning, purpose, and authority of God's statutes. How can the heart be sound in that about which the mind is ignorant, uncertain, or hesitating? A law must be known before it can be obeyed. So with God's statutes. I must know what they are, and assent to their necessity and utility, before they can become governing forces in my life. These statutes "are exceeding broad," and cover the whole field of doctrine and morals. God's statutes are, *e.g.,* the Ten Commandments; but they are more. We read, "Believe also in Me," "Receive ye the Holy Ghost," "Repent ye and believe the Gospel," &c., and these are as much statutes as, "Thou shalt not steal." Why then should orthodoxy in the former be of less moment than orthodoxy in the latter? The only difference is that heterodoxy in the latter is an offence against man, and in the former is a dishonour put upon God, which man naturally prefers. True enough orthodoxy by itself is of little value, just as true ideas of health avail nothing except they are practically applied. But we never hear of objections to orthodoxy in science, &c., objected to on these grounds.

II. Orthodoxy **consists** in soundness of heart in God's statutes—*i.e.,* experimental piety. As it is not merely correctness of intellectual belief on the one hand, neither is it simply correctness of life on the other. A man may have all the elements of the form of godliness, his morality may be very exact, his duties may be performed with the most scrupulous punctuality, and yet he may be like a whited sepulchre or an apple of Sodom, full of rottenness for the want of spiritual life and power,—*e.g.*, the Pharisees. But for a man to be sound at heart, God's statutes must dwell in him (Heb. viii. 10); they must be at the root of the governing forces of his life, transforming him into the image of God, moulding and assimilating him in the form which God would have him take, expelling sin, testifying of the divine favour, and subjecting his whole nature to the will of God. Then is a man orthodox—a living practical rule of faith and practice. If the tree is good the fruit will be good, and if a man is sound at heart he will be sound in his life, and pure and undivided in his allegiance to God and man.

III. The **result** of orthodoxy is that a man whose heart is sound in God's statutes will not be ashamed. Unsoundness is the source of shame everywhere, except in those whose faces are steeled against shame. It is very sad when men glory in their shame, and make a boast of their heterodoxy in life, heart, or creed. But those who are sound have—

1. *No occasion of shame before God.* Soundness of heart will give us confidence in His presence (1 John iii. 21) and boldness of approach to the throne of grace (Heb. xiii. 18, Rom. viii. 1), and before the throne of judgment by and by. It is quite otherwise when the heart is unsound.

2. *No occasion of shame before ourselves.* An unsound heart rouses the indignation of conscience (Rom. vi. 21). As soon as Adam sinned he was ashamed of himself. But the righteous man can approach the tribunal of conscience without fear of shame (2 Cor. i. 12).

3. *No occasion of shame before our fellows.* We shall neither be stumbling-blocks to them, nor be exposed to the contempt of those whose opinion we value.

IN CONCLUSION.—Let those who would be orthodox, in its fullest sense, learn— (i.) *That God alone can make them so* (Isa. li. 10, Eph. iv. 24). (ii.) *That it should be sought with prayer and earnest purpose*, and will be vouchsafed (Ezra viii. 10, Ps. cxxxix. 23, 24). Let not the man of sceptical opinions nurse them under the impression that they evidence soundness of intellect, and are therefore desirable, or the man of unsound life under the impression that it is manly. (iii.) *That a constant sense of God's presence and a careful watchfulness of our ways is necessary* to the maintenance of a sound creed, a sound heart, and a sound life (ver. 168, Jer. xvii. 9, Heb xii. 13).

MAN'S ADVERSITY AND GOD'S SALVATION.

(*Verses* 81-88.)

Our text teaches us—

I. **That man's adversity is often extreme.**

1. *In its intensity.* "My soul fainteth," "Mine eyes fail," "When wilt Thou comfort me?" No figures could convey more powerfully than these the Psalmist's extremity. When man's comfort is gone and dimness covers his sight, and when his heart sinks within him, his case is extreme indeed.

2. *In its duration.* "I am like a bottle in the smoke." "As wineskin in the smoke, my heart is sere and dried."—*Keble.* So long have I been afflicted that I have become dried and wrinkled. God allows many a saint to cry out in his trouble, "*When* wilt Thou comfort me?"

3. *In its danger.* "The proud have *digged pits* for me." "They had almost *consumed* me." They were not successful in their snares and temptations, so they turn to active persecution and almost consume him. This is most frequently the order in which tribulations come. If the wicked are successful in their machinations, they are satisfied; if resisted, all their active malice is aroused.

II. **That God's salvation is the**

remedy for man's adversity. This salvation is presented under four aspects—

1. *"Comfort"* is sometimes salvation. Paul, the martyrs, all reformers are saved in this way. It is not always necessary to be actually delivered. Timely comfort is timely succour.

2. *The execution of judgment on oppressors* (ver. 84). This is sometimes God's way, but not often. Sufficiently often, however, and conspicuous to strike terror in the heart of tyrants, Satan, Pharaoh, the Philistines, Herod, &c.; but not often and conspicuously enough to lead His people to look too much for sanguinary vengeance on their foes.

3. *Personal rescue.* "Help Thou me." Sometimes *immediate*. By the direct exercise of His omnipotence, God effects a complete deliverance for His people. It was so with Israel's redemption from Egypt. It is so in some of those mysterious cases when long sources of trouble are suddenly dried up, and paths of prosperity suddenly opened. Sometimes with the *use of means*. By medicine in diseases, by industrious exertion in poverty. Sometimes God saves *conspicuously* by the unbaring of His arm; sometimes *invisibly* in the course of His providence.

4. *Divine quickening* (ver. 88). The infusion of the divine life of His Spirit, by means of which man is continually renewed and strengthened either to bear his afflictions or to overcome them.

III. **That man's adversity should lead him to cry mightily for God's salvation.** Powerful pleas are here presented and urged why God should save. The Psalmist here—

1. *Expresses his hope in the divine promises.* "I hope on Thy word." This is presented as a reason why God should not disappoint him.

2. *Confesses that God is his only comfort.* "When wilt *Thou* comfort me?" God sometimes waits till we have exhausted every other resource. But when man is led to cry to his soul, "Hope thou in God," that cry will not be in vain.

3. *Urges the brevity of his life* (ver. 84). "Are my days so many as to admit of delay in the manifestations of Thy righteous judgments?"—*Speaker*. "This is not a desire to be told how long he was to live, as if it were an object of desire to know this, but it is a method of saying that He could not live long under these circumstances, and therefore asked that God would save him soon."—*Barnes.*

4. *Mentions the divine faithfulness and loving-kindness* (vers. 86, marg., and 88).

5. *Reminds God of His own steadfastness* (vers. 83, 86, and 87). Happy the man whose adversity has not impaired his memory or loosened his hold of God's law!

IV. **That this remedy should be sought for holy ends.** The Psalmist did not pray for salvation that he might be happy, but that he might be holy (ver. 88).

GOD'S WORKS AND GOD'S WORDS.

(*Verses* 89–91.)

To the devout and intelligent student there is a very close relationship and analogy between God's Word and God's works. Both proceed from the same Author, both teach truth, both answer moral ends, both appeal to man's faith, hope, and love. The Psalmist traces some features of this analogy.

I. The heavens and the earth rest upon **immovable foundations**: so do the promises of God. All have a common basis in the divine faithfulness. If the universe came into existence by chance, or continued to exist by chance, it might cease by chance, and thus our confidence in its stability would end, and the gravest apprehensions would arise. So, if the promises rested on any other basis but God's fidelity and truth; if they were merely imaginations or guesses, or the result of a devout and elevated enthusiasm; our spiritual foundations, all the bases of moral hope and life would be shaken or removed, and what then would the righteous do? But, thank God—

"His every word of grace is strong
As that which built the skies,
The voice that rolls the stars along
Speaks all the promises."

II. The heavens and the earth continue: so do the promises of God, because held together by the divine faithfulness. Many changes have taken place since matter was first consolidated into worlds, but all these changes have been superintended and controlled by the gracious hand of Him "who upholds all things by the word of His power;" and notwithstanding all those changes it is the same universe. So with the promises. Some have been made to one generation, and some to another; some are of one quality and some of another; but they remain the same in power and beneficence to-day. The Psalmist trod the same soil under the same heavens as we do, and the same kind words which supported him are for our service, because maintained by the faithfulness of God.

III. The heavens and the earth are **servants** of the divine faithfulness: so are the promises. They all acknowledge one common Lord, and God employs them all for His children's benefit. The heavens give cheering light, and send down refreshing showers. By the moon our tides are regulated, by the planets our time. The earth yields her increase for the children of men, and all the elements are ministers of the divine pleasure, and hearken unto the voice of His word. Much more so the promises. God has given man a spiritual nature, which requires food, support, and encouragement, and to this end in faithfulness as well as mercy are the divine promises sent on their errands.

IV. The heavens and the earth now so stable, according to the divine faithfulness will some day cease to be ; not so the promises, which by virtue of the same faithfulness "for ever are settled" and are made to "all generations." The universe was made to accomplish a divine but temporary purpose. "Towards that grand far-off divine event the whole creation moves." Having reached it they will have accomplished their mission, and will pass away to make room for that "new heaven and new earth wherein dwelleth righteousness." "Heaven and earth shall pass away, but My word shall never pass away." The words of man, like him who makes them, and his works are subject to revision ; but God's word is above all change, being the unalterable decree of the ever-faithful Jehovah. Learn—

(i.) *To trust in God when the fulfilment of His promises is delayed* (Heb. vi. 12). (ii.) *To trust in God as the sure anchorage of the soul amidst the mutations of earthly things* and when its vanities would entice us away. (iii.) *To trust in the Lord as here revealed so faithful and true*, and not lean to the intuitions of our own fickle and faithless hearts (Luke xxiv. 25, Rom iv. 20).

THE BENEFIT AND OBLIGATION OF THE WORD OF GOD.

(*Verses* 92, 93.)

Learn—

I. That in the order of divine providence God's people are afflicted. This is the teaching of all the Bible and all experience.

II. That affliction unsanctified will damage and destroy the spiritual life. God sends it for beneficent purposes, but man may misapply the means and thus defeat the end. The Psalmist was perilously near doing this, and was thus (ver. 92).

III. That God's law delighted in is the means of sanctifying affliction and saving the soul from death.

1. *It shows the reason for and the beneficence of affliction.*

2. *It affords comfort and support in affliction.*

3. *It reveals and leads us to that life which saves from destruction, and quickens us with its own vitality.*

IV. That these benefits involve duties and responsibilities (ver. 93).

Many a man who has made the Word his constant study in affliction, forgets it altogether in his prosperity.
1. *Don't forget to read it.*
2. *Don't forget what it says* either by *command or promise.*
3. *Don't forget to be grateful for what it has done.*
4. *Don't forget to practise what it enjoins.*

Remember what help it afforded you and the vows you made respecting it during your affliction, now you are well.
IN CONCLUSION.—(i.) *If our delights are in God's Word while we are ill, much more should they be when we are well.* (ii.) *If it can quicken us in affliction, it can maintain us in our health and qualify us with living power for service day by day.*

AN ALL-PREVAILING PLEA.
(*Verse* 94.)

I. The plea. "I am Thine." No plea is so universally prevalent as this. It is the plea of all properties, the plea of all relationships. The reason why things are saved from destruction is because they say to their owner, "We are thine." The reason why a father is solicitous about his offspring is because they cry, "We are thine." And the plea most powerful with man is most powerful with God, and can never be urged in vain. How can we urge this plea? We are God's—1. *By creation* (1 Chron. xxix. 11). 2. *By redemption,* "Ye are not your own." 3. *By covenant* (Hosea ii. 23). 4. *By re-creation* (Eph. ii. 10), and *adoption* (Rom. viii.). 5. *By conquest.* 6. *By self-dedication to His service.* 7. *By assimilation to His likeness.*

II. The prayer based upon this plea. "Save me." Having this plea use it, urge it as a reason why God should save from (1) *Sin,* (2) *Despair,* (3) *Foes,* (4) *Unfaithfulness,* (5) *Hell.*

III. The sources of the Psalmist's information both as to plea and prayer. "For I have sought Thy precepts." From no other source could he have known that he was God's, and that God was willing to save.

IN CONCLUSION.—(i.) *Can we all say when asked,* "To whom belongest thou and whence art thou?" "I am thine." (1.) *When did you take the oath of allegiance?* (Deut. xxvi. 17, 18.) (2.) *Have you the seals and signs of the divine possession?* (ii.) *Acknowledge God's full authority.* God gave Himself for you, and the least you owe Him is yourselves, and by giving Him yourselves you lose nothing but gain everything. (iii.) *Seek upon this basis God's full salvation.*

THE ATTITUDE OF THE WICKED TOWARDS THE RIGHTEOUS, AND THE CONDITION OF THE RIGHTEOUS UNDER OPPRESSION.
(*Verses* 95, 110, 121. 122, 134, 157, 161.)

This Psalm is of peculiar value as exhibiting the characteristic features of wickedness in all ages, and the attitude which evil men will everywhere assume in their opposition to the good. It will be profitable to view all the references to this subject at one glance, and then in their relation to each other. By that means we shall catch many shades of thought we should otherwise miss. In these verses the Christian is informed *all that he* may expect from the enemies of God and man, and instructed how he should comport himself under this special form of trial.

I. The wicked are here described.
1. *Who they are.* (1.) *The wicked,* a general term covering all the rest. Godless, transgressors of God's law and therefore transgressors of man's. (2.) *The oppressors.* Those who put burdens on the helpless, and take advantage of, and crush the little strength of the weak. (3.) *Enemies of the righteous,* necessarily and perpetually. (4.) *Proud.*
2. *What they are.* (1.) "*Many*" in

number. (2.) *Powerful in influence,* "princes." (3.) *Malicious in designs.* (4.) *Subtle in methods of operation.*
3. *What they do.* (1.) *They wait for the righteous for their destruction.* (2.) *They lay snares for their ruin.* (3.) *They oppress.* (4.) *They persecute.*

II. **The righteous are here by the example of the Psalmist counselled—**
1. *To pray.* (1.) *For protection* (vers. 121, 122). (2.) *For deliverance* (ver. 134).

2. *To consider God's testimonies,* (1) *of His goodness, faithfulness, and power,* (2) *against their enemies.*
3. *Not to err from God's statutes by falling into the snare of the wicked.* Hence watchfulness.
4. *To keep God's statutes in spite of oppression.*
5. *Not to decline from God's testimonies.*
6. *To stand in awe of God's word.*

THE FINITE AND THE INFINITE.
(Verse 96.)

The Psalmist relates what was a matter of experience to him. He had seen the end of all "perfection," so may we. All finite things are perishable and perish before our eyes—empires, majesty, learning, art, pleasure, life. The first man and the last, and all those and their belongings who have come between, are of the earth earthy, and fade away. But in the midst of all these mutations the word of God lives on. "All flesh is grass," &c. It has seen the rise and fall of many idolatries, superstitions, infidelities, and persecutions, but it stands to-day unmoved and unshakable. The truth of our text holds good with regard to

I. **Earthly life.** There is a limit to its perfection. "The days of our years are threescore years and ten," &c. Beyond that it cannot pass. It is bounded by the bourne of an undiscovered country, which it cannot pass. But God's commandment is exceeding broad. It covers not only time, but the eternity which bounds it on both sides. It was in God's mind innumerable ages before man breathed the breath of life, and will survive the wreck of matter and the crush of worlds.

II. **Earthly greatness and grandeur.** The limitations to that we see day after day. The popular favour which has built it up may be withdrawn, the friends who contributed it may fall away or die, the enemies who are waiting their opportunity to undermine it may succeed, health may fail, and life. But God's commandment is exceeding broad. It can confer honours which are supernatural and immortal, "crowns of glory which can never fade away."

III. **The development of human cha-**
racter. There is a point to which a man's character without God may reach, beyond which it is impossible to go. And how often do men reach that point and then utterly break down in the line of wisdom, goodness, or charity! But God's commandment is exceeding broad. There is no "hitherto shalt thou go and no farther" to those whose character is based upon that. By following the lines indicated there, and securing the power offered there, a man who has scaled the loftiest height of saintliness there known could still say, "I count not myself to have attained it."

IV. **The acquisition of human knowledge.** The *mind* has limitations beyond which, "madness lies." It can be stretched to a certain tension, but if stretched further it breaks. But God's commandment is exceeding broad. It provides for the indefinite expansion of the mind it has sanctified, and offers subjects which shall occupy without wearying it to all eternity. The *subjects* of human knowledge are bounded, and it is not impossible when scientific instruments reach the perfection that they promise, to imagine the time when the circle of human information will be complete; when our telescopes shall have swept every star, and our microscopes revealed every molecule, and our natural philosophy the details of every element. But God's commandment contains things into which we shall desire to look for ever. The *records* of human knowledge perish; inscriptions become illegible; books and parchments wear out; but God's commandment will endure for ever.

V. Human pleasures and satisfactions. Sensual gratifications soon pall upon the taste. Sinful appetites are soon jaded. The worldling sooner or later comes to the old conclusion, "All is vanity and vexation of spirit." The "pleasures of sin are for a season." Even innocent enjoyments lose their re-creative power. They must be changed again and again, for without variety they cease to satisfy at all. When over indulged, or sought as an end and not a means to an end, they lose their pleasurableness altogether. But God's commandment is exceeding broad. It contains and leads us to fulness of joy and pleasures for evermore.

VI. Human institutions. These are mostly *local*. As a rule the institutions of a country are confined to that country. The manners and customs of a race or clime usually belong only to that race or clime. But God's commandment is exceeding broad. Its institutions and principles are adapted to the whole world. Human institutions are all *temporary*. They are founded to answer passing needs. The institution of God's word will last through the eternity of man's spiritual want. They are the bread and water of his life by which he shall be satisfied for evermore.

IN CONCLUSION.—Why? Because all things merely human are confined to time. God's commandment, covers time and eternity. Things human cannot touch the immortal life and satisfy it, cannot cleanse the sinful conscience, soothe the troubled heart, or give peace to the agitated soul. They cannot aid us in our great concerns, cannot tell us about God, duty, acceptance with heaven, death, preparation for a life to come. God's commandment can and does all this, and therefore is it "exceeding broad." Therefore our text is *a solemn word* for everybody. It is an encouragement to the weak, a warning to the great, a comfort for the old, an exhortation to the young. All perfection has an end, but God's commandment is exceeding broad.

THE SAINT'S ENJOYMENT OF THE LAW OF GOD.

(Verses 97 and 103.)

I. The law of God is **lovable.** It is worthy of notice, that the Psalmist's appreciation was not only of its promises (ver. 103), but of its injunctions (ver. 97).

1. *Because of its author.* It is our Father's legacy. The commandment and promises of Him who sticketh closer than a brother. It is the counsel and loving assurance of our best and truest Friend.

2. *Because of its subject-matter.* (1.) *It is truth divine and infallible.* "Thy word is truth" (Ps. xix. 9, Eph. i. 13). It is necessary truth that would never have been discovered by the unaided use of our understandings. All truth should excite affection, because of its suitability to the mind and its power to satisfy it. (2.) *It is the revelation of perfect love and goodness.* Tells us of our Father's character and the beneficence of His intentions, how sin may be pardoned, the soul sanctified, the whole nature blessed, and heaven gained.

3. *Because of the benefit it confers.* It convinces the sinner of the error of his ways (Jer. xxiii), Paul before Felix. It converts the soul from sin (Ps. xix. 7). It promises comfort in all times of distress. It is a safe guide in the affairs of life. It initiates and increases in the knowledge of God, and is able to make us perfect in every good word and work (2 Tim. iii. 7, 2 Pet. i. 19).

II. **God's saints possess a spiritual taste** which enables them to appreciate the law of God. The soul has faculties which perform the same functions for it as the senses do for the body (Heb. v. 14). Thus it is said to hear, see, handle, feel, speak; and as here and in Psalm xxxiv. 8, *taste*. These are the most acute of all senses. The higher the life, the keener the sense. Animals feel more than plants; men more than animals; spiritual men more than carnal men.

1. *What this taste presupposes.* Soul hunger. A jaded or satisfied appetite more or less impairs the sense of taste. Taste, too, has frequently to be created.

Things which before were noxious then become enjoyable. And to the hungry soul, whose taste has been quickened by God, is God's law sweet (Prov. xxvii., Rom. viii. 5).

2. *What this taste involves*, a relish for the word of God (Jer. xv. 16, Ezek. iii. 3, Rev. x. 10). No man who does not relish God's words can use the language of our text.

III. God's saints exercise that taste continually. "It is my meditation all the day." This is but natural. What we love most, we most desire. What we most delight in, we seek most familiarity with. This holds good all the world over. Fame, pleasure, business, war, &c., so here the saint loves God's Word, delights in it, and hence "meditates upon it all the day."

SUPERIOR UNDERSTANDING.

(*Verses* 98-102, 104.)

I. **What in?** Pre-eminently in holiness. "I have refrained my feet from every evil way;" "I have not departed from Thy judgments." The Psalmist does not mean simply in intellectual matters, although that may hold good. The man who prays is most likely to keep his intellect clear. He who recognises his mental faculties as a solemn and responsible gift of God is most likely to be industrious in their employment. He who devoutly seeks for divine assistance is most likely to gain it, and thus distance his compeers. But the Psalmist seems to contemplate both superiority of subject, and superiority of attainment in that subject.

II. **Over whom?**

1. "*Mine enemies.*" That is most likely from their qualities as mentioned in this Psalm. A man who entertains enmity in his heart is not likely to be an adept in the knowledge of God.

2. "*My teachers.*" Because of his more diligent use of means. It is not seldom that scholars outstrip their teachers by this method. The Psalmist's teachers may have been mere surface or fanciful expositors of the Word of God, or mere sinecurists or ceremonialists?

3. "*The ancients.*" Those older than *himself* (Job xxxii. 7, 8), because he meditated where they only skimmed, and practised where they only theorised. Or his *predecessors*, because he possessed more of the word of inspiration than they. Can we with "all Scripture" use the words of the text?

III. **Through what power?** "Thou hast made me wiser;" "Thou hast taught me."

1. *Not by the use of his unaided faculties, or any superiority of intellect, insight, or industry.* The one thing which he and his brethren earnestly disclaim is originality. But—

2. *By direct divine instruction.* To attain this superiority now we must have it from the same source. All that the unaided understanding can do in this direction has been achieved, and that is nothing. No reflection, thought, or study even of the divine oracles can make us "wise unto salvation," except through "the faith and love which is in Christ Jesus." "They shall be all taught of God."

IV. **By what instrumentality.** "Through Thy precepts."

1. *Continual meditation.* "They are ever with me." Knowledge, like life, must be continually fed.

2. *Consistent practice.* "I keep Thy precepts." Theories can only keep their hold in so far as they are consistently reduced to practice.

3. *Earnest continuance.* "I have not departed," &c.

V. **With what results?**

1. *Distaste for falsehood* (ver. 104).

2. *Unswerving integrity.*

GOD'S WORD A LAMP AND A LIGHT.

(*Verse* 105.)

The Psalmist here employs two powerful and familiar figures to express the enlightening power of the Word of God. In the day it is a light showing us the direction, course, peculiarities, and dangers of our path. At night, when the sun has set and the gloom has settled, and we have to pick our way, it shall be a candle, not perhaps illuminating the entire course, but sufficient to guide our footsteps clear of the stumbling-blocks and difficulties of the way. In the day its light is delightful, displaying all the beauties of the landscape and cheering our onward tread. In the night it is useful, showing us where we may err, where we should tread, and how it is possible to fall.

I. The Word of God is a **light**.

1. *It claims to be a light* (Prov. xvi. 23, 2 Pet. i. 19). Certain types powerfully shadow it forth as such (Exod. xiii. 21, xxvii. 20, 21; Neh. ix. 10).

2. *Reason supports this claim.* It is God's Word (1 John i. 5). Holy men wrote it (2 Pet. i. 21). Moral enlightenment and guidance is the design of it.

3. *Experience warrants it.* Bad men fear and hate it (John iii. 20, 21). Good men have loved and enjoyed it (Ps. xix. 8). Those who have gone without it or rejected it have stumbled. Those who have accepted its guidance have had the light of life.

II. The Word of God is a **clear light**. It is not twilight, or starlight, or moonlight, but daylight.

1. *It is a clear light in the right way* (Ps. xliii. 3). The wisest men have wandered without it.

2. *It is a clear light on the wrong way.* It not only tells us what to do, but what not to do. Warns us against going astray. Informs us where sin and madness lie. Urges us to beware of and shun the magic music of the syren's voice and the pleasant pastures of sin. And, thank God, it shines to lead us back again. It is a revelation of God's way to bad and fallen men (1 Cor. xiv. 24).

3. *It is a clear light in the dark way.* Clouds may settle on the path of God. The sun may hide itself. Our way may lie through dark ravines and the valley of the death-shadow. Trouble may overcast the soul and lead us to say, "Hath God forgotten to be gracious?" But even under circumstances such as these, light breaks forth from God's holy word which makes it a lamp to our path (Isa. l. 10).

III. The Word of God is a **full and perennial light**. It guides by day and it guides by night. It illumines our path, but it enables us to pick *each individual step*.

1. *Generally it tells us the course of life we should pursue,* the grand choice we ought to make, and the sublime destiny we ought to reach (Ps. xxv. 12).

2. *In particular.* Many men are wise in a general way, but sadly fail when they come to details. A man may be a very good mathematician, yet a very bad accountant. A great statesman may be utterly unable to grasp the minor and subordinate details of state policy. So many a man has taken the Bible as the guide for his general course of conduct, who for want of attention to its details has stumbled and fallen. The Bible not only unveils the whole way, but lights up every successive step of the way (1 Pet. i. 15). No man need err respecting any duty, responsibility, or privilege in his path. This applies to men of all ages, and conditions everywhere. This being the case—

(i.) *How thankful we ought to be for the Word of God!*

(ii.) *How diligently we ought to study and practise it!*

RELIGIOUS PROFESSION.

(*Verse* 106.)

Our text suggests—

I. That the profession of religion should be of the **strongest and most binding character**.

1. *This has been the practice of the godly in all ages* (Job xxxi. 1; 2 Chron. xv. 12-14, xxxiv. 31).

2. *The weakness of our own nature demands it.* Our mere purposes and resolutions are like the morning cloud, &c., and require to be bound down under the most solemn obligations.

3. *The character of the subject requires it.* God has sworn with an oath to fulfil

His engagements towards us (Heb. vi. 18), and requires a responsive oath from us (Exod. xxiv. 3). The beneficence and necessity of the laws, in the keeping of which religion consists, demand it.

II. That the profession of religion should be **the result of serious thought.** The resolution to keep God's righteous judgments implies a study of those judgments which has resulted in the conclusion that they are righteous. When a man determines to be a Christian, he should know what he is about. He is making a throw for time and for eternity. God Himself demands that the cost should be counted, so that there may be no afterthoughts, for He has no pleasure in the sacrifice of fools.

III. That the profession of religion should **be made with a free but resolute will.** The individual himself should of himself and for himself say, "I will." Let parents beware how they compel their children to appear religious. Many a moral wreck has been stranded on the shores of eternity through this. Compulsion will breed distaste. Rather guide the judgment, reason, and affections. Show the duty, need, and lovableness of religion, and lead the child to say of himself, "I will keep Thy righteous judgments." The will once bent, fix it. Let nothing alter your decision or make you swerve.

IV. That the profession of religion once made should be **faithfully and consistently kept.** "I will perform it." The strength of the Psalmist's accumulated expressions will be seen at once.

1. *To break our oath is to aggravate our sin.* Better not swear at all than swear and not perform (Eccl. v. 5).

2. *The same motives that urged us to take the vow hold good all the way through.* After the most protracted test and trial of religion, the godly man sees no reason to repent his choice. God is the same, and His judgments lose none of their righteousness by lapse of years.

3. *God is the severe and just avenger of broken fidelity.* Young man! (i.) *Resolve to be religious.* It is the noblest, most reasonable, and safest thing to do. (ii.) *Resolve and fulfil your resolutions, not in your own strength, but in the strength of God.* (iii.) *Resolve and expect God's blessing and reward.*

AFFLICTION.

(*Verses* 107, 109, 120, 124, 135, 143, 153, 154, 156.)

This Psalm is emphatically a psalm for the afflicted. Sorrow and trouble are here delineated in every form in which they may be expected to occur. But not only so: all the consolations and remedies that are at the disposal of the afflicted are here opened up, and also all the obligations which comfort or restoration imposes, and all the results which may be expected to follow. It will be profitable, therefore, to survey the whole field displayed in these verses as briefly as possible.

I. The **characteristics** of affliction.

1. *It is sometimes extreme* (vers. 107, 143).

2. *It is sometimes perilous* (ver. 109). "The image is taken from a traveller carrying precious jewels in his hand through dangerous paths, or from soldiers who carry their lives in their hands, in that their lives depend upon their valour in fight, or perhaps from a game of chance. "Though I play with my life and risk it always," &c. Vaihnger interprets "my soul is in, or upon my hand, apt to fall off and perish, as anything in or upon the hand easily falls off."—*Speaker's Com.*

3. *It is sometimes a judicial infliction* (ver. 120; Lam. iii. 39). (See also Job iv. 15; Isa. ii. 10; Jer. li. 27; Exod. xxxiv. 7.)

II. The **consolations** of affliction.

1. *That God permits it.* This is the assumption of the whole Psalm, and what quiets and comforts the Psalmist's soul. If God permits it, it must be for the bringing about of some beneficent end.

2. *That it does not produce forgetfulness of God's law* (ver. 109). When men do forget God's law, let them not charge affliction with this terrible dis-

comfort. In many cases it is sent to stimulate memory.

3. *That it has opened to him the supports and pleasures of the Word of God* (ver. 143). Happy the man whose affliction has given him time for, and driven him to, the study of God's law.

III. The **remedy** for affliction.
1. *The divine favour* (vers. 124, 156).
2. *The divine promise* (ver. 154).
3. *The divine wisdom* (ver. 156).
4. *The divine assistance* (Ps. xxxv. 1, xliii. 1, lxxiv. 22). "The expression belongs properly to judicial proceedings. The Psalmist is wrongfully accused, and prays to God to be his advocate; but inasmuch as the cause is carried on, not in a court of justice, but in the battle-field, the advocate must be also a champion."—*Speaker's Com.*

IV. The results of affliction.
1. *Quickened vitality* (vers. 154, 156). Painful operations sometimes save life, and life is all the stronger for these operations. The cancer must be cut out, that the life that is being consumed may be spared and made more healthy.
2. *Instruction in God's statutes.* Affliction is what we run into sometimes in our flight from the divine ways. It is beneficial for a child to feel the pain of fire that he may avoid it, and so God's child is made to feel the bitterness of sin, that he may value and be faithful to his Father's law.
3. *The special favour of God* (ver. 135). A parent regards with peculiar complacency and love his child who has been rescued from peril and disease.

Lessons—
(i.) *Let affliction drive us in prayer to God* (ver. 153).
(ii.) *Let no affliction drive us to transgress God's law* (ver. 109, &c.).
(iii.) *Let affliction stimulate us to expect quickened life, a more earnest fidelity, and double favour.*

SPIRITUAL SACRIFICES.

(*Verse* 108.)

This verse appropriately follows the Psalmist's contemplation of his affliction. God had afflicted him in mercy and with judgment. God had wonderfully delivered him. He feels as the Apostle felt centuries afterwards (Rom xii. 1), that in recognition of the Divine beneficence it was incumbent upon him to offer spiritual sacrifices to God. Note comparisons and contrasts, and the word *beseech* in both. We have here—

I. A recognition of the **spiritual priesthood** of believers. The offering presupposes the priesthood. God's people throughout the ages have been members of a royal priesthood. The Jewish nation was such (Exod. xix. 5, 6). The prophets contemplated the time when pious Gentiles would be such (Isa. lxi. 6, lxvi. 21; Mal. i. 11). The New Testament recognises all Christians as such (1 Pet. ii. 9; Rev. i. 6).

II. Spiritual priests must have a **spiritual preparation.** Under the law, the priests were to be separate from the commonalty. Under the Gospel, they are a holy nation and a peculiar people. Under the law they received a special anointing; under the Gospel they receive the unction of the Holy One (1 John ii. 20). Under the law the priests were prepared for their office by a lustration; Christians are baptized with the Holy Ghost (Titus iii. 6). All priestly orders, whether received from Greece or Rome, are invalid, except those conferred by Him who alone can "make" "kings and priests."

III. Spiritual priests must **offer and can only offer spiritual sacrifices.** Not expiatory, but eucharistic; not sin offerings, but peace and thank offerings (Heb. vii. 27, x. 14, xiii. 15). As the priesthood is purely spiritual so must be the sacrifices (John iv. 24; Ps. l. 13-15, lxix. 30, 31). The particular offering here specified includes or presupposes all the rest. Prayer (Ps. cxli. 2). Praise (Ps. liv. 6). Thanksgiving (Ps. l. 1, 4). The body (Rom. xii. 1). Body and spirit (1 Cor. vi. 20). Ourselves (2 Cor. viii. 5). Almsgiving (Phil.

iv. 18; Heb. xiii. 16). Notice, further, that these are sacrifices because they are true to the laws which underlie the whole doctrine of sacrifice — *viz.*, self-denial, recognition of what is due to God (Ps. l. 5), contrition for sin (Ps. li. 17), trust in the Redeemer's sacrifice (Eph. v. 2), acknowledgment of individual undeservedness of the divine favour.

IV. Spiritual offerings must be free-will offerings.

1. *Because God deserves a service that is free.*

2. *Because the spiritual man is upheld by "a free spirit,"* and has been made "willing in the day of God's power."

3. *Because free-will offerings are those which are most likely to be permanent.*

V. Free-will offerings are most acceptable to God. "God loveth the cheerful giver" (Isa. lx. 7; Malachi iii. 4).

VI. God's gracious acceptance of free-will offerings must be regarded as a great blessing, and as therefore incurring corresponding obligations. "Teach me Thy statutes" (Ps. xix. 14).

(*Verse* 109), see *verse* 107.

(*Verse* 110), see *verse* 95.

GOD'S WORD THE HERITAGE OF HIS PEOPLE.

(*Verses* 111, 112.)

Notice—

I. That God's Word is a heritage. A heritage is that which has been specially bequeathed. Heritages are not purchased, but testated. So the Word of God has not been made or purchased by man, but has been freely given to us by our Father God.

II. That God's Word is a valuable heritage. "They are the rejoicings of my heart."

1. *It is an undeserved heritage.* We can lay no natural claim or title to it. When made out for us we were "alienated and enemies in our mind by wicked works."

2. *It is a full heritage.* Nothing can be added to it. It contains all things necessary and profitable to life, godliness, and eternity. The ever-blessed Trinity, providence, grace, earth, heaven, all are there ; and all are his to whom the testimonies of God belong (Ps. xvi. 5 ; 1 Cor. iii. 21 ; 2 Cor. vi. 10).

3. *It is a sure heritage.* There are no flaws in the title (Heb. vi. 17).

4. *It is an abiding heritage.* Estates are valuable in proportion to the time they last. God's Word is not leasehold as are all His temporal gifts. They are the saints' freehold (Ps. lxxiii. 26).

III. It is a responsible heritage.

1. *It is offered to our choice.* "I have taken." It is not forced upon us. We may reject it. If other things are more rejoicing to the heart we are welcome to them—if we can get them—with the consequences.

2. *That choice is the result of a preparation.* "I have inclined." A child's faculties must be developed before he is fit to become the responsible owner of property. So man must incline himself by Divine grace for the duties and responsibilities which devolve upon him as the proprietor of the Word of God.

3. *That choice involves the agent in grand and eternal responsibilities.* "To perform Thy statutes alway even unto the end." Free as is our heritage there is a tax upon it. The same tax that is upon all property—*viz.*, right use. If this is not observed within certain limits in worldly estates, the right is lost. The profligate and spendthrift neglecting to pay this tax squanders an ample portion and is reduced to beggary. The careless heir who neglects it, finds it squandered for him. He who uses it to violate the law of the land has it taken from him. So those who do not carefully and responsibly use this great heritage of God will lose it.

LOVE AND HATE.

(*Verses* 113, 128, 163.)

These verses view the two great and influential affections in their relation to one another. Let us view them first together and then separately. Together observe—

I. Affection is set against affection; hatred against love. Love and hatred are good or evil according to their objects. Nothing is worse than love of the world, sin, and vanity, or hatred of God and holiness; but set upon proper objects, hatred upon evil, and love upon good (Amos v. 15), they exhibit the soul as divinely constituted at the first. For as has been well said, "Man fallen is but an anagram of man in innocency; we have the same affections, but they are misplaced. Love was made for God; hatred for sin. Hatred was put on us that we might fly from evil. Love was given us that we might attach ourselves to God and the things which glorify Him."

II. Object is set against object. As love is opposed to hatred, so are vain thoughts and lying to God's law, and every false way to God's precepts. For as God's Word is solemn, practical, and necessary truth, so it requires solemnity and truth in those who would observe it.

LOVE FOR GOD'S WORD.

(*Verses* 113, 127, 128, 140, 159, 163, 165, 167.)

We have already considered love in contrast with hate, and God's Word in contrast with vain thoughts, lying and every false way. Let us now isolate those passages which regard the supreme affection of man's heart as set upon God's Word.

I. What is it to love God's Word?

1. *Negatively.* Not (1.) *The bare acknowledgment of its divinity.* This many do from the force of external evidence. (2.) *Nor a bare approval of its excellence.* Many admire where they do not trust and follow. (3.) *A mere spasm of delight,* as Herod rejoiced in John's light for a season (Mark vi. 20).

2. *Positively.* (1.) *Such a love as is rooted in the heart* (Jas. i. 21), and stirs all the affections to their inmost depths. (2.) *Such a love as leads us to consult it on all occasions* (Ps. i. 2, xix. 10, 11). (3.) *Such a love as lays its sweet constraint on our obedience* (1 John ii. 4; Rom. vi. 17).

II. What degree of love ought we to have for God's Word?

1. Supreme, "above gold, yea even fine gold." We ought to love God's Word more than riches, because it is more valuable than riches. Wealth is not prized for its own sake, but only for what it represents and can do. The Word of God contains "the unsearchable riches of Christ." This love, then, is such as will render us willing to sell all we have, so that we may obtain "the pearl of great price" (ver. 72).

2. *Intense and abundant.* "Consider *how* I love Thy laws." God only can measure the depth of it. "I love them exceedingly." Not with the transient affection of children for things which excite their passing inclinations, but with a love whose power cannot be broken, and whose ardour many waters cannot quench (vers. 48, 97; 1 John ii. 5).

III. Why should we love God's Word?

1. *Because its precepts concerning all things are right*" (ver. 128). All things, all persons, considered every way, universally, God's Word is right.

2. *Because it is "very pure"* or *"purifying."* (1.) *Pure in itself* (Ps. xix. 8). Refined from all dross, error, or falsehood. (2.) *Pure in the examples it presents* (Heb. vi. 12; 1 John iii. 3; 1 Pet. i. 15). (3.) *Purifying in the influence it exerts* (ver. 9; John xv. 3, xvii. 17). Showing us our impurity (Matt. xvi. 19; Jer. iv. 14). Exhort-

ing us to be clean (ver. 1; Isa. i.; Jas. iv. 8). Revealing the cleansing fountain (Eph. v. 26; Ezek. xxxvi. 25-27). Encouraging to purity (Matt. v. 8; 2 Cor. vii. 1).

2. *Because it is tranquillising* (ver. 165). (1.) *It reveals the " peace of God"* which "keeps the heart and mind." (2.) *Christ the Prince of Peace there confers it* (John xiv. 27). (3.) *The Spirit of Peace through it breathes His own tranquillity* (Rom. xv. 13; Gal. v. 22, vi. 16).

IV. How should we show our love to God's Word?

1. By hating "*vain thoughts*," "*false ways*," and "*lying*."
2. By loving obedience (ver. 167).
3. By prayer for more lively service (ver. 159).

V. What results will follow our love of God's Word?

1. *It will afford a powerful plea in prayer* (ver. 159). This was the confident appeal of one who was conscious that he was truly attached to God (John xxi. 17).

2. *It will stimulate to active service* (ver. 140).

3. *It will afford a powerful protection* (165, marg.). "No event of providence shall be an invincible temptation or powerful affliction, they shall hold fast their integrity and preserve their tranquillity. Nothing shall offend or hurt them, for everything shall work for their good. They will not perplex themselves with needless scruples, nor take offence at their brethren" (1 Cor. xiii. 6, 7).

HOLY HATRED.

(*Verses* 113, 128, 163.)

I. In its nature.
Hate is that passion which is aroused by the presence and antagonism of that which is repugnant, and which is excited to injure or exterminate that to which it is irreconcilably opposed. This is strong language, but justifiable and appropriate when applied to the believer's attitude against sin. Note a few of its attributes—

1. *Implacability.* It is not a passing spasm of indignation; it aims at nothing short of extermination. Those who hate sin pursue it with relentless vigour.

2. *Universality.* Anger is aroused against individuals; hatred against species. So the Christian hates all sin.

3. *Growth.* It is a principle which develops with our own spiritual *strength* (Acts xxiv. 16; 1 John iii. 9).

4. *Intensity* (ver. 163). Mere detestation is not enough. Anything short of abhorrent hatred will not meet the necessities of the case. Resolution will not, nor fear, nor dislike.

II. In its causes.

1. *Spiritual knowledge* (vers. 11, 104; Jer. xxxi. 19).
2. *The love of God* (Ps. xcvii. 10).
3. *Filial fear of God* (Prov. viii. 13).
4. *A spiritual sense of self-preservation.*

III. In its specific objects.

1. "*Vain thoughts.*" The original word with a different punctuation occurs in 1 Kings xviii. 21, "opinions." LXX here have παρανόμους, "lawless men;" Syr., "Perversely-minded men;" Chal., "Thinkers of vain thoughts." "The Psalmist describes mischievous speculations, subtle, useless, and perilous; heterodox pernicious teachings; opposed to truth revealed, and likely to interfere with its acceptance in its simplicity."— *Geier.* "The word is probably concrete and not abstract, 'doubters,' 'sceptics,' 'double-minded men' (Jas. i. 8), ἀνὴρ δίψυχος, a double-minded man divided between two opinions.—*Speaker's Com.*

2. "*False ways.*" "Every course of life not based on truth or a right view of things."—*Barnes.*

3. "*Lying.*" (1.) *The speaking of that which is false with an intention to deceive.* (2.) *The suppression of truth that should be told* (John xii. 42, 43). (3.) *Hypocrisy.* (4.) *Disobedience to the law which we profess to believe and obey.* Lies can be acted as well as told (Hosea xi. 12; 1 John i. 6, ii. 4).

IN CONCLUSION.—We should hate all sin, because it is what it is, and because of what it does. It is the contempt of

God's authority (Exod. v. 4). It is a breach of His righteous law (1 John iii. 4). It separates from God (Isa. lix. 2). It defaces the divine image (Ps. xliv. 12). It is the abominable thing which God hates, and works ruin and damnation to the soul.

THE DIVINE PROTECTION.

(*Verse* 114.)

I. **The divine protection.**
1. *A need implied.* The soul is in continual danger (Eph. vi. 12). It is beset by enemies who excel in craft, malice, pertinacity, numbers, and power. Hence it needs a shield to protect it in active warfare and a hiding-place to render it secure when at rest.
2. *Protection vouchsafed.* God is a shield to keep us in danger, and a hiding-place to keep us out of it. This promise guarantees that danger shall be entirely warded off, or if not, it shall not overwhelm us, but shall the rather make us sensible of the divine defence. (1.) "*Thou art my hiding-place.*" When sorely beset by danger, or unable to defend themselves, or wanting rest from conflict, men run to a hiding-place (1 Sam. iii. 6; Ps. xxxii. 7; Prov. xxxii. 3). A hiding-place must have *capacity.* God has room for us (Ps. xxxi. 20; 2 Tim. i. 12). *Secrecy* (Ps. xxvii. 5); God's protection of His saints is a mystery, hidden from the eyes of men. "Your life is hid with Christ in God." *Comfort* (Ps. xxxiv. 22, xci. 1). *Safety* till trouble is over (Ps. lvii. 1; Isa. xxvi. 20). (2.) "*Thou art my shield*" (Ps. v. 12, xxviii. 7, xci. 4). For a shield to afford safety it must have sufficient *breadth* (Ps. v. 12). *Resistance, impenetrability,* and *power to repel* the missiles that are hurled against it, back upon the foe (Ps. lix. 11).

II. **Where the divine protection is revealed.** In God's Word—
1. *It sets God forth as His people's sure defence* (Ps. lxxxiv. 11; Gen. xv. 1).
2. *It gives infallible assurance of the Divine protection.* Prov. xxx. 5; Ps. xviii. 30).
3. *It invites and encourages us to avail ourselves of that protection.*
4. *It tells us what qualifications he must have who would avail himself of that protection.* Faith (Prov. xxx. 5; Ps. xviii. 30). Obedience (Ps. lxxxiv. 11; Prov. ii. 7; Isa. xxxiii. 15, 16).
5. *It tells us how to enjoy that protection* (Zeph. ii. 3).

III. **The comfort this revelation brings.** "I hope in Thy word."
1. *It tranquillises the soul while it waits for God's own time* (Ps. xxxiii. 20. Isa. xxviii. 16).
2. *It fortifies the heart in present difficulties, and when danger is, or promises to be extreme.* Moses in the wilderness (Ps. xc. 1), David in exile (Ps. iii. 3).
3. *It empowers us cheerfully to do what God would have us do, and go where God would have us go,* fearlessly trusting in God's goodness and power (Ps. xxxi. 5).

IN CONCLUSION.—(1.) *A word of comfort.* No hurt can happen to us without God's leave. (ii.) *A word of warning.* There is no safety for us except behind God's power. (iii.) *A word of exhortation.* Acknowledge God at all times as your protector, and seek Him in every time of need.

SEPARATION AND CONSISTENCY.

(*Verse* 115.)

These two ideas stand or fall with each other. It is impossible to be obedient to the law of God while associating with wicked men, and equally impossible to keep bad company while doing good works. Observe—

I. **The necessity of separation** from evil doers.
1. *Its limitations.* (1.) *Not in mere matters of business* (1 Cor. v. 5), nor while it is possible to do them good. Nor should we renounce Church fellowship

because evil or inconsistent men are there—a most absurd, but, alas! frequent course. There are black or unsound sheep in every flock, tares in every harvest, chaff in every threshing-floor. "I fly from the chaff that I may not be it; but I fly not the floor lest I be nothing." —*Augustine*. But (2) *We are required not to be unequally yoked with them in cordial friendship or matrimonial alliances* (Exod. xxxiv. 15, 2 Cor. vi. 14), not to imitate their manners and customs, and not to partake of their sins (Eph. v. 11). But by virtue of our new nature, our spiritual sonship, our moral inheritance, our communion with God, and our hope of heaven, we are enjoined to come out from among them and be the saintly and peculiar people of God.

2. *Its reasons*. (1.) *Our love of God should prevent us being on terms of amity and fellowship with those who are at enmity with Him.* It would argue but poor patriotism for a soldier to be on terms of cordiality with a rebel or a foe (Ps. cxxxix. 21, 22; 2 Pet. ii. 8). (2.) *Evil communications corrupt good manners* (Ps. i. 1; Isa. vi. 5; Prov. i. 10, 15; 1 Cor. v. 6.) (3.) *Our familiarity will harden them in their sins, while our separation from them may promote reflection* (2 Thess. iii. 6–14). (4.) *Friendship with them will bring a blemish on our fair fame.* A man is known by the company he keeps (2 John ii., Heb. xii. 15, Ps. l. 18). (5.) *We stand in danger of sharing their ruin* (Gen. xiv. 12, Prov. xiii. 20, Rev. xviii. 4).

II. The **duty of keeping God's commandments.**

1. *We are under the most solemn obligations to do so.* They are the commandments of our God. Ours by covenant engagement. He has promised to be ours only on the condition of the fulfilment of our duty (Deut. xxvii. 9, 10).

2. *We owe it as a debt of gratitude to God for revealing them.* Since God has been at the trouble of revealing them, holy and just and good as they are, we ought to be at the trouble of keeping them.

3. *Upon keeping God's commandments our wellbeing absolutely depends.* To transgress them is to transgress the fundamental laws of spiritual life.

4. *Upon our constant obedience depends our hope of heaven.* "Be thou faithful unto death," &c.

III. **The importance of prompt and decisive resolution.** "Depart." "I will."

1. *God has no pleasure in an unstable, double-minded man.*

2. *Without resolute determination all desires are vain.*

3. *Unless we are prompt and decisive, evildoers will take advantage of us and easily win us to their ways.*

GOD'S ATTITUDE TOWARDS THE RIGHTEOUS AND THE WICKED.

(*Verses* 116–119.)

I. **God's attitude towards the righteous.**

1. *What that attitude is.* Twofold. Something to hold. Some one who holds. *Teneo et teneor*. (1.) *God is something to hold.* A prop, a rock, a sure foundation; something clinging to which we shall not be swept away by the surging billows. (2.) *God is some one who holds.* The Psalmist thinks of the strong and tenacious grasp of God; "They shall never perish," &c. This double idea is expressed in Ps. lxxiii. 23.

2. *Upon what that attitude depends.* Twofold again. The divine promise and cheerful obedience. (1.) "*According to Thy word.*" The Bible is full of promises in this direction too numerous to quote. (2.) "*I love Thy testimonies.*" "I will have respect unto Thy statutes continually."

3. *What this attitude implies.* (1.) *Life.* (2.) *Glorious hope.* (3.) *Safety.*

II. **God's attitude towards the wicked.**

1. *What that attitude is.* (1.) *Contempt.* Sept. and Vulg., "Thou dost despise (ver. 118). (2.) *Rejection* (ver. 119). "There is no true metal in them when they are tried by the refining fire, they are burnt up; they fly off in fumes. There is probably an allusion to the

scum or scoriæ at the surface of melting metals, which is swept off previously to casting the metal into the mould."— *Clarke.*

2. *Why that attitude is assumed.* (1.) *Because of their falsehood.* (2.) Because of their worthlessness: "dross." 3. *What that attitude implies.* One word describes it all. "Everlasting destruction from the presence of the Lord and from the glory of His power."

(*Verse 120*), see *verse 107.*
(*Verse 121*), see *verse 95.*
(*Verse 122*), see *verse 95.*

LOFTY ASPIRATIONS.
(*Verses 123–125.*)

I. The **objects** of these aspirations. (1.) *Salvation.* (2.) *The words of God's righteousness.* This may refer to some precious promise, some solemn injunction, or some righteous law. (3.) *Divine teaching.* The Word of God is a sealed word without the illumination of the Divine Spirit.

II. The **quality** of these aspirations. 1. *Intensity.* "Mine eyes fail." "The idea here is that of looking out for a thing—of '*straining* the eyes' so that their power becomes exhausted." 2. *Resignation.* "Deal with Thy servant according to Thy mercy." What is best for me grant. If I ask amiss withhold.

THE LORD'S TIME AND OURS.
(*Verse 126.*)

The Hebrew literally rendered is, "Time to do for Jehovah," and means either that it is time for *the Lord* to work, or time *for us* to work for the Lord. As expositors are divided, its vagueness warrants us to learn the blessed truths taught by both interpretations; for are not we "workers together with God"? Notice—

I. **A time common to both to work.** When man makes void the law of God. When is this time? Alas! when is it not? Men make void the law of God every day, every moment. The time, then, for God and man to work together is *now.* Not to-morrow, not on special days or special occasions, but "now is the accepted time, now is the day of salvation."

II. **A work common for both to do.** The work of salvation. Man saves *instrumentally*, by example, by exhortation, by influence, in leading men to a knowledge of their sins, to repentance, and to trust in Christ. God saves *effectually* by the restraining influences of His grace, by the convictions and regeneration of the Holy Ghost, by cleansing in the precious blood, by pardon.

III. **A time for God alone to work.** Where men have made void God's law, without repentance or remedy. Such a time has often occurred in human history. The iniquities of men and nations have become full, and God has visited them with vengeance. This time occurred to Sodom, Assyria, Babylon, Israel, Rome, &c. Such a time will occur when human history has closed. Of this time and season it is not for man to know.

IV. **A work for God alone to do.** Vengeance and destruction. In this man can and must play no part except as the merest instrument in God's hands. "Vengeance is *Mine.*"

A DANGER AND ITS REMEDY.
(*Verses 126–128.*)

The force of "*therefore*" in verses 127, 128, may be taken in three different ways. 1. It may mean that as a consequence of the evil of the times, the superior value of God's Word was shown by contrast, and that, therefore, the Psalmist loved it intensely. 2. That as the times were so evil, therefore he would do all that he could to counterbalance that evil by a superior religious excellence. But 3. There seems to underlie these latter verses the reason for the general ungodliness of the times as described in verse 126; and viewed in connection with the thought that runs through the whole Psalm, the danger of the Psalmist from the number of his powerful enemies, the *therefore* seems to point to love of God's Word, &c., as a sure protection and remedy from the evil.

I. The **danger**. A time of great religious declension is a time of great danger, because of the difficulties and temptations that are in the way of religious consistency. The question of time now-a-days resolves itself into a question of space. Whenever men live in a neighbourhood of intense ungodliness, they are always in great danger. This danger consists in—

1. *The lust of gain* (ver. 127). To this danger all business men are exposed. In the midst of a community to which "gold" is the one thing needful, there is great danger of succumbing to the prevalent fever, and pursuing the popular but godless course.

2. *Infidelity* (ver. 128). To this danger all reading and thinking men are exposed. Just now the very atmosphere is charged with unbelief. Newspapers and periodicals are published, and societies are founded for the express purpose of trying to show God's precept concerning all things to be *wrong*, and there is a great danger of even Christian men running with this giddy multitude.

3. *Sin*, alas! abounds everywhere. The false way in which men make void God's law is a very broad way, and many men are in it. False sentiments, false judgments, false practices are extremely prevalent, and men are strongly tempted to live *down* to the times and avoid the singularity of walking in the true and narrow way.

This danger is a *present* danger, an *increasing* danger, and often a *subtle* danger.

II. The **remedy** is not at all times or usually flight from danger, but by the "expulsive force of a new affection" to make danger flee. "Therefore," &c. The remedy—

1. *For lust of gain, is to love God's commandments above gold.* Wealth will then sink into its proper and useful place. We have not to be taken out of the world, but to be kept from its evil, and this will do it. It is better to be good than to be rich; for by becoming good a man often makes the best of both worlds, and only the love of God's commandments can make men good.

2. *For infidelity, is to esteem all God's precepts concerning all things to be right.* Let a sincere and intelligent study of those precepts decide. Let history decide. Let the lives of those men who have been without, or who have rejected, God's Word decide; and the lives of those men who have followed its counsels and commands.

3. *For sin, is to hate every false way.* That which we hate we endeavour to injure or destroy; and when this is impossible we avoid it.

III. The **danger is avoided and the remedy applied** by earnest prayer for God to work and by earnest co-operation with God in working (ver. 126). See previous outline.

1. *God only can work in us to will and to do, &c.*

2. *But we must work out what God has worked in*, and (1) *apply ourselves to the earnest love of God's commandments, &c.* (2) *Apply ourselves to the work of grappling with selfishness, infidelity, and sin.* The more we work with God for man's salvation, the more we shall lessen our danger.

GOD'S WORD: DESIRED, INSTRUCTIVE, WONDERFUL, KEPT.

(*Verses* 129–131.)

I. **Desired** (ver. 131). "When under an enforced absence from God's ordinances he longed to be restored to them; when he enjoyed them he greedily sucked in the Word of God as new-born babes desire the milk."—*M. Henry.* "A metaphor taken from an animal in the chase. He runs open-mouthed to take in the cooling air, the heart beating high and the muscular force nearly expended through fatigue. The Psalmist sought for 'God's commandment' as he would run from a ferocious beast for life."—*A. Clarke.*

II. **Instructive** (ver. 130). "As a beam of light illumines a dark chamber. But פֵּתַח lit opening, unfolding, or revelation, LXX. and Vulg. δήλωσις, *declaratio*, means not so much entrance of the word into the soul, but rather its being made open *to us* so that we may perceive its beauty, or may ourselves "enter" into its meaning, its mysteries, and its beauties. Simple, means those who are open to persuasion, or who are easily enticed or seduced. Then it refers to the *credulous* (Prov. xiv. 15), and then to the *inexperienced.*"—*Speaker's Com. and Barnes.*

III. **Wonderful** (ver. 129).
1. *In the character of its revelations.* God, the soul, and the future state.
2. *In its forbearance and benignity towards the lost and the erring.*
3. *In the self-consistency of its separate books, dispensations, &c.*
4. *In its sin-convincing and soul-converting power.*
5. *In its purity and sublimity.*
6. *In its supporting and comforting promises and helps and hopes.*

IV. **Kept** (ver. 129). "'As a treasure of inestimable value that I cannot be without.' We do not keep them to any purpose unless our souls keep them. They must be deposited, as the tables of testimony were in the ark; there they must have the innermost and uppermost place. Those that see God's Word to be admirable, will prize it highly and preserve it carefully, as that which they promise themselves great things from."—*M. Henry.*

PRAYER.

(*Verses* 132-135.)

I. The **character** of prayer. Personal intercourse with a personal God. "Look *Thou* upon *me.*" We cannot worship an abstraction at all. And we cannot worship the living and true God by proxy.

II. The **matter** of prayer.
1. *Supplication of the divine mercy* (ver. 132). (1.) *A sense of personal unworthiness.* (2.) *A recognition of the divine beneficence.* (3.) *An ardent expectation of the divine salvation.*
2. *Petition for practical direction.* "Order my steps in Thy word," "Teach me Thy statutes." (1.) *A confession of ignorance and departure.* (2.) *A desire for restoration.* (3.) *A high valuation of obedience.*
3. *Request for personal deliverance* (ver. 134).
4. *Desire for divine favours* (ver. 135).

III. The **manner** of prayer.
1. *Humble and reverent.* "Look Thou upon me." Permit me to pray.
2. *Confident.* These verses breathe an intense hopefulness.
3. *Sincere.* "So will I keep Thy precepts."

IV. The **plea** to be used in prayer (ver. 132). Marg., "According to the custom towards," &c. Heb., "According to the *judgment.*" What is right, "what is due; or of what is usually determined; *i.e.*, as God usually determines, judges, acts towards those who love Him. The idea is according to the rules which regulate the treatment of Thy people."—*Barnes.*

V. The **purpose** which should sustain prayer (ver. 133). Holiness. For *verse* 134 see also *verse* 95. For *verse* 135 see also *verse* 107.

THE PROPER ATTITUDE OF THE RIGHTEOUS TOWARDS THE UNGODLY.

(*Verses* 136, 139, 155, 158.)

Whatever interpretation we attach to the "Imprecatory Psalms," certainly the

Psalmists do not indiscriminately curse all ungodly men. That David could be susceptible of such forbearance towards his great and influential enemies, and that this Psalmist could be instinct with such evangelical charity as to weep over sinners, and to be consumed with zeal for their reclamation, seems to point to a meaning in the above-named Psalms which perhaps does not lie upon the surface. At any rate the meaning of these verses is clear.

I. The ungodly are **described as—**
1. *Malignant.* "Mine enemies." Opposers of righteous words and persecutors of godly people. They are known everywhere by their antagonism to God's children. The carnal mind being at enmity against God is at enmity with the family of God. Let it not be overlooked that this is not a general classification here. The Psalmist had particular persons in his eye.
2. *Wicked.* From רָשָׁע. To make a wilful mistake. This fixes on the sinner conscious and deliberate guilt.
3. *Transgressors.* בֹּגֵד. Faithless to God and man.

Let these powerful expressions be particularly noted as bringing out the Psalmist's large-hearted charity.

II. The ungodly are the subjects of **the tenderest compassion and the bitterest grief.** "Mine eyes descend in rivers of waters because men despise Thee and destroy themselves. Most of the Easterns shed tears much more copiously than Europeans. I have myself seen Arabs shed tears like streams."—*Speaker's Com.*

1. *This attitude has always characterised the righteous.* Jeremiah (ix. 18, xiii. 17, xiv. 17; Lam. i. 16, ii. 18, iii. 48); *Our Lord* (Mark v., Luke xix. 41); *Paul* (Phil. iii. 8, Rom. ix. 2, 3).
2. *This attitude is right.* Nothing should stir our hearts so deeply as the ruin and degradation of our fellow-men. God's Word singles it out as a conspicuous mark of grace (Ezek. ix. 4, 1 Cor. v. 2). "There is nothing which more certainly indicates true piety, and which is certainly more connected with a work of grace or a revival of religion, than when such deep compassion for men as sinners pervades a church."—*Barnes.*
3. *This attitude is necessary.* (1.) How is it possible for us to contemplate with dry eyes and unmoved heart such sights as are every day seen! Drunkenness, swearing, dishonesty, &c. To see men bent on thwarting the divine providence and damning their own souls. (2.) Because the prevalence of sin deprives God of glory, and spreads ruin and desolation over God's fair world. (3.) Because this is the first step in the direction of zeal for the sinner's reclamation. "Then Christians will pray, labour to save sinners, feel their dependence on God, and then the Spirit will descend and bless the effort put forth." —*Barnes.*

III. The ungodly are the subjects of **zealous evangelisation.**
1. *All the compassion in the world by itself will not only do the sinner no good, but rather perhaps excite his contempt.*
2. *Compassion must receive a practical expression in intense and all-consuming zeal* (ver. 139). This word is elsewhere rendered consumed, cut off, vanished, destroyed. "He pined away; his strength was exhausted; he was sinking under the efforts he had put forth."—*Barnes.* (Ps. lxix. 9; 1 Kings xix. 10.)

IV. The ungodly are **pitied and evangelised not for sentimental but for practical reasons.** *Note*—"It was not because they were *His* foes,—not because He was endeavouring to destroy them, or take vengeance upon them. It is a great triumph when in looking at persecutors and slanderers,—we are more grieved because they violate the law of God, when our solicitude turns from ourselves to God."

The reasons are because—
1. *They have not kept God's laws.* Hence his tears.
2. *They have forgotten God's works and despised His salvation.* Hence His zeal. Would to God, these considerations would produce the same effect in every Christian now.

THE DIVINE RIGHTEOUSNESS.

(*Verses* 137, 138, 142, 144.)

The Psalmist here deals with the righteousness of God from a fourfold point of view. First he declares God to be *absolutely* and *inherently* righteous; then the *judgment* of the righteous God to be righteous, *i.e.*, God is *actively* righteous; then that God has revealed both His active and passive righteousness is His testimonies, *i.e.*, God is *declaratively* righteous. This being the case, he points out that those testimonies are a faithful record of that righteousness, and therefore are to be depended upon by man.

I. God is **absolutely** righteous (ver. 137). From the fundamental principles of His nature the conception is impossible that God in thought, word, or deed, should swerve from the lines of strict and immutable equity.

II. God is **relatively and actively** righteous. "Upright are Thy judgments." This follows upon His absolute righteousness. He cannot do unjustly, but must award every man according to his work (Rom. ii. 5–9; 1 Pet. i. 17), forgiving on confession of sin (1 John i. 9), approving obedience (Heb. vi. 10), rewarding (2 Tim. iv. 8), punishing (Rom. ii. 9; 2 Thess. i. 8; 1 John iii. 18, 19). Hence His active righteousness is everlasting. "Human governments change. New laws are enacted under new administrations. Old dynasties pass away. Custom, opinion, the world, men, all change. But as God Himself never changes, so it is with His law. Founded on eternal truth it can never change."—*Barnes.*

III. God is **declaratively** righteous through those testimonies which are (Marg.) *righteousness*. No truer or sublimer definition could be given of God's Word. It is a perfect delineation of the righteousness of God's character and ways, without admixture of error. "Thy law is the truth." It is founded not on mere arbitrary will, but on the reality of things, and can therefore never change.

IV. Therefore those testimonies **which declare God's righteousness are to be depended on by man.** Thy testimonies are very *faithfulness*.

IN CONCLUSION (ver. 144).—(i.) *Those who would see and enjoy the divine righteousness must pray for understanding.* (ii.) *Those who have that understanding shall live.* How? The just shall live by faith. Faith in what? Rom. iii. 24–26.

(*Verse* 139), see *verse* 126.

GOD'S WORD A TRIED WORD AND A LOVED WORD.

(*Verse* 140.)

The margin renders "tried." P. B. version, "Tried to the uttermost." These words describe the test to which the Word of God in every age has been subjected, and the result. It has come out of the fire as refined gold (Ps. xii.). No error has been proved to be in it or cast from it. Therefore God's people love it. In this age everything is put upon its trial. Modern criticism subjects every institution and relic of antiquity to the keenest tests. Our philosophers place everything in their crucibles, and subject everything to their dissecting knives. Every day we hear of history which has proved to be myth, and belief but exploded superstition. But into whatever alembic the Word of God has been plunged, it has come out without diminution and very pure.

I. The **trial** to which the Word of God has been subjected.
1. *The conflict with sin.*
2. *The contradictions of unbelief.*
3. *The inconsistencies of its apparent friends.*
4. *The experience of saints and sinners.*

II. The **love** with which it is received. "I use the Scriptures not as an arsenal to be resorted to only for arms and weapons . . . but as a matchless temple, where I delight to contemplate the beauty, the symmetry, and the magnificence of the structure; and to increase my awe and excite my devotion to the Deity there preached and adored. . . . Whereas at my entrance I took even the choicest to be at best but like some Indian province, wherein though mines and gems were more abundant than in other countries, yet they were but sparingly to be met with, here and there; after a competent stay, my ensuing perusals presented it to me, if not as a *royal* jewel made of gold and precious stones, yet (which is more glorious) like Aaron's breast-plate, a *sacred* jewel, the particular instructions for which were given by God Himself, and which besides the various number of flaming gems set in fine gold and placed in a mysterious order, was ennobled by that *Urim-ve-Thummim* wherein God vouchsafed to reveal Himself. . . . This experiment keeps me from wondering to find that the poet attributes blessedness to '*delight* in the law of the Lord.'"—*The Hon. Robert Boyle.*

TRUE GREATNESS.

(*Verse* 141.)

Notice—

I. **That true greatness may be consistent with external humiliation.** A man may be very poor and mean in the world's estimation. He may be *small* because he does not aim at political and social greatness. He may be *despised* because all his principles are against that wholesale murder which men denominate valour. He may be *afraid* to do what is wrong and sin against God, and thus be open to the scoffs of the profligate and the sneers of the bravo. But if he does not forget God's precepts he has the essentials of true greatness. True greatness does not consist in those external exhibitions which pass off as such. A man may be a great philosopher and yet be morally small as Bacon. A man may be great in war as Bonaparte and yet have a little soul. True greatness is greatness in the sight of God. And that greatness has he who does not forget God's precepts. He will have power with God, and in the long run with man, as well.

II. **That external humiliation should not be-little a man.** This is a sad and prevalent tendency. When a man is esteemed small and despised, he aspires to what is termed greatness and honour by trying to forget God's precepts. When a man is ashamed of his father's Bible and his mother's piety, he is on the true road to be-little himself in the sight of God, and in the long run, in the sight of man.

(*Verse* 142), see *verse* 137.
(*Verse* 143), see *verse* 107.
(*Verse* 144), see *verse* 137.

EFFECTUAL, FERVENT, AND BELIEVING PRAYER.

(*Verses* 145-152.)

I. **Its object.** "O Lord," "I cried unto Thee." The Psalmist entertained no idea of intervening or interceding saints or angels. He had been taught and believed that worship must be directed to God alone. Therefore all his aspirations ascended to the *personal* God.

II. **Its reasons.**

1. *Affliction.* The whole of this clause breathes out a spirit that was in sore distress.

2. *Personal and imminent danger* (ver. 150). This holds good with every Christian. Satan and all the forces of evil are ever near to work damage to the soul.

3. *Inability to do the will of God.* All Christians share this consciousness. God's "statutes" cannot be kept with-

out the help of God's Spirit, whose presence must be supplicated in prayer.

III. Its petitions.
1. "*Hear me.*" This should be the primary petition. Without God's condescending attention all supplication is vain.
2. "*Save me.*" Those whom God hears He saves. Unless God saves, all ground for hope and prayer is taken away. Salvation is the most urgent petition that man can offer.
3. "*Quicken me.*" Those whom God saves God quickens, and without this quickening, salvation is vain. Salvation is a rescue from danger; quickening is the invigoration of new life, and unless that takes place the end of prayer is unattained.

IV. Its characteristics.
1. *Earnestness.* "I cried." Unless God sees our eagerness and our intense desire to prevail, He will not listen to our prayer.
2. *Undividedness.* "With my whole heart." Unless our whole nature is bent upon securing the answer to our prayer God will not save. The worship of the lips is a mockery in the sight of God. Mind, emotions, will, tongues, must all be engaged in this service.
3. *Importunity* (vers. 147, 148). Sometimes God delays His quickening to test this importunity and to draw it forth (Luke xviii). The ten days which preceded Pentecost: Morning, noon, and night must be spent directly or indirectly in this service.

4. *Faith.* "I hoped in Thy word." Hope based on the promises and expectant of their realisation is the sublimest faith.

V. Its warrants.
1. *The divine loving-kindness* (ver. 149). If God is not gracious and kind, we have no warrant to approach His august and terrible majesty.
2. *The divine nearness* (ver. 151). If God is not near He cannot hear. The Psalmist held this to be one of the primary tenets of the faith (Ps. cxxxix). So do Christians. "Lo, I am with you alway."
3. *The truth of the divine promise* (ver. 147, *cf.* 151). Man may break his promise. There may be no sincerity in his promise. But when God says, "Call upon Me in the day of trouble," &c., we know that He means what He says.
4. *Past experience* (ver. 152). What God has done He can still do; and therefore the Psalmist argues what He did for me of old He will do for me again, and thus—

" Old experience doth attain
To somewhat of prophetic strain."

VI. Its resolutions.
1. *Obedience.* "I will keep Thy *statutes.*"
2. *Witness-bearing.* "I will keep Thy *testimonies.*"

VII. Its basis (ver. 148). By continual meditation on God's Word he was instructed how to pray, what to pray for, and when to pray.

MORNING PRAYER.

(*Verse* 147.)

"I cried unto Thee *early*, *i.e.*, before others, in the gloom, before the dawning of the morning : my fixed hope in Thy promise suffered me not to rest."—*Speaker's Com.*

I. The Bible speaks much of morning prayer (Exod. xxxii. 4; Mark i. 35). "It is full of morning. 'My voice shalt Thou hear in the morning, O Lord; and in the morning will I direct my prayer unto Thee, and will look up.' 'The Lord's mercies are new every morning.' Of old 'the morning stars sang together.'

'I, Jesus, am the bright and morning Star.' Truly the day declines; but at 'eventide there is light,' when in the morning there has been converse with God. The morning makes the day. A morning misspent is a day ruined; a morning saved is a day completed. Lord, awake me at sunrise, and by the beauty of the coming light give hope for the whole day."—*Dr. J. Parker.*

II. Morning is the most favourable time for prayer. It is calm. The cares and anxieties of the day have not broken upon us. Our mind is then clearest; and away from our families and our businesses, we can be alone.

III. **Morning is the time God demands for prayer.** "The *morning* is the time fixed for my meeting with God. What meaning there is in time as well as place! In the morning—then God means me to be at my best in strength and hope. In the night I have buried yesterday's fatigue, and in the morning I take a new lease of energy. Give God all thy strength. In the morning—then He may mean to keep me long that He may make me rich."—*Dr. J. Parker.*

IV. Morning is the **most appropriate time** for prayer. The day is before us, and the day will be wasted if not sanctified by God.

THE CONSTITUENTS OF A COMPLETE AND HOLY DAY.

(*Verses* 146–148.)

I. The day **begins** with prayer. "The first thing he did in the morning, before he admitted any business, was to pray when his mind was most fresh and in the best frame. If our thoughts in the morning be of God, they will help to keep us in His fear all the day long."—*M. Henry.* Observe that this morning prayer stimulated his hope in God's promises, and thus braced and encouraged him for the exercises of the day.

II. The day **continues** with practical obedience. "I shall keep Thy statutes." Beginning well it continues well. Prayer secured the fulfilment of the divine promises in the divine guidance and the divine protection. Hence consistency and holiness.

III. The day **closes** with meditation on God's Word. The crown and completion of a good day. All anxieties are over. The time due to our fellow-men has been spent, and well spent; and now the man of God recognises God's claim upon his eventide.

See also for *verse* 148 on *verse* 55.

GOD'S NEARNESS AND MAN'S.

(*Verses* 150, 151.)

1. Man is near to harass; God is near to help.
2. Man is near to hurt; God is near to protect.
3. Man is near to discourage; God is near to comfort.
4. Man is near to tempt to sin; God is near to save from sin.
5. Man is near to cast doubts; God is near to resolve doubts.
6. Man is near to drag down to the world, flesh, and devil; God is near to lift up to heavenly things, where Christ sitteth at the right hand of God.
7. Man is near to kill; God is near to give life and immortality.

THE DIVINE CONSIDERATION.

(*Verses* 153–157.)

I. The Psalmist's **need** of it.
1. *Personal affliction.*
2. *Numerous persecutors.*

II. The Psalmist's **estimate** concerning it—
1. *Contemplation of his case.* "Take it into thy thoughts and all the circumstances of it, and sit not by as one unconcerned."—*M. Henry.*
2. *Pleading his cause* (ver. 154). "Be Thou my patron and advocate, and take me for Thy client."

3. *Deliverance from his affliction.*
4. *Quickened life.*

III. The Psalmist's **pleas** for it.
1. *His remembrance of the divine law* (ver. 153).
2. *His trust in the divine promises* (ver. 154).
3. *The fact that salvation was for such as he* (ver. 155).
4. *The manifold character of God's tender mercies* (ver. 156).

5. *His love for God's precepts* (ver. 158).
6. *The immutability of the divine word* (ver. 160).

See also for *verses* 153, 154, 156, see *verse* 107; for *verses* 155, 158, see *verse* 136; for *verse* 157, see *verse* 95; for *verse* 159, see *verse* 113.

THE TRUTH AND ENDURANCE OF GOD'S WORD.

(*Verse* 160.)

"Literally, 'The head of Thy Word is truth,'" probably meaning that its principles and basis were truth. It was not *made* truth by the mere will of God, but it was *founded on* essential truth.— Marg., 'The beginning of Thy Word is true.' Its origin, foundation, and essential nature is truth."—*Barnes*. "Does he refer to the *first word* in God's Word, בראשית. 'In the beginning, ראש is the root of that word. Every word that Thou hast spoken from the first in *Bereshith* to the end of the law, and all Thou wilt yet speak, as flowing from the *fountain of truth*, must be true, and all shall have in due time their fulfilment." —*A. Clarke*.

I. God's Word is **based upon truth,** and therefore endures. It does not rest on tentative hypotheses or speculations, but upon the infallible and immutable declarations of God. Everything not built on this solid foundation will not bear the tear and wear and fret of time.

II. God's Word had its **beginning in truth,** and therefore its righteous judgments endure for ever. As the spring so the stream. If the source is tainted so will be the river. But God's Word sprang from Him who is "the Truth," and therefore it continues true all along its course.

III. God's Word is **true all through,** and therefore endures. Man's building may be upon unstable foundations, may be of defective materials, and be erected on a false plan. Earthly rivers may be pure in their source, but may receive poisoned waters from tributary streams. But the Word of God is built on, composed of, and designed by truth, and with its waters errors will not mix. Delitzsch says that truth "is the total number of all the items in the reckoning. The Word of God is reckoned over in its parts and as a whole. Truth is the grand denominator, and truth the result."

IN CONCLUSION.—God's Word is the truth, the whole truth, and nothing but the truth. (i.) *Are you based upon it?* (ii.) *Are you drinking from it?* (iii.) *Are you moulded by it?* (iv.) *Will you continue with it?*

(*Verse* 161), see *verse* 95.

GOD'S WORD THE OBJECT OF REVERENCE AND JOY.

(*Verse* 161, *last clause, and verse* 162.)

I. God's Word the **object of joy.** The expression is as true as it is remarkable.

1. *The joy of victory in conflict*. To gain spoil, fighting is necessary, and success over the foe. So we do not find the unsearchable riches of Christ without contest. We must battle with doubts, drawbacks, disinclinations, &c. The mere obtaining a victory is a cause of joy even when no substantial result is achieved.

2. *The joy of enrichment after victory.* (1.) *Victory over unbelief gains stronger ground for faith.* (2.) *Victory over disinclination is rewarded by some new truth.* (3.) *Victory over darkness is the acquisition of light.* (4.) *Victory over tribulation secures fresh comfort.* (5.) *Victory over sin finds the great spoil of holiness.*

II. God's Word the **object of reverence.** The two clauses are to be united as in cxii. 1. Sometimes the gaining of spoil is worse for an army than defeat. Men are demoralised. Nations become arrogant. And lest man should be lifted up by pride with the knowledge he has of the Word of God, let it be remembered that it is the *Word of God*, and stand in awe of it.

(*Verse* 163), see *verse* 113.

CONSTANT PRAISE.

(*Verse* 164.)

"Not only morning and evening, not thrice only (Ps. lv. 17), but seven times, *i.e.*, again and again, and many times (Ps. xii. 6, lxix. 12; Lev. xxvi. 18, 24; Gen. iv. 15; Prov. xxiv. 16), each day, so as to hallow the day, the Psalmist thanks God for His word."—*Speaker's Com.* "Rabbi Solomon says this is to be understood literally, for they praised God *twice* in the morning before reading the decalogue, and *once* after; *twice* in evening before the same reading, and *twice* after; thus making seven times. The Roman Church has prescribed a similar service."—*A. Clarke.*

I. **Constant praise is demanded, because of the constancy of the divine judgments.** They never fail. By them the universe is held together, society made possible, and human blessedness secured.

II. **Constant praise is due to God for the beneficence of His judgments.** They are given in mercy, not in wrath. They are not impracticable, nor burdens too heavy to be borne. They are made for and given to man for his safety and peace.

III. **Constant praise is due to God for the clearness of His divine judgments.** They are not enveloped in a cloud of mystery, or hidden behind perplexing technicalities, or in such a way as to be out of the reach of the common people. "The way-faring man, though a fool, cannot err therein."

VI. **Constant praise is due to God for the help He vouchsafes to keep His righteous judgments.** The Holy Spirit is given to help our infirmities. We are invited to approach the throne of grace, to obtain grace to help in time of need.

V. **Constant praise is due to God for the forgiveness** He offers when we have broken His righteous judgments. "If we confess our sins," &c. "If any man sin we have an Advocate," &c.

PEACE.

(*Verse* 165.)

Peace is man's highest hope and best inheritance. All other blessings are valued only as they promote it, and the loftiest dignity and wealthiest affluence are worth nothing without it. Obstacles to peace abound, and the largest part of life is spent in overcoming them. Offences and stumblingblocks are the greatest obstacles. Genuine difficulty and hard work promote peace. Let a man know there is a difficulty in the way, or a work to be done, and he composes his mind to grapple with them. But when he meets with a stubborn obstacle, or stumbles over it, his mind is hurt and his peace is gone. So the believer may be unmoved amidst the greatest afflictions and trials, and yet through some unforeseen and insignificant impediment he may stumble and lose all his tranquillity. Notice—

I. **A qualification.** Love of God's law. "To *love* a law may seem strange; but it is the only true divine life. To keep it because we are afraid of its penalties is only a form of fear or prudential consideration. To keep it to preserve a good name may be propriety and respectability. To keep it because it is best for society may be worldly self-interest. To keep it because of physical health may be the policy of epicurean philosophy. To keep it because we love it is to show that it is already part of us—has entered into the moral texture of our being. Sin then becomes distasteful, and temptations lose their power."—*Statham.*

II. **A process.** "Nothing shall offend them," *i.e.*, nothing shall be a stumblingblock to them and so hurt them. Those whose hearts and minds are embued with and thus protected and directed by God's law, although there must needs be stumblingblocks in their way, yet they shall not stumble over them nor be hurt by them.

1. *They will not stumble over apparent discrepancies in God's law.* He who loves God's law will not go to God's Word *to find or make them.* When they come across his path, the Divine Interpreter explains them, and a sanctified insight and experience will discover their true harmony.

2. *They will not stumble at temptations.* Those who are protected by the law of God are safe. Temptations find nothing in common with them on which they can take hold. The world has no equivalent to offer for the pleasures and profit of the law of the Lord.

3. *They will not stumble at circumstances.* If adversity comes, those who love God's law are prepared for that. They know it to be necessary for them or it would not come. If prosperity comes, that prosperity is sanctified by the sanctity of those in whom it meets. God's law teaches that "all things work together for good," &c.

4. *They do not stumble at death.* The law of God has robbed death of its terrors. That law shows that Christ has withdrawn death's sting, that it is now not only harmless, but is pressed into the service of the people of God. "Death is yours." Now your friend to conduct you to a place where its office is at an end. Those who love God's law know that Christ has vanquished "him that had the power of death, and delivered them who through the fear of death were all their lifetime subject to bondage."

III. The **result**. Having no fear of stumblingblocks, and not being hurt by them, the lovers of God's law have great peace. Not mere peace, but great peace.

1. *Great, because divine.* It is the "peace of God." "My peace." "Not as the world giveth."

2. *Great, because powerful.* It "keeps the heart and mind." It eases tremendous anxieties, removes perturbing fears.

3. *Great, because incomprehensible.* "It passeth all understanding." It cannot be defined. The Christian only knows he has it.

4. *Great, because eternal.* "Peace shall flow as a river," unexhausted, always running, yet never running to waste or away.

GOD'S SALVATION.

(*Verses 166–175.*)

The closing verses of this long Psalm are in harmony with all that has gone before. The themes are the same, the prayers are the same, the purposes are the same. The Psalmist's one desire is to taste the fulness and sweetness of God's salvation, to know more of His Word, and to praise His name. Taking as our leading thought God's salvation we have—

I. The **nature** of that salvation (vers. 166–174).

1. *Personal rescue* (ver. 170).

2. *Divine teaching.* It is quite a mistake to suppose that salvation is exclusively a single act. It is a process as well. Man is delivered out of darkness into God's marvellous light; and to be saved from lapsing into darkness again, he must have the Divine Teacher near him, showing him how to walk in the light (ver. 171).

3. *Divine help* (ver. 173). Teaching alone is insufficient. Countless multitudes of even Christian people know the way, who, from lack of the help they ought to have, do not walk with firmness and consistency. Vain is the attempt to work out our own salvation without divine help. Thank God, that help is abundantly vouchsafed.

4. *Soul life* (ver. 175). This is the prime vital and all-essential characteristic of salvation. It is the synonym for it both in the Old Testament and the New. The unsaved soul is like the valley of dry bones, and dead in trespasses and sins. Salvation is not only deliverance from sin. It is the perpetual indwelling of the Divine and quickening Spirit.

II. The **conditions** upon which God saves.

1. *Obedience to God's commandments*

(ver. 166). But this is mere legality! Is it? Who said, "*Repent ye and believe* the Gospel." "Ye are My friends if ye do whatsoever I *command* you.

2. *Keeping and loving God's testimonies* (vers. 167, 168). What do they testify? God's love, God's mercy, God's willingness to save. How can God save? how can man be saved, unless it is the rejoicing of his heart to know and to keep the testimony that "God so loved the world," &c., "that God willeth not the death of the sinner"?

3. *Thankfulness for God's promises* (ver. 172). Unless man has these promises, and is grateful for them, he is unwilling to be saved, and even God cannot save the thankless soul. "The goodness of God" should lead to repentance and trust (Rom. ii. 4, 5).

4. *Choice of the right way and love of it* (vers. 173, 174). Our salvation largely depends on our own choice. God will not force it upon us. This choice must have respect to the ulterior duties of salvation. This choice must not be determined by fear, interest, but intelligent appreciation of what is best and love of it for its own sake.

III. The **characteristics** of the prayer for God to save. Those who desire salvation *must* pray, *will* pray. How?

1. *Hopefully* (ver. 166). Faith enters largely into the composition of evangelical hope. They have the same attributes as well as the same objects. Hope longs (ver. 174) with confident expectation.

2. *Sincerely* (ver. 168). The prayer of the hypocrite is an abomination to God. The man who prays for salvation must be prepared to display all his ways before God. He must conceal nothing, omit nothing.

3. *Intensely* (vers. 169, 170). "Cry." "Supplication."

4. *Availingly* (ver. 170). The divine promise was never pleaded in vain.

IV. The **obligations** of God's salvation. The one word twice uttered by the Psalmist reveals them all, "*Praise*," (vers. 171, 175). It was not personal blessing so much as the Divine glory.

THE LOST SHEEP.

(*Verse* 176.)

"The Psalmist begins with, 'Blessed are the undefiled in the way,' &c. He concludes with, 'I have gone astray,' &c. And thus conscious of the blessedness of those who are in the way of righteousness, he desires to be brought into it, that he may walk in newness of life. Verse *first*. It is a good way, and they are blessed who walk in it. Verse the *last*, 'Bring me into this way that I may be blessed.' And thus the Psalm in sentiment returns into itself; and the latter verse is so connected with the former as to make the whole a perfect circle."—*Dr. A. Clarke.*

The text may be applied with equal propriety to sinners and backsliders.

I. The **wandering**. Men, like sheep, have broken through the hedge of God's law, have forsaken the Shepherd and Bishop of their souls, and have gone astray into the paths of error and sin. "Like a *sheep*," *i.e.*, like a beast, an animal; for sin appeals to the lower instincts of humanity, and develops them, and so man sinks to the level of a brute. Mark, not like a lion or a horse, some noble or gifted creature, but like a poor, silly, unintelligent sheep. Why? Because sin is stupidity, and the sinner is no more a criminal than he is a fool.

1. *The wandering sheep displays the greatest folly.* Its safety, food, very existence, depends upon the shepherd's presence.

2. *The wandering sheep displays the deepest ingratitude.* It owes everything to the vigilance, sympathy, and activity of the shepherd.

3. *The wandering sheep displays but one symptom of intelligence, that of going astray.* If there be but one gap in the hedge he will find it. If the chances are a thousand to one against his straying, he will avail himself of it.

4. *The wandering sheep displays perseverance in straying.* If found to-day it will lose itself again to-morrow if it can. And once out of the fold it wanders on and on and never dreams of

returning till sought, found, and brought back.

Brethren, each one of us must say, "I have gone astray like a lost sheep." We have all gone astray ungratefully and foolishly from Him who alone can, and who alone has, vouchsafed all the benefits that we want and enjoy. In departing from God we have displayed an ingenuity worthy of a better cause. We have wandered where it has been perilous to wander, and have gone farther and farther from God, and from worse to worse, till we have become lost. Straying, men lose their owner, lose their fellows, lose themselves.

II. The **search**. The sheep having gone astray, what more natural than that the shepherd should go in search of it? So God is in search of lost men. "Christ came to seek and to save that which was lost."

1. *This search was the prompting of love.* The relation between the eastern shepherd and his sheep is very different from the western, and is fitly typical of God's relation to man. God loves man with an everlasting love, and cannot afford to lose him, the latest born in His vast household, and therefore preserves him with a love which many waters cannot quench.

2. *This search was pursued by the most wonderful self-sacrifice.* The shepherd seeking the sheep far from home, amidst winter snows, and among prowling beasts, and on dark and dismal nights, is very feeble as a symbol of God's search for man. Christ came to "lay down His life for His sheep." Such was His fixed intention, and such His accomplished purpose. "He loved me, and gave Himself for me."

3. *This search was rewarded by success.* Such was the case with the Psalmist. Such is the case of all who will be found. Here man is unlike a sheep. Its will cannot resist the more powerful will of its owner. Alas! man can resist God.

III. The **recollection**. "In all my wandering, with my consciousness of error, with my sense of guilt, I still *do* feel that I love Thy laws. They are the joy of my heart, and I desire to be recalled from all my wanderings that I may find perfect happiness in Thee and in Thy service evermore. Such is the earnest wish of every regenerated heart. Far as such an one may have wandered from God, yet he is conscious of true attachment to Him and His service; he desires and earnestly prays that he may be 'sought out' and brought back and kept from wandering any more."—*Barnes.*

THE SONGS OF DEGREES.
PSALMS CXX.–CXXXIV.

GENERAL INTRODUCTION.

The principal hypotheses on which to account for the "Songs of Degrees," "Songs of Ascents," "Pilgrim Psalms," and to each of which great names are attached, and each of which has something to say for itself, are as follows:—1. The songs of the pilgrims returning from exile (*Syr. Chrysostom, Theodoret*). 2. The songs chanted by the Temple worshippers on each of the fifteen steps of the Temple (*The Rabbins, Gospel of Mary, Vulg.*—*Luther, Grotius*). 3. Denoting some peculiar structure, a gradation of thought approaching a climax (*Gesenius, Delitzsch*). 4. A musical term denoting some peculiarity of rhythm or music (*Michaelis*, &c.). 5. And most supported songs for pilgrims making their periodical journeys to Jerusalem (*Ewald, Perowne, Hengstenberg*). The true interpretation probably is yet to be given, none of the above hypotheses completely answering the requirements of the case. Characteristics—"Sweetness and tenderness; a sad pathetic tone; an absence generally of the ordinary parallelism; and something of a quick trochaic rhythm."—*Speaker's Com.*

PSALM CXX.

INTRODUCTION.

This Psalm carries on its face the notion of individual and hardly bearable trial, more than that of national distress (opposition of foreigners to the rebuilding of the Temple, &c.). The trial is like that of David (1 Sam. xxi. 7, xxii. 9, &c., mentioned in the contents of A. V.), and is inflicted by a slanderous tongue. It is soothed by the recollection that God hears the cry of the suppliant, and answers it always. A difference of opinion exists respecting almost every word and verse.—*Speaker's Com.*

THE GODLY UNDER MISREPRESENTATION.

(*Verses* 1, 2.)

I. **That the godly are not exempt from misrepresentation.** Rather are they most subject to it. They of all men have characters *to lose*, and from their guilelessness and sincerity are most open to attack. A greater than the Psalmist said, "In the world ye shall have tribulation," and one of the keenest forms of tribulation comes from "lying lips and the deceitful tongue" (Matt. x. 24-28). The motives of the godly are misrepresented, their words, their actions. Misrepresentation exists in many forms, direct lying, suppression, innuendo, &c. No man can expect to be entirely free from it. The thing itself might be endured but for the senseless minds who take it in, and the bad hearts who rejoice to believe it. Misrepresentation in its worst form is that which is covered by professions of friendship to the person misrepresented.

II. **That the godly are distressed by misrepresentation**, and, humanly speaking, they may well be. No circumspection can guard against it. No force can destroy it. Its origin cannot always be traced. Some will even believe it to be true. It reaches those who can never be reached by its refutation. Always leaves its object open to suspicion.

" Whose edge is sharper than the sword;
  whose tongue   [breath
Outvenoms all the worms of Nile; whose
Rides on the posting winds, and doth belie
All corners of the world : kings, queens, and
  states,
Maids, matrons ; nay, the secrets of the grave,
This viperous slander enters."—*Shakespeare.*

III. **That the godly should cry to God in misrepresentation.**

1. *Because God knows all the facts of the case, and therefore judges righteously.* Slander should not affect a man whose conscience is clear in the sight of God. He is the Master to whom man stands or falls. Let men, therefore, commit their case to Him (1 Pet. ii. 24).

2. *Because the slandered and suspected soul naturally yearns to unbosom itself.* This it often dares not do to its dearest friend. Vehement vindication sometimes only gives rise to suspicions that there must have been something in it after all. The soul can tell its troubles to God without fear of this.

IV. **That God clears the godly from misrepresentation.**

1. *God enables His people to live slander down.* This is the only effectual refutation. Men who refuse to listen to the clearest vindication are compelled to recognise the *manifestation* of the truth, and the commendation of ourselves to every man's *conscience* (2 Cor. iv. 2, i. 12).

2. *God will vindicate them before the assembled universe*, when all shall be made manifest; and throughout eternity.

THE SELF-RETRIBUTIVE CHARACTER OF SLANDER.

(*Verses* 3, 4.)

"' What punishment shall be assigned thee, or what shall be done or added to thee, in recompense for misery caused ?' or, ' What shall (God) give unto thee, and what shall (He) add unto thee ?' Answer—'Sharp arrows (Ps. xlv. 5) wielded by a mighty one (Ps. cxxvii. 4 ; Jer. l. 9), and burning coals of juniper' (Ps. cxl. 10 ; Prov. xxv. 22). Thus the punishment of the slanderous tongue is appropriate ; for itself is a *sharp sword* (Ps. lvii. 4), a *pointed arrow* (Jer. ix. 8), and it *burns like hell fire* (Jas. iii. 6). The root of the *retem* or broom is used for fire in the desert, and retains its heat for a year."—*Speaker's Com.*

I. The **work** of slander. Like that which shall destroy it.

1. *To sting.* It is always hurtful, harassing, and annoying. It will always more or less damage the reputation, and inflict a wound on the mind or temper which will take some time to heal. Its sting often remains.

2. *To burn.* It sometimes blasts and utterly destroys. It has frequently undermined a man's character beyond recovery, and brought him down with grief, affliction, and poverty to an untimely grave.

II. **The retribution** of slander. The law of requital holds terribly good here.

1. *It is stung in return.* God's arrows fly thick and sharp upon the slanderous soul. He is ever in fear lest the lie should be traced back to its source, lest it should be proved to be a lie, and lest his calumny should miss its mark. He bears about him, too, the sharpest javelin in God's armoury— CONSCIENCE!

2. *It is consumed.* Society consumes the evil speaker and his speech. It sternly condemns him whether his mischievous tales are true or not, and avoids his company and leaves him in contempt to perish. His accumulated fears consume him; and he that maketh a lie inherits the hottest fire of God's wrath.

THE TRIALS OF THE GODLY.

(*Verses 5-7.*)

I. **Uncongenial neighbours.** The Psalmist's residence in Mesech and Kedar is probably not to be understood literally, as Mesech (Gen. x. 1) inhabited the mountain ranges south of and adjoining Caucasus, and the south-coast borders of the Black Sea, and Kedar was probably an Arabian tribe. They evidently stand for Barbarians. A man can hardly be subjected to a greater trial than to be compelled to mix in society with which he has no sympathy and which has no sympathy with him,—*e.g.*, a scholar with those who despise learning, an artist with those that have no taste, the pure with the impure, the sober with the profligate, and *vice versa*. So the Psalmist felt himself unhappy amongst men with whom he had no spiritual affinity. This is the case with the godly through all time. They dwell in a world that does not acknowledge their God, and with men who cannot appreciate their worth. Heaven is the place where all is harmony, and whose pursuits, &c., are congenial to all. Hell is the opposite.

II. **Unrighteous contradictions.** "They will listen to nothing. They are for discord, variance, strife. All my efforts to live in peace are vain. They are determined to quarrel, and I cannot prevent it. (*a*) A man should separate himself in such a case as the only way of peace. (*b*) If this cannot be done, then he should do nothing to irritate and keep up the strife. (*c*) If all his efforts for peace are vain, and he cannot separate, then he should bear it patiently as divine discipline. There are few situations where piety will shine more beautifully. (*d*) He should look with the more earnestness for the world of peace; and the peace of heaven will be all the more grateful after such a scene of conflict and war."—*Barnes*.

THE NATURE AND DOOM OF CALUMNY.

(*Verses 1-4.*)

The Israelites had returned from Babylon, and were engaged in rebuilding the demolished Temple at Jerusalem. The Samaritans—heathens by extraction, and still continuing heathens at heart — wished to join in the work. The devout Jews, thinking it out of place for any who did not fully acknowledge Jehovah to take part in so sacred an enterprise, quietly but firmly declined their overtures. Exasperated with the repulse, the Samaritans employed every means to annoy the workers, and to hinder the work. They concocted the vilest slanders, and sought to prejudice the mind of the Persian king, by whose permission the liberated Jews were allowed to rebuild the Temple. The Church of God is still assailed by the malice of the wicked. What they cannot accomplish by open violence, they seek to effect by the subtlety of the tongue.

Observe :—

I. That calumny is a terrible instrument of mischief. 1. *It is subtle in its insinuations.* "A deceitful tongue." It affects a reluctance to tell all it knows. It implies more than it openly states. It deals in half truths, or in a small modicum of truth, which it makes the pivot on which a whirlwind of the most pernicious slander revolves. It is eloquent in facial expression. A wink, a shrug of the shoulder, a little hieroglyphic finger-writing on the viewless air, a whispered innuendo, will insinuate more evil into the midst of a community than the most outspoken declamation. Calumny is cheating with the tongue. 2. *It is false in its representations.* "Lying lips." A liar does his mischief openly for the most part. Stung by a well-deserved rebuff, or prompted by a feeling of spontaneous hatred, he circulates the most flagrant falsehoods. The more barefaced the falsehood the less harm it does among the thoughtful. The consummate liar rings his own alarm bell, and the unprejudiced are sufficiently warned. But there is always a large class of people who will believe the most abominable lies : the more confidently and unblushingly they are uttered, the more firmly are they credited. The splenetic detractor is never at a loss for defamatory material. A word is falsely reported, an act misconstrued, a motive misread, and the whole plan of life misconceived. When all else is exhausted, the vile calumniator falls back upon the endless fabrications of a corrupt imagination. 3. *It is dangerous in its use.* It pollutes and debases those who traffic in it.

"Let falsehood be a stranger to thy lips ;
Shame on the policy that first began
To tamper with the heart to hide its thoughts !
And doubly shame on that unrighteous tongue
That sold its honesty and told a lie !"
—*Havard.*

It is pernicious in its effects on individuals, societies, and commonwealths. "A lie," says Carlyle, "should be trampled on and extinguished wherever found. I am for fumigating the atmosphere when I suspect that falsehood, like pestilence, breathes around me." The march of calumny is invisible as the wind, and often more terribly destructive.

II. That calumny is productive of acute suffering. 1. *It fills the soul with anguish.* "In my distress." It wounds the soul as with the barb of an envenomed arrow, and inflicts incredible pain. The distress is aggravated when we discover that the javelin is thrown by the hand of a professed friend. The discovery of treachery in human nature is a painful shock to the confiding. Calumny is not easily traced to its source, and is often difficult to refute. 2. *It mars the happiness of a life.* "Deliver my soul"— my life. The Psalmist felt that his whole life was endangered. Calumny has ruined the fairest reputation, embittered many a life, blasted its prospects, diverted its influence, and injuriously affected its destiny.

III. That calumny drives the soul to seek redress in prayer. 1. *The refuge of the calumniated is in God.* "In my distress I cried unto the Lord. Deliver my soul, O Lord, from lying lips." No man is safe from the shafts of falsehood. He cannot always refute it. He cannot prevent its effects on his reputation. Slanders may penetrate into regions where its refutation never comes. The sufferer can do nothing but commit his case to God, and trust to his own conscious integrity, the lapse of time, and the operations of Divine providence to clear his character. 2. *The cry of the calumniated is not in vain.* "He heard me." Prayer is the surest method of relief. The soul is comforted. Grace is given to act circumspectly, and to live down the false imputations. When Plato was told how his enemies slandered him, he quietly replied, "I fear them not. I will so live that no one shall believe them." In His own way, and at His own time, Jehovah vindicates His suffering people.

IV. **That calumny involves its perpetrators in severest vengeance.**

"What shall be done unto thee, thou false tongue? Sharp arrows of the mighty, with coals of juniper." The juniper sparkles, burns, and crackles more vehemently than any other wood, and is of such a nature that, if covered with ashes, it will continue alive the whole year. Fiery arrows, or arrows wrapped round with inflammable material, were formerly used in sieges to set the place on fire. The *Chaldee* has it:—"The strong sharp arrows are like lightning from above, with coals of juniper kindled in hell beneath." The tongue of the calumniator was often like a sharp, fiery arrow shot by a strong hand, causing intense and prolonged pain; but now the fierce, burning arrow of vengeance, shot by the Mighty One, has pierced the soul, and will rankle there in ever-increasing torture. The future retributive sufferings of the wicked will infinitely exceed anything they ever inflicted on their most helpless victims. Beware of indulging revenge. We may safely leave our oppressors to their merited punishment. "Speak not of vengeance; 'tis the right of God."

LESSONS:—1. *Calumny is the source of many evils.* 2. *The best of characters are liable to its most distressing assaults.* 3. *God will defend, sustain, and vindicate His people, and signally punish their calumniators.*

THE FEROCITY OF THE WICKED A SOURCE OF DISTRESS TO THE GOOD.

(*Verse* 5-7.)

Mesech refers to a barbarous race inhabiting the Moschian regions between Iberia, Armenia, and Colchis. From this people the Muscovites descended. Kedar describes the wild, restless, nomadic offspring of Ishmael, who occupied the territory of Arabia Petræa. The Psalmist did not personally reside in either Mesech or Kedar. The sixth verse gives the key to the sense in which the words are to be understood. He dwelt in the midst of a people as rudely barbarous, and as fiercely contentious, as those in Mesech and Kedar. The Church of God is now situated in the midst of a mass of gross wickedness that surrounds and assails it like an angry sea.

I. **That the Good are brought into Unavoidable Contact with the Wicked.**

There is no spot under heaven into which evil cannot penetrate. Go where we will it presses in upon us from every quarter. *The exigencies of life* will sometimes lead the godly into the company of the wicked. But for this, not only would commercial extension be impossible, but the humanising influence of social intercourse be lost to the world. *The Providence of God* may conduct His people into the midst of the wicked—to testify against their pernicious practices, to moderate their violence, to present a holy and beneficent example, to attract to a better life. The residence of the good among the habitations of the wicked is sometimes *compulsory*. Without any fault of their own they are banished from home and temple, and compelled to mingle with people whose principles they disapprove, and whose practices they detest. It is possible to be encompassed with evil, and yet not participate in it. As the fire-fly will pass through the flame without being singed, as fresh water currents circulate in the sea without partaking of its saline property, as the pearl is unimpaired by the unsightly shell in which it is clasped, so the good may move about in the midst of abounding wickedness without contamination.

II. That the attitude of the wicked is one of fierce antagonism to the good.

They hate peace—they are for war. The presence of the good is a perpetual rebuke to the wicked. Their simple transparency of character makes them conscious of the duplicity and blackness of their own; their pacific temper, instead of soothing, is made an occasion of ungovernable irritability. 1. *The antagonism of the wicked is prompted by a spirit of intense hatred.* "My soul hath long dwelt with him that hateth peace." Hatred is the great mischief-maker. It sets man against himself; against society; against God; against the universe. "A man," says Plato, "should not allow himself to hate even his enemies; because if you indulge this passion, on some occasion it will rise of itself on others; if you hate your enemies, you will contract such a vicious habit of mind, as by degrees will break out upon those who are your friends, or those who are indifferent to you." Hatred in the heart of the wicked is a fiend let loose. 2. *The antagonism of the wicked is unreasonable.* "I am for peace, but when I speak, they are for war." There are some restless, quarrelsome spirits, whom nothing will propitiate or pacify. If no provocation is given, they will invent one. Whatever efforts are made to promote peace, they construe into causes for new hostilities. They are like the Macedonians, of whom it was said, in the time of Philip, "To them peace was war, and war was peace." Such conduct is senseless and unreasonable.

III. That the ferocity of the wicked is a source of distress to the good. "Woe is me."

There is no greater pain to a tender, sensitive spirit, than to be brought in contact with prevalent wickedness. The most pathetic lamentations of Jeremiah were uttered when he beheld the moral degeneracy and violent discord of his countrymen. Evil is abhorrent in any aspect; but when it assumes the fierceness of a reckless, impetuous, and fiendish aggression, it is intolerable. To be compelled to dwell in the midst of the quarrelsome is a miniature pandemonium. Such an experience is often the means of discipline to the good. It teaches forbearance, patience, and self-control. It calls for the exercise of a spirit of god-like forgiveness and charity. It reveals the diabolic character of sin, and its inevitable tendency to transform men into demons.

Learn—1. *The universality of sin.* 2. *The greatest troubles of life are the result of sin.* 3. *A time is coming when the good will be for ever delivered from the assaults of sin.*

PSALM CXXI.

INTRODUCTION.

This "Song of the Ascents"—a title slightly varying from that of each of the other Gradual Psalms—is as suitable as any for the Israelite's use when not leaving his home for the earthly Jerusalem, but only meditating on the circumstances and prospects of his spiritual progress, especially when life is drawing to a close; but its beauties are more apparent if we regard it as bursting from the lips of the pilgrims as after their long, weary, and dangerous march, in spite of Mesech and Kedar, though not yet beyond their reach, they come at last in sight of the mountain range of Moriah and Zion. O joyful! Yonder is Jerusalem! There is the sheen of the Temple! Our journey is nearly over! Jehovah is appealed to by the Church or saint in the first three verses, and in the remainder answers and confirms His believing people.—*The Caravan and Temple.*

JEHOVAH THE REFUGE OF THE DISTRESSED.
(*Verses 1-4.*)

Wherever the devout Hebrew wandered, and whatever might be his condition, his eyes turned towards the mountain heights of his native Judea. In the distance those heights assumed the appearance of one vast mountain, on which there was a particular eminence that arrested the gaze of the eager worshipper, as if held by the spell of an irresistible fascination. This was Mount Zion, the consecrated hill of the Lord—the foundation on which He had built His Church, and the symbol of its permanency—the charmed circle of divinest manifestation — the central fountain from which streams of blessing have issued for the healing of the nations. As the mountaineer, pressed and worsted in the conflict, fled to his native hills for refuge and defence, so the suffering Israelite sought comfort and protection from Him "whose righteousness is like the great mountains."

Note.—I. That the soul is often placed in circumstances of distress.

Suffering is the commonest, yet most mysterious, feature of our human life. None are exempted. Heaven has no dispensations to grant to special favourites. Whatever differences there may be in mental endowments, wealth, or social position, there is, among all the descendants of Adam, an unavoidable, all-levelling communism in suffering. Apparent and numerous as may be the physical sufferings of mankind, there is a depth of mental distress of which the outer world knoweth not, and with which a stranger may not intermeddle. The hope deferred that maketh the heart sick; the collapse of undertakings that have cost days and nights of anxious thought and devoted labour; the wounds inflicted by unjust and mean insinuations, or by words barbed with envy and dipped in the venom of a heartless cruelty; the nameless pang of disappointment occasioned by the faithlessness of one we trusted, and to whom we knew not how far we had surrendered our heart till he flung it from him a pierced and bleeding thing—all these, and infinitely more, are hidden from the great world outside; they are beyond its power to assuage, or even to appreciate.

II. That in every time of distress Jehovah is an ever-available Refuge.

1. *His power is unbounded.* "My help cometh from the Lord, which made heaven and earth." The Creator of all can succour and defend all. The great forces of both worlds are under His control. He restrains their malignant, and multiplies their beneficent, ministries. However complicated our straits and pungent our grief, His power is all-sufficient. With such a refuge despair would be madness.

2. *His defence is invincible.* "He will not suffer thy foot to be moved." The sliding of the foot is an emblem of misfortune frequently used, and a very natural and suggestive one to the dweller in the Hebrew mountains, where a single slip of the foot was often attended with great danger (Psalm xxxviii. 16; lxvi. 9). The foundation on which the believer rests —the Divine power and goodness—is immovable, and while fixed on this basis his foot shall not be moved. The giddy whirl of pleasure; the artful devices of the tempter; the sombre tempest of calamities will, alike, be powerless to harm while he is circled by the Divine defence.

3. *His vigilance is unwearied.* "He that keepeth thee will not slumber. Behold, He that keepeth Israel shall neither slumber nor sleep." Sleep is necessary to repair the waste occasioned by toil. It is an indication of weakness and limitation. All mundane creatures sleep. God never sleeps. He knows no weariness. To Him there is no night; the darkness and the light are both alike to Him. Nothing can escape His eye. No enemy can secrete himself unnoticed; no ambush can surprise Him. The sentinel may slumber at his post; the steersman at the helm; the mother by the sick-bed; but God never slumbers. He is never exhausted; never inattentive to the condition of His people, or the wants of the universe.

III. That the most signal manifestations of Divine help are realised in the sanctuary.

"The hills from whence cometh my help." On those hills the Temple stood—the pride of the Hebrew, the marvel of the ages. There Jehovah localised His presence; there the ineffable glory hovered; there the people held sublime communion with their God; there were witnessed the brightest visions of His face; there were realised the strongest consolations of His love. The fondest, dearest memories of life cluster around the experiences of the sanctuary. The sad heart has there lost its burden; joy has been raised into a purer passion; the holy resolution been confirmed; and the future lit up with the kindling radiancy of hope. Who can estimate the loss to the worshipper of a single careless neglect of the service of the sanctuary!

IV. That the soul is delivered from its distress only as it turns to Jehovah.

"I will lift up mine eyes unto the hills." Help is not to be found in man. We cannot look to idols, or to the mighty, who, like hills, fill the earth, and raise their heads towards heaven. Truly, in vain is salvation hoped for from these hills (Jer. iii. 23). When all human help fails, with God nothing is impossible. To brood over our distress is to increase it. Our greatest distress comes when we wander farthest from God, and vanishes when we turn again to Him with a sincere heart.

LESSONS:—1. *Distress is never far to seek.* 2. *The Divine Refuge is open for all.* 3. *To receive timely help be always in your place in the sanctuary.*

Divine Protection.

(*Verses 5-8.*)

A celebrated traveller—after an absence of three years, during which he had walked across the continent of Africa from east to west, through vast regions never before trodden by the foot of the white man—recently received an enthusiastic welcome home. As he approached the quiet Kentish village where he had spent his boyish days, his first act, before entering his much-loved home, was to pass through the portals of the church where his aged father ministered, and, humbly kneeling, offer his devout thanksgiving to that God who had watched over and preserved him in all his wanderings. Among other appropriate Scriptures, this Psalm was read. It was a touching scene! Many hearts heaved with emotion, and many tears were shed, as the reader, in trembling accents, uttered the words, "The Lord is thy keeper. The Lord is thy shade upon thy right hand. The sun shall not smite thee by day, nor the moon by night. The Lord shall preserve thy going out and thy coming in from this time forth, and even for evermore." It was a graceful and fitting acknowledgment of that Divine Goodness which had safely conducted the weary, sun-burnt traveller through all the perils of his great and adventurous journey. We should be ever ready to acknowledge and adore the Gracious Power that shelters and protects us every moment. Observe—

I. The Divine protection is ample and efficient.

1. *It is ample.* "The Lord is thy shade." He surrounds His people, and guards them at every point of attack. Without His encompassing shadow they are exposed to the fierce onslaught of numberless enemies, and must become an easy prey to their violence. Where the danger is greatest, there the Divine shade is thickest. The foe must be able to pierce the invulnerable, and conquer the invincible, before he can touch the feeblest saint who is sheltered by the wings of God. 2. *It is efficient.* "Upon thy right hand." The right hand is the organ of action, either in aggression or defence. If that is paralysed, man is shorn of his main strength. As the enemies of God's people are ever standing at their right hand to frustrate all their efforts in well-doing, so Jehovah is at their right hand to encourage and sustain those efforts, and restrain their enemies. At the point where the forces of evil most thickly concentrate, there the Divine protection operates most powerfully.

II. The Divine protection shields from the most open assaults. "The sun shall not smite thee by day." To the inhabitants of the East, where the fierce rays of the sun are sometimes fatal in their effects upon the incautious traveller, these words would have a special significance. They also indicate figuratively the open dangers which threaten God's people every day, and the flagrant, cruel, persecuting hatred of their most furious enemies. "Dangers stand thick through all the ground;" but God is present to defend. The worker in the dismal mine, the traveller by road, or rail, or sea, the toiler surrounded by the most destructive materials, is alike under the shadow of the Divine protection.

III. **The Divine protection guards from the effects of the most secret treachery.** "Nor the moon by night." The moon is the ruler of the night; and everything belongs to it which happens during its reign, so that it is not necessary to trace all the evils of the night directly to the influence of the moon. The Lord will protect from all the subtle and invisible attacks of the wicked, though they come upon His people as silently and unseen as the penetrating cold of the moonlight night. He sees the approach of the least suspected danger, estimates the force of the subtlest influence, smiles at the treachery of His enemies, and disconcerts their cleverest combinations. The Divine Sentinel never slumbers. He can never be outwitted by the cunning of the most malicious.

IV. **The Divine protection is a defence against every evil.** "The Lord shall preserve thee from evil: He shall preserve thy soul." He protects from the evil of sin and of suffering. He turns away the evil that is feared, and alleviates and sanctifies the evil He permits. He will preserve the life (the soul) of His saints in war or peace—when the weapons of destruction hurtle through the air, or when disease silently sheds around its noxious poison. He will keep the soul from doing evil, cleanse it from all pollution, and invest it with a purity immaculate and fadeless.

V. **The Divine protection is realised amid the active duties of life.**
"The Lord shall preserve thy going out." The good man is directed in the *beginning* of his undertakings, and shielded by the Divine presence during their active prosecution (Deut. xxviii. 3-6). He is safe wherever his duties carry him—in the workshop, the street, the busy mart, on the restless sea, or in strange and distant countries.

"In foreign realms and lands remote,
  Supported by Thy care,
Through burning climes they pass unhurt,
  And breathe in tainted air.
When on the dreadful tempest borne,
  High on the broken wave,
They know Thou art not slow to hear,
  Nor impotent to save."
                    —*Addison.*

A moment comes when there shall be the last going out—the ebb of life when the soul shall go out with the tide, to return no more! Then shall it be enfolded with the Divine protection, and preserved in endless bliss.

VI. **The Divine protection overshadows the rest and quietness of home.** "And thy coming in." Better is the end of a thing than the beginning thereof. The Divine protection is not less exercised in the *conclusion* of any undertaking than in its commencement. Evening brings all home; and the weary one, after the toils and dangers of the day, enjoys the peace and rest of his home all the more because he knows he is encircled by the Divine guardianship. And when the shadows of life's eventide gather round him, he fears not. The Lord will preserve his coming in—his tranquil entrance into the heavenly home!

VII. **The Divine protection is unremitting.** "From this time forth and even for evermore." He is the continual portion and defence of all who trust in Him, in all places, at all times, in all actions, in life, in prosperity, in adversity, in death, in time, in eternity. No evil shall befall them to endanger their present and ultimate good. The safety of the Church and of every individual member is insured.

LESSONS :—1. *Offer grateful praise for the protection of the past.* 2. *Fear not the most furious assaults of the enemy.* 3. *Put all your confidence in the Divine Protector.*

PSALM CXXII.

INTRODUCTION.

This Psalm, which the title ascribes to David, was probably composed by him after he had settled the Ark in Mount Zion, to encourage the people to resort to Jerusalem to the three annual feasts, or to express his pleasure in observing that they did assemble there in great numbers. With how much greater joy ought Christians to embrace all opportunities of approaching God and assembling with His people in the more rational, spiritual, and edifying worship of the New-Testament Church!

THE JOY OF DIVINE WORSHIP.

(Verses 1, 2.)

This Psalm is a song on the entrance of the Church and State of Israel into a superior habitation. It seems to have been originally written in the interval between the translation of the Ark to Zion by David and the erection of the Temple there by Solomon. We may picture the multitudes of eager worshippers singing this song as they journeyed in companies from different parts of Palestine to the holy sanctuary of Zion. As they leave their homes, as in the morning they resume their march, as they approach the gates of the city, or as they pause within them and prepare to go up in solemn procession with music and song to the sanctuary, they unite in singing these words of joy and gladness. Observe—

I. That the joy of Divine worship is realised in anticipation. "I was glad when they said unto me" (ver. 7). The invitation to worship is met with an eager and joyous response, as though the soul had been pleasantly musing on the theme and was longing for the time of public worship to return. Much of our happiness in life, and of our misery too, are realised by anticipation. The same power by which we forecast the future and fill the mind with sombre pictures of coming calamities, may also be used to portray with the vividness of reality the exquisite pleasures which are yet to come. Prolonged absence from the sanctuary, whether from sickness or distance, gives piquancy to the spiritual appetite, and adds an additional charm to the prospect of soon joining again with the happy worshippers. The joy of the devout emigrant as he returns once more to his native village, is intensified by the hope of again worshipping God in the rustic temple with which are associated the happiest moments of his youth.

II. That the joy of Divine worship is enhanced when shared with others. "Let *us* go." Man can worship God alone, but he can worship Him better in company. The song of the solitary bird does not create such a tempest of tumultuous rapture as when it is blended with the summer-morning chorus of a thousand merry choristers, rising over brake and woodland. The journey of the pilgrim is not so long and tedious when it is prosecuted in the society of kindred spirits and enlivened with songs of gladness. Our worship of God will reach its highest joy when it is rendered in fraternal union with that great multitude which no man can number (Rev. vii. 9–12).

III. That the joy of Divine worship is most fully realised in the sanctuary. "Into the house of the Lord." Here Jehovah dwells, making His home in the hearts of the sincere worshippers. Here His majestic glory is displayed with overwhelming splendour. Here the mysteries of His providential dealings are explained. Here His will is made known with unmistakable plainness and emphasis, illustrated with the commentary of passing events. Here the worshipper has received his most memorable blessings—his fears have been banished, his murmurs silenced, his false ideas corrected, his faith invigorated, his soul tuned to harmony and love. The blissful associations of the sanctuary in the past assist the worshipper every time he visits the loved and sacred shrine. Many are thankful in the recollection of those whose advice and example led them to the sanctuary. The Christian mother of Gregory Nazianzen often begged her Pagan husband to join the Lord's people in their worship, but had to go without him for a long time. At last her remembered words were irresistible music to his spirit. In a dream, he repeated the first words of the Psalm: "I was glad when they said unto me, Let us go into the house of the Lord." The opposite had been the fact; but the dream would come to pass. Such happiness was soon his lot. He felt a longing to accept the Christian religion, and was soon able, when wide awake, to say the same words with literal truth.

IV. **The joy of Divine worship is abiding.** "Our feet shall *stand* within thy gates, O Jerusalem" (ver. 2). The joy of worship is satisfying and permanent: it remains with us when other joys have vanished—vanished like the bloom of a short-lived flower, like the picture of a pleasant dream, like the delicate tints of a lovely scene, like the sweet strain of an entrancing melody. David governed with his harp as much as with his sword and sceptre; and the songs of Zion which he taught his people to sing were a potent and constant influence in the formation and solidifying of the national religious life. The unceasing praise of Jehovah in the Heavenly Jerusalem will be an occasion of unceasing joy.

" In thy gates, O Jerusalem bright,
Have our feet often stood with delight:
And again shall they measure the way,
Till within them, enchanted, we stay."

LESSONS :—1. *The true praise of God is the highest worship.* 2. *The worship in the Church below begets a preparedness and fitness for worship in the Church above.* 3. *The highest worship is the unfailing source of the highest rapture.* 4. *Much spiritual loss is suffered by changing or neglecting the sanctuary.*

JERUSALEM A TYPE OF THE CHURCH OF GOD.

(*Verses* 3–5.)

I. **Because it is securely founded.** "Jerusalem is builded as a city that is compact together" (ver. 3). It was situate on a lofty eminence: it was strengthened till it became an impregnable fortress: it was beautified by a series of princely palaces: it was crowned by the most magnificent Temple: it was circled and invested by the Divine presence. So the Church of God has its basis in invulnerable truth: it is defended by the ablest intellects: it embraces the good of all ages: it has survived the wreck of the mightiest empires, and the rage of the most formidable enemies: it is overshadowed with the glory of God: it is dowered with a fadeless immortality.

II. **Because it is the place of general assembly.** "Whither the tribes go up, the tribes of the Lord" (ver. 4). 1. *There the will of God is made known.* "Unto the testimony of Israel." The ark was there, containing the tables of the law, the testimony of God's will and Israel's duty (Exod. xxv. 21, 22). In the Church of God, as in the Temple of Jerusalem, the Word of God is expounded and the individual path of duty clearly marked out. Obedience is encouraged by promises of blessing, and its failure threatened with corresponding punishment; and the law of God is an awful and imperishable testimony of the Divine faithfulness in each sphere. 2. *There the Name of God is worshipped.* "To give thanks unto the Name of the Lord." The Divine Name is the embodiment of the Divine perfections; and that mysterious Name is the legitimate object of all true worship. Thanksgiving is the essence of acceptable worship. "To give thanks" becometh a creature who is so absolutely dependent on the Divine bounty as man. Thanksgiving should be offered *humbly, fervently, constantly.*

III. **Because it is the seat of uni-**

versal government. "For there are set thrones of judgment, the thrones of the house of David" (ver. 5). It is a picture of combined and quiet strength. The pilgrims do not look upon a solitary throne, exposed and insecure; but see thrones, firm and safe, beneath and around David's, occupied simultaneously by his advisers, administrators, and magistrates, including his sons, all in his royal name and service (2 Sam. viii. 18; 1 Chron. xviii. 17). They behold a broadly organised and settled government. (*Vide* "The Caravan and the Temple.") From this metropolis of power all civil and ecclesiastical mandates must issue, and to it all classes were taught to look for justice. So the Church of God is the seat and centre of government. If justice is not found here, it can be found nowhere. And not justice only, but all that which government exists to promote and conserve—righteousness, peace, joy, love—these are the stable constituents and ornaments of the Divine throne.

LESSONS:—1. *The Church of God is the repository of the greatest mental and moral wealth.* 2. *A secure place in the true Church is gained only by a Divinely implanted moral fitness.* 3. *A member of the true Church is amenable to the Divine laws.*

PEACE AND PROSPERITY.

(*Verses* 6–9.)

I. **That peace and prosperity should be subjects of earnest prayer.** "Pray for the peace of Jerusalem: they shall prosper that love thee" (ver. 6). It is not in mortals to command success, nor is it always in the power of man to maintain peace in either Church or State. It is an Apostolic direction—*As much as lieth in you*, live peaceably with all men. But the best intentions are often misinterpreted, and, such is the perversity of the human mind, the very efforts made to promote peace are often the occasion of strife. The baffled mediator finds his readiest and most potent resource in prayer. All who truly love the Church of God will be constant and fervent in supplication for its peace and prosperity. Prayer succeeds when the most astute diplomacy fails.

II. **That peace and prosperity are correlative blessings.** "Peace be within thy walls and prosperity within thy palaces" (ver. 7). When peace takes its flight from a community or nation, prosperity soon follows: one depends upon the other. Nothing is prosperous with the man who is not at peace. The prosperity of the wicked is but temporary and apparent: it is for the present life only. It sows the seeds of discord and rebellion, and involves thousands in suffering and adversity. The man who strives to promote peace is a benefactor to the race. We should strive with others, as Lord Bacon says, "as the vine with the olive, which of us shall bear the best fruit; not as the briar with the thistle, which is the most unprofitable."

" A peace is of the nature of a conquest :
For there both parties nobly are subdued,
And neither party loses."—*Shakespeare*.

Peace is the condition of a permanent and increasing prosperity.

III. **That peace and prosperity are necessary for the cultivation of fraternal intercourse and affection.** "For my brethren and companions' sakes, I will now say, Peace be within thee" (ver. 8). The unity of a nation depends upon its loyalty to the Church of God; and the welfare of the Church is the measure of a nation's prosperity. Let Jerusalem be secure and blest, and the population generally will be secure and happy. How often is the peace of a home wrecked by the absence of love and harmony. A drunken husband, a scolding wife, a dissipated son, make sad havoc of what might be the happiest of homes. "As hatred by quarrels exposes the faults of others, so love covers them, except in so far as brotherly correction requires their exposure. The disagreements which hatred stirreth up, love allays; and the offences which are usually the causes of quarrel it sees as though it saw them not, and excuses them. It gives to men the forgiveness which it daily craves from God."

> "Love is the happy privilege of mind;
> Love is the reason of all living things.
> A trinity there seems of principles,
> Which represent and rule created life—
> The love of self, our fellows, and our God."
> —*Festus.*

IV. That peace and prosperity should be sought for the sake of the Church of God. "Because of the House of the Lord our God I will seek thy good" (ver. 9). In promoting the good of the Church, we promote our own best interests and those of all mankind. If we love God, we love His Church. We stand very much in the estimation of God according to our worth to His Church. The character of Eli is redeemed from much of its weakness and blame-worthiness, when we discover the tenderness and strength of his attachment. The brave old man bore up heroically when he was told the astounding news from the battle-field, that Israel was defeated and his own sons were among the slain; but when the messenger announced as the climax of his doleful tidings, that *the Ark of God was taken,* a deeper chord was touched than that of the patriot and the father, and, smitten to the heart, he fell backward and expired; and the sublimity that massed itself around the close of the aged prophet's career seemed to overshadow the feebleness and imperfections of his previous life. God will forgive a great deal to the man who helps—in gifts, in work, in witness-bearing, in sacrifices, in suffering—to promote the peace and prosperity of Zion.

LESSONS :— 1. *Sin is the fruitful source of war and poverty.* 2. *It is the mission of Christianity to confer a universal and permanent peace.* 3. *He prospers best who prays the most.*

PSALM CXXIII.

INTRODUCTION.

Since the time when it was produced by its now unknown author, when was not this hymn of hope a favourite with God's people? The pensive individual might use this form of meditation and prayer with comfort and edification in view of his private distresses; the tuneful company might probably beguile the way to or from Jerusalem with its plaintive cry; and it was fit to be chanted in the courts of Zion, in the name of the Church universal. After the afflicted pilgrims of Israel, in their successive generations, troubled Christians have repeated it in all countries; and it still describes the griefs and aspirations of the tempted servants of the Lord, as, in their various degrees, they "climb the steep ascent to heaven."—*The Caravan and Temple.*

THE HEAVENWARD GLANCE.

(*Verses* 1, 2.)

I. Is directed to One who is enthroned in glorious majesty. "Unto Thee lift I up mine eyes, O Thou that dwellest in the heavens" (ver. 1). From God's footstool of hills and altars the suppliant looks up into the face of the Master. "The Lord's throne is in heaven: His eyes behold, His eyelids try, the children of men" (Ps. xi. 4). All the glories of the upper world circle round that lofty throne, and borrow their meaning and their lustre from Him who sitteth thereon. To Him cherubim and seraphim continually do cry, "Holy, holy, holy is the Lord of Hosts." The starry constellations render Him ceaseless homage, and obey His mandate. The heavenly intelligences live in His smile, and rejoice in His service. The splendour of the greatest earthly monarch is extinguished by the glory of the Heavenly King. And it is to this glorious Ruler that man is permitted to direct his inquiring gaze, and from whom he must derive his mightiest help.

II. Is directed to One who has supreme government and power. "Behold, as the eyes of servants look unto the hand of their masters, and as the eyes of a maiden unto the hand of her mistress" (ver. 2). The Divine Hand —(1) *Guides.* The Eastern ruler, reticent and sparing in words, directs his attendants and agents by signs, and they are his best servants and least likely to incur sorrow who, not from fear but love, are swift to notice and obey the slightest movements of his speaking hand. The heart must be in the eyes that wait upon Jehovah.

" Leave to His sovereign sway
To choose and to command,
So shalt thou wondering own His way,
How wise, how strong His hand."

(2) *Supplies.* Servants look to their masters for sustenance (Prov. xxxi. 15). So must we look to God for daily bread, and for needed grace (Ps. cxlv. 16). (3) *Protects.* If the servant meet with opposition in his work, if he is wronged and injured, he looks to his master for protection. God is the shield of His people, not like the martial shield covering a portion of the person, but guarding every part (Gen. xv. 1, Ps. v. 12). When threatened by our spiritual foes, we look to God for shelter and protection. (4) *Corrects.* God smites with the same hand with which He guides and protects. *Harmer* observes—"As a slave ordered by a master or mistress to be chastised for a fault turns his imploring eyes to that superior till the motion of the hand appears which puts an end to the punishment, so our eyes are up to Thee, our God, till Thy hand shall give the signal for putting an end to our sorrows; for our enemies, O Lord, we are sensible, are only executing Thy orders, and chastening us according to Thy pleasure." It is wise for us humbly to submit to the mighty Hand of God. (5) *Rewards.* The hand of the world is filled with tempting rewards, but, like the fabled fruit of Sodom, they turn into bitter dust and ashes between the teeth of its votaries. But the faithful servants of Jehovah are rewarded with satisfying and endless pleasures.

III. **Is directed to One who is rich in mercy.** "The Lord our God, have mercy upon us" (ver. 2). Stung with a sharp sense of guilt, oppressed with the burden of multiplied troubles, and conscious of utter helplessness, the sinner turns a piteous gaze to Him whose mercy as well as righteousness endures for ever. "Lord, in trouble have they visited Thee; they poured out a prayer when Thy chastening was upon them" (Isa. xxvi. 16). The severity of God is tempered with mercy. " He delighteth in mercy."

IV. **Is persevering and triumphant.** "So our eyes wait upon the Lord our God *until* that He have mercy upon us" (ver. 2). The believing soul fixes its eye upon the Divine mercy, and keeps it there *till* the gracious answer comes. We remain unblessed for lack of steady fixedness in our faith. Persevering faith is ever triumphant.

LESSONS:—1. *Man must look heavenward for all true help.* 2. *God never disappoints the humble and sincere suppliant.*

SARCASM THE CAUSE OF PUNGENT SUFFERING.

(*Verses* 3, 4.)

I. **That sarcasm is a common weapon of the enemies of God.** 1. *It is used by the worldly-minded.* " The scorning of those that are at ease." When the Jews, who had returned from captivity, were engaged in rebuilding the Temple and city of Jerusalem, they were much tried by the interference of certain dwellers in Samaria, who seemed ready to declare themselves Israelites or Pagans, as it might suit their interests; and when they were rejected as unfit to engage in so sacred a work, they did all they could to hinder and annoy. They misrepresented the motives of the Jews to the Persian king, who then held rule over Palestine; and poured contempt and derision on the struggling patriots (Comp. Ezra iv. 1-3; Neh. ii. 19, 20;

iv. 1–4). "In every succeeding age the protesting and conservative faithful, the heart and bone of the undying Church, have been first courted, and then bantered and baffled by their worldly-minded and semi-heathen neighbours. The world about and among them, divided by rival idolatries, is united in jealousy, hatred, and scorn of the true Israel. The Samaritans will join the working church, if in so doing they may carnally benefit themselves; but when their help, which would be ruin, is not accepted, they unscrupulously hinder, misrepresent, and despise God's children" (*The Caravan and Temple*). 2. *It is used by the intellectually proud.* "And with the contempt of the proud." The scorner is deluded by the most despicable vanity. He assumes a superiority of knowledge, of virtue, and of authority over all others, of which all the time he is most lamentably destitute. Pride of intellect is the most dangerous form of self-deception, and the most hopeless of reformation.

"He that is proud eats up himself. Pride is
His own glass, his own trumpet, his own chronicle;
And whatever praises itself but in
The deed, devours the deed in the praise."
—*Shakespeare.*

It is easier to sneer than to argue and to scoff at goodness, than to imitate it.

II. **That sarcasm is the cause of pungent suffering to God's people.** "We are exceedingly filled with contempt." It is hard to bear the blame of a wrong of which we are wholly innocent, to have our holiest motives misinterpreted, our failings exaggerated, our best actions maligned, and our God insulted and blasphemed. The suffering is increased when the injured one is powerless to respond or retaliate, and when a sensitive and passionate nature is to be held in check while writhing under a sense of injustice and cruelty. When John Nelson, a vigorous and successful lay-helper of Wesley, was impressed as a soldier, he was subjected to very aggravating insults from a pompous young ensign. "It was very difficult to bear,' said the stalwart Yorkshire mason, "when I knew how easily I could tie the head and heels of the young stripling together." But suffering endured for Christ's sake is a very potent element in moral discipline, and in the perfecting of the Christian character.

III. **That the suffering occasioned by sarcasm is counterbalanced by the consolations of the Divine mercy.** "O Lord, have mercy upon us." The mercy of God never fails. From the inhumanity of man the tortured soul turns to the Divine mercy for comfort and strength. It then learns that the suffering occasioned by sarcasm is only brief in duration, and that it is made the means of attaining a higher righteousness and an ampler reward (Rom. viii. 28).

LESSONS:—1. *The holiest do not escape the attacks of the adversary.* 2. *The bitterness of sarcasm is its unscrupulousness.* 3. *The Divine mercy should be sought in every time of suffering.*

PSALM CXXIV.

INTRODUCTION.

This jubilant song speaks of a sudden peril and narrow escape, and praises God for the great deliverance. We take it to be, according to its title, a Psalm of David, not a hymn founded upon his character, writings, and history. It is full of his force and fire, suits not a few situations in which he shared the lot of Israel as herein described, and contains expressions parallel with words occurring in compositions of which he is the undoubted author. The figures employed describe the situation of God's people in any place or age, when they suddenly find themselves overtaken by calamity as if in the earthquake's jaws, when sorrow bursts upon them like the mountainous waves on a ship, when floods of ungodly men make them afraid, when they seem to feel in their flesh the teeth of slander and malice, when they are unexpectedly entangled in perplexities and difficulties, like the bird in the snare.—*The Caravan and Temple.*

THE INSATIABLE VORACITY OF THE WICKED.

(*Verses* 1-6.)

I. **That the wicked are ever ready to devour the righteous.** "They had swallowed us up quick" (ver. 3). "The Lord hath not given us as a prey to their teeth" (ver. 6). 1. *The righteous are assailed with the anger of the wicked.* "Men rose up against us; their wrath was kindled against us" (vers. 2, 3). The sight of virtue, however modest and inoffensive, will inflame the anger of the wicked. It is said of a certain lady that when the mirror revealed the wrinkles in her face she dashed it to the ground in a fury. So is it with the wicked; they are enraged with the transparency of a character in which they see reflected the moral deformities of their own. The anger of the wicked is *unreasonable*. It springs from the basest passions, and scorns all attempts to control it. It is like a rudderless vessel tossed about in a tempestuous sea. The anger of the wicked *recoils upon themselves*. Says the proverb, "Anger is like ashes which fly back in the face of him who throws them." Pope pithily observes, "To be angry is to revenge others' faults upon ourselves." 2. *The anger of the wicked is insatiable.* "Then the waters had overwhelmed us, the stream had gone over our soul: then the proud waters had gone over our soul" (vers. 4, 5). As the advancing tide carries everything before it, and sucks it back again into the capacious throat of the stormy sea, so the wicked pour out their anger like a flood, and would fain swallow up the righteous, on whom their fury is spent. But the anger of the wicked, though insatiable, is impotent to destroy the good. It is limited by power Divine, and may be made to minister to the Divine praise (Ps. lxxvi. 10).

II. **That the Lord is the Deliverer of the righteous.** "The Lord was on our side" (vers. 1, 2). More than ordinary help was needed on this occasion. The enemies were too fierce and too formidable for any human power to withstand. Jehovah champions the cause of the helpless; and when the last moment of extremity is come, He strikes in for victory. There is no waste of power with Him. When the sinner sinks down in despair, and gives up all for lost, then the Lord stretches forth His hand and saves. In this way He demonstrates the salvation to be Divine.

III. **That thanksgiving should be offered to the Lord for His delivering power.** "Blessed be the Lord, who hath not given us as a prey" (ver. 6). This is the leading sentiment of the Psalm. Let God have all the glory. He only is the Deliverer, and His help is all-sufficient. The grateful heart rejoices in rendering its praise to God; and in proportion to the depth of distress from which we are lifted up will be the reality and fervour of our thankfulness.

LESSONS:—1. *If the wicked had their way, every vestige of righteousness would be utterly destroyed.* 2. *The power of the wicked is divinely restricted.* 3. *The righteous have always some cause for grateful praise.*

THE SOUL'S ESCAPE FROM DANGER.

(*Verses* 7, 8.)

I. **That the soul is surrounded by many dangers.** "As a bird, the snare of the fowlers" (ver. 7). 1. *It is ensnared by worldliness.* One of the most gigantic dangers against which God's people have specially to guard—an enemy to all spirituality of thought and feeling. 2. *It is ensnared by selfish-ness*—a foe to all simple-hearted charity, to all expansive generosity and Christian philanthropy. 3. *It is ensnared by unbelief*—the enemy of prayer, of ingenuous confidence, of all personal Christian effort. These are not imaginary dangers. We meet them in every-day life. They threaten us at every point, and often have we to lament over the havoc they make in our hearts.

II. **That the dangers surrounding the soul are not invincible.** "The snare is broken, and we are escaped" (ver. 7). 1. *May be overcome by watchfulness.* 2. *By prayer.* 3. *By obedience.* And yet all our endeavours will fail, if we depend on *them* rather than on God. We cannot boast of our natural powers. "What pride has a bird in its wings and feathers when once caught in the silken thread, or fast in the golden wire? However splendid their endowments, only God can deliver souls from evil, and keep them free."

III. **That a way is divinely provided for the escape of the soul from all danger.** "Our help is in the name of the Lord, who made heaven and earth" (ver. 8). Here we learn that the name of Jehovah is the source of help, and that this help is omnipotent. He "who made heaven and earth" is infinite in resources: all the forces of the universe are within His view, and obedient to His nod. "We may not see any peril, when our safety is to let our Saviour see for us. We only see beautiful shrubs and shadowy trees. He who is on our side sees the foe behind them in ambush. We only see the pleasing bait on a bosom of shining grass and showy flowers. Our constant Friend sees there the hidden trap. We only see the smooth turf inviting our feet, tired of ruts and stones. He who is yet for us sees the pit artfully concealed. We only see the glancing water and the smiling sky. Our Keeper sees the hurrying squall, and cries, "Beware! take in sail" (*The Caravan and Temple*). As we look back upon the past, we see that our help in extremity has come from Jehovah. In Him, therefore, may we place implicit confidence for the future.

LESSONS:—1. *Our greatest dangers are those we least suspect.* 2. *The utmost vigilance does not always avail.* 3. *The only reliable help is from God.*

PSALM CXXV.

INTRODUCTION.

This Psalm belongs most probably to the times after the Captivity, and has been applied, with apparent propriety, to the opposition which Sanballat the Horonite, Geshem the Arabian, and Tobiah the Ammonite gave to the Jews while employed in rebuilding the walls of Jerusalem and restoring the Temple. It is designed to encourage and comfort God's people in all ages against the plots and malice of their enemies. The three prominent themes are danger, defence, and duty; and every verse contains a word descriptive of those for whom the Songs of Degrees were intended, and of the militant Church in every age and country. They are called Israel, the good, the upright in their hearts, the righteous, the people of Jehovah, they that trust in the Lord.

THE PRIVILEGE AND SECURITY OF THE GOOD.

(*Verses* 1, 2.)

I. **It is the privilege of the good to trust in the Lord.** "They that trust in the Lord." Man cannot trust himself; he is too conscious of personal weakness and infirmity. He cannot trust in others; he has been too often disappointed and deceived. He finds true rest, comfort, and peace by trusting in the Lord, the All-Perfect, the All-Powerful, the All-Sufficient One. This trust should be unhesitating and complete.

"Thy God hath said 'tis good for thee
To walk by faith and not by sight:
Take it on trust a little while,
Soon shalt thou read the mystery right,
In the bright sunshine of His smile."
—*Keble.*

II. **It is the security of the good to be guarded by the Divine Presence.** 1. *The Divine Presence is the guarantee of stability.* "Shall be as Mount Zion, which cannot be removed, but abideth for ever" (ver. 1). Zion was a mountain, built upon and surrounded by other mountains: to all natural appearance it was immovable. But the spiritual Zion is still more stable and enduring. It rests on the mountains of unchallengable truth, and is bound together by the invisible bands of Divine safeguards.

2. *The Divine Presence is an impregnable defence.* "As the mountains are round about Jerusalem, so the Lord is round about His people" (ver. 2). Jerusalem was fortified by nature; it was situated on a rocky elevation, and, with the exception of a small space to the north, was encircled by deep valleys, and these again were protected by an amphitheatre of hills. The situation was such as to be easily rendered impregnable; but the most impenetrable rampart was the Divine presence. While this hovered over the city, it defied the skill and prowess of the mightiest armies; when it was withdrawn, the hills and valleys were of no avail; Jerusalem was laid low by the hand of the Assyrian and the Roman. Jehovah surrounds His people with an unpierceable shield. He is above, beneath, around them; they defy the fury of the foe.

III. **The security of the good is perpetual.** "From henceforth, even for ever" (ver. 2). Mountains may crumble and come to nought, and the rocks be removed out of their place, but God's promise to His obedient people cannot be broken, nor will His protecting care be withdrawn. (Isa. liv. 10). While they keep within it their fortress is impregnable, and they can suffer no evil. The security of the good reaches its highest realisation in the heavenly Jerusalem.

LESSONS:—1. *There is no true goodness apart from trust in God.* 2. *Faith in God will give strength in temptation and victory in conflict.*

THE TYRANNY OF THE WICKED TRANSIENT.

(*Verse 3.*)

I. **That the rule of the wicked is one of tyranny.** "The rod of the wicked upon the lot." When Israel reached its highest point of wealth and influence under David and Solomon, there were many who coveted possession of its rich inheritance. The sceptres of the Babylonians, Romans, and Mohammedans often fell upon Zion, like the rod of a merciless oppressor. "What was signified in their assaults and successes? The rod of sin, in the power and authority of the outward oppressor, often answered to the ascendancy of iniquity in the heart of Jerusalem. The prevalence of spiritual wickedness within Israel attracted the earthly tyranny of heathenism outside. God was working in every instance, using the rods of wickedness for the probation and punishment of those who ought to have been righteous; and He still chastises sinners by means of sin; their own inviting wrath, and that of aliens inflicting it—thus extirpating iniquity, purifying and preserving the Church, and making unfaithfulness and apostacy praise Him."
—*The Caravan and Temple.*

II. **That the tyranny of the wicked is transient.** "The rod of the wicked shall not rest upon the lot of the righteous." The righteous may not always escape the rod of the oppressor. "They that will live godly in Christ Jesus must suffer persecution." The mailed hand that smote shall not *rest* on its victim. The triumph of the wicked is short. The reign of terror cannot be permanent. It wearies and disgusts its most brutal agents. It breeds a rebellion which erelong overthrows its power. The fierceness of tyranny consumes itself.

III. **That the unchecked tyranny of the wicked would be a serious discouragement to the righteous.** "Lest the righteous put forth their hands unto iniquity." If the wicked had absolute sway religion would soon become extinct. The professor would become weary of a cause that involved unmitigated suffering, and would be tempted to give it up. His faith would become demoralised, and he would cast off God, thinking he was forsaken of Him. In a moment of despair he would adopt unlawful means to rid himself of his misery (Eccles. vii. 7). But the Lord proportions trial according to the strength of the sufferer, and never permits it to remain longer than required to accomplish a beneficent purpose (Isa. x. 24–26).

LESSONS:—1. *The policy of the wicked is short-sighted, and defeats itself.* 2. *True goodness cannot be crushed by oppression.* 3. *The Lord knows the right moment in which to deliver from the tyranny of the wicked.*

THE OBEDIENT AND THE APOSTATE CONTRASTED.

(*Verses* 4, 5.)

I. **That the obedient are sustained by a consciousness of personal rectitude.** "Them that are upright in their hearts" (ver. 4). The holy principle imparts uprightness of heart and prompts to uprightness of life. The way of holiness is straightforward; there are no windings and turnings in it. Job was an upright man, one who feared God and eschewed evil; and his conscious integrity bore him up under the unparalleled trials that fell upon himself, his family, and his possessions. When the sense of right becomes dim in the soul, the man gives way and is lost.

II. **That the obedient enjoy the Divine aid and blessing.** 1. *Their goodness is Divinely strengthened.* "Do good, O Lord, unto those that be good" (ver. 4). Goodness intensifies the desire for more; it claims the fulfilment of the Divine promises; it lays hold on the power of God. "Truly God is good to Israel, even to such as are of a clean heart" (Ps. lxxiii. 1). The rod of the oppressor has been used as a trowel by the wise Master Builder in restoring and strengthening His spiritual temple. 2. *Their very troubles shall result in peace.* "But peace shall be upon Israel" (ver. 5). While those who apostatise from God meet with punishment and ruin, the faithful shall find that their distresses will issue in a permanent and more hallowed peace. The calm that succeeds the furious tempest is all the more soothing and refreshing because of the terrors and tumults of the previous storm. The prayer for peace in Psalm cxxii. is here answered. This is what comes of serving God, and trusting in His defence. Peace is an unspeakable blessing to the empire, the church, and the individual. Peace in its widest range of meaning and blessing is the special gift of Christianity (Eph. ii. 14).

III. **That the apostates will be certainly punished.** 1. *By their own tortuous policy.* "As for such as turn aside unto their crooked ways" (ver. 5). The unfaithful get into the spirit of the world, and are warped into its crooked and winding ways. They twist about to conceal their base intentions, to accomplish their sinful purposes, or to elude punishment for their crimes; but disappointment, confusion, and misery overtake them. "No sufferings in God's service are reasons for unfaithfulness and apostacy. His grace makes us able to drink whatever cup His providence administers. At the worst, it is death; and then the worst is best." 2. *By an act of Divine justice.* "The Lord shall lead them forth with the workers of iniquity" (ver. 5). As malefactors are led to the place of execution. The justice of God binds Him to punish sin. The apostate will exchange the lot of the righteous for the heritage of evil-doers.

LESSONS:—1. *There is an eternal distinction between right and wrong.* 2. *Jehovah is the friend of the upright, and the foe of every worker of iniquity.* 3. *The most consummate hypocrite will be exposed and punished.*

PSALM CXXVI.

INTRODUCTION.

This Psalm was penned with reference to some great deliverance of the people of God out of bondage and distress, most likely their return out of Babylon in Ezra's time. It is very beautiful and highly descriptive of the circumstances which it represents. The liberation of the captive Hebrews was a type of the redemption of the human race, and the return to Zion of such as improved their opportunity a figure of the salvation of believers.

DELIVERANCE A THEME FOR JOYOUS SONG.

(*Verses* 1-4.)

I. Because of the misery from which it emancipates. "The Lord turned again the captivity of Zion" (ver. 1). To a free and privileged people it is a painful indignity to be robbed of liberty and treated as slaves. Though the captivity of the Jews in Babylon might not be marked by any acts of cruelty, it was suffering keen enough to feel they were in bondage at all. But, lo! how real, how degrading, how miserable is the slavery of sin. To liberate from sin is a Divine work. The LORD must turn again our captivity.

II. Because of its unexpectedness. "We were like them that dream" (ver. 7). The deliverance was so unlooked for, and came upon them with such a surprise that it seemed more an illusion than a reality. But when the full meaning of the event dawned upon them, their joy knew no bounds. A similar incident is recorded by Livy, when the Romans, having conquered Philip of Macedon, restored liberty to all the Grecian cities. The proclamation was made by the herald in the midst of the circus when a vast multitude of the Greeks were assembled to witness the Isthmian games. The people were so stunned with the news that they could scarcely believe their own ears. They "were like them that dream." But when, at their request, the proclamation was repeated, and the glad tidings thus confirmed, they shouted and clapped their hands with such vigour as showed how heartily they appreciated the blessing of liberty. The Lord often surprises and gladdens His people with His marvellous deliverances.

III. Because of its reviving effects. "Turn again our captivity, O Lord, as the streams of the South" (ver. 4). Accomplish our deliverance, as well in delivering of our brethren which are yet remaining in Babylon, as in fulfilling of ours, who yet lie languishing under grievous burdens; that it may be such a comfort and refreshing to us as watering is to dry and desolate places, which are refreshed and flourish again by the coming in of running streams (*Diodati*). Drought and barrenness disappear under the showers of Divine blessing; and the Church is quickened with new life and hope.

IV. Because of the irrepressible gladness it occasions. "Then was our mouth filled with laughter, and our tongue with singing" (ver. 2). It was like being in a new world. Our deliverance came upon us with such a surprise, that we could not contain ourselves. We burst into a transport of rapture, and laughed and sung in turns with delirious joy. The heathen, who had rejoiced in our captivity, noticed the gladness occasioned by our deliverance, and acknowledged its Divine source. "Then said they among the heathen, The Lord hath done great things for them" (ver. 3). How much more is our deliverance from sin and death the theme of endless rejoicing and praise!

V. Because of its evidence of the Divine mightiness. "The Lord hath done great things for us; whereof we are glad" (ver. 3). The predictions of Isaiah and Jeremiah were fulfilled (Isa. lii. 9, 10; Jer. xxxiii. 10, 11). The Lord has more pleasure in exerting His power to deliver His people than in creating a world, or in sustaining the whole fabric of existing things.

"'Twas great to speak a world from nought,
'Twas greater to redeem."

LESSONS:—1. God is not unmindful of His captive people. 2. Deliverance is near when we least suspect it. 3. Every act of Divine deliverance is an occasion for joyous praise.

SOWING AND REAPING.

(Verses 5, 6.)

Sowing and reaping, tears and laughter, are never far asunder in a world like this. The Jews who escaped the captivity of Babylon were not without their trials. The joy of deliverance was sobered by their toils and difficulties. Their journey to Zion was long, wearisome, and full of peril. When they reached their beloved country it was to find it a wilderness waste—Jerusalem and its Temple in ruins. How great must be the labour and sacrifice, and how long the period before the city could be restored and the Temple once more erected. Pestered by violent enemies, and invaded by bands of roaming robbers, it was with trembling the Hebrew husbandman ventured into the field and hastily buried the grain, not knowing whether he or the enemy would reap the harvest.

It is ever so in every work we do for God—the tears of anxious labour give place to the gladness of success. "Toiling, rejoicing, sorrowing; onward through life we go." Observe—

I. That the time of sowing is often attended with anxiety and sorrow. "They that sow in tears: he that goeth forth and weepeth, bearing precious seed."

1. Because of the high estimate we have formed of the value of the seed sown. "Precious seed." The teacher of God's holy Word, whether from desk or pulpit, cannot be too strongly imbued with the unspeakable value of the Divine treasure which is thus put into earthen vessels. The views that are sometimes caught of the grandeur and appropriateness of the Divine Word are overwhelming; and the human vehicle trembles with fear lest the truth should lose any of its Divine force and meaning in transmission—in the act of sowing.

2. Because of the toil involved in becoming possessed of the seed. The greatest prizes of life are not obtained without pains. The blessing that does the most in elevating and perfecting the human soul, and in conferring the greatest good on others, is secured only after numberless failures and infinite efforts. No wonder that is "precious" to man which has cost him so much. The gardener values the plant the more which has involved so much care in bringing to its present state of perfection and beauty.

3. Because of the meagre results witnessed in comparison with the effort put forth. True worth is not always appreciated. It is the fate of every man who raises himself by his talents and industry above the common level to be abused and hated by those whom he has eclipsed. Joseph was envied by his brethren, and David was persecuted by his. Jeremiah, the weeping prophet, who bewailed the fallen fortunes of Jerusalem, and whose fate was like Cassandra's, always to speak truth but never to be believed, pathetically exclaimed, "O my mother, thou hast borne me a man of strife!" (Jer. xv. 10). And it is often cause of bitterest sorrow to the Christian worker that so few accept his testimony, or understand the nature and drift of his most unselfish labours.

II. That the time of reaping is one of inexpressible joy. "Shall reap in joy: Shall doubtless come again with rejoicing, bringing his sheaves with him."

1. Because it is the realisation of patient hope. The man who blossoms suddenly into a genius has often been toiling and suffering for years in obscurity, though assured in himself his day of triumph would come. There is a kind of prophetic instinct in great minds that tells them of the bright prospects in reserve for them, and whispers to them the secret of their after great-

ness. In early youth, Joseph saw by anticipation his sheaf higher than all the sheaves of the field, and the sun and moon and the eleven stars bowing down to the soles of his feet. Nelson, stung by the neglect of his superiors to his professional claims, said, "I shall one day have a gazette to myself"—and he had. Raffaelle, in youth, triumphantly exclaimed, "I, too, am a painter;" and posterity endorsed the estimate he had formed of himself. It is with every true work, as with every true worker: patient waiting and working will bear fruit in joyous success.

2. *Because it brings blessing to many for whose welfare we have been painfully concerned.*

3. *Because it is an additional evidence of the Divine faithfulness* (Isa. lxi. 11).

LESSONS:—Here is encouragement—1. *To the Christian thinker;* 2, *the true patriot;* 3, *the faithful preacher;* 4, *the Sunday-School teacher;* 5, *the anxious parent.*

PSALM CXXVII.

INTRODUCTION.

Various considerations taken together require the opinion that this middle Song of Degrees was composed by Solomon. It suits the time of peaceful house-building and civil settlement and progress during which he reigned. It uses a word answering to his name Jedidiah, meaning beloved of the Lord, and seems in connection with it to refer to the promise made to him of wisdom, riches, honour, and length of days. "So He giveth His beloved sleep," or to His beloved in sleep (2 Sam. xii. 25; 1 Kings iii. 5-15). It appears to suggest that the claims of the Temple to the efforts of builders are superior to those of any other intended erection. And it agrees with Solomon's sententious style in his proverbs. The ambitious may not boast of their own wisdom and might; and the prosperous may not suppose they are self-sufficient. It is God who gives skill to plan and ability to execute. He is the Source of blessing.—*The Caravan and Temple.*

THE HAPPINESS OF SOCIETY DEPENDENT ON THE DIVINE BLESSING.

(*Verses* 1, 2.)

I. That family greatness should be founded in the Divine blessing. "Except the Lord build the house, they labour in vain that build it" (ver. 1). It has been the ambition of many to found a family and to hand down a name to posterity. The love of posthumous fame is a mania with some men. But if God be ignored and the law of righteousness disobeyed, the most colossal efforts to raise a distinguished and enduring house, though protected by all the laws that the ingenuity of the legislature can invent, will prove futile. The history of the changes that have taken place among the families of some of our old nobility furnishes some of the saddest and most humiliating revelations of social life.

II. That the safety of civil society is secured by the Divine blessing. "Except the Lord keep the city, the watchman waketh but in vain" (ver. 1). It is sometimes a marvel with some how the vast populations of our large cities are *fed*: it is no less a marvel how they are *protected*. Around the masses of society is drawn the strong cordon of Divine law, and over all there rest the ample wings of the Divine protection. If the Lord were to withdraw His presence, the vigilance of the police and the utmost alertness of the civic authorities would not avail. Society would be unendurable, indeed impossible, as at present constituted, but for the action of our Divine Guardian. How much less can a spiritual commonwealth be reared or preserved without the blessing of God!

III. That the prosperity of society is dependent on the Divine blessing.

1. *Labour is useless without the Divine blessing.* "It is vain for you to rise up early, to sit up late, to eat the bread of sorrows" (ver. 2). Labour is the

prime necessity of man and the first condition of prosperity. The most princely fortunes have sprung from toil, and are kept together by it. A wealthy farmer when asked why he should trouble himself to rise so early as he did, replied—"If you want the world you must rise and seek it, and if you have the world you must rise and keep it." Often more anxious labour is involved in taking care of this world's goods than was spent in first acquiring them. And yet no amount of labour, no amount of parsimonious care will suffice, if God withhold His blessing.

"Except the Lord conduct the plan,
The best concerted schemes are vain,
And never can succeed;
We spend our wretched strength for nought:
But if our works in Thee be wrought,
They shall be blest indeed."

2. *Rest is a Divine gift.* "For so He giveth His beloved sleep" (ver. 2). Sleep is half meat; it is the most beneficent medicine of wearied and suffering humanity. "The sleep of a labouring man is sweet, whether he eat little or much; but the abundance of the rich will not suffer him to sleep" (Eccl. v. 12): if he eat much when he ought to eat little, or if his plenty be a load upon his conscience, or if his godless puzzle day and night be how to retain. The man loved of God may lie down in peace and sleep. Prosperity brings no joy to him who cannot sleep.

LESSONS:—1. *Jehovah is the founder, defender, and preserver of the family, the State, and the Church.* 2. *The happiness of society rests, not on the wisdom and toil of its most gifted members, but on the Divine blessing.*

CHILDREN THE GIFT OF GOD.

(*Verses* 3–5.)

I. That children are the gift of God. "Lo, children are an heritage of the Lord; and the fruit of the womb is His reward" (ver. 3). This view is frequently and emphatically stated (Gen. xxx. 2, 18; xxxiii. 5; xlviii. 9; Deut. vii. 13; Prov. xix. 14). The gift of children is an evidence of the Divine favour. They are to be welcomed with joy and affection, and not to be regarded as an encumbrance and a burden. The childless pair, whatever worldly affluence they possess, feel that one of heaven's choicest gifts is withheld. It is a most unenviable home, if *home* it can be called, where a child is unwelcome.

II. That children are to be firmly and judiciously trained. "As arrows are in the hand of a mighty man; so are children of the youth" (ver. 4). They are a sacred trust and solemn responsibility: not to be weakly fondled or foolishly spoilt; but to be wisely, kindly, and strictly disciplined to obedience and duty. "Parents must not trifle with their children, like idiots playing with sharp tools; but as the bowman straightens and polishes his arrow, gives it a solid point and wings it with proper feathers, they must educate their sons and daughters in the name, and with the help of the Rewarder of them that diligently seek Him." The arrows that are not prepared and directed when in the hand, may, when they are gone abroad into the world and all parental training is too late, prove arrows in the heart.

III. That a large family is a source of domestic joy. "Happy is the man that hath his quiver full of them" (ver. 5). The parents live over again the happy period of their youth in the gambols and laughter, and the indescribable "little ways" of their children. It is a dismal house where there is a silent nursery. It may be scrupulously clean and faultlessly prim, but there is a strangely felt absence of life, of voice, of genial humanity. When the father of John Wesley received his son unscathed from the window of the burning parsonage, he exclaimed, "Come, neighbours, let us kneel down; let us give thanks unto God: He has given me all my eight children; let the house go, I am rich enough." The good children of a large family help one another, and are a source of comfort and support to their aged parents.

IV. That children are the strength and defence of the home. "They shall not be ashamed, but they shall speak with the enemies in the gate" (ver. 5). The parents shall courageously plead their cause in courts of judicature, which were held at the gates of cities, not fearing to be crushed by the might of their adversaries, as weak and helpless persons frequently are. Or, as some understand the words, the children shall not be ashamed to plead for their parents in the gates, but will be ready at all times to appear for them, to answer any charge, and to vindicate them in their persons, their good name, or their property. The Chinese have a proverb—"When a son is born into a family, a bow and arrow are hung before the gate." In Eastern books sons are spoken of as the arrows of their fathers. People fear to offend a family where there are many sons, lest the arrows should be sent at them. The training of children has a reflex influence for good upon parents. Many a hint is unconsciously given as to "training up a *parent* in the way he should go."

LESSONS:—1. *A large family has its cares, but it has also its special rewards.* 2. *The training of children is also a training of the parents.* 3. *Children may become the greatest blessing, or the greatest curse.*

PSALM CXXVIII.

INTRODUCTION.

This, like the former, is a Psalm for families. In that, we were taught that the prosperity of our families depends upon the blessing of God; in this, we are taught that the only way to obtain that blessing which will make our families comfortable, is to live in the fear of God, and in obedience to Him. It is thought by many to have been sung at the marriages of the Israelites, as it is a part of the matrimonial service used in modern times.

THE BLESSEDNESS OF THE GOOD.

(*Verses* 1-6.)

I. That the blessedness of the good is the result of a holy life. 1. *A holy life begins in the fear of God.* "Blessed is every one that feareth the Lord" (ver. 1). Not the shuddering fear of conscious guilt. Not the fear of the hypocrite, or the formalist. But the fear that arises out of a profound reverence and love of God. This fear of the Lord is the beginning of wisdom. 2. *A holy life is maintained by constant obedience.* "That walketh in His ways" (ver. 1). As Comber remarks—"He only truly fears God who is afraid to displease Him by forsaking the paths of His commandments." Loving fear is the strongest motive to obedience; and obedience is the practical manifestation of true piety. That is a happy home indeed where the fear of God is the regulating principle.

II. That the blessedness of the good consists in a happy and contented livelihood. "For thou shalt eat the labour of thine hands: happy shalt thou be, and it shall be well with thee" (ver. 2). Some men labour and worry, and all in vain. They are never any better off, and they have no enjoyment in the fruit of their labour. But the good man, though not exempt from toil, is happy in his daily work, and enjoys what he earns. The fruit of his labour is not taken from him and possessed by others, as was threatened to the disobedient Israelites (Deut. xxviii. 33, 38–40; Lev. xxvi. 16). "Noble, upright, self-denying toil," wrote Hugh Miller, "who that knows thy solid worth and value would be ashamed of thy hard hands, thy soiled vestments and thy obscure tasks, thy humble cottage and hard couch and homely fare!" Religion gives dignity to labour, and transmutes what was originally a part of man's curse into a blessing.

III. That the blessedness of the good is found in the joys of domestic life. "Thy wife shall be as a fruitful vine by the sides of thine house: thy children like olive plants round about thy table" (ver. 3). The woman pictured in the Song is not to be seen lounging at the door, an idle gossip, with something to say to every passer-by, but attends to her duties in the interior of the dwelling, and, like her husband, fears the Lord (Prov. ix. 13, 14; Amos vi. 10). The clinging vine is a symbol of attachment, grace and fruitfulness, dressing the props and walls to which its curling tendrils hold with leaves that shade the verandah and cool the house, and enriching them with clusters of juicy fruit that maketh glad the heart of man. The pious and loving wife, the screen, adornment, and crown of the God-fearing husband, who is her support and strength, so smiles and speaks and acts that the master is happy everywhere because most happy when at home. The children are like olive-plants—vigorous, able to stand alone and separate, bright with the promise of goodly fruit and rivers of oil. Rooted to the spot, glad to stay at home, "round about thy table," loving and dutiful, they shall abundantly delight thy heart.—*The Caravan and Temple.*

IV. **That the blessedness of the good is augmented by witnessing the advancing prosperity of Zion.** "Behold, that thus shall the man be blessed," &c. (vers. 4-6). The good man is not only blessed by the Church, he is also a blessing to it. He becomes identified with all its interests; mourns over its reverses and rejoices in its success. A happy home is a blessing both to the Church and to the nation. "It is a circle of blessing, the Lord, the saint, and the neighbour; closet prayer, family worship and temple service; the Home, the Church and the State. Like the cloud falling upon the earth, the river running to the sea, and the ocean rising to the sky, it is a perpetual round of fertility, beauty, and thanksgiving, regarded with complacence by the radiant Artificer enthroned in the heavens." The chief concern of the good is the peace and prosperity of Israel.

LESSONS:—1. *There is no blessedness apart from goodness.* 2. *None are excluded from this blessedness—it is for " every one that feareth the Lord."*

PSALM CXXIX.

INTRODUCTION.

This Psalm was written after the Captivity, and contains a reference to the many tribulations which the Jews passed through from their youth—*i.e.*, the earliest part of their history,—their bondage in Egypt. The intent of the Psalmist is to comfort the Church in affliction, and to stir her up to glorify God for His providence over her, always for her good, and bringing her enemies to confusion and sudden ruin.—*A. Clarke.*

THE AFFLICTIONS OF THE GOOD.

(*Verses* 1-4.)

I. **That the good in all ages have been greatly afflicted.**

1. *The afflictions of the good are manifold.* "Many a time have they afflicted me from my youth" (ver. 1). The Jews had been oppressed by Pharaoh in Egypt, by the tribes north of the wilderness, by the Canaanites, Philistines, and Ammonites, by the Assyrians and Babylonians; and now they were harassed by the time-serving Samaritans. So has it been in all ages. The Church has suffered from a variety of enemies—from the reigning powers for the time being, from the envy and hatred of unbelievers, from the falseness and apathy of professed friends.

2. *The afflictions of the good are marked by unusual severity.* "The plowers plowed upon my back; they made long their furrows" (ver. 3). The sufferings of God's people have been unparalleled. They have been torn as the husbandman tears the ground with his ploughshare. Many martyrs for the truth have been "first lashed with the terrible scorpion and loaded whips; and then, as they hung on the little horse, torn with the hooked rake, which lite-

rally dug deep, long furrows in their bleeding and quivering flesh." But there is One in whom we see all Israel, and in whose sufferings the words of the text received a remarkable fulfilment. The incarnate Son of God gave His back to the smiters (Isa. l. 6).

II. **That the good have always survived the cruelty of their tormentors.** "Yet they have not prevailed against me" (ver. 2). The combined powers of evil have not been able to destroy the Church. A Swedish captain has recently invented a fire-proof dress, the wearer of which is enabled to walk up and down in the fiercest furnace without being injured. So the people of God have outlived the fiery assaults of the wicked, because clothed in the unconsumable panoply of the Divine protection. The afflictions of the Church have tended to its purity and strength. When Ignatius, Bishop of Antioch (A.D. 107), was taken to Rome and cast to the lions, he exclaimed, "I am God's wheat, and must be ground by the teeth of the wild beasts that I may be found His pure bread." The Church of God is unconquerable. "It is," says Trapp, "as the palm tree, which spreadeth and springeth up the more it is oppressed: as the bottle or bladder that may be dipped but not drowned: as the oak that sprouts out the thicker from the maims and wounds it receiveth."

III. **That the afflictions of the good are Divinely limited.**
1. *The character of God is a pledge of timely deliverance.* "The Lord is righteous" (ver. 4). As His people become worldly and unfaithful, He permits them to be afflicted; but when they cry to Him in penitence and faith, he delivers them out of their distresses. They suffer not a moment longer than may be necessary for their more complete consecration to God and holiness.

2. *The power of the wicked to harm is limited.* "He hath cut asunder the cords of the wicked" (ver. 4). Evil is not omnipotent, and it is restrained and defeated by the strong hand of God. The very instrumentalities by which the wicked sought to destroy the rising Church have been used to frustrate their cruel designs, and to effect their own ruin.

LESSONS:—1. *The holiest are not exempt from suffering.* 2. *Affliction may prove a blessed moral discipline.* 3. *The good are Divinely rescued from trial.*

THE LAMENTABLE FATE OF THE CHURCH'S ENEMIES.

(*Verses 5–8.*)

I. **They are signally defeated.**—"Let them all be;" or, "They shall all be confounded, and turned back that hate Zion" (ver. 5). Though advancing in formidable and threatening array, they shall be thrown into confusion and driven into ignominious retreat. They are engaged in an unequal conflict. They are allowed to gain some unimportant conquests, and while full of boastful daring, and reckoning upon certain and final victory, they are "melted like snow in the glance of the Lord" (Job xxxiv. 20, 21; Ps. lxx. 2).

II. **Their wicked life-purpose is abortive.** "Let them be as the grass upon the house tops, which withereth," &c. (vers. 6, 7). On the flat roofs of Eastern houses it is not uncommon to see grass growing, but for want of proper nourishment and soil, it cannot grow to maturity, and speedily withers away. It is sad to see one's life-purpose suddenly collapse and hopelessly perish. But so must it be with the designs of the wicked, after a lifetime of plotting and toiling; so must it be with the wicked themselves (Isa. xxxvii. 27).

III. **They remain unblessed.** "Neither do they which go by say, The blessing of the Lord be upon you: we bless you in the name of the Lord" (ver. 8). An emblem of Israel blessed by the Lord is a wide field of thickly growing corn stirred by gentle breezes under a ripening sun. As the labourers, humming or shouting snatches of cheery song, bind the sheaves and carry load after load away, they receive friendly salutations from people passing by (Ruth

ii. 4). The thought is ridiculous of house-top harvesting occasioning such benedictions. Equally out of question is it for the Church's adversaries to be blessed by God or man. (*The Caravan and Temple.*) It is impossible for nature to furnish an emblem that can sufficiently express the utter confusion, disaster, and misery that will certainly overtake the enemies of God. It is the highest aggravation of their sufferings that they remain for ever unblest.

LESSONS :—1. *A life of sin is a series of disappointments and defeats.* 2. *The enemies of God cannot escape His righteous vengeance.* 3. *The haters of Zion ignore the hope of salvation, which it alone offers.*

PSALM CXXX.

INTRODUCTION.

The Psalm before us, like the other pilgrim-songs, implies circumstances of bitterness; but it is, as in truth is each of them, more than a cry occasioned by outward hardship and danger. The sixth of the seven penitential Psalms, so styled by way of eminence, and not with a meaning that there are no other Psalms of penitence—this is intensely spiritual. It is at once a soliloquy, a petition, a statement, and an exhortation, a hymn for private use and public service, the voice of the soul and of the congregation. The former half is an address to the Lord: the latter is, first a profession of hope and expectation in His mercy, and then an argued invitation to the mind and course described as happily adopted. Throughout it is the language of deep distress on account of sin, a prayer for compassion and forgiveness, and an expression of trust in the promises and provisions of God's love.—*The Caravan and Temple.*

DE PROFUNDIS.

(*Verses* 1-4.)

I. That a consciousness of sin sinks the soul into depths of penitential sorrow. The Psalmist is penetrated with a sense of personal defilement, and measuring sin according to the standard of Divine purity, is plunged as into an abyss of humiliation and despair. "If thou, Lord, shouldest mark iniquities, O Lord, who shall stand?" The light makes manifest the darkness, the beautiful in nature reveals by contrast the ugly and repulsive; so an exalted purity brings out the loathsomeness and deformity of sin. Better to be overwhelmed with a genuine sorrow for sin than with the wrath of God that will certainly overtake the impenitent (2 Thess. i. 7-9).

II. That from the depths of penitential sorrow the soul cries earnestly for pardon. "Out of the depths have I cried unto thee, O Lord. Lord, hear my voice; let Thine ears be attentive to the voice of my supplications" (vers. 1, 2). The distressed soul finds relief in cries and tears. The heart would break if it found no outlet for its pent-up grief. In the darkest, deepest sorrow, it is our privilege to cry to God and to be heard. To cry to God in sorrow for sin is to pray to be delivered from it: it is an appeal for mercy. It is only when we taste the bitterness of sin, only when we are surrounded by its black horrors and the terrible vengeance it merits, that we are truly in earnest in pleading for forgiveness. The wail of despair is transformed into a song of hope when assured that pardon is attainable. "There is forgiveness with Thee." But for this, the soul might cry in vain: answered only by its own mocking echo; despair recoiling upon yet deeper despair.

III. That the penitent soul seeks pardon in order to serve God acceptably. "But there is forgiveness with Thee, *that Thou mayest be feared*" (ver. 4). True religion is justly defined as *the fear of God.* Not the cowering terror of the slave, not the sullen, pouting fear of the culprit, not the half-hope and half-dread of the awakened sinner, but the loving, reverential, obedient fear of the forgiven and accepted child. Pardon is absolutely necessary for acceptable and useful Christian work. God forgives, not simply to deliver from the depths of penitence, not to give license for indulgence in wickedness; but to create a moral fitness for exalted and extensive service (Psalm li. 12, 13).

LESSONS:—1. *From the deepest depths of misery the cry of penitence reaches the heights of heaven.* 2. *The more vivid our sense of sin, the more appreciative are we of the blessing of forgiveness.* 3. *The Lord delivers from sin that we may serve Him with loving fear.*

THE HOPE OF REDEMPTION.

(*Verses 5-8.*)

I. Is based on the revelation of the Divine Word. "I wait for the Lord, my soul doth wait, and in His Word do I hope" (ver. 5). Hope must have a solid foundation to rest upon, else it is mere dreamy conjecture, the rosy bloom of fancy that is shrivelled up by the first rude blast of trial. The Word of God is the foundation of the soul's hope of redemption; and that redemption is the theme which pervades every page of revelation. The word translated to *wait*, properly signifies *the extension of a cord from one point to another.* The Word of God is one point, the soul the other; and the extended cord between both is the earnest believing desire of the soul. This desire, this *hope*, strongly extended from the heart to God, is the active energetic waiting which God requires and which will be successful. God never disappoints: His Word never fails. Myriads have looked to Him for redemption, and not in vain.

II. Rouses the most passionate longings of the human soul. "My soul waiteth for the Lord more than they that watch for the morning: I say, more than they that watch for the morning" (ver. 6). It is an emphatic repetition, indicating that the whole soul is waiting and watching for redemption. "The priest staying in the temple for the moment of the early oblation, the warder on the tower looking for the first streak of day, the benighted traveller unable to take another step till the long darkness shall be over, the sick man sleeplessly longing for the family to be astir, the mariner wanting the light that he may examine the doubtful coast,— not one of them so earnestly hopes for the morning which will end his watch as my soul waits for the Lord, who forgives repented iniquity." The nearer a great blessing appears to us the more eager are we to possess it. The blessing of redemption is worthy of the most ardent and patient hope.

III. Is encouraged by reflecting on the amplitude of the Divine mercy. "Let Israel hope in the Lord: for with the Lord there is mercy, and with Him is plenteous redemption" (ver. 7). The first conception of redemption was the offspring of the Divine pity and compassion. The Lord yearns to deliver man from sin: He delighteth in mercy. (Compare Jer. xxxi. 20; James v. 11; Exod. xxxiv. 6, 7). There can be no true peace, no moral safety, without pardon. How great and condescending is that act of Divine mercy by which the sinner is pardoned, and his soul, wearied and distracted with long and anxious waiting, is set at rest and filled with unutterable peace!

IV. Is strengthened by the assurance of the completeness of redemptive blessings. "And He shall redeem Israel from all his iniquities" (ver. 8). It is no temporary, or indistinct, blessing that is so anxiously sought; it is nothing less than a complete deliverance from all iniquity. Redemption from sin includes redemption from all other evils: it is the greatest and most perfect work of God, and bestows the most exalted blessings on man. "A sacred presence in this Psalm asks the conscience a succession of important questions. Have you been in depths of distress on account of sin? Did you cry to the Lord to deliver you from the deep waters? Have you given up all thought of escaping by your own righteousness? Is all your appeal to God's redeeming mercy? Are you contentedly waiting and watching till He shall give you His promised blessing? Is your heart set upon the full daylight of holiness to the Lord?"

LESSONS :—1. *Redemption is a Divine work.* 2. *The most degraded soul is not beyond the hope of recovery.* 3. *Redemption must be eagerly and prayerfully sought.*

PSALM CXXXI.

INTRODUCTION.

"A Song of Degrees." See introduction to Psalm cxx. In the superscription this Psalm is ascribed to David, and although it is so short, it contains marks of its Davidic origin. "This short Psalm," says Perowne, "one of the most beautiful in the whole Book, assuredly breathes David's spirit. A childlike simplicity, an unaffected humility, the honest expression of that humility as from a heart spreading itself out in conscious integrity before God—this is what we find in the Psalm, traits of a character like that of David."

ASPECTS AND EXPRESSIONS OF HUMILITY.

We have here—

I. Humility in certain of its features. "Lord, my heart is not haughty, nor mine eyes lofty: neither do I exercise myself in great matters, or in things too high for me." Here are three negative features of humility.

1. *The absence of the proud heart.* "Jehovah, my heart is not haughty." In the heart of the truly humble man all high thoughts of self-righteousness, and all notions of self-reliance, are effectually abased. He is "poor in spirit," conscious of spiritual poverty and deep need, and consequently humble before God.

2. *The absence of the "high look."* "Nor mine eyes lofty." Hengstenberg: "Pride has its seat in the heart, and betrays itself especially in the eyes." (Compare Ps. xviii. 27; ci. 5; Prov. vi. 16, 17.) The man of proud heart will look disdainfully upon his fellow-man, as the Pharisee did upon the Publican, in the parable of our Lord. That Pharisee may fairly be regarded as an illustration of spiritual pride, and the Publican of sincere humility.

3. *The absence of ambitious projects.* "Neither do I exercise myself in great matters, or in things too high for me." The marginal reading is the correct one. The Psalmist did not strive with or after things that lay beyond his power or his sphere. (1.) He did not seek *to know* the mysteries of the humanly unknowable. Even if we could "understand all mysteries and all knowledge," that would not give rest to our soul. (2.) He did not attempt *to do* that which was beyond his power. Rest is not attained through the efforts of daring and "vaulting ambition."

"I would not have the restless will
That hurries to and fro,
That seeks for some great thing to do,
Or secret thing to know ;
I would be treated as a child,
And guided where I go."
—*A. L. Waring.*

II. Humility as connected with contentment and rest. "Surely I have behaved and quieted myself as a child that is weaned of his mother ; my soul is even as a weaned child." Perowne's note is excellent : "*I have stilled my soul, i.e.,* the pride and passions which were like the swelling waves of an angry sea. The word is used in Isa. xxviii. 25, of *leveling* the ground after the clods have been broken by the plough. The E. V. uses 'behaved' in the old sense of restraining, managing, as for instance in Shakespeare's *Timon of Athens,* 'He did behave his anger ere 'twas spent.' The next two clauses of the verse would be more exactly rendered:—

'As a weaned child *upon* his mother,' (*i.e.,* as he lies resting upon his mother's bosom) ; ' As the weaned child (I say), lies my soul upon me.' The figure is beautifully expressive of the humility of a soul chastened by disappointment. As the weaned child when its first fretfulness and uneasiness are past no longer cries, and frets, and longs for the breast, but lies still and is content, because it is with its mother ; so my soul is weaned from all discontented thoughts, from all fretful desires for earthly good, waiting in stillness upon God, finding its satisfaction in His presence, resting peacefully in His arms.

"'The weaned child,' writes a mother, with reference to this passage, 'has for the first time become *conscious of grief.* The piteous longing for the sweet nourishment of his life, the broken sob of disappointment, mark the trouble of his innocent heart: it is not so much the *bodily* suffering; he has felt that pain before, and cried while it lasted; but now his *joy and comfort are taken away,* and he knows not why. When his head is once more laid upon his mother's bosom, then he trusts and loves and rests, but he has learned the first lesson of humility, he is cast down, and clings with fond helplessness to his one friend.'"

And M. Henry: "Thus does a gracious soul quiet itself under the loss of that which it loved, and disappointment in that which it hoped for, and is easy whatever happens, lives, and lives comfortably, upon God and the covenant-grace, when creatures prove dry breasts." Pride is never satisfied, never restful, but fretful and discontented. Humility is content with the Divine allotments, and restful in the Divine love. The childlike spirit is simple, docile, modest, and lowly. Such a spirit was the Psalmist's.

III. Humility growing into hope. "Let Israel hope in the Lord from henceforth and for ever." The ancient Hebrews were animated by great hopes. But greater and more exalted are the hopes of the Christian. He hopes for complete triumph over evil, for utter purity of heart, for the vision of God, for transformation into His image, &c. "We are saved by hope." But mark the characteristics of this hope.

1. *It is Divine.* "Hope in the Lord." The Christian's hope rests not in anything transient, changeable, or limited; but in the eternal, unchangeable, infinite, holy God. A true hope resting in Him "maketh not ashamed."

2. *It is common.* "Let Israel hope in the Lord." It was not the exclusive privilege of the poet, the priest, the prophet, or any one class. The whole nation is here called to exercise it, and rejoice in it. In the inspiring and glorious hope of the Christian believer all men may share.

3. *It is present.* "From henceforth." If we have not cherished this hope hitherto, we may begin to do so at once. We should cherish it at all times and under all circumstances.

4. *It is perpetual.* "From henceforth, and for ever." Hope, like faith and charity, is an abiding thing. Earth and time cannot exhaust the hope of the Christian. His being will eternally rest in God. His expectation will be directed to Him for ever. In heaven itself the child of God will have much to hope for; further discoveries of the perfection and glory of God, and further growth of the faculties and capacities of his own being, will for ever invite him onward.

Now, *this glorious hope grows out of humility.* The humble soul claims nothing, yet hopes for everything, from God. Humility is the root of all Christian graces.

"Humility, that low, sweet root,
From which all heavenly virtues shoot."
—*Moore.*

Humility is *becoming in us, agreeable to others,* and *acceptable to God.* Prayerfully and diligently let us cultivate it.

"The bird that soars on highest wing
  Builds on the ground her lowly nest;
And she that doth most sweetly sing
  Sings in the shade when all things rest:
In lark and nightingale we see
What honour hath humility.

"The saint that wears heaven's brightest
  In deepest adoration bends; [crown
The weight of glory bows him down
  The most when most his soul ascends;
Nearest the throne itself must be
The footstool of humility."—*Montgomery.*

EXEMPLARY HUMILITY.

(*Verse* 1.)

If good men cannot always use this language of David, it is their prevailing desire to be able to do so; and if at any time they have been "exalted above measure," like Hezekiah, they will humble themselves for the pride of their hearts (2 Chron. xxxii. 26).

I. The humility he displayed.

1. *This is a grace of the Spirit—the fruit and product of inward religion.* Humility is not a plant that grows in Nature's garden. Of all the evils in our corrupt nature there is none more natural than pride: this is the grand wickedness—self-exaltation in our own or others' esteem. St. Augustine truly said: "That which first overcame man is the last thing he overcomes." Nothing can effectually overcome it but Divine grace. If we imagine that we can humble our own proud hearts by our own strength, we shall be disappointed. That pride, which is the curse of our nature, has struck its roots too deeply within us for any human arm to pluck it thence. We are not able to plant a single grace in our hearts, nor to preserve it when planted; but every spiritual good is God's gift, a gift as freely bestowed as the rain that comes down from heaven. But though we are thus weak and worthless in ourselves, the Holy Spirit generally works His purposes of grace by the use of means, and through these He allows and commands us to seek His grace. He is ready to pour down His richest spiritual gifts, &c.

2. *It is peculiarly acceptable in the sight of God.* The Lord "giveth grace unto the humble." He gives grace to make them humble, to keep them humble, and then honours the grace He has given. There is no mansion He loves so well as a sinner's humble heart. (Comp. Isa. lvii. 15.) "He giveth grace to the humble;" pours it out plentifully upon devout and humble hearts. His sweet dews and showers of grace slide off the mountains of Pride, and fall on the low valleys of humble hearts to make them fertile and prosperous. The law of God's procedure is, that "before honour is humility." He pours the oil of grace into none but broken hearts. God first humbles, then exalts. So David, Abigail, Moses, Luther. As the lower the ebb the higher the tide, so the measure of our humility is often the measure of our exaltation: the lower the foundation of our humility, the higher is the crown of our glory (1 Pet. v. 6).

3. *This grace has shone most brightly in the most eminent saints.* Specify Moses and Elias under the Law; Isaiah and Daniel among the Prophets; and John the Baptist and Paul under the Gospel. But Christ is the great Exemplar and Pattern.

II. **Some of the methods in which the possession of this grace will be shown and attested.**

1. *It will regulate our inquiries after truth.* "I do not exercise myself in things too high for me."

2. *It will be seen in the exercises of devotion.* The Pharisee stood and boasted; the publican smote upon his breast and prayed.

3. *It will prepare us to receive the principles and doctrines of the Gospel as the basis of our acceptance with God.* It led Paul to a simple dependence upon Christ — renouncing everything else. (Comp. Phil. iii. 4–9.) He neither depends upon his graces as a Christian, his attainments as a man, his labours as an Apostle, nor his success as a minister. Dependence on Christ must flow from humility of heart. Nothing but a heartfelt sense of our sinfulness will lead us to the Cross, or keep us there.

4. *It will be seen in practical submission to God's will.*

III. **Some of the means of producing it —**

1. *Meditate upon the greatness and holiness of God.*

2. *Keep near to the Cross of Christ.*

3. *Frequently review your transgressions and sins.*

4. *Think of your obligations to Divine grace.*

5. *Anticipate the Judgment Day.—The Late Samuel Thodey.*

PSALM CXXXII.

INTRODUCTION.

The author of this Psalm and the occasion upon which it was composed are both unknown. The opinion of M. Henry, Perowne, and others, is that it was composed for the dedication of Solomon's Temple. Many ancient expositors held that it was composed by David, either at the time of the bringing of the Ark to Zion, or at the time when it was in his heart to build the

Temple of the Lord. Many modern expositors hold that it was composed for the dedication of the Second Temple. It is quite impossible to arrive at any certain conclusion on the question. "This Psalm," says Perowne, "is a prayer that God's promises made to David may not fail of fulfilment, that He will dwell for ever in the habitation which He chose for Himself in Zion, and that the children of David may for ever sit upon His throne. It opens with a recital of David's efforts to bring the Ark to its resting-place; it ends with a recital of the promises made to David and to his seed."

Homiletically we shall view it as presenting *Lessons for Church-Builders, and Encouragements for Church-Builders.*

LESSONS FOR CHURCH-BUILDERS.

(*Verses* 1-10.)

From these verses we learn—

I. **That when churches are needed their erection is of great importance** (vers. 1-6). Previous to the bringing of the Ark to Mount Zion, the arrangements for religious worship were most unsatisfactory. "The sacred tent was without the Ark of the covenant, a body without a soul; and the Ark was at Kirjath-jearim, deposited as in its grave, without any rites of worship, well-nigh lost sight of." David himself said, "Let us bring again the Ark of our God to us; for we inquired not at it in the days of Saul." He was deeply solicitous for the revival of the national religion, and that arrangements should be made for the worship of Jehovah, with suitable dignity and magnificence. The Psalmist represents him as *tormenting* himself with anxiety to prepare a becoming dwelling-place for the Lord. The intensity of his concern was manifest in—(1.) The *solemnity* of his declaration concerning it. "He sware unto the Lord, and vowed unto the mighty One of Jacob." This solemn vow is not recorded in the history. Nor do we know whether it was made concerning the removal of the Ark to Zion, or the fixing the site of the Temple and the preparation of materials for its erection (1 Chron. xxii. 1-5). But that it was made is an evidence of the anxious care of David that appropriate provision should be made for the worship of the people. This care was manifest in— (2.) The *promptitude* of his declaration. "Surely I will not come into the tabernacle of my house, nor go up into my bed," &c. (vers. 3-5). So in 1 Chron. xxii. 5 David says, "I will *now* make preparation for it." The matter was too important and urgent to admit of any delay; so he resolved to make it his first business and to set about it at once.

Now the lesson we deduce from this is, that when adequate and appropriate provision is not made for religious worship, the building of churches is of great importance. This will appear from the following considerations:—

1. *The religious element in man is the grandest portion of his nature.* Reason, conscience, affections, and that in us which wonders, admires, adores—these are the highest things in us.

2. *The religious element in man needs worship for its right development and growth.* The worship of the Highest humbles, purifies, exalts, enriches our being. Worship transforms the worshipper into the image of the object of worship. The complete and harmonious development of our being is impossible apart from worship.

3. *That churches are needed for the becoming and profitable exercise of worship.* We need the absence of distracting scenes and circumstances, the aid of quiet and of hallowed associations, in order to worship in a becoming manner and with spiritual advantage. These are secured by the erection of churches.

But are not the temple of nature and the sanctuary of home sufficient for the worship of man? They would be if man were not a social being; but man *is* a social being. "It is not good that man should be alone." In work and play, in enjoyment and sorrow, man needs and delights in fellowship. Private and family worship is not enough; we need public worship also to help us to realise our relation to our fellow-men, that we

347

are members of one great family, children of one Divine Father. We need both the closet and the temple, both the quiet and solitude of private worship, and the fellowship and inspiration of public worship. Where adequate provision is not made for the public worship of the people, the building of Christian churches is a work the importance of which it is impossible to exaggerate.

II. That churches should be erected for the worship of God. "We will go into His tabernacles; we will worship at His footstool." We fear that all persons who are zealous in the building of churches do not always regard the worship of God as the great purpose for which they are to be used. The grand use of Christian churches is—

1. *Not the propagation of any ecclesiastical system.* The laudation of "*the church*," or of "*our denomination*," or of "*our body*," seems to be the object for which some churches are built. This is misleading and injurious.

2. *Nor the propagation of any theological system.* Some churches seem to be built chiefly for the propagation of Calvinism, Arminianism, Sacramentarianism, &c. But our interpretations of God and His Word are one thing, while God and His Word are other and sometimes very different things. Even at best "our little systems are but broken lights" of the Most High.

3. *Nor for the delivery of religious addresses or theological lectures, however able or eloquent they may be.* We are far from undervaluing the importance of the preaching of the Word, but it seems to us that the worship of God is a higher use of Christian churches than even that.

4. *Nor for ritualistic display however brilliant, or musical performances however perfect.* When forms and ceremonies, processions and pageants, are the great things in what ought to be Christian churches, intelligent and earnest Christians cannot but regard such a state of things as a prostitution of such edifices.

5. *But for the worship of God.* The grand use of churches is to worship the Lord God in spirit and in truth. This worship should be *humble* and *reverent*.

We are not worthy to approach His throne or look into His face, but we may "worship at His footstool."

III. That in the worship of God in His Church the manifestation of His presence should be earnestly sought. "Arise, O Lord, into Thy rest," &c. (vers. 8, 9). The Lord is here entreated to dwell in His Church—

1. *As an abiding presence.* "Arise, O Lord, into Thy rest." This may have been spoken when the Ark was brought to Zion, and certainly was spoken at the dedication of the Temple. The Ark was no more to be removed from place to place, but was to be fixed there. We need the abiding presence of God in our churches; for without this, however stately and beautiful they may be, they will be but as beautiful corpses.

2. *As a strengthening presence.* "Thou, and the Ark of Thy strength." The Ark was the symbol of the Divine presence and power. When it was taken with them into battle, the people were nerved to courage and endurance and conquest. When God by the Holy Ghost dwells among His people, they are "strengthened with might in the inner man."

3. *As a sanctifying presence.* "Let Thy priests be clothed with righteousness." One of the effects of the abiding presence of God in the Church will be that His ministers will be holy in heart and life. "Righteousness is the best ornament of a minister." It is an essential qualification for the office.

4. *As a joy-inspiring presence.* "Let Thy saints shout for joy." Sincere worshippers of Jehovah are here designated His "saints." They find their highest blessedness in the realisation of His presence. They sing, "In Thy presence is fulness of joy."

Here is the great want of religious assemblies and of the Church of God as a whole in this day—the realisation of His abiding presence. Having this, she will be nerved with might, clothed with righteousness, and inspired with joy.

IV. That in seeking the manifestation of the presence of God in His Church, we have powerful pleas which we may urge. We may, like the Psalmist, plead—

1. *The solicitude of our pious ancestors for His worship.* "Lord, remember David, and all his afflictions." David's anxiety to provide for the becoming celebration of the worship of God is here urged with God on behalf of his descendants. And as we seek the Divine blessing we may surely make mention of the devotion of our godly forefathers.

2. *His covenant relation with our pious ancestors and with us.* "For Thy servant David's sake, turn not away the face of Thine anointed." Perowne: "The anointed here must be Solomon, or some one of David's descendants, who pleads David and the promises made to David as a reason why his prayer should not be rejected." And we in this age plead—

"God of our fathers, be the God
Of their succeeding race."

God will ever be mindful of His covenant, and we shall do well to encourage ourselves in prayer by the remembrance of this.

CONCLUSION.—To build churches for the seeking of the manifestation of the Divine Presence, and for the offering of humble and reverent worship to the Divine Being, is to engage in a work of sacred significance and great importance. Churches consecrated to such purposes are blessings of incalculable worth to society; they aid the spiritual education and growth of the race towards perfection; they promote in a high degree the wellbeing of man, and they honour the Lord God.

BLESSINGS ON THE SANCTUARY.

(*Verses* 8, 9.)

Notice two or three thoughts—

I. The Temple is here called the place of rest, or the abiding place of God. "Arise, O Lord, into Thy rest," &c. The words mark a transition from the nomadic condition of the tribes to the compacted life of the nation, and a transfer of obligation that was suited to the change. In the free, wild life of the desert, with its perpetual migrations, the Sacred Tent might be pitched and struck like the others. But when the city was laid out for man, God would have His honoured house chiefest and costliest of all. . . . The Christian dispensation, although it is a dispensation of universality, and bases all its promises and sanctions upon the fact of spiritual service, has not annulled the seemly and the sacred in connection with the worship of God. It nowhere approves the idea that all places are equally sacred, or that God has ceased to visit Zion, and to dwell in its tabernacles with His manifestations of peculiar regard. If you want to know whether God can manifest His Spirit and His power in connection with the houses that are set apart for Him, you have but to think of the building of the Temple. "It seems as if God had built a Solomon on purpose that Solomon might build a house." And then, underneath that, how all inferior forces were brought into tribute! . . . Has not the Lord Himself proclaimed it,—"The Lord loveth the gates of Zion more than all the dwellings of Jacob"?

II. The Temple, gorgeous as it was, was altogether incomplete and valueless without the Ark. In all ages the Ark in the Temple is its life. Still the quick heart within the man, and you will have the stately skeleton soon. Withdraw the magic vapour, and the wheels whirr no longer, and the most exquisite contrivances are mute and motionless machinery. Take the breath from the great organ's heart, and in vain you bid it discourse its harmonies. And as the heart to the man, as the engine to the machinery, and the breath to the instrument of sound, so is the Ark to the Temple, because it is the symbol of the presence of the Lord.

There is no age that needs to be more impressed with this truth than the age in which we live. Our organisations are multiplied, &c. We are too apt to vaunt of our institutions, of our efforts, of our sacrifices, and thus damage our usefulness fatally by putting the instrument in the place of the power.

III. Look at the other blessings

which are asked for, either obviously or by direct implication in the Psalm. The presence of God is the chief, the all-absorbing object of desire; but then that presence is manifested by the diffusion of itself in blessing.

1. The Ark of God's strength in the Temple implies that *God's power* is in the Temple, and He waits to exert it in the Word, in the ministers' appeals, in the people's prayers. God's power is always in the Temple when God's presence is there. Power "to make the sinner quail," and to "sound the unbelieving heart;" power to send healing to the spirit of the wounded; power to make the selfish bountiful, &c.

2. The prayer proceeds to ask that the priests may be "clothed with righteousness," which is, in fact, a petition for *universal purity*. There is no priesthood now except the priesthood of the Saviour in heaven, and the priesthood of the whole community of the faithful, who are "kings and priests unto God." It is a prayer, therefore, not only for us who minister, but for you who hearken, that we may, all of us, be robed always, robed already, in the new linen, clean and white, in which the saints were seen in heaven. Righteousness is a word of comprehensive import, and it includes all that is alleged of it touching the purification of the soul before God. . . . It is, in fact, Paul's Thessalonian supplication, embodied in a solemn litany, "And the very God of peace sanctify you wholly," &c. (1 Thess. v. 23). If we are to be a strong church, we must be a pure church.

3. The third blessing that is asked for is *holy joy in God*, which has its foundation in oneness with God, both in favour and feeling, and which has its outlet in the appropriate expressions of praise. This will, indeed, be a natural result of the blessings already asked, for if we take hold of God's power, and if we reflect God's purity, be sure we shall never lack materials for praise.

I cannot dwell, except for a moment, upon the beautiful answer which the prayer received — so prompt, so generous, so full. In every case the answer is more large than the request. The prayer is contained in the first ten verses of the Psalm; in the eleventh the answer begins. It is worth looking at. . . .

Mark the ineffable wealth with which He fulfils the promises He makes to His people.—*W. M. Punshon, LL.D.*

ENCOURAGEMENTS FOR CHURCH-BUILDERS.

(*Verses* 11–18.)

The Psalmist, for the encouragement of the people, recalls certain promises which were made to David. The Lord had promised him that the government should be perpetuated in his family (2 Sam. vii. 12–16). But the promise was conditional. The great majority of the Divine promises are so. It was distinctly intimated to David that if the conditions were not fulfilled, though the promise would not be withdrawn, yet its operation would be suspended. The descendants of David failed to comply with the conditions; they violated the covenant; and the sovereignty for a long time passed away from the house of David. But that sovereignty in a higher form, on a vastly wider scale, and with more glorious significance, was resumed by "the Root and Offspring of David," even by Jesus Christ the Lord. In Him the promises made to David have their full and splendid realisation.

Here, in this section of the Psalm, are promises which are richly fraught with encouragement for those who are engaged in the building of churches, or in any other work for the extension of the Redeemer's kingdom. We have here a promise of—

I. **The presence of God in His Church.** "For the Lord hath chosen Zion," &c. (vers. 13, 14). (See *Hom. Com.* on Ps. xlviii. 1, 2; and lxxvi. 2.)

1. *He dwells there by His own choice.* "The Lord hath chosen Zion; He hath desired it," &c. "I have desired it." Hengstenberg translates: "He has selected it for His habitation. . . . I have selected it." God dwells in the Church,

not because of the excellence or worthiness of the members thereof, but because of His own good pleasure.

2. *He dwells there perpetually.* "This is My rest for ever." "Shiloh," says Perowne, "had been abandoned; for a time the Ark was at Bethel (Judg. xx. 27); then at Mizpah (Judg. xxi. 5); afterwards, for twenty years, at Kirjath-jearim (1 Sam. vii. 2); and then for three months in the house of Obed-Edom, before it was finally brought to its last resting-place." The Ark and the Temple have long since passed from Zion; but this Divine assurance finds its fulfilment in the Christian Church. In the darkest days of her history His presence has not been withdrawn; nor will He ever withdraw from His Church. Here then is a most inspiring assurance for all who are interested in His Church. Here is consolation for Christians in the dark and stormy day. Here also is inspiration for the Christian worker.

II. The blessing of God in His Church.

1. *His blessing as an accompaniment of her ordinances.* "I will abundantly bless her provision; I will satisfy her poor with bread." M. Henry interprets this as provision for both body and soul, and applies it to both "the poor of this world" and "the poor in spirit." And Barnes says: "A strong affirmation, meaning that He would do it in every way; that every needed blessing would be imparted; that God would provide abundantly for their support." But it seems to us to refer to spiritual provision. God by His blessing will vitalise the ordinances of the Church; He will make her services means of grace indeed to His people,—channels by which pardon shall flow to the guilty, comfort to the mourner, strength to the weak, holiness to those who long for it, &c.

2. *His blessing upon her ministers.* "I will also clothe her priests with salvation." This is an assurance that the petition in verse 9 should be granted. (See on that verse.) Perhaps the change of the word "righteousness" for "salvation" is meant to indicate that God will not only bless them with holiness of heart and life, but also make them instrumental in saving souls. Usefulness is a result of holiness.

3. *His blessing upon her members.* "And her saints shall shout aloud for joy." This also is a promise that the petition in verse 9 should be granted. (See on that verse.) M. Henry: "It was desired that the saints might *shout for joy;* it is promised that they *shall shout aloud for joy.* God gives more than we ask, and when He gives salvation He will give an abundant joy." Here then is encouragement, &c.

III. The triumph and glory of the Head of the Church. "There will I make the horn of David to bud," &c. (vers. 17, 18). David is here put for the house of David. And we must look to the Christ for the complete fulfilment of these promises. The horn is the symbol of power. To "make the horn to bud" is to make it shoot forth and grow. In Christ God "raised up an horn of salvation in the house of His servant David." He is "mighty to save." We have here an assurance of—

1. *The subjugation of His enemies.* "His enemies will I clothe with shame." God will frustrate their deepest designs, and overthrow their mightiest forces. "He must reign till He hath put all enemies under His feet."

2. *The success and glory of His reign.* "I have ordained a lamp for Mine Anointed." (On the application of this to David, comp. 1 Kings xi. 36.) But the lamp is frequently used in the Scripture as an emblem of prosperity. And so we regard it here in its application to the kingdom of our Lord. We have the same idea in the last clause of the Psalm: "Upon Himself shall His crown flourish," or blossom. The glory of the Redeemer's crown shall never fade; amaranthine are the flowers which adorn His brow.

> "O'er every foe victorious,
> He on His throne shall rest;
> From age to age more glorious,
> All-blessing and all-blest.
> The tide of time shall never
> His covenant remove;
> His name shall stand for ever;
> That name to us is—Love."
>
> —*Montgomery.*

CONCLUSION.—1. *Here is warning to the enemies of the Lord.* If you persist in your opposition to Him He will clothe you with shame, and crush you by His power. 2. *Here is exhortation to the enemies of the Lord.* Submit yourselves to Him, ere His anger wax hot against you. 3. *Here is amplest en-* couragement to His people, and especially to those who heartily labour in His cause. According to His promise He is ever present to enrich His Church with grace and power; and all who labour for the extension of His kingdom will find in the end their labour crowned with complete and glorious success.

THE SONG OF THE BUILDERS.

(*The whole Psalm.*)

Our Psalm has been universally and wisely applied to the Church of these Christian days, and its invocations and promises claimed as expressive of the desires and confidences of Christian people in their work for God. We are God's building, and we are God's builders too. The Psalm is full of strength and encouragement for us in both characters. . . . We may call it the Song of the Builders. . . . For our present purpose it will be most convenient to divide the whole into three sections, in the first of which, extending to the close of the seventh verse, the Church pleads with God the many thoughts and long toil that had laid the foundation for His house.

I. Let us gather from this portion some lessons touching **preparatory work.** "Lord, remember David, and all his afflictions." The Psalmist looks upon the fair dwelling, reared at last for God, and goes back in thought to the days when the design thus happily accomplished was first conceived. It was David's thought which was the parent of this holy and beautiful house, though Solomon was its builder; and his name springs first to the singer's lips. . . . Not the toil of hand and arm which carries out, but the mind which conceives the plan is its true author. "Lord, remember *David.*" Look at the picture which is given of the aged king setting himself to his task. (Comp. 2 Sam. vii. 1 and 2 with vers. 3 and 4 of the Psalm). He was an old man now, wearied with "all his afflictions," &c. And he had the other excuse for repose that he had done much work, as well as suffered many changes. . . . But not so does a true man think. . . . He will put his own comfort second, God's service first. The picture may be a rebuke to the slothfulness of us all, &c. But it should come with a special message to men and women of comparative leisure and freedom from corroding frets and consuming toils, whose lives are only too apt to be frittered away in trifles and dissolved in languid idleness, or corrupted by self-indulgence. To such the lesson from that picture of the old soldier-king is, Brace yourselves for continuous service, &c.

Notice, too, that *David's devotedness does make a plea with God.* The prayer goes upon the supposition that his toil and self-sacrifice will not, cannot, be all in vain. And the prayer is answered. God does not require perfect faithfulness in us ere He blesses us with His smile; He does not need that the temple shall be all complete ere He enters in. He receives, and pardons, and loves an imperfect faith; a wandering heart He still blesses and welcomes; stained services, in which much of the leaven of earthly motives may be fermenting, and many a taint of sloth and selfishness may be found, are not therefore rejected of Him.

And consider, too, *how God's remembrance of such preparatory work is shown.* David saw no result from all his toils to build the Temple. He got together the great store, but it was reserved for another to mould it into completeness, and to see the cloud of glory fill the house. But none the less was it true that God remembered David, and accepted and crowned his work. We all receive unfinished tasks from those who go before; we all transmit unfinished tasks to them who come after. Our vocation is to advance a little the dominion of God's truth, and to be one of the long line who pass on the torch from hand to hand. "One soweth and another reapeth," &c. You may never see the issues of your toils. If you can see them, they will generally not be worth looking at. We work for eternity. We may well wait for the scaffolding to be taken away.

II. **The prayer for God's blessing on the builders' work** (vers. 8–10). Picture to yourselves the moment. The Temple is finished, shining in its new beauty on its hill top. (See 2 Chron. v.–vii.) The Psalmist asks first that God would dwell in the completed Temple, and that the symbol of His presence may now at last, after so many wanderings, rest there, &c.

May we not, from all this, draw needful lessons for ourselves? And first, as to *the one great blessing which all builders for God should desire*. The Temple may be finished. But something more is needed. Not till the Ark is in the Holiest of all, and the cloud of glory fills the house could they say, "It is finished." The lesson is of everlasting importance. We need to guard ourselves most jealously lest we come to put the instrument in the place of the power. You may perfect your machinery, but all its nicely-fitting parts stand motionless—a dead weight; and not a spindle whirrs till the strong impulse, born of fire, rushes in. . . . When we have done all, we have to pray, "Arise, O Lord, into Thy rest," &c.

That presence will surely be given, if we desire it.

And that presence is all which we need to make ourselves strong and our work effectual.

From this fundamental petition all the other clauses of the prayer flow. I can only glance hastily at them.

There is first *power*—"The ark of Thy *strength*." They in whom God dwells will be strong. . . . There is next *righteousness*, with which the Psalmist prays that the priests may be clothed. In the new Israel all the people are priests. Righteousness is to be the robe of every Christian soul. . . . Thank God for that "fine linen, clean and white, the righteousness" with which Christ covers our wounded nakedness. Remember that growing purity in life and deed is the main proof that Christ's righteousness is indeed ours. If we are to do God's work in the world we must be good, true, righteous men. . . . Further, the prayer desires that *gladness* from God's presence and the possession of His righteousness may burst into the shout of praise. All true religion is joyful. . . . Finally, the Psalmist prays that the king of Israel and his people with him may be heard and accepted when they pray. Such are his desires for his nation. What do we desire most for our brethren, and for ourselves?

III. **The Divine answer, which more than fulfils the Psalmist's desires** (vers. 11–18). Throughout these verses there is constant allusion to the preceding petitions. The shape of the response is determined by the form of the desires. (Comp. ver. 2 with ver. 11, and ver. 5 with ver. 13). Not in us, but in Him, lies the motive for His grace, and so it can never change.

Then, notice, that each single petition is enlarged in the answer to something much greater than itself. (Comp. ver. 8 with vers. 14, 15; ver 9 with ver. 16; and ver. 10 with vers. 17, 18.) Put this in its widest form, and what does it come to but that great law of His grace by which He over-answers all our poor desires, and, giving us more than we had expected, shames us out of our distrust? And the law holds for us in all our works and in all our prayers.—*A. Maclaren, D.D.*

ZION A TYPE OF THE CHURCH.

(*Verses* 13–16.)

I. God's delight in Zion.
1. There He dispensed His ordinances.
2. There He vouchsafed His presence.
3. There he communicated His blessings.

II. God's promises to Zion.
1. In respect to its institutions.
2. In respect to its ministers.
3. In respect to all its worshippers.

Infer—
(1.) That formalists do not really belong to the Church. (2.) That the Church cannot be overthrown. (3.) That Christians are bound to serve and honour God.—*George Brooks.*

PSALM CXXXIII.

INTRODUCTION.

In the superscription this Psalm is attributed to David. It has been thought by some that it was composed on the occasion of the coming of the elders of Israel to Hebron to anoint him king over all the tribes of Israel (2 Sam. v. 1–3; 1 Chron. xii. 38–40). Others have opined that the assembling of the people in great multitudes at Zion to celebrate the great religious festivals gave rise to the Psalm. But it is impossible to come to any certain conclusion as to the date or occasion of its composition.

Herder says that this Psalm "has the fragrance of a lovely rose;" and Perowne: "Nowhere has the nature of true unity—that unity which binds men together, not by artificial restraints, but as brethren of one heart—been more faithfully described; nowhere has it been so gracefully illustrated, as in this short ode. True concord is, we are here taught, a holy thing, a sacred oil, a rich perfume which, flowing down from the head to the beard, from the beard to the garments, sanctifies the whole body. It is a sweet morning dew, which lights not only on the lofty mountain-peaks, but on the lesser hills, embracing all, and refreshing all with its influence."

THE EXCELLENCE AND BEAUTY OF FRATERNAL UNITY.

By unity we do not mean uniformity, or the harmony which is brought about by regulations and restrictions. We are unable to discover any beauty worth speaking of in the unity which is the result of artificial and mechanical arrangements. It is the unity of life and activity and variety which is here celebrated. Uniformity is monotonous, wearisome; but unity is refreshing and beautiful. The only unity worth contending for is "the unity of the Spirit." We have seen an orchestra with five thousand musicians and singers playing and singing magnificent choruses with the most inviolate and enrapturing harmony. There was a great diversity of instruments, and of performers upon them, and of voices, yet there was a sublime and splendid unity. Unity of spirit and aim it is that is insisted upon in the Scriptures. (See Eph. iv. 1–16.)

The Psalmist sets before us—

I. **The propriety of this unity.** "Behold how good and pleasant it is for *brethren* to dwell together in unity." Those who form part of one family, should surely live together in peace and harmony. All mankind are children of one father, and are "made of one blood," and should therefore live in peace and harmony. The words of Abram to Lot are applicable between man and man all the world over: "Let there be no strife, I pray thee, between me and thee; for we be brethren." "He that soweth discord among brethren" is "an abomination unto the Lord." This unity is specially binding upon and appropriate amongst Christian brethren. Barnes: "They are redeemed by the same Saviour; they serve the same Master; they cherish the same hope; they are looking forward to the same heaven; they are subject to the same trials, temptations, and sorrows; they have the same precious consolations. There is, therefore, the beauty, the 'goodness,' the 'pleasantness' of obvious fitness and propriety in their dwelling together in unity."

II. **The comprehensiveness of this unity.** Perowne holds that it is this which the poet intends to set forth by the figures of the anointing oil and the dew. He says, "The first figure is taken from the oil which was poured on the head of the high priest at his consecration (Exod. xxix. 7; Lev. viii. 12, xxi. 10). The point of the comparison does not lie in the *preciousness* of the oil, or in its *all-pervading fragrance;* but in this, that being poured on the head, it did not rest there, but flowed to the beard, and descended even to the garments, and thus, as it were, consecrated the whole body in all its parts. *All the members participate in the same blessing.* (Comp. 1 Cor. xii.) This is the point of the comparison. . . . If, as is commonly assumed, the point of comparison lay in the all-pervading fragrance of the oil, the addition to the figure, which descended upon *the beard* . . . which descended to the *edge of his garments,* would be thrown away. But understand this as typifying the consecration of *the whole man,* and the extension of the figure at once becomes appropriate, and full of meaning." Luther remarks :—" In that he saith ' from the head,' he showeth the nature of true concord. For like as the ointment ran down from the head of Aaron, the high priest, upon his beard, and so descended unto the borders of his garment, even so true concord in doctrine and brotherly love floweth as a precious ointment, by the unity of the Spirit, from Christ, the High Priest and Head of the Church, unto all the members of the same. For by the beard and extreme parts of the garment, he signifieth that as far as the Church reacheth, so far spreadeth the unity which floweth from Christ, her Head." Perowne holds that in the figure of the dew, the same idea is conspicuous. "Here, again, it is not the *refreshing* nature of the dew, nor its *gentle, all-pervading* influence, which is the prominent feature. That which renders it to the poet's eye so striking an image of brotherly concord, is the fact that *it falls alike on both mountains:* that the same dew which descends on the lofty Hermon descends also on the humbler Zion. High and low drink in the same sweet refreshment. Thus the image is exactly parallel to the last; the oil descends from the head to the beard, the dew from the higher mountain to the lower."

III. **The joyousness of this unity.** Anointing with oil was practised by the Jews on occasions of rejoicing and festivity. From this custom it became an emblem of prosperity and gladness. (Comp. Ps. xxiii. 5, and Isa. lxi. 3.) As Perowne thinks that the comprehensiveness of the unity is the chief feature in the comparison, so Barnes regards the joyousness of the unity. He says, "There is no other resemblance between the idea of anointing with oil and that of harmony among brethren than this which is derived from the gladness—the joyousness—connected with such an anointing. The Psalmist wished to give the highest idea of the pleasantness of such harmony; and he, therefore, compared it with that which was most beautiful to a pious mind — the idea of a solemn consecration to the highest office of religion." Discord and strife are painful things; peace and concord are delightful.

IV. **The influence of this unity.** This is represented as—

1. *Delightful.* The anointing oil was beautifully perfumed, and, when it was poured forth, it diffused its fragrant odours to the great delight of all who were near. Unity is not only good and pleasant in itself, but it agreeably affects all who behold it. When the world beholds a truly united Church, it will speedily be won to Christ. (John xvii. 21.)

2. *Gentle.* "As the dew." Quiet, yet most mighty, is the influence of unity. We may apply to it the words of Tennyson—

"Right to the heart and brain, though undescried,
Winning its way with extreme gentleness
Through all the outworks of suspicious pride."

3. *Refreshing.* "As the dew." In eastern climes, because of its refreshing effects upon vegetation, the dew is inestimably precious. So unity cheers and invigorates the heart.

4. *Powerful.* "Union is strength." "A threefold cord is not quickly broken." "Separate the atoms which make the hammer, and each would fall on the stone as a snowflake; but welded into one, and wielded by the firm arm of the quarryman, it will break the massive rocks asunder. Divide the waters of Niagara into distinct and individual

drops, and they would be no more than the falling rain; but, in their united body, they would quench the fires of Vesuvius, and have some to spare for the volcanoes of other mountains."—*Dr. Guthrie.*

5. *Securing the Divine blessing.* Where true brotherly unity is, "the Lord commands the blessing, life for evermore." A life of peace and love is Divine and everlasting.

CONCLUSION. — "Behold, how good and pleasant it is," &c. 1. Behold, and admire. 2. Behold, and *imitate.*

CHRISTIAN UNION.

(*Verse 1.*)

Christian union is my theme on this occasion. *Christian union*—not simply the union which should prevail among the members of any particular denomination of Christians, but the love and unity which ought to exist among all the real people of God.

I. Its nature.
1. *Unity in sentiment.*
2. *Union of feeling.*
3. *Union of effort.*

II. **The desirableness, or importance, of Christian union.**

1. *The teachings of Scripture.*
2. *The example of the early Christians.*
3. *The evils of division.*
4. *Christians are engaged in the same cause.*
5. *Union is strength.*
6. *Union is promotive of happiness.*
7. *It is only by the exercise of that love, which is the substratum of union, that one can resemble God and become imbued with the spirit of heaven.*—*W. C. Whitcomb,* in *"The Preachers' Treasury."*

PSALM CXXXIV.

INTRODUCTION.

"Three things," says Delitzsch, "are clear with regard to this Psalm. First, that it consists of a greeting, verses 1, 2, and a reply, verse 3. Next, that the greeting is addressed to those priests and Levites who had the night-watch in the Temple. Lastly, that this Psalm is purposely placed at the end of the collection of Pilgrim Songs in order to take the place of a final blessing." The words of verses 1 and 2 were probably addressed by the people to the priests and Levites, and those of verse 3 by the priests to the people. Both the author of the Psalm and the occasion of its composition are unknown.

DOXOLOGY AND BENEDICTION.

I. **Doxology.** In verses 1 and 2 the people exhort the priests and Levites to praise the Lord. Consider—

1. *The offering to be presented.* "Behold, bless ye the Lord." The ministers of the Temple are called to offer the sacrifice of thanksgiving unto the Lord. Here are two points. (1.) The *nature* of this offering. Praise. "Bless ye the Lord." This should be presented (*a*) because of what *He does* for us. Gratitude urges—"Bless the Lord, O my soul, and forget not all His benefits." And (*b*) because of what *He is* in Himself. He is "glorious in holiness." Admiration and reverence urge us to "Bless His holy Name." (2.) The *importance* of this offering. "Behold." This word calls attention to the exhortation which follows as a thing of importance and urgency. Worship is an engagement of the utmost moment to man. The obligations to it are most binding. And the exercise of it is essential to the right development and to the perfection of the human spirit.

2. *The persons by whom it is to be offered.* "All ye servants of the Lord, which by night stand in the house of the Lord." The priests and Levites are here addressed. But in this Christian dispensation priesthood is a thing of character, not of class. Every believing and reverent soul is a priest unto God by virtue of the highest and holiest consecration. Every Christian is exhorted

to "offer the sacrifice of praise to God continually, that is, the fruit of lips giving thanks to His Name."

3. *The time at which it is to be offered.* "By night." Some of the ministers of the Temple were in attendance there all night. (Compare Exod. xxvii. 20, 21; 1 Chron. ix. 33.) They were there to guard the sacred and precious things of the Temple, and to keep the lamps alight and the fire upon the altar burning. Hengstenberg thinks that when the Pilgrim bands arrived at the Temple in the evening they addressed this exhortation to the servants of the Lord. The rest and quiet of the night render it a suitable season for praising God. When the duties of the day are done, and its busy and confused noises are silenced, the soul may be lifted up in adoration to God without interruption.

4. *The place towards which it is to be offered.* "Lift up your hands in the sanctuary." Margin: "in holiness." Hengstenberg and Perowne regard קֹדֶשׁ as "the accusative of direction," and translate, "to the sanctuary." The most holy place was regarded as the audience-chamber of the Most High, the place where God hears prayer, and whence He communicates answers to His people. The Lord Jesus Christ is the true Shekinah and Holy of Holies. We draw near unto God through Him. He is the meeting-place between God and man. Thus, then, let us offer to God the sacrifice of praise from grateful and adoring hearts.

II. **Benediction.** "The Lord that made heaven and earth bless thee out of Zion." This benediction is taken in part from the form used by the high priest in blessing the children of Israel. This accounts for the use of the singular, "*thee,*" not the plural, *you.* Notice—

1. *The power of God to bless.* "The Lord that made heaven and earth" is omnipotent. He "is able to do exceeding abundantly," &c.

2. *The means by which God blesses man.* "Bless thee out of Zion." God blesses the world through the Church. He employs the Church in communicating spiritual blessings to mankind.

3. *The authority of the servants of God to pronounce His blessing.* The poet represents the priests as authoritatively pronouncing the blessing of God upon the people. And the ministers of the Lord Jesus Christ still possess this authority, not because they are priests, but because they are Christians. Every Christian has the right to pronounce the benediction of God upon devout worshippers; and the minister of Christ has this right not only as being himself a Christian, but as the representative of the Church.

CONCLUSION.—Here are two of the highest privileges to which any created spirit can aspire. Through Christ we may draw near to the great God with ascriptions of honour and praise, being confident of audience, acceptance, and blessing. And by our voice the Divine blessing may be conveyed to the ear and heart of our fellow-men. Let us endeavour to live in the grateful and reverent exercise of these privileges.

PSALM CXXXV.

INTRODUCTION.

"We have now," says Hengstenberg, "a group of twelve Psalms, sung after the prosperous completion of the Temple, and probably at its dedication, consisting of three new Psalms at the beginning, and one at the end, Ps. cxlvi., which enclose in the middle eight Psalms of David. . . . No period was more suitable for the appropriation of this Davidic cycle of Psalms than that in which the Davidic stem was, poorly enough, represented by Zerubbabel, whose humbled condition also gave occasion to the prophets of that period, Haggai and Zechariah, to lay a firmer and deeper hold on the rich promises given to the race of David."

This is one of the Hallelujah Psalms; it was intended for use in the Temple service; it is general in its character, and consists of exhortations to praise Jehovah, with reasons for so doing. This Psalm has much in common with the preceding one. Both are exhortations to worship; both are addressed to the priests and Levites engaged in ministering in the Temple. But this Psalm differs from the preceding in that in it the exhortation to praise the Lord is enforced by several reasons. There is no superscription to the Psalm; and we know neither its author nor the date of its composition.

Incitements to Praise the Lord.

(*Verses* 1–7.)

In this strophe we have a fervent exhortation to celebrate the praise of God, supported by weighty motives to do so. Consider—

I. The persons to whom this exhortation is addressed. "Praise ye the Lord. Praise ye the Name of the Lord," &c. (vers. 1, 2). (See the *Hom. Com.* on Ps. cxxxiv. 1.) The exhortation is addressed "to the Levites who sang psalms and played on the different musical instruments which were used in the service of God, and to the priests who blew with the trumpets and repeated the liturgical prayers and the blessings." In this age we have no priestly class, for all Christians are priests, and the exhortation of the text is applicable to all Christians. Two characteristics of those to whom it is addressed are here specified—

1. *They have access to God.* They "stand in the house of the Lord, in the courts of the house of our God." Every believer in Jesus Christ may "enter into the holiest by His blood." "Through Him we have access unto the Father."

2. *They serve God.* "Servants of the Lord, that stand in the house of the Lord." They stand ministering in His Temple. They wait His behests, and then hasten to obey them. The Christian looks to Christ not only as a Saviour to be trusted, but as a Sovereign to be obeyed. They who are thus admitted into the presence and service of God are under special obligations to praise Him.

II. The reasons by which this exhortation is enforced.

1. *Because of the holiness of God.* "Praise the Lord; for the Lord is good." In Himself God is absolutely perfect. "God is light, and in Him is no darkness at all." In Him the conscience finds the Supremely Righteous; the intellect, the Supremely Intelligent; the heart, the Supremely Kind; the soul, the Supremely Beautiful. Therefore it is fitting that He should be praised, and that with all our powers.

2. *Because of the delight which the exercise yields.* "Sing praises unto His Name; for it is pleasant." Sincere praise to God exalts and exhilarates the spirit of him who presents it, strengthens his faith, increases his strength, and transforms him into the image of God. The reverent and hearty praise of the Divine Being is the heaven of the godly soul.

3. *Because of His special relation to Israel.* (1.) In a special sense they were His people. "For the Lord hath chosen Jacob unto Himself, Israel for His peculiar treasure." As His people they enjoyed *special privileges.* He guided them, sustained them, gave to them a goodly inheritance; many a time He delivered them, &c. As His people they had *special obligations.* They were called to be witnesses to the great truths of His unity, spirituality, and holiness, to the heathen nations. By their civil and religious institutions, and by their life and conduct, they were to testify for the Lord God amongst men. (2.) In His esteem they were *specially precious.* "His peculiar treasure." "The Lord taketh pleasure in His people." "If ye will obey My voice, indeed, and keep My covenant, then ye shall be a peculiar treasure unto Me above all people; for all the earth is Mine." "God is good to all;" but to His people He manifests His special regard. He—

"Keeps with most distinguished care
The man who on His love depends."

(3.) He had *chosen* them for this position. They did not attain it by their own effort, or merit it by their own excellence; but were selected to it by Him in His sovereign favour. This special and privileged relation to Him supplies most cogent reasons for praising Him. And the argument applies with still greater force to the people of God to-day.

4. *Because of His sovereignty in nature.* "For I know that the Lord is great, and that our Lord is above all gods," &c. (vers. 5–7). The poet represents this sovereignty as (1.) *Absolute.*

"Whatsoever the Lord pleased that did He." "He does what He pleases, because He pleases, and gives not account of any of His matters." (2.) *Omnipotent.* Whatsoever in His sovereignty He willed, that by His power He effected. (3.) *Universal.* "In heaven, and in earth, in the seas, and all deep places." By these expressions the Psalmist intends to set forth the entire universe.

"He everywhere hath sway,
And all things serve His might."

The poet represents the Lord as absolutely supreme over all the forces and phenomena of nature. And this representation we regard as (*a*) *Philosophic;* (*β*) *Scriptural;* (γ) *Assuring.* (See the *Hom. Com.* on Ps. cvii. 23–32.) As the universal Sovereign, He has a right to universal praise.

CONCLUSION.—Let us offer to God the sacrifice of praise continually. Let us praise Him not only with the lip, but with the life ; not only in church, but everywhere ; not only on the Lord's day, but every day. Let us seek for a heart of constant praise—

"Not thankful, when it pleaseth me ;
As if Thy blessings had spare days :
But such a heart whose pulse may be
Thy praise."
—*Herbert.*

THE GREATNESS OF GOD AN INCENTIVE TO PRAISE HIM.

(*Verses* 8–14.)

In this strophe the poet presents illustrations of the greatness and supremacy of the Lord to invite the people to praise Him. He illustrates His greatness by—

I. His judgments upon the heathen. "Who smote the firstborn of Egypt, both of man and beast," &c. (vers. 8–11).

1. *His judgments fall upon all classes of men, and even upon the brute creation.* "Who smote the firstborn of Egypt, both of man and beast. Who sent tokens and wonders into the midst of thee, O Egypt, upon Pharaoh, and upon all his servants." Servants suffer for their masters' sins. The consequences of a king's obstinate tyranny over man, and rebellion against God will fall heavily upon his subjects. And even the brute creation feel the smart of the penalty of human transgressions. When the Divine judgments fall upon the land, all classes, from the sovereign to the serf, feel the weight of the stroke.

2. *His judgments reach the mightiest powers.* "Who smote great nations, and slew mighty kings," &c. "Sihon king of the Amorites," was a man of great courage and audacity, and a distinguished military leader. "And Og king of Bashan," was a man of gigantic size and stature, the ruler over sixty proud fenced cities, inhabited by a brave and powerful people. Yet, these great and warlike kings, with their valiant armies, were smitten and slain when the Most High arose against them. His frown strikes with dismay the heart of the most courageous, and the strong arm falls nerveless, and great and powerful nations are brought to nought.

3. *His judgments are lessons.* They are "tokens and wonders." "Wonders" —things calculated to beget surprise and amazement. "Tokens," or "signs "— things calculated to excite inquiry, and to teach inquirers important truths. The plagues of Egypt were significant of important truths concerning the Divine Being and His government. To the "earnest listener" they announced the almighty power of God, His hatred of tyranny and oppression, His regard for the oppressed, &c. These miracles of judgments were parables of the Divine character and procedure towards men. In this great power which is arrayed against tyranny and oppression we have a motive for celebrating the praise of the Lord.

II. His regard for His people.

1. *He makes His judgments upon the heathen an advantage to His people.* He "gave their land for an heritage, an heritage unto Israel His people." (See Ps. cxi. 6.) In His government of the world the Lord has special regard to the interests of His loyal subjects. He makes "all things work together for their good."

2. *He defends the cause of His people.*

"For the Lord will judge His people." (See Deut. xxxii. 36.) He will see that they have that which is right, and in due time will rid them of their oppressors, and avenge them of their adversaries.

3. *He pities them in their distresses.* "He will repent Himself concerning His servants." (See the *Hom. Com.* on Ps. xc. 13.) He will not suffer them to be oppressed beyond their power of endurance, but in His mercy He will visit them in their afflictions and "compass them about with songs of deliverance." Here then is a stirring incentive to praise the Lord; an incentive that should move the dullest heart to joyous and reverent strains.

III. **His eternity and unchangeableness.** "Thy Name, O Lord, endureth for ever; Thy memorial, O Lord, throughout all generations." God's eternity involves His immutability. It is the omnipotent and unchangeable eternity.

All earthly things are transient and mutable; but God abides for ever, and He is for ever the same. In this we have—

1. *An encouragement to faith.* He is still the same as when He wrought mighty wonders and signs on behalf of Israel. Age does not diminish His interest in His people, or His faithfulness to them, or His power to aid them. Therefore they may sing, "Behold, God is my salvation; I will trust, and not be afraid."

2. *An argument for praise.* The constancy of God's love for His people and of His great and glorious doings for them, should constrain them to offer to Him the lowliest adoration and the heartiest praise.

Here, then, in these illustrations of the greatness of God, we have what ought to prove to all who are loyal to Him, irresistible incentives to exalt and magnify His holy Name.

THE VANITY OF IDOLS AN INCENTIVE TO PRAISE THE LORD GOD.

(*Verses* 15–21.)

"To show more fully the propriety of praising God, and Him alone as God, the Psalmist institutes a comparison between Him and idols, showing that the gods worshipped by the heathen lacked every ground of claim to divine worship and homage. They were, after all that could be done to fashion, to decorate, and to adorn them, nothing but silver and gold, and could have no better claim to worship than silver and gold as such."—*Barnes.* Verses 15–20 correspond almost exactly to Ps. cxv. 4–11. And as that passage has already engaged attention in this work, it will be sufficient in this place to indicate briefly a homiletical method of treatment. Here are four main points for consideration—

I. **The innate religiousness of human nature.** The manufacture of idols indicates the religious tendency of human nature. Man must have a god of some kind; he must worship. Without an object of worship there are instinctive desires and cravings of the human soul which find no satisfaction.

1. *Man wants an object of trust.* Man is conscious of insufficiency for the deep meanings and momentous issues of life, and looks for help from beyond and above himself. If he find nothing higher, he will trust even in a dead idol (ver. 18).

2. *Man wants an object of worship.* He has instincts which urge him to pay homage and reverence to a being or beings higher than himself. Worship is not imposed upon human nature, but the development of some of the deepest instincts of that nature. If it be objected that peoples have been discovered amongst whom there was no sign of the religious element, the reply is obvious, that such extreme exceptions prove the rule.

II. **The sad perversion of the religious element in human nature** (vers. 15–18). That which should find its exercise and satisfaction and blessedness in the holy and ever-blessed God is here exhibited as turning to dead idols—vain simulacra—in trust and reverence.

1. *This perversion indicates amazing*

stupidity. How irrational! how absurd to suppose that a wooden, silver, or golden thing can be worthy of homage or of trust!

2. *This perversion indicates moral derangement.* If the conscience and the affections were in their normal condition, idolatry would be impossible. Idolatry is sin as well as folly.

3. *This perversion is deplorably degrading in its effects.* "They that make them are like unto them, so is every one that trusteth in them." "They who, turning away from God's witness of Himself in the visible creation, worshipped the creature rather than the Creator, received in themselves the sentence of their own degradation. 'Their foolish heart became darkened.' They became blind, and deaf, and dumb, and dead, like the idols they set up to worship."—*Perowne.* Worship is transforming. Man becomes like his god. These remarks are applicable to the idolatries of our own land,—the worship of wealth, social status, &c.

III. **The grand Object of worship for man as a religious being.** "Bless the Lord," &c. (vers. 19, 20). Here is an Object—

1. *Suited to the needs of man.* We have pointed out that man wants in his god an object of trust and of worship. The Lord is *supremely trustworthy.* He is unchangeable and infinite in power, kindness, and faithfulness. He is *supremely excellent.* He is "glorious in holiness." "God is light."

2. *Suited to the needs of man as man and of all men.* The "house of Israel," the "house of Aaron," the "house of Levi," and all "that fear the Lord," are here called upon to praise Him. The Lord is the God not of any one class or race, but "the God of the spirits of all flesh."

Here is the grand object of worship for all men. All others are false and vain. Let all men worship the Lord God, and in so doing they will find the satisfaction, perfection, and blessedness of being.

IV. **The chief place of worship for man as a religious being.** "Blessed be the Lord out of Zion, who dwelleth at Jerusalem. Hallelujah." "As in cxxviii. 5, cxxxiv. 3, Jehovah blesses out of Zion, so here, on the other hand, His people bless Him out of Zion. For there they meet to worship Him; there not only He, but they may be said to dwell (Isa. x. 24); and thence accordingly His praise is sounded abroad."—*Perowne.* The church, though not the exclusive, is the chief place of worship. There devout souls meet; there He has promised to meet with them, &c.

To the Lord God, and to Him alone, let the hearty and reverent praise of all men be given. "Praise ye the Lord."

PSALM CXXXVI.

INTRODUCTION.

"This Psalm," says Perowne, "is little more than a variation and repetition of the preceding Psalm. It opens with the same liturgical formula with which the 106th and 118th Psalms open, and was evidently designed to be sung antiphonally in the Temple worship. Its structure is peculiar. The first line of each verse pursues the theme of the Psalm, the second line, 'For His loving-kindness endureth for ever,' being a kind of refrain or response, like the responses, for instance, in our Litany, breaking in upon and yet sustaining the theme of the Psalm: the first would be sung by some of the Levites, the second by the choir as a body, or by the whole congregation together with the Levites. We have an example of a similar antiphonal arrangement in the first four verses of the 118th Psalm; but there is no other instance in which it is pursued throughout the Psalm. The nearest approach to the same repetition is in the 'Amen' of the people to the curses of the Law as pronounced by the Levites (Deut. xxii. 14)."

The subjects mentioned as the ground of the praise of the eternal mercy of God have so frequently engaged our attention in previous Psalms as to require but little additional illustration.

MERCY IN GOD AND IN CREATION.

(*Verses* 1-9.)

I. Mercy in the Divine Being and Character (vers. 1-3). We have here—
1. *A revelation of God in the names applied to Him.* (1.) "O give thanks unto *Jehovah.*" Jehovah = ὁ ὤν = the Self-Existing, the Continuing, the Permanent, the Everlasting. (2.) "O give thanks unto *the God of gods,*"— the Most High God, the Supremely Powerful, who is far above all that is called God or worshipped as God. (3.) "O give thanks to *the Lord of lords,*"— the Ruler of rulers, whose authority is supreme over all governors, princes, and kings. Such, then, are the ideas of God embodied in the names which are applied to Him by the poet—the Self-Existing, the Supremely Powerful, and the Supremely Authoritative.

(2.) *A revelation of God in His character.* "O give thanks unto Jehovah; for He is good." (See *Hom. Com.* on Ps. cvi. 1, and cxxxv. 3.) He is good both in Himself and in His dealings with His people.

3. *A revelation of God in His relation to men.* "His mercy endureth for ever." Mercy is a modification of goodness. It is goodness in its relation to the sinful, the ill-deserving, and the miserable. To men "God is rich in mercy." He delights in showing mercy to them. Connect the mercy of God with those aspects of His Being which are brought into view in the names applied to Him. "Jehovah," the Self-Existing, is essentially merciful. His mercy is eternal as His Being. "The God of gods," the Supreme Deity, the Omnipotent, is merciful. We cannot reverence mere power. Might is sometimes terrible. But the Most High is as tender as He is strong. He is infinite in mercy as in power. "The Lord of lords," the Supreme Ruler over all kings and magistrates, is a merciful Being. His compassion is as wide and deep and lasting as His authority. For these reasons let us praise Him.

II. Mercy in the Divine work in creation (vers. 4-9). To the Psalmist the universe was neither eternal, nor self-originated, but a creation of God.

1. *Creation is a work of wonder to man.* "To Him who alone doeth great wonders." The contrivances and constructions of the universe are wonderful in their skill and in their strength. The more thoroughly man becomes acquainted with the heavens and the earth, the more astonishing are the evidences which he discovers of infinite intelligence in designing and almighty power in creating them.

2. *Creation is an embodiment of the wisdom of God.* "To Him that by wisdom made the heavens." The scientific student discovers design and the most benevolent and beautiful adaptations in every department of nature. Only a being of infinite intelligence could have designed the universe with its indescribable wonders, beauties, and utilities.

3. *Creation is an expression of the mercy of God.* It exhibits the benevolence as well as the wisdom of the Creator. In the devout student it excites not only wonder and admiration, but gratitude and praise. His mercy is manifest *in the heavens.* In their order and harmony and beauty, and in their benign influences, we discover indications of His mercy. It is manifest also *in the earth.* In making the earth fit for human habitation, and a pleasant habitation; in making it so fruitful, so safe, and so varied and beautiful in appearance, we see His kindness. It is manifest *in the sun and the day.* The sun is the source of light, warmth, life, and beauty. The reign of darkness would soon lead to the reign of death. By its light and warmth the sun sustains life and promotes joy. In a great measure the beauties of the universe are produced by his influence, and without his light no gleam of beauty would be discernible. So we see in the sun and the day the kindness of the Creator. His mercy is manifest *in the night and the moon and stars.* Night with

its darkness and silence so eminently adapted for sleep and rest, with its enchanting and refining beauties of moon and stars in the heavens, and their reflection on the rippling surface of rivers and the restless waves of the sea,—for these we have felt deep thankfulness times innumerable. But the Psalmist represents the sun as ordained " to *rule* by day," and " the moon and stars to *rule* by night." (*a*.) They rule by determining the duration of day and night. (See *Hom. Com.* on Ps. civ. 19-23.) (*b.*) Their rule is an illustration of the principle taught by our Lord that he who is chief in service shall be chief in sovereignty,—the true ruler most diligently and heartily serves those whom he governs. (Luke xxii. 25-27.) The mercy of God which is manifested in creation is *eternal*. "His mercy endureth for ever ;" literally : " For unto eternity His mercy." When the heavens and the earth shall have passed away, the mercy which was manifested in them shall continue. We shall need mercy throughout this life, in the hour of death, and in the day of judgment ; and mercy will still endure and meet our need. The generations that shall tread this globe in the future will need mercy as much as we do, and for them also mercy shall remain as free and plenteous as ever. " Unto eternity is His mercy."

Let us—

" Make life, death, and that vast for-ever,
One grand sweet song "

of praise to Him whose mercy, like Himself, is eternal.

MERCY IN THE REVOLUTIONS OF PROVIDENCE.

(*Verses* 10-22.)

There is no difficulty in discovering the kindness of the dealings of God with Israel. But where is mercy manifest in His treatment of the people of Egypt, of Pharaoh, Sihon, and Og ? This we will endeavour to show. There was—

I. Mercy in the judgments upon Egypt. "O give thanks to him that smote Egypt in their firstborn ; for His mercy endureth for ever." The Egyptian oppression of the Israelites was unjust, wicked, cruel ; they had reduced them to slavery ; they treated them with brutality ; they refused to liberate them, although the command to do so was authenticated by extraordinary wonders and signs ; judgments of less severity had produced only a transient and brief effect upon them ; and so the Lord brought upon them the severe stroke of the death of the firstborn, both of man and beast, and of small and great. It is not only right but merciful to compel the strong to respect the rights of the weak, if they will not do so without compulsion. It is merciful to insist upon the doing of justice amongst men.

II. Mercy in the destruction of tyrannical kings. "O give thanks to Him who overthrew Pharaoh and his host in the Red Sea ; for His mercy endureth for ever. To Him who smote great kings," &c. (vers. 15, 17-20). (See *Hom. Com.* on Ps. cxxxv. 8-11.) We hold that it is in mercy that tyrannical and oppressive rulers are swept from the earth.

1. *It is a mercy to themselves.* (1.) Supposing there be no retributory state in the future, then it is a mercy to terminate their existence ; for their life must be tormented by the passions which they cherish in their breasts. Ambition, lust of power, cruelty, impoison their life at its very springs. (2.) Supposing there be a retributory state in the future (and the evidence for the existence of such a state is to us irresistible), then it is a mercy to terminate the earthly existence of the incorrigibly evil ; for while it continues, they are increasing their guilt, and " treasuring up unto themselves wrath against the day of wrath and revelation of the righteous judgment of God." For them prolongation of life in the present will involve corresponding increase of misery in the future, therefore it is merciful to them to cut short their wicked career.

2. *It is a mercy to mankind.* The existence of cruel and tyrannical oppressors afflicts humanity like some terrible

nightmare. When they are removed the race breathes freely once again. Such ambitious tyrants, if unchecked, would convert the fair world into a slaughter-house reeking with human gore. The peace and progress of mankind unite in demanding the removal of ambitious tyrants and cruel oppressors from the face of the earth. To destroy such men is a mercy to the entire human race. Therefore let us "give thanks to Him who smote great kings; for His mercy endureth for ever."

III. **Mercy in the history of Israel.** It was manifest—

1. *In their emancipation from Egypt and its bondage.* This was not accomplished by a single act or effort. It involved a series of Divine interpositions. The poet here mentions :—(1.) *Their deliverance from slavery and from the land of Egypt* (vers. 10–12). It was in mercy to them and to mankind that the Israelites were rescued from the crushing burdens which their oppressors imposed upon them. The greatness of the mercy may be approximately estimated by the severity of the sufferings from which it rescued them, and by the persistency and power exerted in doing so. Blessings have flowed to the entire human race through the deliverance of Israel from Egypt. (2.) *Their deliverance from peril at the Red Sea* (Exod. xiv.). Point out their extremely perilous position. Can they be rescued from it? And how? Jehovah answers (α.) *By dividing the waters of the sea.* "To Him that divided the Red Sea into parts." (β.) *By nerving them to pass through the watery walls.* "And made Israel to pass through the midst of it." He manifested His power over the waters in dividing them, and over the hearts of the dismayed people by giving them courage to travel through a passage so unprecedented, and apparently so perilous. (γ.) *By the destruction of their enemies by the same sea.* "And overthrew Pharaoh and his host in the Red Sea." Thus the Lord completely and gloriously delivered them from the hands of their enemies, and conspicuously displayed His mercy to them.

2. *In leading them through and supporting them in the wilderness.* "To Him which led His people through the wilderness; for His mercy endureth for ever." For the space of forty years He protected them from their enemies, provided for their necessities, and guided them in their wanderings by supernatural agencies; and He did this notwithstanding their oft-repeated unbelief and rebellion against Him. In His dealings with them in the wilderness, we have a most impressive display of His mercy to them.

3. *In giving to them the land of Canaan for an inheritance.* He "slew famous kings; and gave their land for an heritage unto Israel, His servant; for His mercy endureth for ever." (See the *Hom. Com.* on Ps. cxxxv. 12.) The land had been defiled by the wars, the crimes, and the idolatries of the ancient Canaanites, so God overthrew and disinherited them, and gave their land for an heritage to the people of His choice. God manifests His mercy to His people by a special regard to their interests in His providential government of the world.

CONCLUSION.—Inasmuch as the mercy of the Lord is perpetual—1. *Let oppressors take warning.* The constancy of His mercy towards His people is a pledge of the constant course of His justice against their enemies. 2. *Let the oppressed and afflicted take encouragement.* His mercy is far greater than their misery; it is infinite, and it "endureth for ever."

MERCY IN HUMAN REDEMPTION AND PROVISION.

(*Verses* 23–26.)

The poet refers in the 23rd and 24th verses to the deliverance of the Jews from the Babylonish captivity. But this section of the Psalm may appropriately be applied to the spiritual redemption and sustentation of man. Consider—

I. **The mercy of God in redemption** (vers. 23, 24).

1. *The need of redemption.* This arose from (1.) *Man's depressed condition.* "Our low estate." From his high estate man fell by sin; the crown and glory of his being are gone; the completeness of his moral power is broken; he is a degraded, ruined being. (2.) *Man's oppressed condition.* He is troubled from without as well as from within. He is begirt by "enemies." The Chaldeans had taken the Jews into captivity and oppressed them. Man is enslaved by sin, led captive by the devil; his spiritual enemies are many and subtle and strong; and he is unable to cope successfully with them. He needs an emancipator, a redeemer.

2. *The stages of redemption.* The poet mentions two steps in the process of the redemption of man. (1.) *The exercise of Divine thoughtfulness.* He "remembered us in our low estate." It is unspeakably assuring and encouraging to know that the Lord thinketh upon us in our helplessness and need. He is interested in us. He careth for us. We never pass beyond His kindly notice and care. (2.) *The exertion of Divine power.* "He hath redeemed us from our enemies." He set free the Jews from their captivity in Babylon. He has redeemed sinful and lost men by the power of His love, manifested in the teaching and work, the life and death, of the Lord Jesus Christ. "Ye were redeemed with the precious blood of Christ." "We have redemption through His blood," &c.

3. *The source of redemption.* "For His mercy endureth for ever." In the heart of God our redemption took its rise. The streams of mercy by which we are refreshed, strengthened, and saved, flow from the throne of God. Our redemption must be traced to the loving-kindness of the Lord God. "O give thanks unto the Lord; for He is good; for His mercy endureth for ever."

II. **The mercy of God in provision.** "He giveth food to all flesh; for His mercy endureth for ever." "At length," says Calvin, "He extends the fatherly providence of God indiscriminately, not only to the whole human race, but to all animals, so that it might not appear wonderful He should be so kind and provident a Father towards His own elect, since He does not reckon it a burden to provide for oxen and asses, ravens and sparrows." (Comp. Ps. civ. 27, 28.) Two inquiries may fairly be proposed here—

1. *If He giveth food to the beasts, will He be unmindful of the needs of man who is made in His own image?* "How much then is a man better than a sheep?" "Ye are of more value than many sparrows." (Ps. xxxiv. 9, 10.)

2. *If He provides food for man's bodily necessities, will He not much more provide for His spiritual needs?* He who has redeemed us from sin has also promised us strength to empower us for life's duties, and grace to sustain us in life's trials. "The Lord will give grace and glory; no good will He withhold from them that walk uprightly." The mercy to which we owe so many and great blessings, both in the past and in the present, will never fail us. Through all eternity it will continue to enrich us with purest and most precious treasures. "O give thanks unto the God of heaven; for His mercy endureth for ever."

HUMAN WRETCHEDNESS AND DIVINE COMPASSION.

(*Verses* 23, 24.)

Any one would remember us in a *high* estate; but Jesus remembers us in a low one.

I. **To take a view of the wretched condition of mankind, in consequence of their apostacy from God.**

Language does not afford a more emphatic description of complete wretchedness than to say of a man that he is *lost*—a *captive*—a subject of *corruption*—*dead!*

1. *Man has gone astray from the path of life and happiness.* Apart from Revelation, human nature itself bears witness to itself by evident marks of degeneracy and corruption. The passions

which enslave our minds; the diseases that afflict our bodies; the disorders in the natural and moral world around us; the various wretchedness of man; and the universal law of mortality, all proclaim that some unhappy change has passed on our nature since its original formation. Various conjectures have been formed to account for this state of things. But the Bible alone solves the appearances so difficult to be reconciled by unassisted reason. Here we are taught that man, by transgression, has debased himself below the rank originally assigned him in the creation of God; and that the consequences of the sin of our first parents attach to all their offspring, in the evils which arise from a sinful, sorrowful, and mortal condition. Our steps are now voluntarily turned far away from the only path of happiness. (See Job xxi. 14; Jer. ii. 13; Rom. iii. 11, 12.) For this is the habitual state of mind, not of the more grossly profligate and abandoned only, but of mankind generally, however improved by culture and enlightened by education—the active principle of rebellion against God, which Grace alone can subdue.

2. Man has not only left the path of life, but *stands exposed to the fatal effects of Divine displeasure, by actual transgression.* The sentence of the broken law holds in full force (Gal. iii. 10; Col. iii. 6). And who knoweth the power of God's anger? Who can imagine the judgments which God has in store against the enemies of truth and righteousness? (Job xxxiv. 29, xxxviii. 22, 23; Ps. xxxix. 11). If such be the effect of His fatherly chastisement under a dispensation of mercy, how dreadful must His fiery indignation be when Guilt has run its full course, and Justice is compelled to take its unrestricted sway! (Heb. x. 31.) There is not a part of these fleshly tabernacles which He cannot visit with exquisite anguish; and if but a spark of His wrath fall upon the soul, how dreadful is the ruin! Witness Cain, Judas, Simon Magus, Ananias, and Sapphira.

3. *That we are unequal to our own deliverance.*

II. **To admire the method of Divine compassion to man in his rescue from this state of guilt and misery.**

1. *By the incarnation and death of the Son of God.* Throwing a veil over the dazzling glories of Divinity, He came among us in great humility, bearing the attractive character of a kinsman and a friend. He is a *Physician* to heal, a *Shepherd* to seek, and a *Saviour* to restore. (Luke xix. 10.)

To see the nature and importance of His work, look back to the Old Testament. See what a space our redemption has occupied in the Divine counsels; see how all events in Providence were made to prepare for it; see what lofty representations are given of it by the ancient prophets; see how all the types and institutions of the law prefigured His approach, and how all these ancient prefigurations are accomplished in His death.

You become convinced of His high qualifications for this important work, when you observe the perfection of His mediatorial nature, blending the attributes of earth and heaven—all the tenderness of suffering humanity with all the glory of the unapproached Divinity. In magnitude the work of redemption has no rival; and none but the Lord of life and glory was equal to such a work. We know that Infinite Wisdom would not make choice of a weak and ineffectual instrument, or appoint to so important an office one unqualified to perform it. All objections vanish and all fears are banished when we read of Him as "Emmanuel, God with us." (Matt. i. 23; John i. 14; 1. Tim. iii. 16). You may see the ability of Christ to save in the high attestations He received. Thrice did the Voice from heaven proclaim, "This is My beloved Son," &c. On the Cross, when He offered Himself a sacrifice holy and acceptable, all nature was convulsed, and the veil of the Temple was rent in twain. At His resurrection the stone was rolled away from the door of the sepulchre, and He was declared to be the Son of God with power. By His ascension He rose victorious to heaven, that he might fill all things. And He is now exalted at the right hand of power as a Prince and a Saviour.

(Heb. vii. 25). Meditate much, therefore, upon His equal ability and willingness to save. As the merit of His atonement exceeds by infinite degrees the guilt of your sin, so does the power of His grace surpass the strength of your corruption.

2. *By the work and agency of His Blessed Spirit.* He who made your hearts can surely renew them; and He who glorified Christ in the days of the Apostles can glorify Him still in your experience, by applying the testimony of the Word, and raising you from the death of sin to the life of holiness. Commit yourself to Christ, therefore, as the great Physician. He will purify your souls by His Spirit, &c.

3. *By the combined influence of His Providence and Grace.* Christ is engaged to bring many sons to glory; and He overrules all the scenes of their earthly lot and mortal history, to guide their footsteps through time and discipline their hearts for the purity and bliss of heaven. (Isa. xxvi. 7; Psa. xvi. 11.)—*Samuel Thodey.*

PSALM CXXXVII.

INTRODUCTION.

"There can be no doubt whatever," says Perowne, "as to the time when this Psalm was written. It expresses the feeling of an exile who has but just returned from the land of his captivity. In all probability the writer was a Levite, who had been carried away by the armies of Nebuchadnezzar when Jerusalem was sacked and the Temple destroyed, and who was one of the first, as soon as the edict of Cyrus was published, to return to Jerusalem. He is again in his own land. He sees again the old familiar scenes, the mountains and the valleys that his foot trod in youth are before him. The great landmarks are the same, and yet the change is terrible. The spoiler has been in his home, his vines and his fig-trees have been cut down, the house of his God is a heap of ruins. His heart is heavy with a sense of desolation, and bitter with the memory of wrong and insult from which he has but lately escaped.

"He takes his harp, the companion of his exile, the cherished relic of happier days,—the harp which he could not string at the bidding of his conquerors by the waters of Babylon; and now with faltering hand he sweeps the strings, first in low, plaintive, melancholy cadence pouring out his griefs, and then with a loud crash of wild and stormy music, answering to the wild and stormy numbers of his verse, he raises the pæan of vengeance over his foes.

"What a wonderful mixture is the Psalm of soft melancholy and fiery patriotism! The hand which wrote it must have known how to smite sharply with the sword, as well as how to tune his harp. The words are burning words of a heart breathing undying love to his country, undying hate to his foe. The poet is indeed—

"'Dower'd with the hate of hate, the scorn of scorn,
The love of love.'"

PRECIOUS, YET SORROWFUL, RECOLLECTIONS.

(*Verses* 1–6.)

The poet here expresses the deep sorrow of Israel during their exile from the land of their fathers, and their solemn vow never to forget the holy city. No song of praise was heard amongst them, their harps were hung upon the willows, and their recollections of Zion filled them with sadness. Attracted by a common sympathy, a fellowship of suffering, they assembled in companies upon the banks of the Babylonian streams, and expressed their deep grief in sighs and tears. The scene is intensely poetic; it awakens our sympathy, and excites our imagination. But our business is to elicit its teachings.

I. **They wept at the recollection of lost privileges.** "We wept when we remembered Zion."

1. *Their tears express their patriotism.* "If I forget thee, O Jerusalem," &c. (vers. 5, 6). We all know something of love of country. Whatever may be the natural, political, or moral characteristics of the country which gave us birth and education, there is none like unto it in heart attractions. In everything else

it may be greatly surpassed by other countries; but in its hold upon our heart it stands unrivalled. "No power can sever our heart from the land of our birth." But if a country be beautiful or sublime in its scenery, fertile in its soil, wise and liberal in its institutions and government, and rich in historical associations, then its hold upon the heart of its people is more intense and close. Thus stood the case in respect of the Jews and their country. To them there was no land like Canaan. It was a magnificent country, with grand old mountains towering sky-ward, and delicious plains fertile and flower-clad, and watered by delightful streams. "A good land, a land of brooks of water," &c. (Deut. viii. 7–9). Moreover, it was sacred to them by immortal and precious memories,—memories of Abraham and Moses, Joshua and Samuel, David and Solomon, Elijah and Elisha,—memories of the glorious doings of God on behalf of their fathers. Well may these Jews love such a country. But this country they had lost; and these tears bewail their loss.

2. *Their tears express their yearning for freedom.* Once they were free under their glorious theocracy. But their freedom they had lost. They had lost their civil liberty, and were captives; their religious liberty, and were in the land of idolaters. Their tears expressed their sorrow for the loss of their liberty, and their longing for its recovery. Their tears expressing their yearning for liberty tell us that man was not made for bondage, that in proportion to the force and fulness of his manhood will be his unwillingness to submit to bondage in any form. In the same proportion he will feel the degradation and smart of the yoke of the oppressor, and pine and struggle for liberty. God made man to be free. Freedom is the birthright of man as man, and of every man.

3. *Their tears express their love for the house of God and the ordinances of worship.* The loss of their country and of their political privileges was great, and was deeply felt by them; but their spiritual deprivation in being sundered from Zion was a greater loss, and was more deeply felt by them. "We wept when we remembered *Zion.*" (On Zion and its associations, see *Hom. Com.* on Ps. xlviii. 1–3, lxxvi. 2, cxxxii. 13, 14.) Zion was inseparably connected with the supply of their spiritual requirements, and the development of their moral and religious nature. The loss of those things which tend to ennoble and develop our higher nature—our true self—is the greatest of all losses. Having those things upon which the growth and progress of our soul depend we are rich, though in other respects we may be as destitute as Lazarus; without those things we are abjectly poor, though in other respects we may be as rich as he at whose gate Lazarus was laid. These most costly things, these divinest things, the Jews had lost. From Zion, with all its sacred mementoes, and delightful associations, and divine ordinances, and religious privileges, they were ruthlessly torn. They had lost all. Country lost, liberty lost, the Temple lost, the manifestation of God lost,—*all lost!* Well may they weep! Two facts are suggested by this portion of our subject:—(1.) *True love is independent of bodily presence or nearness.* When far removed from Zion the love of the captive Jew for the sacred place became not cold, but more fervent. Material distance cannot quench the holy flame. Moral distance is the only thing which can. (2.) *True love endures through time and all its changes.* Seventy weary years of deprivation and sorrow failed to extinguish the love of the pious and patriotic Jew for Zion. Neither duration nor change can exhaust genuine affection: it is a growing and abiding thing.

II. **They wept at the recollection of privileges which they had lost by reason of their non-appreciation of them.** They were removed from their country and their home because of their sins. They were carried to Babylon in consequence of their neglect of Divine ordinances, their idolatry, rebellion against God, and spiritual apostacy. No people were more favoured, or were so favoured as they were. They had been warned, exhorted, entreated, encouraged, &c. (Comp. Jer. vii. 25, 26,

xxv. 1–11.) They were thoughtless, disobedient, stiff-necked, determined to pursue their own course; and it led them to Babylon with all its sorrows. And now in the sufferings of exile they begin to consider, now recollection plays its part, now their eye is turned upon themselves, and reflection brings self-reproach and added sorrow. How painful must have been their recollections of Zion! Zion which they had neglected, dishonoured, despised; and from which they were justly exiled;—Zion which once in the beauty of its situation they had regarded as "the joy of the whole earth," now ruined and desolated by their Pagan foes, the fertile vales of Palestine all dreary and neglected, the walls of Jerusalem levelled to the ground, the city destroyed, the Temple desecrated —painful, indeed, must have been their recollections! Yet, could they forget their country and Zion? Never! Recollection constantly led them there, and their sins rose darkly before them. When they had their privileges they failed to appreciate them, neglected them; when they lost them they saw their value. "The well is never prized until it is dry."

Observe here three important facts—

1. *We are prone to disparage the ordinary and regular blessings of life.* We see this as regards the blessings of the kind and pious home, the Christian ministry and means of grace, the Bible, and even salvation and the Saviour. Familiarity engenders neglect.

2. *The disparagement of these blessings is an ample cause for their withdrawal.* The Jews disparaged their privileges, and for seventy years God withdrew from them some of His most precious gifts. Let those who neglect the familiar blessings of this Christian land and age be warned. God may withdraw His most precious gifts from you, &c.

3. *Should these blessings be withdrawn their value would then be felt—be felt when it is too late.* The privileges of Zion were valued by the Jews in Babylon; they were valued when lost.

" Like birds whose beauties languish, half concealed,
Till mounted on the wing, their glossy plumes
Expanded shine with azure, green, and gold;
How blessings brighten as they take their flight!"
— *Young.*

Let us be wise and appreciate Heaven's gifts while we have them.

What a solemn view of life this subject presents! Every circumstance and action of life by the operation of memory is endless in its influence. Memory eternalises the records of life. Memory makes the fleeting present everlasting. How important then is life! *Do you love Zion?* Are you wisely estimating and using your religious advantages and opportunities? *Or are you penitently sorrowing at the recollections of the past?* What opportunities neglected, blessings depreciated! &c. Thank God! the blessings are not yet withdrawn; salvation is still offered, &c. Look from the guilty past to Jesus for pardon and life. Then take your harp from the willows, and join in the song of the ransomed, "Unto Him that loved us," &c. *Our responsibilities are proportioned to our privileges.* The Jews were banished from their Temple and country for neglecting their privileges. This was the most bitter ingredient in their sorrow by the rivers of Babylon. How great, then, are the responsibilities of the people of this land and age!

HARPS ON THE WILLOWS.

(*Verse 2.*)

This is a beautiful and pathetic picture of the captive Jews and their sorrows in the land of Babylon. . . .

And is not that a picture of many conditions of your human life? Sorrow has invaded our lives. We wander by the side of some Babylonian stream. We hang our harp upon the willow that bends above it. We weep when we remember the happier moments that have fled.

There are three things that we would learn from this picture of sorrow.

I. **Every man has a harp.**

The harp was the well-known instrument for the accompaniment of song.

Its music was sweet and delightful. When calamity fell upon the nation their harps were silenced, &c. And thus it is with all our lives. We have the elements of joy in them, the powers of song and gladness, and there is no man who has not the capacity and the occasion for delightful mirth.

1. Just *think of the constitution of our nature*, wherein a place is secured for joy. The body is attuned to pleasure. God might have made us with organisations fitted for life, for recreation, for intelligence and activity, and yet altogether without the capacity of experiencing pleasure. Consider the sense of hearing. Sounds might have been so indistinct that to hear would have required the constant exercise of attention, the strain of effort painful and wearying; or they might have been so powerful that a whisper would be shocking, whilst the natural speech of our friends would be like the explosion of cannon close to the ear. And yet how exquisitely has God harmonised the sound and the sense!

2. What a harp man possesses *in physical nature* if he would only let its music be heard. Every sight and sound, every scene and action, all things fair and good, bright and godly, are but fingers of Nature's skilful hand, which will touch the strings of the harp of our being, and wake their perfect tones of rapture.

3. Man has the harp for pleasant accompaniment of happy song *in the region of the immaterial and the intellectual.* What delights there are in intellectual operations! The joy of learning—when it is indeed learning worthy of the name; the discovery of the unknown; the pursuit of the law which underlies obscure phenomena; the search for causes; the enumeration of effects—these and others afford keen and lasting delight.

4. The pleasure which belongs to *the still higher sphere* which we are privileged to enter. I forbear to pursue the delights of our soul in its affections—the raptures of home; the loves of children, &c. Let me now only remind you of *that sacred melody which is attuned when the joys of the spirit are experienced.* The sinner seeks his Saviour, and finds the pardon of Father and of Friend. You remember the hour of forgiveness. Heaven's clouds were cleared, the storm was hushed, the dread was dissipated, and a Father's love received you through the mighty merits of a Saviour's death. The best music of all the Christian poets falls far short of the rapture which dwells within the forgiven heart.

And with what language shall we tell of the occasions for harping that have occurred so often since the first forgiveness! Have there not been Bethels of a Divine covenanting, Horebs of refreshment, and Red Sea passages of deliverance and triumph? Prayer has had its blessed answers, and meditation its holy raptures. Nothing but song could express our heightened feeling; and we felt as if angel-hands were sweeping the cords of our harp of life, and making the glad accompaniment to our joyous mood. (Comp. Isa. li. 11.)

Remember, *this harp must be tuned and practised on.* And yet it is the last thing some Christians think of—tuning their harp. Let Zion re-echo with your songs.

II. But sometimes the harp has to be hung upon the willows. In the land of Babylon the Israelites had no heart to sing. Tears were the only outpourings of which they were capable. And so it is with the harps of life. We have to lay them aside or hang them upon willows that droop over rivers of sadness, by whose banks we sit and wail.

1. It is thus *when disease invades our bodies* or *sorrow smites the soul.* Songs are not suitable to funerals, and harpings in the house of mourning are out of place and impertinent.

2. There are some *silences still more profound* that fall upon the music of our life. The father whose eldest son forswears his father's faith, and throws away his father's virtues, and wins only a name that will be a dishonour among men—such a father has little heart for harpings, and is, indeed, in a silent land of bitter exile.

3. And then how useless is the harp when we ourselves are *in the hours of*

spiritual distress. God is absent, and we know no gladness till He shows His face again. They sang a hymn when the Master was among them, even though when they rose from the supper it was to pass to Gethsemane, and Pilate's bar, and Calvary. But their hearts had no desire for singing in the suspense and numb agony of the hour when the Christ lay dead. And so it is with the Christian still, &c.

III. But though there is no heart or place for song, and *the harp* must be laid aside, it needs not to be cast away.

They had been foolish and wicked men of Israel if they had flung their harps beneath the running river, and thus deprived themselves altogether of the means of melody when the days of joy came back again. (See Ezra iii. 9–13.)

So, brethren, cast not away your harp. The weather will clear and the soul will awake to gladness when the sunshine comes.

And the sickness will depart, and the strengthened frame shall recover its wonted sense of health and vigour. Not always the darkened room, &c.

Yea, and there shall be some hours of gladness even for the wailing weary heart that sickens over the sinfulness of child and friend. It was a sad home when the prodigal was far away. But one day the father saw the returning son, ragged, worn, and disgraced, and that night there was music and dancing in the long silent homestead. Keep your harp, my friend, &c.

And thou, too, depressed and cast down Christian, throw not away thy harp. There shall be peace and joy and fulness of blessing yet for thee. God shall show Himself, and Christ will yet return.

The time when the harp shall be needed may not come until the moment of death. A life of sorrow, doubt, or conflict may not have one hour of leisure or delight, and only swan-like can be the song; and yet, then the harp will be needed, though only one chord may be struck from it upon earth—its strains sounding amid the music of heaven. Then, for all a harp will be gained, for all shall sing the new song of Moses and the Lamb.—*Ll. D. Bevan, LL.B.*

The Diffculty of Singing Songs in Exile.

(*Verse* 4.)

I. What the world is to the Christian. "A strange land." Like Babylon to the Israelites. There they had many comforts; for God "made them to be pitied of all those that carried them captives." They were treated more like colonists than captives; and many of them grew wealthy and were even loth to return. But it was not their home. What Babylon was to Israel such is the present evil world to the Christian. Like a man born in a cottage, the son of a prince, to whom a rich inheritance belongs in another country, when he comes to know the secret of his birth, the rank he sustains, and the possessions that belong to him; then that which was his home ceases to be so, and he longs to cross the river, or climb the mountain, or set sail for his true country: so it is with the Christian who, though born a worldling, and once satisfied with his portion, now learns the secret of his true and nobler birth. Many of the sons of the captives were born in Babylon; but, having the heart of an Israelite, felt it not a home: it was "a strange land" to them.

On earth the Christian feels himself to be an *exile*—distant from his Father's home—distant from near and beloved connections and friends who have got home before him. True, he has many comforts, &c. But still this is not his rest; not his birthplace; not the condition for which his faculties and affections were originally designed. There are times in which his hope is full of immortality, and he has bright glimpses of the better country in his hours of faith and devotion; and then he feels indeed a stranger and a pilgrim; he spurns the yoke; he mourns the chain; and, like a captive minstrel, hangs his harp upon the willows, and cries, "Oh, that I had wings like a dove," &c.

II. Whence arises the difficulty of singing the Lord's song in a world like this? It may be done; it is important that it should be done; provisions are made for doing it, for they had harps and they had the subject of their song, just as Christians have now the means, the materials, and the elements of their spiritual joy. Yet there are obstructions to the full enjoyment of the peace which the Gospel brings. Whence arises the hindrance?

1. *From want of sympathy in those around us.* Their oppressors did not ask for the song from love to the religion, or sympathy with the captives, but to add insult to their misery by holding up their religion to contempt, and mocking at the hope and promise it contained. Here we admire the captives. They did not forget to take their harps with them to Babylon. They did not refuse to sing because they were ashamed of their religion, or would make a secret of it. They did not hide their harps, as if they were afraid of their avowal; and they did not break their harps, as if they were abandoned to despair; but they hung them upon the willows in sight of the foe, and only refused to sing because the company was uncongenial.

And is it not so still? Are not the peace and happiness of the children of Zion grievously diminished by the uncongenial society with which they are called to mingle—sometimes in their own families, when a believing wife is yoked to an unbelieving husband, or a religious husband to an irreligious wife? "Can two walk together, except they be agreed?" (Amos iii. 3). How much less can two sing together? When Christians mingle with irreligious persons in the same house, the same shop, the same workroom, &c.

2. *From the pressure of outward trial and of mental grief.* I know that all the troubles of the wilderness ought not to put us out of tune for singing the songs of Zion; but they sometimes do. We have often observed a counter-effect produced for a season by the calamities of life—that whereas they are both designed and adapted to lead us at once and directly to God, yet under the first and immediate pressure an opposite effect is produced, till principle has time to rally and grace obtains her triumph. The cup intoxicates; the blow stuns. David expresses this in Ps. lx. 3.

But even then the Christian does not break his harp; he only suspends it; and if he cannot find a song, he will at least hush the breath of murmuring and complaint. David corrects his despondency, and at the very worst anticipates brighter times (Ps. xlii. 11). Yet the Lord Jesus anticipates even His sufferings with a song (Matt. xxvi. 30.)

3. *Because our hearts are out of tune for the exercise.* Under the consciousness of spiritual declension it is very difficult to "sing the Lord's song."

III. What answer shall be returned to the inquiry—"How shall we sing the Lord's song"? &c.

1. *If you would sing the Lord's song in adversity, make yourself well acquainted with it in prosperity.* It is bad to have our comforts to seek when we want to enjoy them; our anchor to provide when we want to use it; our song to learn, &c. (Isa. xii. 1).

2. *Live close to God, and exercise renewed acts of faith in Christ.* Retrace your steps if you have wandered. "Repent, and do thy first works."

3. *Be much in prayer.* "Open Thou my lips," &c.

4. *Honour the work and agency of the Holy Spirit.*—*Samuel Thodey.*

SONGS IN A STRANGE LAND.
(*Verse 4.*)

I. The Christian on earth is in a strange land—
1. As to his feelings.
2. As to his supplies.
3. As to his dangers.

II. The Christian on earth, although in a strange land, has songs—
1. Of gratitude.
2. Of penitence.
3. Of resignation.
4. Of hope.—*George Brooks.*

RETRIBUTION.

(*Verses 7-9.*)

We have in these verses—

I. An important feature of the Divine government of the world. The designs of God are sometimes wrought out by wicked men, but this affords no excuse to such men, nor will it secure to them any exemption from the just consequences of their deeds. In the Babylonish captivity this is strikingly exemplified. The Jews were carried into Babylon by the permission of God as a punishment for their many sins, particularly their idolatry. And in one respect, at least, the captivity accomplished its purpose; for the Jews have never since relapsed into idolatry. So far the Babylonians did the work of God. But they did it unintentionally, unconsciously. They had no thought of working out the purposes of God in so doing, but simply of fulfilling their own proud and lawless designs. The captivity was overruled by God for the accomplishment of His designs, yet on the part of Babylon it was unjustifiable and wicked. And did she go unpunished? No. The hour of retribution struck, the strange fingers appeared in the royal banquet hall, the letters of doom with appalling distinctness and mystery were inscribed upon the wall, the enemy even then was close upon the city: "in that night was Belshazzar king of the Chaldeans slain," and Babylon, "the lady of kingdoms," was a kingdom no longer. We see the same principle in operation in the life of Joseph (Gen. 1. 20; Ps. lxxvi. 10).

How magnificent is this aspect of the Divine government! All things in the universe are under the control of the Almighty, and the most malignant powers are used for the accomplishment of His glorious purposes. There is no real triumph of falsehood and evil. Their victories are only brief appearances. All things in the universe are aiding to enthrone the True and the Good.

II. A cry for retribution. "Remember, O Lord, the children of Edom," &c. "Deepest of all," says Dean Stanley, "was the indignation roused by the sight of the nearest of kin, the race of Esau, often allied to Judah, often independent, now bound by the closest union with the power that was truly the common enemy of both. There was an intoxication of delight in the wild Edomite chiefs, as at each successive stroke against the venerable walls they shouted, 'Down with it! down with it! even to the ground!' They stood in the passes to interrupt the escape of those who would have fled down to the Jordan valley; they betrayed the fugitives; they indulged in their barbarous revels on the Temple hill. Long and loud has been the wail of execration which has gone up from the Jewish nation against Edom. It is the one imprecation which breaks forth from the Lamentations of Jeremiah; it is the culmination of the fierce threats of Ezekiel; it is the sole purpose of the short, sharp cry of Obadiah; it is the bitterest drop in the sad recollections of the Israelite captives by the waters of Babylon; and the one warlike strain of the Evangelical Prophet is inspired by the hope that the Divine Conqueror should come knee deep in Idumean blood (Lam. iv. 21, 22; Ezek. xxv. 12–14; Obad. 1–21; Jer. xlix. 7–22; Isa. lxiii. 1–4)."

This cry to the Lord for retribution to Edom implies—

1. *The existence of the sense of justice in the human soul.*
2. *Belief in the righteous government of God.*
3. *Belief in the efficacy of prayer to God.*

III. An illustration of the nature of retribution. "O daughter of Babylon, who art to be destroyed, happy shall he be that rewardeth thee as thou hast served us." Margin: "That recompenseth unto thee thy deed which thou didst to us." Perowne, literally: "The requital wherewith thou hast requited us." "Agreeably to His justice," says Tholuck, "God exercises the *jus* *talionis.* Justice is elastic; the unjust blow I inflict upon another, by the order of the moral world, recoils upon myself." (Comp. Judges i. 6, 7; Jer. li. 54–56.) "God has undertaken," says Bushnell, "to dispense justice by a law of natural consequence. He has connected thus, with our moral and physical nature, a law of reaction, by which any wrong of thought, feeling, disposition, or act, provokes a retribution exactly fitted to it, and to the desert of it. And this law is just like every law of natural order, inviolable, not subject to suspension, or discontinuance, even by miracle itself. And justice is, in this view, a fixed principle of order, as truly as the laws of the heavenly bodies."

IV. The desire for retribution is prone to develop into vindictiveness towards those who have injured us.

"Happy shall he be that taketh and dasheth thy little ones against the rock." In ancient warfare the indiscriminate slaughter of persons of all ages and of both sexes was common. Perhaps the Psalmist in this utterance "only acts as a Divine herald to confirm former predictions." As a matter of fact Cyrus, the conqueror of Babylon, is reckoned amongst the heroes of history. But "there is great need to have the heart well guarded with the fear of God, for, otherwise to allow the dashing of little ones against the stones, might make a man guilty of savage cruelty." Guard earnestly against a vindictive spirit.

"Consider this,—
That, in the course of justice, none of us
Should see salvation: we do pray for mercy;
And that same prayer doth teach us all to render
The deeds of mercy."—*Shakespeare.*

PSALM CXXXVIII.

INTRODUCTION.

"This," says Barnes, "is the first of a series of eight Psalms (Ps. xxxviii.–cxlv.) placed together in this part of the book, and ascribed to David. They appear to be of the nature of a *supplement* to the Book of Psalms, composed of Psalms unknown to the original collector and arranger of the Book, and subsequently discovered and ascertained to be the works of David. It is not to be regarded as strange that there should be Psalms of this nature composed by David at different periods of his life, which might have been preserved in different branches of his family, and which might not have been generally known to exist. It is rare that the works of an author, especially a poet, are collected and published, and that things of this kind—fugitive and occasional pieces—are not subsequently found; nor is it very unusual that such pieces may, after all, be amongst the most tender, touching, and beautiful of his compositions. Burn's 'Highland Mary,' so much admired, and his, 'When wild War's deadly blast was blown,'— a poem which no one can read without tears,—with not a few others of his, are of this description. They are said, in his Biography, to have been 'extracted from the *correspondence* of Burns.'

"The occasion on which this Psalm was composed cannot now be determined."

A DEVOUT RESOLUTION, GRATEFUL RECOLLECTION, AND AN ENCOURAGING ANTICIPATION.

(*Verses* 1–5.)

We have here—

I. **A devout resolution** (vers. 1, 2). The poet resolves to celebrate the praise of God, and to do so—

1. *In the most excellent manner.* (1.) *Heartily.* "I will praise Thee with my whole heart." It is remarkable that he does not say whom he will praise until he comes to the fourth verse. This is significant. "It is as though in the Psalmist's heart there could be but one object of praise, whether named or unnamed." Whole-heartedness and fervour in worship are acceptable unto God. (2.) *Confidently.* "Before the gods will I sing praise unto Thee." "'The gods,'" says Perowne, "are the false gods, the objects of heathen worship, in the very presence of whom, and to the confusion of their worshippers,

the Psalmist will utter his praise of the true God." When our faith in God is strong we shall be neither afraid nor ashamed to praise Him before any person. (3.) *Becomingly.* "I will worship toward Thy holy temple." The Psalmist was not allowed to enter the interior of the tabernacle, which he here designates, "Thy holy temple." The tabernacle was regarded as the special residence of the Most High. Because He specially manifested Himself there, the pious Israelites turned their faces towards it when they worshipped. Thus Daniel in his exile prayed with "his windows open in his chamber toward Jerusalem." There are certain forms and arrangements for worship which are reverent and seemly, and these every devout worshipper will endeavour to conform to. "Keep thy foot when thou goest into the house of God," &c. We must worship reverently through the mediation of Jesus Christ.

2. *For the most excellent reasons.* "I will praise Thy Name for Thy lovingkindness and for Thy truth; for Thou hast magnified Thy word above all Thy Name." The poet resolves to praise the Lord because of the kindness and faithfulness which He had manifested according to His Word. The final clause in the second verse has occasioned considerable difficulty to some expositors. The interpretation of Barnes, Hengstenberg, Henry, Perowne, and others seems to us undoubtedly correct,—that the revelation of Himself which God has given to man in His Word surpasses in clearness and preciousness all the other manifestations which He has made of Himself. Thus Perowne: "*Thy word,* or 'promise.' (Comp. Ps. lvi. 10, lx. 6, lxii. 11.) No particular promise is meant. The same word occurs frequently in Ps. cxix. *Above all Thy Name.* The expression seems to mean that to the soul waiting upon God, and trusting in His word, the promise becomes so precious, so strong a ground of hope, that it surpasses all other manifestations of God's goodness and truth; or in the promise may here also be included the fulfilment of the promise." In His Word God has given many exceeding great and precious promises, and they are all worthy of acceptation; for God in His fulfilment is better even than in His promises. Here then is an excellent reason for praising God, because He has manifested so much of Himself, and especially of His loving-kindness and faithfulness to us in His Word. Our revelation is much fuller and richer than was that of David. "We see Jesus,"

" And, in His face a glory stands,
The noblest labour of Thy hands;
The radiant lustre of His eyes
Outshines the wonders of the skies."
—*Watts.*

Therefore, our praise should be more hearty and confident than was that of David.

II. **A grateful recollection.** "In the day when I cried Thou answeredst me, and strengthenedst me with strength in my soul." Perowne: "Thou madest me courageous with strength in my soul." In time of need the Psalmist had sought the Lord in prayer, and the Lord had heard and graciously answered him. God had answered him—

1. *Speedily.* "In the day when I cried Thou answeredst me." "Before they call, I will answer; and while they are yet speaking, I will hear." (Comp. Dan. ix. 20–24.)

2. *Spiritually.* "Thou madest me courageous with strength in my soul." We pray in time of difficulty, and He gives us wisdom and courage to meet and surmount the difficulty; in time of affliction, and He gives us patience and strength to bear the suffering. "My grace," saith He, "is sufficient for thee." Recollections such as this one of David's stimulate the heart to grateful and joyous praise.

III. **An encouraging anticipation.** The Psalmist confidently anticipates a time when all the kings of the earth shall recognise Jehovah as God, and render to Him devout homage and cheerful obedience.

1. *All kings shall be made acquainted with the highest revelation of God and with His glory.* They shall "hear the words of His mouth," and see that "great is the glory of the Lord." The Gospel shall be preached in all the

world, and the glory of the Divine grace shall be exhibited to all peoples. God in Christ shall be made known to all men.

2. *When all kings are acquainted with "the words" and "the glory of the Lord" they will heartily praise and cheerfully serve Him.* "Shall praise Thee, O Lord," &c. "Yea, they shall sing in the ways of the Lord." "The ways of the Lord" are those of obedience and worship; the ways of reverence towards God and righteousness towards men. They shall tread them with cheerfulness. Obligation will be regarded as a privilege. Duty will be transferred into delight. Statutes will be translated into songs, and set to joyous music. *A true acquaintance with the highest revelation of God is calculated to lead to such a result.* The revelation of God in Christ is fitted to inspire our trust, to captivate our affections, and to secure our enthusiastic obedience. Let the world heartily accept Christ—the Christ not of the creeds and the churches, but of the Evangelists—as the supreme Revelation of God, and it will speedily bow to His authority, resound with His praise, and delight in His service.

GOD'S WORD EXALTED.

(*Verse 2.*)

"Thou hast magnified Thy word above all Thy Name."

I. As the medium of His self-manifestation.
II. As the exposition of His government.
III. As the record of His will.
IV. As the instrument of His power.
V. As the revelation of His love.
—*W. W. Wythe.*

AN EARNEST PRAYER, AND AN IMMEDIATE ANSWER.

(*Verse 3.*)

Consider—

I. The earnestness of his prayer.
"I cried unto Thee." Beautiful description of prayer—crying unto God. "Prayer," says Mrs. More, "is the cry of want, to Him that can relieve it; of guilt, to Him who is able to pardon it; of sorrow, to Him who is able to relieve it." (So Ps. cxix. 145.)

1. *It supposes the pressure of distress*, under the frowns of the world; under the temptations of Satan; under the difficulties of the way; under the exigencies of the Christian conflict. The day of trial, a long day—a dark day—a stormy day—a day that brings God and the soul together. The time of affliction is the time of supplication. God afflicts us that He may hear from us.

2. *It supposes the ready recourse of the Christian to God in prayer.* No sooner does the storm of danger come down than the cry of faith and fervour goes up. It is this spirit of heartfelt continued instancy in prayer that keeps the Christian in the hour of temptation, or in the floods of adversity, and maintains the spiritual life within. But often is the Christian constrained to acknowledge that his heart has little to do with the cry of his lips. Yet in danger still he cries—sometimes with a cry which no words could fully express, that vents itself only in "groanings which cannot be uttered"—a cry that "enters into the ears of the Lord of Sabaoth."

3. *It supposes previous habits of acquaintance with God;* for we do not run to a stranger in distress, much less to an enemy, but to a known and tried friend.

4. *It supposes the union of prayer and thankfulness.* Praise should always follow where prayer is answered. A gracious man is a praising and a grateful man. As answers come down, praises should go up.

II. The effectual relief he gained.
God is a prayer-hearing and a sin-pardoning God.

1. *He obtained an immediate answer.* "In the day when I cried Thou

answeredst," &c. Moses cried at the Red Sea, and had instant help. No needless delay: no indifference to the state and condition of the Church on the part of God. (Compare Ps. xxxii. 3–5.) . . . While the voice of penitent confession was suppressed, his cries and lamentations were disregarded; but upon the first utterance of prayer from his lips, or rather on the first purpose of contrition formed in his heart, the pardon, the full and free pardon, is granted. "I said, I will confess, . . . and Thou forgavest." How prompt was the answer to Jacob's prayer at Jabbok (Gen. xxxii. 24–30); to Gideon's (Judges vi. 36–40; to Daniel's (Dan. ix. 20–23).

2. *He was replenished with inward grace.* "Thou strengthenedst me with strength in my soul." Strength to bear troubles; strength to overcome temptations; strength to war with the powers of evil. Especially was he strengthened in the actings of faith—led to renewed exercises of dependence upon the power and grace of Christ. Weak indeed are our purposes without grace to strengthen them, and worthless our good resolutions without grace to carry them out; but when the grace is enjoyed, difficulties give way, enemies are overcome, and inward peace is attained amidst outward trials. This is God's way of putting life into the soul, when by an inexpressible sweetness and power He allures the soul to Himself. Every step, indeed, to the very end will be a conflict with besetting sin or with remaining enmity and unbelief. But in answer to prayer there will be a continual drawing of the Spirit of God towards high and holy things. The same Hand that gave a new bias to the soul in a heavenward motion, will confirm and strengthen it to the end.

3. *The principle of hope was itself reinvigorated*, that he was not only strengthened for the present, but enabled to anticipate the future. "Though I walk in the midst of trouble, Thou wilt revive me."

III. The force and inspiration of his example upon other minds.

"All the kings of the earth shall praise Thee, O Lord, when they hear the words of Thy mouth," &c. We not only must be religious ourselves, but help others to be so.—*Samuel Thodey.*

GOD'S TREATMENT OF DIFFERENT CLASSES OF CHARACTER.

(*Verses 6–9.*)

I. God's treatment of the humble. "Though the Lord be high, yet hath He respect unto the lowly."

1. *The character.* "The lowly." Not the lowly in outward condition merely, but in inward disposition—the humble. Humility is not a thing of circumstances, but of soul.

2. *The treatment.* "The Lord hath respect unto the lowly." He "looks upon" them. He not only sees them, but regards them graciously. He views them with approving interest, and affords them kindly aid.

3. *The reason.* "Because the Lord is high He hath respect unto the lowly." The A. V. in giving the impression that the Lord looks upon the humble *notwithstanding* His greatness does not represent the poet's meaning. God graciously regards the poor in spirit *because* He is so great. A more correct rendering is, "For the Lord is lifted up, and looks upon the lowly."—*Hengstenberg.* Or: "For lofty is Jehovah, and the humble He sees."—*Barnes.* God is a great Being, and therefore He is condescending. Hengstenberg: "The lofty elevation of the Lord forms the ground, on account of which He lifts up the lowly, brings down the proud; not: and yet; but: and *therefore.*" "Thus saith the high and lofty One that inhabiteth eternity, whose name is Holy; I dwell in the high and holy place, with him also that is of a contrite and humble spirit, to revive the spirit of the humble and to revive the heart of the contrite ones."

II. God's treatment of the proud. "The proud He knoweth afar off."

1. *The character.* "The proud." Not

the exalted in station, but the haughty, the arrogant. Pride is *unbecoming, foolish, sinful.* "Pride," says Sidney Smith, "is not the heritage of man; humility should dwell with frailty, and atone for ignorance, error, and imperfection."

2. *The treatment.* Jehovah knoweth the proud afar off. He regards them only at a distance. Pride is an insuperable barrier between God and man. A haughty man is not regarded by God with favour, nor can he have any communion with Him. "Every one that is proud in heart is an abomination to the Lord."

III. **God's treatment of His afflicted people.** "Though I walk in the midst of trouble," &c. We have here—

1. *A depressing possibility in the life of good men.* The life of a good man may be—(1.) *Surrounded by trouble*—a journey "in the midst of trouble." Piety does not secure a man from the afflictions of life. The godly man is exposed to infirmities and diseases of the body, to losses and difficulties in temporal affairs, to family and social trials and bereavements, to spiritual conflicts and distresses. Like Job, the godly man is sometimes almost overwhelmed with trouble. The life of a good man may be—(2.) *Imperilled by angry enemies.* The Psalmist seems to have been exposed to the wrath of his adversaries when he wrote this Psalm. The godly soul is exposed to the assaults of spiritual foes. The lusts of the flesh, the cares and anxieties, pomps and vanities, shams and dissipations of the world, and the subtlety and power of the devil are arrayed against him. The good man is acquainted with both trouble and peril; he has trials and enemies.

2. *An encouraging confidence in the life of good men.* David was confident of—(1.) *Revival in trouble.* "Thou wilt revive me." He had an unfailing hope that the Lord would quicken and strengthen him to bear his trials. He sustains and comforts His afflicted people. David was confident of—(2.) *Deliverance from enemies.* "Thou shalt stretch forth Thine hand against the wrath of mine enemies, and Thy right hand shall save me." God exerts His almighty power for the protection and salvation of His people. The good are shielded by Omnipotence.

IV. **God's treatment of His trustful people.** "The Lord will perfect that which concerneth me," &c. Notice :—

1. *The inspiring assurance.* The poet was confident that the Lord would accomplish the work which He had begun concerning him. God does not abandon His work in an incomplete state. We are "confident that He which hath begun a good work in you will perform it until the day of Jesus Christ." "Grace will complete what grace begins."

2. *The firm basis of this assurance.* The confidence of the Psalmist was grounded on the unchangeableness of God's everlasting mercy. "Thy mercy, O Lord, endureth for ever." He who bases his trust of complete and glorious salvation on this foundation will never be put to shame.

3. *The humble dependence of this assurance.* "Forsake not the works of Thine own hands." The poet here translates into a prayer what he had just before expressed as a conviction of his soul. Prayer is one of the means whereby the completion of the Divine work in us and for us is secured. The good man is sensible of his own weakness and waywardness, and depends upon God to perfect His own work in his salvation. In the material universe there are no unfinished worlds or systems; no half-made and forsaken works of His hands. And His work in the soul that trusts Him He will continue until it attains full and glorious perfection.

Here, then, is encouragement to His people to trust in Him at all times.

THE MAJESTY AND CONDESCENSION OF GOD.

(*Verse 6.*)

"Though the Lord be high, yet hath He respect unto the lowly."

I. **The majesty of God.**
1. Consider His eternity.
2. Consider His immutability.
3. Consider His power.
4. Consider His goodness.

II. **The condescension of God.**
1. Consider the persons to whom His preference is shown.
2. Consider the special blessings with which He honours them.—*Geo. Brooks.*

PSALM CXXXIX.

INTRODUCTION.

"Nowhere," says Perowne, "are the great attributes of God—His omniscience, His omnipresence, His omnipotence, set forth so strikingly as they are in this magnificent Psalm. Nowhere is there a more overwhelming sense of the fact that man is beset and compassed about by God, pervaded by His Spirit, unable to take a step without His control; and yet nowhere is there a more emphatic assertion of the personality of man as distinct from, not absorbed in the Deity. This is no pantheistic speculation. Man is here the workmanship of God, and stands in the presence and under the eye of One who is his Judge. The power of conscience, the sense of sin and of responsibility, are felt and acknowledged, and prayer is offered to One who is not only the Judge but the Friend; to One who is feared as none else are feared, who is loved as none else are loved.

"Both in loftiness of thought and in expressive beauty of language the Psalm stands pre-eminent, and it is not surprising that Aben Ezra should have pronounced it to be 'the crown of all the Psalms.' The Psalm both in the Hebrew and the LXX. is ascribed to David.

"The rhythmical structure is, on the whole, regular. There are four strophes, each consisting of six verses; the first three strophes containing the proper theme of the Psalm, and the last the expression of individual feeling.

"I. In the first strophe the poet dwells on the omniscience of God, as manifested in His knowledge of the deepest thoughts and most secret workings of the human heart, vers. 1-6.

"II. In the second, on His omnipresence, inasmuch as there is no corner of the universe so remote that it is not pervaded by God's presence, no darkness so deep that it can hide from His eyes, vers. 7-12.

"III. The third strophe gives the reason for the profound conviction of these truths of which the poet's heart is full. No wonder that God should have so intimate a knowledge of man, for man is the creature of God : the mysterious beginnings of life, which none can trace; the days, all of which are ordered before the first breath is drawn,—these are fashioned and ordered by the hand of God, vers. 13-18.

"IV. In the last strophe the Psalmist turns abruptly aside to express his utter abhorrence of wicked men—an abhorrence, no doubt, deepened by the previous meditation on God and His attributes, and called forth probably by the circumstances in which he was placed; and then closes with a prayer that he himself may, in his inmost heart, be right with that God who has searched him and known him and laid His hand upon him, and that he may be led by Him in the way everlasting, ver. 19-24."

GOD'S PERFECT KNOWLEDGE OF MAN.

(*Verses 1-6.*)

Our purpose is not to write on the omniscience of God in general, or to make an attempt to set it forth with completeness and show its relations and bearings; but to call attention to those aspects of it which are mentioned by the Psalmist, and to indicate the practical bearing of these aspects upon human life. The poet sets forth in this strophe the omniscience of God as related to human life.

I. **God knows all men.** David does not write of himself alone. That the Psalm is addressed "to the chief musician" is a proof that it was intended to be set to music for use in public worship. The entire congregation was to use the Psalm. Its utterances were to be adopted by every member of the congregation. Every person in the world may say with truth, "O Lord, Thou hast searched me and known me," &c. Neither is there any creature that is not manifest in His sight; but all things are naked and opened unto the eyes of Him with whom we have to do."

II. God knows all men thoroughly.

1. *He knows all their words and actions.* "Thou art acquainted with all my ways, for there is not a word on my tongue, but lo, O Lord, Thou knowest it altogether." The entire course of every human life, and every step in every individual course, are perfectly known to God, and not a word that is uttered by human tongues escapes His ear.

2. *He knows all their thoughts.* "Thou understandest my thought afar off." However great the distance between God and man may seem to be, yet He is "a discerner of the thoughts and intents of his heart." Calvin: "God is not shut up in heaven, as if He delighted in an idle repose (as the Epicureans feigned), and neglected human affairs; but though we live at a great distance from Him, still He is not far from us." All worthy thoughts and pure and generous feelings He knows, and all evil thoughts and impure and malignant feelings He also knows. "Before men we stand," says Beecher, "as opaque beehives. They can see the thoughts go in and out of us; but what work they do inside of a man they cannot tell. Before God we are as *glass* beehives, and all that our thoughts are doing within us He perfectly sees and understands."

III. God knows all men constantly.

At all times and under all circumstances He is perfectly acquainted with us. He knows us in *work* and in *rest*, in our *daily walk* and in our *nightly repose*. "Thou knowest my downsitting" for rest, "and mine uprising" for action. "Thou compassest my path and my lying down." Perowne: "My path and my bed Thou hast examined." Lit. "Thou hast winnowed," or "sifted." Hengstenberg: "זָרָה, properly, to sift, then poetically, to prove, to know." God knows our "path," our way of active life, and our "couch" or "bed," our thoughts and feelings in our place of rest. We are altogether and always perfectly known unto Him. God's knowledge of us differs from our knowledge of each other not only in its extent and completeness, but in other respects.

First, *His knowledge is underived and independent.* We receive instruction from tutors and information from books. But He receives not his knowledge from anything without Him. His knowledge is as independent as Himself and His own essence. "Who hath directed the Spirit of the Lord, or, being His counsellor, hath taught Him?" "Our knowledge," says Charnock, "depends upon the object, but all created objects depend upon God's knowledge and will: we could not know creatures unless they were; but creatures could not be unless God knew them."

Second, *His knowledge is clear and perfect.* "We see through a glass, darkly;" and only "know in part." He knows all things clearly and distinctly, intimately and thoroughly, infallibly and perfectly. "God is light, and in Him is no darkness at all." "His understanding is infinite."

Let us endeavour to point out the practical bearing of this knowledge on us and on our life. It ought to prove—

1. *An antidote to the pride of intellect.* "Such knowlege is too wonderful for me; it is high, I cannot attain unto it." We cannot comprehend the Divine omniscience. Our attempts to do so end in ignominious failure. We can but cry, "Oh, the depth of the riches both of the wisdom and knowledge of God!" &c. How vain and ridiculous it is for any man to pride himself in his intellectual attainments or acquisitions! What we know is almost as nothing in contrast to what we do not know. "We have a drop of knowledge, but nothing to the Divine ocean. What a vain thing is it fo a shallow brook to boast of its streams before a sea, whose depths are unfathomable!"

2. *An effectual restraint from sins both of heart and of action.* The eye

of man often imposes a restraint upon the evil-doer; and shall the eye of God, which is ever upon us, be disregarded? Men seek to hide their evil doings by the darkness of night, saying, "How doth God know? can He judge through the dark cloud?" But darkness cannot hide from Him. He knows the evil thought, the dark design, the impure feeling. Secret sin is impossible. Let the fact of God's omniscience check evil in its first beginnings.

3. *A solemn warning to the sinner.* Secrecy does not hide from God, hypocrisy does not deceive Him, the lapse of time does not cause Him to forget, all sins are known to Him, and will be visited upon the sinners unless they are pardoned. "What a terrible consideration is it to think that the sins of a day are upon record in an infallible understanding, much more the sins of a week: what a number, then, do the sins of a month, a year, ten or forty years arise to!" Sinner, take warning.

4. *The utter impossibility of any man justifying himself in the sight of God.* God knows all and everything. "Our secret sins are in the light of His countenance." He sees defects and imperfections even in our best deeds. "Enter not into judgment with Thy servant; for in Thy sight shall no man living be justified."

5. *A comfort to the people of God when misjudged by man.* Men frequently mistake the motives of their fellow-men and judge them harshly. But how comforting it is to turn from man unto God. "Behold, my witness is in heaven, and my record is on high. He knoweth the way that I take," &c. Our cause is in the hands of the Omniscient and All-Merciful.

6. *A guarantee of the well-being of the people of God.* God not only knows, but also cares for His people. "As providence infers omniscience as the guide of it, so omniscience infers providence as the end of it." He knows them in their weakness to sustain them, in their need to provide for them, in their dangers to rescue them, in their sorrows to comfort them, &c. Our Lord Himself set forth the Divine knowledge as an encouragement to His people to trust in God. "Your Heavenly Father knoweth that ye have need of all these things," &c. (Matt. vi. 31, 32).

7. *A pledge of the triumph of the Divine government.* All the dark and cunning designs of His enemies are known to Him. Their most secret plans cannot surprise Him. Their most subtle plans cannot baffle Him. He will make their counsel of no effect, and frustrate their deepest schemes. His omniscience assures us of the triumph of His cause. All things are under His control. He, and He alone, can say, "My counsel shall stand, and I will do all My pleasure."

GOD'S OMNIPRESENCE.

(*Verses 7-12.*)

The Psalmist here treats of the omnipresence of God, not as a metaphysical conception, but as a momentous practical truth. This truth he sets forth in language of great force and beauty. In other portions of the Holy Word this truth is clearly and forcibly expressed. 1 Kings viii. 27; Jer. xxiii. 23, 24; Amos ix. 2, 3. According to the representation of David—

I. **God is personally present everywhere.** The Psalm was not written by a Pantheist. He speaks of God as a Person everywhere present in creation, yet distinct from creation. In our text He says, "*Thy* Spirit, . . . *Thy* presence, . . . *Thou* art there, . . . *Thy* hand, . . . *Thy* right hand, . . . darkness hideth not from *Thee.*" God is everywhere, but He is not everything. All things have their being in Him, but He is distinct from all things. He fills the universe, but is not mingled with it. He is the Intelligence which guides, and the power which sustains; but His personality is preserved, and He is independent of the works of His hands. however vast and noble. Charnock: " Where light is in every part of a crystal globe, and encircles it close on every side, do they become one? No; the crystal remains what it is, and the light retains its own nature. God is not in us as a part of us, but as an efficient and preserving cause." "In Him we live, and move, and have our being." "We live and move in God, so we live and move in the air; we are no more God by that than we are mere air because we breathe in it, and it enters into all the pores of our body."

II. **God is influentially present everywhere.** The Psalmist felt that wherever he was—in heaven, in Sheol, or on the utmost verge of creation—he would be led and sustained by God. "Even there shall Thy hand lead me, and Thy right hand shall hold me." He is everywhere present in His *sustaining* energy. "O Lord, Thou preservest man and beast." "By Him all things consist." "He upholds all things by the word of His power." He is everywhere present by His *controlling* energy. He restrains and overrules all evil. He originates and fosters all good. "This influential presence may be compared to that of the sun, which, though at so great a distance from the earth, is present in the air and earth by its light, and within the earth by its influence in concocting those metals which are in the bowels of it, without being substantially either of them."

III. **God is intelligently present everywhere.** The poet felt that, wherever he was and in whatever circumstances, he would be fully known to the Lord.

"And should I say: Only let darkness cover me, and the light about me be night; even darkness cannot be too dark for Thee, but the night is light as the day; the darkness and light (to Thee are) both alike." "The eyes of the Lord are in every place, beholding the evil and the good." "With one single look He beholdeth the whole universe. As I am accounted present in this auditory, because I see the objects that are here, because I am witness of all that passes here; so God is everywhere, because He sees all, because veils the most impenetrable, darkness the most thick, distances the most immense, can conceal nothing from His knowledge. Soar to the utmost heights, fly into the remotest climates, wrap thyself in the blackest darkness, everywhere, everywhere, thou wilt be under His eye."—*Saurin*.

IV. **God's presence is everywhere realised by the godly soul.** To the Psalmist the Divine omnipresence was not a mere opinion, not a mere article of a creed, but a realised fact. "Whither shall I go from Thy Spirit? or whither shall I flee from Thy presence?" He *felt* the presence of God everywhere. At every step and in every circumstance of life he felt himself in that presence. In all the phenomena of nature he recognised that presence. To him all things are full of God, "yet all distinct from Him. The cloud on the mountain is His covering; the muttering from the chambers of the thunder is His voice; that sound on the top of the mulberry trees is His 'going;' in that wind, which bends the forest or curls the clouds, He is walking; that sun is His still commanding eye." The godly soul is possessed by an intense consciousness of the constant presence of God.

"God is a sphere or circle, whose centre is everywhere, and circumference nowhere." So far is His presence from being bounded by the universe itself, that, as we are taught in our text, were it possible for us to wing our way into the immeasurable depths and breadths of space, God would there surround us, in as absolute a sense as that in which He is said to be about our bed and our path, in that part of the world where His will has placed us. As He is larger than all time, so He is vaster than all space.

Let us now point out the practical bearings of this great truth.

1. *It should restrain us from evil.* The eye of a child will effectually check the execution of some evil purposes; more the eye of man or woman; yet more the eye of a holy man or woman. Men chose darkness and secrecy for the perpetration of evil. But "there is no darkness nor shadow of death where the workers of iniquity may hide themselves." God's eye sees all things everywhere. He is in the darkness by the

side of the worker of iniquity. And He is perfectly holy.

2. *It should lead us to hold humble thoughts of ourselves and exalted ideas of God.* How small are we to God! Our existence seems almost as non-existence when placed beside His immensity. Let His greatness excite our reverence. Let our littleness lead us to constant lowliness.

3. *It should comfort and strengthen the people of God in severe trial, in painful loneliness, and in arduous duty.* He accompanies His people into the furnace of affliction, and preserves them from injury. "When thou passest through the waters, I will be with thee," &c. (Isa. xliii. 2). When exiled from friends, or forsaken of friends, or bereaved of friends by death, His presence is never withdrawn. If He call us to some difficult task, He assures us, "My presence shall go with thee." His realised presence is the secret of the success of Moses, Paul, &c.

4. *It should be an incentive to holy action.* The athletes of Greece and Rome were inspired to run or wrestle by the knowledge of the fact that they were surrounded by a vast assembly of spectators. It is said that, at the battle of Prestonpans, a Highland chief of the noble house of M'Gregor was wounded by two balls and fell. Seeing their chief fall, the clan wavered, and gave the enemy an advantage. The old chieftain, beholding the effects of his disaster, raised himself up on his elbow, while the blood gushed in streams from his wounds, and cried aloud, "I am not dead, my children : I am looking at you to see you do your duty." These words revived the sinking courage of the brave Highlanders, and roused them to put forth their mightiest energies ; and they did all that human valour could do to stem and turn the dreadful tide of battle. Oh ! if we but realised God's presence, felt Him near to us, our life would become brave and beautiful and holy. God is not only present everywhere, but everywhere present to inspire, and aid, and bless.

5. *It is of vital importance to all worshippers of God.* The consideration of the Divine omnipresence is calculated to *destroy formality,* to *inspire reverence,* and to *strengthen faith.* "Where two or three are gathered together in My name, there am I in the midst of them."

THE OMNIPRESENCE OF GOD AND ITS IMPRESSIONS UPON MAN.

(*Verses* 7–12.)

There is one circumstance in the text which directs a humble mind how it ought to be treated, and that is with the utmost humility of devotion ; for it is a direct address to God Himself. However discursive the imagination might be on other texts, on this it is quite out of character.

If this thought be powerful on the mind of your preacher, there is another which ought equally to affect the minds of the hearers ; and that is, that you are now in a place where you ought to feel yourself most exposed to His survey. God indeed is about your bed and about your path ; but in the house of prayer you voluntarily expose yourself to His immediate notice, you court His scrutiny. Recollect that God is present ; the King is now come in to see His guests : He knows with what motives you have come hither ; whether you prayed before you came ; whether you listened to the reading of the Scriptures as to the Word of God ; whether you prayed in prayer ; whether you sung with devotion, "making melody in your heart to the Lord." Yes, my brethren, even now you are weighed in the balances of the sanctuary. God grant that you may not be found wanting.

I. **Let us endeavour to realise the grand sentiment which the text contains.**

God is everywhere present. The first thought of the sinner is how he may escape. "Whither shall I go from Thy Spirit ?" &c. How vain ! A reflection upon human nature. Grace is wiser ; it teaches us to seek His presence. "Let him take hold of My strength," &c. "When shall I come and appear before God?"

How many present have never reflected upon the subject; and though always surrounded by God, have never derived comfort from His presence! Without hope, without God — awful thought!

1. *How great must be the Being who possesses such an empire!* These are His attributes; these are not limited. A wing that never tires: an eye that never sleeps.

2. *How melancholy the reflection that the great thought that occurs to the sinner is how he may escape Him!* "Whither shall I go from Thy Spirit?" &c. This is not natural: sin is the cause of it. How false the hope! How miserable the condition!

3. *How valuable is that religion which teaches us to hope in His mercy;* which tells us that over all worlds He exercises a Father's care; that His fostering wing extends to the minutest object; and that He especially discerns the returning sinner.

II. **Let us trace some of the impressions which it ought to produce on individual character.**

1. *The utter hopelessness of a career of crime or of indifference to God.* Wherever you are engaged in guilt, God is there to interrupt, to record, to disappoint, to vex the soul. Think of this in your plans of life, in business, in your families. Examples: Achan (Josh. vii. 16–26). Gehazi (2 Kings v. 20–27).

2. *The strong consolation afforded to the humble penitent.* He sees every desire, hope, effort. "Why sayest thou, O Jacob?" &c. (Isa. xl. 27–31).

3. *The absolute necessity of making this God our Friend.*

4. *The glory of heaven, where His presence is felt only to bless.*

5. *The dreadfulness of that world in which His mercies are "clean gone for ever," and His influence is felt as an unmitigated and insupportable curse.*—*Samuel Thodey.*

MAN A WONDERFUL CREATION OF GOD.

(*Verses* 13–16.)

The connection of these verses with the preceding seems to be this—God must needs have a perfect acquaintance with man because He created him. Hengstenberg suggests that verse 13 refers back to verse 2. "Thou knowest my downsitting and mine uprising. Thou understandest my thought afar off. . . . For Thou hast formed my reins," &c. The Psalmist here states that—

I. **Man is a creation of God.** "Thou hast formed my reins, Thou didst weave me together in my mother's womb."—*Perowne's translation.*

Man was created—

1. *According to God's design.* "In Thy book all my members were written," &c. What the architect is to the edifice God is to man. We existed first as an idea in the Divine mind. And if we read, "In Thy book all of them were written, the days which were ordered when as yet there was none of them," we still have the idea of the Divine design in the life of man. Man's entire being is prearranged by God.

2. *Under God's inspection.* "My substance was not hid from Thee, when I was made in secret," &c. The great Creator superintended the formation of man's bodily frame in the secrecy and obscurity of the womb.

3. *By God's power.* "Thou hast formed my reins, Thou didst weave me together in my mother's womb." God is the Author of our being: our parents are but the instruments thereof. Every human being is a creation of the Divine power.

II. **Man is a wonderful creation of God.** "I am fearfully and wonderfully made; marvellous are Thy works, and that my soul knoweth right well." This is manifest—

1. *In his body.* "The frame of man's body, and the cohesion of its parts," says Lord Herbert, "are so strange and paradoxical, that I hold it to be the

greatest miracle of nature." "An anatomist, as Dr. Paley observes, who understood the structure of the heart, might say beforehand that it would play; but he would expect, I think, from the complexity of its mechanism, and the delicacy of many of its parts, that it should always be liable to derangement, or that it would soon work itself out. Yet shall this wonderful machine go night and day, for eighty years together, at the rate of a hundred thousand strokes every twenty-four hours, having at every stroke a great resistance to overcome; and shall continue this action for this length of time without disorder and without weariness. Each ventricle will at least contain one ounce of blood. The heart contracts four thousand times in one hour, from which it follows, that there passes through the heart every hour four thousand ounces, or two hundred and fifty pounds, of blood. Now the whole mass of blood is said to be about twenty-five pounds, so that a quantity of blood, equal to the whole mass of blood passes through the heart ten times in one hour; which is once every six minutes. When we reflect also upon the number of muscles, not fewer than four hundred and forty-six in the human body, known and named; how contiguous they lie to each other, as it were, over one another; crossing one another; sometimes embedding in one another; sometimes perforating one another; an arrangement which leaves to each its liberty, and its full play; this must necessarily require meditation and council. Dr. Nieuentyt, in the Leipsic Transaction, reckons up a hundred muscles that are employed every time we breathe: yet we take in, or let out, our breath without reflecting what a work is hereby performed—what an apparatus is laid in of instruments for the service, and how many such contribute their assistance to the effect. Breathing with ease is a blessing of every moment; yet of all others, it is that which we possess with the least consciousness."—*Buck.*

"The human body is ever changing, ever abiding; a temple always complete, and yet always under repair; a mansion which quite contents its possessor, and yet has its plans and its materials altered each moment; a machine which never stops working, and yet is taken to pieces in the one twinkling of an eye, and put together in the other; a cloth of gold to which the needle is ever adding on one side of a line, and from which the scissors are ever cutting away on the other. Yes: Life, like Penelope of old, is ever weaving and unweaving the same web, whilst her grim suitors, Disease and Death, watch for her halting; only for her is no Ulysses who will one day in triumph return."—*Dr. G. Wilson.*

Truly we are "fearfully and wonderfully made."

2. *In his rational soul.* That which thinks, feels, desires, resolves, we call the soul. The soul is wonderful *in itself.* We do not know what it is; we cannot apprehend it by any of the senses; it has neither shape nor size; it is a mystery. It is wonderful *in its powers.* How great and marvellous are its powers of memory, reflection, reasoning, anticipation, imagination, &c. And these powers are capable of endless development and increase. How fearfully and wonderfully are we made.

3. *In the union of soul and body.* How dissimilar they are; yet they are united! Man "is sure that he is distinct from the body, though joined to it, because he is one, and the body is not one, but a collection of many things. He feels, moreover, that he is distinct from it because he uses it; for what a man can use he is superior to. No one can mistake his body for himself. It is *his,* it is not he. . . . When two things which we see are united, they are united by some connection which we can understand. A chain or cable keeps a ship in its place. We lay a foundation of a building in the earth, and the building endures. But what is it that unites soul and body? how do they touch? how do they keep together? So far from its being wonderful that the body one day dies, how is it that it is made to live and move at all? how is it that it keeps from dying a single hour?

"Again: the soul is in every part of the body. It is nowhere, yet everywhere. Since every part of his body belongs to him, a man's self is in every part of his body. The hands and feet, the head and trunk, form one body under the presence of the soul within them. Unless the soul were in every part, they would not form one body; so that the soul is in every part, uniting it with every other, though it consists of no part at all."—*J. H. Newman.* This seems contradictory, yet it is true. How mysterious is our being! How fearfully and wonderfully we are made!

III. **Because man is a wonderful creation of God he should celebrate the praise of his Creator.** " I will praise Thee; for I am fearfully and wonderfully made." Man as a creation of God presents many and remarkable illustrations of the *wisdom, power,* and *goodness* of his Creator, and these should excite his wonder, admiration, gratitude, and praise.

The highest praise we can offer to our Creator is to fulfil His design in our creation. He who most completely embodies and most clearly expresses the will of God presents to Him the truest and highest worship.

Verses 1-16 may be taken as the text of one homily and its teachings developed under an arrangement of this kind :—

I. **The Statement of God's perfect knowledge of man** (vers. 1-6).

II. **The Proof of God's perfect knowledge of man.** This is is drawn from—
1. *His Omnipresence* (vers. 7-12); 2. *His Creatorship* (vers. 13-16).

III. **The Effect of this knowledge upon the godly man.** 1. *A deep impression of intellectual limitation* (ver. 6); 2. *An inspiration to celebrate His praise* (ver. 14).

IV. **The Practical uses of this great truth.**

THE PRECIOUSNESS AND NUMBER OF GOD'S THOUGHTS.

(*Verses* 17, 18.)

In forming so wonderful a being as man there must have been much thought. Many thoughts and deep are embodied in man. Yet man is only a small portion of the creation of God. Looking at the universe as an embodiment of Divine ideas, we are almost overwhelmed at the number, profundity, and preciousness of God's thoughts. The thoughts of a being indicate his character. " As a man thinketh in his heart so is he." But in order to be known, thoughts must be expressed. Men express their thoughts by means of *speech, writing,* and *action.* Action is embodied thought. God has unfolded some of His thoughts. What a revelation of wisdom, goodness, beauty we have in the universe! God's thoughts in relation to the human race as sinners are expressed in the Bible. Jesus Christ is a Revelation and Revealer of the thoughts of God. What purity, tenderness, love, righteousness, majesty shine forth in Him! David rejoiced in God's thoughts. We have more of His thoughts and more precious ones than

David had; how much more then should we rejoice! Consider—

I. **The preciousness of God's thoughts.**
" How precious also are Thy thoughts unto me, O God." God's thoughts are precious—

1. *Because of their originality.* If a man be the originator of some new and useful process or machine, or the author of a clever or able book, he is honoured as a genius and a benefactor of the race. But *absolute originality* is not in man. The most original thinkers can only make new groupings of old ideas, or bring old thoughts into new associations and applications. But God's thoughts are absolutely original. The astonishing ideas of the moral restoration of man and the mode of effecting it are God's own original thoughts. There is originality in God's thoughts in nature, in the superintendence of human affairs, and in the great redemptive plan and work.

2. *Because of their moral excellence.* Distinguish between *great* thoughts and *good* ones. The devil is a great

thinker, but his thoughts are not precious. Thoughts must be good to be precious. God's thoughts combine the highest intellectual power with supreme moral excellence. All the ideas of the Divine Mind that have been revealed are perfectly true, righteous, and beautiful.

3. *Because of their practicableness and utility.* Amongst men there are many original and morally excellent thinkers whose ideas are utterly impracticable—they will not work. But God's thoughts are all practicable. See this in *nature*, in *history*, in *redemption*. Ultimately His every plan will be fully developed, His every thought perfectly embodied. His ideas are useful in themselves, and they stimulate others to usefulness. They arouse men to thought and action.

4. *Because of their influence upon our thoughts.* God's thoughts *quicken* ours. See how His thoughts in the Bible have stimulated the minds of men. Poets and artists have obtained from it their grandest subjects and their mightiest and holiest inspirations. Nature and the Bible are of exhaustless significance. They are replete with germs of thought. God's thoughts *correct* ours. Without the thoughts of God ours would be wild, chaotic, conflicting. Our ideas of God, the soul, truth, &c., are regulated by the revealed thoughts of God.

5. *Because of their generosity.* Forgiveness for the guilty, holiness for the depraved, rest for the weary—these are some of His thoughts. "I know the thoughts that I think toward you, saith the Lord, thoughts of peace, and not of evil." "As the heavens are higher than the earth, so are My thoughts higher than your thoughts."

II. **The number of God's thoughts.** "How great is the sum of them! If I should count them, they are more in number than the sand." Many of His thoughts are revealed, and we see them. Many others may be revealed, but we have not yet the capacity to perceive them. And many more may be revealed by Him in the future. His mind is infinite, ever active, ever productive, ever revealing. His thoughts are not only multitudinous in number, but profound in meaning. In our present state we have neither the time, the facilities, nor the capacity fully to number and comprehend the thoughts of God. But in the future, with quickened faculties, increased facilities, and everlasting existence, some of the great thoughts of God will probably be perceived in their completeness by us. "Now we see through a glass darkly, but then face to face," &c. If one of God's ideas is so precious as that of redemption is, how infinitely valuable must be the whole of His thoughts! "Many, O Lord my God, are Thy wonderful works which Thou hast done, and Thy thoughts which are to us-ward," &c.

III. **The realisation of God's presence.** "When I awake, I am still with Thee." "As often as he awakes from sleep, he finds that he is again in the presence of God, again occupied with thoughts of God, again meditating afresh with new wonder and admiration on His wisdom and goodness."—*Perowne.* The poet had an abiding sense of the presence of God with him, which was a comfort, and refreshment, and strength to his soul.

CONCLUSION.—1. *Endeavour to understand God's thoughts.* Examine them, meditate upon them as you find them in nature, the Bible, and Christ.

2. *Rejoice in the preciousness of God's thoughts.* Rejoice in them notwithstanding that many of them are mysterious, and perhaps even painful at present. David said, "Such knowledge is too wonderful for me," &c. Yet he rejoiced. His thoughts may be too great for us, yet they are all wise and kind. Think of a few of His thoughts. Here is one of His thoughts for the *guilty:* "Let the wicked forsake his way," &c. (Isa. lv. 7). For the *suffering:* "Our light affliction which is but for a moment," &c. (2 Cor. iv. 17, 18). For the *perplexed:* "In all thy ways acknowledge Him," &c. (Prov. iii. 6). For the *bereaved:* "I would not have you to be ignorant, brethren, concerning them which are asleep," &c. (1 Thess. iv. 13, 14).

3. *Seek to become embodiments of God's thoughts.* Live them.

The Poet's View of the Wicked.

(*Verses 19-22.*)

"How strangely abrupt," remarks Perowne, "is the turning aside from one of the sublimest contemplations to be found anywhere in the Bible, to express a hope that righteous vengeance will overtake the wicked. Such a passage is startling—startling partly because the spirit of the New Testament is so different; partly too, no doubt, because 'our modern civilisation has been so schooled in amenities' that we hardly know what is meant by a righteous indignation. It is well, however, to notice the fact, for this is just one of those passages which help us to understand the education of the world. Just because it startles us is it so instructive. The 63d Psalm presents us with a similar contrast. There, however, the feeling expressed is of a more directly personal kind. David is encompassed and hard pressed by enemies who are threatening his life. He has been driven from his throne by rebels, and the deep sense of wrong makes him burst forth in the strain of indignation and of anticipated victory. 'They that seek my life to destroy it shall be cast into the pit,' &c. Here, apparently, the prayer for the overthrow of the wicked does not arise from a sense of wrong and personal danger, but from the intense hatred of wickedness as wickedness, from the deep conviction that, if hateful to a truehearted man, it must be still more intensely hateful to Him who searcheth the hearts and trieth the reins. The soul, in the immediate presence of God, places itself on the side of God, against all that is opposed to Him. Still, the prayer, 'Oh that Thou wouldest slay the wicked,' can never be a Christian prayer."

I. **The character of the wicked described.** They are—

1. *Cruel.* "Bloody men." Perowne: "Bloodthirsty men." (Comp. Ps. v. 6, xxvi. 9, lv. 23.)

2. *Rebellious.* "They speak against Thee wickedly.... Those that rise up against Thee." Wicked men rebel against the most righteous and benevolent authority.

3. *Enemies of God.* "Them that hate Thee." It is a terrible thing to hate a Being of infinite wisdom and truth, righteousness and love. Men may, and sometimes do, grow so wicked that they hate the God whose holy law condemns them.

II. **The end of the wicked predicted.** "Surely Thou wilt slay the wicked, O God." We may interpret this in three ways. 1. As expressing the assurance of the Psalmist that God would *destroy the wicked*, that he would "slay" them, bring them to an utter end. Or, 2. As expressing the assurance of the Psalmist that God would *severely punish the wicked*. He might perhaps have used the word "slay" figuratively, to denote the punishment which would be inflicted on cruel and rebellious haters of the Lord. Or, 3. May we not say that God will "*slay the wicked*" *by slaying their wickedness?* You destroy an enemy when you make him your friend. "He must reign till He hath put all enemies under His feet."

III. **The companionship of the wicked avoided.** "Depart from me therefore, ye bloody men." The Psalmist seeks to separate himself from the workers of iniquity. He is moved to this by—

1. *Desire for his own safety.* Dark and threatening are the prospects of evildoers, and therefore David shunned association with them (ver. 19).

2. *Sympathy with God.* "Do not I hate them, O Lord, that hate Thee?" &c. The man who sincerely loves God will find the society of the wicked repugnant to him.

3. *The influence of divergent characters.* "What fellowship hath righteousness with unrighteousness? and what communion hath light with darkness?" &c.

CONCLUSION.—"Let the wicked forsake his way," &c. (Isa. lv. 7). "As I live, saith the Lord God," &c. (Ezek. xxxiii. 11).

A PRAYER OF THE UPRIGHT.

(*Verses* 23, 24.)

We have here—

I. **A request for Divine examination.** "Search me, O God, and know my heart: try me, and know my thoughts." This request implies—

1. *Consciousness of sincerity.* It is not the request of one who was ignorant of his true character and inflated with presumption, but of one who was conscious of his freedom from hypocrisy and of his integrity of heart. To make an appeal like this unto the great Searcher of hearts a man must be thoroughly conscious of his own sincerity, or must have fallen very low indeed.

2. *Distrust of self.* David felt his liability to error, and to self-deception, and therefore he appealed to the Omniscient and the Infallible.

3. *Confidence in God.* We would not that our heart should be completely exposed, that all our thoughts should be fully revealed even to our most trusted friend. "That man," says Calvin, "must have a rare confidence who offers himself so boldly to the scrutiny of God's righteous judgment." There are many things we would not disclose to any fellow-creature, and yet we are thankful that God knows them. This thought is beautifully expressed in Keble's Hymn for the "Twenty-fourth Sunday after Trinity."

II. **A desire for entire freedom from evil.** This seems to be implied in the request, "and see if there be any wicked way in me." The poet was not aware of any wicked way in him. But if any evil tendency or way had escaped his scrutiny, it could not escape that of God. And if God discovered such, the clearly implied desire of the Psalmist was that he might be delivered from it. "Any wicked way." Margin: "Way of pain or grief." "The way of pain is the way which leads to pain." The wicked man *causes pain.* Fürst says that the idea here is the way of "*affliction, injury* which one causes." The wicked man *suffers pain.* "The way of transgressors is hard." David wishes to be free from every evil way. One unguarded entrance to the beleaguered city may admit the invading hosts; one wicked way may ruin a soul.

III. **A request for Divine guidance in the way of righteousness.** "Lead me in the way everlasting." "The one true abiding way which leads to the true and everlasting God." "The way which leads to everlasting life." "The way which leads to the blessed eternity." "The way everlasting" is in contrast to "the way of pain." The one leads to misery; the other leads to joy. Here are two points—

1. *Man's need of guidance.* David felt this. We are exposed to temptation, prone to go astray, &c.

2. *Man's infallible Guide.* David sought the Divine lead. The Lord is perfectly acquainted with both the traveller and the way.

" Lead us, O Father, in the paths of right;
Blindly we stumble when we walk alone,
Involved in shadows of a darksome night,
Only with Thee we journey safely on.

" Lead us, O Father, to Thy heavenly rest,
However rough and steep the path may be,
Through joy or sorrow, as Thou deemest best,
Until our lives are perfected in Thee."
—*W. H. Burleigh.*

A NEEDFUL PRAYER.

(*Verses* 23, 24.)

This is a very *honest* prayer—a very *practical* prayer. The text before us is a very *personal* text. "Search *me,* O God, and know *my* heart," &c. We will consider—

I. **The need there is for such a prayer** as this. You have not to travel far to find out the need for such a prayer. You have but to look within,—to consider the motives and the thoughts and the desires and the purposes which are continually working within your own hearts, and you will find out, if you be honest, the need for such a prayer as this. There may be some amongst you who know that you are cherishing sin in the heart, and who have no desire to part with it. Does not that prove the necessity for such a prayer as this, that God would search your heart, and make you so feel your need of repentance and of a Saviour that you might forsake that sin this very night?

But the prayer is rather the prayer of a true servant of God. There may exist in the heart of a genuine Christian much undetected evil. A conviction of the omniscience and omnipresence of God is quite consistent with the presence of evil in the heart. We have no grander description of those great attributes of Jehovah than in this Psalm; and yet the Psalmist recognised the possibility that evil was lurking within. A conviction of the evil of sin, a deep abhorrence of iniquity, is quite consistent with the presence of evil in the soul. . . . Again, a deep sense of our acceptance in Christ, of our reconciliation to God, of our pardon, and of our blessedness in Christ, is consistent with the presence of evil in the heart. Our acceptance in Christ does not destroy the old nature. That nature remains, and shall be destroyed, but not yet. Once more. We may say also, that an earnest purpose and determination to get rid of all evil is consistent with its presence. The man of God longs for the complete deliverance which shall be the perfect answer to the prayer before us. There is need, then, for such a prayer as this.

II. The manner in which such a prayer as this receives its answer. Let us be well assured that God knows the heart. But the question is, How does God make that known to us which is known so perfectly to Him? How does God search the heart? Take an illustration. After David's great fall, sin certainly was in his heart. For months, apparently, he lived without confession and without forgiveness. . . . (See 2 Sam. xii. 1-14.) "Thou art the man. Thus saith the Lord God." It was God's authoritative word that brought conviction,— which revealed and detected the evil.

David confessed his sin, was pardoned, and restored. Peter denied his Lord, &c. "And Peter remembered the word," &c. (Matt. xxvi. 75). That word searched him, and he went forth and wept bitterly. The Word, then, is that instrument which the Lord God uses to search the depths of the human heart; and bringing home that Word by the power of the Spirit, He reveals the sinner to himself, and so teaches him his need of repentance.

There is no one present who has not a history. There are facts in every life, perhaps, which we would not tell to those nearest and dearest to us. There have been sins cherished in the heart, if not practised in the life. There are secrets unrevealed, scarcely, perhaps, remembered, seldom dwelt upon; but there is a history in each one of us. Now, the Word of God has a wonderful power of fastening upon some critical point in that history, so as to detect the evil—to lay bare the secret—to drag it out, as it were, into light, and, letting the light of truth shine in upon it, to lead the man to know himself. Take, for example, the secret of sin. Illustration: Our Lord and the woman of Samaria (John iv. 1-42).

Or, again, a case the very opposite to the woman of Samaria, a man upright, moral, devout, religious, learned, admired, honoured, respected. You have it in the Nicodemus; and how does the Lord meet that man's conscience? (John iii. 1-13). Or one who was wedded to one particular idol, though all the rest of his life was fair and good and upright (Matt. xix. 16-22). And would you have an example of one who was upright, who feared God, and who eschewed evil, and who yet was brought to confess that he was a grievous sinner? You have it in the well-known case of the patriarch Job. . . . And how are those convictions wrought? By the suspicious silence of his friends? No. By the blunt and open charges of those same friends? No. By the wiser counsel and the more truthful accusations of Elihu? No; but by the solemn word of Jehovah, &c. (Job xxxviii.-xli.). And what is the result? (Job xl. 3-6; xlii. 5, 6).

There are probably few Christians present who do not feel the pointed application of these words to their own hearts. You know that there is evil lying within. What you want to know is how to get rid of that evil. You must get rid of the evil within by the application of the very same principle of faith as that by means of which you have become established in Christ. We are justified by faith; we are sanctified by faith in the Lord Jesus.—*Sir Emilius Bayley.*

THE WICKED WAY WITHIN US, AND THE PRAYER PREFERRED.

(*Verse 24*)—" See if there be any wicked way in me."

This a beautiful and impressive *prayer* for the commencement of every day.

It is, also, a great sentiment to *admonish* us at the beginning or close of each day.

"The law of sin in our members," warring against the law of truth, of holiness, and of God, is still very *powerful*, and often very painfully exemplified.

There is the way of *unbelief* within, to which we are very prone.

There is the way of *vanity* and *pride*, to which we often accustom ourselves—vain of something in connection with the body, the accomplishments of the mind, &c. And then how frequently we show a proud and inflated spirit, instead of the temper of deep humility.

There is the way of *selfishness* in which we frequently walk. We are sometimes quite absorbed in considerations which relate only to our personal advancement or happiness.

There is the way of *worldliness* we often pursue. The empty pleasures, the shadowy honours, &c.

There is the way of *sluggishness*, by which we are often marked, and in connection with which we are sadly injured. What apathy in prayer, in the examination and application of God's Word, we manifest!

There is the way of *self-dependence*, by which we often dishonour God and injure ourselves. There is not simple, unhesitating, unbroken reliance on the perfect work, the infinite merits of our Divine Redeemer always unfolded, which we are bound invariably to exercise.

There is, unhappily, the way of *disobedience* in which we often walk. At any rate, our obedience is cold, reluctant, uncertain—not distinguished by its simplicity, its entireness, its fervency.

Now, each of the "ways" to which reference has been made is radically unsound, radically bad,—to every one of which we are individually prone, and from which we require to be delivered.

How necessary is it, then, to go to God at once, and, with the utmost earnestness, to prefer the petition, "Lord, see if there be any wicked way in me." Anything dark to enlighten, anything erroneous to correct, anything injurious to remove, anything degrading to elevate, anything impure to cleanse, anything deadening to quicken. Let nothing that is wrong, that is opposed to Thy character, repugnant to Thy Word, or injurious and debasing to ourselves, remain, or be harboured within us.

Can anything be more consistent than this? Anything be wiser than this? Can any prayer issue in a larger, richer, or more abiding blessing?

Let us remember that if there be what is holy *within*, there will be nothing that is unholy *without;* if there be irregularity *within*, there must be irregularity and confusion *without*. If the *heart* be unsound, the *life* must inevitably be unsound also.

Can you prefer, with the utmost sincerity, this fine prayer?—*T. Wallace.*

PSALM CXL.

INTRODUCTION.

"This Psalm is a prayer for protection against enemies who were at once violent and crafty, and unscrupulous in the use of their tongues. The general strain of the Psalm is like that of many which occur in the earlier books, and like them it is ascribed to David. In tone and language it resembles Psalms lviii. and lxiv. The chief peculiarity of the Psalm is, that it has several words which occur nowhere else."—*Perowne.*

In ascribing the Psalm to David, the superscription is confirmed by the Davidic style and spirit of the Psalm. The Psalm is addressed "To the chief musician," which shows that it was intended to be set to music for use in the public services. The occasion on which it was composed is not known.

TROUBLE IN LIFE, PRAYER IN TROUBLE, AND CONFIDENCE IN PRAYER.

I. Trouble in life. It is quite clear that the occasion on which the Psalm was written was one of trouble, and that this trouble arose from the enemies of the Psalmist. From what he says of them in the first part of the Psalm we have a clear idea of the character of his enemies. They were—

1. *Malignant.* "The evil man; . . . which imagine mischiefs in their heart; . . . the wicked." Their hostility arose not from any misapprehension, but from malice; not from the suggestions or force of circumstances, but from their depraved souls. Many of the troubles of life spring from the mischievous devices of wicked hearts.

2. *Confederate.* "Continually are they gathered together for war." They had banded themselves into an organisation for the accomplishment of their wicked designs. The archleader of the forces of evil aims at unity of design and effort in the great struggle against the right and true.

3. *Slanderous.* "They have sharpened their tongues like a serpent; adders' poison is under their lips." They invented and published malicious lies against the poet to ruin his reputation. The words of the slanderer are like the poison of the bite of the adder, which is among the most poisonous of serpents. The slanderous tongue is the virulent weapon of the malignant heart.

4. *Violent.* "Preserve me from the violent man." They used not only the slanderous tongue, but the strong arm against the Psalmist. The tongue, the pen, and the sword have all been used at times against the people of God. The reviler, the controversialist, and the persecutor have set themselves against the Church of God.

5. *Determined.* "Who have purposed to overthrow my goings." Their evil thoughts and feelings had led to the formation of an evil design. Their attempted injuries to the poet were the expression of their firm determination to effect his ruin. Men sin not only through weakness, but by settled purpose. There are men who "do evil with both hands earnestly."

6. *Proud.* "The proud have hid a snare for me." They were haughty and arrogant, "conceited of themselves and confident of their success; and herein they resemble Satan, whose reigning ruining sin was pride. The pride of persecutors, though at present it be the terror, yet may be the encouragement of the persecuted, for the more haughty they are the faster are they ripening for ruin. 'Pride goes before destruction.'"

7. *Cunning.* "The proud have hid a snare for me, and cords; they have spread a net by the wayside; they have set gins for me." They employed fraud against him as well as force. They not only made open war against him, but they plotted and schemed to overthrow him suddenly and unawares. "Great persecutors have often been great politicians, which has indeed made them the more formidable." Such is the description which David here gives of his foes. We cannot wonder that they troubled his life. The good man is

still troubled in his life upon earth by outward enemies and inward fears, by bodily sufferings and mental distresses, by social trials and spiritual conflicts. "In the world ye have tribulation."

II. Prayer in trouble. The Psalmist prays for—

1. *Preservation from his enemies.* "Deliver me, O Lord, from the evil man; preserve me from the violent man; keep me from the hands of the wicked." His enemies were endeavouring to blast his reputation, to rob him of his throne, and to take away his life; he knew their malice and cunning and power, and his own peril, and he entreated the Lord for deliverance and looked to Him for protection.

Prayer is the great resource of the righteous in the troubles and perils of life. When every other refuge fails, there is safety at the throne of grace. He whom God protects is inviolably secure. "Call upon Me in the day of trouble: I will deliver thee," &c. "God is our refuge and strength," &c. The Psalmist prays for—

2. *The overthrow of his enemies.* He asks that this may be accomplished by (1.) *The recoil of their evil designs.* "As for the head of those that compass me about, let the mischief of their own lips cover them." His wish is that the mischief which they had designed against him might fall upon their own heads. The cruel and cowardly calumniator, the violent persecutor, and the crafty plotter of the overthrow of his fellow-men, will each find the injury which he has inflicted upon others falling with fury upon himself. There are many Hamans who to-day are building gallows for many Mordecais upon which they will be hung themselves. (2.) *By the infliction of Divine judgments.* "Let burning coals fall upon them; let them be cast into the fire, into deep pits, that they rise not up again. Let not an evil-speaker be established in the earth: evil shall hunt the violent man to overthrow him." Instead of, "into deep pits," Hengstenberg translates, "into water-floods," and Perowne, "into floods of water." We are by no means certain that a retaliative and sinful spirit did not give rise to the tenth verse. But it is inspiring to know that an evil-speaker shall not be established in the earth or anywhere else. A lie cannot live always. The slanderer builds on the sand, and his building shall fall into ruin upon the builder. "'Evil shall hunt the violent man,' as the blood-hound hunts the murderer to discover him, as the lion hunts his prey to tear it to pieces. Mischievous men will be brought to light, and brought to ruin; the destruction appointed shall run them down and overthrow them. 'Evil pursues sinners.'"—*M. Henry.*

III. Confidence in prayer. The prayer of David was neither the cry of despair nor the entreaty of doubt or fear, but a confident appeal to the Lord God. The confidence of the Psalmist was based upon—

1. *His relation to God.* "I said unto the Lord, Thou art my God." In the time of trouble, when we approach God in prayer, it is most inspiring to be able to claim personal relationship to Him, and to cling to Him by faith. If He is "my God," He will not leave me to the might and malice of my foes.

2. *His ideas of God.* "O God the Lord, the strength of my salvation." His appeal is to *Jehovah Adonai.* Jehovah is the Self-Existent One; Adonai is the Supreme Ruler, the Governor of all things and all beings. The possession of an interest in such a Being may well inspire confidence. So the Psalmist looks to Him as the strength of his salvation. "Behold, God is my salvation: I will trust and not be afraid; for the Lord Jehovah is my strength," &c.

3. *His experience of the protection of God.* "Thou hast covered my head in the day of battle." As the helmet shields the head (that vital part) amid the perils of the battle-field, so God had guarded him from the assaults of his enemies. The experience we have had of God's protecting care in the past should inspire us with confidence in the present, and with hope for the future. "Behold, the Lord's hand is not shortened that it cannot save; neither is His ear heavy that it cannot hear." He is "the same yesterday, to-day, and for ever."

4. *His faith in the righteous rule of*

God. "I know that the Lord will maintain the cause of the afflicted, the right of the poor. Surely the righteous shall give thanks unto Thy name; the upright shall dwell in Thy presence." The Psalmist was convinced that the government of God was opposed to wicked oppressors. God is the Champion of His oppressed people. He will vindicate their cause, and give them abundant reason to offer unto Him grateful praise. The wicked shall shrink in dismay from His frown; but the upright shall dwell in His presence, and rejoice in His favour. (Comp. Ps. xi. 7, xvi. 11, lxi. 7.) A faith like this in the government of God is one of the truest and greatest supports of man amid the trials and difficulties of life.

CONCLUSION. — Learn, — 1. *That the true and good are sometimes exposed to severe trials and extreme perils.* 2. *That the true and good have no adequate reason for fear at any time.* 3. *That the resources of the true and good are more than adequate to every trial and peril.* Their security is guaranteed by ONE who is infinite in wisdom, almighty in power, and unchangeable in truth.

THE DAY OF BATTLE AND THE PROTECTION OF GOD.

(*Verse 7.*)

Consider :—

I. The period spoken of.
"The day of battle." Heb. lit. "armour," as in 1 Kings x. 25; 2 Kings x. 2; Ezek. xxxix. 9, 10. "'The day of armour' is not the day of preparation for battle, but the day on which the armour is carried for the battle, consequently the day of battle."—*Moll.*

David had been in many battles; he was well acquainted with their toils and dangers, their excitements and horrors. But let us notice—

1. *What the battle implies.* (1.) *Enemies.* The Psalmist had many foes; and they were bitter and violent, crafty and combined, in their hostility to him. The godly soul has to contend against "the world, the flesh, and the devil"—against evil in society (John xv. 18–21; 1 John iii. 13; iv. 4, 5; v. 4, 5), in our own nature (Rom. vii. 21–23; Gal. v. 7), and in malignant spirits (Eph. vi. 10–18; 1 Pet. v. 8). Our enemies are many, subtle, and strong. (2.) *Peril.* The field of battle is a scene of danger. The day of moral battle has its perils. The godly soul may be injured: There is danger that we may yield to the subtle suggestions, or be overpowered by the vigorous onslaughts of our foes. Good men have received injury in this battle; *e.g.,* Moses and Aaron (Num. xx. 12); David (2 Sam. xi., xii. 7–12; Peter (Matt. xxvi. 69–75). Few, if indeed any, come out of this battle without some wounds or scars. (3.) *Effort.* There is no battle without strenuous exertion. The godly soul has to resist the attacks of his enemies; to watch and ward that he be not surprised by his foes, and to endeavour to overcome them. We have to act not only on the defensive, but on the offensive; not only to guard ourselves, but to conquer the world for Jesus Christ. The maintenance and growth of the Christian life cannot be attained by merely wearing the uniform and carrying the weapons of a soldier, or by appearing in the army on review days only. We must fight if we would conquer; we must fight if we would not sustain defeat.

2. *How long the battle lasts.* "The day of battle." The conflict is only for a brief season. It is severe, but short.

"The strife will not be long;
This day the noise of battle,
The next the victor's song."

The battle is but for a day; the triumph is eternal. Therefore, Christian soldier, fear not, faint not. "Fight the good fight of faith," &c.

II. The protection acknowledged.
"O Jehovah Lord, the strength of my salvation, Thou hast covered my head in the day of battle." God had defended David in many battles, kept him in safety amidst many perils. Gratefully and hopefully he calls this protection to mind in his present dangers.

1. *Protection of a vital part.* "Thou hast covered my head," *i.e.,* as with a helmet. (Comp. Psa. lx. 7.) In the battle of life we may suffer in many things, but our vital interests are safe: we may be wounded, but we shall not be slain: we may suffer loss, but we shall not fall a prey to our adversaries.

2. *Protection by an all-sufficient Being.* "Jehovah, the Lord, the strength of my salvation." Here is a Being of—(1.) *Independent existence.* "Jehovah," the Self-Existing, the Permanent, the Everlasting. He ever lives to guard and save His people. (2.) *Sovereign authority.* "The Lord," the Supreme Governor. "His kingdom ruleth over all." (3.) *Saving power.* "The strength of my salvation." He is "mighty to save."

III. The encouragement to be deduced.

1. *To trust in Him for protection.* What He has done is an earnest of what He will yet do. David was accustomed to argue from the past to the future. "The Lord that delivered me out of the paw of the lion," &c. (1 Sam. xvii. 37). "Because Thou hast been my help, therefore in the shadow of Thy wings will I rejoice." He who has protected us in the past still lives, still He is sovereign in authority, and still He is strong to save, therefore let us trust Him.

2. *To pray to Him for protection.* The Lord will "be inquired of by the house of Israel to do for them." Sincere and believing prayer is a Divinely-appointed condition of blessing. Let His protection in past times inspire our petitions in the present. "Because He hath inclined His ear unto me, therefore will I call upon Him as long as I live." Let our own experience stimulate and strengthen our confidence in Him and our prayers to Him as the God of our salvation.

PSALM CXLI.

INTRODUCTION.

"This Psalm presents," says Perowne; "some peculiar difficulties of interpretation, which, however, are due neither to the words employed nor to the grammatical construction, but to the extreme abruptness with which in vers. 5-7 the thoughts follow one another, and the extreme obscurity which hangs over the allusions. To translate each sentence by itself is no difficult matter, but it is almost hopeless either to link the sentences plausibly together, or to discover in them any tangible clue to the circumstances in which the Psalmist was placed. As all the ancient versions must have had substantially the same text, the deviations in any of them being very slight, it is hardly probable that, as Olshausen and Hupfield maintain, the text is corrupt: it is more likely that our entire ignorance of the circumstances under which the Psalm was written prevents our piercing the obscurity of the writer's words.

"It has been usual to accept the inscription which assigns the Psalm to David, and to assign it to the time of his persecution by Saul. Verse 5 has generally been supposed to allude to David's generous conduct in sparing the life of his foe when he was in his power (see 1 Sam. xxiv.); but it is quite impossible on this supposition to give any plausible interpretation to ver. 7.

"Delitzsch, with more probability, refers the Psalm to the time of Absalom's rebellion. He sees an allusion to David's distance from the sanctuary and the worship of the sanctuary in ver. 2, and he explains ver. 6 of the punishment which shall overtake the rebel leaders, and the return of the people to their allegiance."

It is unmistakably clear from vers. 7-10 that the Psalm was written at a time of trial and peril. And it brings before our notice—

THE CONDUCT OF A GOOD MAN IN A TIME OF TRIAL.

We can trace in this Psalm with considerable clearness the spiritual mood and exercises of the Psalmist in this time of trouble and danger. We have here—

I. Earnest prayer. In his distress David lifted up his voice and his heart to God in prayer. He asks—

1. *For Divine audience.* "Give ear unto my voice, when I cry unto Thee." Not even the whisper of sincere prayer escapes the ear of God; yet it is becom-

ing in us humbly to entreat Him to hear favourably our prayers. Our asking tends to strengthen our faith in His hearing.

2. *For Divine acceptance.* "Let my prayer be set forth before Thee as incense, the lifting up of my hands as the evening sacrifice." "The sacrifice here meant," says Perowne, "is strictly the offering consisting of fine flour with oil and frankincense, or of unleavened cakes mingled with oil, which was burnt upon the altar (Heb. *minchah*, E. V. 'meat-offering:' see Lev. ii. 1–11). This, however, like the 'incense,' was only added to the burnt-offering, the lamb which was offered every morning and evening (Exod. xxix. 34–42; Num. xxviii. 3–8). It would seem, therefore, that these two, 'the incense' and 'the offering of fine flour,' &c., stand for the morning and evening sacrifice; and the sense is, 'Let my daily prayer be acceptable to Thee as are the daily sacrifices of Thine own appointment.'" The incense which ascended in a fragrant cloud was a symbol of acceptable prayer. And the lifting up of the hands was a symbol of the lifting up of the heart. The poet offered his heart to God in prayer. And he asks that his prayer may find acceptance with God.

3. *For speedy Divine assistance.* "Lord, I cry unto Thee, make haste unto me." The burden of his trouble was heavy, and his peril was imminent and his need urgent; therefore he entreats God to appear quickly for his help.

4. *For preservation from sinful speech.* "Set a watch, O Lord, before my mouth; keep the door of my lips." He asks to be kept from the utterance of foolish or bitter words in his time of trial. (See the *Hom. Com.* on Ps. xxxix. 1.)

5. *For preservation from sinful conduct.* "Incline not my heart to any evil thing, to practise wicked works with men that work iniquity; and let me not eat of their dainties." Not for one moment can we entertain the idea that God ever exerts any positive influence to induce men to sin. His holy nature, His revealed will, and all His arrangements are utterly opposed to such an idea. The prayer of the Psalmist is in effect that God would not leave him to himself to go astray, or to any evil influence that would lead him astray. He seeks preservation from (1) sinful practices, that God would keep him from the wicked doings of the workers of iniquity. And from (2) sinful pleasures, that God would keep him from the easy, luxurious, sensual life of the wicked who have their portion in this world, that he may "not eat of their dainties." Two points are worthy of notice here—

First: *This sense of dependence on God, which the Psalmist manifested, would ensure his safety.* "They that trust in the Lord shall be as Mount Zion, which cannot be removed, but abideth for ever."

Second: *In thus taking his trouble to God by prayer the Psalmist would find relief.* The mere utterance of our anxieties or griefs to a Being of perfect love and faithfulness affords us relief. The exercise of prayer to God is itself a helpful and blessed thing.

II. **Noble resolutions.** David expresses his resolution—

1. *To welcome the rebukes of the righteous.* "Let the righteous smite me, it shall be a kindness; and let him reprove me, it shall be an excellent oil, which shall not break my head." Perowne more correctly translates thus: "It shall be as oil upon (my) head, let not my head refuse (it)." The rebuke of the righteous may be painful, but it promotes our well-being. The pain which it causes is, like that which is inflicted by the knife in the hand of the skilful surgeon, for the good of the sufferer. The true friend who, because of his regard for us, faithfully reproves us when we are in fault, is a great blessing. And the man who, like David, is wise and good will welcome his reproofs with joy, though they are painful. He will not only not refuse them, but will receive them as the oil which was poured on the head on festive occasions, "the oil of gladness." "Faithful are the wounds of a friend." "It is better to hear the rebuke of the wise, than for a man to hear the song of fools."

2. *To defend himself by prayer against*

his adversaries. It appears to us that our translation of the last line of ver. 5 does not give the true meaning. Hengstenberg renders it: "If still, then, I shall pray against their wickedness." And Perowne: "For yet is my prayer against their wickedness." The idea seems to be that he would have recourse to prayer as the best defence against the wickedness of his persecutors. He would not seek to retaliate upon them, or meet their wickedness towards him with wickedness towards them, but he would commit his cause unto the Lord in prayer. Surely these resolutions indicate a true and great soul.

III. Confident expectation. The Psalmist expresses his assured hope of deliverance from peril and of the triumph of his cause. His statement of his expectation presents three points:—

1. *That the chief men among his enemies would be overthrown, and that their overthrow would promote his triumph.* "When their judges are overthrown in stony places, they shall hear my words; for they are sweet." Perowne: "This verse, difficult in itself, is still more difficult, because it has no very obvious connection either with what precedes or with what follows. The allusions are so obscure that it is impossible to do more than guess at their meaning." The interpretation which he proceeds to suggest seems to us the most probable. "(When) their judges have been hurled down the sides of the rock, then they shall hear my words that they are sweet." *Their judges* must be the rulers or princes of the wicked adversaries of the poet. The verb *hurled down* is the same which is used of the throwing down of Jezebel from the window (2 Kings ix. 33); and it indicates a punishment which David anticipates will be inflicted upon these rebel rulers (see 2 Chron. xxv. 12). The words *they shall hear* refer not to the judges, but to their followers who have been led astray by them. If the Psalm refers to the rebellion of Absalom or any similar occasion, the sense will be, "when the leaders in the insurrection meet with the fate they deserve, then the subjects of the king will return to their allegiance." And the expression, "they shall hear my words that they are sweet," would be a thoroughly oriental mode of describing the satisfaction with which they would welcome the gracious amnesty pronounced by their offended sovereign.

2. *That his present sufferings would promote his triumph.* "Our bones are scattered at the grave's mouth, as when one cutteth and cleaveth wood upon the earth." The explanation of this verse also is difficult. It seems quite clear that the supplying of the word "wood" as the object of the verb, as in the A. V., is both unnecessary and misleading. Perowne translates: "As when one furroweth the earth (with the plough), our bones have been scattered at the mouth of the grave." The interpretation of Delitzsch and Hengstenberg seems to us correct. It is thus stated by the latter: "As in ploughing the tearing up of the earth is not the ultimate design, but only the means of a fruitful result, only serves the purpose of making the earth yield its produce; therefore, with an equally beneficent design, or in order that, through the present injury, new life may arise, our bones also are scattered about. While the enemies are conducted from life to death (ver. 6), we are conducted from death to life." The sufferings of the present were as the seed from which would grow a plenteous harvest of prosperity and joy. This truth is taught frequently and clearly in the New Testament (Rom. v. 3–5; James i. 2, 3).

3. *That his confidence was reposed in God.* "But mine eyes are unto Thee, O God the Lord; in Thee is my trust." His expectation of deliverance and triumph was fixed in God, — not in the skill of his strategy, or the strength of his forces, but in Jehovah the Lord.

The poet closes the Psalm as he began it, with—

IV. Earnest prayer. He prays—

1. *That he may be protected from his enemies.* "Leave not my soul destitute. Keep me from the snares which they have laid for me, and the gins of the workers of iniquity." Here are three points:—(1.) His enemies had cunningly devised his overthrow. (2.) God was

able to protect him against their deepest designs. (3.) For this protection he prays, in it he trusts. The all-wise and Almighty One will baffle the most subtle plots that are formed against His people.

2. *That the designs of his enemies may be turned against themselves.* "Let the wicked fall into their own nets, whilst that I withal escape." The sinner digs the pit for his own destruction, builds the prison for his own incarceration, collects the fuel for his own hell-fire. The blow which he aims against others recoils upon himself. "No law can be more just than that the architects of destruction should perish by their own contrivances." (See the *Hom. Com.* on Ps. cxl. 9.) When the wicked are overthrown, like Pharaoh and his host, by the waters of that sea into which they have presumptuously and wickedly adventured, the righteous shall pass in safety and triumph unto the other side.

The Sufferings of God's Servants, and the Relief which the Gospel affords.

(*Verses* 7, 8.)

I. **That God's most favoured servants have often been exposed to the utmost extremity and danger.**

"Our bones are scattered," &c. It is an expression denoting the extreme of suffering — hopeless calamity. When the prophet Ezekiel would express the overwhelming ruin under which Israel was sunk, he compares their case to a valley of dry bones, many, and exceeding dry; and explains the allegory thus— "Our bones are dried, and our hope is lost" (Ezek. xxxvii. 11).

A similar destitution of hope and happiness has often characterised God's people. David was hunted like a partridge upon the mountains, whilst Saul was on the throne. Moses was a fugitive and outlaw from Egypt. Paul was in bonds, whilst Festus was on the bench. Job was on the dunghill. Those "of whom the world was not worthy" were "destitute, afflicted, tormented." Christ was a prisoner at the bar, whilst Herod, in royal apparel, sat on the judgment-seat. More remarkable still,— they who possessed miraculous powers could not employ them for the relief of their own wants. Peter's shadow could heal the diseases of others; but he could not release himself from prison.

But why is all this suffered? Certainly not from indifference to their interests; for He calls them His jewels, His children, His flock. Not from inability to help or save; for He has all power in heaven and earth,—and He who conducts them to thrones of glory in the next world could equally enrich them with the treasures of this.

1. *To lead the soul to God, in the immediate exercise of faith and dependence, for better treasure than the world can give.* This was the immediate effect here: "Our bones are scattered; ... but mine eyes are unto Thee." God reveals Himself as the Refuge : He loves to be known and trusted under that character. He is never more present with His people than when the world forsakes. Nothing is more delightful than the view afforded by the Cross of Christ of the revealed character of God. Every creature has its refuge—some place of defence to which it can betake itself in the hour of threatening danger. The lion has its den ; the hunted deer betakes itself to the running stream; the dove flies to the clefts of the rock, &c.; the good man turns to God.

2. *To prove principle and purify character.* These trials are necessary to *prove* grace and to *improve* it. "That the trial of your faith being much more precious," &c. (1 Pet. i. 7). God often chooses His people in the furnace of affliction, but always refines them in it. Whilst you are under affliction you are under a process of cure. The true thought is, that sin introduced suffering, but God, superior at all points to evil, employs suffering as an instrument by which sin may be destroyed in His own people.

It is one means of fulfilling the prayer: "Keep me from the snares they have laid for me" (ver. 9).

3. *To prepare for greater usefulness here, and for endless happiness hereafter.*

II. **That in the most hopeless circumstances the Gospel affords relief.**

1. *From the fact of Divine appointment.* HE causes grief; not an enemy. They come not from the enemy of souls, but the Friend of sinners. The same hand that opens the fountain of our joys opens that of our sorrows too. God administers them. They are the signs of His love. They shall not exceed the measure of your strength, nor be continued a moment longer than needful.

2. *From the sympathy and compassion of Christ.*

3. *From the promises of the Gospel.*

4. *From the bright prospects of future glory.*

III. **That in proportion to the happiness and safety of God's children must be the misery and wretchedness of His enemies.**

. . . .
Samuel Thodey.

PSALM CXLII.

INTRODUCTION.

"A maschil of David," *i.e.*, an instruction or a didactic poem by David. "A prayer when he was in the cave;" "That is," says Barnes, "either a prayer which he composed while there, or which he composed afterwards, putting into a poetic form the substance of the prayer which he breathed forth there. The reference may be either to the cave of Adullam (1 Sam. xxii. 1), or to that in Engedi (1 Sam. xxiv. 3). In both cases the circumstances were substantially the same, for David had fled to the cave to escape from Saul. It is a cry of distress when there was no refuge—no hope—but in God; when there seemed to be no way of escape from his enemies; and when, forsaken by his friends, and pursued by an enemy who sought his life, he seemed now to be in the power of his foe. It may also be used to express the feelings of one now in danger,—as of a sinner under condemnation, seeing no way of escape, exposed to ruin, and shut up entirely to the mercy of God. Such a one feels as David did on this occasion, that there can be no escape but through the interposition of God."

Many of the Psalms give utterance to the same feelings. Over and over again we have Psalms containing an expression of trouble, prayer for relief, and believing expectation of deliverance. With such similarity of sentiment, variety of homiletic treatment is very difficult; if the main points in each Psalm are to be indicated in such treatment. The chief characteristics of this Psalm—distress, prayer, and hope—we have met with repeatedly in our survey of this book.

A PRAYER OF THE GODLY MAN FROM THE DEPTHS OF DISTRESS.

We have here:—

I. **A picture of deep distress.** Several features of the distress of the poet are here set forth.

1. *The persecution of his enemies.* "In the way wherein I walked have they privily laid a snare for me. . . . Deliver me from my persecutors; for they are stronger than I." His enemies were (1) *cunning.* In his path they had hidden a snare for him, with a view to entrap and injure him. Their persecution was not open and manly, but secret and artful. Even in the path of his duty they had concealed their snares for his overthrow. They were (2) *powerful.* "My persecutors are stronger than I." Saul and his emissaries are here referred to. They were more in number, better equipped, and better fitted for warfare than David and his party were. He felt that he was no match for his enemies. There were times in which David suffered the deepest dejection and distress of spirit by reason of the persecutions of Saul (1 Sam. xx. 1, 3, 41, 42; xxvii. 1). Of ourselves we are unable to cope successfully with the enemies of our spiritual life and interests. Our foes are too subtle and too strong for our unaided efforts; but, like David, we can seek help from on high.

2. *The failure of human help.* "I

looked on my right hand and beheld, but there was no man that would know me; refuge failed me; no man cared for my soul." These words are not to be taken as a literal description of the circumstances of David either in the cave of Adullam or in that of Engedi. The meaning is that there was no one to whom he could look for protection, no one on whom he could rely. Those who were with him were not able to protect him; those who were able to do so cared not for his life. Deep and painful was his sense of loneliness. He was in constant peril, yet of those who might perhaps have rendered him effectual aid none were concerned for him. There are times in the life of almost every man when he seems bereft of human sympathy and help. There are some cases in which man might render aid if he would, but he will not. There are others in which man would render aid if he could, but he cannot. There are needs to which only He who is both God and man can minister.

3. *The depression of his outward circumstances and inward condition.* In his outward circumstances he seems to have been greatly reduced. "I am brought very low." And his spiritual state was that of deep distress. "My spirit is overwhelmed within me." His outward condition was almost desperate, and the deep prostration of his spirit corresponded thereto. Darkness seemed to be settling down upon both his soul and his circumstances. Many a godly soul has passed through similar experiences. Darkness and trial to some extent fall to the lot of every good man in this life. It is well that it is so. The gloom of the night is as needful as the glory of the day. "Sweet are the uses of adversity."

II. **A prayer of strong confidence.** The Psalmist manifests his faith in—

1. *God's accessibleness to him.* "I cried unto the Lord with my voice; with my voice unto the Lord did I make my supplication. I poured out my complaint before Him; I showed before Him my trouble." The fact that he thus unfolded the tale of his woes to God, and entreated His mercy, is conclusive evidence that he believed that God may be approached by His creatures in prayer.

2. *God's interest in him.* Unless the Psalmist had believed in God's kind interest in him, he could not have poured out his complaint before Him as he does in this Psalm. God is both accessible to us and interested in us. "The righteous cry, and the Lord heareth, and delivereth them out of all their troubles." "The Lord heareth the prayer of the righteous." "If we ask anything according to His will, He heareth us." "He careth for you."

3. *God's knowledge of him.* "When my spirit was overwhelmed within me, then Thou knewest my path." The dangers that beset the poet and the troubles that distressed him were all known to God. The conviction of this must have been a source of unspeakable comfort and strength to David. This assurance was precious to the afflicted Patriarch of Uz. "He knoweth the way that I take: when He hath tried me I shall come forth as gold." Be comforted, my distressed brother; the Lord knoweth thy path, He is watching over thee, He careth for thee, &c.

4. *God's protection of him.* "I cried unto Thee, O Lord; I said, Thou art my refuge, my portion in the land of the living." The Psalmist found security and comfort in the Lord, who was the source of his help and the God of his salvation. The Lord was his only refuge. There is a well-known picture of a large cross hewn out in the form of a rock standing in the midst of a wild and raging sea to which a struggling form clings with the tenacity of despair. Our Lord is that rock. The floods of this world's strife and sorrow and pain may well-nigh overwhelm us, the seething waves of sin may lash wildly about us, but if we have found Him, He will be to us a sure refuge and rock of defence. God is the *only* sure refuge in the storms of life, and He is a refuge which is *inviolably secure* and *ever available*.

5. *Upon this confidence in God the Psalmist bases his prayer to Him for deliverance.* "Attend unto my cry, for I am brought very low; deliver me from

my persecutors, for they are stronger than I. Bring my soul out of prison, that I may praise Thy name." David seemed imprisoned by difficulties and dangers, encompassed with enemies, and unable to effect his escape, and he cried with well-founded confidence to God for emancipation. We know how glorious an answer he received to his prayer. God granted him complete deliverance and high distinction—translated him, in His own time and way, from the cave of the outlaw to the throne of the king. In this we have an illustration of the way in which He ever answers sincere and believing prayer.

III. An anticipation of a happy issue of his distress.

The poet anticipates—

1. *That God would completely deliver him.* "Thou shalt deal bountifully with me." He anticipated not mere deliverance, but such a deliverance and such blessings as would result from the bountiful dealings of the gracious Lord.

2. *That he would praise God.* "That I may praise Thy name." In the complete deliverance which he anticipated he would have occasion to praise the name of the Lord, and he would joyfully improve the occasion. The benefit of the salvation being his, its glory he would heartily ascribe to God.

3. *That the righteous would rejoice in his deliverance.* "The righteous shall compass me about, for Thou," &c. David anticipated that the righteous would be encouraged by his salvation, and would resort unto him with gladness and with congratulations. Thus in his distress the poet anticipates complete and joyous deliverance,—a deliverance that shall awaken his own heart to glad and grateful praise, and call forth the congratulations of all the godly.

CONCLUSION.—Distress is a common experience in this life. But the resources of men when in distress greatly differ. There is but one true and adequate Refuge. To Him David turned in confidence, and found safety and relief. Let all distressed souls look to Him, and they shall not be disappointed.

THE SORROWS OF THE SOUL AND THE KNOWLEDGE OF GOD.

(*Verse 3.*)

"When my spirit was overwhelmed within me, then Thou knewest my path."

We have here—

I. A figure indicating great sorrow. "My spirit was overwhelmed within me." The expression sets forth the sorest distress.

1. *Distress in that part of man's nature where it is most severely felt.* "My spirit." "The spirit of a man will sustain his infirmity; but a wounded spirit who can bear?" If the spirit be peaceful and blessed, if it be inspired by joy and hope, it enables man to triumph over the severest physical sufferings. Paul and Silas at Philippi, in the inner prison, with their feet fast in the stocks, and their backs torn and tortured by many stripes, rose superior to their circumstances and their sufferings, and caused the prison to resound with their songs of praise. Christian martyrs have exulted in the flames which were consuming their bodies. St. Stephen, who was stoned to death, "fell asleep." Physically his death was a cruel and painful thing; but the faith and hope and vision which animated his spirit made his death a *euthanasia*. But who can rise above the sorrows of the soul? When the spirit suffers, the man himself suffers; when it is overwhelmed, the whole nature is overwhelmed.

2. *Distress of the severest kind.* "My spirit was overwhelmed." Sorrow had submerged him. Great afflictions are frequently represented by the figure of overwhelming floods. "Deep calleth unto deep," &c. (Ps. xlii. 7). "Let me be delivered out of the deep waters," &c. (Ps. lxix. 14, 15). "Thou hast afflicted me with all Thy waves" (Ps. lxxxviii. 7). "When thou passest through the waters, I will be with thee," &c. (Isa. xliii. 2). Such sore distress sometimes befalls the servants

of God. Great saints have great sorrows. "Whom the Lord loveth He chasteneth," &c. (Heb. xii. 6, 7).

II. A fact affording great consolation.

"Then Thou knewest my path." All the painful and perilous wanderings of David were known to God. (Comp. Ps. lvi. 8.)

1. *This fact may be abundantly confirmed.* An infinite Being must know all things. Nothing is so great as to exceed His comprehension; nothing so small as to elude His notice. The Bible asserts God's omniscience (2 Kings xix. 27; Ps. cxxxix. 1–4; Heb. iv. 13). How strikingly our Lord declared God's perfect knowledge of His people! (Matt. vi. 32; x. 30.) The history of good men illustrates it. In the lives of Joseph and Moses, David and Daniel, Paul and John, how clearly does this truth shine forth,—"Thou knewest their path."

2. *This fact is very comprehensive.* It implies much more than it expresses. The knowledge which is here affirmed implies approbation and guidance, protection and provision, kindness and care. Thus David Dickson says: "'Thou knewest my path;' that is, Thou approvedst my part, who was unjustly pursued." And Charnocke: "This knowledge adds to the simple act of the understanding, the complacency and pleasure of the will. 'The Lord knows who are His,' that is, He loves them; He doth not only know them but acknowledge them for His own. It notes not only an exact understanding, but a special care of them. . . . On the contrary, also, whom God doth not approve, He is said not to know (Matt. xxv. 12), 'I know you not,' and (Matt. vii. 23), 'I never knew you;' He doth not approve of their works. It is not an ignorance of understanding, but an ignorance of will; for while He saith He never knew them, He testifies that He did know them, in rendering the reason of His disapproving them, because He knows all their works: so He knows them, and doth not know them in a different manner: He knows them so as to understand them, but He doth not know them so as to love them." "Thou knewest my path" implies, Thou didst approve and direct, sustain and secure, my way.

3. *This fact is very consolatory.* That it was so to David appears from our text, and from Ps. lvi. 8. It was so to the sorely-afflicted Job: "He knoweth the way that I take," &c. (Job xxiii. 10). Amid misrepresentation to be able to make our appeal to Him; amid persecution to be assured of His protection; amid sorrow of soul to know that we have His sympathy; in loneliness to realise His friendly presence,—these afford the richest consolation and the most effective help. To possess these is the privilege of every child of God.

THE DUTY OF CARING FOR SOULS.

(*Verse 4.*)

"No man cared for my soul."

Let us inquire—

I. What it is to care for the souls of others. The care of the soul involves—

1. *A deep and heartfelt conviction of its worth.* The care of an object is generally in proportion to its value. The soul is spiritual in its nature, noble in its capacities, and eternal in its duration.

2. *A deep and thorough sense of the danger to which it is exposed.* We are not in the habit of caring for that which is invaluable if it is secure; but here is an object of inestimable worth exposed to danger the most imminent—to a destruction the most severe.

3. *Tender solicitude for its welfare.* Examples of tender solicitude for souls are not wanting in the inspired volume (Ps. cxix. 136; Jer. ix. 1). But if we want to see true solicitude for souls, we must look for its manifestation in the conduct of Him who, when He beheld the city, wept over it, &c.

4. *Zealous exertion for their salvation.*

If love to souls really exist, it will manifest itself in ardent and continued effort to diffuse the knowledge of Christ among men. In solemn warning, affectionate entreaty, earnest prayer, and liberal contribution.

II. **On whom this duty devolves.**
1. *It is incumbent on the heads of families.* God holds them, to a certain extent, accountable for the souls under their care.
2. *On all the members of the Church.* Collectively and individually. To these is committed the evangelisation of the world.
3. *Pre-eminently on ministers.* The "care of souls" is the minister's province. His studies in private, his discourses in public, his prayers, his visits, his time, his talents, ought all to be devoted to this object.

III. **The great evil of neglecting this duty.**
1. *It is cruel.* A man would be considered cruel who saw one of the "beasts that perish" in danger, and did not attempt its rescue. He is cruel, who, having it in his power to relieve the necessitous, or save the perishing, does not do it. But the cruelty of the man who, knowing the danger of souls, does not care for them, is beyond expression.
2. *It is ungrateful.* If others had not cared for us, we must have perished. And shall we refuse to feel and labour for those who are now what we were once, and for whom the Saviour has, as well as for us, shed His own precious blood?
3. *It is criminal.* We cannot neglect the salvation of others and be innocent. Disobedience to God, and cruelty to men, are joined in neglecting to care for souls.
4. *It is fatal.* Fatal to those who are perishing, and fatal to those who have a name to live; fatal to all genuine piety, fatal to all ardent love to the Saviour's cause, fatal to zealous exertions for others, but especially fatal to our own souls.—N. in *Sketches of Sermons.* Abridged.

HUMAN IMPRISONMENT AND DIVINE EMANCIPATION.

(*Verse* 7.)

"Bring my soul out of prison, that I may praise Thy name."

We shall use these words to illustrate—

I. **Man's imprisonment as a sinner.** Man as a sinner is in bondage, oppressed with guilt, enslaved by carnal passions and evil habits; he is in "prison." Now imprisonment implies—

1. *The criminality of the prisoner.* The prisoner is either awaiting his trial on a charge of crime, or enduring his punishment as a criminal. Man has sinned and is guilty before God. The voice of God, both in the Bible and in his own conscience, condemns him.

2. *Deprivation to the prisoner.* The prisoner is deprived of (1.) *Liberty.* He is confined by massive walls, strong bolts and bars, &c. The sinner is bound by the chain of his sins. (2.) *Light.* Darkness is almost entirely supreme in the prison cells. The soul which is dominated by sin is blind to the beautiful light of the spiritual universe: its "understanding is darkened." (3.) *Society.* The prisoner is secluded from society. The unrenewed soul is a stranger to the highest fellowship; he is self-exiled from the society of true and holy souls.

The imprisonment of the soul is a far greater evil than that of the body. When the body is imprisoned, the soul may be free and joyous. When the bodies of Paul and Silas were in prison at Philippi with "their feet fast in the stocks," their souls went forth in worship, &c. When the body of Bunyan was in Bedford jail, his soul went forth on that glorious pilgrimage to the celestial city. His body was in the jail, but his soul—himself—was in the interpreter's house, and the house beautiful, on the delectable mountains, &c.

"Stone walls do not a prison make,
Nor iron bars a cage;
Minds innocent and quiet take
That for a hermitage.
If I have freedom in my love,
And in my soul am free,
Angels alone that soar above
Enjoy such liberty."—*Lovelace.*

But the imprisonment of the soul is the imprisonment of the man himself. Death terminates the imprisonment of the body, if it is not terminated before. But death has no power to liberate the soul from the prison and the fetters of corrupt passions, sinful habits, &c. "If ye believe not that I am He, ye shall die in your sins."

II. **Man's emancipation by the Saviour.** "Bring my soul out of prison." This prayer implies—

1. *A consciousness of the misery of imprisonment.* This is the first step, and an essential step, to liberation.

2. *A desire for emancipation.* "O wretched man that I am! who shall deliver me?" &c.

3. *A consciousness of inability to effect his own deliverance.* Man is too completely and securely fettered to be able to liberate himself. He must feel this before he can obtain his freedom.

4. *Confidence in the Lord Jesus as the great Emancipator.* He was "anointed to proclaim liberty to the captives, and the opening of the prison to the bound." "If the Son shall make you free, ye shall be free indeed."

III. **Man's praise to the Emancipator.** "That I may praise Thy name."

1. *Imprisonment restrains true praise.* Sin crushes the affections and aspirations of the soul towards God.

3. *Emancipation gives occasion for praise.* It would be such an expression of the goodness of God as would merit grateful and hearty acknowledgment.

3. *Emancipation imparts inspiration to praise.* The sense of freedom, the beauty of light, the pleasures of society, to which the liberated soul is introduced, will constitute an irresistible impulse to praise the Emancipator.

PSALM CXLIII.

INTRODUCTION.

This is the last of what are called the Seven Penitential Psalms. In the Hebrew it has the superscription, "A Psalm of David." And in the Septuagint and the Vulgate there is added, "When Absalom, his son, pursued him." Yet many expositors regard the Psalm as written in subsequent times, after the manner of David. Thus Delitzsch views it as "a later effort to copy after the Davidic Psalm-poetry." And Moll doubts "whether such a poet as David would have so copied himself, as would be the case if the Davidic authorship were proved. One might pray in the same language, but would not repeat himself in different poems." Perowne regards the Psalm as having been written after the exile. "The spirit and the language," he says, "it is true, are not unworthy of David; yet the many passages borrowed from earlier Psalms make it more probable that this Psalm is the work of some later poet." This objection loses sight of the fact that "there are many instances of repetitions in Psalms in the earlier portion of the Psalter, which are acknowledged to be those of David, and they do not occasion any difficulty. . . . At all events, the poem, even with the familiarity of its ideas, forms a complete whole, which is worthy of David, and which no critic need on that score hesitate to assign to him." Alexander, Barnes, Hengstenberg, Henry, Wordsworth, and most English commentators, accept the Davidic authorship.

"The Psalm," says Perowne, "consists of two parts, each of which is of six verses, the conclusion of the first being marked by the Selah. The first portion contains the complaint (vers. 1-6); the second, the prayer founded on that complaint (vers. 7-12)."

Homiletically we regard the Psalm as presenting to us *The cry of a distressed servant of God* (vers. 1-6), and *The prayer of a distressed servant of God* (vers. 7-12).

THE CRY OF A DISTRESSED SERVANT OF GOD.

(*Verses 1-6.*)

In this cry of the troubled poet to the Lord, we have—

I. **A picture of great distress.**

"For the enemy hath persecuted my soul; he hath smitten my life," &c. (vers. 3, 4). He was distressed by—

1. *Malignant outward persecution.* "The enemy hath persecuted my soul; he hath smitten my life down to the ground; he hath made me to dwell in darkness, as those that have long been dead." "The Psalmist," says Moll, "evidently means to say that his enemies are intent upon his utter destruction, and that he would remain without deliverance, unless God in mercy were to take up his defence." With what terrible malignity and untiring persistence did Saul persecute David! And how bitterly David suffered from the rebellion of his son Absalom! (2 Sam. xv. 30.) And the servants of God still suffer from without,—from the persecutions of the world (2 Tim. iii. 12); from the treachery of those whom they had trusted, as David did from Ahithophel; from temporal losses, &c. "In the world ye have tribulation."

2. *Insupportable inward suffering.* "Therefore is my spirit overwhelmed within me; my heart within me is desolate." Thus the poet expresses (1.) *His sore sorrow.* "My spirit is overwhelmed within me." (See a sketch on Ps. cxlii. 3a.) (2.) *His painful perplexity.* "My heart within me is desolate," "or rather, 'is full of amazement,' lit., 'astonies itself;' seeks to comprehend the mystery of its sufferings, and is ever beaten back upon itself in its perplexity: such is the full force of the reflexive conjugation here employed."—*Perowne.*

The mystery of suffering is to many minds, and those not the least noble, its most painful element. The experience of the poet was not a solitary or exceptional one. Good men are still liable to outward persecution and inward anguish; they still suffer both in their circumstances and in their souls. "Beloved, think it not strange concerning the fiery trial which is to try you, as though some strange thing happened unto you," &c. "My son, despise not thou the chastening of the Lord," &c. (Heb. xii. 5-11).

II. **An exercise indicating great wisdom.**

"I remember the days of old; I meditate on all Thy works; I muse on the work of Thy hands."

1. *The distinguished mental powers exercised.* (1.) *Recollection.* "I remember the days of old." The poet recalled the past; made it live again before his "mind's eye." (2.) *Meditation.* He reflected upon the scenes which recollection reproduced; and thus endeavoured to ascertain their significance, learn their lessons, &c.

2. *The great subjects on which these mental powers were exercised.* (1.) "*The days of old.*" What a wondrous volume is the past! How marvellous are its revelations! how instructive its contents! how wise its lessons! To this volume the poet turned his attention. (2.) *The doings of God.* "All Thy works, . . . the work of Thy hands." How vast a theme for meditation is this! and how sublime! how fitted to inspire the soul with confidence and hope! (For a fuller treatment of the hints given under this head, see on Ps. lxxvii. 3-6, 11, 12; vol. i., pp. 431-437.) Now, in all this the Psalmist seems to act with great wisdom. In turning his mind from the restless present to the calm past, and from the cruel doings of his enemies and the sore troubles of his heart to the glorious deeds of ancient date which God had done, he adopted a course calculated to calm his fears, strengthen his faith in God, arouse his courage, and inspire his hope.

III. **An appeal of great power.**

"Hear my prayer, O Lord; give ear to my supplications," &c. This appeal is—

1. *Directed to the best Being.* "O Jehovah, hear my prayer," &c. He never turns away His ear from the cry of the troubled heart; He is merciful and gracious; He is able to succour all suffering and needy souls; and "His love is as great as His power."

2. *For real blessings.* He solicits from Jehovah—(1.) *Acceptance of his prayer.* "Hear my prayer, O Jehovah; give ear to my supplications: in Thy faithfulness answer me, and in Thy righteousness." No utterance of man escapes the Divine ear. The Psalmist prays not for a mere hearing, but for a gracious audience, and a favourable answer to his appeal. (2.) *Forgiveness of his sins.* "And enter not

into judgment with Thy servant; for in Thy sight no man living is righteous." The poet here manifests—(α) His consciousness of sin. "He traces his suffering to his sin: the malice of his enemies is the rod of God's chastisement, calling him to repentance." (β) His conviction of the Divine holiness. He who appears quite righteous before man, appears sinful before the infinite purity of God. "What is man, that he should be clean?" &c. (Job xv. 14–16). "How can man be justified with God?" &c. (Job xxv. 4–6). (γ) His belief in the Divine judgment of man. "Enter not into judgment," &c. "God shall bring every work into judgment," &c. (δ) His earnest desire for Divine forgiveness. The petition that God would not enter into judgment with him implies his longing for mercy and pardon of his sins. Here is a need which is common to all men in this world. Our hope must ever be in the forbearing and forgiving mercy of God. (3.) *Deliverance from his enemies and distresses*. This, though not directly expressed in this section of the Psalm, is the great object of the Psalmist's appeal to God. Such were the blessings which the distressed poet sought, &c.

3. *Enforced by the strongest pleas*. (1.) The sore need of the suppliant (vers. 3, 4). (2.) The relation sustained by the suppliant to God. "Thy servant." The phrase, "Thy servant," in ver. 2, "is not a mere oriental circumlocution for the person speaking, and not merely a term of polite address," as appears from the way in which it is used in ver. 12. "The expression, 'with Thy servant,' contains," says Hengstenberg, "the grounding of the prayer; with His servants God *cannot* go into judgment; He chastens them indeed, but He does not give them over to death." (3.) The revealed character of God. "In Thy faithfulness answer me, and in Thy righteousness." "The faithfulness of God," says Moll, "is His faithfulness to His promises, or the truthfulness of His nature, in conformity with which everything that He has spoken or ordained is reliable and unchangeable. His righteousness is the corresponding course of action by which His ordinances are firmly established and fulfilled in the world, so that there is rendered to every man according to his works. God's faithfulness and righteousness are thus assured, as in 1 John i. 9, and the repenting receive the forgiveness of their sins, but the impenitent, judgment." This is the most powerful plea that we can use with God. He cannot be untrue to His promise or to His character. "He cannot deny Himself."

IV. **A desire of great fervour.**

"I stretch forth my hands unto Thee; my soul thirsteth after Thee as a thirsty land." Notice:—

1. *The Object of his desire*. "Unto Thee; . . . after Thee." "Observe how he binds himself to God alone, cuts off every other hope from his soul, and, in short, makes his very need a chariot wherewith to mount up to God." (On this and on the next point see on Ps. xlii. 1, 2; lxiii. 1; vol. i. pp. 206, 207, 314.)

2. *The fervour of his desire*. "I stretch forth my hands unto Thee," "as the weary child stretches forth its hands to its mother, that on her bosom it may be hushed to rest."—*Perowne*. "My soul thirsteth after Thee as a thirsty land." "As a parched land," says Hengstenberg, "stands related to the rain, so my soul to Thee, and to Thy salvation." And Calvin: "In great heat we see the earth cracking and gaping, as though with open mouth she asked for the rain from heaven." So fervently the soul of the poet craved the help and joy of the presence of God.

CONCLUSION.—Exhibit the Psalmist in this cry to God in his distress as *an example to the servants of God in times of* (1) *severe spiritual suffering*, and (2) *tribulation from without*.

Divine Judgment Deprecated.

(*Verse 2.*)

Let us consider—

I. The truths which are here implied.

1. *That the Psalmist was conscious of sin.* So far as his enemies were concerned he felt that they were persecuting him without cause; he was innocent in relation to them; but in relation to God he felt that he was not innocent. The persecutions of his enemies he regarded as the chastisement of God because of his sins.

2. *That the Lord is the Judge of man.* The poet regards Him as having authority to enter into judgment with His creatures. This truth is frequently expressed in the Psalms. "God is Judge Himself." "God is the Judge; He putteth down one," &c. "Lift up Thyself, Thou Judge of the earth," &c. "The Lord will judge His people," &c.

3. *That the Lord is a righteous Judge.* He cannot pass by unrepented sin. If sin be not forgiven and forsaken, He will visit with His judgments because of it, and His judgments are true and righteous. "He shall judge the world in righteousness; He shall minister judgment to the people in uprightness." "He shall judge the people righteously." "He shall judge the world with righteousness, and the people with His truth."

II. The petition which is here offered.

"Enter not into judgment with Thy servant." This is a petition for—

1. *Forbearing mercy.* It is a request that God will not call him to render a strict account for his offences against Him. "If Thou, Lord, shouldest mark iniquities, O Lord, who shall stand?" We need the forbearance of God, because of our imperfections, omissions, and transgressions.

2. *Forgiving mercy.* Though not directly expressed, this is sought by implication in this petition. Even a faithful servant of the Lord needs the forgiveness of sins arising from remaining depravity and moral weakness. And it is an encouragement to know that "there is forgiveness with Him; . . . with the Lord there is mercy, and with Him is plenteous redemption." "He will abundantly pardon." Freely, graciously, and completely He forgives all those who in sincere penitence seek Him.

III. The reasons which are here urged.

"With Thy servant; for in Thy sight shall no man living be justified." Perowne more correctly translates: "For before Thee no man living is righteous." Here are two pleas by which the Psalmist strengthens his petition—

1. *The universal sinfulness of man.* "Before Thee no man living is righteous." "No one of the race, no matter what his rank, his outward conduct, his gentleness, his amiableness, his kindness—no matter how just and upright he may be towards his fellow-men," he is not righteous before the holy God. Before man we may appear righteous; but not before a Being of infinite holiness. Most clear is the testimony of the Bible on this point. "There is no man than sinneth not." "There is none that doeth good, no, not one." "Who can say, I have made my heart clean, I am pure from my sin?" "There is not a just man upon earth that doeth good and sinneth not." "If we say that we have no sin, we deceive ourselves, and the truth is not in us." Hence if God were swift to judge and strict to punish, all men must perish.

2. *The relation of the Psalmist to God.* "Thy servant." David was a distinguished servant of God, yet he felt that he was a sinner before Him. Even a sincere and faithful servant of God cannot stand before Him in judgment; cannot plead any merits of his own, or appeal to God on the ground of His justice. "When ye shall have done all those things which are commanded you, say, We are unprofitable servants;" &c. But when a man can sincerely speak of himself to the Lord as His servant, he has good ground upon which to base his hope of protection and salvation

from Him in His mercy. "When a man resolves with heart and soul to be and remain a servant of God, God will not forsake him; but where He is, there will also His servant be."

CONCLUSION :—

1. *If a true servant of God cannot stand before Him in judgment, how shall the wicked appear at His bar?* "The ungodly are like the chaff which the wind driveth away," &c. (Ps. i. 4–6).

2. *Let every man seek an interest in the infinite mercy of God.* "Let the wicked forsake his way," &c. (Isa. lv. 7). "Return, thou backsliding Israel, saith the Lord," &c. (Jer. iii. 12). "God is rich in mercy." "The Lord is merciful and gracious," &c. (Ps. ciii. 8–12). "Who is a God like unto Thee, that pardoneth iniquity," &c. (Mic. vii. 18, 19).

THE PRAYER OF A DISTRESSED SERVANT OF GOD.

(*Verses* 7-12.)

Notice :—

I. **The blessings which are here sought.**

The Psalmist first solicits the Divine favour in general, and a speedy answer to his prayer : "Hear me speedily, O Lord ; my spirit faileth : hide not Thy face from me," &c. (ver. 7). He then proceeds to specify certain blessings in particular, and to entreat the Lord to bestow them. He asks for—

1. *The lovingkindness of God.* "Cause me to hear Thy lovingkindness in the morning." It is a petition for an early assurance of the mercy of God. Divine lovingkindness is the root of which all other blessings are branches—the fountain from which all other blessings flow. It is also the crown of all other blessings. "Thy lovingkindness is better than life."

2. *Deliverance from his distresses.* (1.) From *outward enemies.* "Deliver me, O Lord, from mine enemies. . . . And of Thy mercy cut off mine enemies, and destroy all them that afflict my soul." Perowne translates : "And of Thy lovingkindness cut off mine enemies, and destroy all the adversaries of my soul." On this verse Barnes says, "The destruction of the wicked is a favour to the universe ; just as the arrest and punishment of a robber or a pirate is a mercy to society, to mankind ; just as every prison is a display of *mercy* as well as of *justice :*—mercy to society at large ; justice to the offenders." There is truth in this ; but the prayer for the destruction of our enemies is not becoming in the lips of a Christian. "I say unto you, Love your enemies, bless them that curse you," &c. (Matt. v. 44, 45). "Bless them which persecute you," &c. "If thine enemy hunger, feed him," &c. Such is the Christian rule. But we may petition God for deliverance from our adversaries. (2.) From *inward sufferings.* "For Thy righteousness' sake bring my soul out of trouble." The poet was in sore distress of soul ; he looks to the faithfulness and mercy of God for deliverance from the same. Let the godly in all times of spiritual trial and sorrow direct their prayer to the same gracious Being. "Call upon Me in the day of trouble ; I will deliver thee," &c.

3. *Inward and spiritual blessings.* In the view of the Psalmist his salvation requires both external deliverances and internal communications of Divine grace. "The way of deliverance," says Moll, "is to the servant of God no external one, but a way of salvation, which the commandments of God point out, in which the Spirit of God, who is good, is the Guide." So the Psalmist petitions for—(1.) *Divine teaching ;*—(*a.*) That he might *know* the way which God would have him to pursue. "Cause me to know the way wherein I should walk." Even the most experienced and holy of men need the direction of God in life. (β.) That he might *do* the will of God. "Teach me to do Thy will." Correct knowledge alone cannot save man from sin or suffering ; correct conduct must be added thereto. Mere theories, however true and good, never raised a life into sanctity and strength.

To do this, theories must be reduced to practice—embodied in life. Most needful and important is the petition, "Teach me to *do* Thy will." (2.) *Divine help.* "Thy Spirit is good; lead me into the land of uprightness." Perowne: "'Let Thy good Spirit lead me in a plain country,' lit., 'in a level land,' or 'on level ground,' where there is no fear of stumbling and falling." Conant translates: "Let Thy good Spirit guide me on even ground." The poet desires to be led into a way of safety. It is a request not simply for enlightenment; but for the Holy Spirit's help, His guiding, guarding, and strengthening influence. Hengstenberg's note is to the point: "David's proper regard is directed to the obtaining of deliverance, which is the object of all his prayers in the preceding and following verses. But he shows himself throughout deeply penetrated with the conviction, that the foundation of the deliverance is righteousness—that it never *can* come, where this foundation is wanting, but that it of necessity *must* come where this foundation exists. He knew, also, that nothing could be done here by one's own power (Comp., for example, Ps. xix.; li.) Hence he prays here, expanding his views farther, that the Lord would (internally) teach him to do His will, convinced that this first gift must necessarily draw the second in its train, that of salvation; so he prays that the good Spirit of God would make him good, and consequently would guide him upon the path of salvation.... The good Spirit *works* good in those who partake of the gift." (3.) *Divine life.* "Quicken me, O Lord, for Thy name's sake." Here the poet prays for an increase of spiritual life and strength. In the way of the Divine commands there is salvation; and the teaching, the guidance, the life, and the strength which are necessary to tread that way, God alone can bestow. Like the Psalmist, let us seek them from Him.

II. **The grounds upon which these blessings are sought.**

1. *The sore need of the Psalmist.* "Hear me speedily, O Lord; my spirit faileth; hide not Thy face from me, lest I be like unto them that go down into the pit." "The pit" is the grave. Apart from the help of God, the Psalmist despairs even of life itself. The greatness of his misery is a touching and forcible appeal to the tender and infinite mercy of God.

2. *The personal relations of the Psalmist to God.* (1.) *Confidence in God.* In various ways does the Psalmist give expression to this: "For in Thee do I trust.... I flee unto Thee to hide me." Margin: "Heb., 'Hide me with Thee.'" Perowne: "'Unto Thee have I fled to hide me;' lit., 'Unto Thee have I hidden (myself).' But the phrase is very peculiar, and its meaning doubtful." Conant: "With Thee I hide myself." "The notions of covering and refuge," says Moll, "are united in the intermediate one of hiding." The expression undoubtedly indicates strong confidence. (Comp. Ps. xxvii. 5; xxxi. 20.) Hengstenberg says admirably, "The allusion points in this direction, that God must conceal those who conceal themselves with Him." Could He fail to deliver one who so utterly confided in Him? (2.) *Prayer to God.* "For I lift up my soul unto Thee." This language denotes earnest desire and confident expectation. "Prayer is the ascent of the soul to God." "Where the soul is really *directed* towards God, it is full of *seeking for help,* and *longing for salvation.*" "To lift up the *soul* to God is to begin the lifting of the *entire* man out of all need." Could God disregard such a desire, or disappoint such an expectation as this? (3.) *Consecration to God.* "For Thou art my God; ... for I am Thy servant." If we have sincerely taken the Lord for our God, and consecrated ourselves to Him as His servants, we may be sure that He will guide and defend us, sustain and save us. (See on ver. 2.)

3. *The revealed character of God.* The Psalmist pleads (1.) *His righteousness.* "For Thy righteousness' sake, bring my soul out of trouble." (See notes on ver. 1.) (2.) *His grace.* "And of Thy mercy cut off mine enemies." He pleads that, in the lovingkindness which He had declared to His people, He would interpose for his deliverance. (3.) *His*

honour. "Quicken me, O Lord, for Thy name's sake." This is a bold and powerful plea. Moses used it with remarkable results (Exod. xxxii. 11–14; Num. xiv. 13–20). So also did Joshua: "What wilt Thou do unto Thy great name?" (Jos. vii. 6 *seq.*) And frequently David urged it with God. Assuredly God will not fail to maintain the honour of His holy name. Thus cogent are the arguments with which the Psalmist entreats God for salvation.

III. **The urgency with which these blessings are sought.** "Hear me speedily, O Lord; my spirit faileth," &c. Perowne translates: "Make haste to answer me, O Jehovah; my spirit faileth," &c. "Matters had now come with the Psalmist to an extremity. Where this is the case with the servants of God, there the Divine help cannot be longer withheld." The poet manifests similar urgency in the petition, "Cause me to hear Thy lovingkindness in the morning," *i.e.*, soon, speedily. "The idea is not that He would wait for another day, but that He would interpose as the very first act,—as when one enters on a day." A prayer like unto this, with such powerful pleas and such urgency of entreaty, is itself a sign of the nearness of the interposition and salvation of the Lord.

A GOOD MAN'S PRAYER FOR GRACE AND GUIDANCE.

(*Verse 8.*)

Value of the Book of Psalms as presenting a test of religious character and experience. Shows what religion is—what religion can do: what it once was, it always is—what it has once done, it can always do.

I. **David prays for God's distinguishing favour as a God of grace.** "Cause me to hear Thy lovingkindness," &c.

1. *The blessing itself is very emphatic.* "Thy lovingkindness." Not God's general benevolence as it shines in nature; not His general protection as it is seen in Providence; but His special manifestation of mercy as it shines in the covenant of grace. "Remember me, O Lord, with the favour of Thy people." "Look Thou upon me, and be merciful unto me, as Thou usest to do unto those that love Thy name."

This he desires beyond created good—beyond his crown as a monarch—beyond his eminent distinction as a man of genius—beyond his highest estimation as a gifted prophet, he values God's favour; just as Moses did "the goodwill of Him that dwelt in the bush" beyond "the chief things of the ancient mountains and the precious things of the lasting hills." These desires are common to all the saints. In New Testament phrase—the love of the Father, the grace of the Son, and the fellowship of the Spirit. Judge of your character by your habitual desires.

2. *The period in which it is desired.* "In the morning." It is sought first in point of *time*—first in point of *importance.* "Seek ye first the kingdom of God," &c. "In the morning" of the day, that we may begin it with God. "In the morning" of the week—the Sabbath. "In the morning" of life—youth. "In the morning" of the resurrection. "Cause me:" Divine influence needful.

II. **For God's daily guidance as a God of Providence.** "Cause me to know the way," &c.

1. *Prompted by a sense of our weakness and ignorance.* How much we need a guide! We have as much need of daily guidance as of daily bread. We cannot get safely through a world of sin and danger without the Presence and Grace of Christ. It is not a matter of indifference to the Christian how he passes through life. Not enough to say, "What shall I eat?" &c.; but, "Lord, lift Thou up the light of Thy countenance upon us." The soul has wants as well as the body. The Christian has moral interests to secure; he has a race to run—a battle to fight—a prize to gain—a God to glorify—a soul to be lost or saved. He is in a world where the great destroyer has his seat. He knows that the interests of others are linked in with his own: cannot stand or fall alone. Hence he prays, "Cause me to know," &c.

2. *Prompted by knowledge of the character of Christ as a Guide.* Wise, powerful, gracious. "The Shepherd and Bishop of your souls." Having had large experience of the conduct of sinners.

III. **For the constant acceptance of his devotions as a prayer-hearing God.** "In Thee do I trust; . . . I lift up my soul unto Thee." This is partly a profession of his daily faith and experience, and partly a plea for the exercise of God's mercy. "In Thee do I trust:" Thou wilt not disappoint.

God is a perfect circle of wonders and miracles; a good perfectly adapted to our moral nature. They who know anything of Him are anxious to know more. —*Samuel Thodey.*

DIVINE GUIDANCE.

(*Verse 8.*)

"Cause me to know the way wherein I should walk; for I lift up my soul unto Thee."

Life is like a heath with paths stretching in various directions. Many appear pleasant and safe that lead astray. Man is often bewildered. He often chooses wrongly. How important this prayer.

I. **This was the prayer of one who felt his need of Divine guidance.**

Many will be their own guides. They are self-reliant; like wayward children, or foolish Alpine travellers, forgetting their own ignorance and liability to error. Some are wise; they will not take a step without God. They feel their need of His guiding hand. This sense of need may arise—

1. *From seeing the errors of others.* Men, however, are seldom wise enough to learn from the sorrows that attend the wanderings of others. Second-hand experiences do not teach much.

2. *From bitter experiences gained in self-chosen paths.* God does not always save us *from* erroneous ways, but often *through* them. Our freedom is part of our discipline.

3. *From Divine enlightenment.* Seldom will a man be humble enough to seek God until he sees *what he is* by the light of God's Spirit. Bitter experiences fail to teach us without grace.

II. **This was the prayer of one who believed that God had a way marked out for him.**

Life is not a pathless wilderness. God has a way laid down for every man. He regards the individual life. Laws are general, but the progress of each life is a speciality. There is a way in which every man *should* walk.

1. *This is true morally.* Right is straight, wrong is zigzag. Right is distinct from wrong,—a Divine way, clear to those who will see it.

2. *This is true intellectually.* Truth is the Divine path for the intellect. Truth, as a narrow way, lies often in the midst of the devious windings of error; but they who are guided by God shall not fail to discover it.

3. *This is true circumstantially.* From the cradle to the grave God has a way for every man. The prayerless miss it; the prayerful find it.

III. **This was the prayer of one who believed that God could reveal His way to him.**

The days of Divine revelations are not over. "There is a spirit in man; and the inspiration of the Almighty giveth him understanding." He causes us to know His way—

1. *By His Holy Spirit.* God is nigh to every man. He can act directly upon each man's spirit. He often leads men when they know it not. His saints are often conspicuously guided.

2. *By His Word.* Its precepts instruct, its revelations enlighten, its examples encourage and warn us.

3. *By the incarnate life of His Son.* He is the way. Those who follow Him do not walk in darkness.

4. *By the force of events.* Way after way is hedged up, and only God's way is left to us. By this God causes us to know the way wherein we should walk.

IV. **This was the prayer of one who**

had placed himself in the right attitude to receive Divine guidance. Attitude is important. Some are listless, others fanatical, others unbelieving. This was—
1. *An attitude of expectancy.* Faith was stretching out the soul-hands to receive (ver. 6). Every faculty was awake and eager. God would find a receptive nature, a waiting heart.
2. *The attitude of ardent desire.* Desire had raised the soul out of its ordinary life. It was rising to meet God. It was lifted up to take hold of Him.
3. *The attitude of importunate prayer.*

He would not be denied the light he sought. He would continue before Him until the mists rolled away, and the Divine path shone out as light in the midst of obscurity. Such an attitude is sure to obtain a knowledge of God's way.

Learn :—
1. *To distrust self.*
2. *To take no step until God makes known His way.*
3. *For in His way there will be found safety, peace, and ultimately heaven.*—W. O. LILLEY. From "*The Homiletic Quarterly.*"

PSALM CXLIV.

INTRODUCTION.

"This is a singularly composite Psalm. The earlier portion of it, to the end of ver. 11, consists almost entirely of a cento of quotations, strung together from earlier Psalms; and it is not always easy to trace a real connection between them. The latter portion of the Psalm, vers. 12-15, differs completely from the former. It bears the stamp of originality, and is entirely free from the quotations and allusions with which the preceding verses abound. It is hardly probable, however, that this concluding portion is the work of the poet who compiled the rest of the Psalm : it is more probable that he has here transcribed a fragment of some ancient poem, in which were portrayed the happiness and prosperity of the nation in its brightest days, under David, it may have been, or at the beginning of the reign of Solomon. His object seems to have been thus to revive the hopes of his nation, perhaps after the return from the exile, by reminding them how in their past history obedience to God had brought with it its full recompense."

Thus Dean Perowne writes—rejecting the Davidic authorship, and bestowing no notice whatever on the superscription, which ascribes the Psalm to David. And Moll says, "It is doubtful whether it should be assigned to David himself." But Hengstenberg says "that it is one of David's peculiarities to derive from his earlier productions a foundation for new ones. . . . This Psalm *can* only have been composed by David." And Alexander : "The Davidic origin of the Psalm is as marked as that of any in the Psalter." And Perowne, notwithstanding the passage above quoted, says, "The language of vers. 1-4, as well as the language of ver. 10, is clearly only suitable in the mouth of a king, or some powerful and recognised leader of the nation ; and it is difficult to find a person of rank in the later history in whose mouth such a Psalm as this would be appropriate." For ourselves we are inclined to accept the superscription, and regard the Psalm as a composition or compilation of David's.

"The Psalmist recounts glorious victories in the past, complains that the nation is now beset by strange, *i.e.*, barbarous enemies, so false and treacherous that no covenant can be kept with them, prays for deliverance from them by an interposition great and glorious as had been vouchsafed of old, and anticipates the return of a golden age of peace and plenty."

INSPIRING ASPECTS OF THE DIVINE BEING.

(*Verses* 1, 2.)

These verses are taken almost verbatim from different portions of Ps. xviii. We regard them as presenting to us the Divine Being in certain inspiring aspects.

I. **As the Author of human skill.**
"He teacheth my hands to war, my fingers to fight." The skill which the poet had in the use of the weapons of war, he attributes to the Lord. The abilities by which battles are planned and victories won come from Him. All beauty of design, and dexterity in labour, and success in achievement in human works, must be attributed to the Great God.

II. **As the Protector of human life.** In several different forms the poet expresses this. "Jehovah my *rock*." Two Hebrew words, which slightly differ in meaning, are translated by the word rock. The one which is employed here (צוּר) suggests the ideas of strength and fixedness; Jehovah is a strong and steadfast refuge. "My *fortress*," *i.e.*, a strong place, generally difficult of access, and thus a secure retreat. "My *high tower*," *i.e.*, a place so high as to be out of the reach of danger, or some almost inaccessible crag affording safety to those who reached it. "My *deliverer*," who rescues me from the power of my enemies. "My *shield*," protecting me from the arrows of the enemies on the field of battle. Now these figures set forth a protection which is—
1. *Unchangeable*, as a rock.
2. *Enduring*, as a rock.
3. *Inviolable.* The various figures which the poet employs suggest this fact. "On the heaping together of epithets and titles of God Calvin remarks, that it is not superfluous, but designed to strengthen and confirm faith; for men's minds are easily shaken, especially when some storm of trial beats upon them. Hence, if God should promise us His succour in one word, it would not be enough; in fact, in spite of all the props and aids He gives us, we constantly totter and are ready to fall, and such a forgetfulness of His lovingkindness steals upon us, that we come near to losing heart altogether."—*Perowne.* So these various figures are used to impress us with the invincibility of the Divine protection, and to inspire our confidence therein.
4. *Ever available.* "The name of the Lord is a strong tower; the righteous runneth into it and is safe." By prayer, by the exercise of faith in Him, we can at any time avail ourselves of the inviolable protection of Jehovah. "If God be for us, who can be against us?"

III. **As the Source of human authority.**
"Who subdueth my people under me." "The Psalmist is not triumphing in the exercise of despotic power, but gratefully acknowledges that the authority he wields comes from God." David was chosen to be king by God, and in His providence all the tribes were led to submit to his government. "Let every soul," saith St. Paul, "be subject unto the higher powers. For there is no power but of God: the powers that be are ordained of God." "For promotion cometh neither from the east, nor from the west, nor from the south. But God is the Judge; He putteth down one, and setteth up another."

IV. **As the Object of human trust.**
"And He in whom I trust." Perowne translates: "He in whom I find refuge." The idea is that the Psalmist confided in Him, sought unto Him for protection in times of peril, fled unto Him as His refuge in trouble. The Lord is an adequate object of trust for man, and the only one. "They that trust in the Lord shall be as Mount Zion, which cannot be removed, but abideth for ever." "Blessed are all they that put their trust in Him."

V. **As the Supreme Good of human life.**
"My goodness." Margin: "My mercy." Perowne: "My lovingkindness." So also Conant. The idea seems to be that the Psalmist regarded the Lord as his Chief Good, as the Source of all his blessings. David frequently gives expression to this sentiment. "There be many that say, Who will show us any good? Lord, lift Thou up the light of Thy countenance upon us." "In His favour is life." "Thy lovingkindness is better than life." And Asaph also: "Whom have I in heaven but Thee?" &c. In Him we have the supreme truth for the intellect, the supreme righteousness for the conscience, the supreme love for the heart, the supreme beauty for the soul.

VI. **As the Recipient of human praise.**
"Blessed be Jehovah my rock," &c. The Psalmist here praises Jehovah for what He is to him, and for what He does for him.
1. *Gratitude urges to this.* Its language is, "What shall I render unto the Lord for all His benefits toward me?"
2. *Reason urges to this.* It is in the

highest degree rational that He who is Supremely Good should be reverenced and loved; that our greatest Benefactor should be praised by us, &c.

3. *This is blessed.* He who sincerely blesses God finds blessing in so doing. True worship tends to purify and strengthen, to sanctify and gloriously transform the worshipper.

CONCLUSION.—The people of God in this world are still a militant people; but the Lord their God is still their omnipotent Protector and their Supreme Good. Let them loyally trust Him, and heartily worship Him, and soon and for ever they shall become a triumphant people over all foes.

THE INSIGNIFICANCE AND GREATNESS OF MAN.

(*Verses* 3, 4.)

The connection of these verses with the preceding is correctly pointed out by Calvin: " David remembers all that God has done for him, and then, like Jacob, thinks: Lord, I am too little for all Thy lovingkindness, and so contrasts his own nothingness and that of mankind generally with the greatness of such a gracious God." Thus the goodness of God produced humility in the poet; and the truest, deepest humility is always produced by the *grace* of God. The poet sets before us—

I. **The insignificance of human life.**
" Lord, what is man? . . . Man is like to vanity; his days are as a shadow that passeth away." Here are two ideas:—

1. *Human life is unsubstantial.* It is here compared to " vanity "—more correctly, "a breath"—and "a shadow." St. James also speaks of human life as " a vapour." How unsubstantial are a " breath " and a " shadow " ! So is human life. We may see this—(1.) *In the objects for which men live.* " All the fret and stir," says Perowne, " all the eager clamour and rivalry of men, as they elbow and jostle one another to obtain wealth and rank, and the enjoyments of life, are but a breath." " With what idle dreams, what foolish plans, what vain pursuits, are they for the most part occupied ! They undertake dangerous expeditions and difficult enterprises in foreign countries, and they acquire fame; but what is it?—*Vanity!* They pursue deep and abstruse speculations, and give themselves to that ' much study which is a weariness of the flesh,' and they attain to literary renown, and survive in their writings; but what is it?—*Vanity!* They rise up early, and sit up late, and eat the bread of anxiety and care, and thus they amass wealth; but what is it?—*Vanity!* They frame and execute plans and schemes of ambition—they are loaded with honours and adorned with titles—they afford employment for the herald, and form a subject for the historian; but what is it?—*Vanity!* In fact, all occupations and pursuits are worthy of no other epithet, if they are not preceded by, and connected with, a deep and paramount regard to the salvation of the soul, the honour of God, and the interests of eternity. . . . Oh, then, what phantoms, what airy nothings are those things that wholly absorb the powers and occupy the days of the great mass of mankind around us ! Their most substantial good perishes in the using, and their most enduring realities are but ' the fashion of this world that passeth away.'"—*Dr. Raffles.* The great majority of those who seek these things do not attain them; and the few who do attain them find them utterly unsatisfactory. (2.) *In life itself.* How unsubstantial is our life as it appears here ! How easily is the vital flame extinguished ! A breath of air laden with disease may soon lay the most robust frame low in death. A draught of tainted water may quench the vital spark in the most beautiful body. A very little accident may still for ever the brain of the wisest man. Men " dwell in houses of clay, whose foundation is in the dust, which are crushed before the moth. They are destroyed from morning to evening; they perish for ever without any regarding it. Doth not their excel-

lency which is in them go away? They die, even without wisdom."

2. *Human life is transitory.* "As a shadow that passeth away." "Come like shadows, so depart," seems to be a law of human life. (1.) "A shadow passeth away" *constantly.* It is never stationary. As the sun advances the shadow moves onward. It cannot rest. So is it with human life.

> "Whate'er we do, where'er we be,
> We're travelling to the grave."

(2.) "A shadow passeth away" *rapidly.* How soon the sun sets, and the shadow is gone! But the sun may be obscured by clouds long before his setting; then also the shadow is gone. A striking illustration of the brevity of human life. If, like Jacob, a man lived an hundred and thirty years, like Jacob he would say, "Few and evil have the days of the years of my life been." But the great majority of men do not live half so long as that. Much more rapidly do they pass away. (3.) "A shadow passeth away" *completely.* The departing shadow leaves not a trace behind. Is it not so with almost all men? How few of all the millions that have lived in the past have any memorial upon earth now!

> "Some sink outright,
> O'er them and o'er their names the billows close,
> To-morrow knows not they were ever born.
> Others a short memorial leave behind;
> Like a flag floating when the bark's engulfed,
> It floats a moment, and is seen no more.
> One Cæsar lives; a thousand are forgot."
> —*Young.*

This aspect of life should humble human pride. Life is unsubstantial and transitory, as a mere "breath" or a passing "shadow." "It is even a vapour, that appeareth for a little time, and then vanisheth away."

> "Life's but a walking shadow—a poor player,
> That struts and frets his hour upon the stage,
> And then is heard no more: it is a tale
> Told by an idiot, full of sound and fury,
> Signifying nothing."—*Shakespeare.*

II. **The greatness of human life.** "Lord, what is man, that Thou takest knowledge of him? A son of man, that Thou makest account of him?" Man is thought of, cared for, graciously regarded by God. This invests human nature with great importance and dignity. God's regard for man is manifest—

1. *In the provision which He has made for us in nature.* He has created all nature to minister to man's needs. Earth and sea, air and sky, all serve us. (Comp. Gen. i. 28, 29.)

2. *In His care over us in Providence.* It was this protecting and sustaining providential care which led the Psalmist to inquire, "Lord, what is man?" &c. He guides and guards and sustains with tenderest care and infinite wisdom. (Comp. Ps. xl. 17.)

3. *In the redemption which He has wrought for us.* "He remembered us in our low estate," &c. (Ps. cxxxvi. 23, 24). "God so loved the world," &c. "God commendeth His love," &c.

4. *In the home which He has provided for us.* "In My Father's house are many mansions," &c. "He hath begotten us again unto an inheritance incorruptible," &c. When man passeth away like a shadow, it is to enter upon an immortal and glorious life.

CONCLUSION.—Let our lives harmonise with God's regard for us.

MAN.

(*Verse 3.*)

"Lord, what is man?"

I. **What was man as he came from the hands of his Creator?**
1. Rational.
2. Responsible.
3. Immortal.
4. Holy and happy.

II. **What is man in his present condition?**
1. He is fallen.
2. He is guilty.
3. He is sinful.
4. He is miserable, and helpless in his misery.

III. What is man when he has believed in Christ?
1. He is restored to a right relation to God.
2. He is restored to a right disposition toward God.
3. He enjoys the influences of the Holy Spirit.
4. He is in process of preparation for the heavenly world.

IV. What shall man be when he is admitted into heaven?
1. Free from sin and sorrow.
2. Advanced to the perfection of his nature.
3. Associated with angels.
4. Near to his Saviour and his God.
—*George Brooks.*

HUMAN LIFE A SHADOW.

(*Verse 4.*)

Man and his days are here compared to "a shadow;" and the propriety of the similitude is attested by the experience of all mankind. The resemblance lies in the following particulars:—

I. **A shadow is compounded of light and darkness**; for when no object intercepts the light of the sun, or when the light of the sun is withdrawn, no shadow is produced. In like manner, the state of man in the present world is made up of joy and sorrow; while, as in the emblem, the latter greatly preponderates.

II. **A shadow seems to be something, when in reality it is nothing.** If you grasp it, you prove its emptiness. The pleasures, riches, and honours of the present world seem important to the eye of the carnal mind when viewed at a little distance; they attract attention, excite desire, and are eagerly pursued. But when, the object being attained, they are closely examined, how empty and unsatisfactory do they prove!

III. **A shadow is the subject of continual changes, till at length it finally and suddenly ceases.** In the morning, when the sun first rises above the horizon, it is weak and extended to a great length. Towards noon it gains strength, and is contracted in its dimensions. From thence to sunset it gradually becomes less distinct, and at last suddenly and wholly disappears. Man, survey in this emblem thy life! How lively and affecting the description! (Comp. Job xiv. 1, 2; James iv. 14.)

IV. **A shadow cannot exist longer than the sun's continuance above the horizon, and is every moment liable to annihilation by the intervention of a cloud.** In like manner, human life generally lasts but three score years and ten, or four score years; and may, by a sudden accident or the power of disease, be much curtailed. We have no security for the protraction of life through another day or hour; and the probability that our life will not reach its customary limit is as great as that the shadow will cease before the evening arrives.

V. **A shadow, when gone, leaves no track of its existence behind.** This also is the case with the riches, pleasures, and honours of the world. "We brought nothing into the world, and it is certain we can carry nothing out." This world is no further substantial, or of importance, than as it stands connected with the next.—"*The Christian Guardian.*"

A PRAYER OF THE GODLY FOR DELIVERANCE FROM THEIR ENEMIES.

(*Verses 5–11.*)

In these verses we have the Psalmist's prayer for the overthrow of his enemies, and for his own victory. Let us notice—

I. **His description of his enemies.**
1. *They were foreigners.* The Psalmist speaks of them as "strange children;" or, taking Perowne's rendering, "sons of the alien" (ver. 7), and "strange persons" (ver. 11). It seems that at this time David was engaged in warfare with some of the heathen nations; but with what people or peoples we know not. The spiritual enemies of the people of God are

strangers both to Him and to them. "If ye were of the world, the world would love his own," &c. (John xv. 18-21; xvi. 1-3.)

2. *They were deceivers.* "Whose mouth speaketh vanity, and their right hand is a right hand of falsehood." "Deception," or "falsehood," would be a better rendering of the Hebrew than "vanity." The right hand amongst the Jews was uplifted towards heaven in taking an oath. These enemies swore falsely; they were covenant-breakers; their most solemn engagements were not reliable. In the present day falsehood is rife. On every hand and in almost every province of life we are confronted with shams. The great enemy of God and man is the original liar, the arch deceiver. "The devil abode not in the truth, because there is no truth in him," &c. (John viii. 44). "Satan himself is transformed into an angel of light." Let the godly be on their guard, "lest Satan should get an advantage of us; for we are not ignorant of his devices." Let them be true in word and deed and life.

3. *They caused him great trouble.* The Psalmist represents himself as in "great waters." This is a Scriptural figure for deep distress. "All Thy waves and Thy billows are gone over me." "Thou hast afflicted me with all Thy waves." "When Thou passest through the waters," &c. (Isa. xliii. 2). The people of God sometimes suffer sorely from their spiritual enemies.

II. **His prayer for deliverance from his enemies.** This is expressed in language which is vigorously and strikingly poetical; and which is very natural in so strong-winged a poet as David. "Bow Thy heavens, O Jehovah, and come down," &c. "The Psalmist longs for a Theophany, a coming of God to judgment, which he describes in language again borrowed from xviii. 9, 14-16." These poetic figures having been dealt with there, we need not dwell upon them here. He prays that he may be delivered—

1. *With Divine majesty.* "Bow Thy heavens, O Jehovah, and come down," &c. (ver. 5). The ideas are doubtless those of awful majesty and irresistible power.

2. *By Divine power.* "Cast forth lightnings, and scatter them; shoot out Thine arrows, and destroy them. Send Thine hand from above," &c. The lightnings are the Lord's arrows. The poet prays that his deliverance may be accomplished by Divine power, as verily effected by the immediate presence and finger of God as if He had come down in visible form to accomplish it.

3. *With Divine completeness.* "Scatter them; . . . destroy them," or "discomfit them." They whom God scatters and discomfits are utterly overthrown; they whom He delivers are triumphantly saved. The Lord is the glorious Deliverer of His people from their spiritual foes. "The God of peace shall bruise Satan under your feet shortly." "We are more than conquerors through Him that loved us." "Thanks be to God, which giveth us the victory through our Lord Jesus Christ."

III. **His resolution to praise God for deliverance from his enemies.**

"I will sing a new song unto Thee, O God," &c. (vers. 9, 10). Notice here—

1. *The assurance of deliverance.* He speaks of God as a present Deliverer to him (ver. 10), and he looks forward with confidence to singing the new song for the new victory. The people of God may well be assured of victory in their moral conflicts; for the purposes, the promises, and the power of God in Christ Jesus, unite to guarantee it unto them.

2. *The basis of this assurance of deliverance.* The Psalmist seems to have grounded His confidence upon God's wonted doings. "He giveth salvation unto kings; who delivereth David His servant from the hurtful sword." God was the great giver of victory to kings; many a time had He delivered David from the sword of his enemies. What He has done in the past, we may expect Him to do again in similar circumstances and to similar characters. Let His past deliverances be to us so many pledges of our full and final triumph.

3. *The promised song of deliverance.* "I will sing a new song unto Thee, O God; upon a psaltery, an instrument of ten strings, will I sing praises unto Thee." More correctly: "Upon a ten-stringed

lute will I make music unto Thee." The goodness of God in the new victory shall be celebrated in a new song; and the new song shall be accompanied with the sweet strains of music. Let new mercies evoke new gratitude; and let the new gratitude be expressed in new songs. Let us through our Lord Jesus Christ anticipate with confidence the new song of heaven: "And they sang a new song, saying, Thou art worthy," &c. (Rev. v. 9–14).

A Picture of a Happy People.

(*Verses 12–15.*)

We regard these verses as presenting a picture of prosperity which the poet desired for Israel. Let us look at its main features—

I. **The blessing of a noble offspring.**

1. *Sons characterised by strength.* "That our sons may be as plants grown up in their youth." The idea is that of young men of vigorous and well-proportioned growth. But the Psalmist certainly could not mean strength of body simply. We interpret his meaning to be vigorous young manhood, including physical, mental, and moral strength. (1.) Physical strength is good. (2.) Intellectual strength is better. (3.) Moral strength is best. The strength of righteous principles, virtuous habits, holy attachments, and devout aspirations—this it is which ennobles manhood. What greater blessing can be desired for any nation than that its manhood should be of this order?

2. *Daughters characterised by beauty.* "Our daughters as corner-stones polished after the similitude of a palace." Conant translates: "Our daughters as corner-pillars, sculptured after the structure of a palace." And Perowne: "Our daughters as corner-pillars, sculptured to grace a palace." Some expositors discover here the idea of *usefulness*: useful as pillars supporting a building, or as corner-stones uniting an edifice. But the main idea is undoubtedly that of the gracefulness and beauty of the maidens. The Psalmist cannot mean external beauty merely. (1.) Beauty of feature and of form is desirable. It is a gift of God. (2.) Beauty of mind and of manner is much more desirable. It is of a higher order, and more lasting than that of feature and form. (3.) Beauty of soul and temper is pre-eminently desirable. This is the highest, the divinest, the unfading, and immortal beauty. This is an unmixed, a pure blessing. Beauty of form and feature, when associated with mental weakness and vacuity, appears misplaced and incongruous; when associated with moral deformity it becomes repulsive and loathsome even. The highest visible beauty is that of the soul manifesting itself in the "human face divine." "I have come to the conclusion," says Professor Upham, "if man, or woman either, wishes to realise the full power of personal beauty, it must be by cherishing noble hopes and purposes; by having something to do, and something to live for, which is worthy of humanity, and which, by expanding the capacities of the soul, gives expansion and symmetry to the body which contains it."

'What's female beauty, but an air divine
Through which the mind's all-gentle graces shine?
They, like the sun, irradiate all between;
The body charms, because the soul is seen."
—*Young.*

Who does not wish that our daughters may shine in the beauty of meekness, gentleness, purity, piety, and love?

II. **The blessing of secular prosperity.**

"That our garners may be full," &c. (vers. 13, 14). Several rare expressions occur in these verses, which are of very doubtful interpretation. It is certain that it is intended to set forth great temporal prosperity; and the entire picture contains three prominent features:—

1. *Well-stored granaries.* "Our garners full, affording all manner of store."

Heb. as in Margin: "From kind to kind." Conant: "Supplying of every kind." The idea is, abundance of all kinds of produce.

2. *Fruitful flocks.* "Our sheep bringing forth thousands and ten thousands in our streets." More correctly, "In our fields." A great part of the wealth of eastern peoples consisted of flocks of sheep.

3. *Laden oxen.* "Our oxen strong to labour." Margin: "Able to bear burdens, or loaden with flesh." The Hebrew is simply: "Our oxen laden." But with what? (1.) With fat and flesh, say some, and therefore strong to labour. (2.) With young, say others, and interpret the clause as descriptive of the fruitfulness of the herds. (3.) With the abundant produce of the fields, say others. "Laden oxen presuppose a rich abundance of produce." The exact meaning is doubtful; but the interpretation last named appears to us the most probable. This however is certain, that the poet is setting forth the great temporal prosperity of an eastern people.

III. **The blessing of settled peace.**

"No breaking in, nor going out, and no complaining in our streets." Perowne translates: "No breach and no sallying forth, and no cry (of battle) in our streets." He says, "'No sallying forth,' lit., 'going out,' which has been interpreted either of 'going forth to war,' or 'going forth into captivity.' This and the previous expression, taken together, most naturally denote a time of profound peace, when no enemy lies before the walls, when there is no need to fear the assault through the breach, no need to sally forth to attack the besiegers." There are other interpretations of these clauses; but this seems to us the most probable. "The image is that of security, peace, order, prosperity."

IV. **These blessings are viewed as flowing from the favour of God.**

"Happy is the people that is in such a case; happy is the people whose God is Jehovah." It was common amongst the ancient Hebrews to regard temporal prosperity as an evidence of the Divine favour. "National piety," says Matthew Henry, "commonly brings national prosperity; for nations, in their national capacity, are capable of rewards and punishments only in this life." And Barnes: "The worship of Jehovah—the religion of Jehovah—is *adapted* to make a people happy, peaceful, quiet, blessed. Prosperity and peace, such as are referred to in the previous verses, are, and must be, the result of pure religion. Peace, order, abundance, attend it everywhere, and the best security for a nation's prosperity is the worship of God; that which is most certain to make a nation happy and blessed, is to acknowledge God and to keep His laws."

But the Christian view of the evidences of the Divine blessing is truer, deeper, nobler than that of the ancient Hebrew. God has granted unto us a fuller and clearer revelation of Divine truth. We look for the evidences of His favour in our souls rather than in our circumstances; in inward joy rather than in outward happiness; not in well-stored granaries, but in the abounding "fruit of the Spirit, in all goodness and righteousness and truth."

SOLICITUDE ON BEHALF OF SONS AND DAUGHTERS.

(*Verse* 12.)

I. **The objects of this solicitude.**

First: *Our sons are objects of solicitude.* "That our sons may be as plants grown up in their youth." The desire is—

1. *That our sons may be as plants of the right kind.* We desire that they may possess right knowledge, right principles, right habits, and be found truly righteous in all they think, say, and do.

2. *That our sons may be as plants in a good situation.* There are honourable situations: such are the lawful callings of life, all stations of virtuous industry. There is one situation we covet for our

sons. We mean that described in Ps. xcii. 13. We desire that our sons may value and enjoy religious ordinances, &c.

3. *That our sons may be as plants rightly cultivated.* Our sons, left to themselves, will grow wild, and bring forth the fruit of a depraved heart. A change of heart is indispensable before our youth can grow up as plants of righteousness. Training is absolutely necessary (Prov. xxii. 6). And with their training pruning is requisite.

4. *That our sons may be as plants that flourish well.* A good profession, with consistency, is a great ornament to character. They will flourish most who make God's Word their study, &c. (Ps. i. 2, 3).

5. *That our sons may be as plants most fruitful and useful.* The plants most admired are fruit-bearing. We would have our sons abound in good works, ready to distribute, willing to communicate, doing good to all men as they have means and opportunity.

6. *That our sons may be as plants of perennial verdure and perpetual stability.* The Psalmist speaks of the blessedness of those whose "leaf shall not wither." He speaks also of the righteous bringing forth fruit in old age. So the prophet Jeremiah says, "Blessed is the man that trusteth in the Lord," &c. (Jer. xvii. 7, 8). Here is the perennial verdure and stability we desire. We would have piety adorn both youth and age. We would have our sons grow in grace as they grow in years.

Second: *Our daughters are objects of solicitude.* "That our daughters may be as corner-stones, polished after the similitude of a palace."

1. *That our daughters may be polished with sound education.* "If either of the sexes ought to have superior training, that privilege should be especially ceded to women. If you have ignorant women, you must have a large mass of foolish and depraved men; but, on the contrary, make the female portion of any nation intellectual, and the other sex must also be mentally improved."

2. *That our daughters may be polished with good manners.* Beauty of person, without good manners, is worthless.

"Favour is deceitful," &c. (Prov. xxxi. 30). Grace and affability are adornments to the female character. Urbanity, tenderness, sympathy, charity, a constant desire to promote universal happiness,—are embellishments above the most splendid attire.

3. *That our daughters may be polished with true piety.* Piety is an adornment which all our daughters may possess. A polished education, and polished manners, in the sense in which these terms are understood in the fashionable and polite world, can be the lot of but few. But true piety is open to all (James ii. 5). Religion refines and elevates the character when all merely secular education fails. It adorns with a meek and quiet spirit, &c.

4. *That our daughters may, as cornerstones, cement and adorn our families.* Benjamin Parsons observes justly: "In the character of companions, friends, sisters, wives, mothers, nursemaids, nurses, and domestic servants, there is a sphere of usefulness assigned to women which angels might envy. In a majority of cases the minds of youth of both sexes are formed by females. Girls are generally educated by their own sex, and boys, in most instances, have their character stamped before they leave the guardianship of mothers and governesses." Sisters may make home to be home to our sons, &c.

5. *That our daughters may, as cornerstones, support and beautify the fabric of the state.* "Verily, it is of more importance to have an intelligent and moral population, than to have great capitalists or landowners. Wealth cannot make any nation great. Enlightened moral principle is the true glory of any kingdom or empire; but this dignity cannot be obtained apart from the due cultivation of all the powers of the human soul, and to accomplish this we must have the agency of mothers."

6. *That our daughters may be as cornerstones in the Church of the living God.* Our Sabbath-schools, our ignorant and destitute neighbourhoods, our sick-chambers, our walks of benevolence, can all yield spheres of usefulness for our daughters. . . . But all this is prepara-

tory to a higher state. The stones that are polished here are preparing to be built up in the heavenly Temple. Whilst, therefore, we may aim to promote their temporal interest, let us not overlook the infinitely more valuable inheritance of personal salvation and eternal glory.

II. **The subjects of this solicitude.** This desire may be considered as,—

First: The cherished anxiety of *all right-minded parents.*

Second: That of *the friends of the young.* Among these are the Sabbath-school teachers of our land, &c.

Third: That of *true patriots and genuine philanthropists.*

Let us remember that without the Divine blessing all our efforts are in vain.—*J. Sayer.*

THE GOD IN WHOM MAN IS BLESSED.

(*Verse 15.*)

"Happy is that people whose God is Jehovah."

Our text warrants two observations—

I. **That all peoples have a god.**

This is clearly implied in the text. Man *must* have a god. The need of a god is constitutional, it is innate, in the case of man.

1. *Man must trust.* Every man does trust in some being or in some thing. The credulousness of man is amazing; and is often a great curse. Men are trusting in idols, in wealth, in friends, in priests, in themselves, in Jehovah.

2. *Man must love.* "Some one to love" is perhaps the deepest cry of the human heart. Every man loves, at least, some person or some thing,—*e.g.*, wealth, honour, self, friends, God. Every man loves some person or something pre-eminently; has some object of supreme love.

3. *Man must worship.* There are in each of us at times feelings of wonder, awe, and reverence, which compel us to worship. You hold your breath in the felt presence of mystery; you are silent in the presence of death; the realisation of the sublime fills you with awe—these are signs of the working of the religious element and instincts of your being. Now, that which man chiefly trusts, supremely loves, and truly worships, is his god. All history testifies with unmistakable clearness to the fact that man must have a god.

II. **That that people only is blessed whose God is Jehovah.**

"Happy is the people whose God is Jehovah."

1. *He is the only adequate Object of trust.* Idols, wealth, friends, priests, ourselves, each and all are terribly insufficient as objects on which the soul may repose its confidence. They are unstable, transient, and equal only to very few of the emergencies of life. Jehovah is all-sufficient;—eternal, unchangeable, equal to every emergency, infinite in His resources, &c.

2. *He is the only worthy Object of our supreme love.* To love material things is degrading to the lover. To love relatives or friends or any created person supremely, is to seek our own disappointment and sorrow, because they are changeable, mortal, imperfect, &c. The object of our chief love should be a person perfectly lovable, true, good, beautiful, unchangeable, and ever-living. Jehovah is all this.

3. *He is the only worthy Object of our worship.* The worship of Jehovah is the only worship which purifies, strengthens, ennobles, and crowns our nature. The old idolatries were terribly degrading; they produced terror, cruelty, uncleanness, and other evils in the worshippers. Worship wealth, and you will degrade your being, &c. Make a relative or friend your god, and you are lost to progress, &c. Make self your god, and you forego all that is noble, &c. The object of our worship should be such as tends to educate, exalt, satisfy, and perfect our spiritual nature. In Jehovah, and in Him alone, have we such a God.

"Happy the people whose God is Jehovah;" because He is supremely good, unchangeable, and eternal, and He stands in covenant relation with His people. His wisdom and power, His goodness and faithfulness, are all pledged to them. "If God be for us, who can be against us?"

THE HAPPY PEOPLE.

(*Verse 15.*)

"Happy is that people whose God is Jehovah." Let us—

I. **Examine what is comprehended in the relation referred to.** It refers—

1. To God as the Object of religious worship.

2. To Him as the Author of every blessing.

3. To the covenant relation in which He condescends to stand to His people—including Divine acceptance, delightful intercourse, pleasing satisfaction.

II. **Confirm and illustrate the declaration itself.** They are happy—

1. Because all the Divine perfections are engaged in their behalf. Mercy to pardon their sins, and deliver them from guilt. Wisdom to direct and guide them through the intricate mazes of the world to heaven. Omnipotence to guard and defend them. Omnipotence to survey them in all conditions. Consummate goodness to supply their needs. And faithfulness to perform all that He has spoken.

2. Because in Him they are assured of finding a refuge in time of need.

3. Because they are warranted to expect every needful supply.

4. Because in Him they have "a Friend that sticketh closer than a brother."

5. Because all the promises of the Gospel are "yea and Amen" in Christ Jesus.

6. Because they have a sure prospect of being with Him for ever.

LEARN.—1. How mistaken the men of the world are with respect to the people of God. 2. How insignificant is the worldling's portion. 3. How dangerous is the condition of those who have not the Lord for their portion. —*L . . . s.*

PSALM CXLV.

INTRODUCTION.

"This is the last of the Alphabetical Psalms," says Perowne, "of which there are eight in all, if we reckon the ninth and tenth Psalms as forming one. Like four other of the Alphabetical Psalms, this bears the name of David, although there can in this case be no doubt that the inscription is not to be trusted. As in several other instances, so here, the acrostic arrangement is not strictly observed. The letter *nun* (נ) is omitted." In the Septuagint, a verse which begins with נ is supplied between vers. 13 and 14. But this is unquestionably an interpolation, and is borrowed from ver. 17, with the exception of the first word, which is taken from the *nun*-strophe of the Alphabetical Psalm cxi.

While Perowne, in the passage quoted above, pronounces so positively against the trustworthiness of the superscription, Hengstenberg is equally firm in asserting "the originality of the superscription," which, he holds, does not admit of doubt. Barnes, David Dickson, M. Henry, and others, accept the Davidic authorship.

"This is the only Psalm which is called a *Tehillah, i.e.*, 'Praise' or 'Hymn,' the plural of which word, *Tehillim*, is the general name for the whole Psalter." The word is admirably descriptive of the contents of the Psalm, which is laudatory throughout.

"The Ancient Church employed this Psalm at the mid-day meal, and ver. 15 at the Passover. The Talmud assures us (Berachoth, 4 b.) that every one who repeats this Psalm three times daily may be satisfied that he is a child of the future world. The Gemarra adduces in support of this the curious reason, that it is not only written in Alphabetical order, like Ps. cxix. and others, and not only praises the Divine care over all creatures, like Ps. cxxxvi. 25, but combines both these important characteristics in itself."

This Psalm "admits of no analysis, being made up of variations on a single theme, the righteousness and goodness of God to men in general, to His own people in particular, and more especially to those that suffer."

THE PRAISE OF THE DIVINE GREATNESS.

(*Verses* 1-7.)

Here are two main lines of thought for us to pursue—

I. **The reasons of the Divine praise.** The grand reason of praise in this section of the Psalm seems to be the greatness of God. "Great is Jehovah, and greatly to be praised; and His greatness is unsearchable." Jehovah is great in Himself; His being is underived, independent, eternal, infinitely perfect. "God's greatness—His infinity—is in itself a just ground of praise, for we should rejoice that there is One Infinite Eternal Being; and as all that greatness is employed in the cause of truth, of law, of good order, of justice, of kindness, of mercy, it should call forth continued praise in all parts of His dominions."—*Barnes.*

1. *He is great in His deeds.* "Thy mighty acts;... Thy wondrous works;... The might of Thy terrible acts." "We must see God," says Matthew Henry, "acting and working in all the affairs of this lower world. Various instruments are used, but in all events God is the supreme director; it is He that performs all things. Much of His power is seen in the operations of Providence (they are 'mighty acts,' such as cannot be paralleled by the strength of any creature), and much of His justice—they are 'terrible acts,' awful to saints, dreadful to sinners. These we should take all occasions to speak of, observing the finger of God, His hand, His arm, in all, that we may marvel."

2. *He is great in His majesty.* "I will speak of the glorious honour of Thy majesty." "By this accumulation of words," says Geier, "the incomparable glory and majesty of God are set forth." The Psalmist is "striving after a suitable mode of expression for his exuberant feeling." Or, as Barnes puts it: "This accumulation of epithets shows that the heart of the Psalmist was full of the subject, and that he laboured to find language to express his emotions. It is beauty; it is glory; it is majesty;—it is all that is great, sublime, wonderful—all combined—all concentrated in one Being."

3. *He is great in His goodness.* "They shall abundantly utter the memory of Thy great goodness." "Great goodness," says Moll, "is not referred to in the sense of abundant mercy (most), but in the sense of the universal excellence of His attributes, His goodness in every relation." Hengstenberg: "The essential goodness."

4. *He is great in righteousness.* "They shall sing of Thy righteousness." The goodness of God is not that weak, molluscous quality which is sometimes called goodness in man: it is a strong thing, a righteous thing. He ever manifests the strictest regard for justice and truth. How great is God! supremely, infinitely great!

II. **The characteristics of the Divine praise.**

1. *It is constant.* "Every day will I bless Thee." Hengstenberg translates: "Continually will I praise Thee." The translation of the A. V. is more faithful to the letter; but Hengstenberg seems to us to present the idea of the poet, that he will offer to God constant worship. Praise with the godly man is not an occasional exercise of the voice, but a continual disposition of the soul. "Praising God must be our daily work; no day must pass, though ever so busy a day, without praising God. We ought to reckon it the most needful of our daily employments, and the most delightful of our daily comforts. God is every day blessing us, doing well for us; there is therefore reason that we should be every day blessing Him, speaking well of Him."—*Henry.*

2. *It is perpetual.* "I will extol Thee, my God, O King; and I will bless Thy name for ever and ever.... 1 will praise Thy name for ever and ever." Here are two aspects of the perpetuity of the praise of God:—(1.) The devout soul will praise God for ever. "So

long as his being lasted in the loving-kindness of God, he must also continue to give praise."

> "Through all eternity to Thee
> A joyful song I'll raise :
> But oh! eternity's too short
> To utter all Thy praise."—*Addison.*

(2.) Every succeeding generation shall praise God. "One generation shall praise Thy works to another, and shall declare Thy mighty acts." "The generation that is going off shall tell them to that which is rising up, shall tell what they have seen in their days and what they have heard from their fathers; and the generation that is rising up shall follow the example of that which is going off: so that the death of God's worshippers shall be no diminution of His worship, for a new generation shall rise up in their room to carry on that good work to the end of time, when it shall be left to that world to do it in in which there is no succession of generations."

3. *It is fervent.* "Greatly to be praised. . . . They shall abundantly utter the memory of Thy great goodness," &c. Conant translates: "Let them pour forth the memory," &c. The idea is that the heart is filled to overflowing with thoughts of the great goodness of God, and that it pours forth its feelings in grateful and fervent praise. God shall be praised with glowing enthusiasm.

4. *It is songful.* "They shall sing aloud of Thy righteousness." His praise is celebrated by His people openly and publicly; not in cold and measured prose, but in glowing and rapturous poetry; not in ordinary speech, but with music's highest and sweetest strains. Their adoring joy pours itself forth in holy and exultant songs.

Let our hearts and voices be much engaged in this holy and delightful service.

The Praise of Time.

(*Verse* 4.)

We may consider this—

I. As the decree of God.

He who made the world has willed that it should praise Him. The *works* of God carry out His decree. The sun and moon proclaim His power. Day and night utter His wisdom. The seasons declare His bounty and His faithfulness. And the *history* of man, even yet more strikingly, sets forth God's glory. This truth is ever written—"The Lord is King." *He* rules. "None can stay His hand, or say unto Him, What doest Thou?" Look at Pharaoh; . . . Nebuchadnezzar. Or call to mind the history of Joseph, Balaam, Jonah, Sennacherib, Cyrus, Saul of Tarsus. Or the Jewish rulers who crucified the Lord of glory, &c. (Acts iv. 27, 28). The mysteries of *affliction* teach the same lesson. The erring has been thus brought back, or the faithful confirmed, or God's power displayed (John ix. 3). And the *Church* of Christ is a standing witness of the same great truth. "The gates of hell shall not prevail against it." Man's opposition has proved the wave that has wafted the truth onward (Acts iv. 31; xi. 19; xiii. 51; xiv. 20; xvii. 15; xxv. 11; xxviii. 31).

What a contrast is there in all this to the name and acts of men! How does every annual revolution of time find human propositions annulled, human names forgotten, human greatness brought low. But each succeeding year finds one Name unchanged; one arm still mighty to deliver; one King ruling, as ever; one Lord still faithful to His promise; one memorial enduring through all generations. The decree of God is kept. All time sets forth His praise.

II. As expressing the resolution and work of Christ's Church.

Praise is the rightful attitude of the redeemed (Ps. cvii. 2). Mercy felt, love appreciated, salvation embraced and enjoyed, is sure to beget true thanksgiving. God hath chosen His people to praise Him (Isa. xliii. 21; 1 Pet. ii. 9). And even angels cannot sing the new song which belongs to the saved from earth alone (Rev. xiv. 3). And the people of God have ever claimed their holy privilege. They have sung of creation and of providence, and the wonders of redeeming love. God has never left Himself without this witness in the world. In every age, however corrupt, there have been those who rejoiced to declare His mighty acts. Even before the Flood, there was Noah ; in the time of idolatrous Ahab, Elijah ; in Babylon, Daniel. In New Testament days we have the same history. Every martyr, from Stephen onward, bore in his blood the testimony of praise. If Job said, "Though He slay me, yet will I trust in Him," Paul answered, "I am willing . . . to die for the Name of the Lord Jesus." If David said, "I will bless the Lord at all times," Paul, again, added, "Rejoice in the Lord alway." If Elijah showed himself to Ahab, Luther did not shrink from meeting those who sought to take his life. If the Apostles went forth, in obedience to the Lord's command, and preached the Gospel, hazarding their lives for the Saviour's Name, this noble act of praise has been re-echoed in later days in Sierra Leone, in New Zealand, in India, in the Sandwich Islands, in Central Africa, by those who have gone forth to brave every danger in making known the same good tidings. Thus in all time the resolution of the Church of Christ is one and the same. "One generation shall praise Thy works to another."

Three thoughts seem to arise in conclusion :—

1. *What are* WE *doing to make our generation one of praise?* We have received from the generations before a glorious light; are we sending it onward and around?

2. *Do we possess in ourselves that salvation which alone enables us truly to praise?* Have we tasted that the Lord is gracious?

3. *How glorious shall be the praise of heaven!* Now one age to another, one land to another, praise God. What shall be the glory of the song when every age and every land shall *join* in the song of Moses and the Lamb!—*W. S. Bruce, M.A.* From "The Homiletic Quarterly."

THE PRAISE OF THE DIVINE GOODNESS.

(*Verses* 8–10.)

In these verses the poet celebrates the praise of God as a good or benevolent Being. Three leading considerations claim our attention :—

I. The various manifestations of God's goodness.

The goodness or benevolence of God is here clearly stated. "Jehovah is gracious . . .; Jehovah is good to all." And it seems to us that the expressions used by the Psalmist suggest certain manifestations of this goodness. Here is an indication of His—

1. *Pity for suffering men.* "Jehovah is full of compassion." Perowne : "Of tender compassion is Jehovah." It presents to us the goodness of God in its attitude towards the wretched. How great and manifold are the sufferings and sorrows of human life! God regards all sufferers with tenderest pity. In all their afflictions He is afflicted. He is "touched with the feeling of our infirmities ;" and touched deeply, for He is "full of compassion." "The Lord is very pitiful, and of tender mercy."

2. *Patience with sinful men.* "Slow to anger." He holds back the outgoings of His wrath. He has great patience with perverse rebels. "The Lord is long-suffering to us-ward, not willing that any should perish, but that all should come to repentance."

3. *Pardon for penitent men.* "Of great mercy ;" or, "great in mercy." How freely and fully in His great mercy does God forgive all who penitently seek Him ! His "mercy is great unto the heavens." "His mercy is everlasting." The greatness of His mercy is seen—(1.) In the immense *numbers* to which it extends. "His tender mercies are over all His works." He is "not willing that any should perish."

(2.) In the *characters* to which it extends. It reaches to the chief of sinners. It offers pardon to the most guilty. It "saves unto the uttermost." (3.) In the *sacrifice* which its exercise involved. "God commendeth His love toward us, in that while we were yet sinners Christ died for us." "God who is rich in mercy, for His great love wherewith He loved us," &c. "He spared not His own Son," &c. (4.) In the *blessings* which flow from it. The free and full forgiveness of sins is but the beginning of its blessings. Holiness, peace, joy, heaven, are all bestowed upon believers in Christ Jesus, in the exercise of the Divine mercy. The blessings which flow from it are rich, inexhaustible, everlasting, and unspeakably precious. Truly God is "great in mercy." "He delighteth in mercy."

II. **The universality of God's goodness.**

"Jehovah is good to all, and His tender mercies are over all His works." It has been well observed that "this is a saying which does not seem as true in the winter as in the summer of life. Spoken in the quiet church, amid all the accompaniments of prayer and praise, with the quietude of the holy place to calm us, and music and memory and hope to bear us company, it is a saying that men will let pass as something they do not think of questioning; but, spoken to a poor woman who has just lost the stay of her home; spoken to a hard-working man who has just seen the hopes of years disappear; spoken to little children who have just been thrown on the world without father, or mother, or friend, or home; spoken to a good man whose earthly reward seems nothing but disappointment and trouble and loss,— I do not wonder that it sounds to some like a mockery: and I do not wonder that men have turned away and said that these things are all very well in the church, but that they break down when men go into the open world.

"Let us look at these words, then, that we may, if possible, find some solid ground for this saying that God is 'good to all.' And here the fact we have to master is this:—That we must judge of God's dealings towards us with reference to some system or order under which we live. The system under which we live is something like this:—

"1. *A vast, complicated, and beneficent set of laws are at work, which apply in common to all.* We are in a world the central principle of which is the universality and certainty of every prevailing law—this necessitating that God shall *not* come forth to accommodate the facts and the laws of the universe to every individual need, but that He shall provide for the steadfast abiding of everything in its place, and for the constancy of that thing to the law of its being. In this very thing, then, which has seemed so hard, inexorable, and cruel; in this *steadfastness* of the laws of the universe, I find the first proof of the universal goodness of God—a goodness which would *not* be increased, which would indeed be marred and spoiled and thwarted if He made the connection between cause and effect uncertain; and if, by special interferences on behalf of individuals, He brought uncertainty into the common life of the race. For if He specially came forth, to interfere in particular cases, to reverse or suspend the ordinary laws of life, or to save men from the effects of causes, every man would look for such interferences on his behalf; and recklessness, and presumption, and indolence, with all their attendant miseries and disappointments, would be increased a thousandfold. Here, then, where God's goodness seems to be *defective*, we find an abiding *proof* of it.

"2. We see that in the Divine administration of the laws of the universe, *there is no partiality: all these great laws are steadfast, whoever applies to them.* God is good to all in working by beautiful and beneficent laws that are as generous and as steadfast as Himself. A man who has just denied the very existence of God goes into his field, and sows his seed; and, in a moment, all the wonderful laws of God leap to obey and bless him, and to give him the result of his seed-sowing, quite as readily, quite as speedily, as in the case where the sower thanks God and sows his seed with prayer. God is clearly no partial administrator of His laws. His sun shines and His rain falls on the evil and on the unthankful. He holds all the myriad laws of the universe to their appointed place, for He is 'good to all.'

"3. Then, closely connected with that, is *His impartial bestowment of all the common mercies of life for all.* God distributes His mercies, not to bless this man or that, any more than He maintains His beautiful laws to advantage this man or that; but He scatters His mercies as men scatter seed, as though He reflected not which should prosper, this or that, or which was good or which was thorny ground. God's sun shines; but if the sinner opens his eyes first, he will first behold it. God's pure air comes on the wings of the morning; but if the impious one goes out first to breathe it, he will first be invigorated by it. God's rain falls on every field, and if the sinner's seed is in, it will first get the sweet enrichments of it. It is the same with *everything*. The mercies of God come to all, are open to all. It is only when sin makes a man naturally unable to find or keep a mercy of God that he finds the mercy disappear; but in every case there is a natural connection between the sin and the deprivation. Thus, again, if a man be pure, and wise, and good, he may be blest above the man who is impure, and foolish, and debased; but if so, it will be because there is a necessary and natural connection between his virtue and the blessing he finds, the one growing out of the other, and not because God selects him for rewards.

"4. We may find His universal goodness in *that wonderful law of our being, by which, as a rule, men are so easily and insensibly adapted to their condition.* Thus, we find that a condition of life which would be insupportable to one, has become quite bearable or even satisfactory to another. The back adjusts itself to the burden; and the mind, the temperament, the tastes, the habits, the hopes, the likes and dislikes of a man, all, as a rule, naturally fall into harmony with his state; and this without his knowing it, or planning it, or striving after it. Thus, it is really quite an open question, whether men who are very rich enjoy life more than men who are moderately poor; or whether the palaces have contained more pleasure than the cottages of the world. You have heard men express their love for occupations that you would despise, and their contentment in habitations that made you shudder, and even their delight in *persons* from whom you shrink. You wonder how they can do without this or that — how they can bear with this or that; but the want is not felt by them, the burden galls them not. To this I might add the touching and most significant fact, that time seems to have a gentle healing virtue in it to soothe and comfort men; so that not only to our general condition in life, but to our special griefs, this blessed law applies. It is not that we forget; for often, as time goes on, memory only brightens and deepens with the passing years; but a gracious hand seems to steal over us, smoothing down the wrinkles of the spirit, and healing the wounds of the heart, and in this we may see a touching proof that God is 'good to all.'

"5. We may look for a closing proof of this statement to *the results that follow much of what we call not good and not merciful in this world.* Much that seems not good, much that seems not merciful, is the best part of the discipline of life— or sometimes even the best guide to the 'still waters' and the 'green pastures.' A vast number of the ills of life are incentives to action, calls to duty, motives for exertion, wonderful schoolmasters to give us the needed mastery of the knowledge of good and evil. Many of the results of hardships are beneficent.

"God is *indeed* good to all; to *every* creature—to the lowest, the saddest, the meanest, the sinfullest; and His tender mercies are over all His works."

III. **The praise of God's goodness.**

"All Thy works shall praise Thee, O Jehovah; and Thy saints shall bless Thee." Concerning this praise two points require notice:—

1. *Its universality.* "All Thy works

praise Thee, O Jehovah." "All God's works do praise Him, as the beautiful building praises the builder, or the well-drawn picture praises the painter." All His works combine in setting forth His perfections; they manifest His power, and wisdom, and goodness. "The heavens declare the glory of God," &c.

2. *Its diversity.* "Thy works praise Thee; and Thy saints bless Thee." "His saints praise Him actively, while His other works praise Him only objectively." Angels and glorified saints in heaven, and His people upon earth, praise Him with their will and affections, their reverence and loving obedience.

"Bless the Lord, O my soul; and all that is within me bless His holy name," &c.

ERRORS RESPECTING THE DIVINE BEING.

(*Verse 9.*)

Right views of God are most important. Our religion will necessarily be a reflection of them. Our spirit, our hopes or fears, will be influenced, &c. Nations always are as the gods they worship. For the moral character of God we must go to His Word. Our text is an epitome.

I. **Let us see what it means.**

The goodness or benevolence of God is that which makes Him the source of blessing to His creatures. It takes in kindness, goodwill, love, benignity, &c. In our text it includes mercy, kindness to the guilty and miserable. Now, observe, this view of God is the doctrine of all dispensations—

1. *See God as man's creator* (Gen. i. 26-28).

2. *Hear God under the law* (Exod. xxxiii. 18, 19; xxxiv. 6).

3. *In the age of Solomon and the Temple* (2 Chron. v. 13).

4. *The prophet Nahum saying*, "The Lord is good; a stronghold," &c. (Nah. i. 7).

5. *Now, hear the Apostles.* John: "God is love." Paul: "God is rich in mercy" (Eph. ii. 4). James: "The Lord is very pitiful and of tender mercy" (James v. 11). Peter: "If so be ye have tasted that the Lord is gracious," &c. (1 Pet. ii. 3-9). Now, before we leave this view of God, see the extent of the Divine goodness. "To all." "Over all." It must be so. God is infinite, and His goodness and love are thus unbounded. "A sea without a bottom, or a shore," &c. And see its duration. "From everlasting to everlasting." "Endureth for ever." Unchanging and eternal.

II. **What views of God are inconsistent with this portrait, and therefore necessarily erroneous.**

1. The view that represents *God as possessing implacable wrath*. This is the opposite pole; never can harmonise; and thus is, of necessity, false. He hateth all evil; but His mercy embraces all sinners.

2. Views which represent *God's goodness as partial and limited*. Flatly contradicting the text and the passages we have quoted.

3. Views of the *Divine reprobative decrees*. By which men have been unconditionally appointed, or left by God, to perish for ever. This is at total variance with the text.

4. Views which represent *God's goodness as only attainable through sacrifice*. That God would not be good to sinners until Christ appeased His wrath, &c. "God so loved the world, that He gave His only begotten Son," &c. Christ is the effect, not the cause, of the Divine mercy. The channel through which it flows, not the spring from whence it rises.

5. *That God can be made good by some acts or ceremonies of ours.* Tears, penance, &c. How futile! We may come to it by tears, repentance, and faith; but there it was in God before we wept, &c.

6. *That God will only be good in the highest sense to a very few.* But the Scriptures say: "The earth is full of His goodness." "He delighteth in

mercy." "Not willing that any should perish." Such, then, is the great goodness of God; His true merciful character. Application. If so—
1. Then even *reason says, Adore Him.*
2. *Gratitude says, Love, praise, and serve Him.* We say to all—
3. *Come to Him by faith.* Trust Him with all your hearts, and evermore, &c.

4. *Love says, Delight in Him;* be filled with His complacent favour.
5. *Wonder marvels at it.* "Herein is love," &c. "God commendeth His love to us," &c. It "passeth knowledge." Here is redemption's rock — eternal, immutable, &c. "Oh give thanks," &c.
6. *Jesus is the grand unspeakable manifestation of it.* "God in Christ reconciling the world unto Himself," &c. (2 Cor. v. 19, *seq.*).—*Jabez Burns, D.D.*

THE PRAISE OF THE DIVINE REIGN.

(*Verses* 11–13.)

The Psalmist here celebrates the greatness and goodness of God as a King in His kingdom. The suggestions of this part of the Psalm may be grouped under two heads :—

I. The characteristics of the reign of the Lord.

The poet here speaks of it as—
1. *Glorious.* "They shall speak of the glory of Thy kingdom; . . . to make known to the sons of men the glorious majesty of His kingdom." The glory of Jehovah's kingdom is not in external pomp and pageantry, but in its moral perfections. In its goodness, its righteousness, its beneficence; in the fact that He reigns to bless His subjects. "Where," asks Perowne, "is the conspicuous excellence of that kingdom seen? Not in the symbols of earthly pride and power, but in gracious condescension to the fallen and the crushed, in a gracious care which provides for the wants of every living thing." (See our remarks on "the blessings of His reign" in vol. i. pp. 383, 384.)
2. *Mighty.* "They shall talk of Thy power; to make known to the sons of men His mighty acts." Barnes refers this to His power "as put forth in the works of creation; as manifested in the dispensations of His providence; as evinced in the conversion of sinners; as displayed in carrying His truth around the world; as exhibited in sustaining the sufferer, and in giving peace and support to the dying." The might of the reign of Jehovah is moral, the power of truth, righteousness, goodness.

3. *Perpetual.* "Thy kingdom is an everlasting kingdom, and Thy dominion endureth throughout all generations." (On "the perpetuity of His reign" see vol. i. pp. 224 and 385.)

II. The conversation on the reign of the Lord.

"They shall speak of the glory of Thy kingdom, and talk of Thy power; to make known," &c. Three homiletical points are here :—
1. *Delight in His reign.* This is here clearly implied. "Out of the abundance of the heart the mouth speaketh." We talk of the things in which we are interested, and of those which afford us pleasure. The reign of the Lord is to His people a delightful theme of meditation and discourse.
2. *Praise of His reign.* The poet here celebrates its perfection and perpetuity. The saints speak of it because they feel that it is worthy of praise and honour. It is one of the reasons for which His saints do bless Him. (On "the praise of His reign" see vol. i. p. 385.)
3. *Desire for the extension of His reign.* The saints speak of its glory and power "to make known to the sons of men His mighty acts, and the glorious majesty of His kingdom." They are solicitous that others should understand and appreciate the perfections of His reign; that they might be led "to yield themselves His willing subjects, and so put themselves under the protection of such a mighty potentate." "The Lord,"

says David Dickson, "will have His saints to instruct such as are not converted to know His glory, power, and majesty, that they may be brought in and made subjects of His special kingdom of grace."

What is our relation to this glorious King?

THE GLORY OF CHRIST'S KINGDOM.

(*Verse* 11.)

As the kingdom of Christ is so conspicuous an object in both Testaments, and is the only one among men by whose government their happiness can be secured, it cannot be improper, from the words before us, to direct your attention to some particulars relating to the nature, extent, and durability of its glory.

I. The glory of this kingdom is manifested in its origin.

It had its origin in infinite mercy and grace. It entered into the councils of the Eternal before the foundation of the world was laid.

In order to establish this kingdom, it was necessary that the Son of God should become incarnate. . . . The foundation of the kingdom was laid in the incarnation and atonement of the Son of God; a foundation proportionate to the grandeur and beauty of the edifice that was to be erected.

The doctrines of the Gospel were, and are, the grand instruments in the hand of the Lord Jesus for bringing souls into subjection to His sceptre. The warfare is entirely spiritual; it is carried on by the light of truth and the burning of conviction. This is a glorious manner of raising a kingdom, worthy of Him who is a Spirit, and who reigns by spiritual and intellectual means in the hearts of His people.

II. The glory of Christ's kingdom is manifested in the manner and spirit of its administration.

The last words of David describe the manner of administering this government; "The anointed of the God of Jacob," &c. (2 Sam. xxiii. 1-4).

The most essential quality in the administration of any government is justice; and justice is most conspicuous in this administration. "With righteousness shall He judge the poor," &c. (Isa. xi. 4, 5). He will render to each of His subjects, not *for* their works, yet *according* to their works.

The administration of His kingdom is also benign and gracious—it is indeed a kingdom of grace. He revealeth His grace, which is His glory; and thus He captivates the hearts of His people. "He delivers the poor when he cries, the needy, and him that hath no helper." "When the poor and needy seek water," &c. (Isa. xli. 17, 18).

In earthly kingdoms the subjects are governed by general laws, which must necessarily be very inadequate to the variety of cases and occurrences. But our King is intimately acquainted with all hearts, and being present in all places, He can apply His acts to individual examples, and appropriate smiles and frowns to each, as if there were no other beings that participated in His attention. In human administrations, the law extends only to outward acts; it relates only to objects of sense: but the kingdom of heaven is a spiritual one—it extends to the heart; it is "within you," and relates to "righteousness, peace, and joy in the Holy Ghost."

It is justly considered a high excellence in a ruler, that he is disinterested, that he pursues no interest of his own apart from the general good of the empire. But never was any one so disinterested as the King of Zion, who laid down His life for His people, while they were yet enemies. The glory of the Father, and the good of man: these engaged His heart, these brought Him from heaven, &c.

III. The glory of the kingdom of Christ appears in the character of His subjects.

1. These subjects are *enlightened.* They form right estimates of objects, as

they are holy or sinful, temporal or eternal, &c.

2. The subjects of this kingdom are *renewed*. They are made, imperfectly, yet truly holy. It is in this kingdom that patience, purity, humility, faith, and love to God and men, reside.

3. The subjects of this kingdom *have in them a preparation for perfect blessedness*. They have that which renders them meet "to be partakers of the inheritance of the saints in light." All the love and joy that glow with celestial fervour before the throne of the Heavenly Majesty, is only the consummation of seeds like those which are sown in the hearts of believers.

IV. The glory of the kingdom of Christ is manifest in the privileges that are attached to it.

1. *Peace* is a peculiar blessing of this kingdom. This begins in reconciliation with God. The consequence of peace with God is peace with one another.

2. The *dignity* of the subjects of this kingdom is another privilege. To "as many as receive Him," &c. (John i. 12; Rom. viii. 16, 17; 1 John iii. 1, 2).

3. *Immortality* shall be the blessing of this kingdom; the subjects shall partake of endless life (John vi. 54, 58). Believers receive in them the embryo of eternal life; the spiritual life rises up into eternal life, and will be displayed in its perfection in the world of glory. These terms include everlasting felicity in the presence of God.

I might mention other properties of this kingdom, which, though they do not enter into the essence of it, are very important.

It is a *growing* kingdom. "Of its increase there shall be no end."

The *perpetuity* of this kingdom must endear it to a good man. It shall *never* be taken away to be given to any other people.

Let us, while we live here, sincerely pray and labour for the advancement and glorious increase of this kingdom.

Finally, let us look to ourselves, that, while we hear these things, we may possess a personal interest in this glorious and happy kingdom.—*Robert Hall, A.M.*

THE PRAISE OF THE DIVINE RELATION TO DIFFERENT CHARACTERS.

(Verses 14–21.)

In these verses Jehovah is praised because of the attitude He sustains and the blessings He bestows upon persons in different classes of character.

I. His relation to the weak and the burdened.

1. *He sustains the weak.* "Jehovah upholdeth all them that fall." The weak and the sinking are here meant; those who by reason of their feebleness are ready to fall. Many are ready to sink beneath life's sorrows, many are almost falling before temptations to sin; but the Lord is their Sustainer: He upholds them.

2. *He relieves the burdened.* "And raiseth up all those that be bowed down." The Psalmist means those who are heavily laden with the duties, the cares, and the trials of life; to whom these things are a heavy burden, bowing them down. Such persons the Lord relieves:—(1.) By removing the burden. In answer to prayer He sometimes takes away the load of care or trial. (2.) By increasing the strength of those who are burdened. By giving more grace the weight and painfulness of the burden are taken away—the burden ceases to be a burden. Let the weak and the heavy-laden trust in Him.

II. His relation to the dependent. "The eyes of all wait upon Thee," &c. (vers. 15, 16). We have here—

1. *Universal dependence.* "The eyes of all wait upon Thee; . . . Thou satisfiest the desire of every living thing." Every creature in the universe is a dependent one. God alone is independent. All creatures depend upon Him. "By Him all things consist." Dependent creatures should be humble.

2. *Divine provision.* "Thou givest them their meat in due season," &c. Here are three points—(1.) The *season-*

ableness of the Divine provision. "In due season." God's gifts are always timely. He will not bestow them too soon; He will not withhold them one moment after their due time. (2.) The *ease* of the Divine provision. To supply the needs of the universe does not tax the resources of God, or cause Him any anxiety or effort. He has but to open His hand, and the countless and endlessly diversified needs of His creatures are supplied. "Thou openest Thine hand," &c. (3.) The *sufficiency* of the Divine provision. "And satisfiest the desire of every living thing." "This," says Barnes, "is to be taken in a general sense. It cannot mean that absolutely no one ever wants, or ever perished from want, but the idea is that of the amazing beneficence and fulness of God in being able and willing to satisfy such multitudes; to keep them from perishing by cold, or hunger, or nakedness. And, in fact, how few birds perish by hunger; how few of the infinite number of the inhabitants of the sea; how few animals that roam over deserts, or in vast plains; how few men; how few even of the insect tribes—how few in the world revealed by the microscope—the world beneath us—the innumerable multitudes of living things too small even to be *seen* by the naked eye of man!"

All this implies unlimited resources in God; and should inspire the hearty confidence of man in Him.

III. His relation to the prayerful.

"The Lord is nigh unto all them that call upon Him," &c. (vers. 18, 19). Notice—

1. *The character indicated.* This is marked by—(1.) *Prayerfulness.* "Them that call upon Him." Here we have not simply dependence, but dependence felt and acknowledged; dependence rising into prayer. We have also an interesting and true view of prayer; it is here presented to us as expressed longing, the cry of desire. "He will fulfil the desire of them that fear Him; He also will hear their cry," &c. (2.) *Sincerity.* "All that call upon Him in truth." Sincerity is utterly indispensable to acceptable approach unto God. (3.) *Reverence.* "Them that fear Him." This fear is not the terror of a slave, but the filial reverence of a child.

2. *The blessings promised.* (1.) The manifestation of His presence. "Jehovah is nigh unto all them that call upon Him," &c. He is near unto all men; but His true worshippers feel Him near unto them, they have communion with Him. "The Lord is nigh unto them that are of a broken heart," &c. (2.) The granting of their desires. "He will fulfil the desire of them that fear Him." "Delight thyself in the Lord, and He shall give thee the desires of thine heart." The desires of godly souls accord with the holy will of God. (3.) The bestowment of His help. "He also will hear their cry, and will save them." Perowne: "And when He heareth their cry He helpeth them." "Call upon Me in the day of trouble, and I will deliver thee," &c. The unanimous testimony of the history of His people confirms these assurances.

IV. His relation to His saints.

"The Lord preserveth all them that love Him."

1. *The human character.* "Them that love Him." They have confidence and complacency in Him; they have given their hearts unto Him. Their language is, "Whom have I in heaven but Thee?" &c. "The chiefest among ten thousand . . . . He is altogether lovely."

2. *The Divine keeping.* "Jehovah preserveth," or "keepeth them." It is implied that they are exposed to danger. They are beset by spiritual enemies; they are weak and liable to receive injury; their spiritual interests are threatened. But Jehovah keepeth them. They "are kept by the power of God, through faith unto salvation." "He preserveth the souls of His saints; He delivereth them from the hand of the wicked." By curbing the power of temptation; by restraining from evil by His Holy Spirit; by quickening the conscience, and strengthening the will, and increasing the spiritual life and activity by the same Holy Spirit, the Lord keepeth His people.

V. His relation to the wicked.

"But all the wicked will He destroy." See here—

1. *A sad character.* This character is the opposite of the godly in all those aspects which have come under our notice. The wicked do not love God, do not reverence Him, do not pray to Him; but the evil of their character is positive and deep rooted; they have fitted themselves for destruction.

2. *A dread destiny.* "Will He destroy." "The enemies of the Cross of Christ; whose end is destruction." They "shall be punished with everlasting destruction from the presence of the Lord, and from the glory of His power."

VI. His righteousness and kindness in all His relations.

"Jehovah is righteous in all His ways, and holy in all His works." Instead of "holy," the Margin has "merciful, or bountiful." Conant: "kind." Perowne: "loving." In His relations to all His creatures, whatever may be their character, He is just and merciful, righteous and kind. He wrongs no one; He requires of no one services which would be unjust. Even to the rebellious and wicked He is kind. "He maketh His sun to rise on the evil and on the good, and sendeth rain on the just and on the unjust." He is slow to anger even with the greatest sinners, and swift to save them when they turn to Him.

VII. His praise because of all His relations.

"My mouth shall speak the praise of the Lord; and let all flesh bless His holy name for ever and ever." We have here—

1. *A resolution to offer personal praise.* "My mouth shall speak the praise of Jehovah."

2. *A desire that He might be praised universally.* "Let all flesh bless His holy name." The godly soul intensely desires that all men should worship the Lord.

3. *A desire that He might be praised perpetually.* "For ever and ever."

UNIVERSAL DEPENDENCE AND DIVINE SUPPORT.

(*Verses* 15, 16.)

The Psalmist here teaches—

I. The universality of dependence amongst creatures.

"The eyes of all wait upon Thee." We depend upon God for "life, and breath, and all things." "He giveth breath to the people upon earth, and spirit to them that walk therein." "Every good gift and every perfect gift is from above," &c. Entire dependence should beget deep humility. "What hast thou that thou didst not receive? now if thou didst receive it, why dost thou glory, as if thou hadst not received it?"

II. The infinitude of the Divine resources.

"Thou givest them their meat in due season; . . . and satisfiest the desire of every living thing." This indicates the possession of resources—

1. *Infinitely vast.* "Every beast of the forest is Mine, the cattle upon a thousand hills." "The silver is Mine, and the gold is Mine, saith the Lord of hosts." His resources are adequate to the abundant supply of all the wants of all creatures. His riches are unsearchable.

2. *Infinitely various.* They are not only more than sufficient for all necessities, but adapted to every variety of need.

III. The timeliness of the Divine communications.

"In due season." The Divine Being is punctual in the fulfilment of every engagement. His gifts are bestowed at that time which infinite wisdom and infinite goodness adjudges to be the "due season." In this we have a reason for patience if His interpositions or communications seem to be delayed.

IV. The sublime ease of the Divine communications.

"Thou openest Thine hand, and satisfiest the desire of every living thing." To satisfy the innumerable needs of the myriads of His creatures does not tax His resources, or challenge an exertion of His power. He has but to open His hand, and the countless needs of the universe are satisfied. What an encouragement is this to believing prayer! He "is able to do exceeding abundantly above all that we ask or think."

V. The sufficiency of the Divine communications.

"And satisfiest the desire of every living thing." "God giveth to all liberally." The provisions of His table are both bounteous and free. He gives "bread enough" for all His creatures, "and to spare." So in spiritual things, His "grace is sufficient." "God is able to make all grace abound toward you; that ye, always having all sufficiency in all things, may abound to every good work: being enriched in everything to all liberality."

Our subject urges all men to—

1. *Gratitude.* Constant provision should lead to constant thankfulness and consecration.

2. *Trust.* (1.) *For temporal supplies.* "Be not careful for your life, what ye shall eat, and what ye shall drink," &c. (Matt. vi. 25–34.) (2.) *For spiritual supplies.* "Grace to help in time of need" will surely be given to all who look to Him.

ATTRIBUTES AND ADVANTAGES OF ACCEPTABLE PRAYER.

(*Verses* 18, 19.)

What is prayer? According to ver. 18, it is a sincere calling upon God. According to ver. 19, it is the cry of the desire of the godly soul. In our text we have—

I. Some attributes of acceptable prayer.

1. *Sincerity.* "All that call upon Him in truth." "God is a Spirit; and they that worship Him must worship Him in spirit and in truth." All unreality is known unto Him, and is abhorred by Him. Words and forms of prayer without the heart are an abomination in His sight.

2. *Reverence.* "Them that fear Him." This is not dread, but reverence,—a devout, trustful, filial spirit. Religiousness of spirit is an essential condition of acceptable prayer.

There are other attributes of acceptable prayer, which are not expressed here, although they are perhaps implied. Of these, two are of prime importance, viz.,—*Faith.* "Without faith it is impossible to please Him." And, *Accordance with the Divine will.* "If we ask anything according to His will, He heareth us; and if we know that He hear us, whatsoever we ask, we know that we have the petitions that we desired of Him."

II. Some advantages of acceptable prayer.

1. *The realisation of His presence.* "Jehovah is nigh unto all them that call upon Him," &c. In His omnipresence and omnipotence He is near unto all men, but in gracious fellowship He is near only to devout souls. Locally, He is everywhere present; but sympathetically, He is present only with the truly pious. "To this man will I look, even to him that is poor and of a contrite spirit," &c. In gracious interest and tenderest regard He is nigh unto them; they realise His blessed presence. "Our fellowship is with the Father, and with His Son Jesus Christ."

2. *The fulfilment of their desires.* "He will fulfil the desire of them that fear Him." God does not promise to grant the desire of the irreligious, the worldly, or the wicked. It would be neither kind nor right to do so. But He pledges His word to grant the desire of the godly. Their desires are pure, unselfish, spiritual, in harmony with His will; and to fulfil them will promote both His own glory and the good of His universe. This truth is very clearly stated in the book of Job xxii. 21–23, 26, 27; and by David: "Delight thyself in the Lord; and He shall give thee the desires of thine heart." (See also John xv. 7; Jas. v. 16.)

3. *The obtainment of His salvation.* "He also will hear their cry, and will save them." "There is no rhetoric, nothing charming, in a cry, yet God's

ears are open to it, as the tender mother's to the cry of her sucking child, which another would take no notice of." In answer to prayer He helps His people in all their need, and ultimately saves them from all evil into perfect purity and joy.

CONCLUSION.—"Oh, fear the Lord, ye His saints; for there is no want to them that fear Him." "Trust in Him at all times; ye people, pour out your heart before Him: God is a refuge for us."

PSALM CXLVI.

INTRODUCTION.

In the Hebrew this Psalm has no superscription. The Septuagint has the superscription, "Hallelujah. Of Haggai and Zechariah;" and is followed in this respect by the Vulgate and the Syriac. This is based perhaps on ancient tradition; but has no higher authority. Modern expositors are generally agreed that the Psalm was composed after the exile. Thus Perowne: "The Psalm bears evident traces, both in style and language, and also in its allusions to other Psalms, of belonging to the post-exile literature." All that can be determined concerning the occasion of its composition is well expressed by Hengstenberg: "That the Psalm was composed in a period of depression for the people of God, is indicated by the predicates given to God, which are all of a kind fitted to elevate the distressed, to console the afflicted, and give them confidence in their God."

This is the first of a series of five Hallelujah Psalms, with which the Psalter is closed. At a later time this series was used in the daily morning prayers, in conjunction with portions of other Psalms and Books of the Old Testament.

The Psalm is chiefly an exhortation and an argument to trust not in man, but in Jehovah.

TRUST AND PRAISE.

Let us notice—

I. The trust prohibited.

"Put not your trust in princes, in a son of man, in whom there is no help," &c. Trust even in the most exalted and powerful of men is here prohibited; and reasons are given for the prohibition. Trust them not, because of—

1. *Their inability.* "Put not your trust in princes, in a son of man, in whom there is no help," or "salvation." We are prone to confide in the great and the high ones of the earth, who seem able to do for us, able to help us, to promote us to rank and wealth, and to establish our state, therefore the Psalmist declares that no man, not even the mightiest, has power to save either himself or others. Prince and pauper are alike destitute of salvation in themselves; alike they must receive it from God, or remain without it. "He giveth salvation to kings."

2. *Their mortality.* "His breath goeth forth, he returneth to his earth; in that very day his thoughts perish." Here are three points:—(1.) The termination of bodily life. "His breath goeth forth."

Without respiration, *i.e.*, without inspiration and expiration, we cannot live. While there is breath there is life. But the time comes when expiration takes place, and is not followed by inspiration; when "his breath goeth forth" and returns not again, and life has ceased. Death

"Is the cessation of our breath;
Silent and motionless we lie,
And no one knoweth more than this.
I saw our little Gertrude die;
She left off breathing, and no more
I smooth'd the pillow beneath her head."

(2.) The destiny of the body. "He returneth to his earth." Barnes says, "The earth—the dust—is *his:*—(*a.*) It is *his*, as that from which he was made: he turns back to what he was (Gen. iii. 19). (*b.*) The earth—the dust—the grave is *his*, as it is his home—the place where he will abide. (*c.*) It is *his*, as it is the only property which he has in reversion. All that a man—a prince, a nobleman, a monarch, a millionaire—will soon have will be his grave—his few feet of earth. *That* will be his by right of possession; by the fact that, for the time being, he will occupy it, and not another man. But that, too, may soon become another man's grave, so that even there he is a tenant only for a time; he has no permanent possession *even of a grave.* How poor is the richest man!" (3.) The failure of temporal projects. " In that very day his thoughts perish." All man's plans and purposes which relate only to time and this world are cut off by death. The patriarch Job gives striking utterance to this truth : "My days are past, my purposes are broken off, even the thoughts of my heart." When the breath goeth forth, "however grand the conception, however masterly the execution, all come to an end. The science, the philosophy, the statesmanship of one age is exploded in the next. The men who are the masters of the world's intellect to-day are discrowned to-morrow. In this age of restless and rapid change they may survive their own thoughts : their thoughts do not survive them." This truth has a very dread aspect to those whose thoughts and purposes are wholly or even chiefly of the things of sense and time; and this aspect our Lord brings into prominence in Luke xii. 16–21. But the practical aspect of this truth with which we have now to do is that which shows the utter vanity of man as an object of human trust. All the kind purposes and designs which man has for us come to an end when he dies ; and all the hopes that are placed on him perish at his death. Therefore, " Trust not in princes, in a son of man, in whom there is no help," &c. " Cursed is the man that trusteth in man," &c. (Jer. xvii. 5–8).

II. **The trust encouraged.** " Happy is he that hath the God of Jacob for his help," &c. (vers. 5–10). We regard the word " Jacob" as denoting in this place the whole people of Israel ; and " the God of Jacob" as the Lord Jehovah whom they worshipped, in contradistinction to the gods of the heathen. The position of the Psalmist is, that they are blessed who trust in Him ; and that for the following reasons :—because of—

1. *His almighty power.* " Who made heaven and earth, the sea, and all that therein is." The creation of the world manifests the omnipotence of God, and this is engaged on behalf of them whose hope is in Him. The Divine name which is here used (אֵל = God) is also expressive of strength. He is strong to succour and help His people.

2. *His unchangeable fidelity.* " Who keepeth truth for ever." Perowne holds that this is " the central thought of the Psalm. For on this ground beyond all others is God the object of trust. He is true, and His word is truth, and that word He keeps, not for a time, but for ever." " Heaven and earth shall pass away, but My words shall not pass away."

3. *His righteous judgment.* " Who executeth judgment for the oppressed." " The Lord executeth righteousness and judgment for all that are oppressed." By His Providence He calmly and steadfastly works for the vindication of the injured. And in the last judgment He will redress every wrong, &c.

4. *His bountifulness to the needy.* " Who giveth food to the hungry." " He satisfieth the longing soul, and filleth the hungry soul with goodness." " The hungry," says Hengstenberg, "represents generally all who stand in need of help." Jehovah is the liberal benefactor of all the necessitous, and especially those of them who trust in Him.

5. *His compassion for the afflicted.* The poet mentions several classes of distressed or troubled men, and of God's gracious dealings with each class. (1.) " Jehovah looseth the prisoners." By the prisoners we understand captives— those that are bound, and those also who are in the prison of distress. He thus set Israel free from their bondage in Egypt, and afterwards from their captivity in Assyria. Christ is the great Emancipator. It is His "to proclaim liberty to the captives, and the opening of the prison to the bound." " If the Son shall make you free, ye shall be free indeed." (2.) " Jehovah openeth the eyes of the blind." Heb., lit. : " Jehovah openeth the blind." Hengstenberg: " The blind are the naturally blind, and such as cannot discern the way of salvation without wisdom and help ; blind-

ness occurs as an image of want of wisdom and support in Deut. xxviii. 29; Isa. lix. 10; Job xii. 25." (Comp. also Ps. cxix. 18; Isa. xxxv. 5.) (3.) "Jehovah raiseth up them that are bowed down." Those who are weighed down and crushed by the burden of anxiety, trial, or sorrow, He sustains and cheers. (See our remarks on Ps. cxlv. 14.) (4.) "Jehovah preserveth the strangers, He relieveth the fatherless and widow." Instead of "relieveth" Hengstenberg translates, "raises up;" and Perowne, "setteth up." "The stranger, the widow, and the fatherless are representatives of persons in a miserable condition;" they are "the three great examples of natural defencelessness." The Lord succours all the helpless; He has a gracious regard for all who stand in special need of His care; He espouses the cause of the destitute and the weak. "A Father of the fatherless, and a Judge of the widows, is God in His holy habitation." In Him "the fatherless findeth mercy."

6. *His complacency in His people.* "Jehovah loveth the righteous." Starke says, "What a sweet word: the Lord loves thee! I would not take a kingdom for that word. Love unites God's heart to mine." And how broad and firm is the basis of trust which it supplies!

7. *His righteous retribution to the wicked.* "The way of the wicked He turneth upside down." Perowne: "He turneth aside." Conant: "He subverteth." The projects of the wicked Jehovah defeats. Under His government their way leads down to ruin. Moll: "The crooked way of the wicked in which death lies (Prov. xii. 28) is turned by Jehovah down towards hell (Prov. xv. 24; comp. ii. 18, Ps. i. 6)." Delitzsch: "There is only a single line devoted to Jehovah's punitive justice. For He rules in love and wrath, but delights most to rule in love."

8. *His everlasting reign.* "The Lord shall reign for ever; thy God, O Zion, unto all generations." No opposition can shake His throne. All the subtlety and strength of His enemy is utterly powerless against Him. (On the everlasting reign of Jehovah, see vol. i. pp. 224 and 385.) In the perpetuity of His reign we have another evidence of the blessedness of those who trust in Him. Surveying all these reasons for confidence, are we not prepared with the accent of conviction to say with the Psalmist, "Happy is he that hath the God of Jacob for his help, whose hope is in the Lord his God"? (Comp. Ps. ii. 12; lxxxiv. 12; Jer. xvii. 7, 8.)

III. The praise celebrated.

"Praise ye the Lord. Praise the Lord, O my soul," &c. Here is—

1. *A declaration of personal praise.* The poet determines to praise God— (1.) *Spiritually.* "Praise Jehovah, O my soul." "For discharging the duty of praise," says David Dickson, "all the powers of the soul must be stirred up; the mind, to meditate; the memory, to bring forth former observations; the heart and affections, for discharging the duty of praise in the best manner." (2.) *Perpetually.* "While I live will I praise Jehovah; I will sing praises unto my God while I have any being."

"I'll praise my Maker with my breath,
And when my voice is lost in death,
 Praise shall employ my nobler powers;
My days of praise shall ne'er be past,
While life and thought and being last,
 Or immortality endures."—*Watts.*

"Not in this song only will he utter his praise, but 'his life shall be a thanksgiving unto the Power that made him.'"

2. *A summons to others to praise Him.* "Praise ye the Lord." Heb., as in Margin: "Hallelujah." Thus the Psalm begins, and thus also it closes. "As one light kindles another," says Starke, "so a believing heart seeks to awaken others and excite them to the righteous praise of God."

THE PHILOSOPHY OF DEATH.

(*Verses* 4, 5.)

The text refers—
I. To the destiny of all.
1. *To a special day.* "In that very day." This is the day of death. There are many important days in a man's history. Often days of great moment.

Each perhaps the crisis of some eventful period of our history. But the day of death is peculiarly momentous: it is invested with unusual solemnity. It is the termination of probation, and the entrance on the unchanging realities of a future world.

The aspect of this day depends entirely on the moral condition of the individual, whether it be bright or dark—a day of bliss or woe—of exaltation to heaven or degradation even to the lowest abyss of hell. It would be well to read and meditate on this day; to look at it in all lights, and in all its consequences; and especially for this reason,—it is a day which we, every one, must personally realise. "It is appointed unto men once to die," &c. "I know Thou wilt bring me to death," &c. Our text refers—

2. *To a striking view of death.* "His breath goeth forth." When God made man, He "breathed," &c. Life is a succession of breathings. By the act of inspiration we take in the air, which supplies the blood with a fresh supply of oxygen, and thus makes it wholesome and nutritious to the system. By the act of expiration, the breath which has become impure is thrown off. Now, this ceasing to breathe is the extinction of life, and this may be produced by a variety of causes,—impure air, organic disease of the heart, affections of the lungs, &c. Oh think of this, and remember every instant there is but one step between us and death. The text refers—

3. *To man's last earthly home.* "He returneth to his earth." From that our first parents sprung. On that we move and live. It yields our supplies of food. We at length return to it. "Dust thou art," &c. "*His* earth"—every man has a claim on the earth for a sepulchre. The poorest have this, and the richest only this. "I know Thou wilt bring me to death, and to the house appointed," &c. "If I wait, the grave is mine house," &c. The text refers—

4. *To the cessation of mental activity.* "In that very day his thoughts perish." His worldly plans and schemes; his anxieties and cares; his purposes and projects; even his religious thoughts of repentance and serving God. His resolutions and vows, &c., all perish—all die with him. Whether king or peasant, philosopher or rustic. Not his soul—no, that still lives. Our text refers—

II. **To the peculiar privileges and happiness of a certain description of character.**

The character introduced is represented under two interesting features.

1. *As sustained by the God of Jacob.* "The God of Jacob for his help." Man requires Divine help. This help Jesus obtained by His obedience and sacrifice. Even the Old Testament saints enjoyed this help by prospective faith in the Redeemer. How God helped Jacob! delivering him from the wrath of his brother, and the oppression of Laban. Helped him to sustain his domestic troubles; helped him in all his trials and difficulties, and led him at last to dwell in the rich and fruitful land of Goshen. God is the help of all the spiritual posterity of Jacob—all who like Jacob are distinguished for prayer, faith, and obedience to His word. God is a help at hand; all-sufficient; unchangeable; everlasting. This character is represented—

2. *As expecting all good in and from God.* "Whose hope is in the Lord his God." The hope of the pious has respect to God's wisdom, truth, goodness, mercy, fidelity, &c. Hope is the balm of life, the very joy of existence. What would man do in the sorrows and trials of his present state, or what in looking towards the eternal future, without hope? He alone can sustain, deliver, bless, and save. Hence, notice—

3. *The blessedness of this character.* "Happy is he," &c. We are often struck most forcibly by contrasts. Contrast the godly man who hath Jehovah for his help with the poor benighted pagan, dwelling in the region of death—anxious, wretched, despairing. Contrast him with the sceptic, who is all doubt and uncertainty. With the worldly, whose hope and happiness are identified with gold and silver. With the neglector of religion, who trifles away opportunities, and mercies, and privileges, until "the

harvest is past," &c. Oh, yes, the godly man is happy—happy in the enjoyment of heavenly knowledge—happy in the enjoyment of Divine peace, internal tranquillity—happy in the prospect of immortality and eternal life. "They shall return and come to Zion with songs," &c.

Our subject contains matter—

1. *For solemn admonition.* Think of the day of death, &c.
2. *For rejoicing, to those who have God for their help.* What a privilege! Oh, value it—often praise God for it.
3. *For exhortation.* Who will consecrate himself to the Lord ?—*Jabez Burns, D.D.*

THE LORD THE LIBERATOR.

(*Verse 7.*)

"The Lord looseth the prisoners."

The text suggested to the preacher to go through the corridors of the great world-prison in which prisoners were confined.

I. The common prison—the ward of sin.
II. The solitary cell—the place of penitence, where was a secret spring, called faith, which, if a man could touch, he could go forth.
III. The silent cell, where he met with people who could not pray.
IV. The cell of ignorance.
V. The prison of habit.
VI. The hard-labour room.
VII. The low dungeon of despondency.
VIII. The inner prison—the hold of despair.
IX. The devil's torture-chamber.
X. The condemned cell.—*C. H. Spurgeon.* From "Lamps, Pitchers, and Trumpets," by *E. P. Hood.*

PSALM CXLVII.

INTRODUCTION.

"Like the last Psalm, and like those which follow it, this is evidently an anthem intended for the service of the Second Temple. It celebrates God's almighty and gracious rule over His people and over the world of nature, but mingles with this a special commemoration of His goodness in bringing back His people from their captivity and rebuilding the walls of Jerusalem. In the allusions to these events in vers. 2, 3, and vers. 13, 14, we shall probably be justified in seeing the occasion of the Psalm. It may have been written for the dedication of the wall at Jerusalem, which, as we learn from Neh. xii. 27, was kept 'with gladness, both with thanksgivings and with singing, with cymbals, psalteries, and with harps.' It is indeed not improbable, as Hengstenberg suggests, that not this Psalm only, but the rest of the Psalms to the end of the Book, are all anthems originally composed for the same occasion. The wall had been built under circumstances of no ordinary difficulty and discouragement (Neh. ii. 17; iv. 23); its completion was celebrated with no common joy and thankfulness; 'for God had made them rejoice with great joy; the wives also and the children had rejoiced: so that the joy of Jerusalem was heard even afar off.' (See Neh. xii. 27-43.)

"The Psalm cannot be said to have any regular strophical arrangement, but the renewed exhortations to praise, in vers. 7, 12, suggest a natural division of the Psalm. It is a *Trifolium* of praise."—*Perowne.*

THE EXCELLENCE OF PRAISE TO GOD.

(*Verses 1-6.*)

The Psalm opens with the summons to praise Jehovah, and proceeds to adduce motives for praising Him. We may arrange these under two heads :—

1. The praise of God is excellent in itself.

"Praise ye the Lord, for "—

1. "*It is good* to sing praises unto

our God." The adjective here used is a very comprehensive one — בוֹט, καλός, *pulcher*, beautiful; or, ἀγαθός, *bonus*, good; or, useful, profitable, beneficent. The same word is applied to the praise of God in Ps. xcii. 1. (See our remarks on that verse, vol. ii. pp. 63, 64.)

2. "*It is pleasant.*" To the godly soul praising God is a delightful thing; a thing affording purest satisfaction, and real joy to the heart. This truth is expressed also in Ps. cxxxv. 3: "Sing praises unto His name, for it is pleasant."

3. *It "is comely."* This clause is probably taken from Ps. xxxiii. 1. "Praise is comely for the upright." To praise God is a most seemly thing. Nothing can be more appropriate than that man, who owes to God so much, and is to some extent capable of appreciating the perfections and glories of His character, should pay to Him humble and hearty worship. It is a becoming thing in man; an honour and an ornament to him.

II. **The praise of God is excellent in its reasons.**

"Jehovah doth build up Jerusalem," &c. (vers. 2–6). God is here praised because of—

1. *His relation to His Church.* "Jehovah doth build up Jerusalem; He gathereth together the outcasts of Israel." There are references here to the rebuilding of the walls and the city of Jerusalem after the Captivity, and to the restoration of the exiled people to their own land. (Comp. Isa. xi. 12; lvi. 8.) The Lord is the builder of His Church. "Upon this rock will I build My Church." "Ye are God's building." He hews the stones out of the quarries of nature, cuts them into shape, works them into the glorious edifice, and carves them into grace and beauty. "The Lord added to the Church daily such as should be saved." He will carry onward the building to splendid completeness. And when His people have been scattered by persecution, or famine, or strife, He brings them together again. "As a shepherd seeketh out his flock in the day that he is among his sheep that are scattered, so will I seek out My sheep, and will deliver them out of all places where they have been scattered in the cloudy and dark day."

2. *His relation to troubled souls.* "He healeth the broken in heart, and bindeth up their wounds." There is much sorrow of heart in the world. It is probable that broken hearts are more frequent amongst men than is generally supposed. Broken hearts are not paraded; they are rather carefully concealed. Hearts are broken by sorrow for sin, by painful disappointments, by wicked calumnies, by distressing bereavements, by severe afflictions, by heavy losses. The Lord is the comforter and healer of such suffering souls. He heals the troubled penitent with His gracious forgiveness of sin; to the disappointed He presents new and brighter and well-assured hopes; to the calumniated He gives the assurance of a splendid vindication (Ps. xxxvii. 5, 6); before the bereaved He holds out the prospect of everlasting and joyful reunion with the beloved departed in our Father's house; He transforms afflictions into angels laden with blessings; and out of temporal losses He evolves eternal gains. "He heals the broken in heart," &c. It is His "to comfort all that mourn, to appoint unto them that mourn in Zion," &c. (Isa. lxi. 2, 3). "As one whom his mother comforteth, so will I comfort you," &c.

3. *His relation to heavenly hosts.* "He telleth the number of the stars; He calleth them all by their names," &c. (vers. 4, 5). "This is adduced," says Perowne, "as a proof of the omniscience and omnipotence of God, and hence as a ground of consolation to His people, however they may have been scattered, and however they may have been oppressed. Surely He must know, He must be able to succour, human woe, to whom it is an easy thing to count those stars which are beyond man's arithmetic (Gen. xv. 5). The argument is precisely the same as in Isa. xl. 26–29: 'Lift up your eyes,' &c. . . . Evidently the words of the prophet were in the mind of the Psalmist." It is stated that in

our sky there are one hundred millions of stars visible by the aid of a telescope, each of which is the centre of a cluster of tributary stars, making altogether "a great multitude which no man can number." "If we ask," says Dr. Chalmers, "the number of suns and of systems, the unassisted eye of man can take in a thousand, and the best telescope which the genius of man has constructed can take in eighty millions.* But why subject the dominions of the universe to the eye of man, or to the powers of his genius? Fancy may take its flight far beyond the ken of eye or of telescope. It may expatiate in the outer regions of all that is visible—and shall we have the boldness to say, that there is nothing there? that the wonders of the Almighty are at an end, because we can no longer trace His footsteps? that His omnipotence is exhausted, because human art can no longer follow Him? that the creative energy of God has sunk into repose, because the imagination is enfeebled by the magnitude of its efforts, and can keep no longer on the wing through those mighty tracts, which shoot far beyond what eye hath seen, or the heart of man hath conceived —which sweep endlessly along, and merge into an awful and mysterious infinity?"

Yet God counts all these stars; marshals all these stars. What an illustration we have in this of—(1.) His unlimited *might!* What power is involved in marshalling the countless hosts of stars, in guiding and keeping them in their spheres! "Great is our Lord, and of great power." (2.) His infinite *knowledge.* "He calleth them all by their names." Perowne: "He giveth names unto them all." The expression indicates "the most intimate knowledge and the most watchful care, as that of a shepherd for his flock (John x. 3)." Or the figure has been interpreted thus: "' He calleth them all by their names '—as if each one had a name, and God could call them forth one by one by their names, like the muster-roll of an army." "His understanding is infinite." Margin: "Of His understanding there is no number."

In the Hebrew there is a play upon the word which is translated "number" in ver. 4. Unlimited is the number both of His understanding and of the stars. The limit of human knowledge is soon reached, but "there is no searching of His understanding." Now this infinite intelligence and almighty power of God should prove an encouragement and an inspiration to all who trust in Him. The idea has been well expressed by Dr. Chalmers: "The God who sitteth above, and presides in high authority over all worlds, is mindful of man; and though at this moment His energy is felt in the remotest provinces of creation, we may feel the same security in His Providence as if we were the objects of His undivided care. It is not for us to bring our minds up to this mysterious agency. But such is the incomprehensible fact, that the same Being, whose eye is abroad over the whole universe, gives vegetation to every blade of grass, and motion to every particle of blood which circulates through the veins of the minutest animal; that, though His mind takes into its comprehensive grasp immensity and all its wonders, I am as much known to Him as if I were the single object of His attention—that He marks all my thoughts—that He gives birth to every feeling and every movement within me—and that with an exercise of power which I can neither describe nor comprehend: the same God who sits in the highest heaven, and reigns over the glories of the firmament, is at my right hand to give me every breath which I draw, and every comfort which I enjoy."

4. *His retributive relation to men.* "Jehovah lifteth up the meek; He casteth the wicked down to the ground." He who "rules the stars in their courses, rules also the world of man." (1.) He exalts the humble and the oppressed. "Jehovah lifteth up the meek," or "the afflicted." (See our remarks on Ps. cxlv. 14; cxlvi. 8.) (2.) He abases the wicked. (See our remarks on Ps. cxlvi. 9.) "His rule and His order are a correction of man's anarchy and disorder."

"Praise ye the Lord; for it is good," &c.

---
* The number is now said to be one hundred millions or more.

The Greatness and Gentleness of God.

(*Verses* 2–5.)

The text reveals *the constructive side of the Divine government.*

I. As shown in the building of the Church.

"The Lord doth build up Jerusalem," &c. That He should do so shows (1) that the Church is *self-demolished;* (2) that it is *self-helpless;* and (3) that God is the Gatherer, the Redeemer, and the Builder of the Church.

It is not God's purpose to *destroy.* It is His very nature to preserve, extend, complete, and glorify. He *does* destroy, but never *willingly.* His arm does not become terrible until His heart has been grieved, until His patience has been exhausted, and until the vital interests of the universe have been put in peril.

II. As seen in the gentle care of human hearts.

"He healeth the broken in heart, and bindeth up their wounds." Still, you see how constructive and preservative is God. His work is edification, not destruction. Who cares for broken-hearted men? Who has patience with the weak and faint? The greater the nature, the greater the compassion. "It is better to fall into the hands of God than into the hands of men." Learn from this gentle care of human hearts—

1. *The personality of God's knowledge.* He knows every bruised reed. Hearts suffer in *secret;* there is nothing hidden from God!

2. *The infinite adaptations of Divine grace.* Every heart, whatever its grief, may be healed! There is "a sovereign balm for every wound." Are we wounded on account of *sin?* Are we writhing under the agonies of *penitence?* Are we tortured by circumstances over which we have no control—the waywardness of children, physical prostration, the opposition of bad men, and the like? For *every* wound there is healing in the grace of God.

3. *The perfectness of Divine healing.* Other healers say, "Peace, peace, when there is no peace." Others, "Heal the hurt of the daughter of My people slightly." We are *not* healed until God heals us. God *offers* to heal us; our disease and our sorrow are challenges to prove His grace. What of the responsibility of *refusal?*

III. As seen in the order, the regularity, and the stability of creation.

"He telleth the number of the stars; He calleth them all by their names." Creation is a volume open to all eyes. Read it, and see the might and gentleness, the wisdom and patience, of God. "Lift up your eyes on high, and behold who hath created these things, that bringeth out their host by number: He calleth them all by names by the greatness of His might, for that He is strong in power; not one faileth." Jesus Christ taught us to reason from the natural to the spiritual: "Consider the lilies," &c.; "Behold the fowls of the air," &c.

(1.) God takes care of the great universe, may I not trust Him with my life?

(2.) Where God's will is unquestioned, the result is light, beauty, music: why should I oppose myself to its gracious dominion?

Let the Church be of good courage. "When the Lord shall build up Zion, He shall appear in His glory." "The gates of hell shall not prevail."

Are we truly broken in heart? Hear, then, the Saviour: "He hath sent Me to bind up the broken-hearted,"—sent His *Son* to heal us.

Are we contrite, humble, penitent? "Thus saith the high and lofty One that inhabiteth eternity, whose name is Holy: I dwell in the high and holy place, with him also that is of a contrite and humble spirit, to revive the spirit of the humble, and to revive the heart of the contrite ones." Our brokenness attracts Him. The cry of our sorrows brings Him down from heaven.—*Joseph Parker, D.D.*

THE SUPREMELY GREAT.

(*Verse 5.*)

Here are three aspects of the Divine greatness:—

I. God is great in His essence.
"Great is the Lord." He is great by reason of—

1. *His spirituality.* "God is a Spirit." Spiritual substances are more excellent than material. "The more perfect anything is in the rank of creatures, the more spiritual and simple it is, as gold is the more pure and perfect that hath least mixture of other metals." So God is a pure and perfect Spirit: He "is light, and in Him is no darkness at all." In Him there is "spirituality without any matter, perfection without any shadow or taint of imperfection."

2. *His self-existence.* His Being is underived and independent. With Him life is essential. He is the "I AM." His name is Jehovah, the Self-Existent One.

3. *His infinity.* (1.) He is infinite as regards *duration.* "From everlasting to everlasting Thou art God." He is eternal in the largest sense of that word. He endures always. He "inhabiteth eternity." (2.) He is infinite as regards *space.* He is present everywhere, from infinity to infinity. "There is no part of the universe, no portion of space, uninhabited by God, none wherein this Being of perfect power, wisdom, and benevolence is not essentially present. Could we with the swiftness of a sunbeam dart ourselves beyond the limits of the creation, and for ages continue our progress in infinite space, we should still be surrounded with the Divine presence, nor ever be able to reach that space where God is not." (Comp. Ps. cxxxix. 7–12 ; Jer. xxiii. 23, 24.)

4. *His unity.* There is but one God. "The Lord our God is one Lord." "If God be an infinitely-perfect Being," says Bishop Wilkins, "it is impossible to imagine two such beings at the same time, because they must have several perfections or the same. If the former, neither of them can be God, because neither of them has all possible perfections. If they have both equal perfections, neither of them can be absolutely perfect, because it is not so great to have the same equal perfections in common with another as to be superior to all others." Well did Massillon exclaim, "God alone is great!"

II. God is great in power.
"And of great power." "The power of God is that ability and strength whereby He can bring to pass whatsoever He please ; whatsoever His infinite wisdom can direct, and whatsoever the infinite purity of His will can resolve." This power is manifested—

1. *In the creation and sustentation of the universe.* "He spake, and it was done," &c. "He is mighty in strength," &c. (Job ix. 4–10). "He stretcheth out the north over the empty place," &c. (Job xxvi. 7–14). "By Him all things consist."

2. *In the government of the universe.* He rules over holy angels. "He maketh His angels spirits," &c. He presides over human governments. He "bringeth the princes to nothing," &c. (Isa. xl. 23, 24). "He putteth down one, and setteth up another." "He doeth according to His will in the army of heaven, and among the inhabitants of the earth," &c. He rules even over His enemies. "Surely the wrath of man shall praise Thee," &c. "The angels which kept not their first estate," &c. (Jude 6).

3. *In the redemption of mankind.* We see here the power of infinite wisdom and truth and love overcoming the antagonism of rebellious wills, the alienation of estranged hearts, &c. This is the grandest, sublimest display of the power of God. He is "mighty to save."

The consideration of the almightiness of God should (1.) prove a *warning to the wicked.* He has power to fulfil His threatenings. "Hast thou an arm like God?" (2.) *Awaken awe in all men.* We should reverently fear so great a Being. (3.) *Encourage faith in His people.* Omnipotence is pledged for their help and keeping. "The Lord is the strength of my life ; of whom shall I be afraid?" "If God be for us, who can be against us?"

III. God is great in knowledge.
"His understanding is infinite."

1. *He knows Himself.* "The Spirit searcheth all things, yea, the deep things of God," &c. (1 Cor. ii. 10, 11).

2. *He knows all creatures.* Angels, men, and even the meanest creatures. (Comp. Job xxxviii. 41; Ps. l. 11; Luke xii. 6, 7.) And He knows them clearly and completely. Thus He is perfectly acquainted with man's thoughts (Ps. cxxxix. 2; Ezek. xi. 5), and secret sins (Ps. xc. 8), and necessities (Matt. vi. 32), and circumstances, and works, and ways (Ps. cxxxix. 1–6).

3. *He knows all events.* (1.) All *past* events. He never forgets anything. This knowledge is clearly implied in Eccles. xii. 14; Rev. xx. 12. (2.) All *present* events. Nothing escapes the vigilance of His eye (Heb. iv. 12, 13). (3.) All *future* events (Isa. xli. 21–26; Acts xv. 18). (4.) All *possible* events. All the possibilities of all things, and beings, and worlds must be present to Him "whose understanding is infinite."

The consideration of this infinite knowledge of the holy God should (i.) *Check sin both in thought and in deed.* You cannot sin in secret. "There is no darkness nor shadow of death where the workers of iniquity may hide themselves." (ii.) *Humble all pride of intellect.* As compared with God, what does even the most intelligent man know? "We are but of yesterday, and know nothing," &c. (iii.) *Destroy all notions of our self-righteousness.* In the presence of this holy and heart-searching Being, "Who can say, I have made my heart clean, I am pure from my sin?" (iv.) *Inspire confidence in the triumph of His cause.* His enemies cannot outwit Him. His designs are formed in infinite knowledge and wisdom. "The gates of hell shall not prevail against" His Church. (v.) *Inspire confidence in His providential dealings with us.* His infinite knowledge is pledged to all who trust in Him. He knows their trials and dangers and sorrows, their wants and ways; and He will guide and support them, &c. "He knoweth our frame," &c.

THE PROVIDENCE AND PLEASURE OF GOD A REASON FOR PRAISING HIM.
(*Verse* 7–11.)

Let us consider—

I. The providence of God.
The Psalmist exhibits the providential agency of God in—

1. *Presiding over the elements.* "He covereth the heaven with clouds, He prepareth rain for the earth." (Comp. Job v. 10; xxviii. 25, 26; xxxvi. 27, 28; Ps. civ. 13.) The clouds do not cover the heavens, neither does the rain descend upon the earth by chance; both are governed by fixed laws; and these laws were appointed and are controlled by God. He is sovereign over all the arrangements and forces of nature.

2. *Creating vegetation.* "He maketh grass to grow upon the mountains." The mountains are mentioned because Palestine was a mountain-land. "A land of hills and valleys, and drinketh water of the rain of heaven" (Deut. xi. 11). And these, which are not watered by the rivers, God clothes with verdure and beauty. (Comp. Ps. civ. 14; Acts xiv. 17.)

3. *Providing for the wants of His creatures.* "He giveth to the beast his food, and to the young ravens which cry." (See our remarks on Ps. civ. 21, 27, 28; cxlv. 15, 16.) The ravens are mentioned here rather than other birds probably because they are offensive birds, in order to show that no creature, however regarded by man, is uncared for by God. Seeing that He supplies the needs of the ravens, is not the conclusion irresistible that He will provide for His children? (Comp. Matt. vi. 26; Luke xii. 6, 7.)

II. The pleasure of God.

1. *It is not in those who trust in their own resources.* "He delighteth not in the strength of the horse; He taketh not pleasure in the legs of a man." Horse and foot soldiers are here meant; the cavalry and infantry of an army.

God has no delight in armies great and strong, or in those who trust in them. Perowne expresses his idea of the meaning of the verse thus: "His delight is not in those who trust in their own strength and swiftness." It is one thing to trust in great and mighty armies and skilful generals; it is another, and in the sight of God a far nobler thing, to say with Jehoshaphat, "O our God, we have no might against this great company," &c. (2 Chron. xx. 12).

2. *It is in those who reverence and trust in Him.* "The Lord taketh pleasure in them that fear Him, in those that hope in His mercy." "A holy fear of God," says Matthew Henry, "and hope in God, not only may consist, but must concur. In the same heart, at the same time, there must be both a reverence of His majesty and a complacency in His goodness, both a believing dread of His wrath and a believing expectation of His favour; not that we must hang in suspense between hope and fear, but we must act under the gracious influences of hope and fear. Our fear must save our hope from swelling into presumption, and our hope must save our fear from sinking into despair." God delights in the man who looks to Him for all good, who reverences Him in all things, and who leans upon Him at all times and in all circumstances. Man's confidence in God is a pleasure to Him. He loves to be trusted by His creatures.

III. The praise of God.

"Sing unto Jehovah with thanksgiving; sing praise upon the harp unto our God." The praise which man offers unto God is here represented as—

1. *A response for Divine favours.* "Sing unto the Lord." The fundamental signification of the word here translated "sing" is to reply, to answer; and, according to Fürst, as used here it means "always *to sing in reply,* not *to sing* merely." Conant translates: "Answer Jehovah with thanksgiving." And Moll: "'Answer to Jehovah.' There is no allusion here to an antiphonal choral song, as in Exod. xv. 21, but a song of praise is called for as the answer of grateful men, to the honour of the Divine Giver (Exod. xxxii. 18; Num. xxi. 17; Isa. xxvii. 2)." The idea seems "to be, that we are to make a suitable *response* or *answer* to the manifold favours which we have received at the hand of God." God blesses man by the bestowal of His gifts, and man responds to God by the presentation of praise to Him.

2. *An expression of gratitude for Divine favours.* "Answer unto Jehovah with thanksgiving," &c. A grateful recollection of the goodness of God to us should find expression in our songs to Him. In our hymns of praise His blessings to us should be thankfully acknowledged, and the glory of them should be given to Him alone.

In the spirit of such worship let us endeavour to live.

GRASS, AND ITS MORAL ANALOGIES.

(*Verse 8.*)

"He maketh grass to grow upon the mountains."

Mr. Ruskin in his *Modern Painters* (III. Pt. iv. ch. xiv. § 51, 52) says some beautiful and suggestive things concerning grass.

"Gather a single blade of grass, and examine for a minute, quietly, its narrow sword-shaped strip of fluted green. Nothing, as it seems there, of notable goodness or beauty. A very little strength, and a very little tallness, and a few delicate long lines meeting in a point—not a perfect point neither, but blunt and unfinished, by no means a creditable or apparently much-cared-for example of Nature's workmanship; made, as it seems, only to be trodden on to-day, and to-morrow to be cast into the oven; and a little pale and hollow stalk, feeble and flaccid, leading down to the dull brown fibres of roots. And yet, think of it well, and judge whether of all the gorgeous flowers that beam in summer air, and of all strong and goodly trees, pleasant to the eyes or good for food—stately palm and pine, strong ash and oak, scented citron, burdened vine—there be any by man so deeply loved, by God so highly graced, as that narrow point of feeble green. . . . . Consider what we owe merely to the meadow grass, to the covering of the dark ground by that glorious enamel, by the companies of those soft, and countless, and peaceful spears. The fields ! Follow but forth for a little time the thoughts of all that we ought to recognise in those words. All spring and summer is in them—the walks by silent, scented paths — the rests in noonday heat—the joy of herds and flocks—the power of all shepherd life and meditation —the life of sunlight upon the world, falling in emerald streaks, and failing in soft blue shadows, where else it would have struck upon the dark mould, or scorching dust — pastures beside the pacing brooks—soft banks and knolls of lowly hills—thymy slopes of down overlooked by the blue line of lifted sea —crisp lawns all dim with early dew, or smooth in evening warmth of barred sunshine, dinted by happy feet, and softening in their fall the sound of loving voices : all these are summed in those simple words ; and these are not all. We may not measure to the full the depth of this heavenly gift, in our own land ; though still, as we think of it longer, the infinite of that meadow sweetness, Shakespeare's peculiar joy, would open on us more and more, yet we have it but in part. Go out in the spring time, among the meadows that slope from the shores of the Swiss lakes to the roots of their lower mountains. There, mingled with the taller gentians and the white narcissus, the grass grows deep and free ; and as you follow the winding mountain paths, beneath arching boughs all veiled and dim with blossom,—paths that for ever droop and rise over the green banks and mounds sweeping down in scented undulation, steep to the blue water, studded here and there with new-mown heaps, filling all the air with fainter sweetness,— look up towards the higher hills, where the waves of everlasting green roll silently into their long inlets among the shadows of the pines ; and we may, perhaps, at last know the meaning of those quiet words of the 147th Psalm, 'He maketh grass to grow upon the mountains.'

"There are also several lessons symbolically connected with this subject, which we must not allow to escape us. Observe, the peculiar characters of the grass, which adapt it especially for the service of man, are its apparent *humility and cheerfulness*."

We discover in the grass an illustration of—

I. Christian humility.

It illustrates—

1. *The usefulness of humble service.* Grass "seems created only for lowest service,—appointed to be trodden on and fed upon." Yet of what great use and value it is ! In like manner the lowly services of humble souls are indispensably necessary and unspeakably precious.

2. *The beauty of humble service.* To a person of pure and refined taste grass is very beautiful. To gaze upon it is in the highest degree restful and grateful to the tired eye. How beautiful is a life of humble service ! Our Lord "came not to be ministered unto, but to minister." He said, "I am among you as He that serveth." He "made Himself of no reputation, and took upon Him the form of a servant," &c.

3. *The divine acceptance of humble service.* "Whosoever shall give to drink unto one of these little ones a cup of cold water," &c. The Most High has declared His special regard for the humble. (See Prov. xvi. 19 ; xviii. 12 ; xxii. 4 ; xxix. 23 ; Isa. lvii. 15 ; 1 Pet. v. 5.)

Let us cultivate lowly thoughts of ourselves ; for—(1.) They are most likely to be true. (2.) They will promote our usefulness. (3.) They attract the Divine regard.

II. Christian cheerfulness.

Grass illustrates—

1. *Cheerfulness in the prosperity of others.* When spring comes the grass "rejoices with all the earth,—glowing with variegated flame of flowers,—waving in soft depth of fruitful strength." The Christian rejoices with them that

rejoice; he looks "not on his own things, but also on the things of others;" he is animated by the charity which "seeketh not her own."

2. *Cheerfulness in the midst of adversity.* When winter comes, the grass, "though it will not mock its fellow-plants by growing then, it will not pine and mourn, and turn colourless or leafless as they. It is always green, and is only the brighter and gayer for the hoar frost." In like manner the Christian "glories in tribulation," &c. (Rom. v. 3–5). He "reckons that the sufferings of this present," &c. (Rom. viii. 18). Thus the truly pious are cheerful in the midst of adversity.

3. *Cheerfulness increased by adversity.* Grass "seems to exult under all kinds of violence and suffering. You roll it, and it is stronger the next day; you mow it, and it multiplies its shoots, as if it were grateful; you tread upon it, and it only sends up richer perfume." Thus afflictions increase the serenity and cheerfulness and strength of humble souls. The proud are hardened and embittered by them; the humble are enriched and blessed. Their "chastening yieldeth the peaceable fruit of righteousness." (Comp. James i. 2, 3; 1 Pet. i. 6–9.)

Let us learn the lessons which the grass may teach us (Matt. vi. 28–30).

Let us cultivate humility of spirit.

PRAISE FROM EXCELLENT SOCIETY AND FOR EXCELLENT REASONS.

(*Verses* 12–20.)

We have here another paragraph in this hymn of praise, in which the poet appeals especially to Jerusalem to celebrate the praise of Jehovah; and mentions the special reasons which its inhabitants had for doing so. Here are two main lines of thought—

I. **Praise from excellent society.**

"Praise Jehovah, O Jerusalem; praise thy God, O Zion." By Jerusalem and Zion the Psalmist means the chosen people of God, the ancient Church. The people of God are under special obligations to praise Him.

1. *They have a clearer knowledge of Him than others.* They have His revealed mind and will. He manifests Himself unto them as He does not unto the world. He bestows upon them His Holy Spirit for their instruction and sanctification.

2. *They have a closer relation to Him than others.* "Thy God" (ver. 12). Jehovah was in covenant relation with Israel. He speaks of them as "My people Israel." "I will walk among you, and will be your God, and ye shall be My people." "Say unto Zion, Thou art My people." Christians, in like manner, are now spoken of as the people of God. (See Acts xv. 14; Tit. ii. 14; Heb. viii. 10; 1 Pet. ii. 9, 10.) Into this relationship they were called with a view to the praise of God, as Peter distinctly states (1 Pet. ii. 9).

3. *They receive richer blessings from Him than others.* This is a result of their closer relation to Him. It was so in the case of Israel (Lev. xxvi. 1–13). It is so in the case of Christians. They are guided by Him (Rom. viii. 14); heirs of Him (Ibid. 17); interceded for by His Spirit (Ibid. 26); have all good guaranteed by Him (Ibid. 32); have communion with Him (1 John i. 3); are called and kept by Him unto a glorious inheritance (1 Pet. i. 3–5). Therefore they are under special obligation to praise Him.

II. **Praise for excellent reasons.**

1. *For the blessings of His providence.* "He hath blessed thy children within thee." Three of these blessings are specified by the poet. (1.) *Protection.* "He hath strengthened the bars of thy gates." The reference is to the restoration of the walls of Jerusalem and the setting up of the gates by Nehemiah (Neh. vii. 1–3). God had enabled them to succeed in this, notwithstanding crafty and determined opposition. "God's almighty protection is the true defence of a country; without it all other defences can neither help or en-

dure." God is the guardian of His people and of His Church. (2.) *Peace.* "He maketh peace in thy borders." The Margin is correct: "Who maketh thy border peace." (Comp. Isa. lx. 17, 18: "I will also make thy officers peace," &c.) "If there be trouble anywhere," says Matthew Henry, "it is in the borders, the marches of a country; the frontier towns lie most exposed, so that, if there be peace in the borders, there is a universal peace, a mercy we can never be sufficiently thankful for." Peace in the soul, in society, and in the world is the gift of God. The universal supremacy of the spirit and principles of Christ would result in universal peace. (3.) *Plenty.* "He filleth thee with the finest of the wheat." The literal rendering is, "He satisfieth thee with the fat of wheat." (Comp. Ps. lxxxi. 16.) God gave them abundance of provisions, and those of the best kind. Here, then, we have reasons for praising God.

2. *For His agency in nature.* "He sendeth forth His commandment upon earth," &c. (vers. 15–18). He is here represented as—(1.) The *controller* of Nature. All its changes are ordered and effected by Him. And they are effected with *ease.* "He sendeth forth His commandment," and it is at once fulfilled. "He spake, and it was done," &c. (Ps. xxxiii. 9). They are effected also with *rapidity.* "His word runneth very swiftly." Snow, frost, ice, cold, warmth, wind, all obey Him without reluctance and without delay. (2.) The *proprietor* of Nature. It is "*His* ice, *His* cold, *His* wind." God is still the sovereign Proprietor of His universe. (3.) The *instructor of man* by means of Nature. (α) His sovereignty over the changes of Nature illustrates His control over the changes of the life of His people. Hengstenberg: "In vers. 15–18 there is probably not only an allusion to the omnipotence of God as manifested in Nature not less than in the government of His people, but at the same time an allegorical representation of this government, so that the Psalmist perceived in the operations of God in Nature the image of His administration in Grace—in the snow, hoar-frost, and frost, an image of the now no longer existing time of trouble; in the spring (ver. 18) an image of the returning salvation. (Comp. the similar figurative representations in Ps. cvii.)" He regulates the vicissitudes of their life, and causes them to "work together for good to them that love God." (β) His agency in nature shows the futility of opposing Him. "Who can stand before His cold?" "If we cannot stand before the cold of His frosts, how can we stand before the heat of His wrath?" (γ) The ready obedience of Nature to Him is both a rebuke and an example to man. The immediate and universal obedience of Nature is a reproach to disobedient man. He alone is rebellious, &c. He may profitably imitate winds and stars, heat and cold, in their prompt fulfilment of the Creator's will.

3. *For the blessings of His revelation.* "He showeth His word unto Jacob," &c. (vers. 19, 20). "God's works in Nature," says Perowne, "are for all men; 'He maketh His sun to rise on the evil and on the good, and sendeth rain on the just and on the unjust' (Matt. v. 45); but there is a special privilege belonging to His chosen people. They, and they alone in the world, have received the lively oracles of His mouth. (Comp. Rom. iii. 1, 2.)" Delitzsch: "The joyful Hallelujah is not sounded because these other nations do not possess such a positive knowledge of God's judgments, but because Israel does possess it. It is declared abundantly in other places that this knowledge of Israel shall be the means of making salvation the common property of the whole world of nations." And Barnes: "There is no nation now so favoured as the nation that has the revealed will of God—the Bible. The possession of that Book gives a nation a vast superiority in all respects over all others. In laws, customs, morals, intelligence, social life, purity, charity, prosperity, that Book elevates a nation at once, and scatters blessings which can be derived from nothing else. The highest benevolence that could be showed to any nation would be to put it in pos-

session of the Word of God in the language of the people."
Here, then, we have abundant and excellent reasons for uniting in the praise of God. Let us praise Him not only occasionally with our voice, but constantly by the loyal obedience of our life.

WINTER, AND ITS MORAL SUGGESTIONS.

(*Verses* 16, 17.)

The Psalmist believed in *God's supremacy over Nature*. He saw His hand in all its various changes. The more we discover of law and order in Nature the more should we be impressed with the wisdom and power of God; and so we should render to Him a more intelligent worship, and exercise in Him a firmer trust.

The Psalmist also believed in *the moral significance of Nature*. So also did David: "The heavens declare the glory of God," &c. Our great dramatist speaks of finding

"Tongues in trees, books in the running brooks,
Sermons in stones, and good in everything."

And the Supreme Teacher read and pointed out the significance of Nature: "Consider the lilies of the field," &c.

The seasons of the year are full of instruction. Spring is a manifestation of the beauty and tenderness and love of God; summer, with its light and heat, speaks of His glory; autumn proclaims His bountifulness; and winter indicates the stern aspects of His character. Let us consider some of the suggestions of winter.

I. **Winter indicates the severity of God.**

It hints that there is wrath as well as love in God. Nor is it alone in its testimony in this respect. Earthquakes, floods, storms, also testify to a terrible power in Nature, and to something answering to it in the God of Nature. (Comp. Rom. xi. 22; Rev. vi. 16, 17.)

II. **Winter suggests the retributiveness of the Divine arrangements.**

Many of those who during the preceding seasons have been guilty of indolence, intemperance, or extravagance, will find the bitter result now. It is in winter that the defective garment is painfully felt, and the dreary home seems utterly intolerable. "Whoso breaketh an hedge, a serpent shall bite him." These retributive laws are at work in the spiritual realm also.

III. **Some of the things which are peculiar to this season have special instruction for us.**

1. *Snow illustrates the wisdom and tastefulness of God.* "Snow is congealed vapour formed in the air by the vapour being frozen there before it is collected into drops large enough to form hail. In the descent of the vapour to the earth it is frozen, and descends in the numerous variety of crystallised forms in which the flakes appear. Perhaps there is nothing more fitted to excite pleasing conceptions of the wisdom of God—not even the variety of beauty in flowers—than the various forms of crystals in which snow appears. These crystals present an almost endless variety of forms. Captain Scoresby, who gave much attention to the subject and to other Arctic phenomena, says that, 'The extreme beauty and the endless variety of the microscopic objects perceived in the animal and vegetable kingdoms are perhaps fully equalled, if not surpassed, in both particulars of beauty and variety, by the crystals of snow. Some of the general varieties in the figures of the crystals may be referred to the temperature of the air; but the particular and endless modification of the same classes of crystals can only be referred to the will and pleasure of the First Great Cause, whose works, even the most minute and evanescent, and in regions the most remote from human observation, are altogether admirable.'" The Divine wisdom and love of beauty are everywhere manifest.

2. *Snow illustrates the power of God.* "Not the thunder itself speaks God's power more than the snow. It bears

His omnipotence, soft and beautiful as it seems. While it is yet in the air, it is lord of the ocean and the prairies. Ships are blinded by it. It is a white darkness. All harbours are silent under this plashy embargo. The traveller hides. The prairies are given up to its behest, and woe to him that dares to venture against the omnipotence of soft-falling snow upon those trackless wastes! . . . But when flake is joined to flake, and the frosts within the soil join their forces to the frosts descended from the clouds, who shall unlock their clasped hands? Who shall disannul their agreement? or who shall dispossess them of their place? Gathered in the mountains, banked and piled till they touched the very clouds again in which once they were born and rocked, how terrible is their cold, and more terrible their stroke when, slipping, some avalanche comes down the mountain-side, the roar and the snow-stroke loud as thunder and terrible as lightning! God gives to the silent snow a voice, and clothes its innocence and weakness with a power like His own."

3. *Snow also illustrates "the power of littles."* Small, insignificant, and feeble in the extreme is the snow-flake when alone; but when multitudes of them are united and firmly frozen, their power is dreadful—sometimes irresistible and terribly destructive.

IV. **Winter is an emblem of old age.**

Poets and artists in personifying winter have generally pictured it as an aged man or woman. Spring is an emblem of youth; summer of young manhood; autumn of mature manhood; and then our life passes into the winter of old age. How frequently does old age seem like winter—cold, cheerless, barren! But as spring is being prepared in winter, and winter shall pass into spring, so the aged Christian is preparing for eternal youth, and the winter of his age shall pass into the "everlasting spring" of heaven.

V. **Winter is an emblem of the present state of the bodies of the departed.**

In winter Nature is not dead; it only seems so. It is full of life and activities; and the result will be manifest in spring. So also with the bodies sown in "God's acre." God shall awake them from their deep wintry slumbers. "All that are in the graves shall hear His voice," &c.

VI. **Winter is an emblem of the present moral state of the world as it often appears to us.**

We see much of evil and suffering, much of darkness and mystery, much of madness and more of sin amongst men. But it will not be so always. God is at work; and out of the darkness He will educe light, &c.

"Ye noble few who here unbending stand
Beneath life's pressure, yet bear up awhile,
And what your bounded view, which only saw
A little part, deemed evil is no more;
The storms of wintry time will quickly pass,
And one unbounded spring encircle all."
—*Thomson.*

THE DIVINE GOODNESS IN NATURE, PROVIDENCE, AND GRACE.

(*Verse* 18.)

We owe much to Divine revelation for the more exalted views we entertain of the character, the perfections, and the grace of God. It was the distinction of the Jews that they possessed "the lively oracles." Hence the superiority of their faith and worship over those of neighbouring nations.

Men mould their idols in their own shape and image: and the worshipper soon reflects the character of the idols he adores. God condemns this. The controversy between Him and man has been,—"Thou thoughtest that I was altogether as thyself."

I. **We see much of the Divine goodness in the vast economy of Nature and Providence.**

"He sendeth out His word, and melteth them," &c. God changes the times and seasons—

1. *In an unexpected moment.* When the frost was at its height.

The wintry season was sometimes very severe in Judea and Palestine; usually lasted about six weeks; though sometimes intermingled with casual mitigations. Severe about Jerusalem—having both hail and snow. But when the sky is agitated by those tempestuous winds called Levanters, the cold is so piercing, the conflict so great of hail, ice, snow, and rain, that many of the poor people and their cattle perish. And it is dreadful to be at the mercy of armed bands at those times. An Oriental describing a defeated army near Ascalon says: "In haste they threw away their armour and clothes, but soon sunk under the cold, together with want of food, slippery and rugged roads, which were everywhere furrowed and broken up by torrents, that they were taken captives in the woods and on the mountains, and threw themselves into the hands of their enemies rather than perish." How welcome, then, the sudden and unexpected change in the text! "He causeth His wind," &c.

2. *By very simple means.* The south wind particularly;—for then the waters, before still and motionless, flow abundantly. So it is by very slight means that God in His Providence relieves trial and restores peace. (Comp. Ps. cxxvi. 1, 4.) A word of advice from a friend may change our plans—a letter —or an accidental interview with a stranger, &c.

II. **We owe much to God in the economy of Grace.**

God has His softening dispensations.

1. *In the conversion of the sinner* it is not all terror, but much mildness. The Lord opened the heart of Lydia. By nature the heart of man is hard and impenetrable, like the earth beneath the frost; cold and stubborn; without any warmth of love to God and Christ and spiritual things. But when God sends His word, accompanied with Divine power, it melts them. When the south wind of His blessed Spirit penetrates the heart, they are convinced of sin and righteousness and judgment.

2. *In the edification of believers* it is not all terror. They owe much to Barnabas the son of Consolation, as well as to Boanerges the son of Thunder. The strong wind, earthquake, and fire were succeeded by the "still small voice." When the Sun of Righteousness arises on them, it is with healing in His wings. "Awake, O north wind; and come, thou south" . . . to show that every wind may blow kindly to the Christian.

3. *In the descent of the Dark Valley* it is not all terror. Death comes with gentle step. We tread on velvet. Stephen pleading, &c. (Acts vii. 59, 60.)

III. **We shall owe much to God in a future world.**

The curse banished. A more favouring constitution of things. "Long nights and darkness dwell below."—*Samuel Thodey.*

PSALM CXLVIII.

INTRODUCTION.

"In this splendid anthem the Psalmist calls upon the whole creation, in its two great divisions (according to the Hebrew conception) of heaven and earth, to praise Jehovah. Things with and things without life, beings rational and irrational, are summoned to join the mighty chorus. The Psalm is an expression of the loftiest devotion, and embraces at the same time the most comprehensive view of the relation of the creature to the Creator. Whether it is exclusively the utterance of a heart filled to the full with the thought of the infinite majesty of God, or whether it is also an anticipation, a prophetic forecast, of the final glory of creation, when, at the manifestation of the sons of God, the creation itself shall also be redeemed from the bondage of corruption (Rom. viii. 18–23), and the homage of praise shall indeed be rendered by all things that are in heaven and earth and under the earth, is a question into which we need not enter. The former seems to my mind the more probable view; but the other is as old as Hilary, who sees the end of the exhortation of the Psalm to be, '*Ut ob depulsam sæculi vanitatem creatura omnis, ex magnis officiorum suorum laboribus absoluta, et in beato regno æternitatis*

aliquando respirans, Deum suum et læta prædicat et quieta, et ipsa secundum Apostolum in gloriam beatæ æternitatis assumpta.'
"The Psalm consists of two equal parts—
"I. The praise of God in heaven (vers. 1-6).
"II. The praise of God on earth (vers. 7-12)."—*Perowne.*

GOD'S PRAISE IN THE HEAVENS.

(*Verses* 1-6.)

The opening verse of the Psalm "is not to be restricted merely to the angels. It is the prelude comprising all afterwards enumerated, angels, sun, and moon," stars, highest heavens, and waters above the heavens. Notice—

I. **The praise of God by heavenly beings.**

"Praise ye Him, all His angels; praise ye Him, all His hosts." "His hosts" we understand as signifying His angels, as in 1 Kings xxii. 19. The expression indicates (1.) *Their immense number.* "The number of them was ten thousand times ten thousand, and thousands of thousands" (Rev. v. 11). (2.) *Their disciplined order.* Like a vast army they execute the commands of the Lord, their great Leader. The praise which they offer to God is—

1. *Voluntary.* They are intelligent beings, and possess moral freedom; and their worship is free, fervent, and joyous. The hosts of stars praise God without will; the hosts of angels praise Him in full and hearty exercise of their will.

2. *Constant.* The praise of God is the vital breath of their being. "Their worship no interval knows." "They have no rest day and night, saying, Holy, holy, holy," &c. And yet they ever rest; for all their service is refreshing and rapturous.

3. *Thorough.* They praise God with all their powers,—with their songs and their services; with their lips and their lives; with their reverent adoration (Isa. vi. 2, 3), and their ready obedience (Ps. ciii. 20, 21; Dan. ix. 21-23).

II. **The praise of God by heavenly bodies.**

"Praise ye Him, sun and moon," &c. (vers. 3-6). "The heaven of heavens" is the highest heavens. "The waters above the heavens" are, we think, the clouds. (Comp. Gen. i. 7.) Thus in the first member of ver. 4 the highest region of heaven is spoken of, and in the second member the lowest region of heaven. These heavenly bodies and places are called upon to praise Jehovah because they were,

1. *Created by Him.* "Let them praise the Name of Jehovah; for He commanded, and they were created." How great is the power that created all these, and that with such perfect *ease!* He merely uttered His commands; and they came at once into existence. (Comp. Gen. i. 3; Ps. xxxiii. 6, 9.)

2. *Sustained by Him.* "He hath also stablished them for ever and ever." Perowne: "And He made them to stand (fast) for ever and ever." The stability and permanence of the heavenly bodies are owing to the omnipotent will of God. He commands, and they stand fast. "By Him all things consist."

3. *Governed by Him.* "He hath made a decree which shall not pass." Perowne: "'He hath given them a decree, and they transgress it not:' lit., 'And none of them transgresses it;' for the verb is in the singular, and therefore distributive. . . . The verb is never used elsewhere of the passing away of a law, but always of the transgression of a law." "The *law*," says Hengstenberg, "is the sphere of being which is appointed to each part of creation, and in which it is held by the Divine omnipotence; as, for example, the stars must pursue their course, the upper and lower waters must remain continually distinct." He has marked out the orbits in which the heavenly bodies "move; He has so bound them that they perform their revolutions with unerring accuracy in the very path which He has prescribed. So accurate are their movements that they can be predicted with exact precision; and so uniform, that any succession of ages does not vary or affect them."

In thus fulfilling their course, and answering so perfectly the design of their Creator, they praise Him. As a faithful and masterly rendering of *The Messiah* is the most eloquent tribute to the splendid genius of Handel; as St. Paul's cathedral is the grandest memorial of Sir Christopher Wren; so the stability and order, the serviceableness and beauty of God's creations praise Him. They exhibit His power, and wisdom, and goodness, &c. "All Thy works shall praise Thee." "The heavens declare the glory of God," &c. (See Exposition of Ps. xix. 1–6; cxlv. 10.)

III. **The interest of godly men in God's praise in the heavens.**

The devout Psalmist calls upon the heavenly beings and bodies to praise Jehovah. We may not infer from this that they need any incitements from us to awaken their praise to God; but it is an evidence that pious souls would have Him praised universally. "When we call upon the angels to praise God," says Matthew Henry, "we mean that we desire God may be praised by the ablest hands and in the best manner,—that we are sure it is fit He should be so,—that we are pleased to think He is so,—that we have a spiritual communion with those that dwell in His house above and are still praising Him,—and that we have come by faith, and hope, and holy love, to the 'innumerable company of angels.'"

GOD'S PRAISE ON THE EARTH.

(*Verses 7–14.*)

Let us consider—

I. **The variety of God's praise on earth.**

"Praise Jehovah from the earth, ye dragons, and all deeps," &c. The Psalmist calls upon every province of our world and every variety of life to celebrate the praise of God. He summons—

1. *The inorganic creation.* "Fire and hail, snow and vapour, stormy wind fulfilling His word; mountains and all hills." "Mountains and hills" are mentioned probably because they are the most conspicuous objects on earth, and rise nearest to the heavens. The "stormy wind" is named, because in its wild course it seems to spurn all law, and to defy all control, and yet it fulfils the will of God and faithfully performs His behests. The "fire" is probably the lightning, and the "vapour" is not mist, but smoke, answering to fire as snow answers to hail.

2. *The vegetable creation.* "Fruitful trees, and all cedars." Fruit-trees are mentioned in distinction from forest trees, and because of their usefulness. "The cedars are named because they especially proclaim the creative power of God through their greatness and majesty; on which account they are called the cedars of God in Ps. lxxx. 10."

3. *The animal creation.* "Praise Jehovah from the earth, ye dragons and all deeps. . . . Beasts, and all cattle, creeping things, and flying fowl." The sea-monsters are named in particular, because "by their gigantic size they more especially proclaim the omnipotence of God's creative power. The same end is served by the description of leviathan in the Book of Job." By "beasts and all cattle" the poet probably intended to set forth wild and tame beasts; "those which roam the forests, and those which have been domesticated for the service of man." "Creeping things and winged fowl" "are grouped together for a reason similar to that for which fruitful trees and cedars, and beasts and cattle, are grouped together, to embrace the whole. The expression embraces the loftiest and lowest; those which ascend farthest above the earth, and those which creep upon its surface."

All these—the whole of the inorganic, of the vegetable, and of the animal creation—are summoned by the Psalmist to praise God. According as they fulfil the purposes for which they were created they may be said to unite in the great chorus of praise to God, inasmuch as in their sphere and measure they manifest the power, and wisdom, and goodness of God. (See Exposition of the preceding verses, and of Ps. xix. 1–6; cxlv. 10.)

4. *The rational creation.* "Kings of the earth, and all peoples," &c. (vers. 11–13). Perowne: "Man is mentioned last, as the crown of all. The first step (see ver. 7) and the last are the same as in Gen. i." The Psalmist clearly intends to include all men in His summons to praise God. (1.) Persons of all ranks. "Kings of the earth, and all people; princes, and all judges of the earth." The rulers and the ruled; those who have much authority and those who have none; the high and the low. Those high in position and in authority are under special obligations to praise God, and those in the lowest position are not exempt from this obligation. (2.) Persons of both sexes. "Young men and maidens." Men by their strength and skill, women by their trust and tenderness, &c., must praise God. (3.) Persons of all ages. "Both young men and maidens; old men and children." "Those in the morning of life," says Barnes, "just entering on their career; just forming their character — with ardour, elasticity, cheerfulness, hope;—let them consecrate all this to God :—let all that there is in the buoyancy of their feelings, in the melody of their voices, in their ardour and vigour, be employed in the praise and the service of God. Old men, with what remains of life, and children, with all that there is of joyousness—let all unite in praising God. Life as it closes, life as it begins, let it all be devoted to God."

As the unreasoning creation praises God unconsciously, the rational creation should praise Him intelligently and voluntarily. By the songs of their voices, by the affections of their hearts, by the adoration of their spirits, and by the obedience of their lives, all men should praise God.

II. **The universality of God's praise on earth.**

The Psalmist calls for universal praise. In the first part of the Psalm he summons all the heavens and the heavenly bodies, and in the latter part of the Psalm everything upon earth, to join the grand anthem to the honour of God. The lower ranks of creation never fail to praise God. "The material world, with its objects sublimely great or meanly little, as we judge them; its atoms of dust, its orbs of fire; the rock that stands by the seashore, the water that wears it away; the worm, a birth of yesterday, which we trample under foot; the streets of constellations that gleam perennial overhead; the aspiring palm-tree fixed to one spot, and the lions that are sent out free;—these incarnate and make visible all of God their natures will admit," and thus they praise Him. Man alone fails in the tribute of praise to God. But this summons to universal praise may be regarded as a declaration of—

1. *God's right.* The homage of the universe is due to Him.

2. *The good man's desire.* The cry of the heart of the godly man is, "Be Thou exalted, O God, above the heavens; Thy glory above all the earth." "Give unto the Lord, O ye kindreds of the people," &c. (Ps. xcvi. 7–9).

3. *A fact which will be realised in the future.* "All the ends of the world shall remember," &c. (*Ibid.* xx. 27). "All the earth shall worship Thee," &c. (*Ibid.* lxvi. 4). "The earth shall be full of the knowledge," &c. (Isa. xi. 9). "Unto Me every knee shall bow," &c. (*Ibid.* xlv. 23; Rom. xiv. 11).

III. **The rationality of God's praise on earth.**

It is manifestly and sublimely reasonable that universal worship should be offered to God. The Psalmist adduces certain reasons for praising Him.

1. *The glorious majesty of God.* "Let them praise the Name of Jehovah; for His Name," &c. (1.) His majesty is *supreme.* "His Name alone is exalted." "Who in the heaven can be compared unto Jehovah?" &c. (Ps. lxxxix. 6). (2.) His majesty is *universal.* "His glory is above the earth and heaven." As His majesty is universally manifest, His praise also should be universal.

2. *The great goodness of God.* (1.) In bestowing prosperity upon His people. "He also exalteth the horn of His people,—the praise of all His saints." The lifting up of their horn is the

bestowment of power and prosperity upon His people. The line, "a praise for all His saints," is of doubtful interpretation. Perowne: "This may either be (1) in apposition with the whole previous sentence, viz., the lifting up of the horn is 'a praise,' a glory to His beloved (comp. Isa. lxi. 3–11; lxii. 7); or (2) in apposition with the subject of the previous verb, God Himself is 'a praise (*i.e.*, object of praise) to,' &c. So the LXX., ὕμνος, Jerome, *laus*. So the P. B. V. gives the sense: 'All His saints shall praise Him.'" The latter seems to us the more probable interpretation. God had so blessed His people that praise to Him was especially binding upon them, and appropriate from them. (2.) In bringing His people near to Himself. "The children of Israel, a people near unto Him." The Israelites were blessed spiritually above other nations. "Unto them were committed the oracles of God." "Israelites; to whom pertaineth the adoption, and the glory," &c. "But now in Christ Jesus ye" (Gentiles) "who sometimes were far off are made nigh by the blood of Christ." In these things we have the most cogent reasons for praise to God. That man should praise Him is more than reasonable; it is obligatory; it is sacredly binding. Not to praise Him is to manifest an utter want of reverence, and to be guilty of basest ingratitude. "Praise ye the Lord."

A Summons to Universal Praise.
(Verses 11–13.)

We regard these verses as suggesting three aspects of God's revelation of Himself:—

I. **As adapted to persons of all ranks, and of the most varied duties.**

"Kings of the earth, and all people; princes, and all judges of the earth." God's revelation of His mind and will must be adapted to these, or this summons to praise Him would be unreasonable. It is so adapted—

1. *Because of its provision for the needs which they have in common.* Kings and their subjects alike need pardon, long for immortality, &c. God reveals these, and the conditions upon which they may be obtained.

2. *Because of its provision for the needs which pertain to their respective ranks and duties.* It has messages for both kings and subjects, rich and poor, &c.

II. **As adapted to persons of all ages.**

"Both young men, and maidens; old men, and children." He reveals Himself as moral Governor, wise and kind Father, infallible Guide, abiding and unchanging Friend, &c. "Children" can understand fatherhood; "young men and maidens" need guidance; "old men" can appreciate the Friend that knows neither change nor death; and to all beings of conscience moral government is intelligible.

III. **As fitted to inspire the praises of persons of all ranks and ages.**

"Let them praise the Name of Jehovah; for," &c. Men of all ranks and ages are here called to praise God, because of—

1. *The incomparable excellence of His character.* "For His Name alone is exalted."

2. *The conspicuous display of His majesty.* "His glory is above the earth and heaven." And, we may add—

3. *Because He confers rich and abundant blessings upon persons of all ranks and ages.* No man can refuse to praise Him without incurring the guilt of blackest ingratitude. With heart, and voice, and life, let us praise the Lord.

A People Near unto the Lord.
(Verse 14.)
"A people near unto Him."

I. **They are near to Him because they are reconciled to Him by faith in Christ.**

II. **They are near to Him because they live in habitual communion with Him.**

III. They are near to Him because they seek conformity to Him.
IV. They are near to Him because they enjoy His protection.
V. They are near to Him because they shall be with Him for ever.—*George Brooks.*

PSALM CXLIX.

INTRODUCTION.

This Psalm, like the others of the series of which it forms a part, bears evident traces both in style and language, and in the feelings which it expresses, of belonging to the post-exile literature. It was probably composed soon after the return from the captivity in Babylon. "It breathes," says Perowne, "the spirit of intense joy and eager hope which must have been in the very nature of things characteristic of the period which succeeded the return from the Babylonish captivity. Men of strong faith and religious enthusiasm and fervent loyalty must have felt that in the very fact of the restoration of the people to their own land was to be seen so signal a proof of the Divine favour, that it could not but be regarded as a pledge of a glorious future yet in store for the nation. The burning sense of wrong, the purpose of a terrible revenge, which was the feeling uppermost when they had first escaped from their oppressors (as in Ps. cxxxvii.), was soon changed into the hope of a series of magnificent victories over all the nations of the world, and the setting up of a universal dominion. It is such a hope which is expressed here. The old days of the nation and the old martial spirit are revived. God is their King (ver. 2), and they are His soldiers, going forth to wage His battles, with His praises in their mouth, and a two-edged sword in their hands. A spirit which now seems sanguinary and revengeful had, it is not too much to say, its proper function under the Old Testament, and was not only natural but necessary, if that small nation was to maintain itself against the powerful tribes by which it was hemmed in on all sides. But it ought to require no proof that language like that of vers. 6-9 of this Psalm is no warrant for the exhibition of a similar spirit in the Christian Church."

THE JUBILANT PEOPLE OF GOD.

(*Verses* 1-5.)

The summons to praise in this Psalm is addressed to the people of God. He is to be praised "in the congregation of saints. Let Israel rejoice in Him," &c. The tone of the Psalm is intensely joyous. Let us notice—

I. The reasons of their rejoicing.

1. *The mercies received by them from God.* That they had received recent and great mercies from God is implied in the summons to "sing unto Him a new song." The new song was for some new and special occasion for praise. Probably the mercies to be thus celebrated were the return from captivity, and the rebuilding of the walls of Jerusalem and of the Temple. And these blessings had awakened new hopes which were also to find expression in the new song. In the life of the people of God new mercies are ever calling for new songs. His goodness should enkindle the gratitude and joy of His people.

2. *The relationships sustained by them to God.* (1.) They are His *subjects.* "Let the children of Zion be joyful in their King." Barnes: "In God as their King. (*a.*) That they have a King, or that there is One to rule over them. (*b.*) That they have such a King; One so wise, so powerful, so good. (*c.*) That He administers His government with so much efficiency, impartiality, equity, wisdom, goodness." Perowne: "Such a King will not leave them under foreign rule; He will break the yoke of every oppressor from their neck." Let the Christian rejoice that he is a subject of the Lord Jesus. (2.) They are His *saints.* "The congregation of saints. Let Israel rejoice in Him that made him. Jehovah taketh pleasure in His people. Let the saints be joyful in glory." They are His people and His saints because He has made them what they are. He selected and called the Israelites to their high spiritual privileges; He made them His own covenant-people. Christians are now made by Him. "All that they have and are is to be traced to Him, as really as the universe of matter is to be traced to His

power. Their condition is not one of development, or one which is the result of their own wisdom, grace, or power;" but of His grace and power. (3.) They are His *delight*. "Jehovah taketh pleasure in His people." He regards them with complacency. He taketh pleasure (*a*) in their progress and prosperity; (*b*) in their worship and service; (*c*) in their future destiny. He has provided heaven for them, and He is preparing them for heaven. "So shall we ever be with the Lord."

3. *The adorning wrought in them by God.* "He beautifieth the meek with salvation." The primary significance of these words is well expressed by Moll: "The help which God vouchsafes to His oppressed people against their oppressors is not merely manifested to the world as deliverance and salvation generally, but serves also as an ornament and honour to that people themselves, so that, coming forth arrayed in it, they gain for it recognition and praise (Isa. lv. 5; lx. 7, 9, 13; lxi. 3; lxii. 7)." God's spiritual salvation is a beautifying of the human character and life. The lowly and meek He clothes with Divine grace. "The beauty of the Lord our God is upon them." "Beholding as in a glass the glory of the Lord, they are changed into the same image, from glory to glory, as by the Spirit of the Lord." For all these reasons let the people of God rejoice in Him.

II. **The character of their rejoicing.**
1. *It is religious.* They are called to "sing unto Jehovah;" to "rejoice in Him;" and to "praise His Name." Their exultation is not sinful or selfish, but holy and in honour of God.
2. *It is constant.* Both by day and "in the congregation of saints," and also by night and "upon their beds." They are to cultivate an abiding spirit of pious gladness; to "rejoice evermore."
3. *It is intense.* The number of times and the various forms of expression employed by the Psalmist in calling upon them to rejoice, and the various modes in which he calls upon them to express their joy, show that the joy is deep and full, active and abounding.

III. **The expression of their rejoicing.**

The poet calls upon Israel to express their joy—
1. *With "a new song."* The exultant soul naturally speaks the language of poetry in the tones of music. New mercies demanded "a new song." They required "a new song" also to express "all the new hopes and joys of a new era, a new spring of the nation, a new youth of the Church bursting forth into a new life."

"Thus far His arm hath led us on;
Thus far we make His mercy known:
And while we tread this desert land,
New mercies shall new songs demand."

2. *With music and dancing.* "Let them praise His Name in the dance; let them sing praises unto Him with the timbrel and harp." "The dance," says Dr. Hayman, "is spoken of in Holy Scripture universally as symbolical of some rejoicing, and is often coupled for the sake of contrast with mourning, as in Eccles. iii. 4, 'a time to mourn and a time to dance' (comp. Ps. xxx. 11; Matt. xi. 17). In the earlier period it is found combined with some song or *refrain* (Exod. xv. 20; xxxii. 18, 19; 1 Sam. xxi. 11); and with the tambourine (A. V., 'timbrel'), more especially in those impulsive outbursts of popular feeling which cannot find sufficient vent in the voice or in gesture singly. . . . Women among the Hebrews made the dance their especial means of expressing their feelings." But, as Barnes remarks, "there is much in the Hebrew mode of worship which cannot be transferred to the forms of Christian worship without an obvious incongruity and disadvantage; and because a thing has been done, and is not in itself wrong, we should not infer that it should always be done, or that it would be always best." Yet whatever is seemly and suitable in music may be employed as an aid in the expression of religious joy.

3. *Both in public and in private.* "In the congregation of saints," and "upon their beds." In the public assemblies for religious worship we should extol our King and our God. And in the quiet of the night our holy joy may rise to Him in songs of praise. The

godly man praises God both in the chamber and in the church.

Let Christians see their privilege, and cultivate and exhibit a spirit of religious thankfulness and joy. "Rejoice in the Lord alway: again I say, Rejoice."

THE PEOPLE AND PLEASURE OF THE LORD.

(*Verse* 4.)

"For the Lord taketh pleasure in His people."

I. **The people.**
1. They have a special relation to God.
2. They are regenerated and sanctified by His Spirit.
3. They are conformed to His image.
4. They are zealous for His glory.

II. **The pleasure.**
1. In their persons.
2. In their welfare.
3. In their services.
4. In their graces.
5. In their fellowship.

(1.) Are we the Lord's people? (2.) Do we realise our privilege as the objects of the Divine delight? (3.) Do we delight in God?—*George Brooks.*

"THE BEAUTIES OF HOLINESS."

(*Verse* 4.)

"He beautifieth the meek with salvation."

"Salvation" is a word which is used by men to represent very different things. The lowest conception of it is that miserably selfish one of deliverance from punishment and the realisation of happiness. The highest is perhaps this, the attainment of spiritual beauty, becoming like Christ, finding our heaven in God. Salvation beautifies human character and life. I fear we are not sufficiently alive to the importance of beauty in the culture of character. God has made the soul receptive of the beautiful, capable of appreciating it, and profiting by it; and "He hath made everything beautiful in its time," to minister to man's thirst for beauty. The beautiful in character is for many reasons the highest beauty. This God promises to the meek. How many blessings come to the meek which the proud never receive! "The meek will He guide in judgment, and the meek will He teach His way." "The meek shall inherit the earth, and shall delight themselves in the abundance of peace." "The Lord lifteth up the meek." "The High and Lofty One that inhabiteth eternity dwelleth with him that is of a contrite and humble spirit, to revive the spirit of the humble and to revive the heart of the contrite ones." "Thus saith the Lord, To this man will I look, even to him that is poor and of a contrite spirit." "Blessed are the meek, for they shall inherit the earth." "Jehovah beautifieth the meek with salvation."

Meekness in itself is beautiful. Who does not love the modest violet? "The ornament of a meek and quiet spirit is in the sight of God of great price." Our Lord Jesus is "meek and lowly in heart." Haughtiness repels; meekness attracts.

Meekness is further beautified with salvation. Salvation is the transforming of our morally disfigured natures into glorious and unfading beauty.

I. **Salvation promotes physical beauty.**

Sin is moral ugliness; and it tends to produce physical ugliness. The sins of the drunkard, and glutton, and sensualist, banish refinement, purity, and beauty from the features, and make them coarse, vulgar, and brutal. Every debauch thickens the lips, dims the fire of the eye, effaces something of the spiritual from the countenance, and stamps it with something animal or even brutal. Now, as salvation promotes temperance, chastity, and spirituality, it also promotes physical beauty. Purity of heart will gradually and silently mould even coarse features into refinement and comeliness. Again, evil passions deform their victims I once saw three portraits of one man, taken at different periods of his life. There was that of youth—fair, beautiful, and apparently ingenuous; there was that of young manhood, still fair and beautiful, but with more of maturity and less of ingenuousness; there was that of the man still young in years, but old in passion, old in sin; and now the features are hard, cynical, bitter, repulsive, reminding one of his own words—

"To be thus—
Grey-hair'd with anguish, like these blasted pines,
Wrecks of a single winter, barkless, branchless,
A blighted trunk upon a cursed root,
Which but supplies a feeling to decay—
And to be thus, eternally but thus,
Having been otherwise!"

But while evil passions darken and scar the features, salvation, which curbs and conquers evil passion, and imparts calmness and peace and love, gives repose and sweetness and beauty of countenance. If truth and purity, spirituality and meekness, peace and love are ours, they will inform the features with a spiritual and divine beauty.

II. **Salvation is spiritual beauty.**
"Beauty is the robe of holiness: the more holiness, the more beauty."

1. *The beauty of salvation resembles the beauty of God Himself.* Moses prayed, "Let the beauty of the Lord our God be upon us." Meekness and patience, truth and righteousness, purity and love,—these constitute the infinite loveliness of the ever-blessed God; and these are the beauties with which He adorns the meek. All human beauty is but a reflection of "the beauty of the Lord our God." Every grace that adorns human character is a ray from the splendours of the loveliness of the Infinite.

2. *This beauty is varied.* The beauty of creation is varied. Each of the seasons has its own peculiar charm. There are the beauties of the sea and shore, the beauties of wild mountain districts, and the beauties of quiet, fertile, pastoral scenes. So spiritual beauty is varied. In Mary we have the beauty of a receptive, meditative, deep, deathless love; in Martha that of an active, careful, ministering, and equally deathless love; in Job we have the beauty of trust in God sorely tested and sublimely triumphant; in Paul the beauty of a self-surrender and earnestness which has never been surpassed by man, &c.

The totality of beauty is found only in Jesus Christ. He is the "Altogether Lovely."

3. *This beauty is immortal.* The beauty of flowers soon perishes. The beauty of "the human face divine" is short-lived even at the longest. As our great dramatist says—

"Beauty is but a vain and doubtful good,
A shining gloss that fadeth suddenly;
A flower that dieth when first it 'gins to bud;
A brittle glass that's broken presently;
A doubtful good, a gloss, a glass, a flower,
Lost, faded, broken, dead within an hour."

But spiritual beauty is a pure good, and it never perishes. "Truth, love, and holiness are Divine, and always young and beautiful. The beauties with which they invest the soul have nothing temporal about them; they are the beauties of eternity." The beauties of salvation are unfading.

4. *This beauty is ever-increasing.* The meek, rejoicing in perpetual youth, will increase in loveliness through all eternity. The redeemed soul will become invested with more and more of the Divine beauty for evermore.

Let us seek to be *beautified* with salvation. We have not sufficiently thought of salvation as an adornment, a thing of light and loveliness. We have not sufficiently sought to add sweetness to strength, and tenderness to integrity of character. Too often the thought of our safety has filled our mind to the exclusion of the nobler solicitude to be beautiful with Divine grace and radiance. Yet we are being saved only "so as by fire" if we are not growing in amiability and loveliness. Oh, seek to be "beautified with salvation"!

The Militant People of God.

(*Verses 6–9.*)

In interpreting this portion of the Psalm we shall do well to heed the words of Delitzsch: "The dream that it was possible to use such a prayer as this, without a spiritual transubstantiation of the words, has made them the signal for some of the greatest crimes with which the Church has ever been stained. It was by means of this Psalm that Casper Sciopius in his 'Clarion of the Sacred War' (*Classicum Belli Sacri*), a work written, it has been said, not with ink, but with blood, roused and inflamed the Roman Catholic Princes to the Thirty Years' War. It was by means of this Psalm that, in the Protestant community, Thomas Münzer fanned the flames of the War of the Peasants. We see from these and other instances that when in her interpretation of such a Psalm the Church forgets the words of the Apostle, 'the weapons of our warfare are not carnal' (2 Cor. x. 4), she falls back upon the ground of the Old Testament, beyond which she has long since advanced, — ground which even the Jews themselves do not venture to maintain, because they cannot altogether withdraw themselves from the influence of the light which has dawned in Christianity, and which condemns the vindictive spirit. The Church of the Old Testament, which, as the people of Jehovah, was at the same time called to wage a holy war, had a right to express its hope of the universal conquest and dominion promised to it, in such terms as those of this Psalm; but, since Jerusalem and the seat of the Old Testament worship have perished, the national form of the Church has also for ever been broken in pieces. The Church of Christ is built up among and out of the nations; but neither is the Church a nation, nor will ever again one nation be the Church, κατ' ἐξόχην. Therefore the Christian must transpose the letter of this Psalm into the spirit of the New Testament."

We may use these verses as suggesting certain features of the spiritual warfare of the Church of Christ.

I. The true spirit of the Church militant.

The people of God in this world are a combatant people. They have enemies which they must war against. They have to contend against evil (1) in themselves. "The flesh lusteth against the spirit," &c. "I keep under my body, and bring it into subjection," &c. Starke: "Wage a good warfare against thyself above all; take vengeance and inflict punishment upon the heathenish desires of thy heart; strike down with the sword of the Spirit what contends against God and His honour." They have to contend against evil (2) in the world. Satan is active in human society. Wicked men are arrayed against the cause of God. Sinful principles and practices are mighty upon earth. Against these Christians have to do battle. They have to conquer the world to Christ by the power of His grace and truth. The spirit in which they should wage this warfare is indicated in the text: With "the high praises of God in their mouth, and a two-edged sword in their hand." Let them go into the conflict with songs; let their spirit be that of triumphant trust in God. The victories of truth and grace are never won either by cowards or by the self-confident, but by those whose strength is in God, and whose courage is inspired by Him. Not with craven fears, but with confident hopes, let the soldiers of Christ war their warfare.

II. The trusty weapon of the Church militant.

"A two-edged sword in their hand." The grand weapon in Christian warfare is "the sword of the Spirit, which is the Word of God." "The Word of God is quick and powerful, and sharper than any two-edged sword." The only weapon which can slay error is truth. The only power which can convert men to God is His own power in the Gospel. "The weapons of our warfare are not carnal, but mighty through God," &c. Many and glorious victories have already been won by this weapon, and yet wider and more brilliant triumphs will be achieved by it in the future.

III. The Divine warrant of the Church militant. "To execute upon them the judgment written." Various interpretations have been given to these words; some of which we need not mention here. The correct view, we think, will be found in this brief quotation from Perowne: "Others understand by 'a judgment written' one in accordance with the Divine will as written in Scripture, as opposed to selfish aims and passions (so Calvin). But perhaps it is better to take it as denoting a judgment fixed, settled—as committed to writing, so as to denote its permanent, unalterable character—written thus by God Himself. As in Isa. lxv. 6, God says, 'Behold, it is written before Me,' &c." Christians have a Divine commission for their holy warfare. That warfare accords with the purposes and plans of God. "As Thou hast sent Me into the world, even so have I also sent them into the world." "Go ye, make disciples of all the nations," &c. "Go ye into all the world, and preach," &c. And He who thus sends them forth, promises to be with them, and to conduct them to complete victory.

IV. The grand design of the Church militant. "This honour have all His saints." More correctly, "It is an honour for all His saints." "That is," says Perowne, "the subjection of the world described in the previous verses. But perhaps it is better to take the pronoun as referring to God: 'He is a glory to all,' &c. : *i.e.*, either (1) His glory and majesty are reflected in His people; or (2) He is the author and fountain of their glory; or (3) He is the glorious object of their praise." The latter seems to us the true interpretation. The glory of the victory of the Church in the subjection of all the world to God will be entirely His in the eyes of all His people. All the praise and honour they will ascribe to Him. The glory of God is the grand end of the work and warfare of the Church. God shall "be all in all." "It should lead us to shout '*Hallelujah*,' that we are permitted to be employed in any way, however humble, in carrying out the Divine plans, or in accomplishing those great designs which He contemplates toward our race." "Praise ye Jehovah."

PSALM CL.

INTRODUCTION.

Dean Perowne speaks of this Psalm as "the great closing Hallelujah, or Doxology, of the Psalter, in which every kind of musical instrument is to bear its part as well as the voice of man, in which not one nation only, but 'everything that hath breath,' is invited to join. It is one of those Psalms which 'declare their own intention as anthems, adapted for that public worship which was the glory and delight of the Hebrew people; a worship carrying with it the soul of the multitude by its simple majesty and by the powers of music, brought in their utmost force to recommend the devotions of earth in the ears of heaven.' 'Take it,' says Isaac Taylor, 'as a sample of this class, and bring the spectacle and the sounds into one, for the imagination to rest in. It was evidently to subserve the purposes of *music* that these thirteen verses are put together; it was no doubt to give effect first to the human voice, and then to the alternations of instruments,—loud and tender and gay,—with the graceful movements of the dance, that the anthem was composed and its chorus brought out,

"'Let everything that hath breath praise the Lord !
Praise ye the Lord !

"'And so did the congregated thousands take up their part with a shout, even as the voice of many waters.'"

THE DOXOLOGY.

I. The sphere of the Divine praise. "Praise ye the Lord. Praise God in His sanctuary, praise Him in the firmament of His power."

1. *In His temple upon earth.* "Praise God in His sanctuary." We understand this of the earthly temple, the place which He had chosen for the special

manifestation of His presence and bestowment of His grace.

2. *In the heavens.* "Praise Him in the firmament of His power;" or "in the expanse of His power." "The call here is on all that dwell above that expanse, in heaven, to unite with those on earth in His praise. It is called 'the expanse *of His power*' because it is in the heavens—in the sun, the moon, the stars—that the power of God seems to be principally displayed." The earthly temple and heaven are mentioned together probably to indicate the universality of His praise. (Comp. 1 Kings viii. 39, 43, 49 ; Ps. xi. 4.)

II. **The reason of the Divine praise.**
"Praise Him for His mighty acts."
1. *In creation.* "By the word of Jehovah were the heavens made," &c. (Ps. xxxiii. 6-9).
2. *In providence.* What marvellous and mighty acts He had wrought on behalf of the Israelites!
3. *In redemption.* In this the power of His wisdom and grace is most clearly and impressively displayed.

III. **The measure of the Divine praise.**
"Praise Him according to His excellent greatness." Hebrew: "The multitude of His greatness." Conant: "His abundant greatness." We are to endeavour to praise Him in a manner which shall be in proportion to His greatness and glory. Man's praise should correspond with God's perfections, as far as this is possible. But when the most perfect praise is offered by the whole universe to God, it will still fall below His infinite greatness and glory. "He who will review only his own life will discover so many of God's deeds that he will not be able to thank Him sufficiently through eternity."

IV. **The manner of the Divine praise.**
"Praise Him with the sound of the trumpet," &c. (vers. 3-5). These verses suggest the following observations as to the manner in which God should be praised :—
1. The praise of God should be *joyous.* "Beyond doubt," says Hengstenberg, "the pipe" (A. V., "organ"), "which otherwise did not belong to the Temple service, was brought into requisition here only because the feast had at the same time the character of a popular rejoicing. In like manner also timbrels and dances. . . . The cymbals were used only at festivals of a joyful kind. (Comp. 2 Sam. vi. 5 ; Ezra iii. 10 ; Neh. xii. 27.)" Joyful worship is acceptable to God and honours Him.
2. The praise of God should be *as perfect as possible.* "Everything pertaining to worship should surely indicate a reverent solicitude to bring to God the best that we can proffer—an offering perfect in every appliance that can give emphasis to its adoration, intensify its rapture, or beautify its love. Hence, the devoutest worshippers will provide for their praise hymns of the highest poetry, and music of the richest harmony."—*Dr. H. Allon.*
3. The praise of God should *thoroughly engage the powers of our spirits.* It behoves us to stir up our warmest and holiest affections to praise God. Where these are not engaged, the most perfect poetry and music will not find acceptance with God. "The finest music before God is the harmonious praise and glorifying of God by the soul united in all its powers, with all the senses and all the members."

V. **The offerers of the Divine praise.**
"Let everything that hath breath praise the Lord." "The very ambiguity of '*all breath*' gives," says Alexander, "an extraordinary richness of meaning to the closing sentence. From the simple idea of wind-instruments mentioned in the context, it leads us by a beautiful transition to that of vocal, articulate, intelligent praise, uttered by the breath of living men, as distinguished from mere lifeless instruments. Then, lastly, by a natural association, we ascend to the idea expressed in the common version, '*everything that hath breath,*' not merely all that lives, but all that has a voice to praise God. There is nothing in the Psalter more majestic or more beautiful than this brief, but most significant, *finale,* in which solemnity of tone predominates, without, however, in the least disturbing the exhilaration which the close of the Psalter seems intended to produce, as if in emblemati-

cal allusion to the triumph which awaits the Church and all its members, when, through much tribulation, they shall enter into rest." All living creatures are summoned to unite in celebrating the praises of God,—all in the air and in the waters, all on earth and all in heaven,—let everything according to its capacity and power join in the universal anthem. "All creatures," says Moll, "should join their voices to the praise of God; but the members of His Church should lead the choir."

The Subjects and Expressions of Praise.

Gospel worship should be joyful worship. "Speaking to yourselves in Psalms and hymns and spiritual songs." The Gospel was sung at Bethlehem before it was preached. We may well say with Greg. Nazianzen: "Lord, I would be a musical instrument for Thee to touch, that I may show forth Thy praise."

I. **Some subjects of praise in which we should unite,** derived from these closing Psalms. Praise the great Head of the Church—

1. *For what He is in Himself.* "Praise Him according to His excellent greatness;" and according to the display of that greatness in each succeeding dispensation. (1.) *Rejoice in the plenitude of His Divine perfections.* The inspired writers always speak of Christ as of One who was far greater than any description that could be given of Him. God has given Him as Mediator, "a Name which is above every name"—above every name on earth or in heaven. For power: He has all power in heaven and on earth. For wisdom: in Him are hid all the treasures of wisdom and knowledge. For love: His love passeth knowledge. For unchanging truth and faithfulness: His righteousness is like the great mountains. "Thy faithfulness hast thou established in the very heavens." (2.) *Rejoice in the tenderness of His human sympathies.* It is remarkable that those who have suffered the most for the cause of Christ, replete with His consolations, have spoken the most loudly of His name. As David's Psalms in the wilderness are the sweetest of his psalms, so Paul's letters in prison are the most delightful of his epistles.

2. *For the wonders of His Providence in the defence and preservation of His Church.* "Praise Him for His mighty acts." Some of these are enumerated in these last five Psalms; *e.g.*, the bringing back of Israel from the Babylonish captivity; the rebuilding and the fortification of Jerusalem; the erection of the second Temple, which was a wonderful thing for a colony of returned exiles to attempt. All Providence is subordinated to the interests, and to the Church, of the Messiah. The government of earth and heaven is upon His shoulder. (Comp. Isa. ix. 6.) The world was built by Him and for Him, for this very purpose, that it might be the scene and theatre of His Divine and gracious government in the great economy of human salvation. (Comp. John i. 1–3, 16.) With the work of Redemption in promise, the Psalmist might well say, and with the work of Redemption in fulfilment, we may well add with him, "Praise Him for His mighty acts; praise Him according to His excellent greatness."

3. *For the special relation in which He stands to us;* that is, to all who bow to His sceptre, and experience the efficacy of His redeeming grace. He is their King; and they have the greatest reason to rejoice in Him.

II. **In what way our love and loyalty to Christ should be made manifest.**

1. *In a more full and frequent contemplation of His infinite excellence, His ineffable love.* In Ps. cxlviii. 14 He is said to be "The praise of all His saints,—a people near unto Him." Especially should this be the case with us when we are called to contemplate the great mystery of redemption, "wherein He hath abounded toward us in all wisdom and prudence." In other events and providential deliverances we see the putting forth of the power of His arm; but here we see unveiled the movements of His heart. Think

then of the mighty acts of our all-glorious Redeemer, &c. . . . These are the trophies of Christ's power; these the putting forth of the resources of His boundless and ineffable love.

2. *By a careful study of His Providences*—towards the Church in general, or towards ourselves in particular. A great cluster of Providences is referred to in these Psalms. Great and signal revolutions of empire among the Persians, the Babylonians, and the Medes, brought about their return from captivity;—their conquerors being moved only by political considerations, as our public men are this day, and not at all about God's designs. He girded Cyrus with his might, though Cyrus knew Him not (Isa. xlv. 5). So the great Reformation in Germany was backed by reasons of state, as they are called; it being the interest of many princes there to countenance Luther's doctrines to stop the growing greatness of Charles V., who designed to enslave them. How wonderful that the building and the fortification of Jerusalem should have been consented to and brought about by their original enemies and enslavers, and even at the cost of their conquerors! . . . How much we may see the hand of God in our national history! in the Norman Conquest—the encouragement of the Reformation by Henry VIII.—the defeat of the Spanish Armada—and the glorious Revolution by William III.

3. *In zealous efforts for the extension of His kingdom.* "Let everything that hath breath praise the Lord."

III. What great losers they are who have no part in these benefits!
—*Samuel Thodey.*

UNIVERSAL PRAISE.

(*Verse 6.*)

This summons to praise Jehovah with which the Book of Psalms closes, is not Jewish, but human; not narrow or exclusive, but broad and catholic. Let us look at universal praise—

I. As the grand prerogative of God. Praise is due to Him from all His creatures because—

1. *Of the perfections of His Being.* We should praise Him for what He is in Himself—the Supremely Great and Good. His character is fitted to awaken the devout admiration, and inspire the reverent affection, and enkindle the hearty praise of all His intelligent creatures.

2. *Of his relations to the universe.* (1.) *Creator.* "Of old hast Thou laid the foundations of the earth, and the heavens are the work of Thy hands." "All things were made by Him, and without Him was not anything made that was made." "We are also His offspring." (2.) *Sustainer.* Constantly and completely all things depend upon Him. "By Him all things consist." "Everything that hath breath" draws that breath from Him. "He giveth to all life, and breath, and all things. . . . For in Him we live and move and have our being." (3.) *Sovereign.* All things are ordered by Him. "He doeth according to His will in the army of heaven, and among the inhabitants of the earth; and none can stay His hand, or say unto Him, What doest Thou?" Therefore, "everything that hath breath" should praise Him. The lower orders of creation praise Him as embodiments of His ideas, and by fulfilling in their existence His purpose concerning them. And the intelligent orders of creation should praise Him by their loyal obedience, reverent worship, and supreme affection. This is due to Him. He has a most righteous and powerful claim upon this.

3. *Praise is due to Him especially from man.* Man's creation is a higher thing than that of other creatures, and brings him into closer relations with God. "Man's origin as to his essential inward being, the intellectual, moral, and spiritual, is not so much a *creation* as an *outbirth*." "The Lord God breathed into his nostrils the breath of life, and man became a living soul." "There is a spirit in man; and the inspiration of the Almighty giveth them under-

standing." "The God of the spirits of all flesh." Hence man's increased obligation to praise God. The position assigned to man still further increases his obligation to honour God. The Creator made man sovereign over the lower ranks of creatures; and gave the earth to him for his sustentation and service (Gen. i. 28, 29; Ps. cxv. 16). And man, as a sinner, was redeemed by God at an immense cost. "Ye were not redeemed with corruptible things," &c. (1 Pet. i. 18, 19). The obligations of man to praise God are of the most sacred and binding character. Universal worship belongs by right to God: it is His prerogative. "Give unto the Lord the glory due unto His Name," &c.

II. As the precious privilege of man.

To contribute to the universal worship of God is not only the binding duty, but the exalted privilege of man.

1. *Because of the acceptance of our praise by Him.* That we are permitted to approach God with our praises, and assured of a gracious welcome, is surely great condescension on His part, and a great privilege on ours. Holy angels worship Him with intensest ardour and humblest reverence (Isa. vi. 3); yet He deigns to hear and receive the praises of such ignorant and sinful beings as we are.

2. *Because of the influence of our praise upon us.* The worship of God has the most blessed effect upon the true worshipper. (1.) Worship is *joy-giving.* It affords richest and purest delight to the devout spirit. One of the highest joys of heaven is the joy of worship. (Comp. Rev. iv. 10, 11; v. 9–14; vii. 9–12.) (2.) Worship is *transforming.* Man becomes like unto the thing or the being whom he really worships. The worship of God promotes in the worshipper the attributes of humility, reverence for all that is true and holy, self-forgetfulness, sanctity, and the highest spiritual beauty. They who worship God in spirit and in truth are changed into likeness to Him "from glory to glory, as by the Spirit of the Lord."

Brothers, behold your privilege! To worship God doubtless is your duty; but it is much more than that: more beautiful and blessed than a mere duty; it is a sacred, precious, exalted privilege. Regard it as such; practise it as such.

III. As the fervent desire of the good.

It is the wish of all godly souls that "everything that hath breath would praise the Lord." They manifest their desire by—

1. *Praising Him themselves.* To praise Him is to them a rich delight. By their songs and by their services, by their profession and by their practice, they honour Him.

2. *Calling upon others to praise Him.* "Let everything that hath breath praise Jah. Praise ye Jah." The godly soul would incite others to join in this blessed service, and would have all creatures to unite in the melodious and mighty chorus to the praise and glory of God. This is the best mode of attaining to this universal praise to God. The time advances when "everything that hath breath will praise the Lord." We may contribute to its advent by sincerely praising Him ourselves, and by inducing others to join us in praising Him.

"Dear Lord, our God and Saviour! for Thy gifts
The world were poor in thanks, though every soul
Should nought but breathe them; every blade of grass,
Yea, every atomic of earth and air
Should utter thanks like dew.
. . . .
Wherefore let us Him ceaselessly adore;
Praise Him, ye chosen of the earth and skies;
Ye visible raylets of invisible Light,
Blend with the universal Heavens your lays!
Immortal leaflets of Love's holy flower,
Breathe forth the perfume of eternal praise."
—*Bailey.*

"LET EVERYTHING THAT HATH BREATH PRAISE JAH!

HALLELUJAH!"

www.ingramcontent.com/pod-product-compliance
Lightning Source LLC
Chambersburg PA
CBHW021420300426
44114CB00010B/569